2025
BIG ROAD ATLAS
BRITAIN

Scale 1:190,000
or 3 miles to 1 inch

33rd edition June 2024 © AA Media Limited 2024
Original edition printed 1991.

All cartography in this atlas edited, designed and produced by the Mapping Services Department of AA Media Limited (A05867).

This atlas contains Ordnance Survey data © Crown copyright and database right 2024. Contains public sector information licensed under the Open Government Licence v3.0. Ireland mapping and Distances and journey times contains data available from openstreetmap.org © under the Open Database License found at opendatacommons.org

Published by AA Media Limited, whose registered office is Grove House, Lutyens Close, Basingstoke, Hampshire RG24 8AG, UK.
Registered number 06112600.

ISBN: 978 0 7495 8395 8 (spiral bound)
ISBN: 978 0 7495 8394 1 (paperback)

A CIP catalogue record for this book is available from The British Library.

Disclaimer: The contents of this atlas are believed to be correct at the time of the latest revision, it will not contain any subsequent amended, new or temporary information including diversions and traffic control or enforcement systems. The publishers cannot be held responsible or liable for any loss or damage occasioned to any person acting or refraining from action as a result of any use or reliance on material in this atlas, nor for any errors, omissions or changes in such material. This does not affect your statutory rights.

The publishers would welcome information to correct any errors or omissions and to keep this atlas up to date. Please write to the Atlas Editor, AA Media Limited, Grove House, Lutyens Close, Basingstoke, Hampshire RG24 8AG, UK.
E-mail: roadatlasfeedback@aamediagroup.co.uk

Acknowledgements: AA Media Limited would like to thank the following for information used in the creation of this atlas: Cadw, English Heritage, Forestry Commission, Historic Scotland, National Trust and National Trust for Scotland, RSPB, The Wildlife Trust, Scottish Natural Heritage, Natural England, The Countryside Council for Wales. Award winning beaches from 'Blue Flag' and 'Keep Scotland Beautiful' (summer 2023 data): for latest information visit www.blueflag.org and www.keepscotlandbeautiful.org. Road signs are © Crown Copyright 2024. Reproduced under the terms of the Open Government Licence. Ireland mapping: Republic of Ireland census 2016 © Central Statistics Office and Northern Ireland census 2016 © NISRA (population data); Irish Public Sector Data (CC BY 4.0) (Gaeltacht); Logainm.ie (placenames); Roads Service and Transport Infrastructure Ireland
Printed by 1010 Printing International Ltd, China

* Nielsen BookScan Total Consumer Market (UK Standard scale atlases) 1–39 weeks to 2 October 2023.

Contents

Map pages	**inside front cover**
Route planning	**II–XVI**
Route planner	II–V
London district	VI–VII
Restricted junctions	VIII
Smart motorways	IX
Caravan and camping sites in Britain	X–XI
Traffic signs and road markings	XII–XIII
Ferries and port plans	XIV–XVI
Atlas symbols	**1**
Road maps 1:190,000 scale	**2–112**
Channel Islands 1:135,000 scale	6–7
Isle of Man 1:190,000 scale	60
Orkney and Shetland Islands 1:709,000 scale	106
Skye & The Small Isles 1:340,000 scale	100
Western Isles 1:709,000 scale	106

Ferry ports

Aberdeen Harbour........XVI	Harwich International	Liverpool Docks............XVI	Port of Tyne.................XVI
Calais XIV	Port XVI	Newhaven Harbour XV	Portsmouth Harbour.....XIV
Channel Tunnel.............XV	Heysham Harbour XVI	Pembroke Dock XVI	Southampton, Port of...XIV
Dover, Port of XV	Holyhead Harbour XVI	Plymouth, Port of XIV	
Fishguard Harbour........XVI	Hull, Port of XVI	Poole, Port of XIV	

Tourist sites with satnav friendly postcodes	**113**
Ireland road maps 1:1 million scale	**114–115**

Town plans

Aberdeen.....................99	Dundee 117	Liverpool.........................54	Plymouth 121
Aberystwyth 32	Durham 118	Llandudno 53	Portsmouth 121
Bath 116	Edinburgh...................118	London..........................119	Salisbury 121
Birmingham 116	Exeter.........................118	Manchester 120	Sheffield 121
Blackpool 116	Glasgow......................118	Middlesbrough 71	Southampton 121
Bradford 116	Great Yarmouth 51	Milton Keynes...............120	Southend-on-Sea..........23
Bristol..........................116	Harrogate 118	Newcastle upon	Stratford-upon-Avon.....122
Cambridge 116	Inverness.....................118	Tyne...........................120	Sunderland....................71
Canterbury 117	Ipswich.........................119	Newquay..........................3	Swansea 122
Cardiff.........................117	Kingston upon Hull......119	Norwich........................120	Swindon 122
Chester 117	Leeds 119	Nottingham 120	Wolverhampton 122
Coventry......................117	Leicester......................119	Oxford 120	Worcester.....................122
Derby 117	Lincoln.........................119	Peterborough 121	York..............................122

Index to place names	**123–144**
County, administrative area map	123
Place name index	124–144
Distances and journey times	**inside back cover**

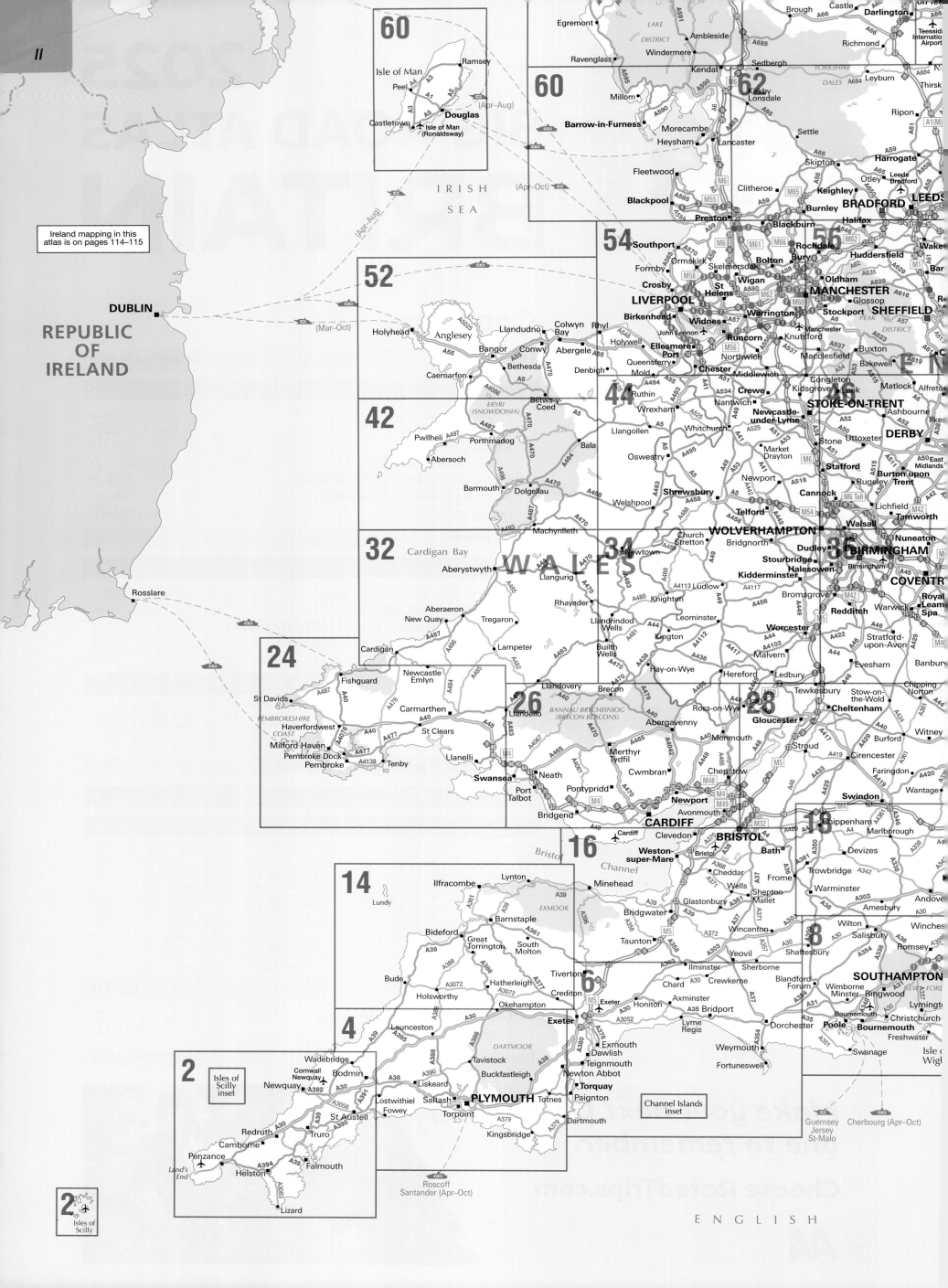

EMERGENCY DIVERSION ROUTES

In an emergency it may be necessary to close a section of motorway or other main road to traffic, so a temporary sign may advise drivers to follow a diversion route. To help drivers navigate the route, black symbols on yellow patches may be permanently displayed on existing direction signs, including motorway signs. Symbols may also be used on separate signs with yellow backgrounds.

FERRY INFORMATION

Information on ferry routes and operators can be found on pages XIV–XVI.

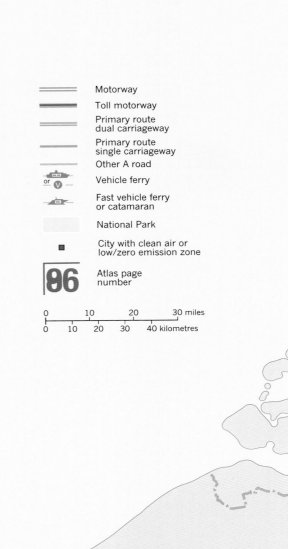

Motorway	
Toll motorway	
Primary route dual carriageway	
Primary route single carriageway	
Other A road	
Vehicle ferry	
Fast vehicle ferry or catamaran	
National Park	
City with clean air or low/zero emission zone	
96 Atlas page number	

0   10   20   30 miles
0   10   20   30   40 kilometres

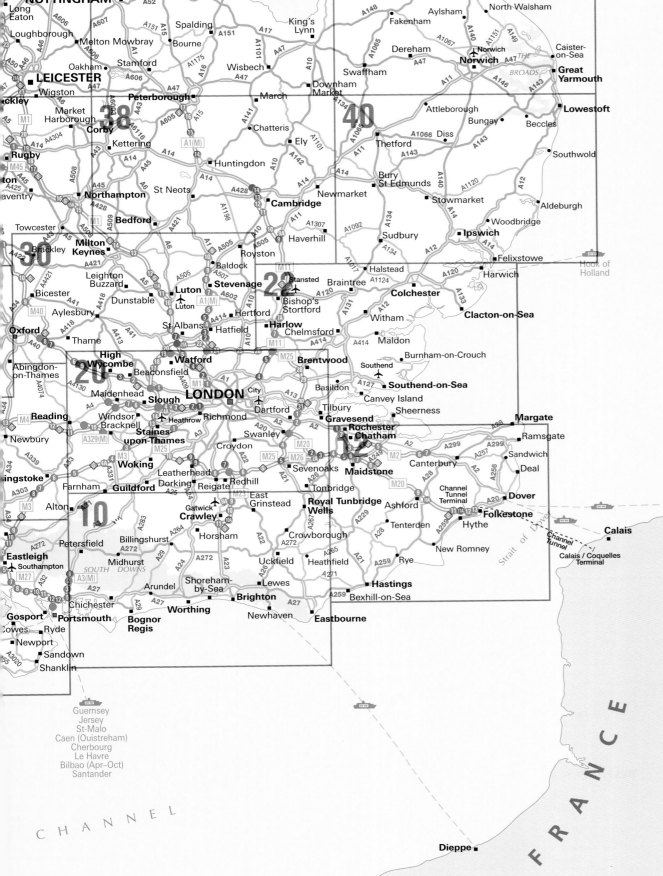

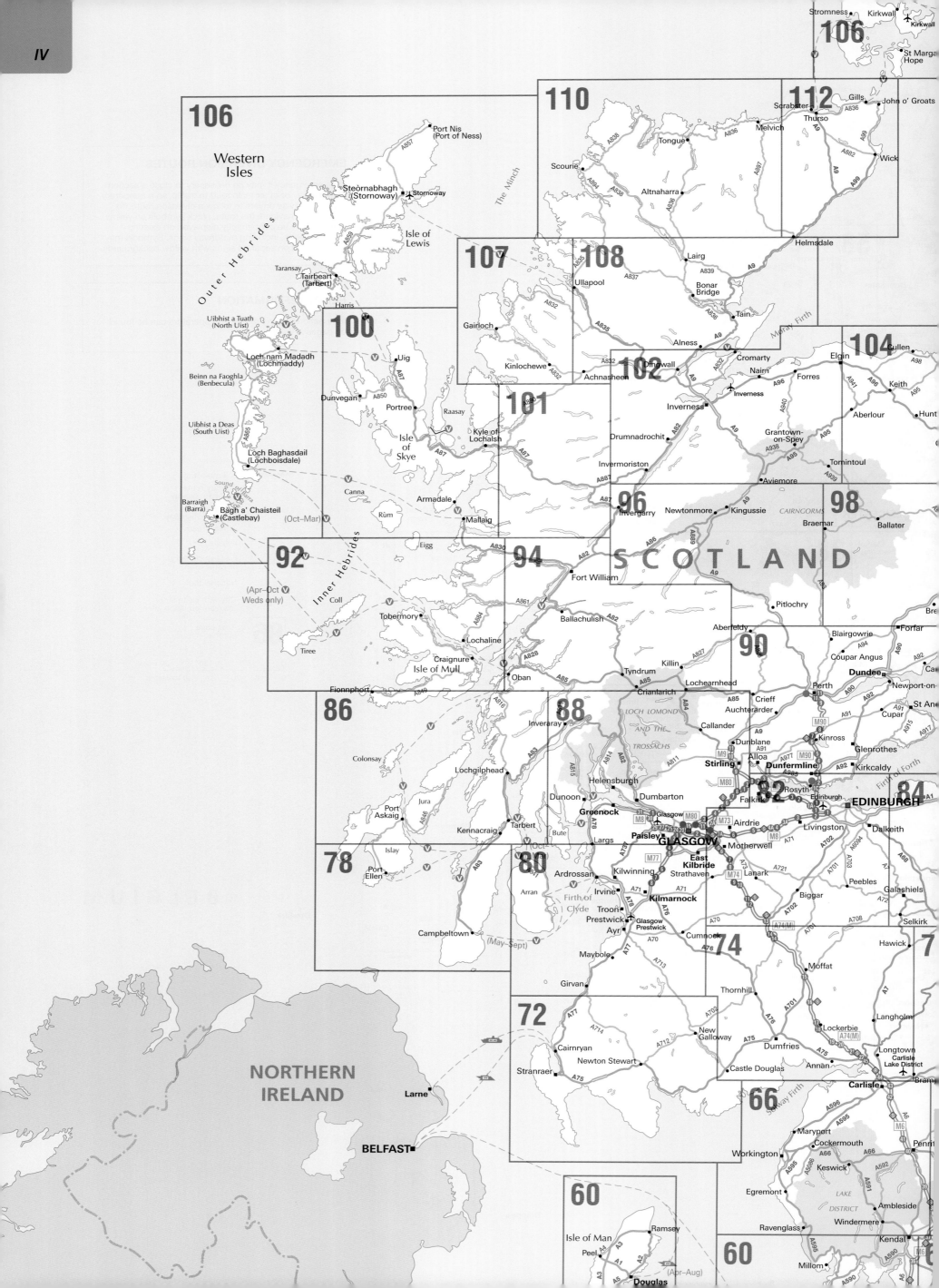

106

Western
Isles

110

112
106

107

108

100

104

102

101

96

98

SCOTLAND

92

94

90

88

86

84

82

80

78

74

7

72

66

NORTHERN
IRELAND

60

60

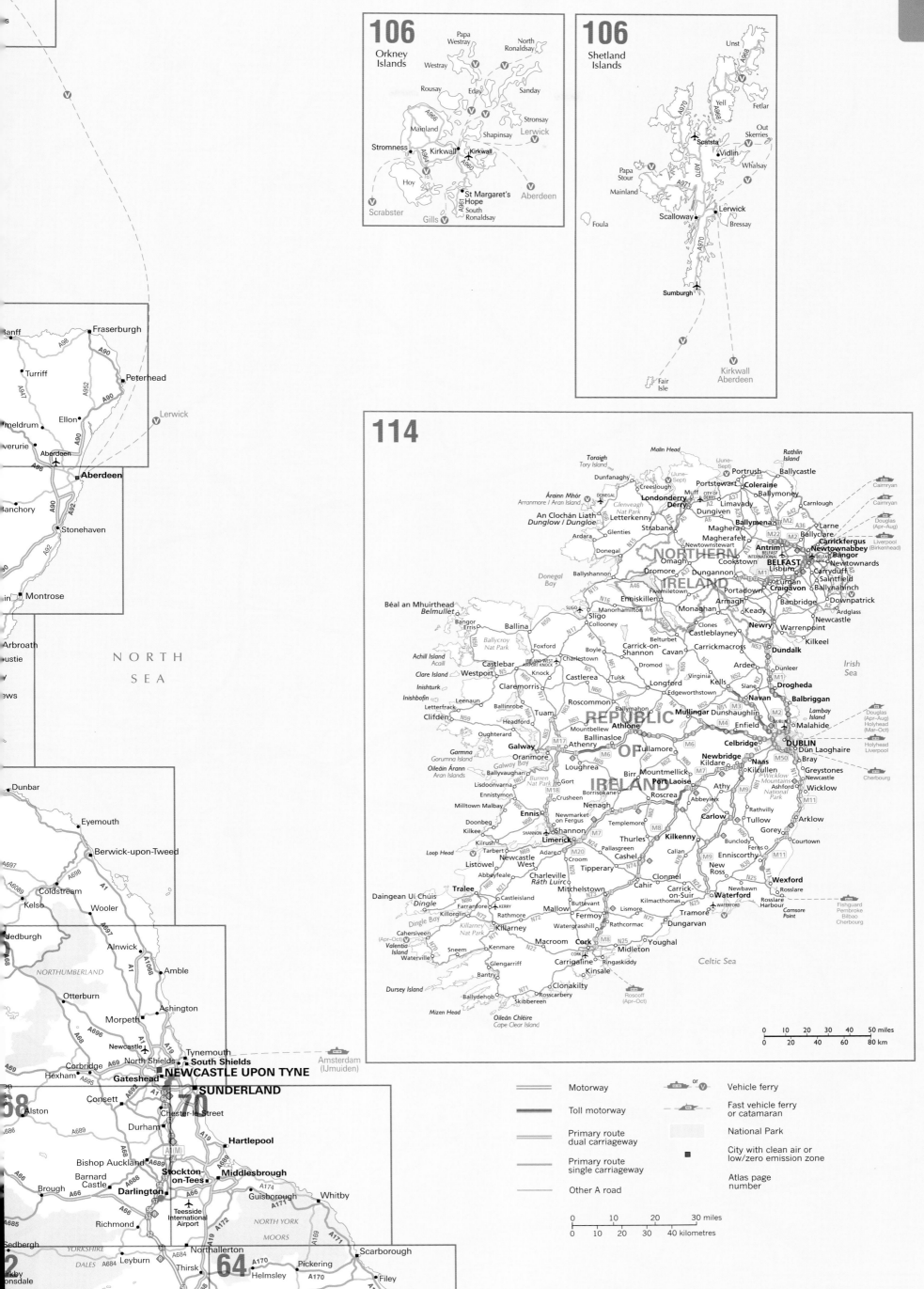

106 Orkney Islands

106 Shetland Islands

114

Motorway
Toll motorway
Primary route dual carriageway
Primary route single carriageway
Other A road

Vehicle ferry
Fast vehicle ferry or catamaran
National Park
City with clean air or low/zero emission zone
Atlas page number

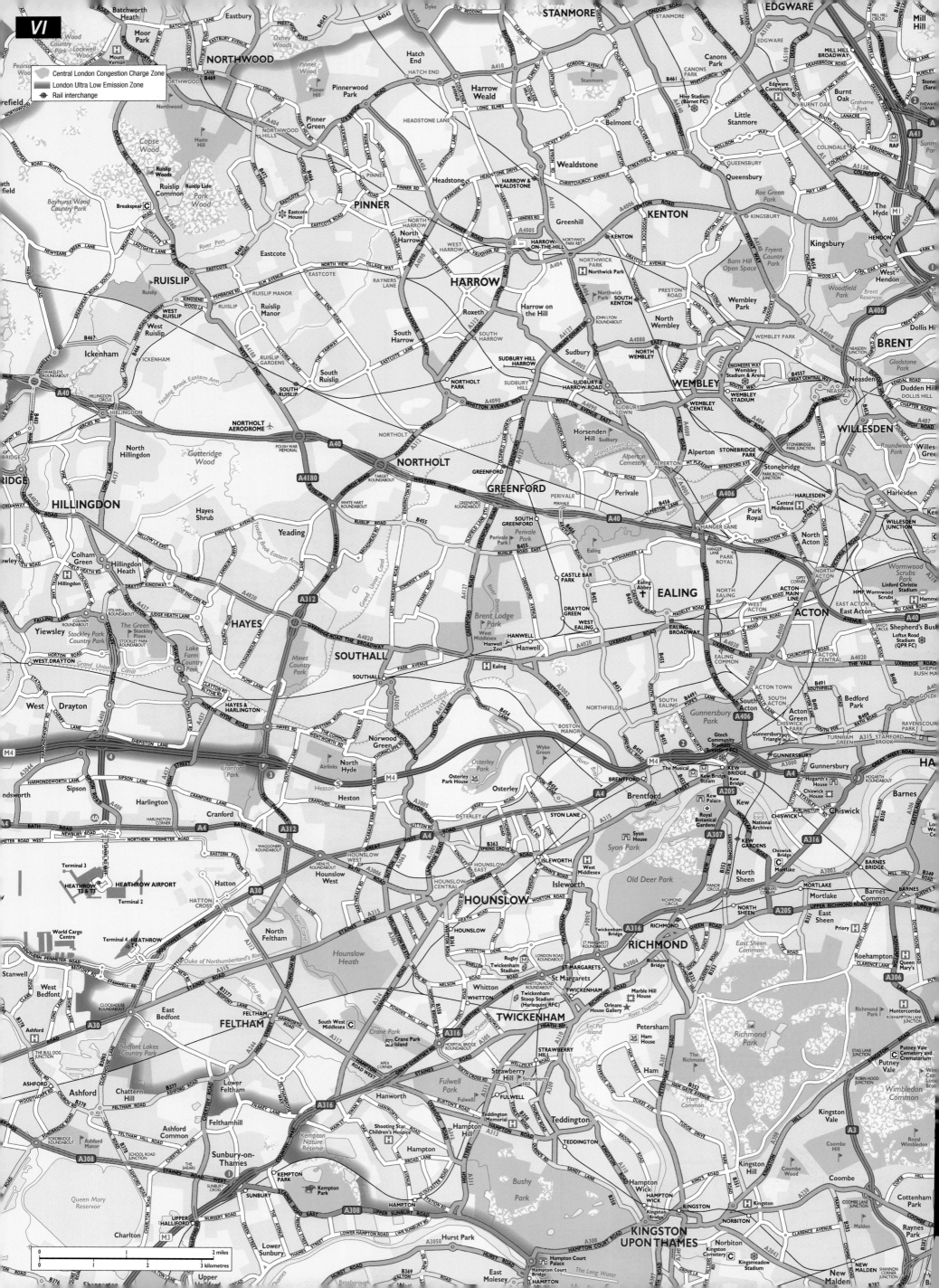

Restricted junctions

Motorway and primary route junctions which have access or exit restrictions are shown on the map pages thus:

M1 London - Leeds

Junction	Northbound	Southbound
2	Access only from A1 *(northbound)*	Exit only to A1 *(southbound)*
4	Access only from A41 *(northbound)*	Exit only to A41 *(southbound)*
6A	Access only from M25 (no link from A405)	Exit only to M25 (no link from A405)
7	Access only from A414	Exit only to A414
17	Exit only to M45	Access only from M45
19	Exit only to M6 *(northbound)*	Exit only to A14 *(southbound)*
21A	Exit only, no access	Access only, no exit
24A	Access only, no exit	Access only from A50 *(eastbound)*
35A	Exit only, no access	Access only, no exit
43	Exit only to M621	Access only from M621
48	Exit only to A1(M) *(northbound)*	Access only from A1(M) *(southbound)*

M2 Rochester - Faversham

Junction	Westbound	Eastbound
1	No exit to A2 *(eastbound)*	No access from A2 *(westbound)*

M3 Sunbury - Southampton

Junction	Northeastbound	Southwestbound
8	Access only from A303, no exit	Exit only to A303, no access
10	Exit only, no access	Access only, no exit
14	Access from M27 only, no exit	No access to M27 *(westbound)*

M4 London - South Wales

Junction	Westbound	Eastbound
1	Access only from A4 *(westbound)*	Exit only to A4 *(eastbound)*
2	Access only from A4 *(westbound)*	Access only from A4 *(eastbound)*
21	Exit only to M48	Access only from M48
23	Access only from M48	Exit only to M48
25	Exit only, no access	Access only, no exit
25A	Exit only, no access	Access only, no exit
29	Exit only to A48(M)	Access only from A48(M)
38	Exit only, no access	No restriction
39	Access only, no exit	No access or exit
42	Exit only to A483	Access only from A483

M5 Birmingham - Exeter

Junction	Northeastbound	Southwestbound
10	Access only, no exit	Exit only, no access
11A	Access only from A417 *(westbound)*	Exit only to A417 *(eastbound)*
18A	Exit only to M49	Access only from M49
18	Exit only, no access	Access only, no exit

M6 Toll Motorway

Junction	Northwestbound	Southeastbound
T1	Access only, no exit	No access or exit
T2	No access or exit	Exit only, no access
T5	Access only, no exit	Exit only to A5148 *(northbound)*, no access
T7	Exit only, no access	Access only, no exit
T8	Exit only, no access	Access only, no exit

M6 Rugby - Carlisle

Junction	Northbound	Southbound
3A	Exit only to M6 Toll	Access only from M6 Toll
4	Exit only to M42 *(southbound)* & A446	Exit only to A446
4A	Access only from M42 *(southbound)*	Exit only to M42
5	Exit only, no access	Access only, no exit
10A	Exit only to M54	Access only from M54
11A	Access only from M6 Toll	Exit only to M6 Toll
with M56 (jct 20A)	No restriction	Access only from M56 *(eastbound)*
20	Exit only to M56 *(westbound)*	Access only from M56 *(eastbound)*
24	Access only, no exit	Exit only, no access
25	Exit only, no access	Access only, no exit
30	Access only from M61	Exit only to M61
31A	Exit only, no access	Access only, no exit
45	Exit only, no access	Access only, no exit

M8 Edinburgh - Bishopton

Junction	Westbound	Eastbound
6	Exit only, no access	Access only, no exit
6A	Access only, no exit	Exit only, no access
7	Access only, no exit	Exit only, no access
7A	Exit only, no access	Access only from A725 *(northbound)*, no exit
8	No access from M73 *(southbound)* or from A8 *(eastbound)* & A89	No exit to M73 *(northbound)* or to A8 *(westbound)* & A89
9	Access only, no exit	Exit only, no access
13	Access only from M80 *(southbound)*	Exit only to M80 *(northbound)*
14	Access only, no exit	Exit only, no access
16	Exit only to A804	Access only from A879
17	Exit only to A82	No restriction
18	Access only from A82 *(eastbound)*	Exit only to A814
19	No access from A814 *(westbound)*	Exit only to A814 *(westbound)*
20	Exit only, no access	Access only, no exit
21	Access only, no exit	Exit only to A8
22	Exit only to M77 *(southbound)*	Access only from M77 *(northbound)*
23	Exit only to B768	Access only from B768
25	No access or exit from or to A8	No access or exit from or to A8
25A	Exit only, no access	Access only, no exit
28	Exit only, no access	Access only, no exit
28A	Exit only to A737	Access only from A737
29A	Exit only to A8	Access only, no exit

M9 Edinburgh - Dunblane

Junction	Northwestbound	Southeastbound
2	Access only, no exit	Exit only, no access
3	Exit only, no access	Access only, no exit
6	Access only, no exit	Exit only to A905
8	Exit only to M876 *(southwestbound)*	Access only from M876 *(northeastbound)*

M11 London - Cambridge

Junction	Northbound	Southbound
4	Access only from A406 *(eastbound)*	Exit only to A406
5	Exit only, no access	Access only, no exit
8A	Exit only, no access	No direct access, use jct 8
9	Exit only to A11	Access only from A11
13	Exit only, no access	Access only, no exit
14	Exit only, no access	Access only, no exit

M20 Swanley - Folkestone

Junction	Northwestbound	Southeastbound
2	Staggered junction; follow signs - access only	Staggered junction; follow signs - exit only
3	Exit only to M26 *(westbound)*	Access only from M26 *(eastbound)*
5	Access only from A20	For access follow signs - exit only to A20
6	No restriction	For exit follow signs
10	Access only, no exit	Exit only, no access
11A	Access only, no exit	Exit only, no access

M23 Hooley - Crawley

Junction	Northbound	Southbound
7	Exit only to A23 *(northbound)*	Access only from A23 *(southbound)*
10A	Access only, no exit	Exit only, no access

M25 London Orbital

Junction	Clockwise	Anticlockwise
1B	No direct access, use slip road to jct 2 Exit only	Access only, no exit
5	No exit to M26 *(eastbound)*	No access from M26
19	Exit only, no access	Access only, no exit
21	Access only from M1 *(southbound)* Exit only to M1 *(northbound)*	Access only from M1 *(southbound)* Exit only to M1 *(northbound)*
31	No exit (use slip road via jct 30), access only	No access (use slip road via jct 30), exit only

M26 Sevenoaks - Wrotham

Junction	Westbound	Eastbound
with M25 (jct 5)	Exit only to clockwise M25 *(westbound)*	Access only from anticlockwise M25 *(eastbound)*
with M20 (jct 3)	Access only from M20 *(northwestbound)*	Exit only to M20 *(southeastbound)*

M27 Cadnam - Portsmouth

Junction	Westbound	Eastbound
4	Staggered junction; follow signs - access only from M3 *(southbound)*. Exit only to M3 *(northbound)*	Staggered junction; follow signs - access only from M3 *(southbound)*. Exit only to M3 *(northbound)*
10	Exit only, no access	Access only, no exit
12	Staggered junction; follow signs - exit only to M275 *(southbound)*	Staggered junction; follow signs - access only from M275 *(northbound)*

M40 London - Birmingham

Junction	Northwestbound	Southeastbound
3	Exit only, no access	Access only, no exit
7	Exit only, no access	Access only, no exit
8	Exit only to M40/A40	Access only from M40/A40
13	Exit only, no access	Access only, no exit
14	Access only, no exit	Exit only, no access
16	Access only, no exit	Exit only, no access

M42 Bromsgrove - Measham

Junction	Northeastbound	Southwestbound
1	Access only, no exit	Exit only, no access
7	Exit only to M6 *(northwestbound)*	Access only from M6 *(northwestbound)*
7A	Exit only to M6 *(southeastbound)*	No access or exit
8	Access only from M6 *(southeastbound)*	Exit only to M6 *(northwestbound)*

M45 Coventry - M1

Junction	Westbound	Eastbound
Dunchurch (unnumbered)	Access only from A45	Exit only, no access
with M1 (jct 17)	Access only from M1 *(northbound)*	Exit only to M1 *(southbound)*

M48 Chepstow

Junction	Westbound	Eastbound
21	Access only from M4 *(westbound)*	Exit only to M4 *(eastbound)*
23	No exit to M4 *(eastbound)*	No access from M4 *(westbound)*

M53 Mersey Tunnel - Chester

Junction	Northbound	Southbound
11	Access only from M56 *(westbound)* Exit only to M56 *(eastbound)*	Access only from M56 *(westbound)* Exit only to M56 *(eastbound)*

M54 Telford - Birmingham

Junction	Westbound	Eastbound
with M6 (jct 10A)	Access only from M6 *(northbound)*	Exit only to M6 *(southbound)*

M56 Chester - Manchester

Junction	Westbound	Eastbound
1	Access only from M60 *(westbound)*	Exit only to M60 *(eastbound)* & A34 *(northbound)*
2	Exit only, no access	Access only, no exit
3	Access only, no exit	Exit only, no access
4	Exit only, no access	Access only, no exit
7	Exit only, no access	No restriction
8	Access only, no exit	No access or exit
9	No exit to M6 *(southbound)*	No access from M6 *(northbound)*
15	Exit only to M53	Access only from M53
16	No access or exit	No restriction

M57 Liverpool Outer Ring Road

Junction	Northwestbound	Southeastbound
3	Access only, no exit	Exit only, no access
5	Access only from A580 *(westbound)*	Exit only, no access

M60 Manchester Orbital

Junction	Clockwise	Anticlockwise
2	Access only, no exit	Exit only, no access
3	No access from M56	Access only from A34 *(northbound)*
4	Access only from A34 *(northbound)*. Exit only to M56	Access only from M56 *(eastbound)*. Exit only to A34 *(southbound)*
5	Access and exit only from and to A5103 *(northbound)*	Access and exit only from and to A5103 *(southbound)*
7	No direct access, use slip road to jct 8. Exit only to A56	Access only from A56. No exit, use jct 8
14	Access from A580 *(eastbound)*	Exit only to A580 *(westbound)*
16	Access only, no exit	Exit only, no access
20	Exit only, no access	Access only, no exit
22	No restriction	Exit only, no access
25	Exit only, no access	No restriction
26	No restriction	Exit only, no access
27	Access only, no exit	Exit only, no access

M61 Manchester - Preston

Junction	Northwestbound	Southeastbound
3	No access or exit	Exit only, no access
with M6 (jct 30)	Exit only to M6 *(northbound)*	Access only from M6 *(southbound)*

M62 Liverpool - Kingston upon Hull

Junction	Westbound	Eastbound
23	Access only, no exit	Exit only, no access
32A	No access to A1(M) *(southbound)*	No restriction

M65 Preston - Colne

Junction	Northeastbound	Southwestbound
9	Exit only, no access	Access only, no exit
11	Access only, no exit	Exit only, no access

M66 Bury

Junction	Northbound	Southbound
with A56	Exit only to A56 *(northbound)*	Access only from A56 *(southbound)*
1	Exit only, no access	Access only, no exit

M67 Hyde Bypass

Junction	Westbound	Eastbound
1A	Access only, no exit	Exit only, no access
2	Exit only, no access	Access only, no exit

M69 Coventry - Leicester

Junction	Northbound	Southbound
2	Access only, no exit	Exit only, no access

M73 East of Glasgow

Junction	Northbound	Southbound
1	No exit to A74 & A721	No exit to A74 & A721
2	No access from or exit to A89. No access from *(eastbound)*	No access from or exit to A89. No exit to M8 *(westbound)*

M74 Glasgow - Abington

Junction	Northbound	Southbound
3	Exit only, no access	Access only, no exit
3A	Access only, no exit	Exit only, no access
4	No access from A74 & A721	Access only, no exit to A74 & A721
7	Access only, no exit	Exit only, no access
9	No access or exit	Exit only, no access
10	No restriction	Access only, no exit
11	Access only, no exit	Exit only, no access
12	Exit only, no access	Access only, no exit

M77 Glasgow - Kilmarnock

Junction	Northbound	Southbound
with M8 (jct 22)	No exit to M8 *(westbound)*	No access from M8 *(eastbound)*
4	Access only, no exit	Exit only, no access
6	Access only, no exit	Exit only, no access
7	Access only, no exit	No restriction
8	Exit only, no access	Exit only, no access

M80 Glasgow - Stirling

Junction	Northbound	Southbound
4A	Exit only, no access	Access only, no exit
6A	Access only, no exit	Exit only, no access
8	Exit only to M876 *(northeastbound)*	Access only from M876 *(southwestbound)*

M90 Edinburgh - Perth

Junction	Northbound	Southbound
1	No exit, access only	Exit only to A90 *(eastbound)*
2A	Exit only to A92 *(eastbound)*	Access only from A92 *(westbound)*
7	Access only, no exit	Exit only, no access
8	Exit only, no access	Access only, no exit
10	No access from A912. No exit to A912 *(southbound)*	No access from A912 *(northbound)* No exit to A912

M180 Doncaster - Grimsby

Junction	Westbound	Eastbound
1	Access only, no exit	Exit only, no access

M606 Bradford Spur

Junction	Northbound	Southbound
2	Exit only, no access	No restriction

M621 Leeds - M1

Junction	Clockwise	Anticlockwise
2A	Access only, no exit	Exit only, no access
4	No exit or access	No restriction
5	Access only, no exit	Exit only, no access
6	Exit only, no access	Access only, no exit
with M1 (jct 43)	Exit only to M1 *(southbound)*	Access only from M1 *(northbound)*

M876 Bonnybridge - Kincardine Bridge

Junction	Northeastbound	Southwestbound
with M80 (jct 5)	Access only from M80 *(northeastbound)*	Exit only to M80 *(southwestbound)*
with M9 (jct 8)	Exit only to M9 *(eastbound)*	Access only from M9 *(westbound)*

A1(M) South Mimms - Baldock

Junction	Northbound	Southbound
2	Exit only, no access	Access only, no exit
3	No restriction	Exit only, no access
5	Access only, no exit	No access or exit

A1(M) Pontefract - Bedale

Junction	Northbound	Southbound
40	Exit only to A162 (M62), No access	Access only, no exit
41	No access to M62 *(eastbound)*	No restriction
43	Access only from M1 *(northbound)*	Exit only to M1 *(southbound)*

A1(M) Scotch Corner - Newcastle upon Tyne

Junction	Northbound	Southbound
57	Exit only to A66(M) *(eastbound)*	Access only from A66(M) *(westbound)*
65	No access Exit only to A194(M) & A1 *(northbound)*	No exit Access only from A194(M) & A1 *(southbound)*

A3(M) Horndean - Havant

Junction	Northbound	Southbound
1	Access only from A3	Exit only to A3
4	Exit only, no access	Access only, no exit

A38(M) Birmingham, Victoria Road (Park Circus)

Junction	Northbound	Southbound
with B4132	No exit	No access

A48(M) Cardiff Spur

Junction	Westbound	Eastbound
29	Access only from M4 *(westbound)*	Exit only to M4 *(eastbound)*
29A	Exit only to A48 *(westbound)*	Access only from A48 *(eastbound)*

A57(M) Manchester, Brook Street (A34)

Junction	Westbound	Eastbound
with A34	No exit	No access

A58(M) Leeds, Park Lane and Westgate

Junction	Northbound	Southbound
with A58	No restriction	No access

A64(M) Leeds, Clay Pit Lane (A58)

Junction	Westbound	Eastbound
with A58	No exit (to Clay Pit Lane)	No access (from Clay Pit Lane)

A66(M) Darlington Spur

Junction	Westbound	Eastbound
with A1(M) (jct 57)	Exit only to A1(M) *(southbound)*	Access only from A1(M) *(northbound)*

A74(M) Gretna - Abington

Junction	Northbound	Southbound
18	Exit only, no access	Access only, no exit

A194(M) Gateshead

Junction	Northbound	Southbound
with A1(M) (jct 65)	Access only from A1(M) *(northbound)*	Exit only to A1(M) *(southbound)*

A12 M25 - Ipswich

Junction	Northeastbound	Southwestbound
13	Access only, no exit	No restriction
14	Exit only, no access	Access only, no exit
20A	Exit only, no access	Access only, no exit
20B	Access only, no exit	Exit only, no access
21	No restriction	Access only, no exit
23	Exit only, no access	Access only, no exit
24	Access only, no exit	Exit only, no access
27	Exit only, no access	Access only, no exit
Dedham & Stratford St Mary (unnumbered)	Exit only	Access only

A14 M1 - Felixstowe

Junction	Westbound	Eastbound
with M1/M6 (jct19)	Exit only to M6 and M1 *(northbound)*	Access only from M6 and M1 *(southbound)*
4	Exit only, no access	Access only, no exit
21	Access only, no exit	Exit only, no access
22	Exit only, no access	Access only from A1 *(southbound)*
23	Access only, no exit	Exit only, no access
31	No restriction	Access only, no exit
34	Access only, no exit	Exit only, no access
36	Exit only to A11, access only from A1303	Access only from A11
38	Access only from A11	Exit only to A11
39	Exit only, no access	Access only, no exit
61	Access only, no exit	Exit only, no access

A55 Holyhead - Chester

Junction	Westbound	Eastbound
8A	Exit only, no access	Access only, no exit
23A	Access only, no exit	Exit only, no access
24A	Exit only, no access	No access or exit
27A	No restriction	No access or exit
33A	Exit only, no access	No access or exit
33B	Exit only, no access	Access only, no exit
36A	Exit only to A5104	Access only from A5104
39	Access only, no exit	Exit only, no access

Since Britain's first motorway (the Preston Bypass) opened in 1958, motorways have changed significantly. A vast increase in car journeys over the last 65 years has meant that motorways quickly filled to capacity. To combat this, the recent development of smart motorways uses technology to monitor and actively manage traffic flow and congestion.

How they work

Smart motorways utilise various active traffic management methods, monitored through a regional traffic control centre:

- Traffic flow is monitored using CCTV
- Speed limits are changed to smooth traffic flow and reduce stop-start driving
- Capacity of the motorway can be increased by either temporarily or permanently opening the hard shoulder to traffic
- Warning signs and messages alert drivers to hazards and traffic jams ahead
- Lanes can be closed in the case of an accident or emergency by displaying a red X sign

- Emergency refuge areas are located regularly along the motorway where there is no hard shoulder available

The map shows the main motorway network with the three different types of smart motorway in operation. Following a government review in 2023, no new smart motorways will be built.

— **Controlled motorway**
Variable speed limits without hard shoulder (the hard shoulder is used in emergencies only)

— **Dynamic hard shoulder**
Variable speed limits with part-time hard shoulder (the hard shoulder is open to traffic at busy times when signs permit)

— **All lane running**
Variable speed limits with hard shoulder as permanent running lane (there is no hard shoulder); this is standard for all new motorway schemes since 2013

— **Standard motorway**

Quick tips

- Never drive in a lane closed by a red X

- Keep to the speed limit shown on the gantries
- A solid white line indicates the hard shoulder – do not drive in it unless directed or in the case of an emergency
- A broken white line indicates a normal running lane
- Exit the smart motorway where possible if your vehicle is in difficulty. In an emergency, move onto the hard shoulder where there is one, or the nearest emergency refuge area
- Put on your hazard lights if you break down

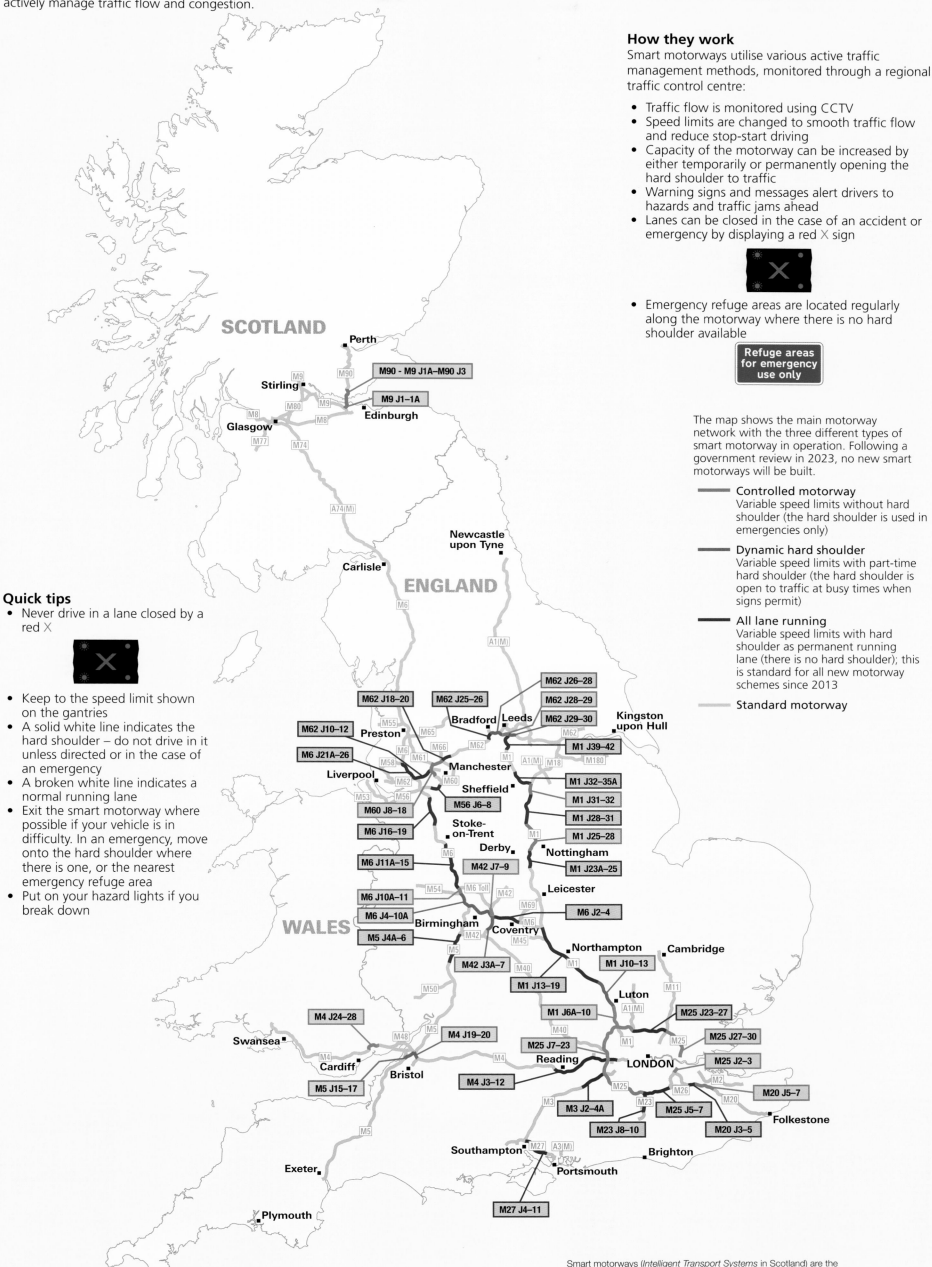

Smart motorways (*Intelligent Transport Systems* in Scotland) are the responsibility of National Highways, Transport Scotland and Transport for Wales

Caravan and camping sites in Britain

These pages list the top 300 AA-inspected Caravan and Camping (C & C) sites in the Pennant rating scheme. **Five Pennant Premier sites are shown in green,** Four Pennant sites are shown in blue.

Listings include addresses, telephone numbers and websites together with page and grid references to locate the sites in the atlas. The total number of pitches is also included for each site, together with the type of pitch available.
The following abbreviations are used: **C = Caravan CV = Campervan T = Tent**

To discover more about the AA-rated caravan and camping sites not included on these pages please visit **RatedTrips.com**

ENGLAND

Alders Caravan Park
Home Farm, Alne, York
YO61 1RY
Tel: 01347 838722 64 C6
alderscaravanpark.co.uk
Total Pitches: 87

Andrewshayes Holiday Park
Dalwood, Axminster
EX13 7DY
Tel: 01404 831225 6 H5
andrewshayes.co.uk
Total Pitches: 150

Atlantic Bays Holiday Park
Padstow, Cornwall
PL28 8PY
Tel: 01841 520855 3 M2
atlanticbaysholidaypark.co.uk
Total Pitches: 70

Ayr Holiday Park
St Ives, Cornwall
TR26 1EJ
Tel: 01736 795855 2 E8
ayrholidaypark.co.uk
Total Pitches: 100

Back of Beyond Touring Park
234 Ringwood Road, St Leonards, Dorset
BH24 2SB
Tel: 01202 876968 8 G8
backofbeyondtouringpark.co.uk
Total Pitches: 80

Bagwell Farm Touring Park
Knights in the Bottom, Chickerell, Weymouth
DT3 4EA
Tel: 01305 782575 7 R8
bagwellfarm.co.uk
Total Pitches: 320

Bardsea Leisure Park
Priory Road, Ulverston
LA12 9QE
Tel: 01229 584712 61 P4
bardsealeisure.co.uk
Total Pitches: 83

Bath Chew Valley Caravan Park
Ham Lane, Bishop Sutton
BS39 5TZ
Tel: 01275 332127 17 Q5
bathchewvalley.co.uk
Total Pitches: 45

Bay View Farm C & C Park
Croyde, Devon
EX33 1PN
Tel: 01271 890501 14 K5
bayviewfarm.co.uk
Total Pitches: 70

Bay View Holiday Park
Bolton le Sands, Carnforth
LA5 9TN
Tel: 01524 732854 61 T6
holgates.co.uk
Total Pitches: 100

Beacon Cottage Farm Touring Park
Beacon Drive, St Agnes
TR5 0NU
Tel: 01872 552347 2 J6
beaconcottagefarmholidays.co.uk
Total Pitches: 60

Beaconsfield Holiday Park
Battlefield, Shrewsbury
SY4 4AA
Tel: 01939 210370 45 M10
beaconsfieldholidaypark.co.uk
Total Pitches: 60

Beech Croft Farm C & C Park
Beech Croft, Blackwell in the Peak, Buxton
SK17 9TQ
Tel: 01298 85330 56 H12
beechcroftfarm.co.uk
Total Pitches: 30

Bellingham C & C Club Site
Brown Rigg, Bellingham
NE48 2JY
Tel: 01434 220175 76 G9
campingandcaravanningclub.co.uk/bellingham
Total Pitches: 64

Beverley Park C & C Park
Goodrington Road, Paignton
TQ4 7JE
Tel: 01803 843887 6 A13
beverley-holidays.co.uk
Total Pitches: 125

Birchwood Tourist Park
Bere Road, Coldharbour, Wareham
BH20 7PA
Tel: 01929 554763 8 C10
birchwoodtouristpark.co.uk
Total Pitches: 175

Blue Rose Caravan & Country Park
Star Carr Lane, Brandesburton
YO25 8RU
Tel: 01964 543366 65 Q10
bluerosepark.com
Total Pitches: 58

Briarfields Motel & Touring Park
Gloucester Road, Cheltenham
GL51 0SX
Tel: 01242 235324 28 H3
briarfields.net
Total Pitches: 72

Bridge House Marina & Caravan Park
Nateby Crossing Lane, Nateby, Garstang
PR3 0JJ
Tel: 01995 603207 61 T10
bridgehousemarina.co.uk
Total Pitches: 50

Broadhembury C & C Park
Steeds Lane, Kingsnorth, Ashford
TN26 1NQ
Tel: 01233 620859 12 K8
broadhembury.co.uk
Total Pitches: 100

Brook Lodge Farm C & C Park
Cowslip Green, Redhill, Bristol, Somerset
BS40 5RB
Tel: 01934 862311 17 N4
brooklodgefarm.com
Total Pitches: 29

Burns Farm Caravan, Camping & Glamping
St Johns in the Vale, Keswick
CA12 4RR
Tel: 017687 79225 67 M8
burns-farm.co.uk
Total Pitches: 32

Burrowhayes Farm C & C Site & Riding Stables
West Luccombe, Porlock, Minehead
TA24 8HT
Tel: 01643 862463 15 U3
burrowhayes.co.uk
Total Pitches: 120

Burton Constable Holiday Park & Arboretum
Old Lodges, Sproatley, Kingston upon Hull
HU11 4LJ
Tel: 01964 562508 65 R12
burtonconstableholidaypark.co.uk
Total Pitches: 105

Caistor Lakes
99a Brigg Road, Caistor
LN7 6RX
Tel: 01472 859626 58 K6
caistorlakes.co.uk
Total Pitches: 28

Cakes & Ale
Abbey Lane, Theberton, Leiston
IP16 4TE
Tel: 01728 831655 41 R8
cakesandale.co.uk
Total Pitches: 55

Camping Caradon Touring Park
Trelawne, Looe
PL13 2NA
Tel: 01503 272388 4 G10
campingcaradon.co.uk
Total Pitches: 75

Capesthorne Hall
Congleton Road, Siddington, Macclesfield
SK11 9JY
Tel: 01625 861221 55 T12
capesthorne.com/caravan-park
Total Pitches: 50

Carlyon Bay C & C Park
Bethesda, Cypress Avenue, Carlyon Bay
PL25 3RE
Tel: 01726 812735 3 R6
carlyonbay.net
Total Pitches: 180

Carnevas Holiday Park
Carnevas Farm, St Merryn, Cornwall
PL28 8PN
Tel: 01841 520230 3 M2
carnevasholidaypark.com
Total Pitches: 195

Cartref C & C
Cartref, Ford Heath, Shrewsbury, Shropshire
SY5 9GD
Tel: 01743 821688 44 K11
cartrefcaravansite.co.uk
Total Pitches: 44

Carvynick Holiday Park
Summercourt, Newquay
TR8 5AF
Tel: 01872 510716 3 M5
carvynick.co.uk
Total Pitches: 47

Castlerigg Hall C & C Park
Castlerigg Hall, Keswick
CA12 4TE
Tel: 017687 74499 67 L8
castlerigg.co.uk
Total Pitches: 68

Cheddar Mendip Heights C & C Club Site
Townsend, Priddy, Wells
BA5 3BP
Tel: 01749 870241 17 P6
campingandcaravanningclub.co.uk/cheddar
Total Pitches: 90

Clippesby Hall
Hall Lane, Clippesby, Great Yarmouth
NR29 3BL
Tel: 01493 367800 51 R11
clippesbyhall.com
Total Pitches: 120

Cofton Holidays
Starcross, Dawlish
EX6 8RP
Tel: 01626 890111 6 C8
coftonholidays.co.uk
Total Pitches: 450

Concierge Camping
Ratham Estate, Ratham Lane, West Ashling, Chichester
PO18 8DL
Tel: 01243 573118 10 C9
conciergecamping.co.uk
Total Pitches: 27

Coombe Touring Park
Race Plain, Netherhampton, Salisbury
SP2 8PN
Tel: 01722 328451 8 F3
coombecaravanpark.co.uk
Total Pitches: 50

Cornish Farm Touring Park
Shoreditch, Taunton
TA3 7BS
Tel: 01823 327746 16 H12
cornishfarm.com
Total Pitches: 48

Cosawes Park
Perranarworthal, Truro
TR3 7QS
Tel: 01872 863724 2 K9
cosawes.co.uk
Total Pitches: 59

Cote Ghyll C & C Park
Osmotherley, Northallerton
DL6 3AH
Tel: 01609 883425 70 G13
coteghyll.com
Total Pitches: 77

Country View Holiday Park
Sand Road, Sand Bay, Weston-super-Mare
BS22 9UJ
Tel: 01934 627595 16 K4
cvhp.co.uk
Total Pitches: 190

Crealy Theme Park & Resort
Sidmouth Road, Clyst St Mary, Exeter
EX5 1DR
Tel: 01395 234888 6 D6
crealy.co.uk
Total Pitches: 120

Crows Nest Caravan Park
Gristhorpe, Filey
YO14 9PS
Tel: 01723 582206 65 P3
crowsnestcaravanpark.com
Total Pitches: 43

Deepdale Camping & Rooms
Deepdale Farm, Burnham Deepdale
PE31 8DD
Tel: 01485 210256 50 D5
deepdalecamping.co.uk
Total Pitches: 80

Dibles Park
Dibles Road, Warsash, Southampton, Hampshire
SO31 9SA
Tel: 01489 575232 9 Q7
diblespark.co.uk
Total Pitches: 11

Easewell Farm Holiday Village
Mortehoe Station Road, Mortehoe, Woolacombe
EX34 7EH
Tel: 01271 872302 15 L3
woolacombe.co.uk
Total Pitches: 328

East Fleet Farm Touring Park
Chickerell, Weymouth
DT3 4DW
Tel: 01305 785768 7 R9
eastfleet.co.uk
Total Pitches: 400

Eastham Hall Holiday Park
Saltcotes Road, Lytham St Annes, Lancashire
FY8 4LS
Tel: 01253 737907 61 R14
easthamhall.co.uk
Total Pitches: 113

Eden Valley Holiday Park
Lanlivery, Nr Lostwithiel
PL30 5BU
Tel: 01208 872277 3 R5
edenvalleyholidaypark.co.uk
Total Pitches: 56

Exe Valley Caravan Site
Mill House, Bridgetown, Dulverton
TA22 9JR
Tel: 01643 851432 16 B10
exevalleycamping.co.uk
Total Pitches: 48

Eye Kettleby Lakes
Eye Kettleby, Melton Mowbray
LE14 2TN
Tel: 01664 565900 47 T10
eyekettlebylakes.com
Total Pitches: 130

Fernwood Caravan Park
Lyneal, Ellesmere, Shropshire
SY12 0QF
Tel: 01948 710221 44 K7
fernwoodpark.co.uk
Total Pitches: 60

Fields End Water Caravan Park & Fishery
Benwick Road, Doddington, March
PE15 0TY
Tel: 01354 740199 39 N2
fieldsendwater.co.uk
Total Pitches: 80

Flaxton Meadows
York Lane, Flaxton, York
YO60 7QZ
Tel: 01904 393943 64 F7
flaxtonmeadows.co.uk
Total Pitches: 35

Flower of May Holiday Park
Lebberston Cliff, Filey, Scarborough
YO11 3NU
Tel: 01723 584311 65 P3
flowerofmay.com
Total Pitches: 300

Forest Glade Holiday Park
Near Kentisbeare, Cullompton, Devon
EX15 2DT
Tel: 01404 841381 6 F3
forest-glade.co.uk
Total Pitches: 80

Freshwater Beach Holiday Park
Burton Bradstock, Bridport
DT6 4PT
Tel: 01308 897317 7 N6
freshwaterbeach.co.uk
Total Pitches: 500

Globe Vale Holiday Park
Radnor, Redruth
TR16 4BH
Tel: 01209 891183 2 J8
globevale.co.uk
Total Pitches: 138

Glororum Caravan Park
Glororum Farm, Bamburgh
NE69 7AW
Tel: 01670 860256 85 T12
northumbrianleisure.co.uk
Total Pitches: 43

Golden Cap Holiday Park
Seatown, Chideock, Bridport
DT6 6JX
Tel: 01308 422139 7 M6
wdlh.co.uk
Total Pitches: 108

Golden Coast Holiday Park
Station Road, Woolacombe
EX34 7HW
Tel: 01271 872302 15 L4
woolacombe.com
Total Pitches: 89

Golden Sands Holiday Park
Quebec Road, Mablethorpe
LN12 1QJ
Tel: 01507 477871 59 S9
haven.com/goldensands
Total Pitches: 172

Golden Square C & C Park
Oswaldkirk, Helmsley
YO62 5YQ
Tel: 01439 788269 64 E4
goldensquarecaravanpark.com
Total Pitches: 129

Golden Valley C & C Park
Coach Road, Ripley, Derbyshire
DE55 4ES
Tel: 01773 513881 47 M3
goldenvalleycaravanpark.co.uk
Total Pitches: 45

Goosewood Holiday Park
Sutton-on-the-Forest, York
YO61 1ET
Tel: 01347 810829 64 D7
flowerofmay.com
Total Pitches: 100

Greenacre Place Touring Caravan Park
Bristol Road, Edithmead, Highbridge
TA9 4HA
Tel: 01278 785227 16 K7
greenacreplace.com
Total Pitches: 10

Green Acres Caravan Park
High Knells, Houghton, Carlisle
CA6 4JW
Tel: 01228 675418 75 T13
caravanpark-cumbria.com
Total Pitches: 35

Greenhill Farm C & C Park
Greenhill Farm, New Road, Landford, Salisbury
SP5 2AZ
Tel: 01794 324117 8 K5
greenhillfarm.co.uk
Total Pitches: 160

Greenhills Holiday Park
Crowhill Lane, Bakewell, Derbyshire
DE45 1PX
Tel: 01629 813052 56 J13
greenhillsholidaypark.co.uk
Total Pitches: 172

Grouse Hill Caravan Park
Flask Bungalow Farm, Fylingdales, Robin Hood's Bay
YO22 4QH
Tel: 01947 880543 71 R12
grousehill.co.uk
Total Pitches: 175

Gunvenna Holiday Park
St Minver, Wadebridge
PL27 6QN
Tel: 01208 862405 4 B5
gunvenna.com
Total Pitches: 75

Haggerston Castle Holiday Park
Beal, Berwick-upon-Tweed
TD15 2PA
Tel: 01289 381333 85 Q10
haven.com/haggerstoncastle
Total Pitches: 140

Hallsdown Farm Touring Park
Arlington, Barnstaple
EX31 4SW
Tel: 01271 850847 15 P4
hallsdownfarm.co.uk
Total Pitches: 30

Harbury Fields
Harbury Fields Farm, Harbury, Nr Leamington Spa
CV33 9JN
Tel: 01926 612457 37 L8
harburyfields.co.uk
Total Pitches: 59

Harford Bridge Holiday Park
Peter Tavy, Tavistock
PL19 9LS
Tel: 01822 810349 5 N5
harfordbridge.co.uk
Total Pitches: 125

Haw Wood Farm Caravan Park
Hinton, Saxmundham
IP17 3QT
Tel: 01502 359550 41 R6
hawwoodfarm.co.uk
Total Pitches: 72

Heathfield Farm Camping
Heathfield Road, Freshwater, Isle of Wight
PO40 9SH
Tel: 01983 407822 9 L11
heathfieldcamping.co.uk
Total Pitches: 81

Heathland Beach Holiday Park
London Road, Kessingland
NR33 7PJ
Tel: 01502 740337 41 T3
heathlandbeach.co.uk
Total Pitches: 63

Heligan C & C Park
Pentewan, St Austell
PL26 6BT
Tel: 01726 842714 3 P7
heligancampsite.com
Total Pitches: 89

Hendra Holiday Park
Newquay
TR8 4NY
Tel: 01637 875778 3 L4
hendra-holidays.com
Total Pitches: 548

Herding Hill Farm Touring & Camping Site
Shield Hill, Haltwhistle, Northumberland
NE49 9NW
Tel: 01434 320175 76 E12
herdinghillfarm.co.uk
Total Pitches: 22

Hidden Valley Park
West Down, Braunton, Ilfracombe, Devon
EX34 8NU
Tel: 01271 813837 15 M4
hiddenvalleypark.com
Total Pitches: 114

Highfield Farm Touring Park
Long Road, Comberton, Cambridge
CB23 7DG
Tel: 01223 262308 39 N9
highfieldfarmtouringpark.co.uk
Total Pitches: 120

Highlands End Holiday Park
Eype, Bridport, Dorset
DT6 6AR
Tel: 01308 422139 7 N6
wdlh.co.uk
Total Pitches: 195

Hillside Caravan Park
Canvas Farm, Moor Road, Knayton, Thirsk
YO7 4BR
Tel: 01845 537349 63 U2
hillsidecaravanpark.co.uk
Total Pitches: 60

Holiday Resort Unity
Coast Road, Brean Sands, Brean
TA8 2RB
Tel: 01278 751235 16 J6
hru.co.uk
Total Pitches: 453

Hollins Farm Holiday Park
Far Arnside, Carnforth
LA5 0SL
Tel: 01524 701767 61 S4
holgates.co.uk
Total Pitches: 12

Homing Park
Church Lane, Seasalter, Whitstable
CT5 4BU
Tel: 01227 771777 13 L3
homingpark.co.uk
Total Pitches: 43

Hutton-le-Hole Caravan Park
Westfield Lodge, Hutton-le-Hole
YO62 6UG
Tel: 01751 417261 64 G2
huttonleholecaravanpark.co.uk
Total Pitches: 42

Hylton Caravan Park
Eden Street, Silloth
CA7 4AY
Tel: 016973 32666 66 H2
stanwix.com
Total Pitches: 90

Island Lodge C & C Site
Stumpy Post Cross, Kingsbridge
TQ7 4BL
Tel: 01548 852956 5 S11
islandlodgesite.co.uk
Total Pitches: 30

Isle of Avalon Touring Caravan Park
Godney Road, Glastonbury
BA6 9AF
Tel: 01458 833618 17 N9
avaloncaravanpark.co.uk
Total Pitches: 120

Jasmine Caravan Park
Cross Lane, Snainton, Scarborough
YO13 9BE
Tel: 01723 859240 65 L3
jasminepark.co.uk
Total Pitches: 68

Kennford International Holiday Park
Kennford, Exeter
EX6 7YN
Tel: 01392 833046 6 B7
kennfordinternational.co.uk
Total Pitches: 22

Killiwerris Touring Park
Penstraze, Chacewater, Truro, Cornwall
TR4 8PF
Tel: 01872 561356 2 K7
killiwerris.co.uk
Total Pitches: 17

King's Lynn C & C Park
New Road, North Runcton, King's Lynn
PE33 0RA
Tel: 01553 840004 49 T10
kl-cc.co.uk
Total Pitches: 150

Knight Stainforth Hall Caravan & Campsite
Stainforth, Settle
BD24 0DP
Tel: 01729 822200 62 G6
knightstainforth.co.uk
Total Pitches: 100

Ladycross Plantation Caravan Park
Egton, Whitby
YO21 1UA
Tel: 01947 895502 71 P11
ladycrossplantation.co.uk
Total Pitches: 130

Lady Heyes Holiday Park
Kingsley Road, Frodsham
WA6 6SU
Tel: 01928 788557 55 M11
ladyheyespark.com
Total Pitches: 65

Lady's Mile Holiday Park
Dawlish, Devon
EX7 0LX
Tel: 01626 863411 6 C9
ladysmile.co.uk
Total Pitches: 570

Lakeland Leisure Park
Moor Lane, Flookburgh
LA11 7LT
Tel: 01539 558556 61 R5
haven.com/lakeland
Total Pitches: 177

Lamb Cottage Caravan Park
Dalefords Lane, Whitegate, Northwich
CW8 2BN
Tel: 01606 882302 55 P13
lambcottage.co.uk
Total Pitches: 45

Langstone Manor C & C Park
Moortown, Tavistock
PL19 9JZ
Tel: 01822 613371 5 N6
langstonemanor.co.uk
Total Pitches: 40

Lanyon Holiday Park
Loscombe Lane, Four Lanes, Redruth
TR16 6LP
Tel: 01209 313474 2 H9
lanyonholidaypark.co.uk
Total Pitches: 25

Lickpenny Caravan Site
Lickpenny Lane, Tansley, Matlock
DE4 5GF
Tel: 01629 583040 46 K2
lickpennycaravanpark.co.uk
Total Pitches: 80

Lime Tree Park
Dukes Drive, Buxton
SK17 9RP
Tel: 01298 22988 56 G12
limetreeparkbuxton.com
Total Pitches: 106

Lincoln Farm Park Oxfordshire
High Street, Standlake
OX29 7RH
Tel: 01865 300239 29 S7
lincolnfarmpark.co.uk
Total Pitches: 90

Littlesea Holiday Park
Lynch Lane, Weymouth
DT4 9DT
Tel: 01305 774414 7 S9
haven.com/littlesea
Total Pitches: 141

Little Trevothan C & C Park
Trevothan, Coverack, Helston, Cornwall
TR12 6SD
Tel: 01326 280260 2 K13
littletrevothan.co.uk
Total Pitches: 80

Long Acres Touring Park
Station Road, Old Leake, Boston
PE22 9RF
Tel: 01205 871555 49 N3
long-acres.co.uk
Total Pitches: 40

Long Hazel Park
High Street, Sparkford, Yeovil, Somerset
BA22 7JH
Tel: 01963 440002 17 R11
longhazelpark.co.uk
Total Pitches: 46

Longnor Wood Holiday Park
Newtown, Longnor, Nr Buxton
SK17 0NG
Tel: 01298 83648 56 G14
longnorwood.co.uk
Total Pitches: 47

Lynmouth Holiday Retreat
Lynton, Devon
EX35 6LD
Tel: 01598 753349 15 R3
channel-view.co.uk
Total Pitches: 76

Manor Farm Holiday Centre
Charmouth, Bridport
DT6 6QL
Tel: 01297 560226 7 L6
manorfarmholidaycentre.co.uk
Total Pitches: 400

Manor Wood Country Caravan Park
Manor Wood, Coddington, Chester
CH3 9EN
Tel: 01829 782990 44 K3
cheshire-caravan-sites.co.uk
Total Pitches: 45

Marsh House Holiday Park
Marsh House Farm, Carnforth, Lancashire
LA5 9JA
Tel: 01524 732854 61 T5
holgates.co.uk/our-parks/marsh-house
Total Pitches: 74

Marton Mere Holiday Village
Mythop Road, Blackpool
FY4 4XN
Tel: 01253 767544 61 Q13
haven.com/martonmere
Total Pitches: 82

Mayfield Park
Cheltenham Road, Cirencester
GL7 7BH
Tel: 01285 831301 28 K6
mayfieldpark.co.uk
Total Pitches: 105

Meadowbank Holidays
Stour Way, Christchurch
BH23 2PQ
Tel: 01202 483597 8 G10
meadowbank-holidays.co.uk
Total Pitches: 41

Mena Farm: Touring, Camping, Glamping
Bodmin, Lanivet
PL30 5HW
Tel: 01208 831845 3 Q4
menafarm.co.uk
Total Pitches: 25

Mill Farm C & C Park
Fiddington, Bridgwater, Somerset
TA5 1JQ
Tel: 01278 732286 16 H8
millfarm.biz
Total Pitches: 275

Mill Park Touring C & C Park
Mill Lane, Berrynarbor, Ilfracombe, Devon
EX34 9SH
Tel: 01271 882647 15 N3
millpark.com
Total Pitches: 125

Minnows Touring Park
Holbrook Lane, Sampford Peverell
EX16 7EN
Tel: 01884 821770 16 D13
minnowstouringpark.co.uk
Total Pitches: 59

Monkey Tree Holiday Park
Hendra Croft, Scotland Road, Newquay
TR8 5QR
Tel: 01872 572032 3 L6
monkeytreeholidaypark.co.uk
Total Pitches: 511

Monkton Wyld Holiday Park
Scott's Lane, Charmouth, Dorset
DT6 6DB
Tel: 01297 631131 6 K5
monktonwyld.co.uk
Total Pitches: 155

Moon & Sixpence
Newbourn Road, Waldringfield, Woodbridge
IP12 4PP
Tel: 01473 736650 41 N11
moonandsixpence.co.uk
Total Pitches: 50

Moss Wood Caravan Park
Crimbles Lane, Cockerham
LA2 0ES
Tel: 01524 791041 61 T10
mosswood.co.uk
Total Pitches: 25

Naburn Lock Caravan Park
Naburn
YO19 4RU
Tel: 01904 728697 64 E10
naburnlock.co.uk
Total Pitches: 115

New Lodge Farm C & C Site
New Lodge Farm, Bulwick, Corby
NN17 3DU
Tel: 01780 450493 38 E1
newlodgefarm.com
Total Pitches: 72

Newberry Valley Park
Woodlands, Combe Martin
EX34 0AT
Tel: 01271 882334 15 N3
newberryvalleypark.co.uk
Total Pitches: 110

Newlands Holidays
Charmouth, Bridport
DT6 6RB
Tel: 01297 560259 7 L6
newlandsholidays.co.uk
Total Pitches: 240

Ninham Country Holidays
Ninham, Shanklin, Isle of Wight
PO37 7PL
Tel: 01983 864243 9 R12
ninham-holidays.co.uk
Total Pitches: 140

Northam Farm Caravan & Touring Park
Brean, Burnham-on-Sea
TA8 2SE
Tel: 01278 751244 16 K5
northamfarm.co.uk
Total Pitches: 350

North Morte Farm C & C Park
North Morte Road, Mortehoe, Woolacombe
EX34 7EG
Tel: 01271 870381 15 L3
northmortefarm.co.uk
Total Pitches: 180

Oakdown Holiday Park
Gatedown Lane, Weston, Sidmouth
EX10 0PT
Tel: 01297 680387 6 G6
oakdown.co.uk
Total Pitches: 150

Old Hall Caravan Park
Capernwray, Carnforth
LA6 1AD
Tel: 01524 733276 61 U5
oldhallcaravanpark.co.uk
Total Pitches: 38

Old Oaks Touring & Glamping
Wick Farm, Wick, Glastonbury
BA6 8JS
Tel: 01458 831437 17 P9
theoldoaks.co.uk
Total Pitches: 88

Orchard Farm Holiday Village
Stonegate, Hunmanby, Filey, North Yorkshire
YO14 0PU
Tel: 01723 891582 65 Q4
orchardfarmholidayvillage.co.uk
Total Pitches: 91

Ord House Country Park
East Ord, Berwick-upon-Tweed
TD15 2NS
Tel: 01289 305288 85 P8
maguirescountryparks.co.uk
Total Pitches: 79

Otterington Park
Station Farm, South Otterington, Northallerton, North Yorkshire
DL7 9JB
Tel: 01609 780656 63 T2
otteringtonpark.com
Total Pitches: 62

Oxon Hall Touring Park
Welshpool Road, Shrewsbury
SY3 5FB
Tel: 01743 340868 45 L11
morris-leisure.co.uk
Total Pitches: 105

Park Cliffe C & C Estate
Birks Road, Tower Wood, Windermere
LA23 3PG
Tel: 015395 31344 61 R1
parkcliffe.co.uk
Total Pitches: 60

Park Foot Holiday Park
Howtown Road, Pooley Bridge
CA10 2NA
Tel: 017684 86309 67 Q8
parkfootullswater.co.uk
Total Pitches: 323

Parkers Farm Holiday Park
Higher Mead Farm, Ashburton, Devon
TQ13 7LJ
Tel: 01364 654869 5 T6
parkersfarmholidays.co.uk
Total Pitches: 100

Parkland C & C Site
Sorley Green Cross, Kingsbridge
TQ7 4AF
Tel: 01548 852723 5 S11
parklandsite.co.uk
Total Pitches: 50

Pebble Bank Caravan Park
Camp Road, Wyke Regis, Weymouth
DT4 9HF
Tel: 01305 774844 7 S9
pebblebank.co.uk
Total Pitches: 40

Perran Sands Holiday Park
Perranporth, Truro
TR6 0AQ
Tel: 01872 573551 2 K5
haven.com/perransands
Total Pitches: 341

Petwood Caravan Park
Off Stixwould Road, Woodhall Spa
LN10 6QH
Tel: 01526 354799 59 L14
petwoodcaravanpark.com
Total Pitches: 98

Piccadilly Caravan Park
Folly Lane West, Lacock
SN15 2LP
Tel: 01249 263164 18 D7
piccadillylacock.co.uk
Total Pitches: 41

Plough Lane Touring Caravan Site
Plough Lane, Chippenham, Wiltshire
SN15 5PS
Tel: 01249 750146 18 D5
ploughlane.co.uk
Total Pitches: 52

Polladras Holiday Park
Carleen, Breage, Helston
TR13 9NX
Tel: 01736 762220 2 G10
polladrasholidaypark.co.uk
Total Pitches: 39

Polmanter Touring Park
Halsetown, St Ives
TR26 3LX
Tel: 01736 795640 2 E9
polmanter.com
Total Pitches: 294

Porthtowan Tourist Park
Mile Hill, Porthtowan, Truro
TR4 8TY
Tel: 01209 890256 2 H7
porthtowantouristpark.co.uk
Total Pitches: 80

Presingoll Farm C & C Park
St Agnes
TR5 0PB
Tel: 01872 552333 2 J7
presingollfarm.co.uk
Total Pitches: 90

Primrose Valley Holiday Park
Filey
YO14 9RF
Tel: 01723 513771 65 Q4
haven.com/primrosevalley
Total Pitches: 35

Ranch Caravan Park
Station Road, Honeybourne,
Evesham
WR11 7PR
Tel: 01386 830744 36 F12
ranch.co.uk
Total Pitches: 120

Ripley Caravan Park
Knaresborough Road, Ripley,
Harrogate
HG3 3AU
Tel: 01423 770050 63 R7
ripleycaravanpark.com
Total Pitches: 60

River Dart Country Park
Holne Park, Ashburton
TQ13 7NP
Tel: 01364 652511 5 S7
riverdart.co.uk
Total Pitches: 170

River Valley Holiday Park
London Apprentice, St Austell
PL26 7AP
Tel: 01726 73533 3 Q6
rivervalleyholidaypark.co.uk
Total Pitches: 45

Riverside C & C Park
Marsh Lane, North Molton Road,
South Molton
EX36 3HQ
Tel: 01769 579269 15 R7
exmoorriverside.co.uk
Total Pitches: 58

Riverside Caravan Park
High Bentham, Lancaster
LA2 7FJ
Tel: 015242 61272 62 D6
riversidecaravanpark.co.uk
Total Pitches: 61

Riverside Caravan Park
Leigham Manor Drive, Plymouth
PL6 8LL
Tel: 01752 344122 5 S10
riversidecaravanpark.com
Total Pitches: 259

Robin Hood C & C Park
Green Dyke Lane, Slingsby
YO62 4AP
Tel: 01653 628391 64 G5
robinhoodcaravanpark.co.uk
Total Pitches: 46

Rose Farm Touring & Camping Park
Stepshort, Belton,
Nr Great Yarmouth
NR31 9JS
Tel: 01493 738292 51 S13
rosefarmtouringpark.com
Total Pitches: 145

Rosedale Abbey Caravan Park
Rosedale Abbey, Pickering
YO18 8SA
Tel: 01751 417272 71 M13
rosedaleabbeycaravanpark.co.uk
Total Pitches: 100

Rudding Holiday Park
Follifoot, Harrogate
HG3 1JH
Tel: 01423 870439 63 S9
ruddingholidaypark.co.uk
Total Pitches: 86

Run Cottage Touring Park
Alderton Road, Hollesley, Woodbridge
IP12 3RQ
Tel: 01394 411309 41 Q12
runcottage.co.uk
Total Pitches: 45

Rutland C & C
Park Lane, Greetham, Oakham
LE15 7FN
Tel: 01572 813520 48 D11
rutlandcaravanandcamping.co.uk
Total Pitches: 130

St Helens in the Park
Wykeham, Scarborough
YO13 9QD
Tel: 01723 862771 65 M3
sthelenscaravanpark.co.uk
Total Pitches: 250

St Ives Bay Beach Resort
73 Loggans Road, Upton Towans,
Hayle
TR27 5BH
Tel: 01736 752274 2 F9
stivesbay.co.uk
Total Pitches: 240

Salcombe Regis C & C Park
Salcombe Regis, Sidmouth
EX10 0JH
Tel: 01395 514303 6 G7
salcombe-regis.co.uk
Total Pitches: 100

Sand le Mere Holiday Village
Southfield Lane, Tunstall
HU12 0JF
Tel: 01964 670403 65 U13
sand-le-mere.co.uk
Total Pitches: 72

Scratby Hall Caravan Park
Scratby, Great Yarmouth
NR29 3SR
Tel: 01493 730283 51 T10
scratbyhall.co.uk
Total Pitches: 85

Searles Leisure Resort
South Beach Road, Hunstanton
PE36 5BB
Tel: 01485 534211 49 U6
searles.co.uk
Total Pitches: 255

Seaview Holiday Park
Preston, Weymouth
DT3 6DZ
Tel: 01305 832271 7 T8
haven.com/parks/dorset/seaview
Total Pitches: 82

Severn Gorge Park
Bridgnorth Road, Tweedale, Telford
TF7 4JB
Tel: 01952 684789 45 R12
severngorgepark.co.uk
Total Pitches: 12

Shrubbery Touring Park
Rousdon, Lyme Regis
DT7 3XW
Tel: 01297 442227 6 J6
shrubberypark.co.uk
Total Pitches: 120

Silverdale Caravan Park
Middlebarrow Plain, Cove Road, Silverdale,
Nr Carnforth
LA5 0SH
Tel: 01524 701508 61 T4
holgates.co.uk
Total Pitches: 80

Skegness Holiday Park
Richmond Drive, Skegness
PE25 3TQ
Tel: 01754 762097 49 S1
haven.com/parks/lincolnshire/skegness-holiday-park
Total Pitches: 49

Skelwith Fold Caravan Park
Ambleside, Cumbria
LA22 0HX
Tel: 015394 32277 67 N12
skelwith.com
Total Pitches: 150

Skirlington Leisure Park
Driffield, Skipsea
YO25 8SY
Tel: 01262 468213 65 R9
skirlington.com
Total Pitches: 280

Sleningford Watermill Caravan Camping Park
North Stainley, Ripon
HG4 3HQ
Tel: 01765 635201 63 R4
sleningfordwatermill.co.uk
Total Pitches: 150

Southfork Caravan Park
Parrett Works, Martock, Somerset
TA12 6AE
Tel: 01935 825661 17 M13
southforkcaravans.co.uk
Total Pitches: 27

South Lytchett Manor C & C Park
Dorchester Road, Lytchett Minster, Poole
BH16 6JB
Tel: 01202 622577 8 D10
southlytchettmanor.co.uk
Total Pitches: 150

South Meadows Caravan Park
South Road, Belford
NE70 7DP
Tel: 01668 213326 85 S12
southmeadows.co.uk
Total Pitches: 169

Stanmore Hall Touring Park
Stourbridge Road, Bridgnorth
WV15 6DT
Tel: 01746 761761 35 R2
morris-leisure.co.uk
Total Pitches: 129

Stanwix Park Holiday Centre
Greenrow, Silloth
CA7 4HH
Tel: 016973 32666 66 H2
stanwix.com
Total Pitches: 121

Summer Valley Touring Park
Shortlanesend, Truro, Cornwall
TR4 9DW
Tel: 07933 212643 2 K7
summervalley.co.uk
Total Pitches: 55

Sumners Ponds Fishery & Campsite
Chapel Road, Barns Green, Horsham
RH13 0PR
Tel: 01403 732539 10 J5
sumnersponds.co.uk
Total Pitches: 86

Swiss Farm Touring & Camping
Marlow Road, Henley-on-Thames
RG9 2HY
Tel: 01491 573419 20 C6
swissfarmhenley.co.uk
Total Pitches: 140

Tanner Farm Touring C & C Park
Tanner Farm, Goudhurst Road, Marden
TN12 9ND
Tel: 01622 832399 12 D7
tannerfarmpark.co.uk
Total Pitches: 120

Tehidy Holiday Park
Harris Mill, Illogan, Portreath
TR16 4JQ
Tel: 01209 216489 2 H8
tehidy.co.uk
Total Pitches: 18

Tencreek Holiday Park
Polperro Road, Looe
PL13 2JR
Tel: 01503 262447 4 G10
dolphinholidays.co.uk
Total Pitches: 254

The Inside Park
Down House Estate, Blandford Forum,
Dorset
DT11 9AD
Tel: 01258 453719 8 B8
theinsidepark.co.uk
Total Pitches: 125

The Laurels Holiday Park
Padstow Road, Whitecross, Wadebridge
PL27 7JQ
Tel: 01208 813341 3 P2
thelaurelsholidaypark.co.uk
Total Pitches: 30

The Old Brick Kilns
Little Barney Lane, Barney, Fakenham
NR21 0NL
Tel: 01328 878305 50 H7
old-brick-kilns.co.uk
Total Pitches: 65

The Orchards Holiday Caravan Park
Main Road, Newbridge, Yarmouth,
Isle of Wight
PO41 0TS
Tel: 01983 531331 9 N11
orchards-holiday-park.co.uk
Total Pitches: 120

The Quiet Site
Ullswater, Watermillock
CA11 0LS
Tel: 07768 727016 67 P8
thequietsite.co.uk
Total Pitches: 100

Thornwick Bay Holiday Village
North Marine Road, Flamborough
YO15 1AU
Tel: 01262 850569 65 S5
haven.com/parks/yorkshire/thornwick-bay
Total Pitches: 67

Thorpe Park Holiday Centre
Cleethorpes
DN35 0PW
Tel: 01472 813395 59 P5
haven.com/thorpepark
Total Pitches: 134

Tollgate Farm C & C Park
Budnick Hill, Perranporth
TR6 0AD
Tel: 01872 572130 2 K6
tollgatefarm.co.uk
Total Pitches: 102

Treago Farm Caravan Site
Crantock, Newquay
TR8 5QS
Tel: 01637 830277 2 K4
treagofarm.co.uk
Total Pitches: 90

Treloy Touring Park
Newquay
TR8 4JN
Tel: 01637 872063 3 M4
treloy.co.uk
Total Pitches: 223

Trencreek Holiday Park
Hillcrest, Higher Trencreek, Newquay
TR8 4NS
Tel: 01637 874210 3 L4
trencreekholidaypark.co.uk
Total Pitches: 194

Trethem Mill Touring Park
St Just-in-Roseland, Nr St Mawes, Truro
TR2 5JF
Tel: 01872 580504 3 M9
trethem.com
Total Pitches: 84

Trevalgan Touring Park
Trevalgan, St Ives
TR26 3BJ
Tel: 01736 791892 2 D9
trevalgantouringpark.co.uk
Total Pitches: 135

Trevarrian Holiday Park
Mawgan Porth, Newquay, Cornwall
TR8 4AQ
Tel: 01637 860381 3 M3
trevarrian.co.uk
Total Pitches: 185

Trevarth Holiday Park
Blackwater, Truro
TR4 8HR
Tel: 01872 560266 2 J7
trevarth.co.uk
Total Pitches: 30

Trevedra Farm C & C Site
Sennen, Penzance
TR19 7BE
Tel: 01736 871818 2 B11
trevedrafarm.co.uk
Total Pitches: 100

Trevornick
Holywell Bay, Newquay
TR8 5PW
Tel: 01637 830531 2 K5
trevornick.co.uk
Total Pitches: 575

Trewan Hall
St Columb Major, Cornwall
TR9 6DB
Tel: 01637 880261 3 N4
trewan-hall.co.uk
Total Pitches: 200

Tudor C & C
Shepherds Patch, Slimbridge,
Gloucester
GL2 7BP
Tel: 01453 890483 28 D7
tudorcaravanpark.com
Total Pitches: 75

Twitchen House Holiday Village
Mortehoe Station Road, Mortehoe,
Woolacombe
EX34 7ES
Tel: 01271 872302 15 L4
woolacombe.co.uk
Total Pitches: 252

Two Mills Touring Park
Yarmouth Road, North Walsham
NR28 9NA
Tel: 01692 405829 51 N8
twomills.co.uk
Total Pitches: 81

Ulwell Cottage Caravan Park
Ulwell Cottage, Ulwell, Swanage
BH19 3DG
Tel: 01929 422823 8 E12
ulwellcottagepark.co.uk
Total Pitches: 77

Upper Lynstone Caravan Park
Lynstone, Bude
EX23 0LP
Tel: 01288 352017 14 F11
upperlynstone.co.uk
Total Pitches: 65

Vale of Pickering Caravan Park
Carr House Farm, Allerston, Pickering
YO18 7PQ
Tel: 01723 859280 64 K3
valeofpickering.co.uk
Total Pitches: 120

Waldegraves Holiday Park
Mersea Island, Colchester
CO5 8SE
Tel: 01206 382898 23 P5
waldegraves.co.uk
Total Pitches: 126

Waleswood C & C Park
Delves Lane, Waleswood, Wales Bar,
Wales, South Yorkshire
S26 5RN
Tel: 07825 125328 57 Q10
waleswood.co.uk
Total Pitches: 163

Wareham Forest Tourist Park
North Trigon, Wareham
BH20 7NZ
Tel: 01929 551393 8 B10
warehamforest.co.uk
Total Pitches: 200

Waren C & C Park
Waren Mill, Bamburgh
NE70 7EE
Tel: 01668 214366 85 T12
meadowhead.co.uk/parks/waren
Total Pitches: 150

Warren Farm Holiday Centre
Brean Sands, Brean,
Burnham-on-Sea
TA8 2RP
Tel: 01278 751227 16 J5
warrenfarm.co.uk
Total Pitches: 575

Waterfoot Caravan Park
Pooley Bridge, Penrith,
Cumbria
CA11 0JF
Tel: 017684 86302 67 Q8
waterfootpark.co.uk
Total Pitches: 34

Watergate Bay Touring Park
Watergate Bay, Tregurrian
TR8 4AD
Tel: 01637 860387 3 M3
watergatebaytouringpark.co.uk
Total Pitches: 171

Waterrow Touring Park
Wiveliscombe, Taunton
TA4 2AZ
Tel: 01984 623464 16 E11
waterrowpark.co.uk
Total Pitches: 42

Waters Edge Country Park
River Road, Stanah,
Thornton-Cleveleys, Blackpool
FY5 5LR
Tel: 01253 823632 61 R11
knepsfarm.co.uk
Total Pitches: 40

Wayfarers C & C Park
Relubbus Lane, St Hilary,
Penzance
TR20 9EF
Tel: 01736 763326 2 F10
wayfarerspark.co.uk
Total Pitches: 32

Wells Touring Park
Haybridge, Wells
BA5 1AJ
Tel: 01749 676869 17 P7
wellstouringpark.co.uk
Total Pitches: 56

Westbrook Park
Little Hereford,
Herefordshire
SY8 4AU
Tel: 01584 711280 35 M7
westbrookpark.co.uk
Total Pitches: 53

Whitefield Forest Touring Park
Brading Road, Ryde,
Isle of Wight
PO33 1QL
Tel: 01983 617069 9 S11
whitefieldforest.co.uk
Total Pitches: 90

Whitehill Country Park
Stoke Road, Paignton,
Devon
TQ4 7PF
Tel: 01803 782338 5 V9
whitehill-park.co.uk
Total Pitches: 260

Whitemead Caravan Park
East Burton Road, Wool
BH20 6HG
Tel: 01929 462241 8 A11
whitemeadcaravanpark.co.uk
Total Pitches: 105

Widdicombe Farm Touring Park
Marldon, Paignton, Devon
TQ3 1ST
Tel: 01803 558325 5 V8
widdicombefarm.co.uk
Total Pitches: 180

Willow Valley Holiday Park
Bush, Bude, Cornwall
EX23 9LB
Tel: 01288 353104 14 F11
willowvalley.co.uk
Total Pitches: 41

Willowbank Holiday Home & Touring Park
Coastal Road, Ainsdale,
Southport
PR8 3ST
Tel: 01704 571566 54 H4
willowbankcp.co.uk
Total Pitches: 87

Wolds View Country Park
115 Brigg Road, Caistor
LN7 6RX
Tel: 01472 851099 58 K6
woldsviewtouringpark.co.uk
Total Pitches: 60

Wooda Farm Holiday Park
Poughill, Bude
EX23 9HJ
Tel: 01288 352069 14 F11
wooda.co.uk
Total Pitches: 200

Woodclose Caravan Park
High Casterton,
Kirkby Lonsdale
LA6 2SE
Tel: 01524 271597 62 C4
woodclosepark.com
Total Pitches: 22

Woodhall Country Park
Stixwold Road,
Woodhall Spa
LN10 6UJ
Tel: 01526 353710 59 L14
woodhallcountrypark.co.uk
Total Pitches: 141

Woodlands Grove C & C Park
Blackawton,
Dartmouth
TQ9 7DQ
Tel: 01803 712598 5 U10
woodlandsgrove.com
Total Pitches: 350

Woodland Springs Adult Touring Park
Venton,
Drewsteignton
EX6 6PG
Tel: 01647 231648 5 R2
woodlandsprings.co.uk
Total Pitches: 93

Woodovis Park
Gulworthy, Tavistock
PL19 8NY
Tel: 01822 832968 5 L6
woodovis.com
Total Pitches: 50

Woolsbridge Manor Farm Caravan Park
Three Legged Cross,
Wimborne
BH21 6RA
Tel: 01202 826369 8 G8
woolsbridgemanorcaravanpark.co.uk
Total Pitches: 60

Yeatheridge Farm Caravan Park
East Worlington,
Crediton,
Devon
EX17 4TN
Tel: 01884 860330 15 S10
yeatheridge.co.uk
Total Pitches: 103

York Caravan Park
Stockton Lane, York,
North Yorkshire
YO32 9UB
Tel: 01904 424222 64 E9
yorkcaravanpark.com
Total Pitches: 55

York Meadows Caravan Park
York Road, Sheriff Hutton, York,
North Yorkshire
YO60 6QP
Tel: 01347 878508 64 E6
yorkmeadowscaravanpark.com
Total Pitches: 45

SCOTLAND

Auchenlarie Holiday Park
Gatehouse of Fleet
DG7 2EX
Tel: 01556 506200 73 N9
swalwellholidaygroup.co.uk
Total Pitches: 49

Barrhill Holiday Park
Barrhill, Girvan
KA26 0PZ
Tel: 01465 821355 72 G3
barrhillholidaypark.com
Total Pitches: 20

Beecraigs C & C Site
Beecraigs Country Park,
The Visitor Centre, Linlithgow
EH49 6PL
Tel: 01506 284516 82 K4
westlothian.gov.uk/stay-at-beecraigs
Total Pitches: 36

Belhaven Bay C & C Park
Belhaven Bay, Dunbar,
East Lothian
EH42 1TS
Tel: 01368 865956 84 H3
meadowhead.co.uk
Total Pitches: 52

Blair Castle Caravan Park
Blair Atholl,
Pitlochry
PH18 5SR
Tel: 01796 481263 97 P10
blaircastlecaravanpark.co.uk
Total Pitches: 184

Brighouse Bay Holiday Park
Brighouse Bay, Borgue,
Kirkcudbright
DG6 4TS
Tel: 01557 870267 73 Q10
gillespie-leisure.co.uk
Total Pitches: 190

Cairnsmill Holiday Park
Largo Road,
St Andrews
KY16 8NN
Tel: 01334 473604 91 Q9
cairnsmill.co.uk
Total Pitches: 62

Craigtoun Meadows Holiday Park
Mount Melville,
St Andrews
KY16 8PQ
Tel: 01334 475959 91 Q8
craigtounmeadows.co.uk
Total Pitches: 56

Faskally Caravan Park
Pitlochry
PH16 5LA
Tel: 01796 472007 97 Q12
faskally.co.uk
Total Pitches: 300

Glenearly Caravan Park
Dalbeattie,
Dumfries & Galloway
DG5 4NE
Tel: 01556 611393 74 F13
glenearlycaravanpark.co.uk
Total Pitches: 39

Glen Nevis C & C Park
Glen Nevis,
Fort William
PH33 6SX
Tel: 01397 702191 94 G4
glen-nevis.co.uk
Total Pitches: 380

Hoddom Castle Caravan Park
Hoddom, Lockerbie
DG11 1AS
Tel: 01576 300251 75 N11
hoddomcastle.co.uk
Total Pitches: 200

Huntly Castle Caravan Park
The Meadow, Huntly
AB54 4UJ
Tel: 01466 794999 104 G7
huntlycastle.co.uk
Total Pitches: 90

Invercoe C & C Park
Ballachulish,
Glencoe
PH49 4HP
Tel: 01855 811210 94 F7
invercoe.co.uk
Total Pitches: 60

Linwater Caravan Park
West Clifton,
East Calder
EH53 0HT
Tel: 0131 333 3326 83 M5
linwater.co.uk
Total Pitches: 60

Milton of Fonab Caravan Park
Bridge Road, Pitlochry
PH16 5NA
Tel: 01796 472882 97 Q12
fonab.co.uk
Total Pitches: 154

Sands of Luce Holiday Park
Sands of Luce, Sandhead,
Stranraer
DG9 9JN
Tel: 01776 830456 72 E9
sandsofluce.com
Total Pitches: 80

Seal Shore Camping and Touring Site
Kildonan, Isle of Arran,
North Ayrshire
KA27 8SE
Tel: 01770 820320 80 E8
campingarran.com
Total Pitches: 43

Seaward Holiday Park
Dhoon Bay, Kirkudbright
DG6 4TJ
Tel: 01557 870267 73 R10
gillespie-leisure.co.uk
Total Pitches: 25

Seton Sands Holiday Village
Longniddry
EH32 0QF
Tel: 01875 813333 83 T3
haven.com/setonsands
Total Pitches: 40

Shieling Holidays Mull
Craignure, Isle of Mull,
Argyll & Bute
PA65 6AY
Tel: 01680 812496 93 S11
shielingholidays.co.uk
Total Pitches: 90

The Paddocks Motorhome Site
Ingliston Estate & Country Club,
Old Greenock Road, Bishopton,
Renfrewshire
PA7 5PA
Tel: 01505 864333 88 K11
ingliston.com
Total Pitches: 30

Thurston Manor Leisure Park
Innerwick,
Dunbar
EH42 1SA
Tel: 01368 840643 84 J4
thurstonmanor.co.uk
Total Pitches: 120

Witches Craig C & C Park
Blairlogie, Stirling
FK9 5PX
Tel: 01786 474947 89 T6
witchescraig.co.uk
Total Pitches: 60

WALES

Beach View Caravan Park
Bwlchtocyn,
Abersoch
LL53 7BT
Tel: 01758 712956 42 F8
beachviewabersoch.co.uk
Total Pitches: 47

Bron Derw Touring Caravan Park
Llanrwst
LL26 0YT
Tel: 01492 640494 53 P10
bronderw-wales.co.uk
Total Pitches: 48

Caerfai Bay Caravan & Tent Park
Caerfai Bay, St Davids,
Haverfordwest
SA62 6QT
Tel: 01437 720274 24 C6
caerfaibay.co.uk
Total Pitches: 106

Cenarth Falls Resort Limited
Cenarth, Newcastle Emlyn
SA38 9JS
Tel: 01239 710345 32 E12
cenarth-holipark.co.uk
Total Pitches: 30

Daisy Bank Caravan Park
Snead, Montgomery
SY15 6EB
Tel: 01588 620471 34 H2
daisy-bank.co.uk
Total Pitches: 64

Deucoch Touring & Camping Park
Sarn Bach, Abersoch
LL53 7LD
Tel: 01758 713293 42 F8
deucoch.com
Total Pitches: 70

Dinlle Caravan Park
Dinas Dinlle, Caernarfon
LL54 5TW
Tel: 01286 830324 52 F11
thornleyleisure.co.uk
Total Pitches: 175

Eisteddfa
Eisteddfa Lodge, Pentrefelin,
Criccieth
LL52 0PT
Tel: 01766 522696 42 K6
eisteddfapark.co.uk
Total Pitches: 100

Fforest Fields C & C Park
Hundred House, Builth Wells
LD1 5RT
Tel: 01982 570406 34 D10
fforestfields.co.uk
Total Pitches: 120

Fishguard Bay Resort
Garn Gelli, Fishguard
SA65 9ET
Tel: 01348 811415 24 G3
fishguardbay.com
Total Pitches: 50

Greenacres Holiday Park
Black Rock Sands, Morfa Bychan,
Porthmadog
LL49 9YF
Tel: 01766 512781 42 K6
haven.com/greenacres
Total Pitches: 39

Hafan y Môr Holiday Park
Pwllheli
LL53 6HJ
Tel: 01758 612112 42 H6
haven.com/hafanymor
Total Pitches: 75

Hendre Mynach Touring C & C Park
Llanaber Road, Barmouth
LL42 1YR
Tel: 01341 280262 43 M10
hendremynach.co.uk
Total Pitches: 240

Home Farm Caravan Park
Marian-glas, Isle of Anglesey
LL73 8PH
Tel: 01248 410614 52 G6
homefarm-anglesey.co.uk
Total Pitches: 102

Islawrffordd Caravan Park
Talybont, Barmouth
LL43 2AQ
Tel: 01341 247269 43 L9
islawrffordd.co.uk
Total Pitches: 105

Kiln Park Holiday Centre
Marsh Road, Tenby
SA70 8RB
Tel: 01834 844121 24 K10
haven.com/kilnpark
Total Pitches: 146

Lakeside Caravan Park
Llangors, Brecon
LD3 7TR
Tel: 01874 658226 27 L2
llangorselake.co.uk
Total Pitches: 40

Pencelli Castle C & C Park
Pencelli, Brecon
LD3 7LX
Tel: 01874 665451 26 K3
pencelli-castle.com
Total Pitches: 80

Penisar Mynydd Caravan Park
Caerwys Road, Rhuallt, St Asaph
LL17 0TY
Tel: 01745 582227 54 C11
penisarmynydd.co.uk
Total Pitches: 71

Plassey Holiday Park
The Plassey, Eyton, Wrexham
LL13 0SP
Tel: 01978 780277 44 H4
plassey.com
Total Pitches: 90

Pont Kemys C & C Park
Chainbridge, Abergavenny
NP7 9DS
Tel: 01873 880688 27 Q6
pontkemys.com
Total Pitches: 65

Presthaven Beach Holiday Park
Gronant, Prestatyn
LL19 9TT
Tel: 01745 856471 54 C10
haven.com/presthaven
Total Pitches: 50

Red Kite Touring and Lodge Park
Van Road, Llanidloes
SY18 6NG
Tel: 01686 412122 33 T3
redkitetouringpark.co.uk
Total Pitches: 66

Riverside Camping
Seiont Nurseries, Pont Rug, Caernarfon
LL55 2BB
Tel: 01286 678781 52 H10
riversidecamping.co.uk
Total Pitches: 73

The Trotting Mare Caravan Park
Overton, Wrexham
LL13 0LE
Tel: 01978 711963 44 J6
thetrottingmare.co.uk
Total Pitches: 54

Trawsdir Touring C & C Park
Llanaber, Barmouth
LL42 1RR
Tel: 01341 280999 43 L10
barmouthholidays.co.uk
Total Pitches: 70

Tyddyn Isaf Caravan Park
Lligwy Bay, Dulas, Isle of Anglesey
LL70 9PQ
Tel: 01248 410203 52 G5
tyddynisaf.co.uk
Total Pitches: 80

White Tower Holiday Park
Llandwrog, Caernarfon
LL54 5UH
Tel: 01286 830649 52 G11
whitetowerpark.co.uk
Total Pitches: 52

CHANNEL ISLANDS

La Bailloterie Camping
Bailloterie Lane, Vale,
Guernsey
GY3 5HA
Tel: 01481 243636 6 e2
campinginguernsey.com
Total Pitches: 100

Traffic signs

Signs giving orders
Signs with red circles are mostly prohibitive.
Plates below signs qualify their message

 Entry to 20mph zone

 End of 20mph zone

 Maximum speed

 National speed limit applies

 School crossing patrol

 Stop and give way

 Give way to traffic on major road

 Manually operated temporary STOP and GO signs

 No entry for vehicular traffic

No vehicles except bicycles being pushed

No cycling

No motor vehicles

No buses (over 8 passenger seats)

No overtaking

No towed caravans

No vehicles carrying explosives

No vehicle or combination of vehicles over length shown

No vehicles over height shown

No vehicles over width shown

Give priority to vehicles from opposite direction

No right turn

No left turn

No U-turns

No goods vehicles over maximum gross weight shown (in tonnes) except for loading and unloading

No waiting

No stopping (Clearway)

 WEAK BRIDGE — No vehicles over maximum gross weight shown (in tonnes)

 Permit holders only — Parking restricted to permit holders

 RED ROUTE No stopping at any time except buses — No stopping during period indicated except for buses

 URBAN CLEARWAY Monday to Friday am 8.00-9.30 pm 4.30-6.30 — No stopping during times shown except for as long as necessary to set down or pick up passengers

Signs with blue circles but no red border mostly give positive instruction.

Ahead only

Turn left ahead (right if symbol reversed)

Turn left (right if symbol reversed)

Keep left (right if symbol reversed)

Vehicles may pass either side to reach same destination

Mini-roundabout (roundabout circulation - give way to vehicles from the immediate right)

Route to be used by pedal cycles only

Segregated pedal cycle and pedestrian route

Minimum speed

End of minimum speed

 Only Buses and cycles only

 Only Trams only

 TRAMWAY LOOK BOTH WAYS Pedestrian crossing point over tramway

One-way traffic (note: compare circular 'Ahead only' sign)

With-flow bus and cycle lane

Contraflow bus lane

With-flow pedal cycle lane

 Note: The signs shown in this road atlas are those most commonly in use and are not all drawn to the same scale. In Scotland and Wales bilingual versions of some signs are used, showing both English and Gaelic or Welsh spellings. Some older designs of signs may still be seen on the roads. A comprehensive explanation of the signing system illustrating the vast majority of road signs can be found in the AA's handbook Know Your Road Signs. Where there is a reference to a rule number, this refers to The Highway Code.

Warning signs
Mostly triangular

STOP 100 yds — Distance to 'STOP' line ahead

Dual carriageway ends

Road narrows on right (left if symbol reversed)

Road narrows on both sides

GIVE WAY 50 yds — Distance to 'Give Way' line ahead

Crossroads

Junction on bend ahead

T-junction with priority over vehicles from the right

Staggered junction

Traffic merging from left ahead

The priority through route is indicated by the broader line.

Double bend first to left (symbol may be reversed)

Bend to the right (or left if symbol reversed)

Roundabout

Uneven road

REDUCE SPEED NOW — Plate below some signs

Two-way traffic crosses one-way road

Two-way traffic straight ahead

Opening or swing bridge ahead

Low-flying aircraft or sudden aircraft noise

Falling or fallen rocks

 Traffic signals not in use

Traffic signals

Slippery road

Steep hill downwards 10%

Steep hill upwards 20%

Gradients may be shown as a ratio i.e. 20% = 1:5

Tunnel ahead

Trams crossing ahead

Level crossing with barrier or gate ahead

Level crossing without barrier or gate ahead

Level crossing without barrier

Patrol — School crossing patrol ahead (some signs have amber lights which flash when crossings are in use)

Frail (or blind or disabled if shown) pedestrians likely to cross road ahead

No footway for 400 yds — Pedestrians in road ahead

Zebra crossing

Safe height 16'6" (5.0m) — Overhead electric cable; plate indicates maximum height of vehicles which can pass safely

 14'6" 4.4m — Available width of headroom indicated

Sharp deviation of route to left (or right if chevrons reversed)

STOP when lights show — Light signals ahead at level crossing, airfield or bridge

Red STOP Green Clear IF NO LIGHT - PHONE CROSSING OPERATOR — Miniature warning lights at level crossings

Cattle

Wild animals

Wild horses or ponies

Accompanied horses or ponies

Cycle route ahead

Ice — Risk of ice

Queues likely — Traffic queues likely ahead

Humps for ½ mile — Distance over which road humps extend

Hidden dip — Other danger; plate indicates nature of danger

Soft verges for 2 miles — Soft verges

Side winds

Hump bridge

Ford — Worded warning sign

Quayside or river bank

Risk of grounding

Direction signs
Mostly rectangular
Signs on motorways - blue backgrounds

 Nottingham M1 — At a junction leading directly into a motorway (junction number may be shown on a black background)

 Nottingham A52 — On approaches to junctions (junction number on black background)

 M1 The NORTH Sheffield 32 Leeds 59 — Route confirmatory sign after junction

 A404 Marlow — Birmingham, Oxford M40 — Downward pointing arrows mean 'Get in lane'. The left-hand lane leads to a different destination from the other lanes.

 A46 (M69) Leicester, Coventry (E) — The NORTH WEST, Birmingham, Coventry (N) M6 — The panel with the inclined arrow indicates the destinations which can be reached by leaving the motorway at the next junction.

Signs on primary routes - green backgrounds

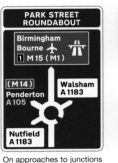 PARK STREET ROUNDABOUT Birmingham Bourne M15 (M1) (M14) Penderton A105 Walsham A1183 Nutfield A1183 — On approaches to junctions

 Lampton Axtley A11 14'6" 1 mile — At the junction

A38 THE SOUTH WEST (M5 South) 5 Gloucester 11 — Route confirmatory sign after the junction

 Swansea Abertawe A483 — On approaches to junction in Wales (bilingual)

TURPIN'S CROSSROADS Biggleswick A11 Lampton (M1) Dorfield A123 Axtley B1991 Steam railway — On approaches to junctions

Blue panels indicate that the motorway starts at the junction ahead.
Motorways shown in brackets can also be reached along the route indicated.
White panels indicate local or non-primary routes leading from the junction ahead.
Brown panels show the route to tourist attractions.
The name of the junction may be shown at the top of the sign.
The aircraft symbol indicates the route to an airport.
A symbol may be included to warn of a hazard or restriction along that route.

 Port Lever Hartleby A666 Ring road Ring road Maverton A6604 Doncastle A6604

Primary route forming part of a ring road

 R

Signs on non-primary and local routes - black borders

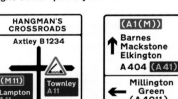 HANGMAN'S CROSSROADS Axtley B1234 (M11) Lampton A11 Townley A11 — On approaches to junctions

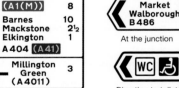 (A1(M)) 8 Barnes 10 Mackstone 2½ Elkington 1 A404 (A41) Millington Green (A4011) 3

 Market Walborough B486 — At the junction

WC — Direction to toilets with access for the disabled

Green panels indicate that the primary route starts at the junction ahead.
Route numbers on a blue background show the direction to a motorway.
Route numbers on a green background show the direction to a primary route.

Signs on non-primary and local routes - black borders

 150 yds — Picnic site

Wrest Park — Ancient monument in the care of English Heritage

 Saturday only P — Direction to a car park

 Zoo — Tourist attraction

300 yds — Direction to camping and caravan site

(A33) (M1) — Advisory route for lorries

Route for pedal cycles forming part of a network

Marton 3 — Recommended route for pedal cycles to place shown

Public library Council offices — Route for pedestrians

Emergency diversion routes

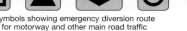 Symbols showing emergency diversion route for motorway and other main road traffic

Northtown — Diversion route

In an emergency it may be necessary to close a section of motorway or other main road to traffic, so a temporary sign may advise drivers to follow a diversion route. To help drivers navigate the route, black symbols on yellow patches may be permanently displayed on existing direction signs, including motorway signs. Symbols may also be used on separate signs with yellow backgrounds.

Information signs

All retangular

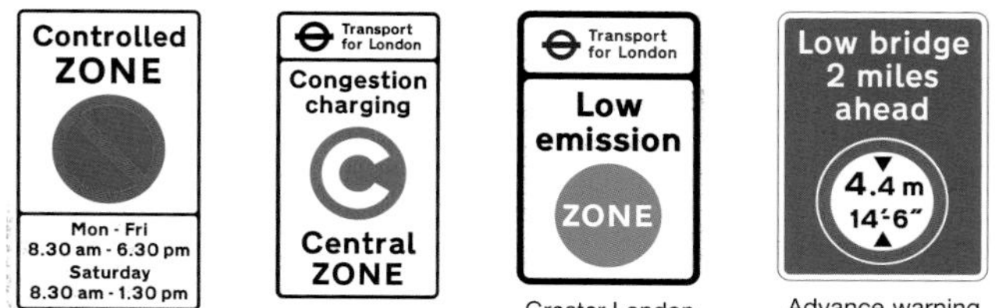
Controlled ZONE
Mon - Fri 8.30 am - 6.30 pm Saturday 8.30 am - 1.30 pm
Transport for London
Congestion charging
Central ZONE
Low emission
ZONE
Low bridge 2 miles ahead
4.4 m
14'6"

Entrance to controlled parking zone

Entrance to congestion charging zone

Greater London Low Emission Zone (LEZ)

Advance warning of restriction or prohibition ahead

P
local
taxi
2+
Mon - Fri 7 - 9 am 4 - 6 pm
2+ lane
For vehicles with 2 or more persons
&
No HGVs over 7.5T

Parking place for solo motorcycles

With-flow bus lane ahead which pedal cycles and taxis may also use

Lane designated for use by high occupancy vehicles (HOV) - see Rule 142

Vehicles permitted to use an HOV lane ahead

M62
Except buses

End of motorway

Start of motorway regulations

Appropriate traffic lanes at junction ahead

200 yards

Traffic on the main carriageway coming from right has priority over joining traffic

Additional traffic joining from left ahead. Traffic on main carriageway has priority over joining traffic from right hand lane of slip road

Traffic in right hand lane of slip road joining the main carriageway has priority over left hand lane

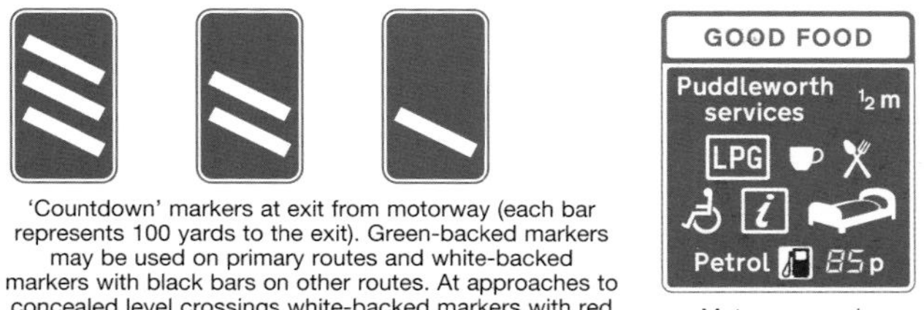
GOOD FOOD
Puddleworth services
½ m
LPG
Petrol
85p

'Countdown' markers at exit from motorway (each bar represents 100 yards to the exit). Green-backed markers may be used on primary routes and white-backed markers with black bars on other routes. At approaches to concealed level crossings white-backed markers with red bars may be used. Although these will be erected at equal distances the bars do not represent 100 yard intervals.

Motorway service area sign showing the operator's name

Priority over oncoming vehicles
H
A & E
not 24 hrs
Tourist information

Traffic has priority over oncoming vehicles

Hospital ahead with Accident and Emergency facilities

Tourist information point

No through road for vehicles

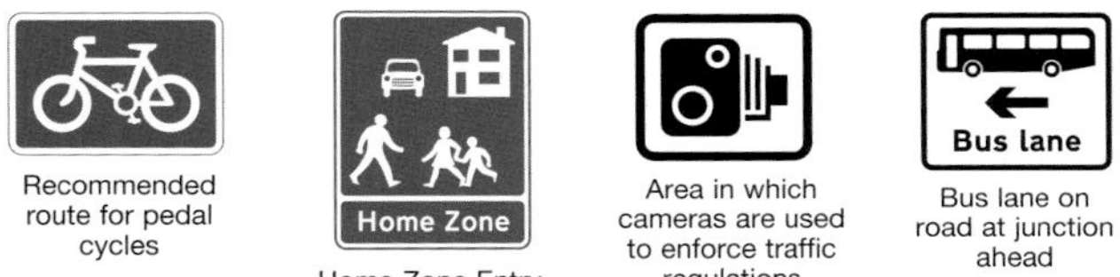
Home Zone
Bus lane

Recommended route for pedal cycles

Home Zone Entry

Area in which cameras are used to enforce traffic regulations

Bus lane on road at junction ahead

*Home Zone Entry – You are entering an area where people could be using the whole street for a range of activities. You should drive slowly and carefully and be prepared to stop to allow people time to move out of the way.

Roadworks signs

SLOW
WET TAR
800 yards

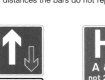

Road works

Loose chippings

Temporary hazard at roadworks

Temporary lane closure (the number and position of arrows and red bars may be varied according to lanes open and closed)

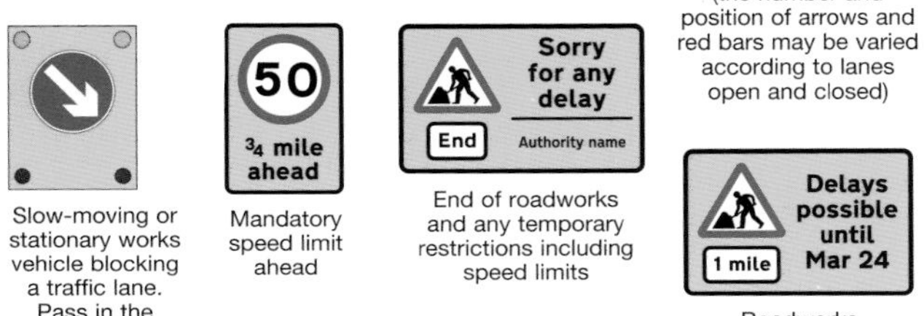
50
¾ mile ahead
Sorry for any delay
End
Authority name
Delays possible until Mar 24
1 mile

Slow-moving or stationary works vehicle blocking a traffic lane. Pass in the direction shown by the arrow

Mandatory speed limit ahead

End of roadworks and any temporary restrictions including speed limits

Roadworks 1 mile ahead

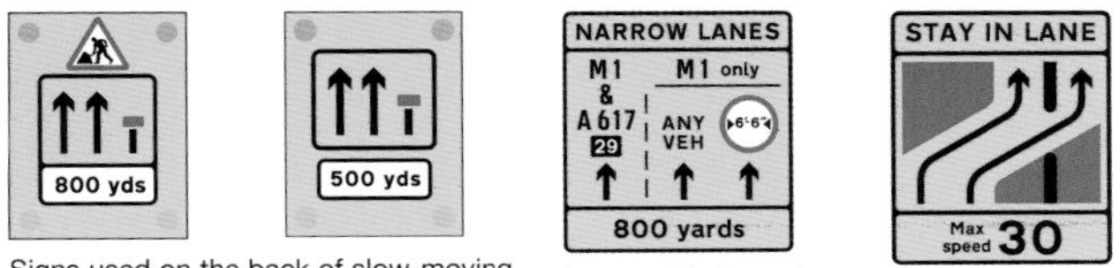
800 yds
500 yds
NARROW LANES
M1
M1 only
& A617
29
ANY VEH
6'6"
800 yards
STAY IN LANE
Max speed
30

Signs used on the back of slow-moving or stationary vehicles warning of a lane closed ahead by a works vehicle. There are no cones on the road

Lane restrictions at roadworks ahead

One lane crossover at contraflow roadworks

Road markings

Across the carriageway

Stop line at signals or police control

Stop line at 'Stop' sign

Stop line for pedestrians at a level crossing

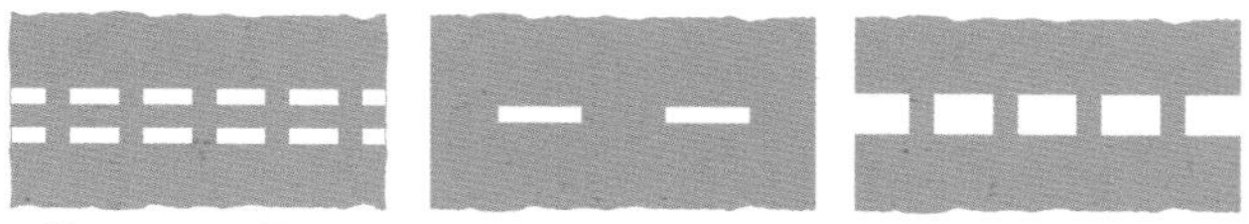

Give way to traffic on major road (can also be used at mini roundabouts)

Give way to traffic from the right at a roundabout

Give way to traffic from the right at a mini-roundabout

Along the carriageway

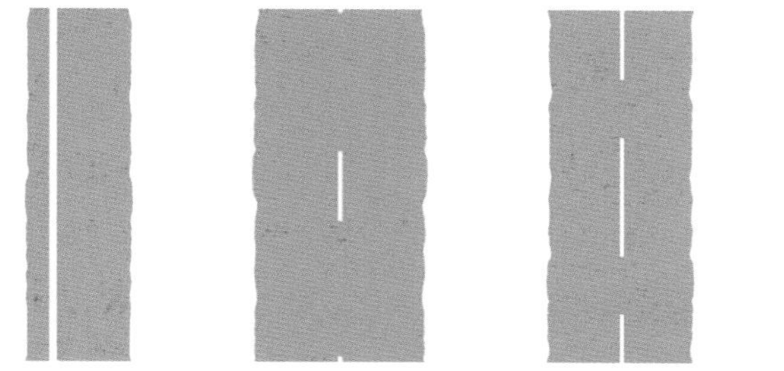

Edge line

Centre line See Rule 127

Hazard warning line See Rule 127

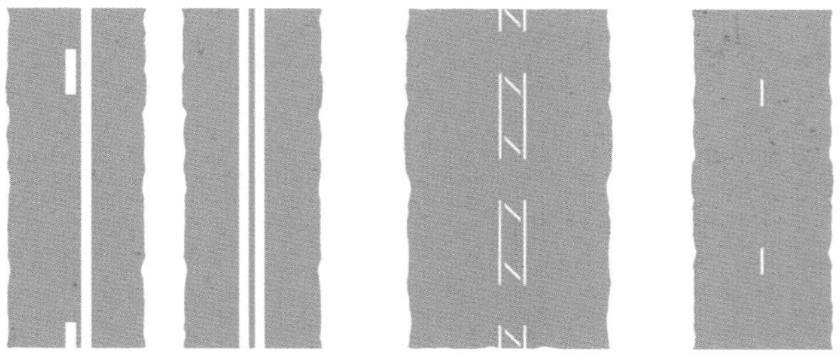

Double white lines See Rules 128 and 129

See Rule 130

Lane line See Rule 131

Along the edge of the carriageway

Waiting restrictions

Waiting restrictions indicated by yellow lines apply to the carriageway, pavement and verge. You may stop to load or unload (unless there are also loading restrictions as described below) or while passengers board or alight. Double yellow lines mean no waiting at any time, unless there are signs that specifically indicate seasonal restrictions. The times at which the restrictions apply for other road markings are shown on nearby plates or on entry signs to controlled parking zones. If no days are shown on the signs, the restrictions are in force every day including Sundays and Bank Holidays. White bay markings and upright signs (see below) indicate where parking is allowed.

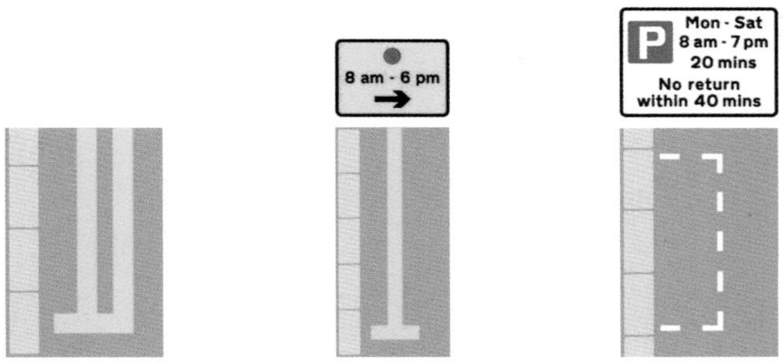
8 am - 6 pm
P
Mon - Sat
8 am - 7 pm
20 mins
No return within 40 mins

No waiting at any time

No waiting during times shown on sign

Waiting is limited to the duration specified during the days and times shown

Red Route stopping controls

Red lines are used on some roads instead of yellow lines. In London the double and single red lines used on Red Routes indicate that stopping to park, load/unload or to board and alight from a vehicle (except for a licensed taxi or if you hold a Blue Badge) is prohibited. The red lines apply to the carriageway, pavement and verge. The times that the red line prohibitions apply are shown on nearby signs, but the double red line ALWAYS means no stopping at any time. On Red Routes you may stop to park, load/unload in specially marked boxes and adjacent signs specify the times and purposes and duration allowed. A box MARKED IN RED indicates that it may only be available for the purpose specified for part of the day (e.g. between busy peak periods). A box MARKED IN WHITE means that it is available throughout the day.

RED AND SINGLE YELLOW LINES CAN ONLY GIVE A GUIDE TO THE RESTRICTIONS AND CONTROLS IN FORCE AND SIGNS, NEARBY OR AT A ZONE ENTRY, MUST BE CONSULTED.

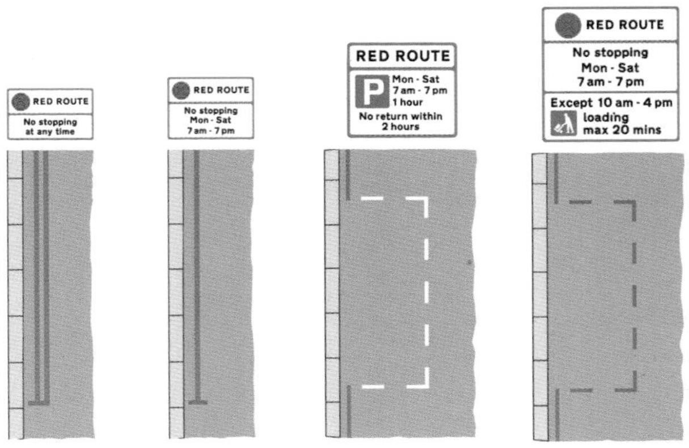
RED ROUTE
No stopping at any time
RED ROUTE
No stopping Mon - Sat 7 am - 7 pm
RED ROUTE
P
Mon - Sat 7 am - 7 pm 1 hour
No return within 2 hours
RED ROUTE
No stopping Mon - Sat 7 am - 7 pm
Except 10 am - 4 pm loading max 20 mins

No stopping at any time

No stopping during times shown on sign

Parking is limited to the duration specified during the days and times shown

Only loading may take place at the times shown for up to a maximum duration of 20 mins

On the kerb or at the edge of the carriageway

Loading restrictions on roads other than Red Routes

Yellow marks on the kerb or at the edge of the carriageway indicate that loading or unloading is prohibited at the times shown on the nearby black and white plates. You may stop while passengers board or alight. If no days are indicated on the signs the restrictions are in force every day including Sundays and Bank Holidays.

ALWAYS CHECK THE TIMES SHOWN ON THE PLATES.

Lengths of road reserved for vehicles loading and unloading are indicated by a white 'bay' marking with the words 'Loading Only' and a sign with the white on blue 'trolley' symbol. This sign also shows whether loading and unloading is restricted to goods vehicles and the times at which the bay can be used. If no times or days are shown it may be used at any time. Vehicles may not park here if they are not loading or unloading.

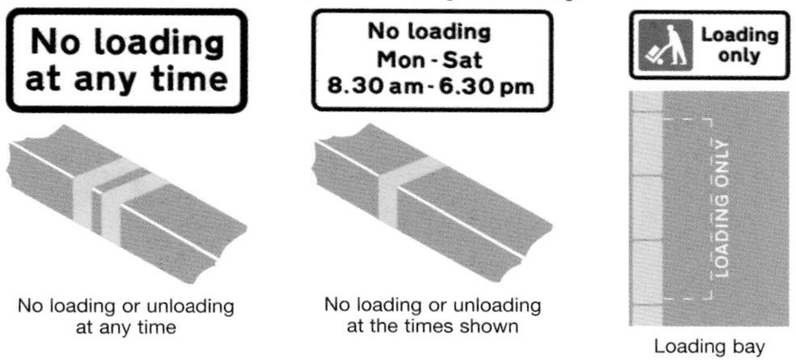
No loading at any time
No loading Mon - Sat 8.30 am - 6.30 pm
Loading only
LOADING ONLY

No loading or unloading at any time

No loading or unloading at the times shown

Loading bay

Other road markings

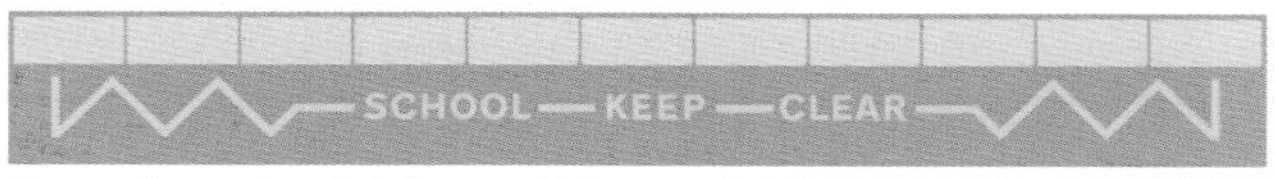
SCHOOL — KEEP — CLEAR

Keep entrance clear of stationary vehicles, even if picking up or setting down children

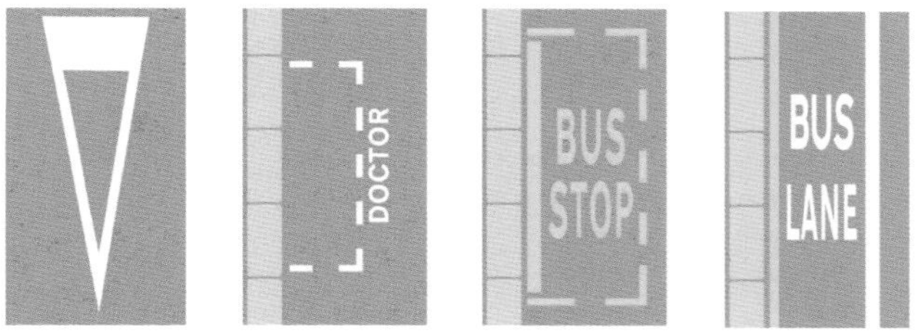
DOCTOR
BUS STOP
BUS LANE

Warning of 'Give Way' just ahead

Parking space reserved for vehicles named

See Rule 243

See Rule 141

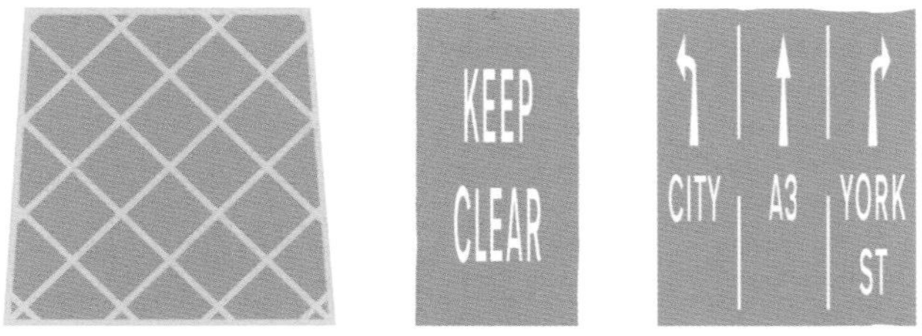
KEEP CLEAR
CITY
A3
YORK ST

Box junction - See Rule 174

Do not block that part of the carriageway indicated

Indication of traffic lanes

Light signals controlling traffic

Traffic Light Signals

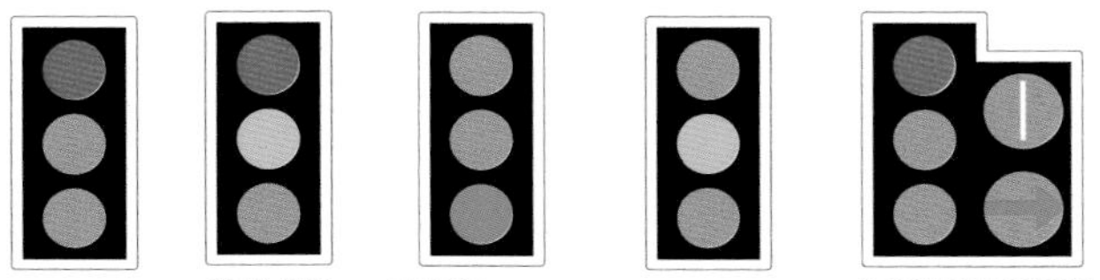

RED means 'Stop'. Wait behind the stop line on the carriageway

RED AND AMBER also means 'Stop'. Do not pass through or start until GREEN shows

GREEN means you may go on if the way is clear. Take special care if you intend to turn left or right and give way to pedestrians who are crossing

AMBER means 'Stop' at the stop line. You may go on only if the AMBER appears after you have crossed the stop line or are so close to it that to pull up might cause an accident

A GREEN ARROW may be provided in addition to the full green signal if movement in a certain direction is allowed before or after the full green phase. If the way is clear you may go but only in the direction shown by the arrow. You may do this whatever other lights may be showing. White light signals may be provided for trams

Flashing red lights

Alternately flashing red lights mean YOU MUST STOP

At level crossings, lifting bridges, airfields, fire stations, etc.

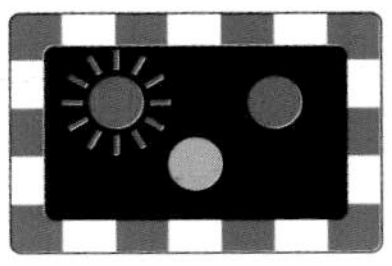

Motorway signals

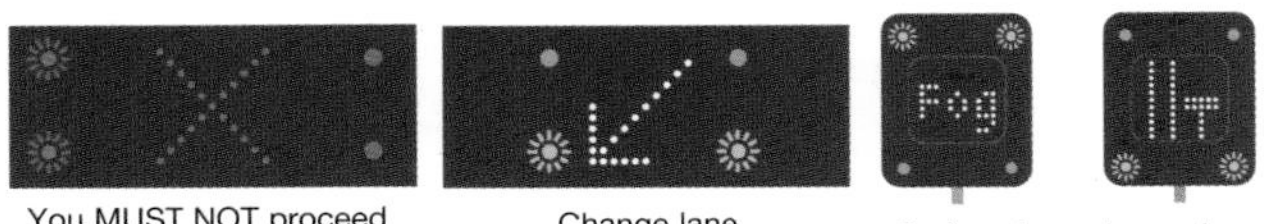
Fog

You MUST NOT proceed further in this lane

Change lane

Reduced visibility ahead

Lane ahead closed

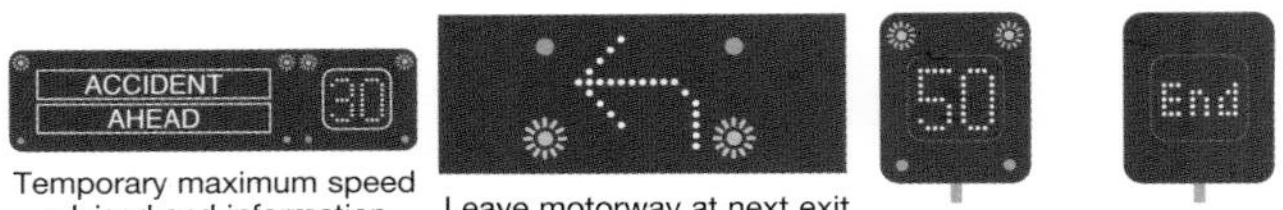
ACCIDENT AHEAD
30
50
End

Temporary maximum speed advised and information message

Leave motorway at next exit

Temporary maximum speed advised

End of restriction

Lane control signals

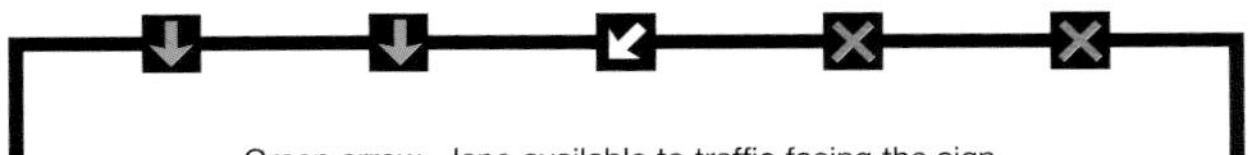

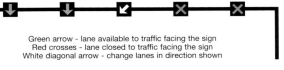

Green arrow - lane available to traffic facing the sign
Red crosses - lane closed to traffic facing the sign
White diagonal arrow - change lanes in direction shown

Channel hopping and the Isle of Wight

For business or pleasure, hopping on a ferry across to France, the Channel Islands or Isle of Wight has never been easier.

The vehicle ferry services listed in the table give you all the options, together with detailed port plans to help you navigate to and from the ferry terminals. Simply choose your preferred route, not forgetting the fast sailings (see ).
Bon voyage!

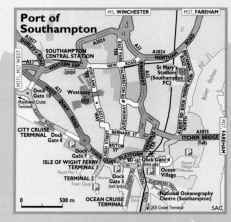

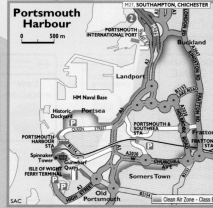

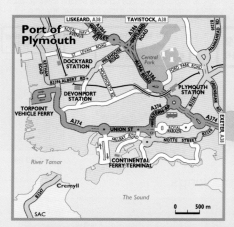

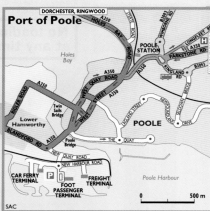

ENGLISH CHANNEL AND ISLE OF WIGHT FERRY CROSSINGS

From	To	Journey time	Operator website
Dover	Calais	1 hr 30 mins	dfdsseaways.co.uk
Dover	Calais	1 hr 30 mins	poferries.com
Dover	Dunkirk	2 hrs	dfdsseaways.co.uk
Folkestone	Calais (Coquelles)	35 mins	eurotunnel.com
Lymington	Yarmouth (IOW)	40 mins	wightlink.co.uk
Newhaven	Dieppe	4 hrs	dfdsseaways.co.uk
Plymouth	Roscoff	5 hrs 30 mins	brittany-ferries.co.uk
Poole	Cherbourg	4 hrs 30 mins (Apr–Oct)	brittany-ferries.co.uk
Poole	Guernsey	3 hrs 🚢	condorferries.co.uk
Poole	Jersey	4 hrs 🚢	condorferries.co.uk
Poole	St-Malo	6 hrs 20 mins–12 hrs (via Channel Is.) 🚢	condorferries.co.uk
Portsmouth	Caen (Ouistreham)	5 hrs 45 mins–7 hrs	brittany-ferries.co.uk
Portsmouth	Cherbourg	8 hrs	brittany-ferries.co.uk
Portsmouth	Fishbourne (IOW)	45 mins	wightlink.co.uk
Portsmouth	Guernsey	7 hrs	condorferries.co.uk
Portsmouth	Jersey	8–11 hrs	condorferries.co.uk
Portsmouth	Le Havre	5 hrs 30 mins–8 hrs	brittany-ferries.co.uk
Portsmouth	St-Malo	11 hrs	brittany-ferries.co.uk
Southampton	East Cowes (IOW)	1 hr	redfunnel.co.uk

The information listed is provided as a guide only, as services are liable to change at short notice and are weather dependent. Services shown are for vehicle ferries only, operated by conventional ferry unless indicated as a fast ferry service (). Please check sailings before planning your journey.

Travelling further afield? For ferry services to Northern Spain see *brittany-ferries.co.uk.*

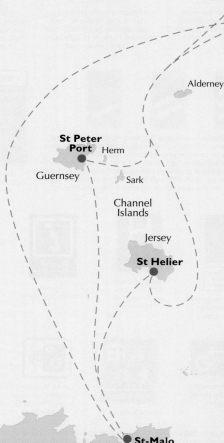

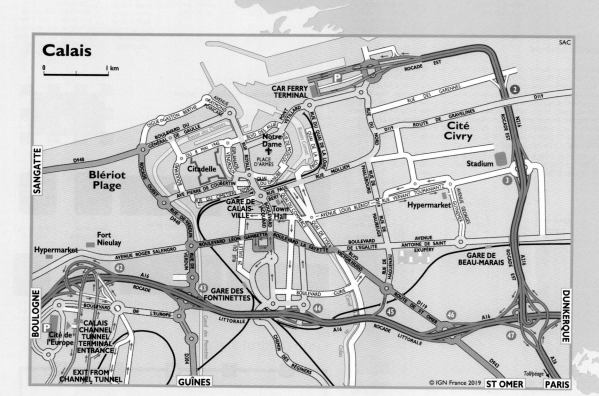

© IGN France 2019

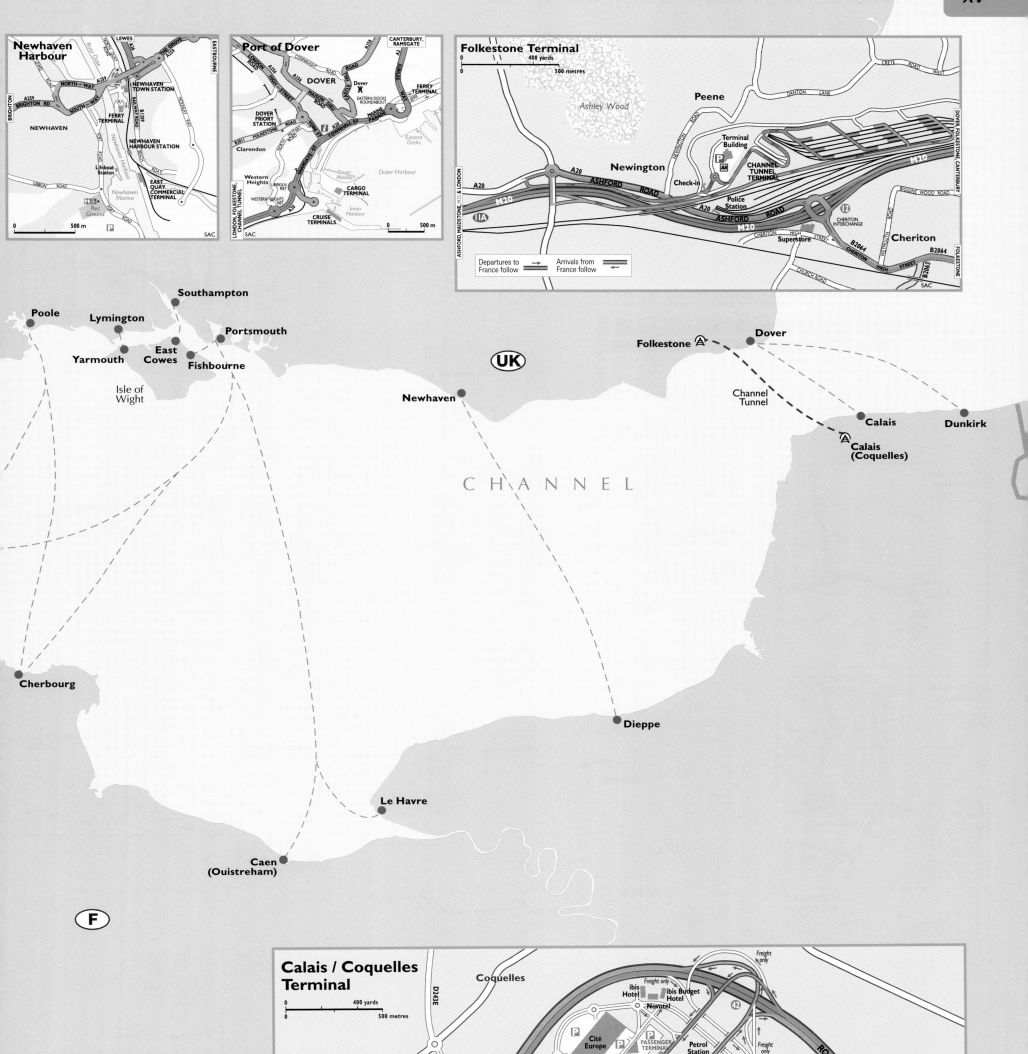

Newhaven Harbour

LEWES
River Ouse
EASTBOURNE
A26
THE DROVE
NORTH WAY
A259 Brighton Rd
SOUTH WAY
NEWHAVEN TOWN STATION
FERRY TERMINAL
B1299
NEWHAVEN
NEWHAVEN HARBOUR STATION
Lifeboat Station
Newhaven Marina
Rec Ground
EAST QUAY COMMERCIAL TERMINAL
CHERRY ROAD
0   500 m
SAC

Port of Dover

CANTERBURY, RAMSGATE
A256
A258
CASTLE STREET
YORK STREET
DOVER
Dover
EASTERN DOCKS ROUNDABOUT
FERRY TERMINAL
TERMINAL EF
MARINE PARADE
DOVER PRIORY STATION
A20 FOLKESTONE ROAD
Clarendon
Eastern Docks
Western Heights
WESTERN HEIGHTS
A20
LINCOLN RD
Dover Marina
Outer Harbour
CARGO TERMINAL
Inner Harbour
CRUISE TERMINALS
LONDON, FOLKESTONE, CHANNEL TUNNEL
0   500 m
SAC

Folkestone Terminal

0   400 yards
0   500 metres
Ashley Wood
Peene
DANTON LANE
Newington
Terminal Building
Check-in
CHANNEL TUNNEL TERMINAL
P
A20
M20
ASHFORD ROAD
Police Station
A20
M20
ASHFORD ROAD
CHERITON INTERCHANGE
12
Superstore
CHERITON HIGH STREET
B2064
B2064
Cheriton
BIGGINS WOOD ROAD
DOVER, FOLKESTONE, CANTERBURY
CHURCH ROAD
ASHFORD, MAIDSTONE, M25 & LONDON
FOLKESTONE
11A

Departures to France follow →
Arrivals from France follow ←

SAC

Poole
Lymington
Southampton
Yarmouth
East Cowes
Fishbourne
Portsmouth
Isle of Wight
UK
Newhaven
Folkestone ⛺
Dover
Channel Tunnel
Calais
Dunkirk
Calais (Coquelles) ⛺

C H A N N E L

Cherbourg
Dieppe
Le Havre
Caen (Ouistreham)

F

Calais / Coquelles Terminal

0   400 yards
0   500 metres
Coquelles
D243E
Freight only
ibis Hotel
ibis Budget Hotel
Novotel
Cité Europe
P
PASSENGER TERMINAL
Petrol Station
Check-in
Frontier Controls
A16 (E402) ROCADE LITTORALE
BOULOGNE
A16 (E402) ROCADE LITTORALE
DE L'EUROPE
BOULEVARD DE LA CÔTE D'OPALE
BOULEVARD DE L'EUROPE
HGV Fuel Station
Freight Terminal
Eurotunnel Administration Headquarters
Parc d'activités les Terrasses
Arrivals Platforms
Departures Platforms
Freight only
Freight only
Freight only
CALAIS
DUNKERQUE A26 (PARIS)
D304
13

Departures to England follow →
Arrivals from England follow ←

SAC

SCOTLAND FERRIES

From	To	Journey time	Operator website
Scottish Islands/west coast of Scotland			
Gourock	Dunoon	20 mins	western-ferries.co.uk
Glenelg	Skye	20 mins (Easter–Oct)	skyeferry.co.uk

Numerous and varied sailings from the west coast of Scotland to Scottish islands are provided by Caledonian MacBrayne. Please visit calmac.co.uk for all ferry information, including those of other operators.

From	To	Journey time	Operator website
Orkney Islands			
Aberdeen	Kirkwall	6 hrs–7 hrs 15 mins	northlinkferries.co.uk
Gills	St Margaret's Hope	1 hr	pentlandferries.co.uk
Scrabster	Stromness	1 hr 30 mins	northlinkferries.co.uk
Lerwick	Kirkwall	5 hrs 30 mins	northlinkferries.co.uk

Inter-island services are operated by Orkney Ferries. Please see orkneyferries.co.uk for details.

From	To	Journey time	Operator website
Shetland Islands			
Aberdeen	Lerwick	12 hrs	northlinkferries.co.uk
Kirkwall	Lerwick	7 hrs 45 mins	northlinkferries.co.uk

Inter-island services are operated by Shetland Island Council Ferries. Please see shetland.gov.uk/ferries for details.

Please note that some smaller island services are day and weather dependent. Reservations are required for some routes. Book and confirm sailing schedules by contacting the operator.

NORTH SEA FERRY CROSSINGS

From	To	Journey time	Operator website
Harwich	Hook of Holland	6 hrs 30 mins	stenaline.co.uk
Kingston upon Hull	Rotterdam (Europoort)	11 hrs	poferries.com
Newcastle upon Tyne	Amsterdam (IJmuiden)	15 hrs 30 mins	dfdsseaways.co.uk

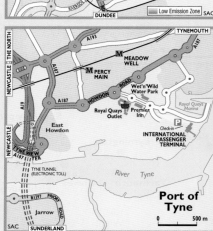

Aberdeen Harbour

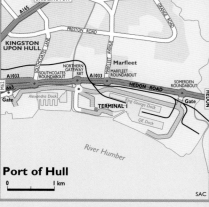

Port of Tyne

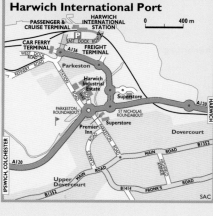

Port of Hull

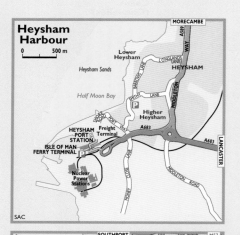

Heysham Harbour

Liverpool Docks

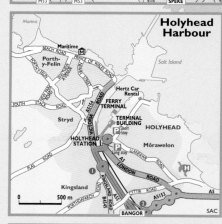

Holyhead Harbour

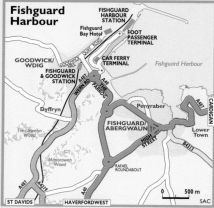

Fishguard Harbour

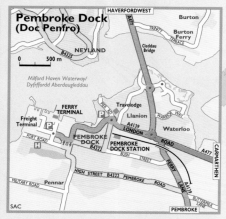

Pembroke Dock (Doc Penfro)

IRISH SEA FERRY CROSSINGS

From	To	Journey time	Operator website
Cairnryan	Belfast	2 hrs 15 mins	stenaline.co.uk
Cairnryan	Larne	2 hrs	poferries.com
Douglas (IOM)	Belfast	2 hrs 45 mins (April–Aug)	steam-packet.com
Douglas (IOM)	Dublin	2 hrs 55 mins (April–Aug)	steam-packet.com
Fishguard	Rosslare	3 hrs 15 mins	stenaline.co.uk
Heysham	Douglas (IOM)	3 hrs 45 mins	steam-packet.com
Holyhead	Dublin	2 hrs (Mar–Oct)	irishferries.com
Holyhead	Dublin	3 hrs 15 mins	irishferries.com
Holyhead	Dublin	3 hrs 15 mins	stenaline.co.uk
Liverpool	Douglas (IOM)	2 hrs 45 mins (Apr–Oct)	steam-packet.com
Liverpool	Dublin	8 hrs–8 hrs 30 mins	poferries.com
Liverpool (Birkenhead)	Belfast	8 hrs	stenaline.co.uk
Pembroke Dock	Rosslare	4 hrs	irishferries.com

The information listed is provided as a guide only, as services are liable to change at short notice and are weather dependent. Services shown are for vehicle ferries only, operated by conventional ferry unless indicated as a fast ferry service (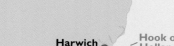). Please check sailings before planning your journey.

Motoring information

Symbol	Description
M4	Motorway with number
Toll	Toll motorway with toll station
6	Motorway junction with and without number
5	Restricted motorway junctions
Fleet / Todhills	Motorway service area, rest area
	Motorway and junction under construction
A3	Primary route single/ dual carriageway
1	Primary route junction with and without number
3	Restricted primary route junctions
S	Primary route service area
BATH	Primary route destination
A1123	Other A road single/ dual carriageway
B2070	B road single/ dual carriageway
	Minor road more than 4 metres wide, less than 4 metres wide
	Roundabout
	Interchange/junction
	Narrow primary/other A/B road with passing places (Scotland)
	Road under construction
	Road tunnel
Toll	Road toll, steep gradient (arrows point downhill)
5	Distance in miles between symbols
or	Vehicle ferry (all year, seasonal)
	Fast vehicle ferry or catamaran
or	Passenger ferry (all year, seasonal)
	Railway line, in tunnel
	Railway station, tram stop, level crossing
	Preserved or tourist railway
	Airport (major/minor)
H	Heliport
F	International freight terminal
H	24-hour Accident & Emergency hospital
C	Crematorium
P•R	Park and Ride (at least 6 days per week)
	City, town, village or other built-up area
628	Height in metres
637 Lecht Summit	Mountain pass
	Snow gates (on main routes)
	National boundary
	County or administrative boundary
	City with clean air zone, low/zero emission zone

Touring information

To avoid disappointment, check opening times before visiting

Symbol	Description
	Scenic route
i	Tourist Information Centre
i	Tourist Information Centre (seasonal)
V	Visitor or heritage centre
	Picnic site
	Caravan site (AA inspected)
△	Camping site (AA inspected)
	Caravan & camping site (AA inspected)
	Abbey, cathedral or priory
	Ruined abbey, cathedral or priory
	Castle
	Historic house or building
M	Museum or art gallery
	Industrial interest
	Aqueduct, viaduct
	Vineyard
	Brewery or distillery
	Garden
	Arboretum
	Country park
	Showground
	Theme park
	Farm or animal centre
	Zoological or wildlife collection
	Bird collection
	Aquarium
	RSPB site
	National Nature Reserve (England, Scotland, Wales)
	Local nature reserve
	Wildlife Trust reserve
	Forest drive
	National trail
	Viewpoint
	Waterfall
	Hill-fort
	Roman antiquity
	Prehistoric monument
1066	Battle site with year
	Preserved or tourist railway
	Cave or cavern
	Windmill, monument or memorial
	Beach (award winning)
	Lighthouse
	Golf course
	Football stadium
	County cricket ground
	Rugby Union national stadium
	International athletics stadium
	Horse racing, show jumping
	Motor-racing circuit
	Air show venue
	Ski slope (natural, artificial)
	National Trust site
	National Trust for Scotland site
	English Heritage site
	Historic Scotland site
	Cadw (Welsh heritage) site
★	Other place of interest
	Boxed symbols indicate attractions within urban area
	World Heritage Site (UNESCO)
	National Park and National Scenic Area (Scotland)
	Forest Park
	Sandy beach
	Heritage coast
	Major shopping centre

Town plans

Symbol	Description
2	Motorway and junction
4	Primary road single/ dual carriageway and numbered junction
37	A road single/ dual carriageway and numbered junction
	B road single/ dual carriageway
	Local road single/ dual carriageway
	Other road single/dual carriageway, minor road
	One-way, gated/ closed road
	Restricted access road
	Pedestrian area
	Footpath
	Road under construction
	Road tunnel
	Level crossing
	Railway station
	Tramway
	London Underground station
	London Overground station
	Rail interchange
	Docklands Light Railway (DLR) station
o	Light rapid transit system station
	Airport, heliport
R	Railair terminal
P•R	Park and Ride (at least 6 days per week)
P P	Car park, with electric charging point
	Bus/coach station
H H	Hospital, 24-hour Accident & Emergency hospital
	Toilet, with facilities for the less able
	Building of interest
	Ruined building
	City wall
	Cliff lift
	Escarpment
	River/canal, lake
	Lock, weir
	Park/sports ground
	Cemetery
	Woodland
	Built-up area
	Beach
i	Tourist Information Centre
V	Visitor or heritage centre
	Post Office
	Public library
	Shopping centre
	Shopmobility
	Theatre or performing arts centre
	Cinema
M	Museum
	Castle
	Castle mound
•	Monument, memorial, statue
	Viewpoint
†	Abbey, chapel, church
✡	Synagogue
☾	Mosque
	Golf course
	Racecourse
	Nature reserve
	Aquarium, zoological or wildlife collection
	World Heritage Site (UNESCO)
	English Heritage site
	Historic Scotland site
	Cadw (Welsh heritage) site
	National Trust site
	National Trust for Scotland site

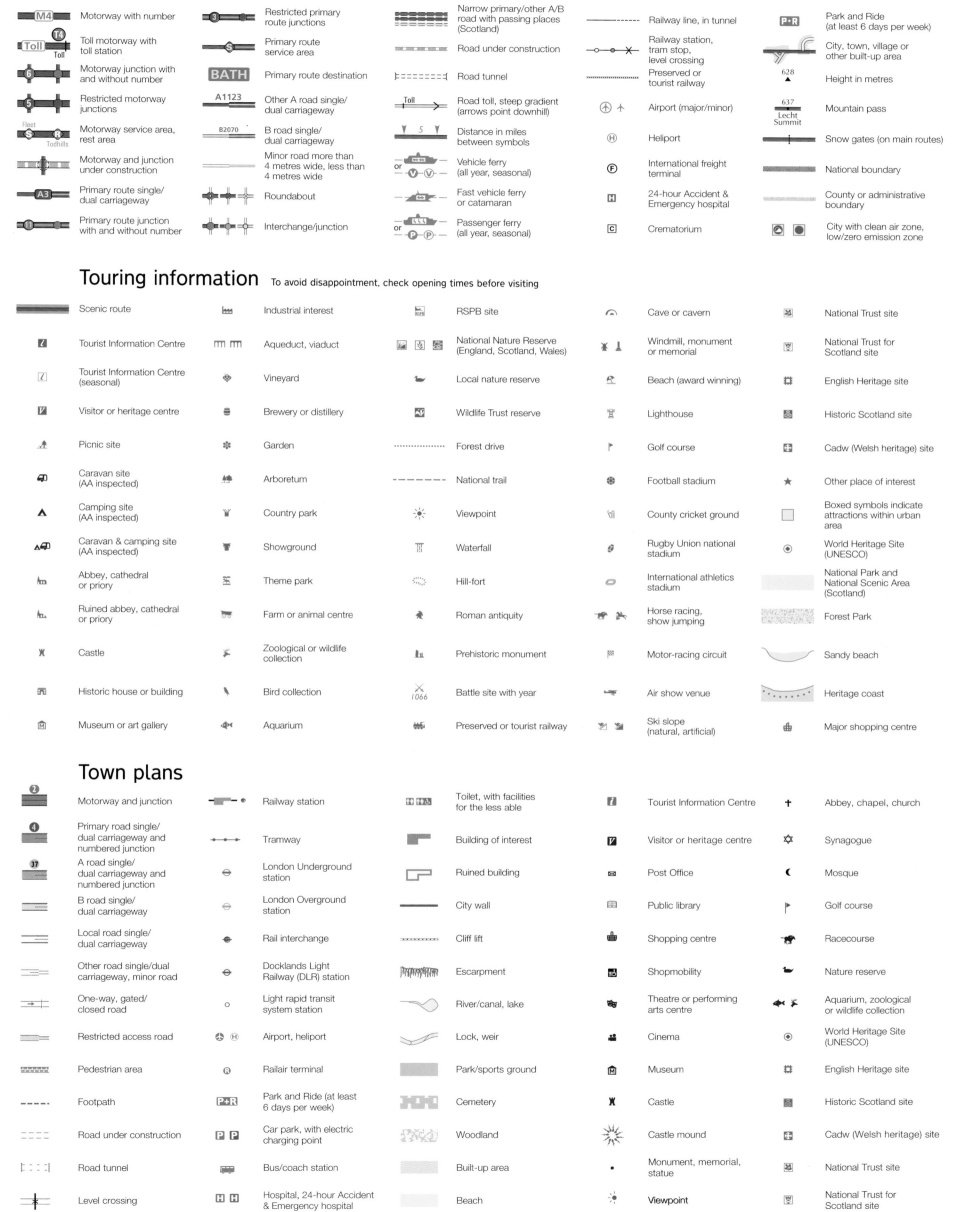

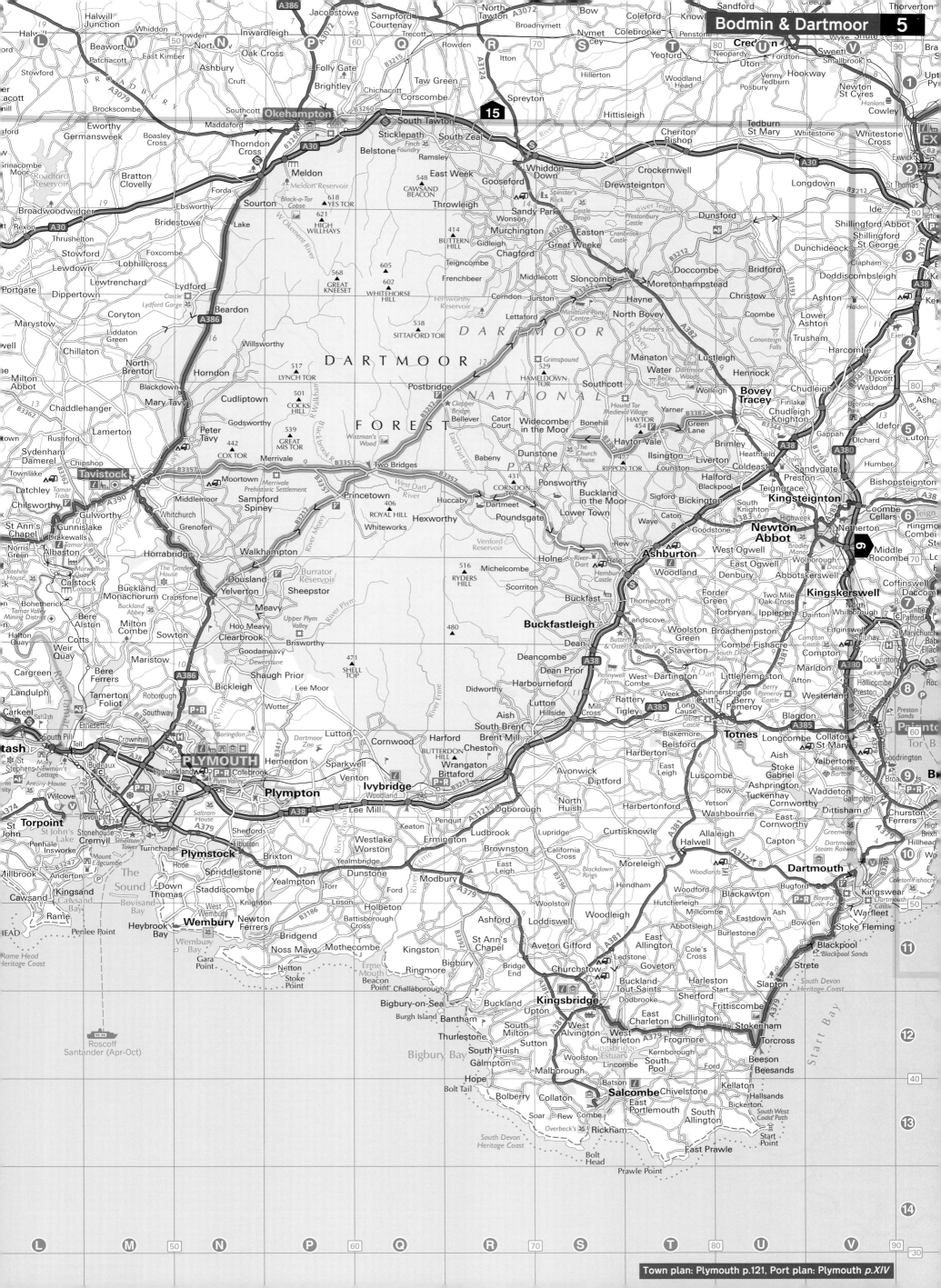

Folkestone Terminal

0   400 yards
0   500 metres

Departures to France follow →
Arrivals from France follow ⇐

Calais / Coquelles Terminal

0   400 yards
0   500 metres

Departures to England follow ←
Arrivals from England follow ⇒

Town plan: Canterbury p.117, **Port plan:** Dover *p.XV*

North West Point
Lundy Heritage Coast
LUNDY
▲142
Marine Reserve
Shutter Point
Surf Point
(Apr-Oct) ℗

SS

Rock Ba
Morte Point
Woolac
Morte Bay

Baggy Point
Putsborou
Croyde Bay
Ge
Croyde Bay
North Devon Heritage Coast
(Apr-Oct) ℗

BARNSTAPLE
OR
BIDEFORD BAY

Northam Burrows
Westward Ho!
N
Appl

HARTLAND POINT
Shipload Bay
Abbotsham
Bide

Damehole Point
Titchberry
Brownsham
The Big Sheep
Ford
Bide

Hartland Quay
Hartland Abbey & Gardens
Stoke
Velly
Clovelly
Buck's Mills
Fairy Cross
Woodtown
Yeo Vale

Speke's Mill Mouth
Hartland
B3248
4
Higher Clovelly
Horns Cross
Littlehar
Saltre

Milford
Docton Mill
Philham
Milky Way
Buck's Cross
A39
10
Goldworthy

Elmscott
Edistone
Tosberry
Woolfardisworthy
Cranford
Parkham
Cabbacott
Monkle

Hardisworthy
South Hole
Parkham Ash
Buckland Brewer
Frith

Welcombe
Ashmansworthy
Melbury
Frithelstock Sto

Mead
Darracott
Gooseham Mill
Woolley
Meddon
East Putford
Thornehillhead

Morwenstow
Gooseham
Eastcott
East Youlstone
Dinworthy
Gnome Reserve ★
West Putford
Haytown
Lang

Higher Sharpnose Point
West Youlstone
16
Bradworthy
Colscott
Stibb Cross

Shop Woodford
A39
Kimworthy
Abbots Bickington
Bulkworthy
A388

Lower Sharpnose Point
Tamar Lakes
Sutcombe
Newton St Petrock

Steeple Point
Kilkhampton
Alfardisworthy
Sutcombemill
River
Venngreen

Stibb
Thurdon
Soldon Cross
Milton Damerel
Shebbear

Sandy Mouth
Soldon
Holsworthy Beacon
Thornbury
Woodacott
Bradford

Northcott Mouth
Maer
Poughill
B3254
Bush 1643
Hersham
Dunsdon
Brendon
Lashbrook
Priestace

Crooklets
Flexbur
Summerleaze
Castle Bude
Stratton
Grimscott
Lana
Chilsworthy
Cookbury
Lash

Bude
Bude
Lynstone
Launcells
Launcells Cross
Kingford
Pancrasweek
Anvil Corner
Cookbury Wick
Holemoor

Bude Bay
Upton
Buttspear Cross
Red Post
10
Derril
Derriton
A3072
Holsworthy
Brandis Corner

Helebridge
Marhamchurch
Bridgerule
Pyworthy
Chasty
Whimble
Hollacombe
Chilla

Widemouth Bay
Titson
Leworthy
Headon

Box's Shop
Coppathorne
19
R Claw
Buckhorn
Halwill

Millook
Kitleigh
Langaford

Dizzard Point
Poundstock
Bangors
Whitstone
East Balsdon
Clawton
A388
Quoditch
Stowford

Dizzard
Penlean
Treskinnick Cross
Week St Mary
North Tamerton
Tetcott
Higher Prestacott

St Gennys
Tregole
Nethercott
Lana
Ashwater
Ashmill

Crackington Haven
Cambeak
Coxford
Penhallam Manor
Greena Moor
R Deer
14
Luffincott

Rosecare
Jacobstow
West Peeke
Henford
Bradaford

Sweets
Southcott
Maxworthy
West Curry
Clubworthy
Bennacott
Copthorne
Boyton
Northcott
East Panson
Virginstow

Wainhouse Corner
4
Trengune
South Wheatley
Chapmans Well
Frankaborough
Sitcott
Grinacombe Moor
Roadfor
Reservoir

Beeny
B3263
A39
Marshgate
Canworthy Water
Troswell
South Beer
West Panson
Gr

Pentire Point - Widemouth Heritage Coast
Witchcraft & Magic
15
19
Billacott
Brazacott
Langdon
Bridgetown
Downcare
K30

Boscastle
Treworld
Tresparrett
Otterham
Trebu
Trel
Warw
Trillacott
Broadwoodwi

Tr
ga
Lesnewth
Otterham Station
20
Trel
Tremaine
North Petherwin
Petherwin Gate
Ladycross
Rexon

Dog...y
Treneglos
Splatt
Hellescott
Crossgate

0 1 2 3 4 5 miles
0 1 2 3 4 5 6 7 8 kilometres
B3266

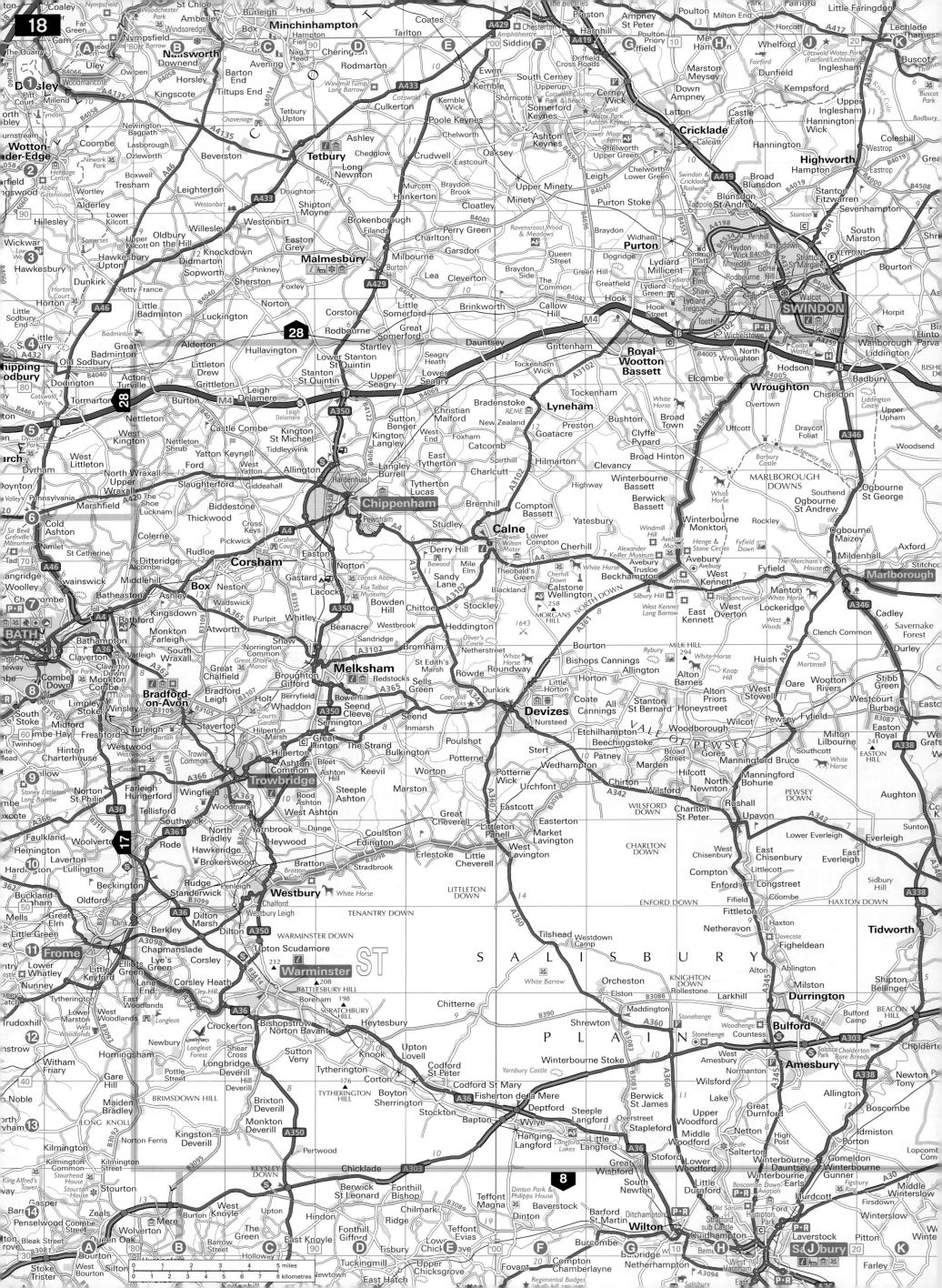

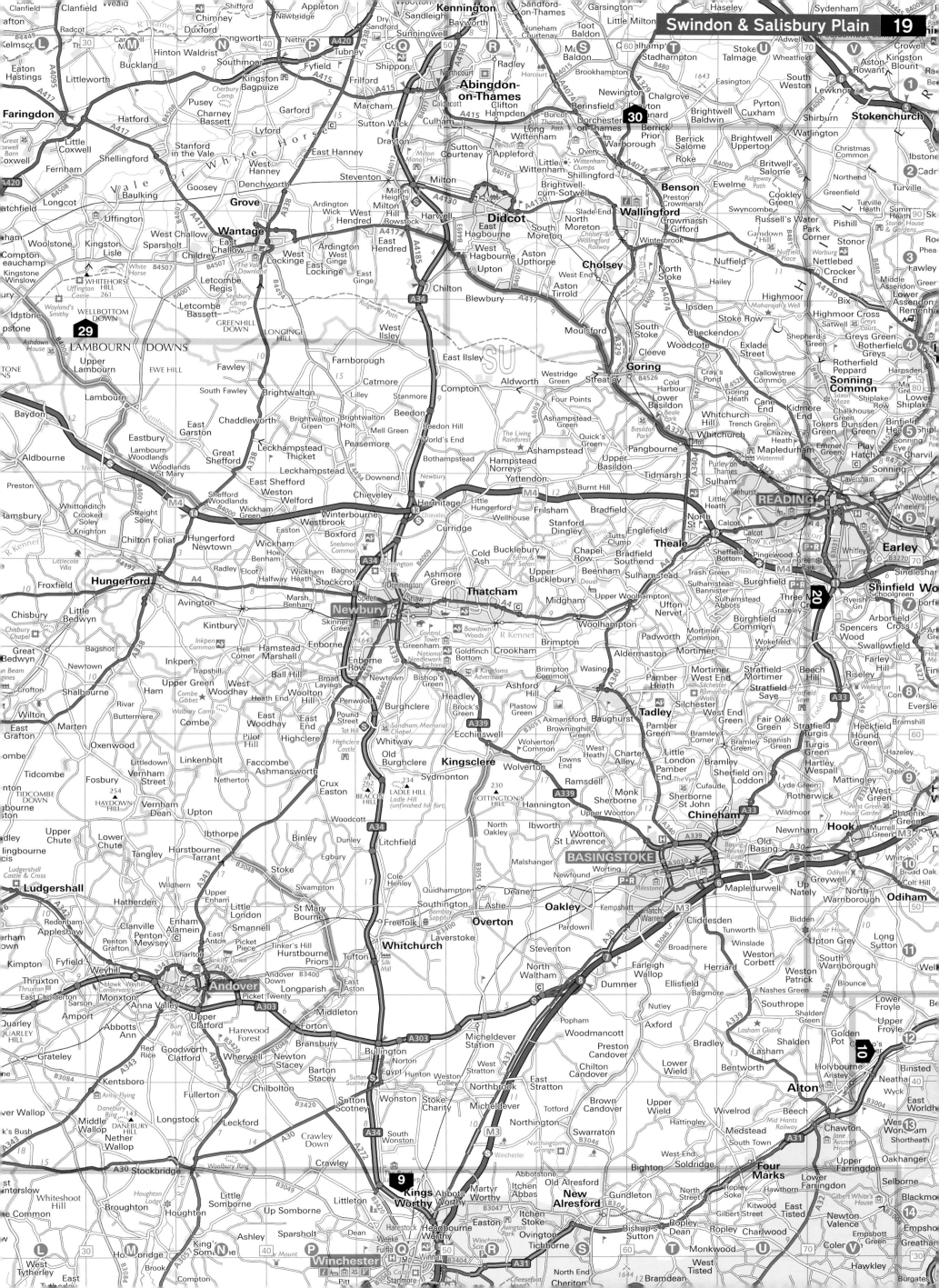

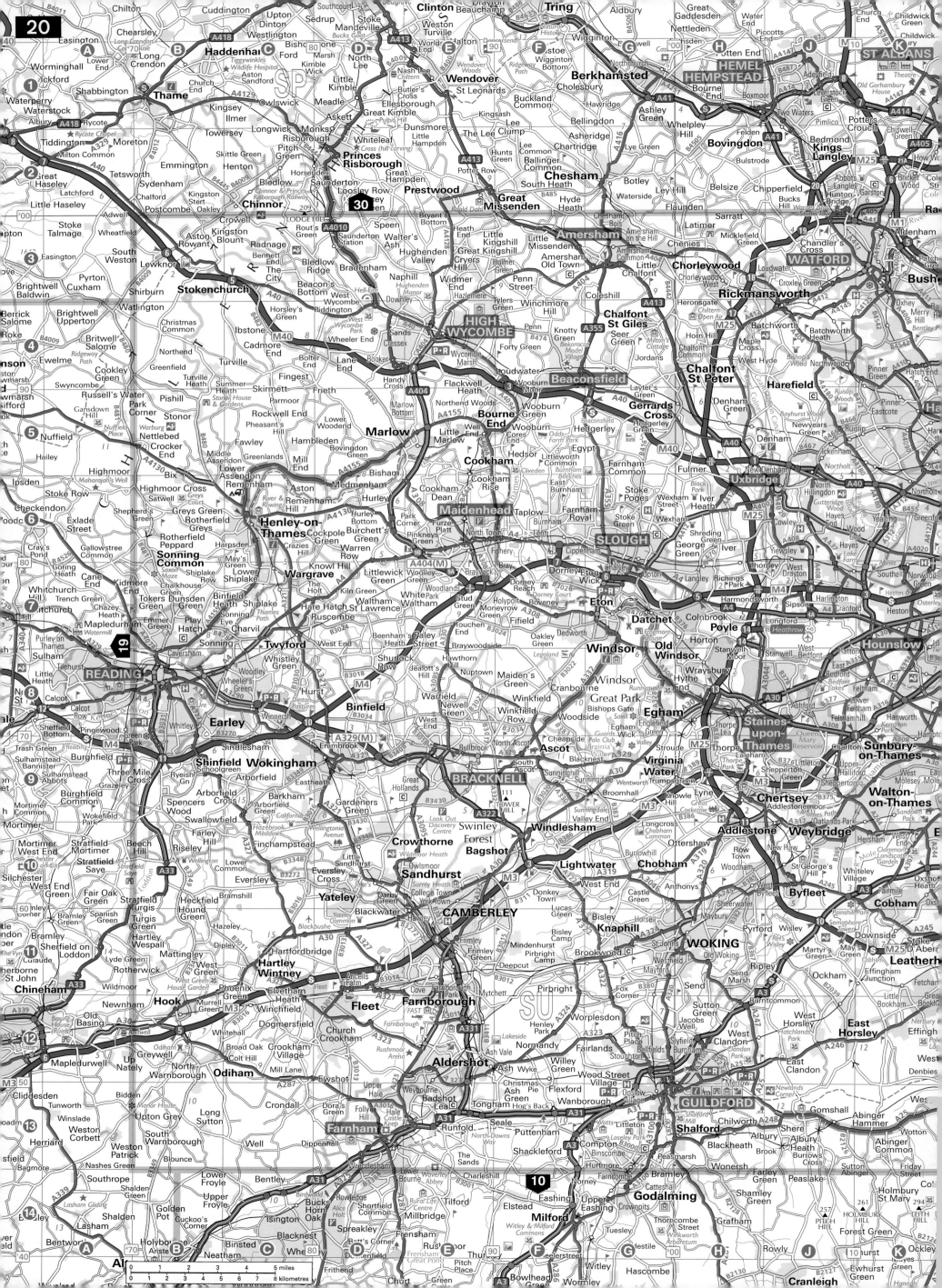

Harwich International Port

PASSENGER & CRUISE TERMINAL
HARWICH INTERNATIONAL STATION
CAR FERRY TERMINAL
FREIGHT TERMINAL
Parkeston
Harwich Industrial Estate
Superstore
PARKESTON ROUNDABOUT
ST NICHOLAS ROUNDABOUT
Superstore
Premier Inn
Dovercourt
IPSWICH, COLCHESTER
A120
HARWICH
A136
Upper Dovercourt
SAC

Southend-on-Sea

LONDON, BASILDON
Beecroft Art Gallery
HM Customs & Excise
Museum & Planetarium
SOUTHEND VICTORIA STATION
Superstore
The Victoria
South Essex College
Surgery
Travelodge
The Forum
University of Essex
South Essex College
SOUTHEND CENTRAL STATION
County Court
Leisure Centre
Porters Civic House
Porters Grange School
Kingdom Hall
Sacred Heart Sch
Salvation Army
Uni of Essex
Cliftown Telephone
Naval & Military Club
Royal Hotel
The Royals
St John's
Victoria Statue
Palace Hotel
Kursaal
Three Shells
Adventure
Island
Pier Museum
SeaLife Adventure
SAC
SHOEBURY
QUEENSWAY
SOUTHCHURCH ROAD
All Saints

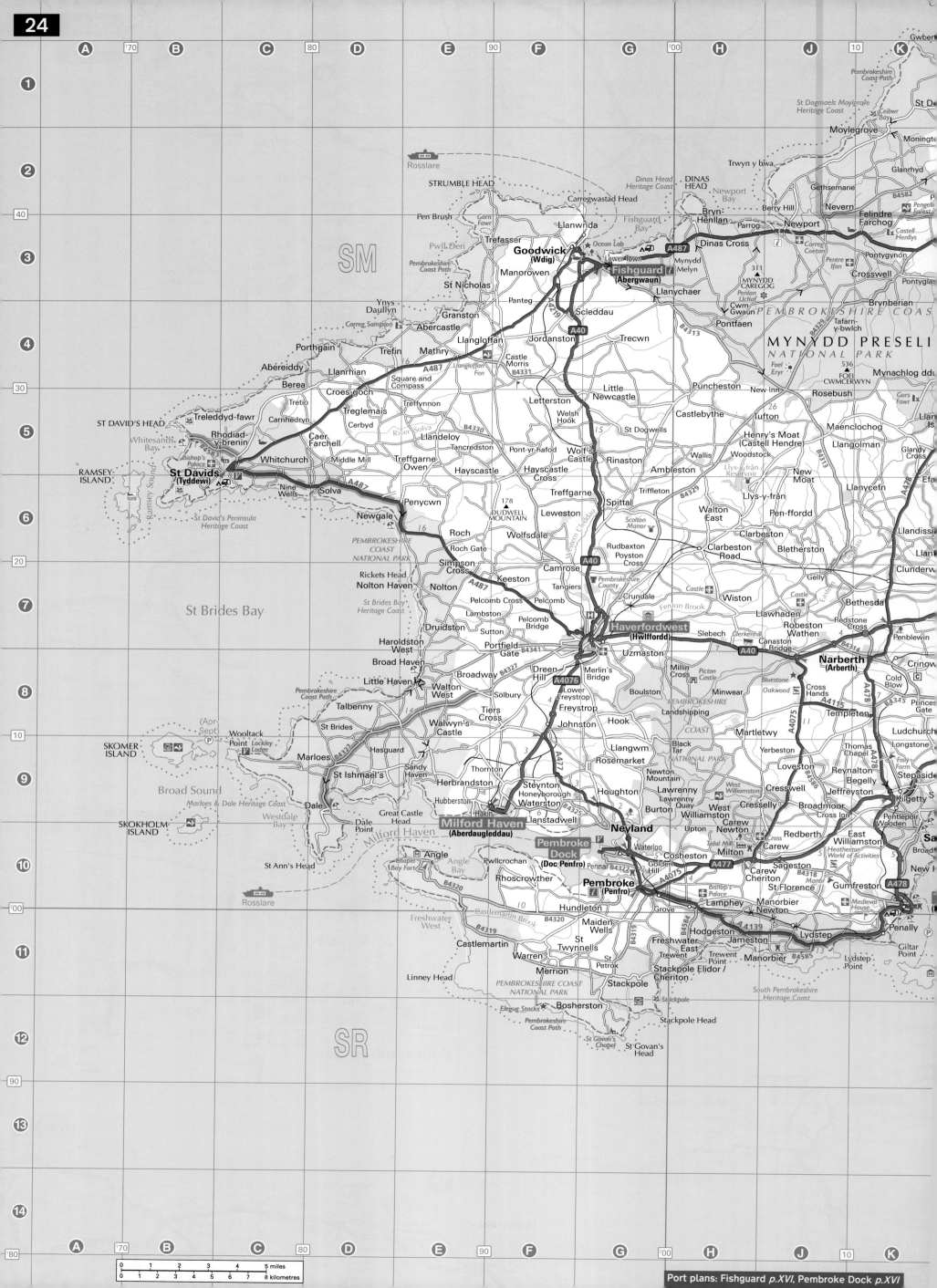

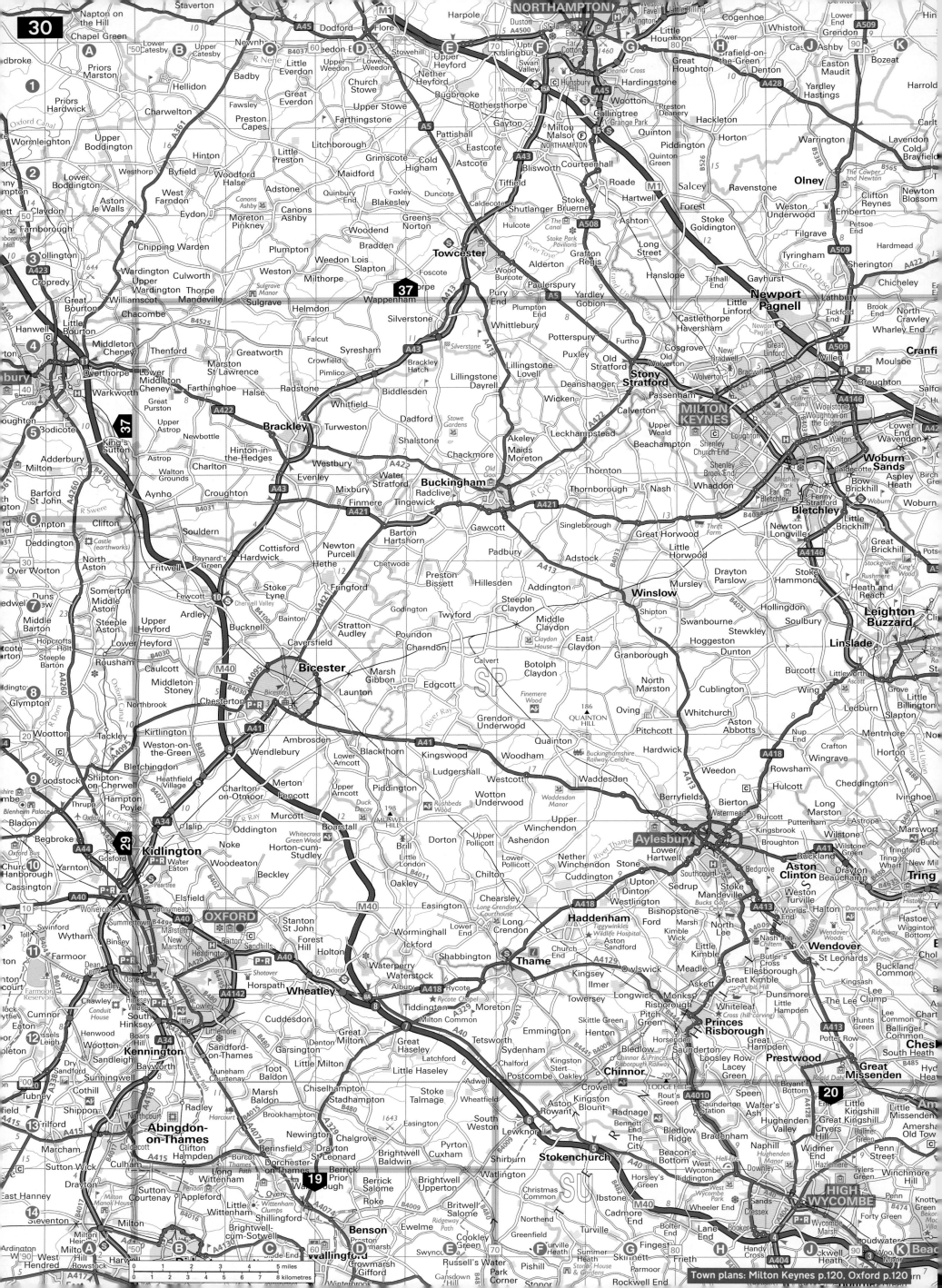

A B C D E F G H J K

Aberystwyth

0   200 m

Cardigan Bay

Bandstand
St Paul Methodist
St David's URC
The Morlan Centre
Capel y Morfa
Surgery
Ceredigion
Bethel
Royal Pier
National Library of Wales
A487
CAB
Coastguard Station
University (Old College)
Clock Tower
Market Hall
Salvation Army
Castle
Monument
Aberystwyth Castle (ruins)
St Michael's
Eglwys y Santes Fair
Holy Trinity
ABERYSTWYTH STATION
St Padarn's Primary School
University (School of Art)
Aberystwyth South Beach
Superstores
Ystwyth Retail Park
Rheidol
Trefechan Bridge
Slipway
Vale of Rheidol Steam Railway Station
River Rheidol
Ro-fawr
Justice Centre
Park Avenue (Aberystwyth Town FC)
Plascrug CP School
Marina
Fire Station
Police Station
Recreation Ground
Lifeboat Station
TA Centre
SAC
CARDIGAN
Aqua Terra

MACHYNLLETH, LLANGURIG
PENGLAIS ROAD
LLANBADARN
PENPARCAU ROAD

CARDIGAN BAY

SN
Ceredigion Heritage Coast

Llanrhystud
A487
Llansantffraid
Llanon
Rhos Haminiog
Aberarth
Aberaeron
Pennant
Monachty
Cilcennin
New Quay (Ceinewydd)
Marine
Henfynyw
Foss-y-ffin
Llyswen
Llwyncelyn
A482
Newbridge
Maen-y-groes
Gilfachrheda
Llanarth
Oakford
Ciliau-Aeron
Cwmtydu
Llanina
Cross Inn
Caerwedros
Dihewyd
Ystrad Aeron
Nanternis
Llwyndafydd
Mydroilyn
Talsarn
Ynys-Lochtyn
Pendinas Lochtyn
Pentre'rbryn
Synod Inn
A487
Temple Bar
Langrannog
Pontgarreg
Plwmp
Ffynnonddewi
Cae Hir
Penbryn
Morfa
B4334
Pentregat
Talgarreg
Gorsgoch
Ffynnonddewi
Cribyn
Parcllyn
Sarnau
Brynhoffnant
B4338
Tresaith
Aberporth
Tan-y-groes
Glynarthen
Capel Cynon
Bwlchyfadfa
Cardigan Island
Blaenannerch
Rhydlewis
Ffostrasol
Cwrtnewydd
Llanwnnen
Cardigan Island Coastal Farm
Mwnt Beach
Y Ferwig
Blaenporth
Capel Cynon
Pontsian
Cwmsychbant
Gwbert on Sea
Poppit Sands
Bettws Ifan
Hawen
Penrhiwpal
Tre-groes
Drefach
Alltyblaca
Pembrokeshire Coast Path
Penparc
Tremain
Beulah
Troedyraur
Maesllyn
Prengwyn
A486
Llanwenog
St Dogmaels Moylgrove Heritage Coast
Abbey & Coach House
Cilgerran
Brongest
Coed-y-Bryn
Croes-lan
Rhydowen
Llanybydder
Ceibwr Bay
St Dogmaels
Bridgend
Llangoedmor
Welsh Wildlife Centre
Ponthirwaun
Llangynllo
Gorrig
Pentrellwyn
Rhuddlan
Moylegrove
A484
Llechryd
Castle
TIVY SIDE
Cwm-cou
Aber-banc
Penrhiwllan
Capel Dewi
Cardigan (Aberteifi)
Pen-y-bryn
Llantood
Bridell
Glanrhyd
Llandygwydd
Horeb
Llandysul
Llanfihangel ar-arth
Trwyn bwa
Pontgarreg
Abercych
Cenarth
National Coracle Centre
Adpar
Llandyfriog
Teifi Valley Railway
Llandysul
Aber-gior
Newport Bay
Gethsemane
Pengelli Forest
Rhoshill
Pen-rhiw
Newcastle Emlyn (Castell Newydd Emlyn)
Henllan
Llangeler
Pontwelly
Mynydd Llanllwni
Berry Hill
Nevern
Felindre Farchog
A487
Newchapel
Penrherber
Aber-arad
Pentre-Cagel
National Wool Museum
Drefach
Pentre-cwrt
B4336
A485
Parrog
Carreg Coetan
Castell Henllys
25
Pentre-Cagel
Drefelin
Saron
Banc-y-ffordd
Pencader
Newport
Cross
Pontygynon
Eglwyswrw
Boncath
Cwmhiraeth
Glynteg
New Inn
Mynydd Caregog
Penlan Uchaf
Pentre Ifan
Blaenffos
Capel Iwan
Felindre
Gwyddgrug
Tafarn-y-bwlch
Crosswell
Whitechurch
Star
Cwmpengraig
Rhos
Dol-gran
Brynberian
Pontyglasier
Bwlch-y-groes
Clydey
Cilrhedyn
Cwm Morgan
Cwmduad
Alltwalis
PEMBROKESHIRE COAST
Foel Eryr
Crymych
Foel Drygarn
Llwyn-drain
Tegryn
Cwmduad
MYNYDD PRESELI NATIONAL PARK
Mynachlog ddu
Pentregalar
Hermon
Llanfyrnach
Hermon
A485
Gwernogle
New Inn
Rosebush
CWMC
Brechfa
Tufton

0   1   2   3   4   5 miles
0 1 2 3 4 5 6 7 8 kilometres

A B C D E F G H J K

Llanpumsaint

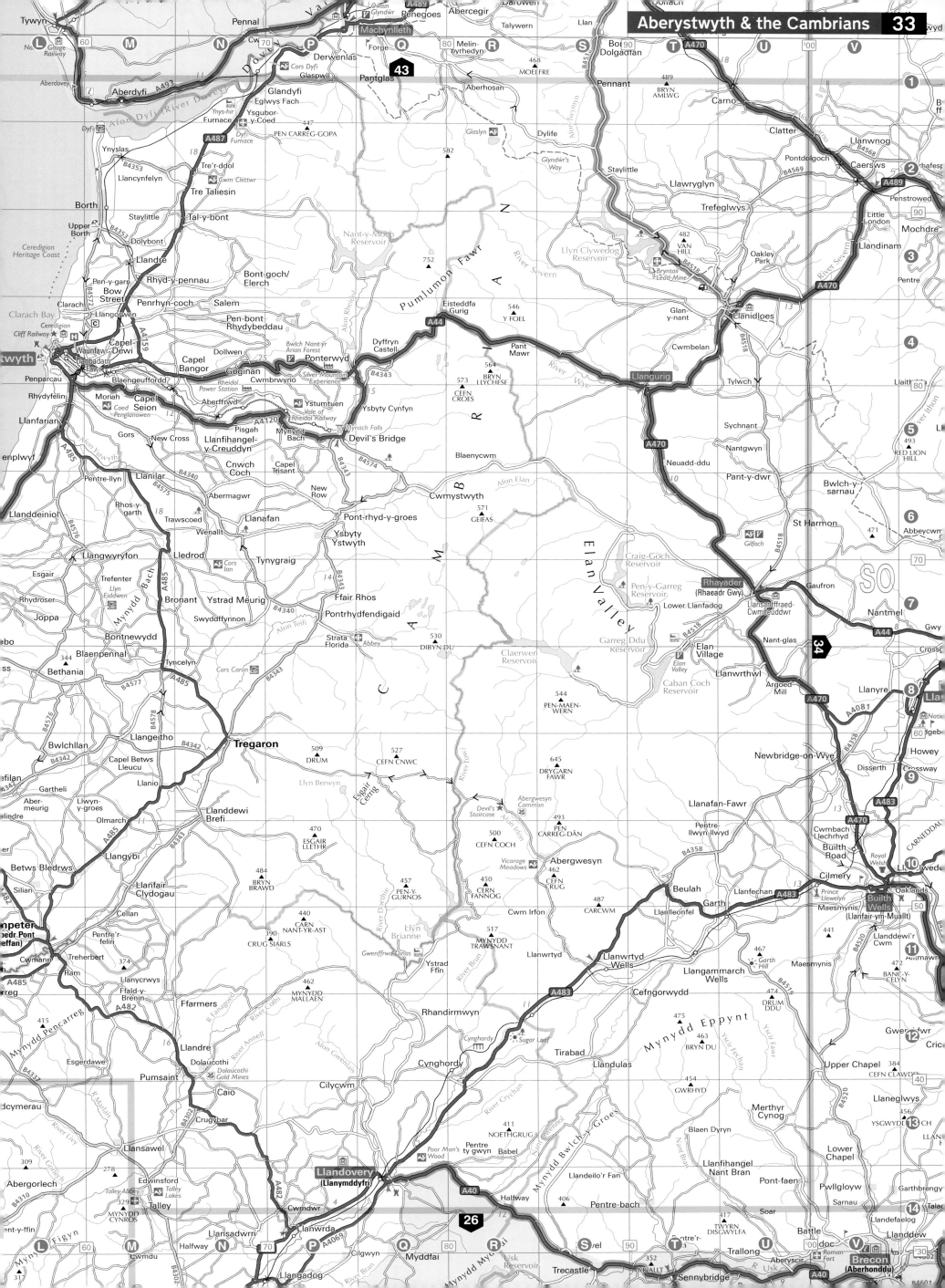

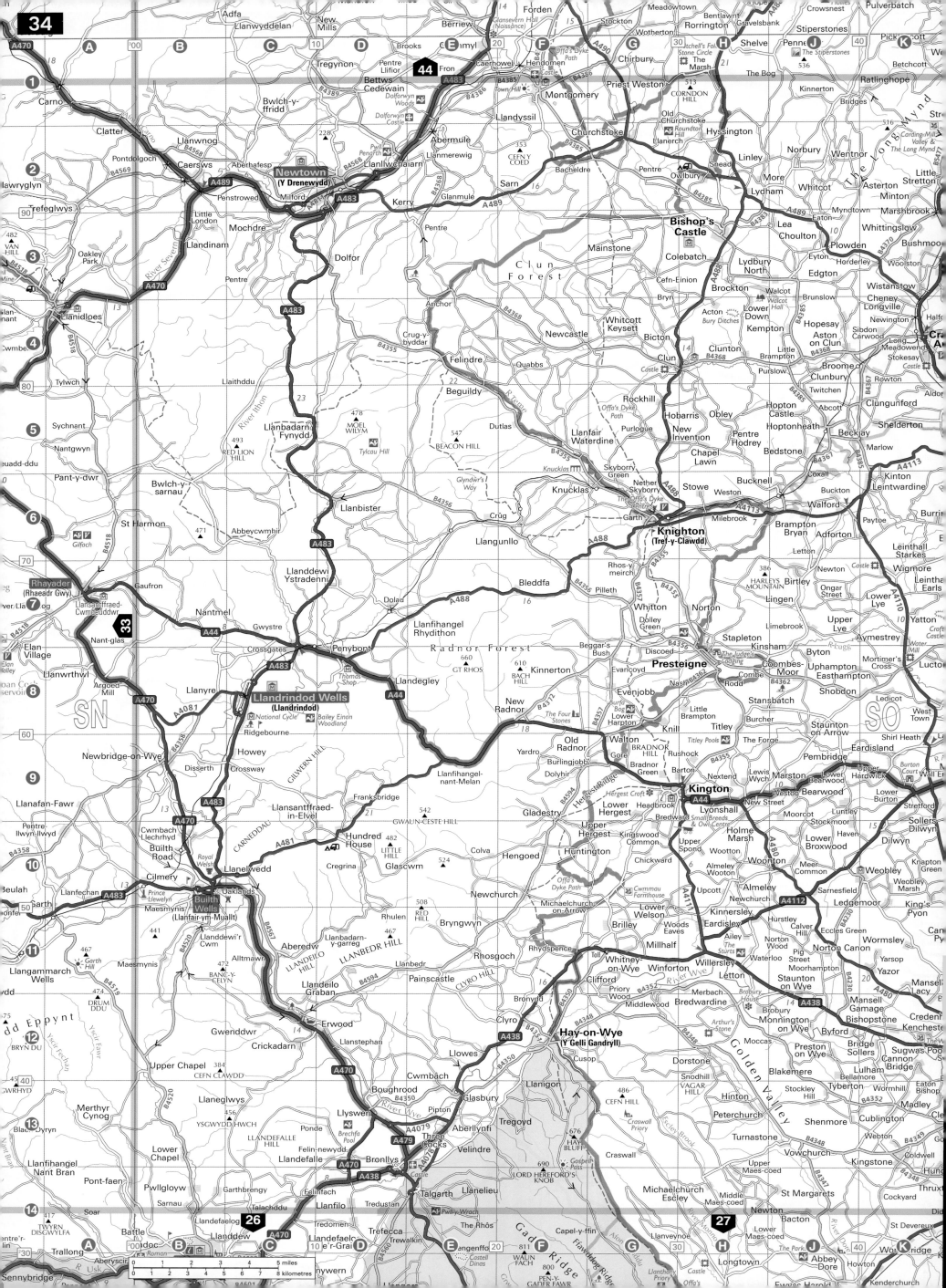

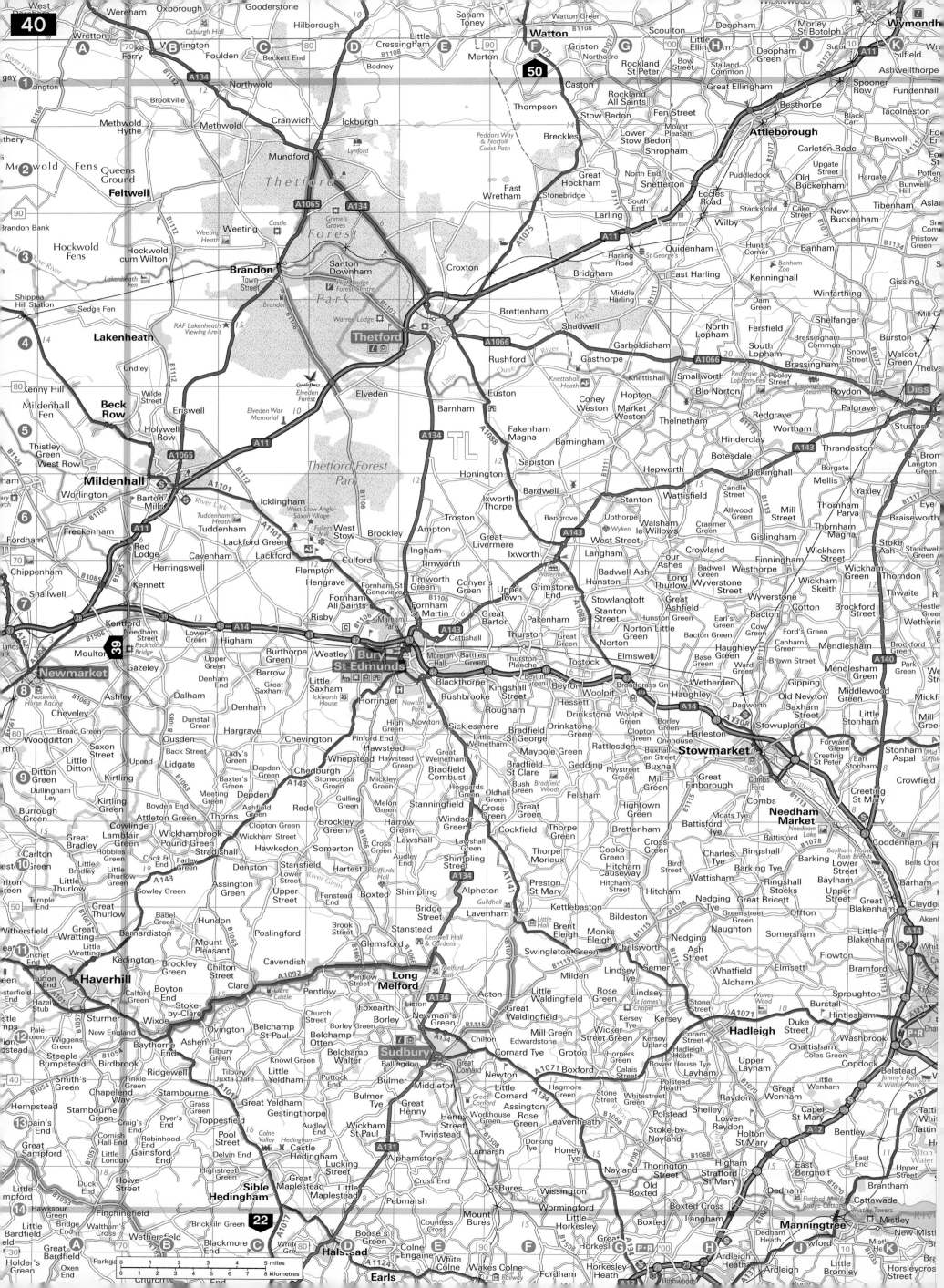

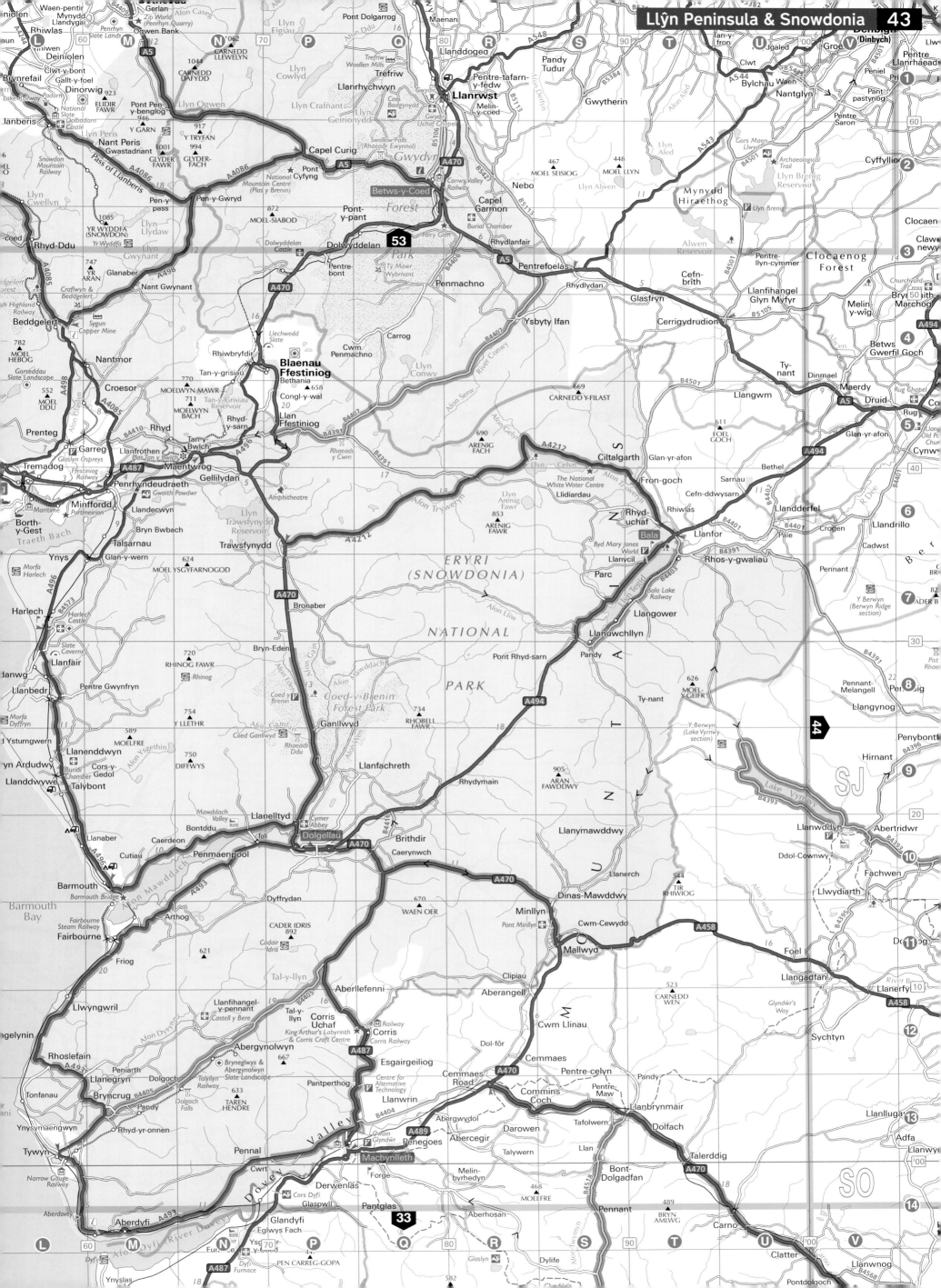

Great Yarmouth

Town plan: Norwich p.120

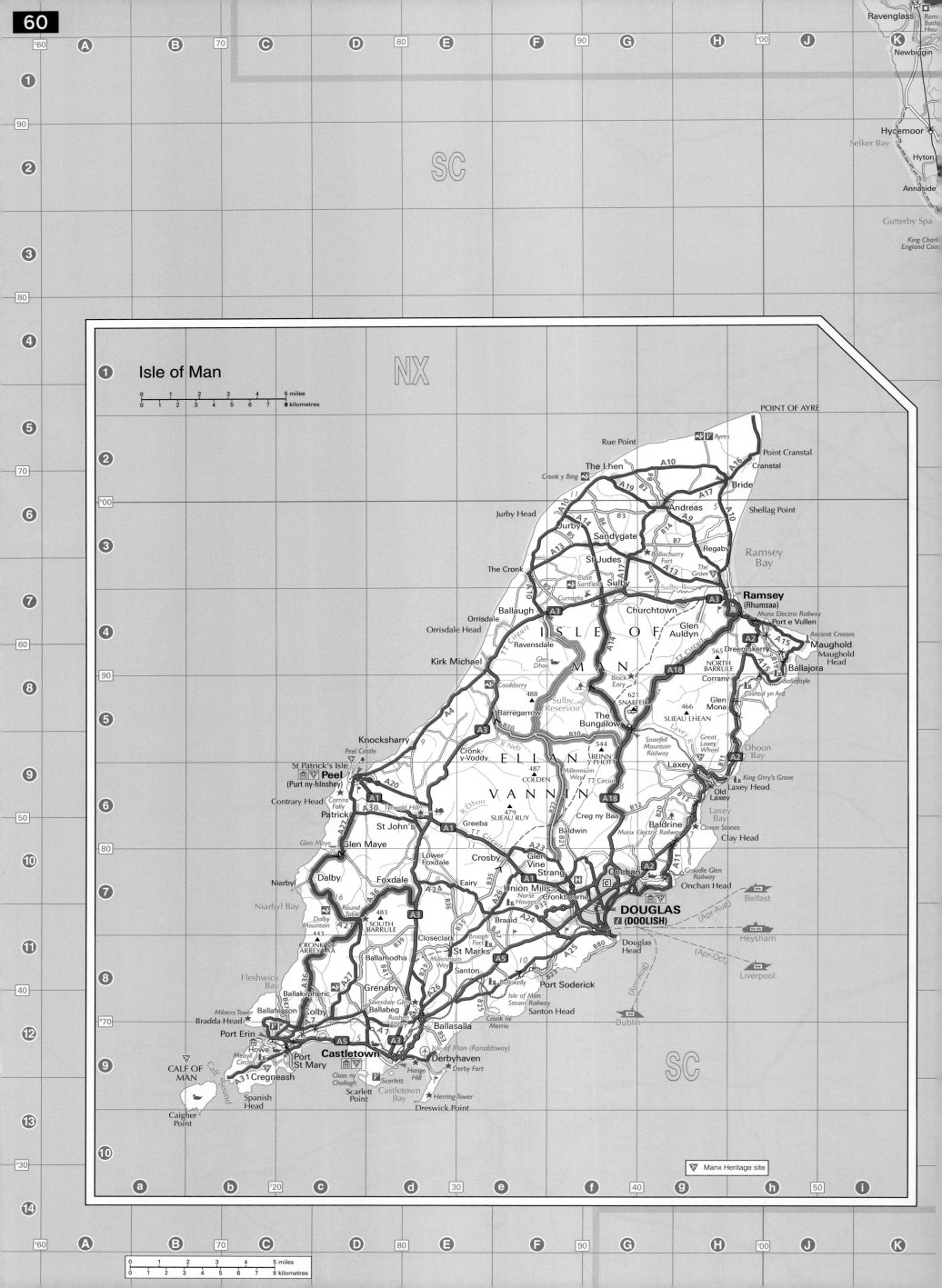

Isle of Man

0 1 2 3 4 5 miles
0 1 2 3 4 5 6 7 8 kilometres

NX

POINT OF AYRE

Ravenglass
Newbiggin
Hycemoor
Selker Bay
Hyton
Annaside
Gutterby Spa
King Charl
England Coa

Rue Point
'Ayres
Point Cranstal
Cranstal
The Lhen
A10
A16
Cronk y Bing
A19
B7
Bride
A17
Jurby Head
A14
Andreas
A9
A10
Shellag Point
Jurby
B5
B3
Sandygate
B14
Regaby
A17
St Judes
Ballachurry Fort
B7
A13
The Grove
Ramsey Bay
The Cronk
A10
Close Sartfield
B9
Sulby
Sulby-R
B14
Sulby-R
Curraghs
Churchtown
Ramsey (Rhumsaa)
A3
A2
Manx Electric Railway
Port e Vullen
Ballaugh
A10
Glen Auldyn
A15
Ancient Crosses
Orrisdale
A14
ISLE OF
Maughold
Orrisdale Head
Ravensdale
Glen Dhoo
A18
NORTH BARRULE
565 Dreemskerry
Maughold Head
Kirk Michael
MAN
Block Eary
Corrany
Ballajora
A4
Cooildarry
488
Barregarrow
Sulby Reservoir
621 SNAEFELL
466 SLIEAU LHEAN
Glen Mona
Cashtal yn Ard
Ballafayle
A3
B10
The Bungalow
Snaefell Mountain Railway
Great Laxey Wheel
A3
B10
544 BEINN Y PHOTT
Laxey
Dhoon Bay
Knocksharry
R Neb
Cronk-y-Voddy
ELLAN
Millennium Way
King Orry's Grave
B11
Peel Castle
St Patrick's Isle
487 COLDEN
TT Circuit
Old Laxey
Laxey Head
Peel (Purt ny-hInshey)
VANNIN
A18
Laxey Bay
Contrary Head
Corrins Folly
A20
479 SLIEAU RUY
Creg ny Baa
B20
B12
Clay Head
Patrick
A1
A30
Tynwald Hill
R Dhoo
Baldrine
Cloven Stones
St John's
A1
Greeba
Manx Electric Railway
Glen Maye
A1
Lower Foxdale
Crosby
Glen Vine
Onchan
Graudle Glen Railway
Glen Maye
TT Circuit
Strang
A2
Onchan Head
Niarbyl
Dalby
Foxdale
Eairy
Union Mills
H
C
Belfast
Niarbyl Bay
A24
Norse House
Cronkbourne
(Apr-Aug)
Round Table
483 SOUTH BARRULE
B39
Braaid
A24
DOUGLAS (DOOLISH)
Dalby Mountain
A27
Closeclark
Brough Fort
Douglas Head
Heysham
443 CRONK NY ARREY LAA
Ballamodha
St Marks
A5
A25
B80
(Apr-Oct)
Fleshwick Bay
Millennium Way
Santon
Liverpool
Ballakilpheric
A27
Grenaby
Silverdale Glen
A26
Ballakelly
Port Soderick
Isle of Man Steam Railway
(Apr-Aug)
Colby
Ballabeg
Rushen Abbey
Cronk ny Merriu
Santon Head
Milners Tower
Ballafesson
Ballasalla
Bradda Head
A7
A3
Dublin
Port Erin
A5
A3
Derbyhaven
SC
Howe
Meayll Circle
Port St Mary
Castletown
Close ny Chollagh
Hango Hill
Derby Fort
CALF OF MAN
A31 Cregneash
Scarlett
Scarlett Point
Castletown Bay
Herring Tower
Spanish Head
Dreswick Point
Caigher Point
Isle of Man (Ronaldsway)

SC

Manx Heritage site

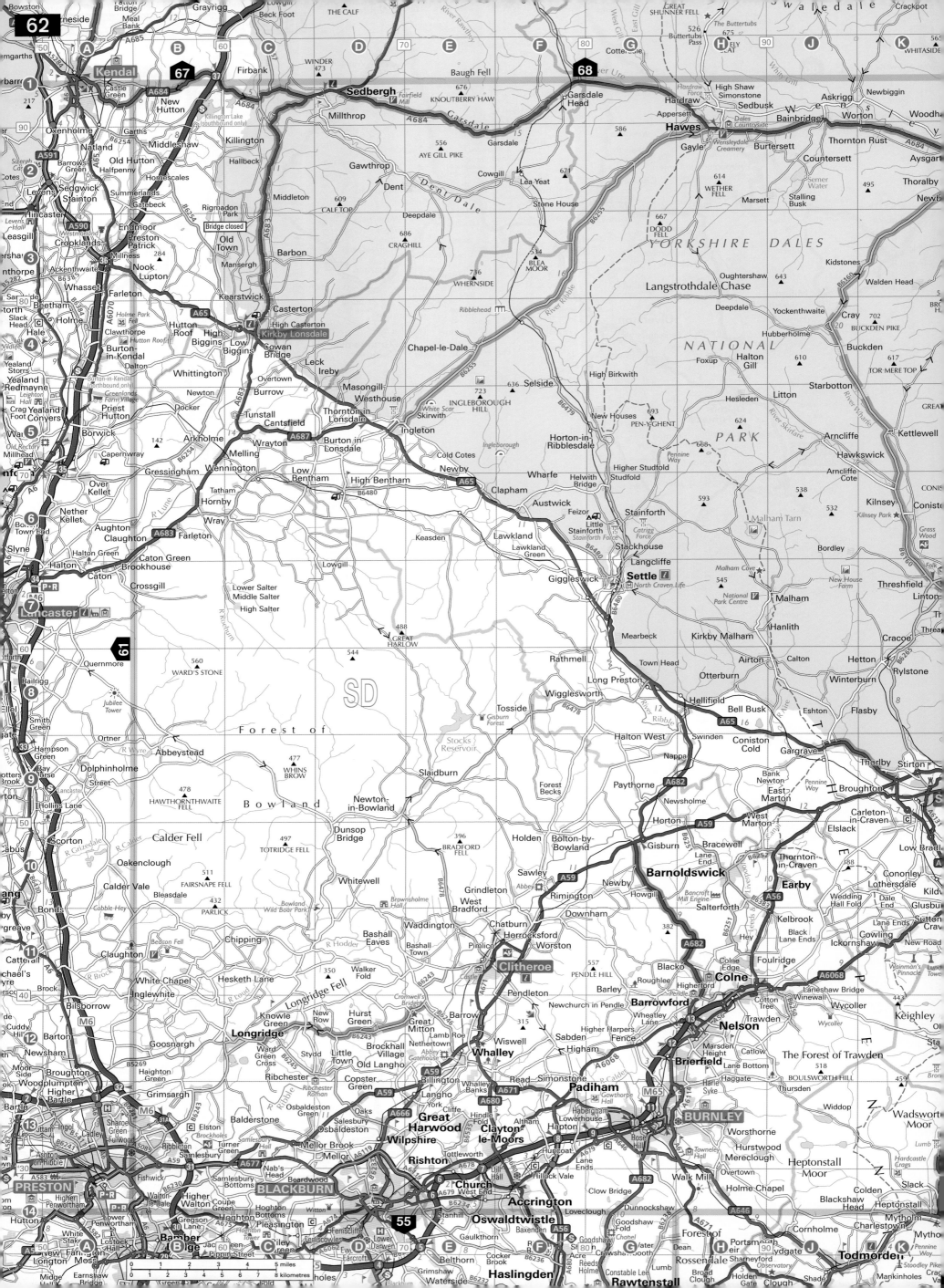

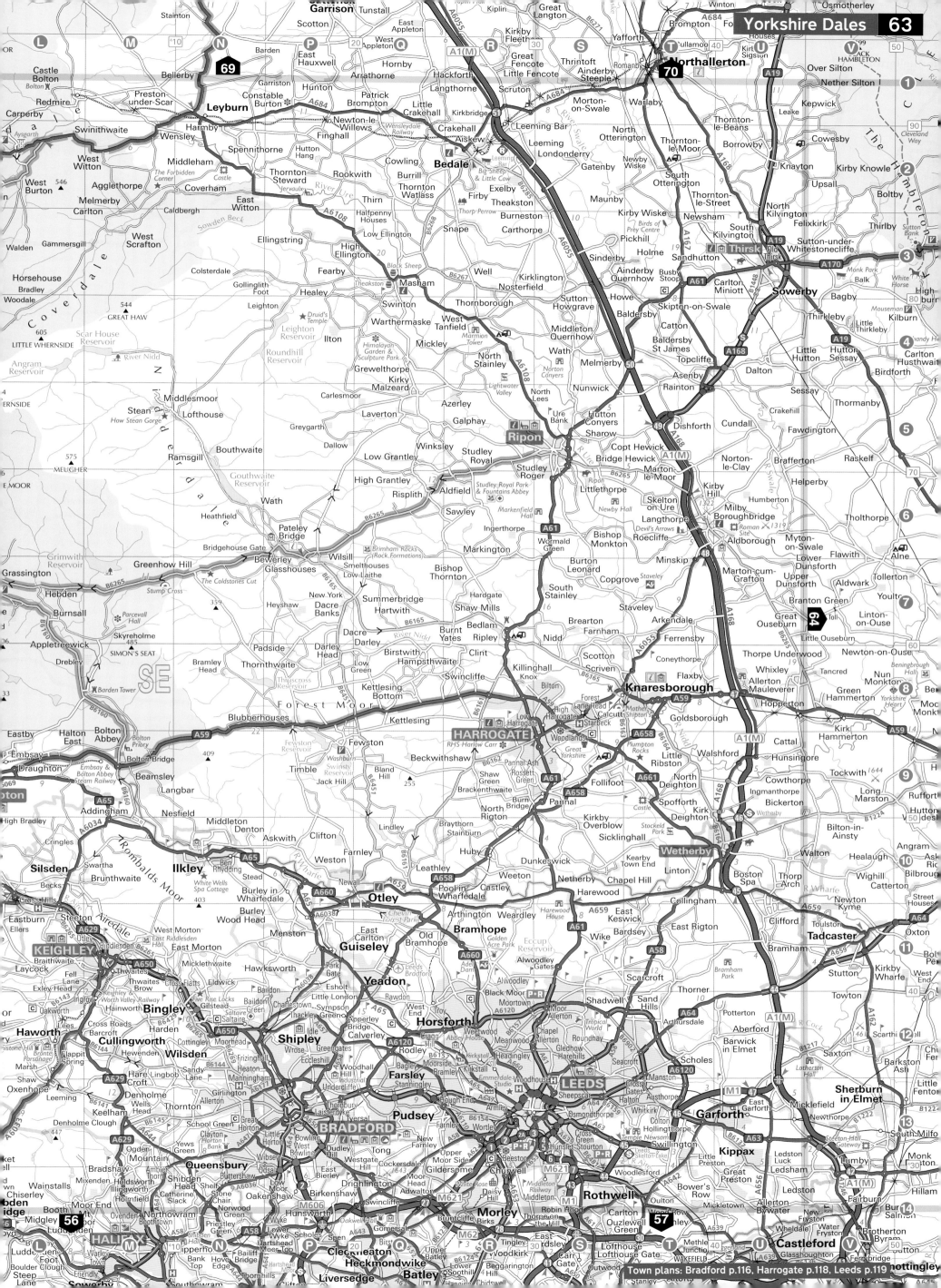

Town plan: Kingston upon Hull p.119

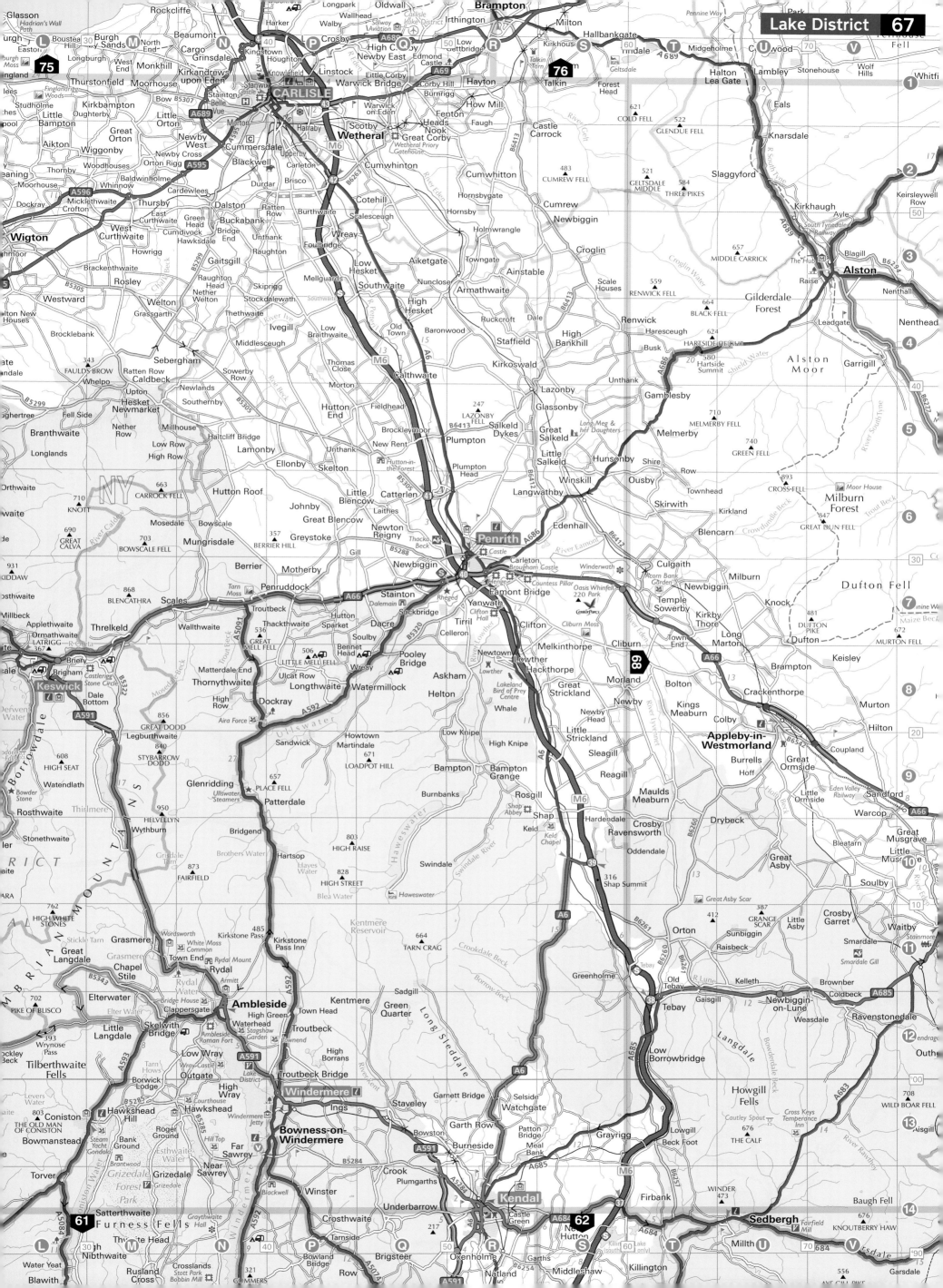

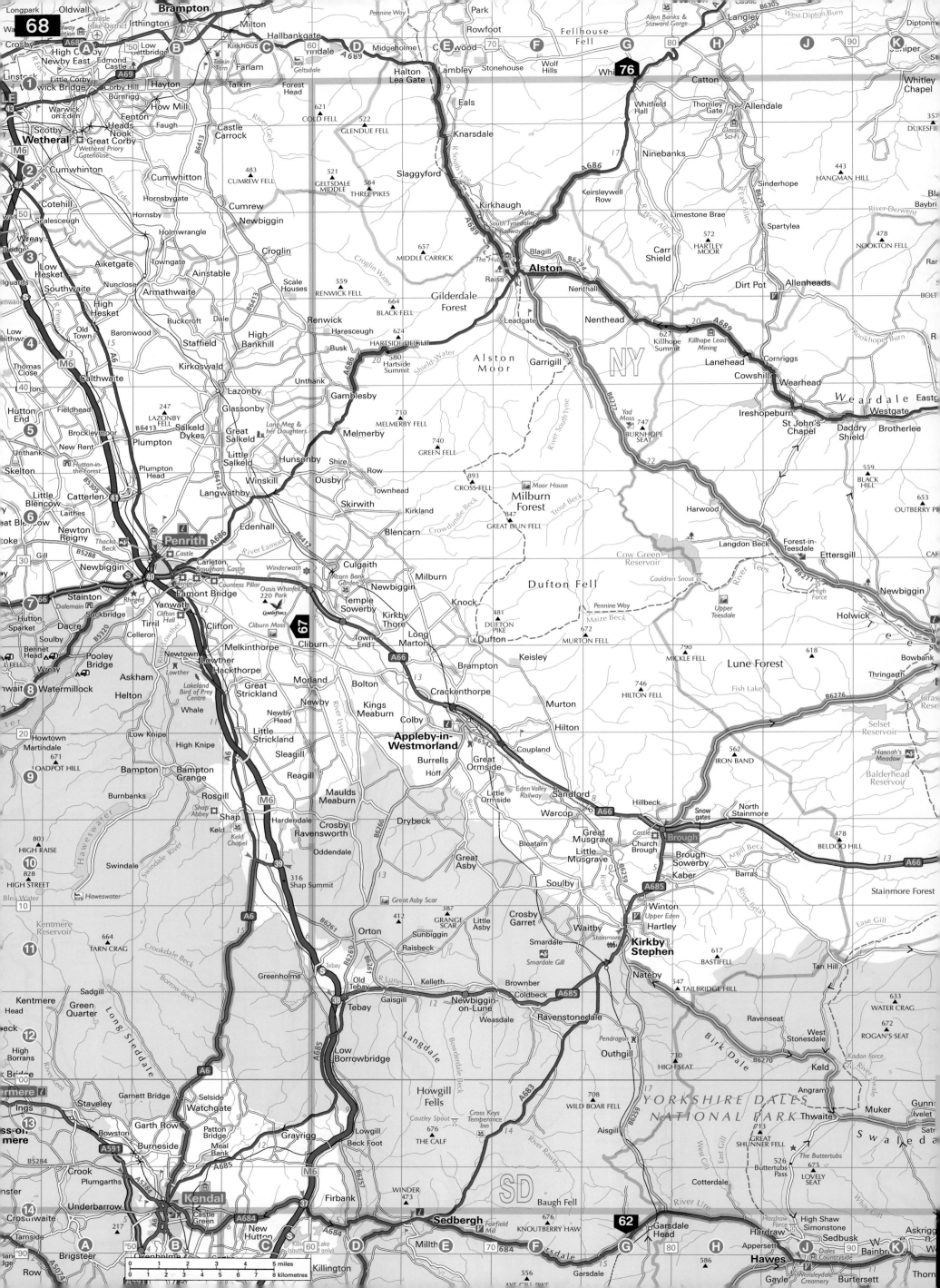

Sunderland

SOUTH SHIELDS
GATESHEAD, NEWCASTLE
Metro station
River Wear
Wearmouth Bridge
Riverside Park
Superstore
Superstore
St Mary's
City Hall & Register Office
WEST WEAR STREET
Empire
St Mark's
Fire Station
Premier Inn
University of Sunderland (City Campus)
Sunderland Minster
Travelodge
SUNDERLAND STATION
The Bridges
Arts Centre
County Court
Sunderland Museum & Winter Gardens
Mowbray Gardens
Hudson Road School
University of Sunderland
Uni
Sunderland College
War Memorial
Surgery
Transport Interchange
Royalty
CHESTER-LE-STREET
BURN PARK ROAD
Kingdom Hall
Bowling Green
SALEM RD
Statue
Surgery
St Anthony's Girl's Academy
St George's
Masonic Hall
Statue
Thornhill Park School
Argyle House School
PARK ROAD
Thornhill Academy
DURHAM
TEESSIDE, (A19)

Middlesbrough

CHARLOTTE ST   NILE ST
Police HQ
TRANSPORTER BRIDGE
BRIDGE STREET WEST
MIDDLESBROUGH STATION
Middlesbrough College
METZ BRIDGE ROAD
MARSH ROAD
Superstore
Hillstreet
Dundas
Town Hall
Jurys Inn
Empire
Leisure Park
Northern School of Art
Cleveland Centre
Council Offices
Combined Court Centre
Travelodge
MIMA Art Gallery
Cannon Park Ind Est
All Saints
Newport Primary School
Teesside University
Abingdon Primary School
Surgery
Newport South Business Park
Sikh Temple
Salvation Army
Teesside University (Campus Heart)
Christadelphian Hall
Teesside University
Ayresome Primary School
Teesside University
Archibald Primary School
Ayresome Gardens
Surgery
Sacred Heart RC Primary School
Meml
Meml
Dorman
Surgery
Albert Park
Fountain
Boathouse
St Joseph's RC Primary School
Ambulance Station
Surgery
RC Church of the Sacred Heart
Lower Lake
Fire Station
STOKESLEY

North Yorkshire and Cleveland Heritage Coast

Saltburn-by-the-Sea
Brotton
Skinningrove
Hummersea Scar
Upton
Boulby
Staithes
Captain Cook & Staithes
Skelton
Carlin How
Loftus
Dalehouse
Port Mulgrave
New Skelton
North Skelton
Kilton
Liverton Mines
Easington
Runswick Bay
Lingdale
Kilton Thorpe
Hinderwell
Roxby
Newton Mulgrave
Runswick
Kettleness
Liverton
Handale
Borrowby
Goldsborough
Overdale Wyke
Stanghow
Moorsholm
Scaling
Ellerby
Lythe
Sandsend
Sandsend Wyke
Gerrick
Mickleby
West Barnby
East Barnby
Raithwaite
Dunsley
Whitby
Scaling Dam
Ugthorpe
Newholm
Abbey
Saltwick Bay
Danby
The Moors National Park Centre
Stonegate
Hutton Mulgrave
Ruswarp
King Charles III England Coast Path
Castleton
Ainthorpe
Lealholm Side
Lealholm
Egton
Aislaby
Briggswath
Sneaton
Stainsacre
High Hawsker
The Green
Glaisdale
Grosmont
Sleights
Iburndale
Ugglebarnby
Low Hawsker
Ness Point or North Cheek
Danby Bottom
Egton Bridge
Key Green
Sneatonthorpe
Robin Hood's Bay
Street
Blue Bank
Littlebeck
Raw
Old Coastguard
Beck Hole
Falling Foss
Fylingthorpe
Robin Hood's Bay
NORTH YORK MOORS
Goathland
Mallyan Spout
Old Peak or South Cheek
PIKE HILL
Ravenscar
Church Houses
NATIONAL PARK
North Yorkshire Moors Railway
Eller Beck
Staintondale
Hayburn Wyke
Thorgill
Low Bell End
Wheeldale Roman Road
Cloughton Newlands
Rosedale Abbey
NORTH YORK MOORS
Harwood Dale
Cloughton
THE YORK MOORS
North Riding
Stape
Cromer Point
Forest Park
Hole of Horcum
Blakey Topping
Cleveland Way
Hartoft End
Bickley
Broxa
Silpho
Burniston
Hutton-le-Hole
Lastingham
Newto Rawcliffe
Levisham
Cow Camp
Bridestones
Dalby Forest Drive
Hackness
Suffield
Scalby
North Bay Railway
Gillam
Ryedale Folk
Spaunton
Cawthorn
Cropton
Lockton
Langdale End
Wrench Green
Everley
Castle
Appleton
North Riding Forest Park
Scarborough

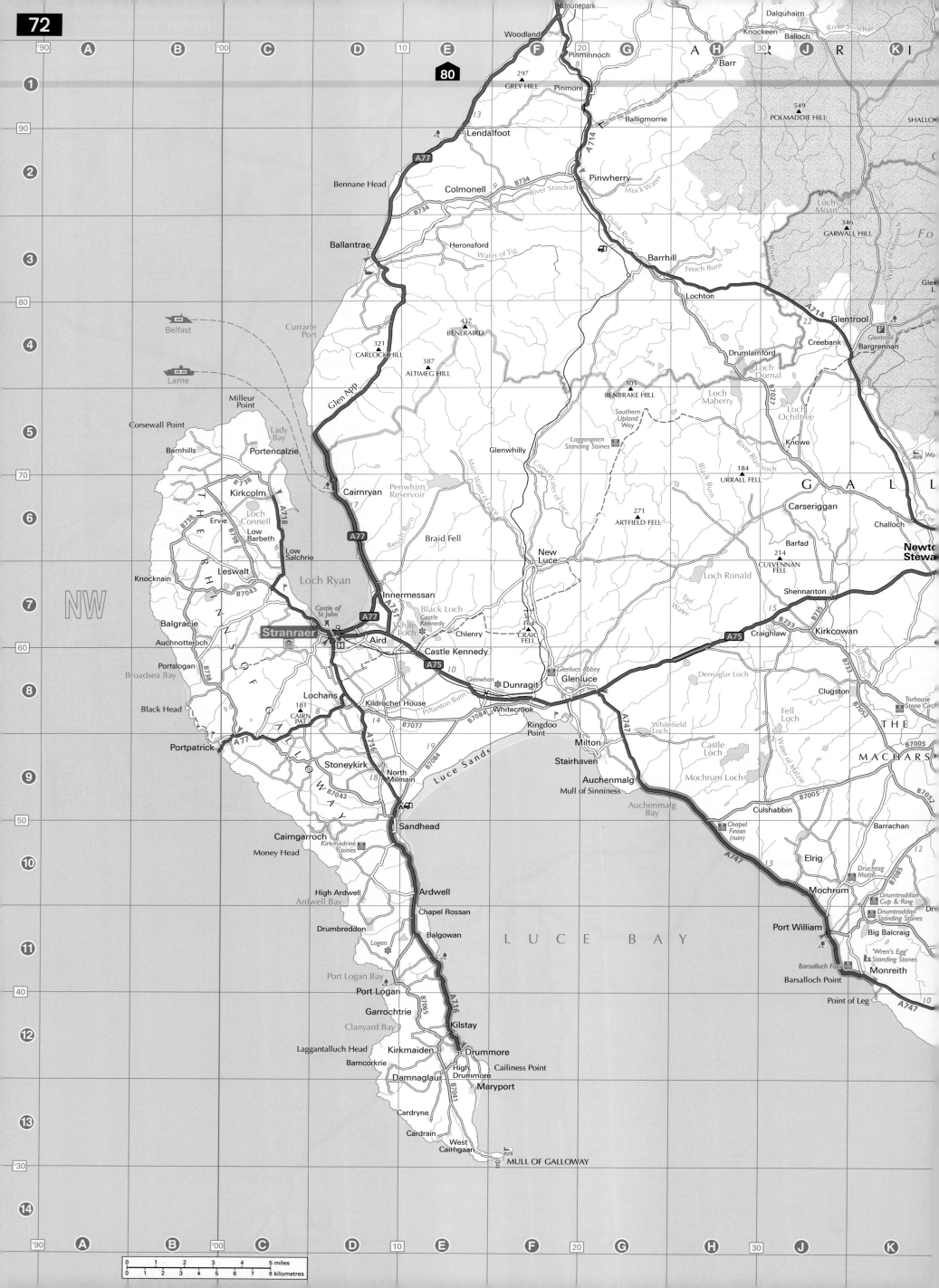

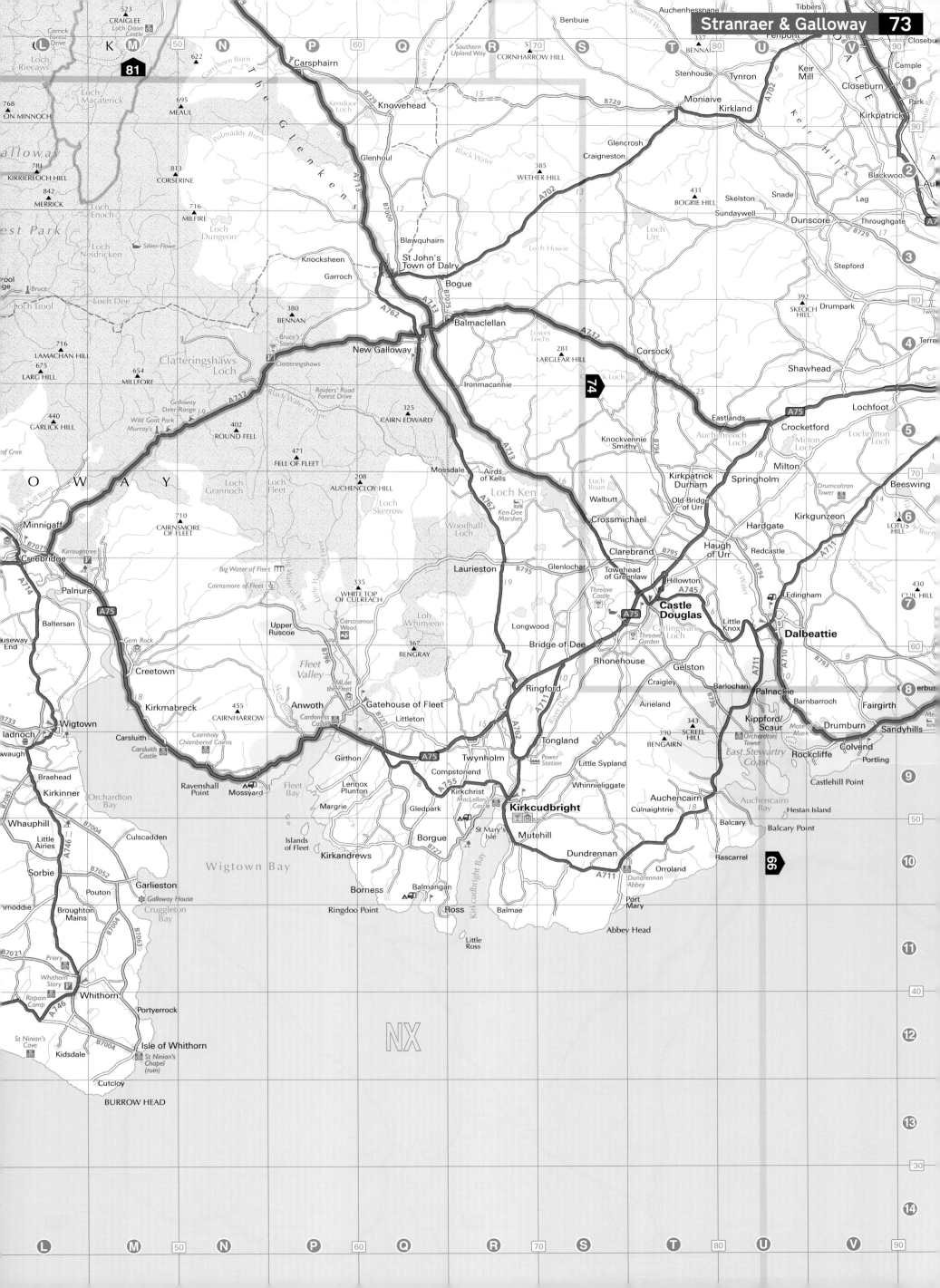

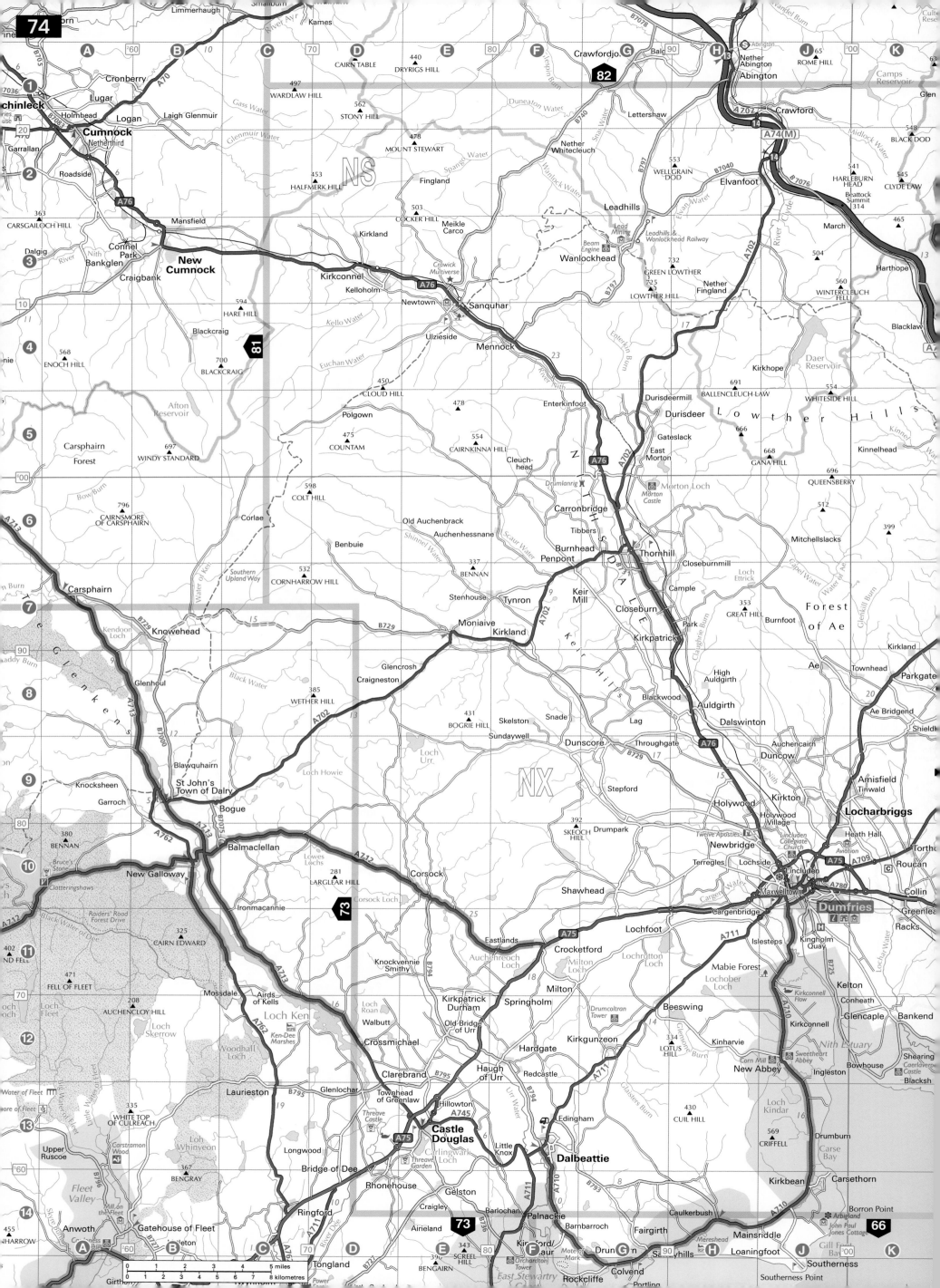

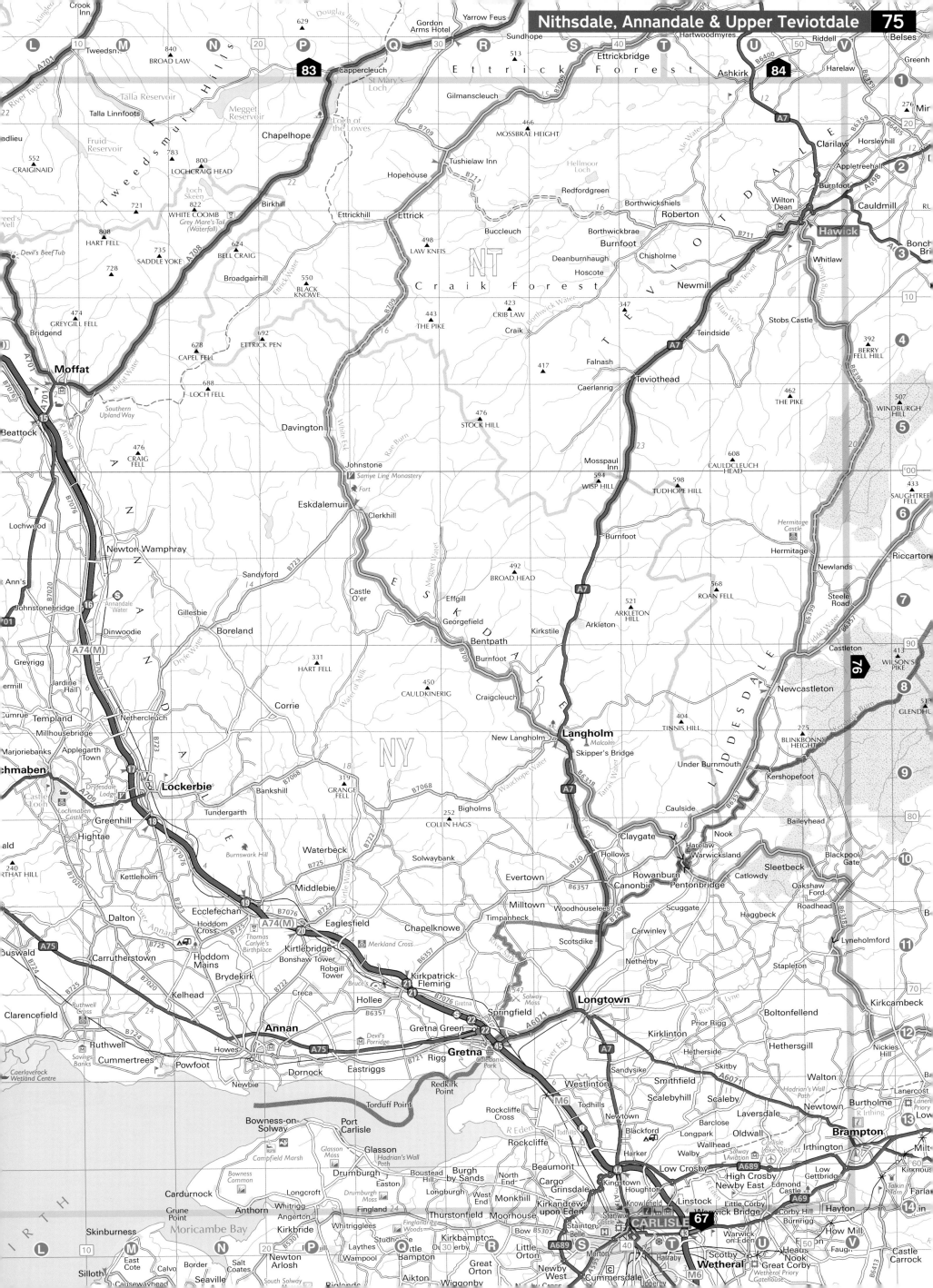

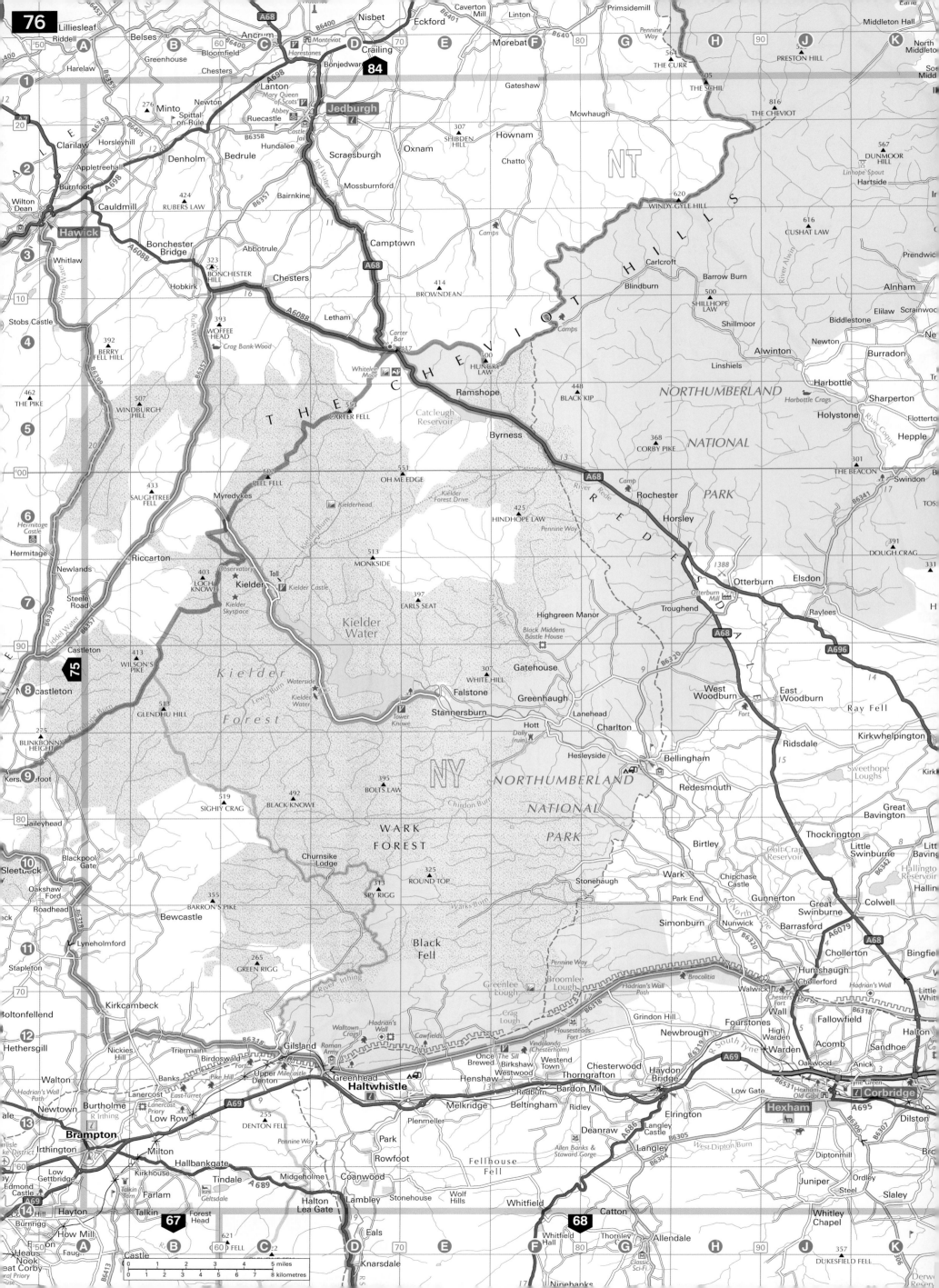

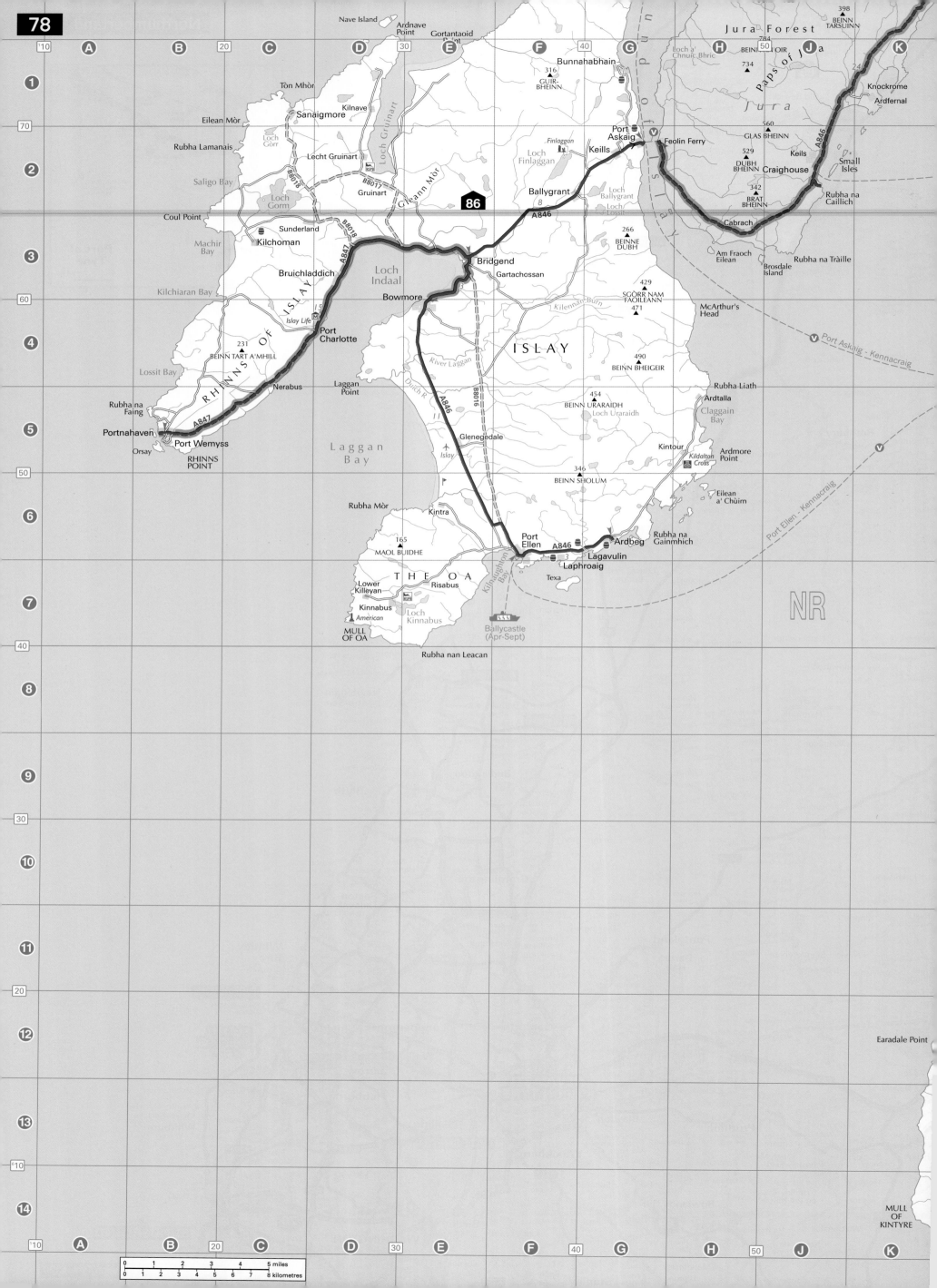

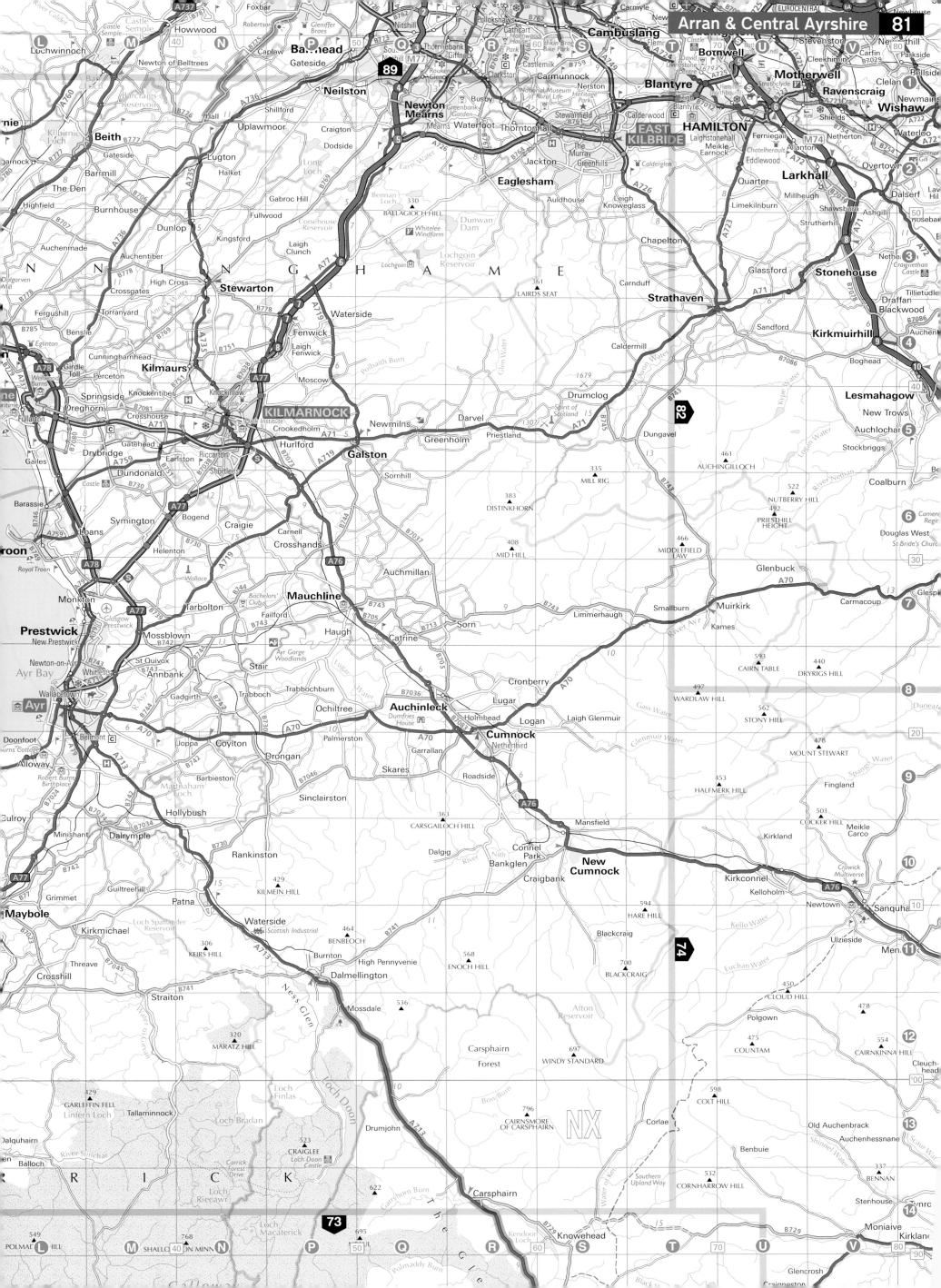

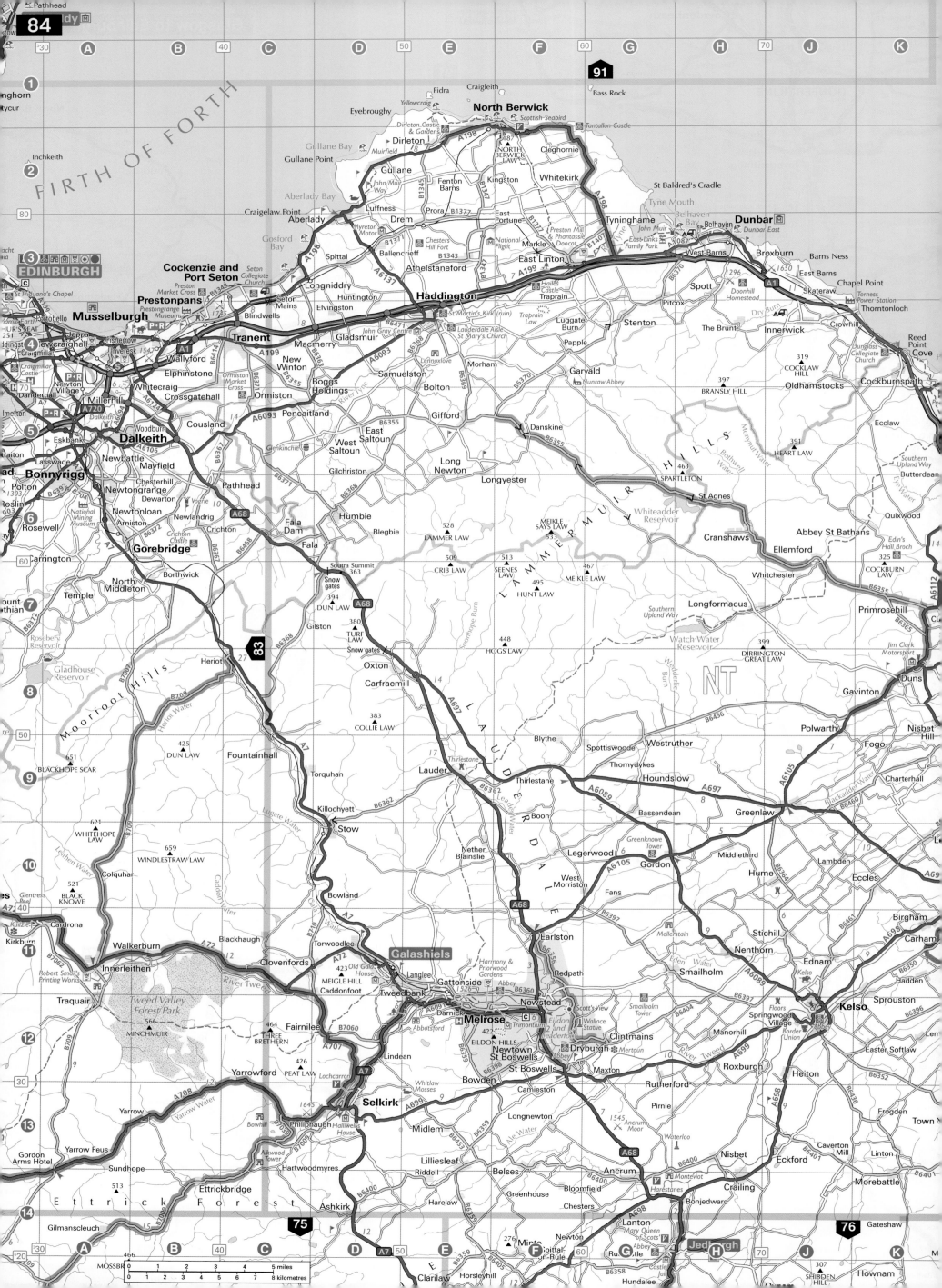

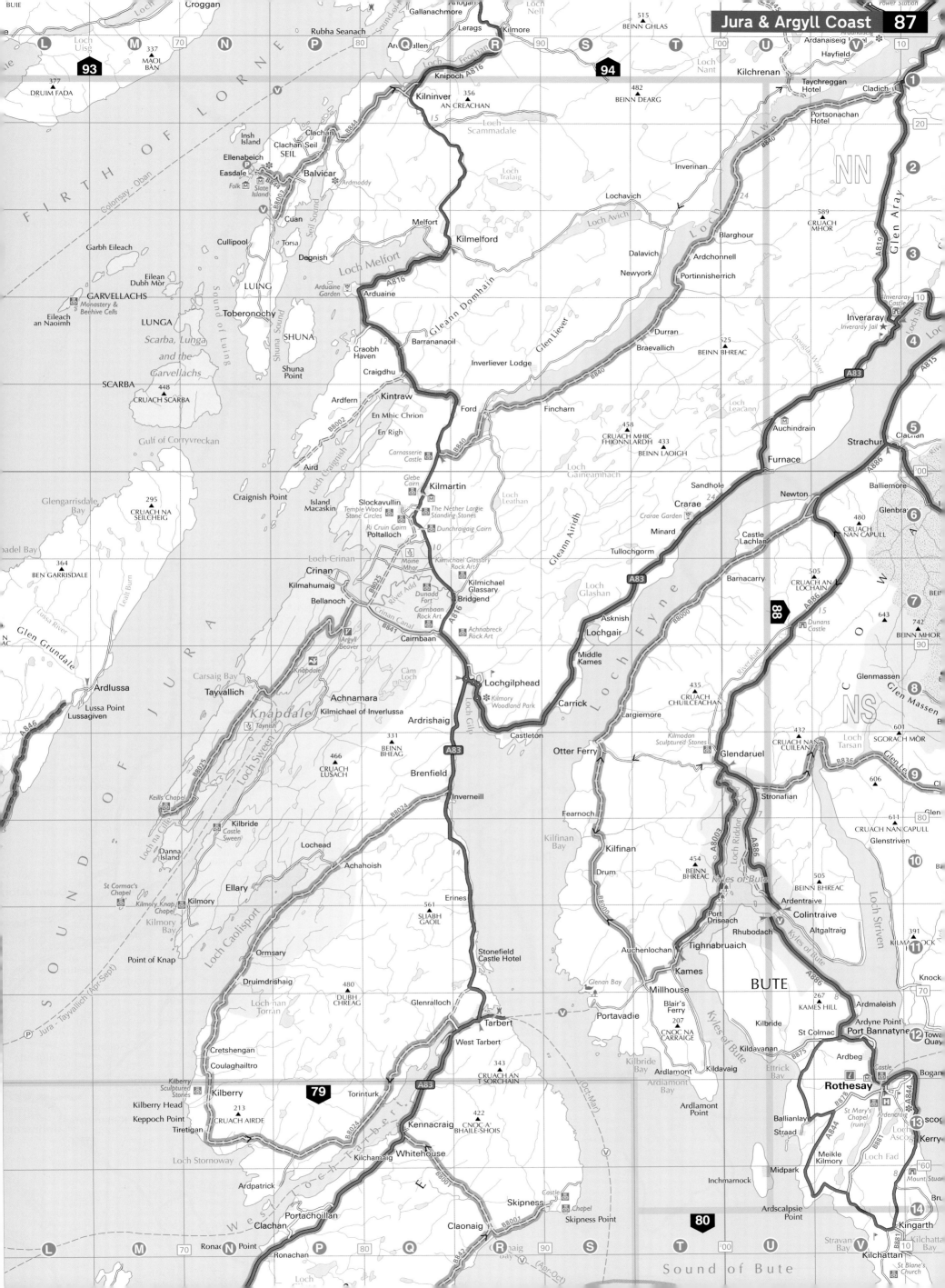

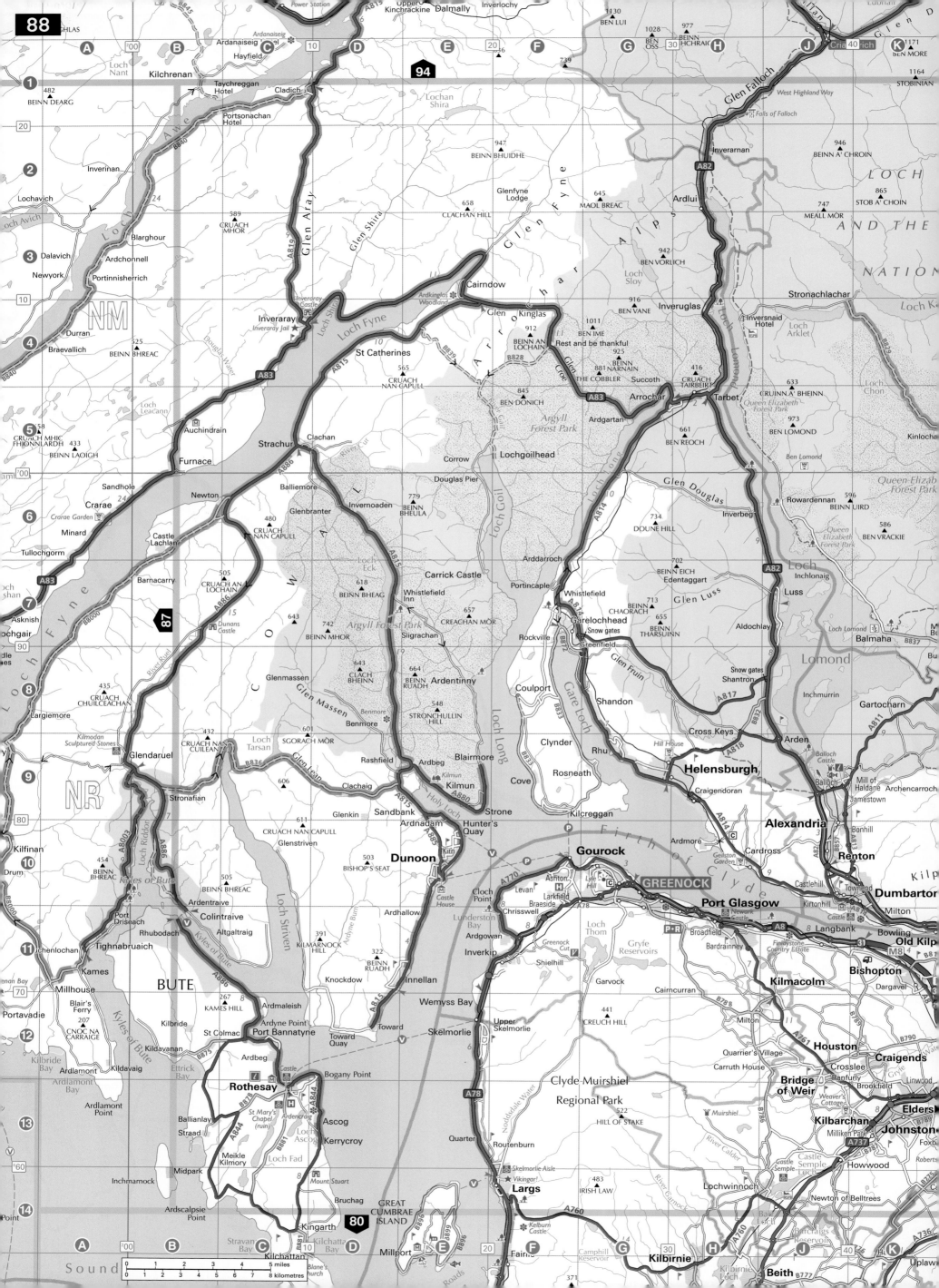

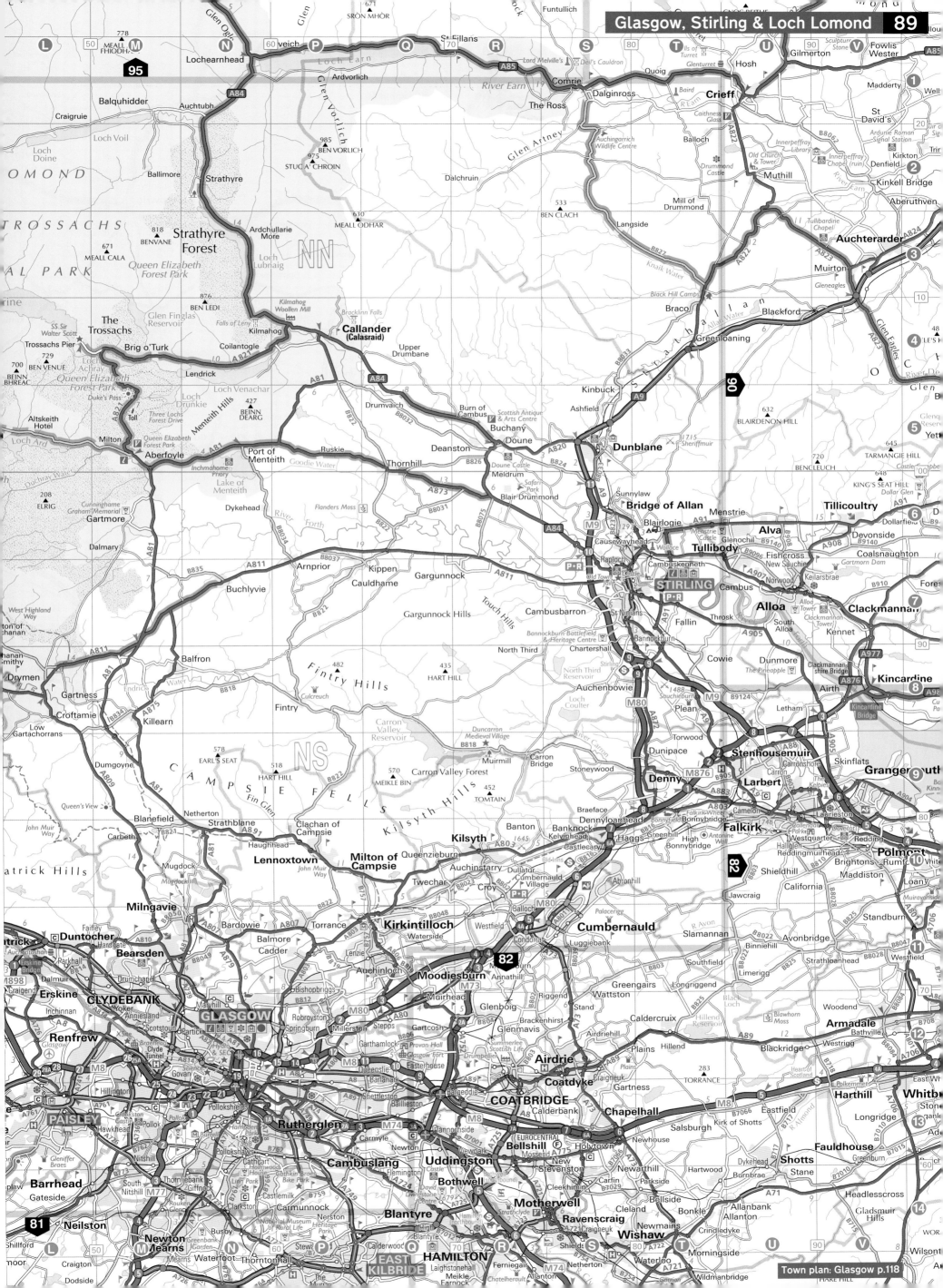

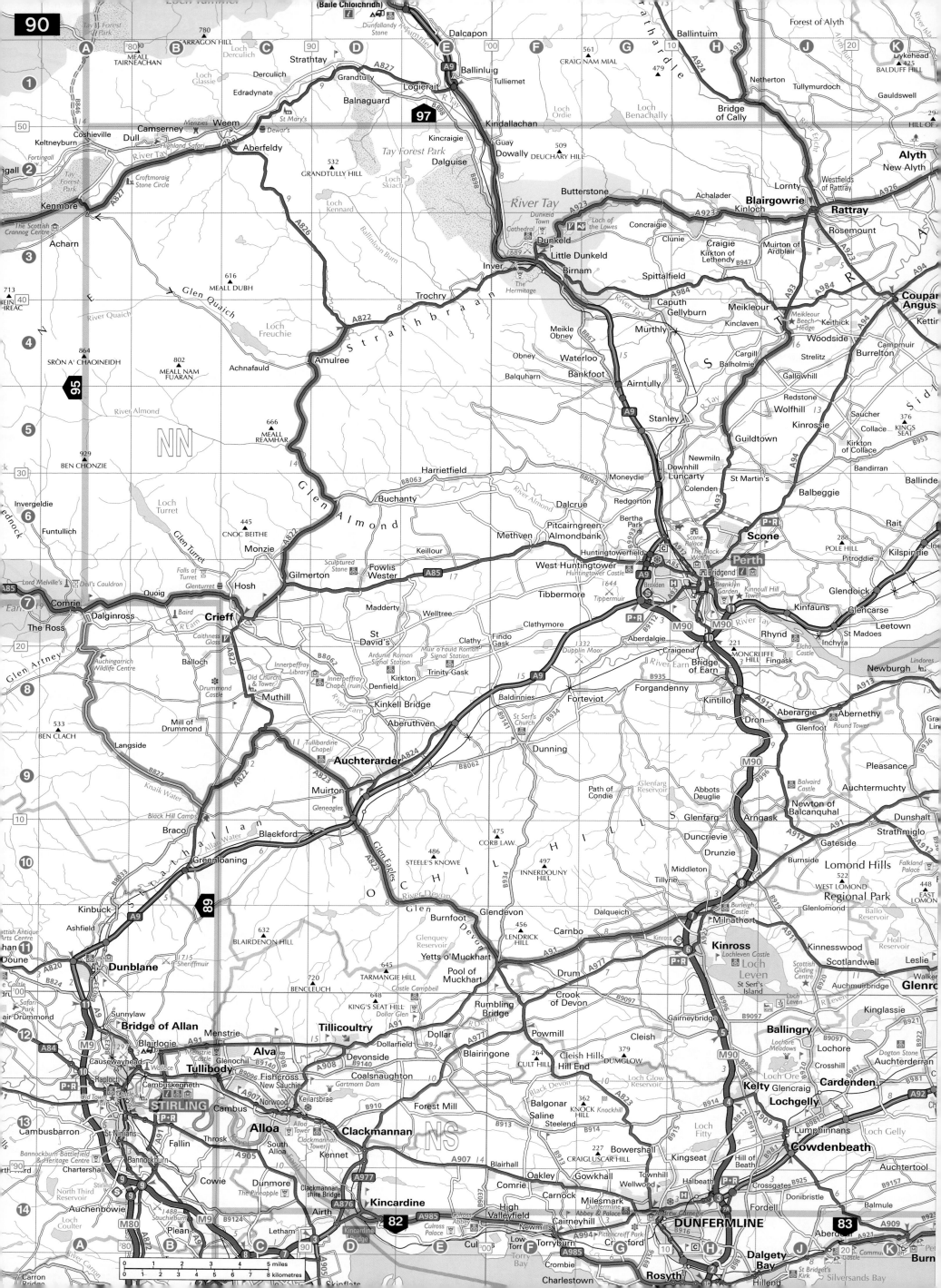

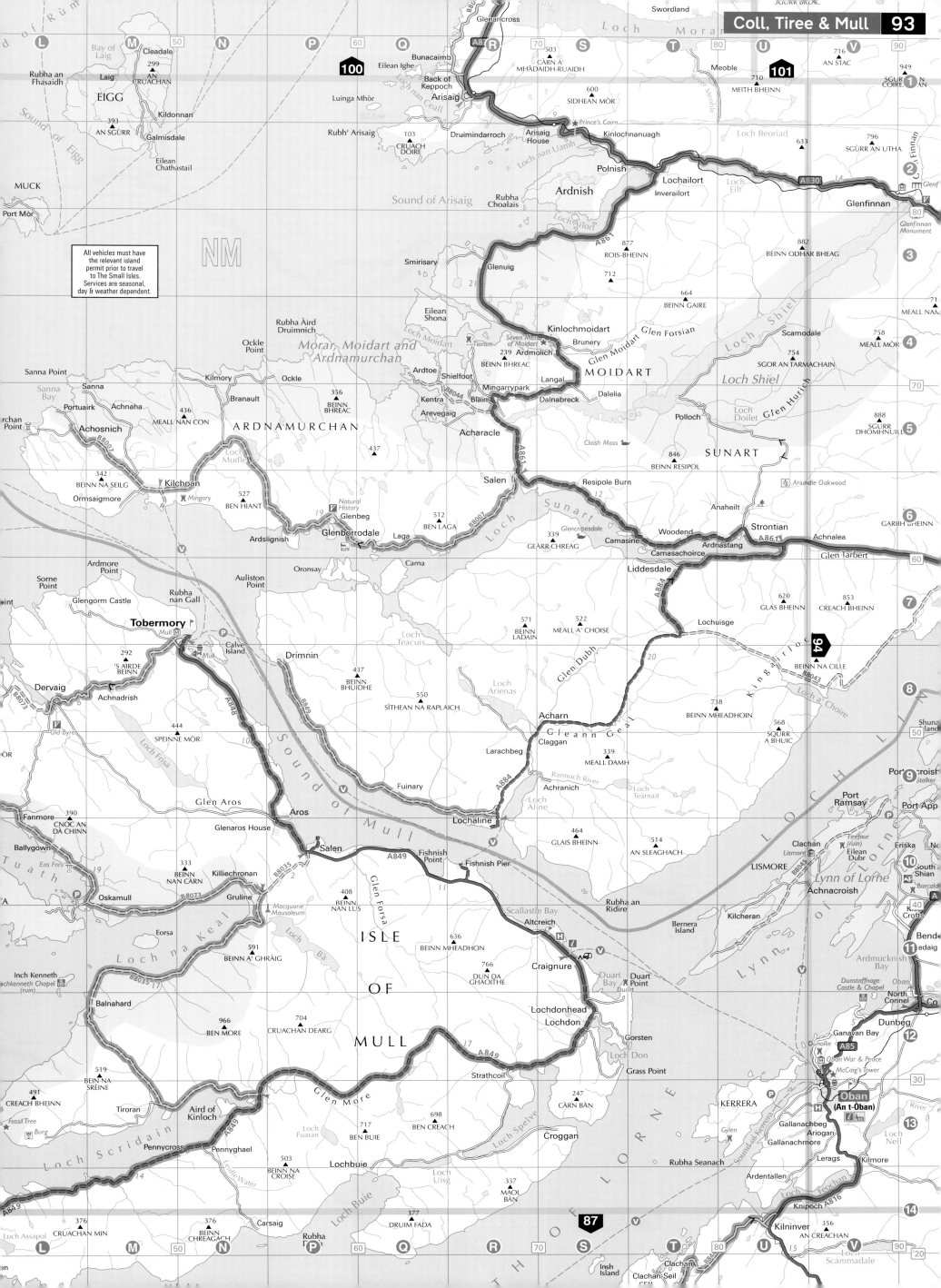

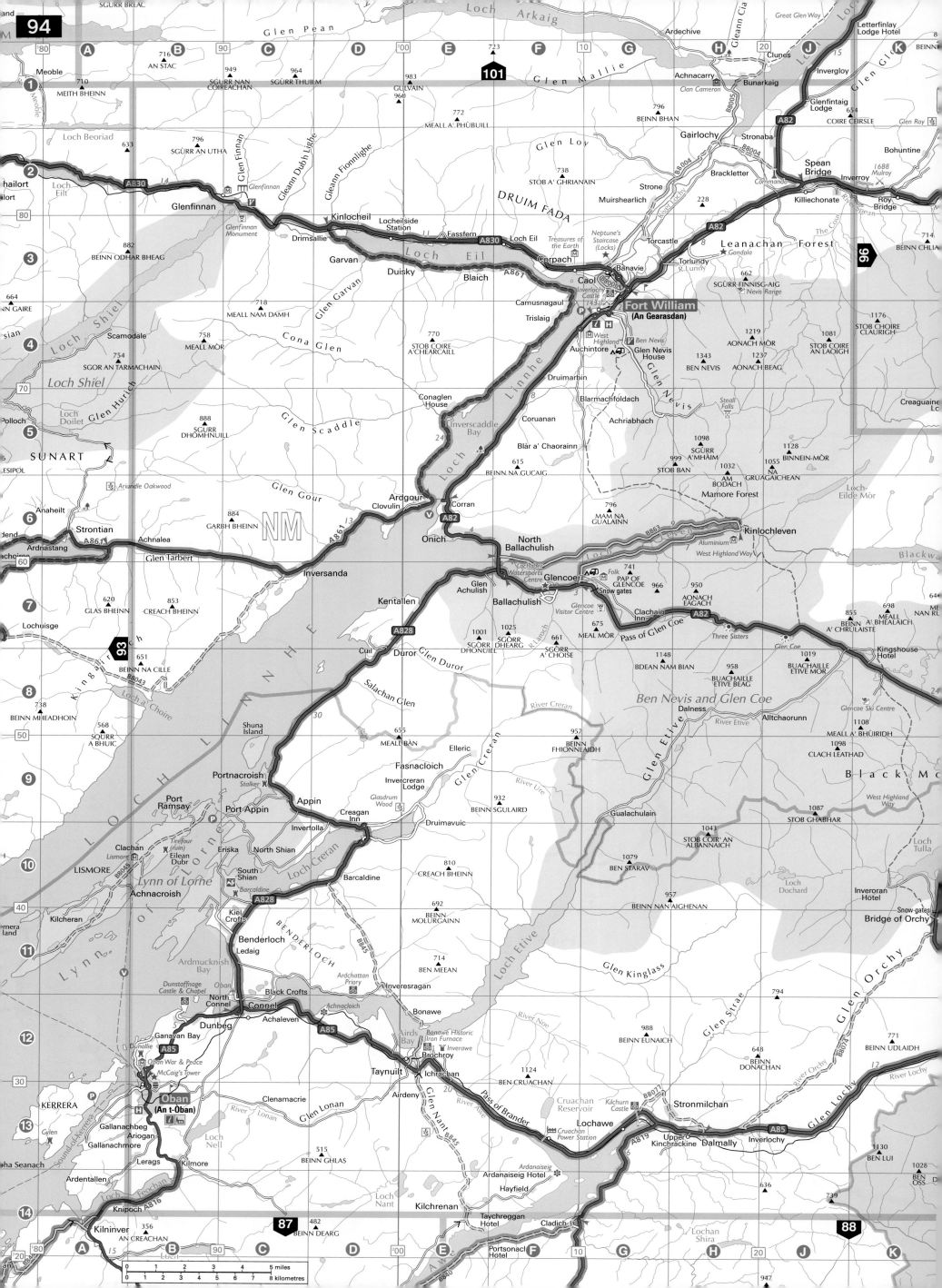

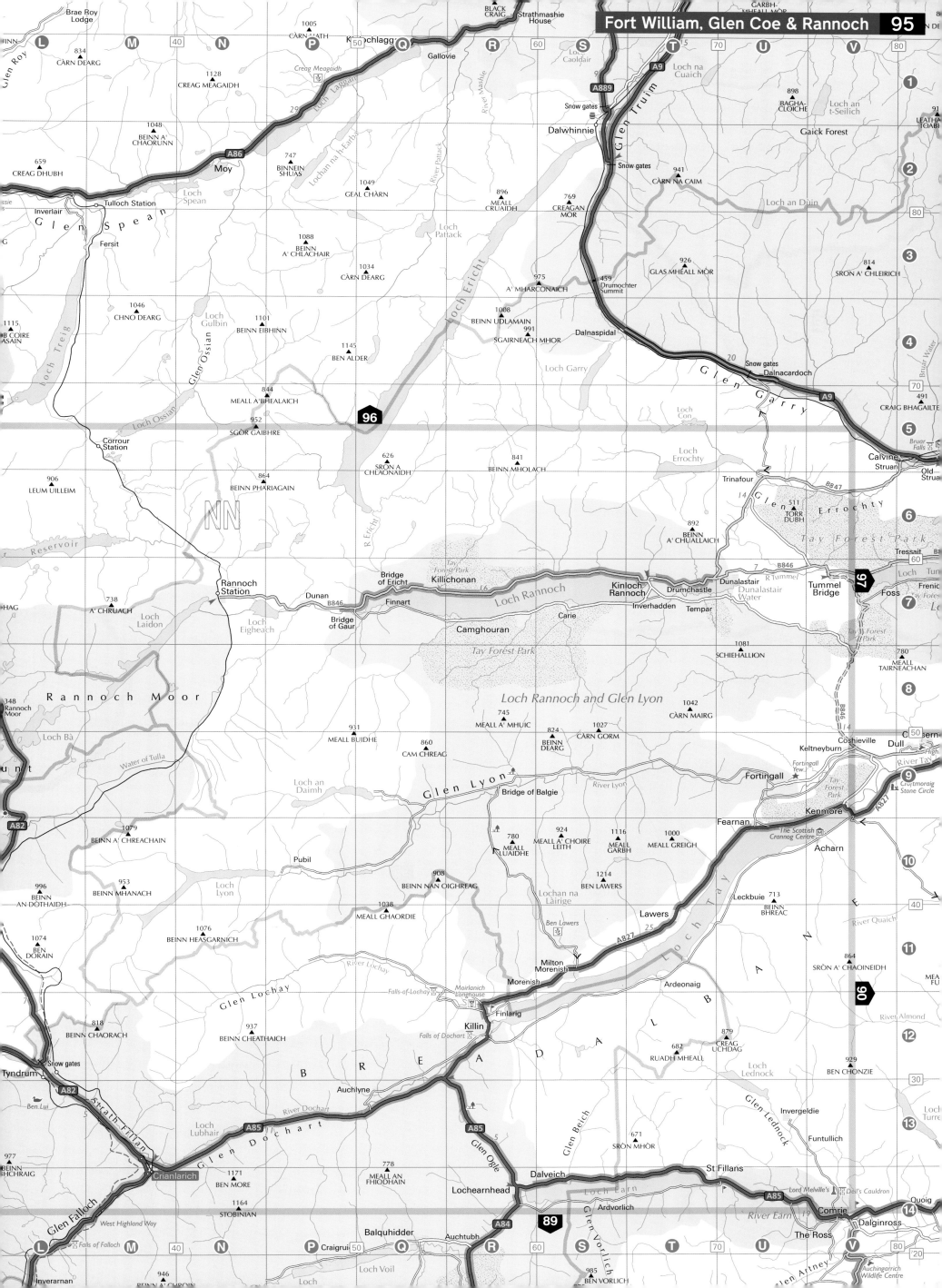

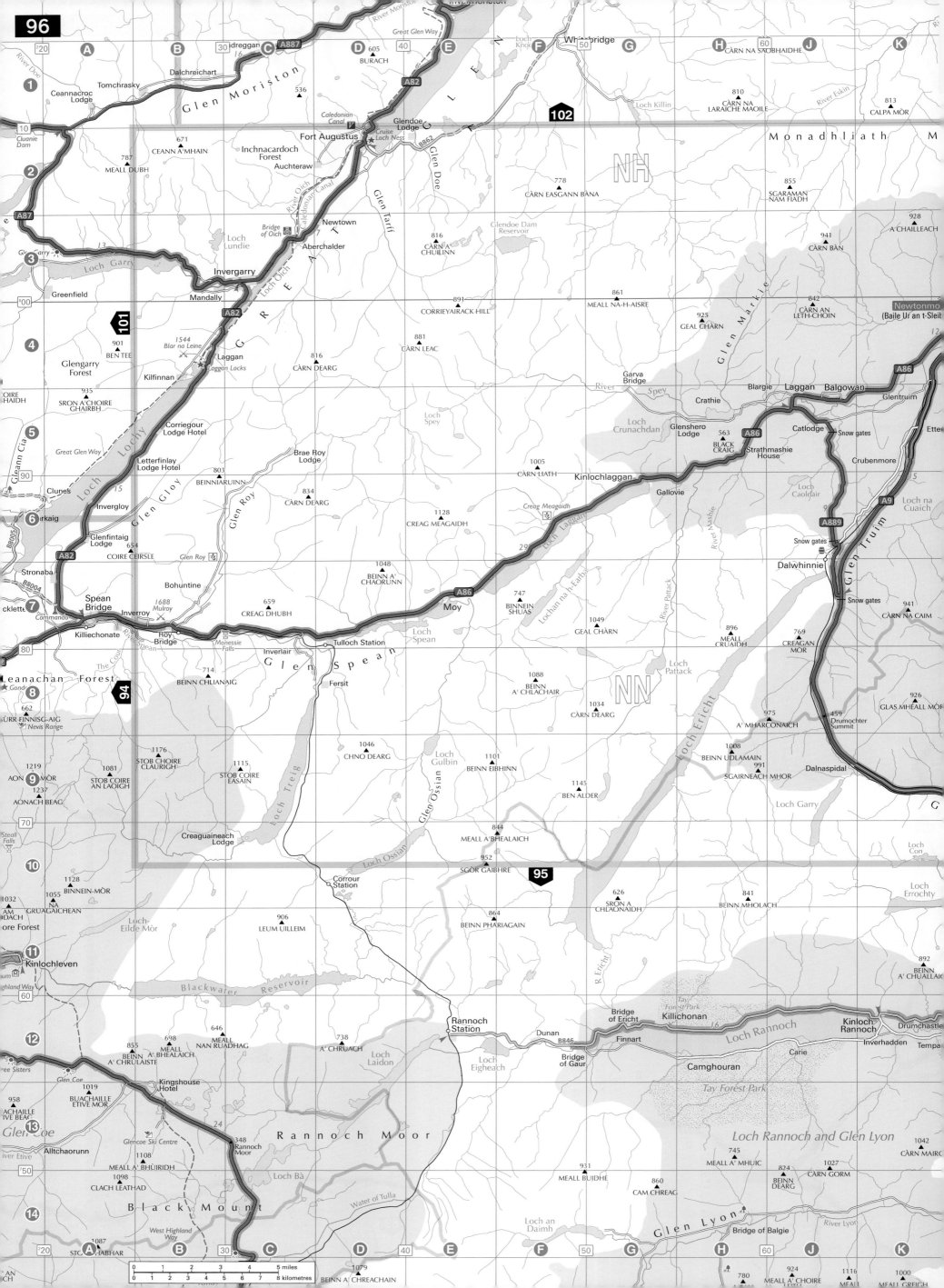

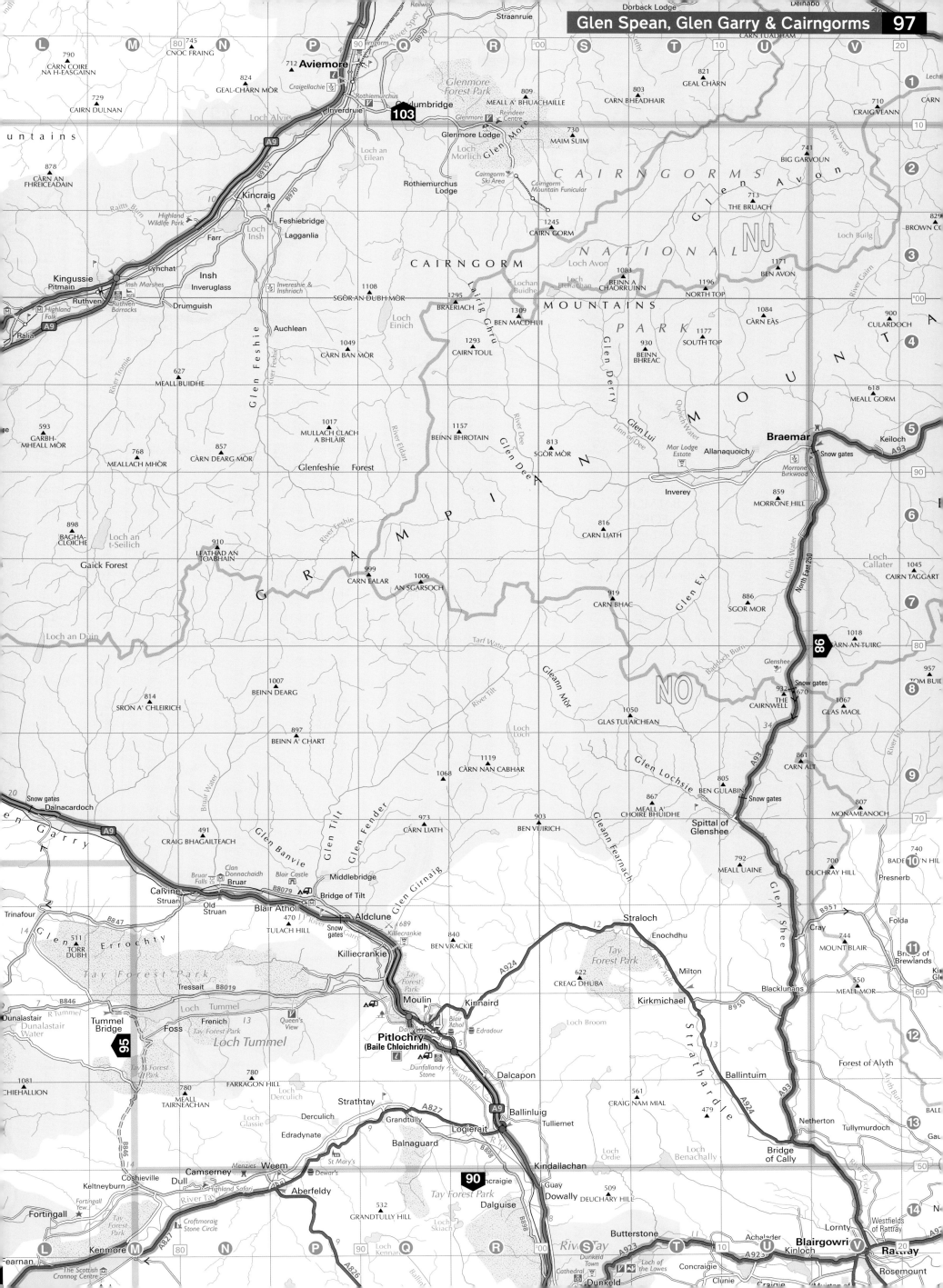

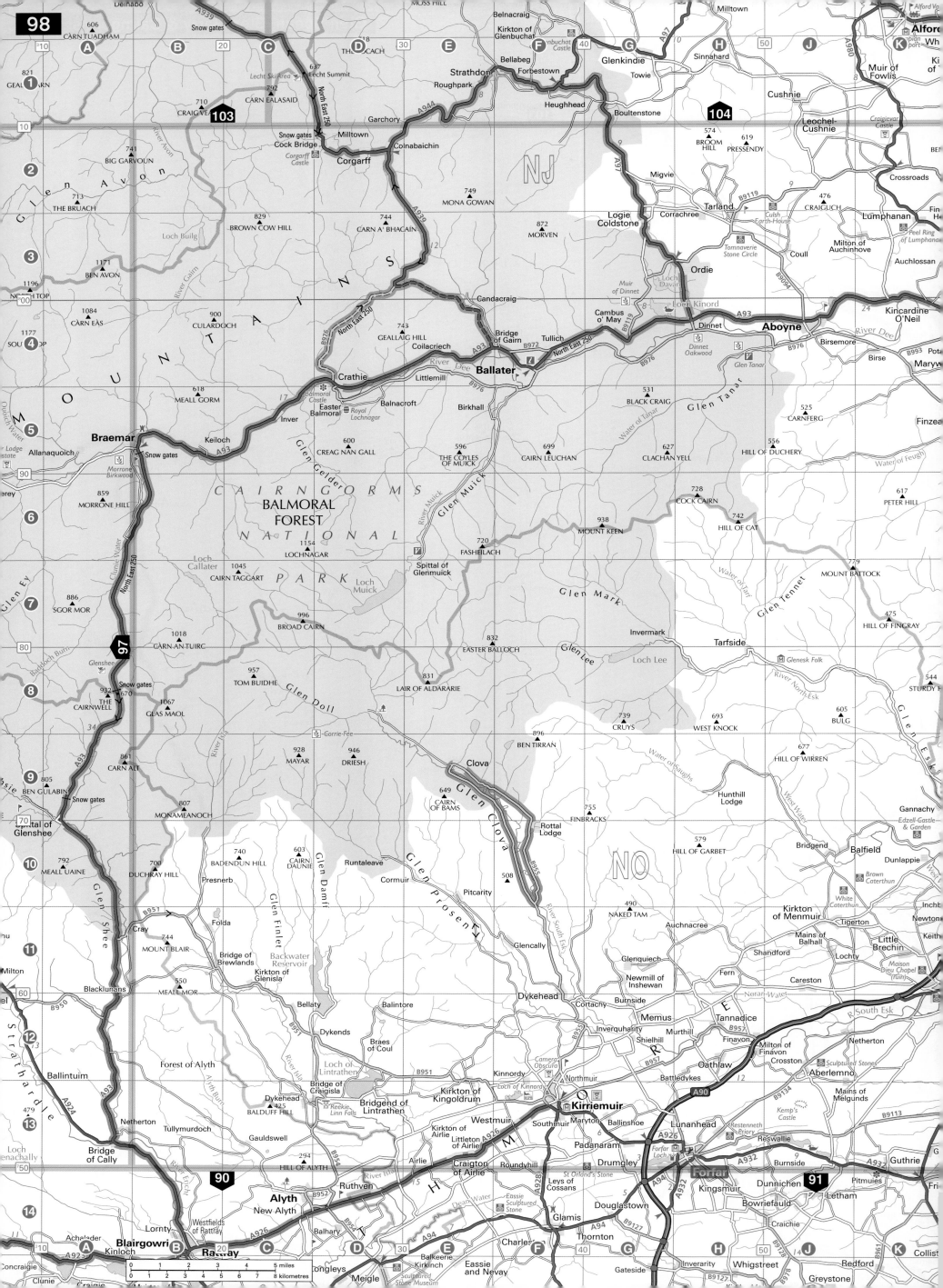

Pitfichie
Monymusk
Kemnay
Kintore
Kinmundy
Benelvie
Kirkwall
Lerwick
house
L
A944
M
Pitmunie
B993
N
Naigearn
Leylodge
Cottown
80
Q
R.Don
Cothal
R
90
Potterton
Blackdog
T
Kirkwall
Lerwick
V
10
ugh
Tillyfourie
Ordhead
Sauchen
Lyne of Skene
Blackburn
A96
A90
Overton
Dyce
Stonewood
Middleton Park
Denmore
Bridge of Don
P·R
1
10

Dunecht
Skene House
Millbuie
B9126
B979
BRIMMOND HILL
265
Bucksburn
Northfield
Botanic
Buckburn
Botanic
Corsindae
Comers
Tillybirloch
Marionburgh
Loch of Skene
Kirkton of Skene
Carnie
Elrick
Kingsford
Westhill
Kingswells
Kittybrewster
Old Aberdeen
2
10

Drumlasie
Echt
Redhill
Cullerlie
B9125
Gullerlie Stone Circle
A944
ABERDEEN
Ruthrieston
Torry
Nigg Bay
3
00

494
QUHALLIE
471
HILL OF FARE
Landerberry
Benthoul
Easter Ord
Blacktop
A90
Cults
Mannofield
Kincorth
Nigg
Altens Haven
rnaveen
Drumlasie
Learney
rphins

Milltown of Campfield
Hirn
Craiglug
Milltimber
Bieldside
Milton of Murtle
Banchory-Devenick
Charlestown
Cove Bay
4
00

B993
Mid Beltie
A980
Brathens
Drumfrennie
Myrebird
Drumoak
Drum Castle
River Dee
North East 250
West Park
Kirkton of Maryculter
A956
Hillside
Marywell
Findon
Portlethen
Old Portlethen
Cammachmore Bay

Bridge of Canny
Banchory
General Burnett's
Upper Lochton
The Neuk
Crathes Castle
Royal Deeside
Crathes
Kirkton of Durris
Denside of Durris
Woodlands of Durris
A90
Cammachmore
Auchlee
Portlethen
Downies
4

310
TOM'S CAIRN
Baulds
336
299
SCOLTY HILL
Bridge of Feugh
B9077
Crossroads
Durris Forest
Cookney
Netherley
Chapelton
Skateraw
Newtonhill
5

B976
Waulkmill
Strachan
376
MONGOUR
Muchalls
A92
Bridge of Muchalls
Doonie Point
5
90

Water of Avon
Glen Dye
532
KERLOCH
Hill of Trusta
Ury
Garron Point
Stonehaven Bay
6

579
LACHNABEN
507
MOUNT SHADE
Bridge of Dye
Snow gates
FETTERESSO
FOREST
320
HILL OF TRUSTA
Kirktown of Fetteresso
Stonehaven
Tolbooth
6

B974
Water of Dye
390
LEACHIE HILL
Elfhill
Tannachie
A90
Dunnottar
7
80

465
GOYLE HILL
Goosecruives
New Mill
Temple of Fiddes
Fowlsheugh
454
Cairn O'Mount
Snow gates
Glen of Drumtochty
Glenbervie
Drumlithie
Mondynes
Crawton
Catterline
7

414
AUCHENBLAE
FINELLA HILL
Auchenblae
Fordoun
B967
Redmyre
Arbuthnott
Grassic Gibbon Centre
A92
Todhead Point
8

Mains of Balnakettle
Fettercairn
B9120
Mains of Haulkerton
Pittarrow
Redmyre
Arbuthnott
Inverbervie
8
80

Bogmuir
Sauchieburn
Edzell
Woods
Luthermuir
Edzell
A90
B974
A937
Laurencekirk
Redford
Benholm
Bervie Bay
Gourdon
Maritime Museum
9
70

Trinity
Logie Pert
Craigo
Lochside
Logie
Morphie
Dykelands
Johnshaven
10

Brechin
A935
Dun
House of Dun
Bridge of Dun
Marykirk
Bush
St Cyrus
Milton Ness
11
60

Caledonian Railway
Haughs of Kinnaird
Barnhead
Maryton
Montrose Basin
Scurdie Ness
Ferryden
Montrose
Montrose Air Station
12

132
WUDDY LAW
Bolshan
terlaw
Farnell
Craig
Usan
13

Kinnell
A934
Boysack
Inverkeilor
Lunan
Boddin Point
Red Head
Lunan Bay
14
50

B965
Chapelton
Cauldcots
Letham Grange
Leysmill
L
70
M
N
80
P
Q
80
R
90
S
T
00
U
V
10
Kinneff
St Vigeans
Auchmithie
Marywell

Aberdeen
200 m
ELGIN
PETERHEAD
ALFORD
WESTBURN ROAD
A944
HUTCHEON STREET
Royal Cornhill
Skene Square School
Sandman Signature Hotel
Aberdeen College Gallowgate Centre
NORTH
City
KING STREET
Jasmine Way
St Andrew's Cathedral
Hanover St School
Robert Gordon's College
Bon Accord
City Council (Marischal College)
Arts Centre
Aberdeen Grammar School
Art Gallery RGU
St Mark's
His Majesty's
Police HQ
Sheriff Court
Provost Skene's House
Gilcomston School
Kingdom
YMCA
Union Bridge
St Nicholas
Market
Maritime Museum
ibis Hotel
Harbour Office
Terminal Building
Music Hall
St Mary's Cathedral
Trinity Centre
Leonardo Hotel
Northlink Ferries
Coastguard
HMRC Surgery
ALFORD
SKENE STREET
Harlaw Academy
St Margaret's School
Union Square
Aberdeen Station
Fish Market
BANCHORY
GREAT WESTERN RD
A93
Nellfield Cemetery
Ferryhill School
Willowbank
Victoria Bridge
Pavilion
River Dee
Hall
■ Low Emission Zone
SAC
DUNDEE, PERTH

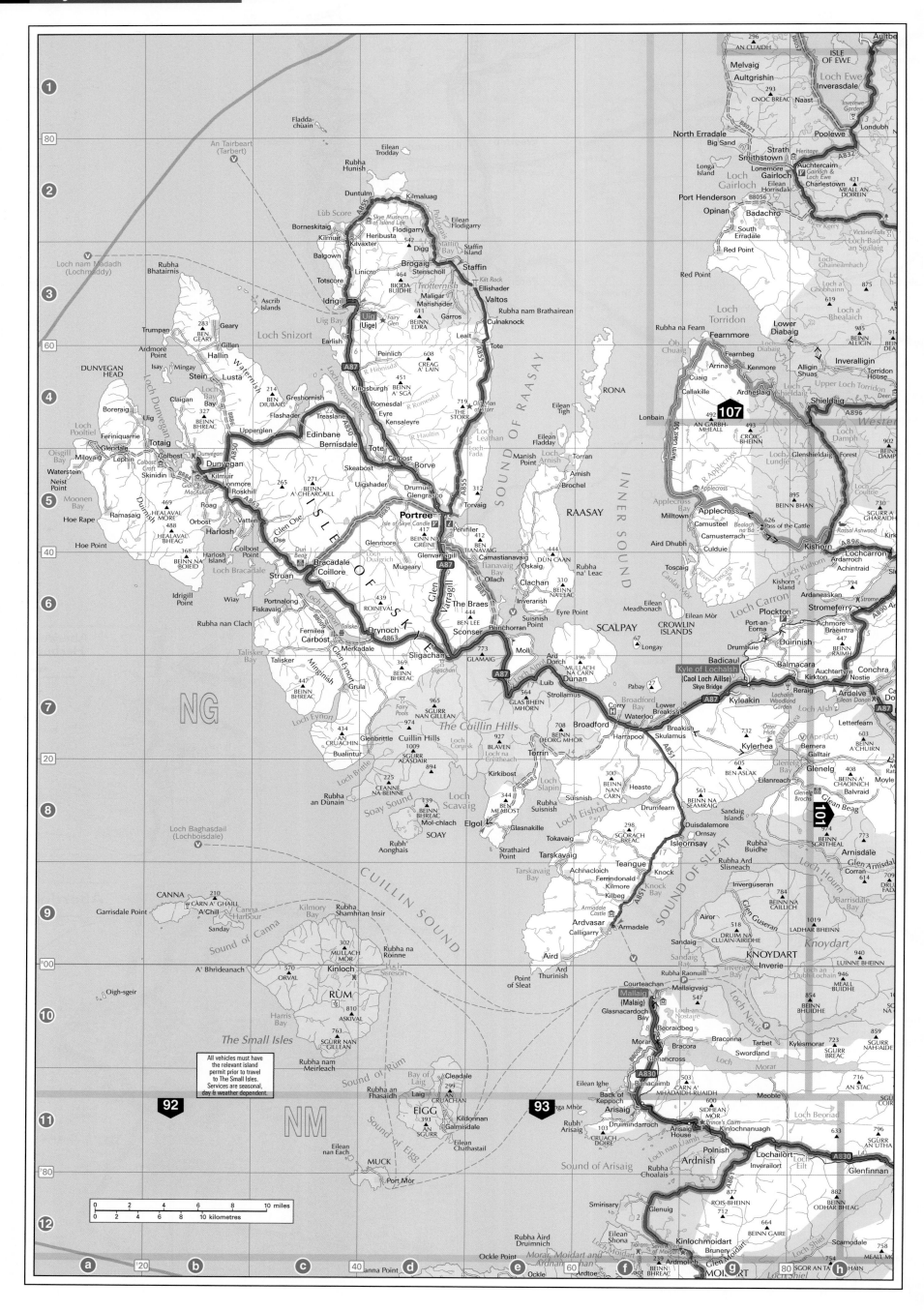

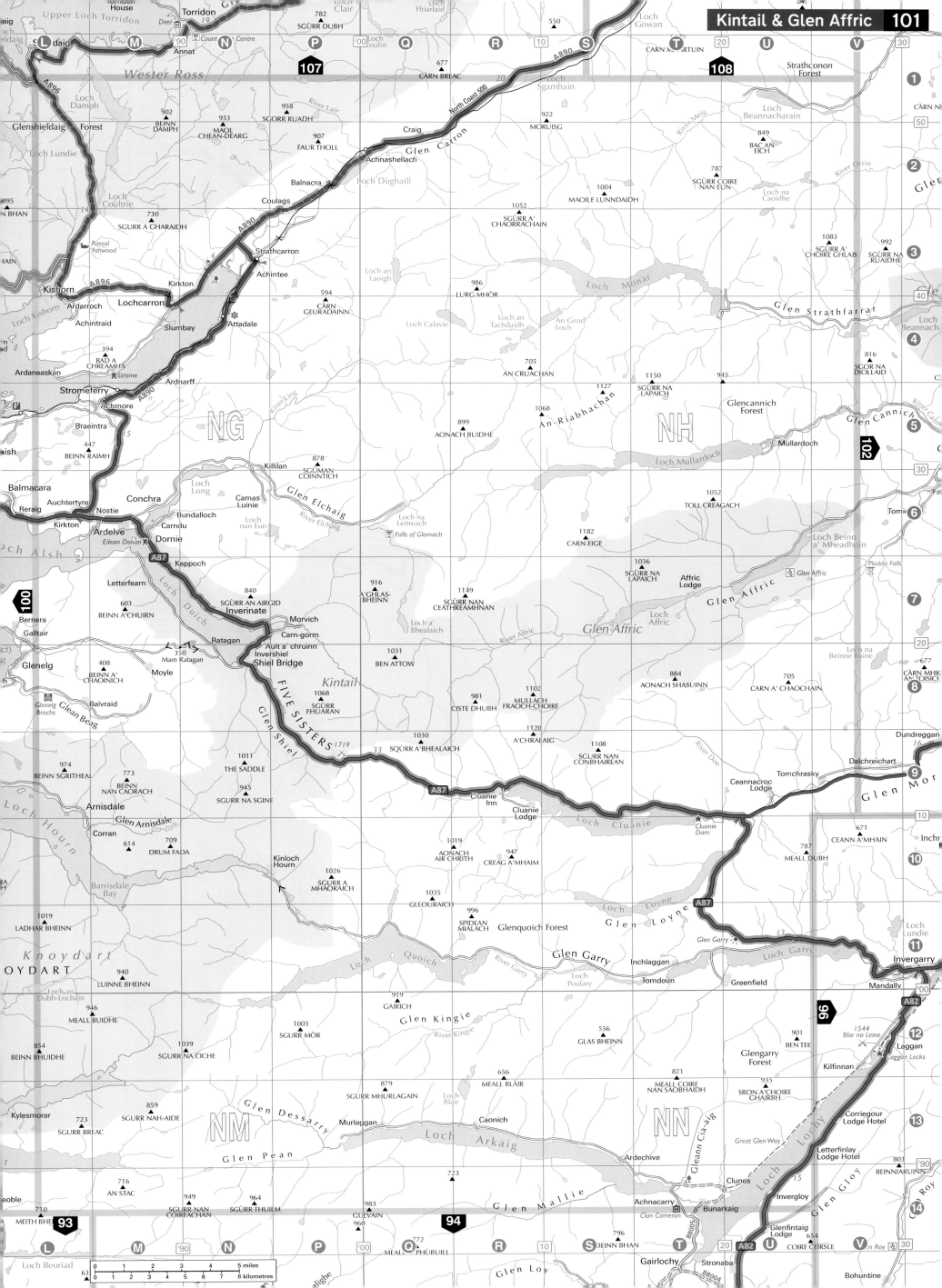

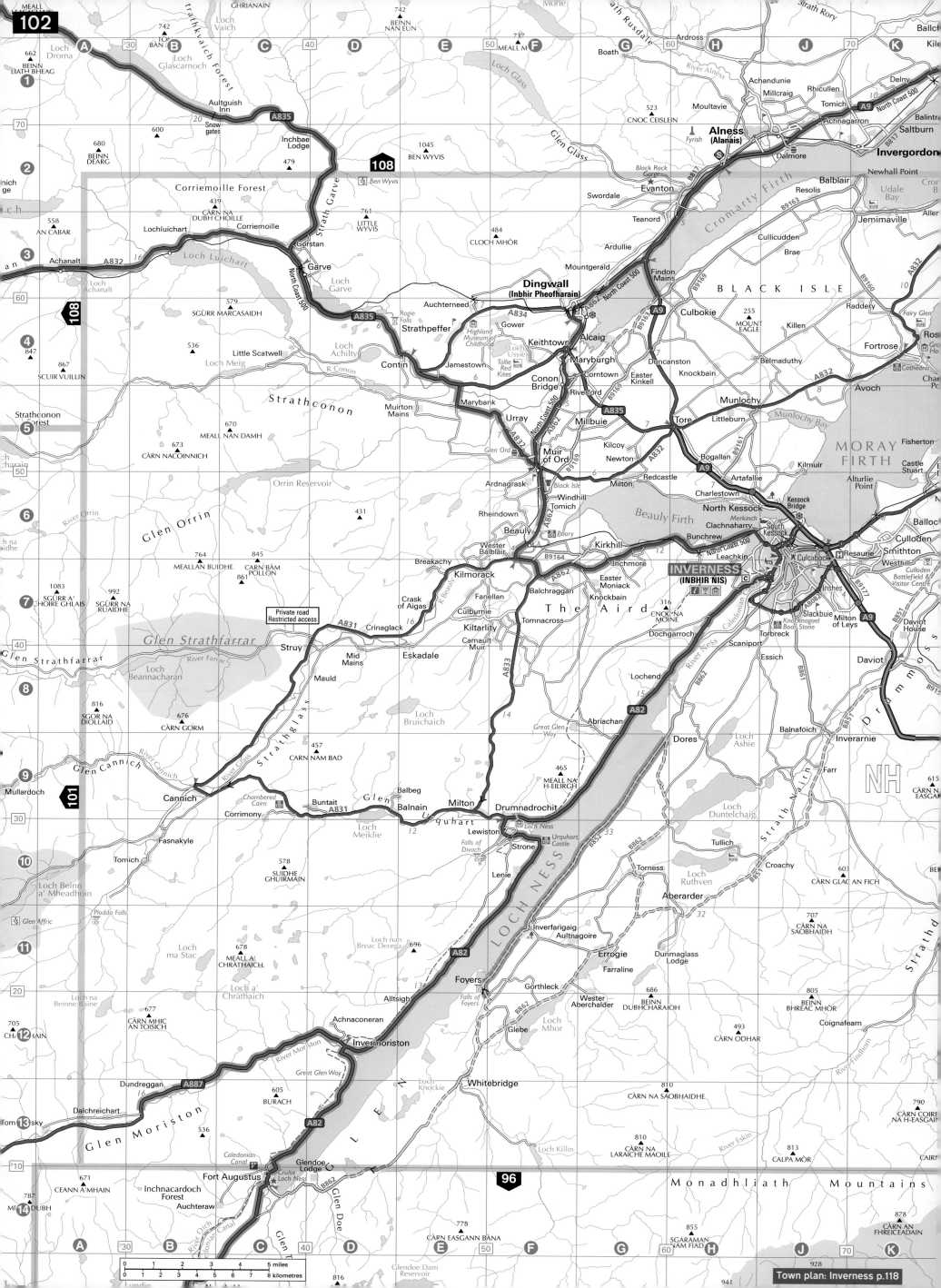

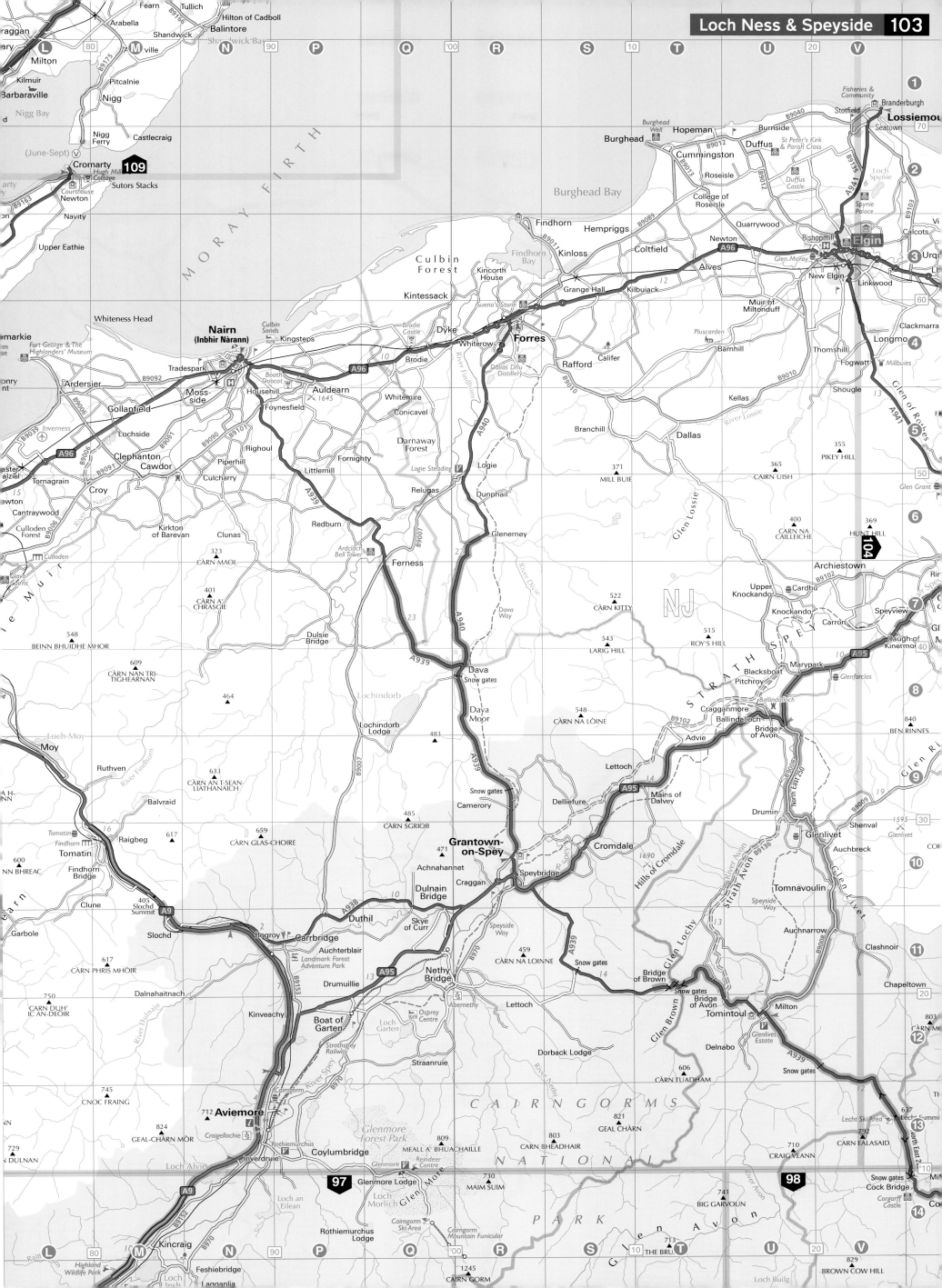

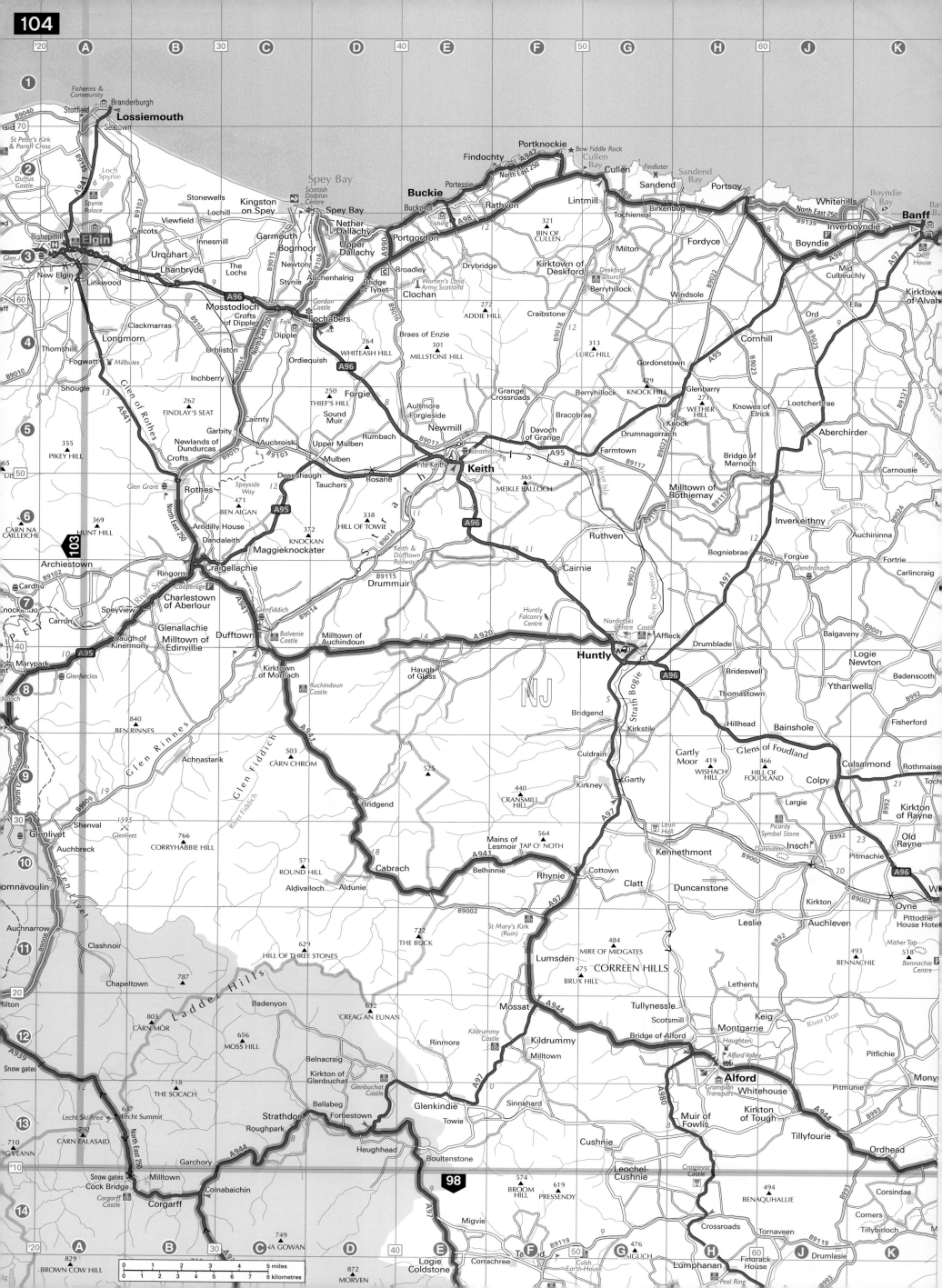

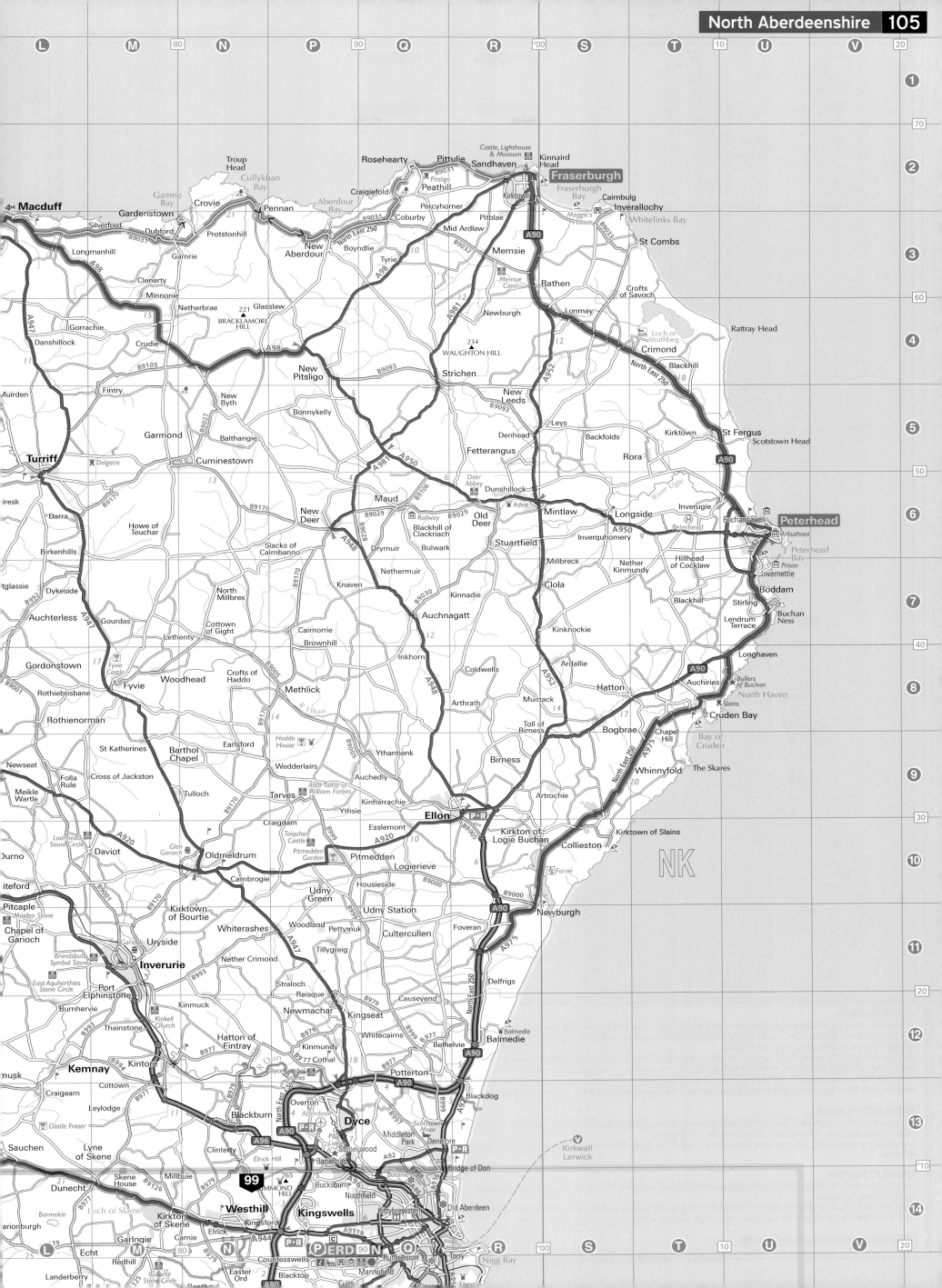

Macduff
Troup Head
Cullykhan Bay
Gardenstown
Silverford
Dubford
Longmanhill
Gamrie
Crovie
Pennan
Protstonhill
New Aberdour
Aberdour Bay
Rosehearty
Pittulie
Peathill
Craigiefold
Coburby
Percyhorner
Sandhaven
Kirktown
Kinnaird Head
Fraserburgh
Fraserburgh Bay
Maggie's Hoosie
Cairnbulg
Inverallochy
Whitelinks Bay
St Combs

Clenerty
Minnonie
Netherbrae
Glasslaw
BRACKLAMORE HILL 221
Danshillock
Gorrachie
Crudie
New Pitsligo
Bonnykelly

Mid Ardlaw
Pitblae
Memsie
Memsie Cairn
Rathen
Newburgh
WAUGHTON HILL 234
Strichen
New Leeds
Leys
Backfolds
Crimond
Blackhill
Rattray Head
Crofts of Savoch
Lonmay
St Fergus
Scotstown Head

Turriff
Muirden
Fintry
New Byth
Garmond
Balthangie
Cuminestown
Darra
Birkenhills
Howe of Teuchar
Slacks of Cairnbanno
New Deer
Maud
Railway
Blackhill of Clackriach
Old Deer
Deer Abbey
Dunshillock
Fetterangus
Denhead
Rora
Kirktown
Longside
Inverugie
Peterhead
Buchanhaven
Arbuthnot
Peterhead Bay
Prison
Invernettie
Mintlaw
Inverquhomery
Nether Kinmundy
Hillhead of Cocklaw
Boddam
Stirling
Buchan Ness
Lendrum Terrace
Longhaven
Bullers of Buchan
North Haven
Slains
Cruden Bay
Bay of Cruden
The Skares
Whinnyfold

Drymuir
Bulwark
Nethermuir
Stuartfield
Clola
Millbreck
Blackhill
Knaven
Kinnadie
Auchnagatt
Kinknockie
North Millbrex
Cairnorrie
Brownhill
Inkhorn
Coldwells
Ardallie
Hatton
Auchiries
Cottown of Gight
Arthrath
Muirtack
Bogbrae
Chapel Hill
Artrochie

Fyvie Castle
Fyvie
Woodhead
Crofts of Haddo
Methlick
Rothiebrisbane
Gourdas
Lethenty
Rothienorman
St Katherines
Barthol Chapel
Earlsford
Wedderlairs
Auchedly
Ythanbank
Birness
Toll of Birness
Colliston
Kirktown of Slains

Auchterless
Dykeside
Gordonstown
Newseat
Folla Rule
Meikle Wartle
Cross of Jackston
Tulloch
Tarves
Ythsie
Kinharrachie
Ellon
Esslemont
Kirkton of Logie Buchan
Forvie
NK

Loanhead Stone Circle
Daviot
Glen Garioch
Oldmeldrum
Carnbrogie
Craigdam
Tolquhon Castle
Pitmedden Garden
Pitmedden
Logierieve
Newburgh

Pitcaple
Maiden Stone
Chapel of Garioch
Kirkton of Bourtie
Whiterashes
Udny Green
Housieside
Udny Station
Woodland
Pettymuk
Cultercullen
Foveran

Brandsbutt Symbol Stone
Inverurie
Uryside
Nether Crimond
Tillygreig
East Aquhorthies Stone Circle
Port Elphinstone
Burnhervie
Kinmuck
Newmachar
Kingseat
Whitecairns
Delfrigs

Kemnay
Thainstone
Kinkell Church
Kintore
Straloch
Reisque
Causeyend
Balmedie

Craigearn
Cottown
Leyolge
Castle Fraser
Blackburn
Hatton of Fintray
Kinmundy
Cothal
Belhelvie
Potterton
Blackdog

Sauchen
Lyne of Skene
Skene House
Millbuie
Dyce
Stoneywood
Middleton Park
Denmore
Scotstown Moor
Kirkwall
Lerwick

Dunecht
GRAMMOND HILL
Loch of Skene
Westhill
Kingswells
Kittybrewster
Old Aberdeen
Bridge of Don
Bucksburn
Northfield

99

Echt
Redhill
Kirkton of Skene
Garlogie
Elrick
ABERDEEN
Countesswells
Ruthrieston
Torry
Nigg Bay

Landerberry
Easter Ord
Blacktop
Mannofield
Culls

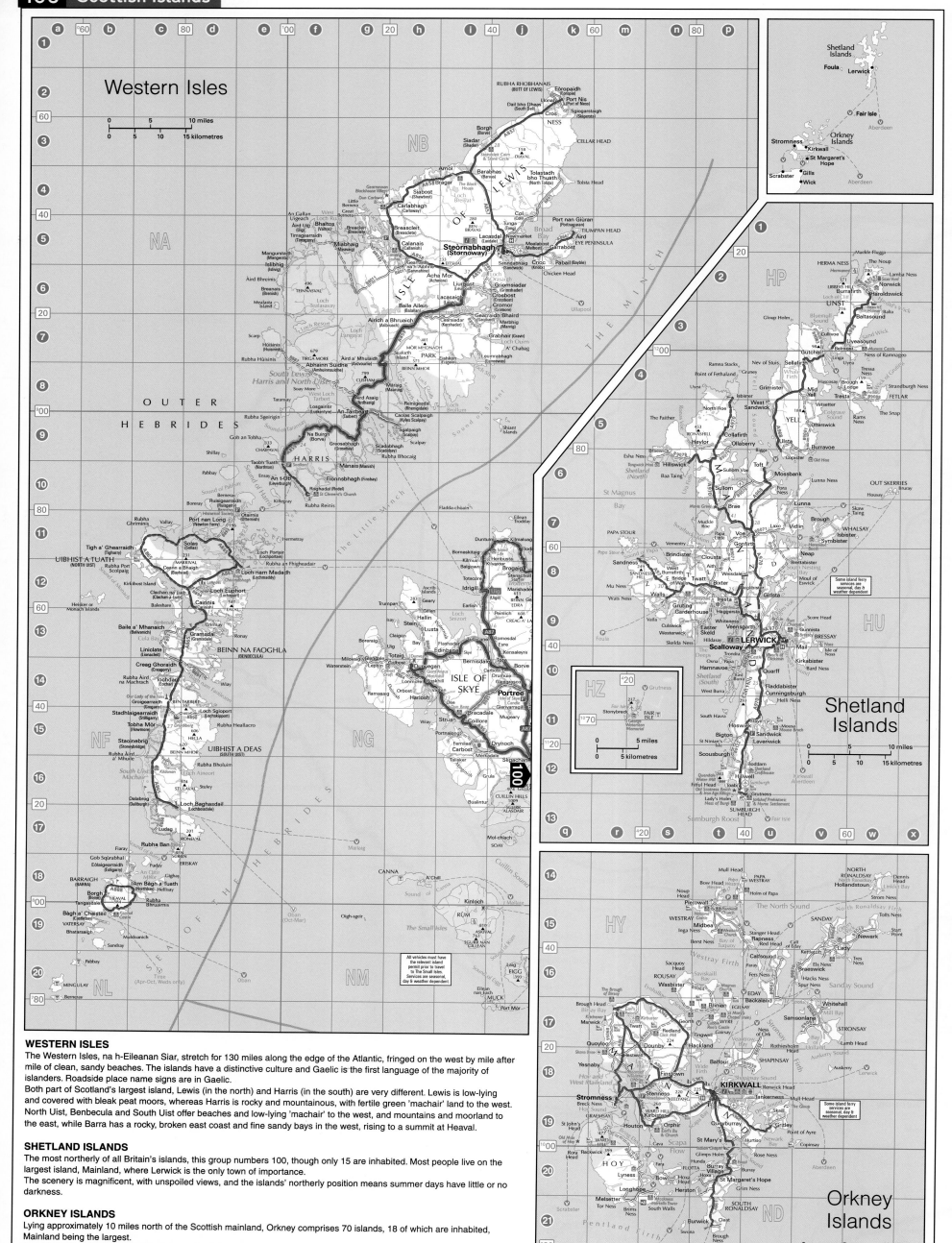

WESTERN ISLES
The Western Isles, na h-Eileanan Siar, stretch for 130 miles along the edge of the Atlantic, fringed on the west by mile after mile of clean, sandy beaches. The islands have a distinctive culture and Gaelic is the first language of the majority of islanders. Roadside place name signs are in Gaelic.

Both part of Scotland's largest island, Lewis (in the north) and Harris (in the south) are very different. Lewis is low-lying and covered with bleak peat moors, whereas Harris is rocky and mountainous, with fertile green 'machair' land to the west. North Uist, Benbecula and South Uist offer beaches and low-lying 'machair' to the west, and mountains and moorland to the east, while Barra has a rocky, broken east coast and fine sandy bays in the west, rising to a summit at Heaval.

SHETLAND ISLANDS
The most northerly of all Britain's islands, this group numbers 100, though only 15 are inhabited. Most people live on the largest island, Mainland, where Lerwick is the only town of importance.
The scenery is magnificent, with unspoiled views, and the islands' northerly position means summer days have little or no darkness.

ORKNEY ISLANDS
Lying approximately 10 miles north of the Scottish mainland, Orkney comprises 70 islands, 18 of which are inhabited, Mainland being the largest.
Apart from Hoy, Orkney is generally green and flat, with few trees. The islands abound with prehistoric antiquities and rare birds. The climate is one of even temperatures and 'twilight' summer nights, but with violent winds at times.

For information on ferry services see page XVI.

Inverkirkaig

NB

NC

Enard Bay

Rubha Còigeach
Rubha Mòr
Reiff
Achnahaird
Altandhu
Polbain
Badentarbet
Achiltibuie
Polglass

SUMMER ISLES

Eilean Mullagrach
Isle Ristol
Glas-leac Mòr

Tanera Beg
Tanera Mòr

Horse Island
Horse Sound

Eilean Dubh

Priest Island

Steòrnabhagh (Stornoway)
Glas-leac Beag

COIGACH

732 SÙILVEN
Fionn Loch

849 CÙL MÒR

769 CÙL BEAG

STAC POLLAIDH
Loch Sionascaig

612

Loch Bad a' Ghaill
Loch Osgaig

Loch Lurgainn

743 BEN MORE COIGACH
Ben Mor Coigach

Achduart
Culnacraig

Strathcanaird

Strath Canaird

A835

110

108

Greenstone Point
Rubha Beag

Mellon Udrigle
Achgarve

GRUINARD ISLAND

Cailleach Head

Leac Dhonn

Scoraig

Annat Bay

Isle Martin

Rhue

Ardmair

Ullapool (Ulapul)

A835

North Coast 500

Foura

Rubha Rèidh

Cove
Rubha nan Sasan
Mellon Charles
Ormiscaig
Aultbea

Laide

Badluarach

A832

Gruinard Bay

Gruinard

North Coast 500

Badcaul

Badrallach

Ardessie

Camusnagaul

Dundonnell

Little Loch Broom

BEINN GHOBHLACH

635

Ardindrean

Lett

Braes of Ullapool

558 BEINN EILIDE

A835

ISLE OF EWE

Melvaig
Aultgrishin

Inverasdale

Loch Ewe

Naast

296 AN CUAIDH

293 CNOC BREAC

Loch a' Bhaid-luachraich

Inverewe Garden

Loch Fada

250 MEALL NA MEINE

681 BEINN A' CHAISGEIN BEAG

Little Gruinard River

Gruinard River

764 SÀIL MHÒR

Lochan Gaineamhaich

347 CREAG-MHEAL BEAG

1062 AN TEALLACH

Fisherfield Forest

Loch na Sealga

Strathnasheallag Forest

Dundonnell Forest

1062

507 CARN A' BHIORAIN

Croftown

601 MEALL AN T-SITHE

North Erradale

B8021

Big Sand

Smithstown
Strath
Lonemore
Gairloch
Auchtercairn

Londubh
Poolewe

A832

Heritage

Gairloch & Loch Ewe

Charlestown

421 MEALL AN DOIREIN

Longa Island

Loch Gairloch

Eilean Horrisdale

Port Henderson

B8056

Badachro
Opinan

South Erradale

River Kerry

Loch Bad an Sgalaig

Victoria Falls 19

Talladale

791 BEINN AIRIDH CHARR

859 BEINN LÀIR

Letterewe Forest

Letterewe

Loch Garbhaig

Fionn Loch

Dubh Loch

906 BEINN DEARG MHOR

Wester Ross

974 SGÙRRBÀN
1019 MULLACH COIRE MHIC FHEARCHAIR

Lochan Fada

Loch a' Bhraoin

999 A' CHAILLEACH

Red Point

Red Point

NG

Loch Maree Islands

Loch Maree

A832

981 SLIOCH

Maree

Loch Ghaineamhach

Loch a' Ghodhainn

875 BAOSBHEINN

855 BEINN AN EOIN

724

680 BEINN A' MHÙINIDH

North Coast 500

Kinlochewe Forest

711 BEINN NAN RAMH

NH

619 BEINN BHREAC

Loch a' Bhealaich

985 BEINN ALLIGIN

914 BEINN DEARG

1009 RUADH-STAC MÒR

972

Beinn Eighe

Incheril

Kinlochewe

Glen Docherty

933 FIONN BHEINN

Rubha na Fearn

Fearnmore
Fearnbeg
Arrina
Kenmore

Cuaig

Callakille

Lonbain

Òb Chuaig

Lower Diabaig

Loch Diabaig

Alligin Shuas

Inveralligin

Torridon House

Upper Loch Torridon

Ardheslaig

Loch Torridon

Craig River

1024

1053 LIATHACH

Glen Torridon

BEINN EIGHE

A896

North Coast 500

A832

Loch a' Chroisg

Achn

782 SGÙRR DUBH

Loch Clair

Loch Fhiarlaid

550

Loch Gowan

A890

492 AN GARBH-MHEALL

493 CRÒIC-BHEINN

Deer

Torridon

Countryside Centre

Annat

Shieldaig

100

101

677 CÀRN BREAC

CÀRN M

North Coast 500

0   1   2   3   4   5 miles
0   1   2   3   4   5   6   7   8 kilometres

Glenshieldaig Forest

902 BEINN DAMPH

907 MAOL CHEAN-DEARG

958 SGORR RUADH

907 FUAR THOLL

Wester Ross

River Lair

Craig

Glen Carron

MORUISG

Loch Coulin

Loch Sgamhain

A890

Loch Damph

L M N P Q R S T U V

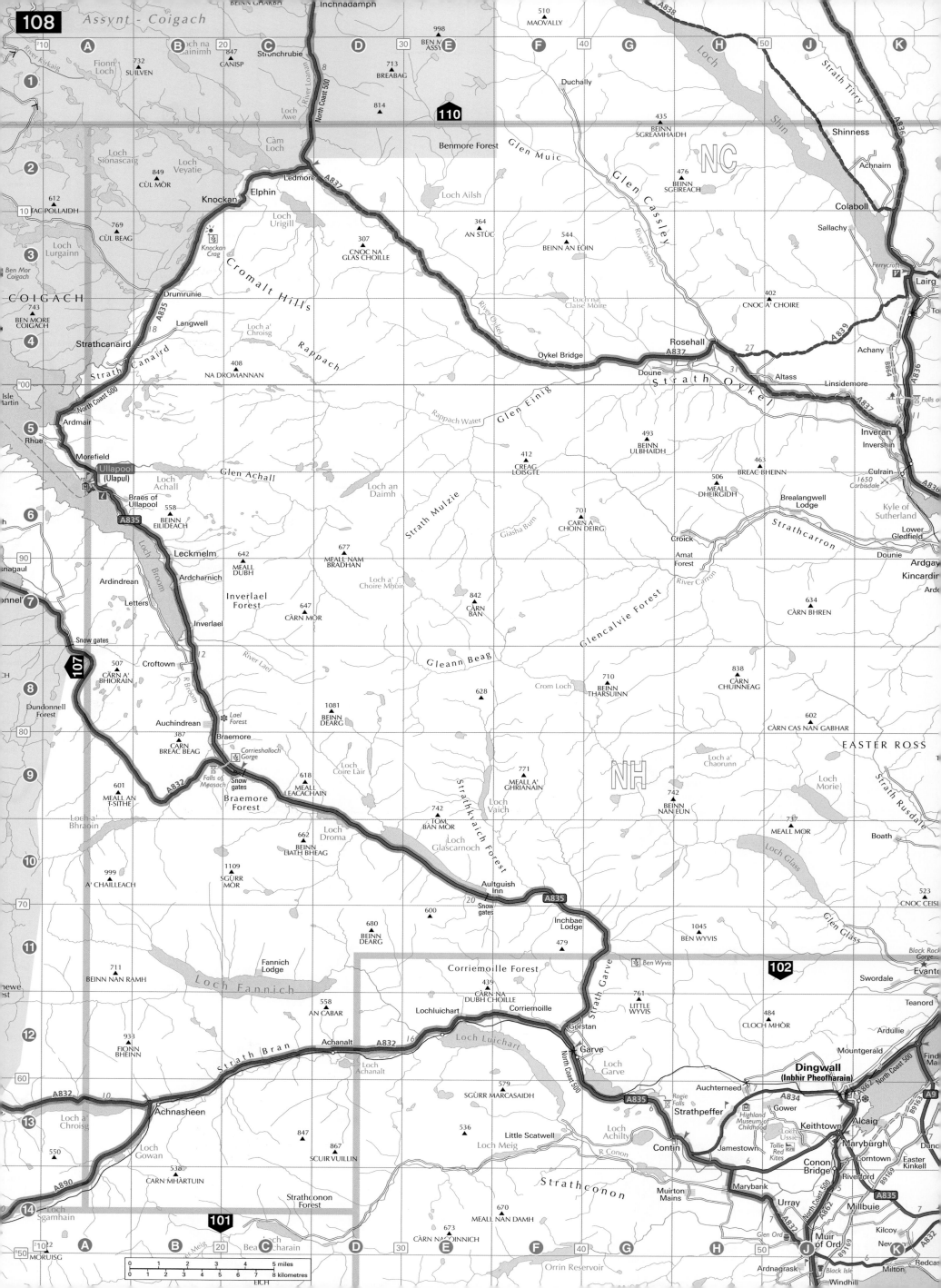

Ben Armine Forest

Strath Skinsdale

L   M   70   N   P   80   Q   R   90   S   A897   T   '00   U   A9 V   10

3   CNOC NA H-
INNSE MOIRE

Kildonan   416
BEINN
DUBHAIN

River Helmsdale

Torrish

404
CREAG
THORARAIDH

Coast S.

10

Badbea
istoric Villa

Ord of Caithness

1

462
MEALLAN
LIATH MOR

111

CNOC NAN CRÙBAG MÒR

624
BEINN
DHORAIN

591
BEINN
MHEALAICH

Glen Loth

Navidale

Timespan

West
Helmsdale

Snow gates

East Helmsdale   112

Helmsdale

Gartymore

Portgower

ND

2

10

Loch
eannach   317
SITHEAN
ACHADH NAN EUN

293
CNOC
LEAMHNACHD

River Brora

Balnacoil

539
COL-BHEINN

Lothmore

Lothbeg

Lothmore

3

323
BEN DOULA

Strath Brora

Loch
Brora

520
BEN
HORN

Dalchalm

Clynelish

Brora

21

Tomich

A839   14

Dalreavoch

Loch
Horn

Doll

A9

520
BEN
HORN

Pittentrail

Rogart

Golspie Burn   378
CAGAR FEOSAIG

Backies

Dunrobin
Castle

Carn
Liath

4

'00

313
CREAGAN GLAS

446
BEN LUNDIE

383
BEN BHRAGGIE

Rhives

Golspie

333
MEALL
EACHAINN

Loch Buidhe

Torboll

North Coast 500

Loch Fleet

5

in   349
BEINN DONUILL

Cambusavie

Skelbo

Littleferry

Sleasdairidh

Badninish

Skelbo Street

River Evelix

Achvaich

Birichin

7

Fourpenny

Embo

6

Bonar
Bridge

Migdale

Rearquhar

Astle

B9168

Embo Street

90

Loch
Migdale   A949

Spinningdale   10

Whiteface

Evelix   A949

Pitgrudy

Royal Dornoch

ie   A836

Clashmore   A9

Camore

3

Dornoch

Dornoch Firth

477
BEINN CLACH
AN FHEADAIN   19

Meikle Ferry

Cuthill

Historylinks

7

Dornoch
Point

Innis Mhor

Tarbat Ness

Wilkhaven

Ardmore

Cambuscurrie
Bay

Ferry
Point

Struie Hill

Dornoch Firth
Bridge

Dornoch Firth

Edderton

A836

Glenmorangie

Portmahomack

Tarbat Discovery
Centre

8

80

692
EINN
RSUINN

Morangie

Inver

Rockfield

Aultnamain

284

Tain
(Baile Dhubhthaich)

Lower Arboll

B9165

Toulvaddie

MORANGIE
FOREST

379
CNOC AN
T-SABHAIL

Loch
Eye

Lochslin

Rhynie

Balmuchy

NJ

9

B9176

Strath Rory

Newfield

B9165

Hill of
Fearn

Hilton of Cadboll
Chapel (ruin)

Ardross

6

Fearn

Tullich

Hilton of Cadboll

Ballchraggan

B9166

Arabella

Shandwick

Balintore

River Alness

Kildary

Shandwick Bay

10

Ardross

Milton

B9175

Ankerville

Moultavie

Achandunie

Rhicullen

Delny

Kilmuir

Pitcalnie

Millcraig

Tomich   A9   North Coast 500

Barbaraville

Nigg

70

Achnagarron

Balintraid

Fyrish

Alness
(Alanais)

Saltburn

B817

Balintraid

Nigg Bay

Castlecraig

Burghead

11

Dalmore

Invergordon

Nigg
Ferry

(June–Sept)

Cromarty

Hugh Miller's
Cottage

Burghead Bay

Newhall Point

Cromarty
Bay

Courthouse

Sutors Stacks

103

Balblair

Udale
Bay

Newton

MORAY FIRTH

Resolis

B9163

Allerton

Navity

B9160

Jemimaville

Findhorn   Hemprigg

B9089

Cullicudden

Brae

B9163

Upper Eathie

Culbin
Forest

Kinloss

12

60

Culbokie

255
MOUNT
EAGLE

Raddery

Fairy Glen

B9160   10

Whiteness Head

Kincorth
House

Kintessack

Sueno's Store

Grange Hall

Coltfield

Kilbuiack

BLACK ISLE

Killen

Rosemarkie

Brodie
Castle

Dyke

Whiterow

Forres

13

on   Belmaduthy

Fortrose

Groam
House

Fort George & The
Highlanders' Museum

Nairn
(Inbhir Nàrann)

Culbin
Sands

Brodie

Dallas Dhu
Distillery

Rafford   Califer

Knockbain

Cathedral

Chanonry
Point

Kingsteps

A96   10

River Findhorn

A940

Munlochy

Avoch

Ardersier

B9092

Tradespark

Auldearn

Whitemire

Branchill

Littleburn

Munlochy Bay

MORAY
FIRTH

Mossside

Househill

Conicavel

14

Tore

Bogallan

Fisherton

B9039

Gollanfield

Foynesfield

Darnaway
Forest

A940

371
MILL BUIE

Artafallie

A   L   Muir   M   N   Castle   P   A96   Q   R   S   T   U   V

70   Charlestown   Easter
Dalziel   Tornagrain   80   90   Fornighty   '00   10

Kessock   Croy   B9090   Culchorny   Logie Stead

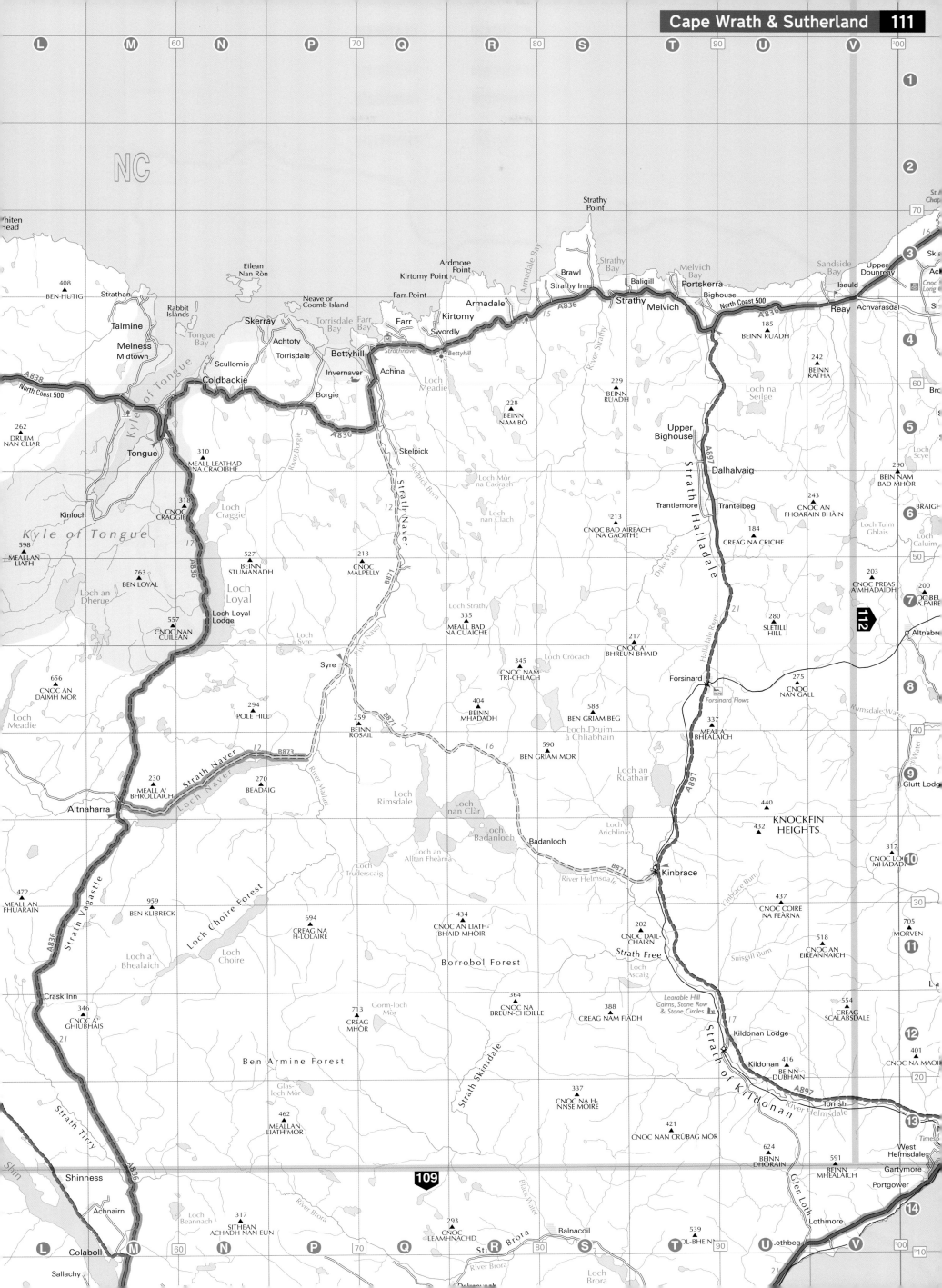

NC

408
BEN-HUTIG
Strathan
Rabbit
Islands
Eilean
Nan Ròn
Neave or
Coomb Island
Ardmore
Point
Kirtomy Point
Farr Point
Strathy
Point
Strathy
Bay
Brawl
Strathy Inn
Baligill
Portskerra
Melvich
Bay
Bighouse
Sandside
Bay
Upper
Dounreay
Isauld
Whiten
Head
Talmine
Melness
Midtown
Skerray
Achtoty
Torrisdale
Bay
Torrisdale
Bay
Farr
Bay
Farr
Kirtomy
Swordly
Armadale
Strathy
Melvich
North Coast 500
Reay
Achvarasdal
185
BEINN RUADH
Tongue
Bay
Sullomie
Bettyhill
Inn
Invernaver
Achina
242
BEINN
RATHA
A836
North Coast 500
Coldbackie
Borgie
13
A836
Loch
Meadie
229
BEINN
RUADH
Upper
Bighouse
Loch na
Seilge
Kinloch
Tongue
310
MEALL LEATHAD
NA CRAOIBHE
Skelpick
228
BEINN
NAM BÒ
Dalhalvaig
A897
290
BEIN NAM
BAD MHOR
Kyle of Tongue
318
CNOC
CRAGGIE
Loch
Craggie
12
Strath Naver
Loch Mòr
na Caoraigh
Loch
nan Clach
213
CNOC BAD AIREACH
NA GAOITHE
Trantlemore
Trantelbeg
243
CNOC AN
FHOARAIN BHÀIN
Loch Tuim
Ghlais
BRAIGH
598
MEALLAN
LIATH
527
BEINN
STUMANADH
213
CNOC
MALPELLY
184
CREAG NA CRICHE
Loch
Caluim
763
BEN LOYAL
Loch
Loyal
335
MEALL BAD
NA CUAICHE
203
CNOC PREAS
A'MHADAIDH
200
BEL
A' FAIRE
Loch an
Dherue
Loch Loyal
Lodge
Loch
Syre
Loch Strathy
217
CNOC A'
BHREUN BHAID
280
SLETILL
HILL
557
CNOC NAN
CUILEAN
Syre
Loch Cròcach
345
CNOC NAM
TRI-CHLACH
112
Altnabre
656
CNOC AN
DÀIMH MÒR
294
POLE HILL
259
BEINN
ROSAIL
B871
404
BEINN
MHADADH
588
BEN GRIAM BEG
Loch Druim
à Chliabhain
Forsinard
Forsinard Flows
275
CNOC
NAN GALL
Rumsdale Water
Loch
Meadie
Strath Naver
12
B873
Loch Naver
230
MEALL A'
BHROLLAICH
270
BEADAIG
River Mallart
16
590
BEN GRIAM MOR
Loch an
Ruathair
337
MEAL A'
BHEALAICH
Glutt Lodg
Altnaharra
Loch
Rimsdale
Loch
nan Clàr
Loch an
Alltan Fheàrna
Loch
Badanloch
Badanloch
Loch
Arichlinie
440
KNOCKFIN
HEIGHTS
432
317
CNOC LO
MHADAD
472
MEALL AN
FHUARAIN
Strath Vagastie
959
BEN KLIBRECK
Loch Choire Forest
694
CREAG NA
H-LOLAIRE
434
CNOC AN LIATH-
BHAID MHÒR
River Helmsdale
B871
Kinbrace
437
CNOC COIRE
NA FEÀRNA
30
705
MORVEN
346
CNOC A'
GHIUBHAIS
Loch a'
Bhealaich
Loch
Choire
202
CNOC DAIL-
CHAIRN
Strath Free
Loch
Ascaig
518
CNOC AN
EIREANNAICH
Crask Inn
21
A836
364
CNOC NA
BREUN-CHOILLE
388
CREAG NAM FIÀDH
Learable Hill
Cairns, Stone Row
& Stone Circles
17
Kildonan Lodge
554
CREAG
SCALABSDALE
713
CREAG
MHÒR
Gorm-loch
Mòr
Ben Armine Forest
Borrobol Forest
Strath Skintsdale
Kildonan
416
BEINN
DUBHÀIN
Strath of Kildonan
A897
401
CNOC NA MAOI
20
Glas-
loch Mòr
462
MEALLAN
LIATH MOR
337
CNOC NA H-
INNSE MOIRE
421
CNOC NAN CRÙBAG MÒR
River Helmsdale
Torrish
West
Helmsdale
Times
Strath Tirry
624
BEINN
DHORAIN
591
BEINN
MHEALAICH
Glen Loth
Gartymore
Portgower
Shinness
Shin
109
293
CNOC
LEAMHNACHD
Balnacoil
539
DL-BHEIN
Lothmore
Achnairn
Colaboll
Sallachy
317
SITHEAN
ACHADH NAN EUN
Loch
Beannach
River Brora
Black Water
Strath Brora
River Helmsdale
othbeg
Loch
Brora
21

ENGLAND

- Acorn Bank Garden CA10 1SP W & F 68 D7
- Aldborough Roman Site YO51 9ES N York 63 U6
- Alfriston Clergy House BN26 5TL E Susx 11 S10
- Alton Towers ST10 4DB Staffs 46 E5
- Anglesey Abbey CB25 9EJ Cambs 39 R8
- Anne Hathaway's Cottage CV37 9HH Warwks 36 G10
- Antony House PL11 2QA Cnwll 5 L9
- Appuldurcombe House PO38 3EW IoW 9 Q13
- Apsley House W1J 7NT Gt Lon 21 N7
- Arlington Court EX31 4LP Devon 15 P4
- Ascott LU7 0PS Bucks 30 J8
- Ashby-de-la-Zouch Castle LE65 1BR Leics 47 L10
- Athelhampton House & Gardens DT2 7LG Dorset 7 U6
- Attingham Park SY4 4TP Shrops 45 M11
- Audley End House & Gardens CB11 4JF Essex 39 R13
- Avebury SN8 1RD Wilts 18 G6
- Baconsthorpe Castle NR25 6LN Norfk 50 K6
- Baddesley Clinton Hall B93 0DQ Warwks 36 H6
- Bamburgh Castle NE69 7DF Nthumb 85 T11
- Barnard Castle DL12 8PR Dur 69 M9
- Barrington Court TA19 0NQ Somset 17 L13
- Basildon Park RG8 9NR W Berk 19 T5
- Bateman's TN19 7DS E Susx 12 C11
- Battle of Britain Memorial Flight Visitor Centre LN4 4SY Lincs 48 K2
- Beamish - The Living Museum of the North DH9 0RG Dur 69 R2
- Beatrix Potter Gallery LA22 0NS W & F 67 N13
- Beaulieu (National Motor Museum/Palace House) SO42 7ZN Hants 9 M8
- Belton House NG32 2LS Lincs 48 D6
- Belvoir Castle NG32 1PE Leics 48 B7
- Bembridge Windmill PO35 5SQ IoW 9 S11
- Beningbrough Hall YO30 1DD N York 64 C8
- Benthall Hall TF12 5RX Shrops 45 Q13
- Berkeley Castle GL13 9PJ Gloucs 28 C8
- Berrington Hall HR6 0DW Herefs 35 M8
- Berry Pomeroy Castle TQ9 6LJ Devon 5 U8
- Beth Chatto's Plants & Gardens CO7 7DB Essex 23 Q3
- Biddulph Grange Garden ST8 7SD Staffs 45 U2
- Bishop's Waltham Palace SO32 1DH Hants 9 Q5
- Blackpool Zoo FY3 8PP Bpool 61 Q12
- Blenheim Palace OX20 1PX Oxon 29 T4
- Bletchley Park Museum MK3 6EB M Keyn 30 J6
- Blickling Estate NR11 6NF Norfk 51 L8
- Blue John Cavern S33 8WA Derbys 56 H10
- Bodiam Castle TN32 5UA E Susx 12 E10
- Bolsover Castle S44 6PR Derbys 57 Q12
- Boscobel House and The Royal Oak ST19 9AR Staffs 45 T12
- Bowes Castle DL12 9LD Dur 69 L10
- Bradford Industrial Museum BD2 3HP W Yorks 63 P13
- Bradley TQ12 6BN Devon 5 U6
- Bramber Castle BN44 3WW W Susx 10 K8
- Brinkburn Priory NE65 8AR Nthumb 77 N6
- Brockhampton WR6 5TB Herefs 35 Q9
- Brough Castle CA17 4EJ W & F 68 G10
- Buckfast Abbey TQ11 0EE Devon 5 S7
- Buckingham Palace SW1A 1AA Gt Lon 21 N7
- Buckland Abbey PL20 6EY Devon 5 M7
- Buscot Park SN7 8BU Oxon 29 P8
- Byland Abbey YO61 4BD N York 64 C4
- Cadbury World B30 1JR Birm 36 D4
- Calke Abbey DE73 7LE Derbys 47 L9
- Canons Ashby NN11 3SD W N Nthn 37 Q10
- Canterbury Cathedral CT1 2EH Kent 13 N4
- Carisbrooke Castle PO30 1XY IoW 9 P11
- Carlyle's House SW3 5HL Gt Lon 21 N7
- Castle Drogo EX6 6PB Devon 5 S2
- Castle Howard YO60 7DA N York 64 G5
- Castle Rising Castle PE31 6AH Norfk 49 U9
- Charlecote Park CV35 9ER Warwks 36 J9
- Chartwell TN16 1PS Kent 21 S12
- Chastleton GL56 0SU Oxon 29 P2
- Chatsworth DE45 1PP Derbys 57 L12
- Chedworth Roman Villa GL54 3LJ Gloucs 29 L5
- Chessington World of Adventures KT9 2NE Gt Lon 21 L10
- Chester Cathedral CH1 2HU Ches W 54 K13
- Chester Zoo CH2 1EU Ches W 54 K12
- Chesters Roman Fort & Museum NE46 4EU Nthumb 76 J11
- Children's Country House at Sudbury DE6 5HT Derbys 46 G7
- Chiswick House & Gardens W4 2RP Gt Lon 21 M7
- Chysauster Ancient Village TR20 8XA Cnwll 2 D10
- Claremont Landscape Garden KT10 9JG Surrey 20 K10
- Claydon MK18 2EY Bucks 30 F7
- Cleeve Abbey TA23 0PS Somset 16 D8
- Clevedon Court BS21 6QU N Som 17 M2
- Cliveden SL6 0JA Bucks 20 F5
- Clouds Hill BH20 7NQ Dorset 7 V6
- Clumber Park S80 3AZ Notts 57 T12
- Colchester Zoo CO3 0SL Essex 23 N3
- Coleridge Cottage TA5 1NQ Somset 16 G9
- Coleton Fishacre TQ6 0EQ Devon 6 B14
- Compton Castle TQ3 1TA Devon 5 V8
- Conisbrough Castle DN12 3BU Donc 57 R7
- Corbridge Roman Town NE45 5NT Nthumb 76 K13
- Corfe Castle BH20 5EZ Dorset 8 D12
- Corsham Court SN13 0BZ Wilts 18 C6
- Cotehele PL12 6TA Cnwll 5 L7
- Cotswold Wildlife Park & Gardens OX18 4JP Oxon 29 P6
- Coughton Court B49 5JA Warwks 36 E8
- Courts Garden BA14 6RR Wilts 18 C8
- Cragside NE65 7PX Nthumb 77 M5
- Crealy Theme Park & Resort EX5 1DR Devon 6 D6
- Crich Tramway Village DE4 5DP Derbys 46 K2
- Croft Castle HR6 9PW Herefs 34 K7
- Croome WR8 9DW Worcs 35 U12
- Deddington Castle OX15 0TE Oxon 29 U1
- Didcot Railway Centre OX11 7NJ Oxon 19 R2
- Dover Castle CT16 1HU Kent 13 R7
- Drayton Manor Resort B78 3SA Staffs 46 G13
- Dudmaston WV15 6QN Shrops 35 R3
- Dunham Massey WA14 4SJ Traffd 55 R9
- Dunstanburgh Castle NE66 3TT Nthumb 77 R1
- Dunster Castle & Watermill TA24 6SL Somset 16 C8
- Durham Cathedral DH1 3EH Dur 69 S4
- Duxford IWM CB22 4QR Cambs 39 Q11
- Dyrham Park SN14 8HY S Glos 28 D12
- East Riddlesden Hall BD20 5EL Brad 63 M11
- Eden Project PL24 2SG Cnwll 3 R6
- Eltham Palace & Gardens SE9 5QE Gt Lon 21 R8
- Emmetts Garden TN14 6BA Kent 21 S12
- Exmoor Zoo EX31 4SG Devon 15 Q4
- Farleigh Hungerford Castle BA2 7RS Somset 18 B9
- Farnborough Hall OX17 1DU Warwks 37 M11
- Felbrigg Hall Gardens & Estate NR11 8PR Norfk 51 L6
- Fenton House & Garden NW3 6SP Gt Lon 21 N5
- Finch Foundry EX20 2NW Devon 5 Q2
- Finchale Priory DH1 5SH Dur 69 S3
- Fishbourne Roman Palace PO19 3QR W Susx 10 C10
- Flamingo Land Resort YO17 6UX N York 64 H4
- Forde Abbey House & Gardens TA20 4LU Somset 7 L3
- Fountains Abbey & Studley Royal HG4 3DY N York 63 R6
- Gawthorpe Hall BB12 8UA Lancs 62 G13
- Gisborough Priory TS14 6HG R & Cl 70 K9
- Glendurgan Garden TR11 5JZ Cnwll 2 K11
- Goodrich Castle HR9 6HY Herefs 28 A4
- Great Chalfield Manor & Garden SN12 8NH Wilts 18 C8
- Great Coxwell Barn SN7 7LZ Oxon 29 Q9
- Greenway TQ5 0ES Devon 5 V10
- Haddon Hall DE45 1LA Derbys 56 K13
- Hailes Abbey GL54 5PB Gloucs 29 L1
- Ham House & Garden TW10 7RS Gt Lon 21 L8
- Hampton Court Palace KT8 9AU Gt Lon 21 L9
- Hanbury Hall WR9 7EA Worcs 36 B8
- Hardwick S44 5QJ Derbys 57 Q14
- Hardy's Cottage DT2 8QJ Dorset 7 T6
- Hare Hill SK10 4PY Ches E 56 C11
- Hatchlands Park GU4 7RT Surrey 20 J12
- Heale Garden SP4 6NU Wilts 18 H13
- Helmsley Castle YO62 5AB N York 64 E3
- Hereford Cathedral HR1 2NG Herefs 35 M13
- Hergest Croft Gardens HR5 3EG Herefs 34 G9
- Hever Castle & Gardens TN8 7NG Kent 21 S13
- Hidcote GL55 6LR Gloucs 36 G12
- Hill Top LA22 0LF W & F 67 N13
- Hinton Ampner SO24 0LA Hants 9 R3
- Holkham Hall NR23 1AB Norfk 50 E5
- Housesteads Roman Fort NE47 6NN Nthumb 76 F12
- Howletts Wild Animal Park CT4 5EL Kent 13 N4
- Hughenden HP14 4LA Bucks 20 E3
- Hurst Castle SO41 0TP Hants 9 L11
- Hylands Estate CM2 8WQ Essex 22 G7
- Ickworth IP29 5QE Suffk 40 D8
- Ightham Mote TN15 0NT Kent 21 U12
- Ironbridge Gorge Museums TF8 7DQ Wrekin 45 Q13
- Kedleston Hall DE22 5JH Derbys 46 K5
- Kenilworth Castle & Elizabethan Garden CV8 1NE Warwks 36 J6
- Kensington Palace W8 4PX Gt Lon 21 N6
- Kenwood NW3 7JR Gt Lon 21 N5
- Killerton EX5 3LE Devon 6 C4
- King John's Hunting Lodge BS26 2AP Somset 17 M6
- Kingston Lacy BH21 4EA Dorset 8 D8
- Kirby Hall NN17 3EN N Nthn 38 D2
- Knightshayes EX16 7RQ Devon 16 C13
- Knole TN13 1HU Kent 21 T12
- Knowsley Safari Park L34 4AN Knows 55 L8
- Lacock SN15 2LG Wilts 18 D7
- Lamb House TN31 7ES E Susx 12 H11
- Lanhydrock PL30 5AD Cnwll 3 R4
- Launceston Castle PL15 7DR Cnwll 4 J4
- Leeds Castle ME17 1PB Kent 12 F5
- Legoland SL4 4AY W & M 20 F8
- Lightwater Valley Family Adventure Park HG4 3HT N York 63 R4
- Lindisfarne Castle TD15 2SH Nthumb 85 S10
- Lindisfarne Priory TD15 2RX Nthumb 85 S10
- Little Moreton Hall CW12 4SD Ches E 45 T2
- Liverpool Cathedral L1 7AZ Lpool 54 J9
- London Zoo ZSL NW1 4RY Gt Lon 21 N6
- Longleat BA12 7NW Wilts 18 B12
- Loseley Park GU3 1HS Surrey 20 G13
- Ludgershall Castle & Cross SP11 9QR Wilts 19 L10
- Lydford Castle & Saxon Town EX20 4BH Devon 5 N4
- Lyme SK12 2NX Ches E 56 E10
- Lytes Cary Manor TA11 7HU Somset 17 P11
- Lyveden PE8 5AT N Nthn 38 E3
- Maiden Castle DT2 9PP Dorset 7 S7
- Mapledurham Estate RG4 7TR Oxon 19 U5
- Marble Hill TW1 2NL Gt Lon 21 L8
- Marwell Zoo SO21 1JH Hants 9 Q4
- Melford Hall CO10 9AA Suffk 40 E11
- Merseyside Maritime Museum L3 4AQ Lpool 54 H9
- Minster Lovell Hall & Dovecote OX29 0RR Oxon 29 R5
- Mompesson House SP1 2EL Wilts 8 G3
- Monk Bretton Priory S71 5QD Barns 57 N5
- Montacute House TA15 6XP Somset 17 N13
- Morwellham Quay PL19 8JL Devon 5 L7
- Moseley Old Hall WV10 7HY Staffs 46 B13
- Mottisfont SO51 0LP Hants 9 L3
- Mottistone Manor & Garden PO30 4ED IoW 9 N12
- Mount Grace Priory DL6 3JG N York 70 F13
- Muckleburgh Military Collection NR25 7EH Norfk 50 K5
- National Maritime Museum SE10 9NF Gt Lon 21 Q7
- National Memorial Arboretum DE13 7AR Staffs 46 G11
- National Motorcycle Museum B92 0ED Solhll 36 H4
- National Portrait Gallery WC2H 0HE Gt Lon 21 N6
- National Railway Museum YO26 4XJ York 64 D9
- National Space Centre LE4 5NS C Leic 47 Q12
- Natural History Museum SW7 5BD Gt Lon 21 N7
- Needles Old Battery & New Battery PO39 0JH IoW 9 L12
- Nene Valley Railway PE8 6LR Cambs 38 H1
- Netley Abbey SO31 5FB Hants 9 P7
- Newark Air Museum NG24 2NY Notts 48 B2
- Newquay Zoo TR7 2NL Cnwll 3 L4
- Newtown National Nature Reserve & Old Town Hall PO30 4PA IoW 9 N10
- North Leigh Roman Villa OX29 6QB Oxon 29 S4
- Norwich Cathedral NR1 4DH Norfk 51 M12
- Nostell WF4 1QE Wakefd 57 P3
- Nunnington Hall YO62 5UY N York 64 F4
- Nymans RH17 6EB W Susx 11 M5
- O2 Arena SE10 0DX Gt Lon 21 Q6
- Old Royal Naval College SE10 9NN Gt Lon 21 Q7
- Old Sarum SP1 3SD Wilts 8 G2
- Old Wardour Castle SP3 6RR Wilts 8 C3
- Oliver Cromwell's House CB7 4HF Cambs 39 R4
- Orford Castle IP12 2ND Suffk 41 R10
- Ormesby Hall TS3 0SR R & Cl 70 H9
- Osborne PO32 6JX IoW 9 Q9
- Osterley Park & House TW7 4RB Gt Lon 20 K7
- Overbeck's Garden at Sharpitor TQ8 8LW Devon 5 S13
- Oxburgh Hall PE33 9PS Norfk 50 B13
- Packwood House B94 6AT Warwks 36 G6
- Paignton Zoo TQ4 7EU Torbay 6 A13
- Paultons Park SO51 6AL Hants 9 L5
- Paycocke's House & Garden CO6 1NS Essex 22 K3
- Peckover House & Garden PE13 1JR Cambs 49 Q12
- Pendennis Castle TR11 4LP Cnwll 3 L10
- Petworth House & Park GU28 9LR W Susx 10 F6
- Pevensey Castle BN24 5LE E Susx 11 U10
- Peveril Castle S33 8WQ Derbys 56 J10
- Pleasurewood Hills NR32 5DZ Suffk 41 T1
- Polesden Lacey RH5 6BD Surrey 20 K12
- Portland Castle DT5 1AZ Dorset 7 S10
- Portsmouth Historic Dockyard PO1 3LJ C Port 9 S8
- Powderham Castle EX6 8JQ Devon 6 C8
- Prior Park Landscape Garden BA2 5AH BaNES 17 U4
- Prudhoe Castle NE42 6NA Nthumb 77 M13
- Quarry Bank Mill & Styal SK9 4HP Ches E 55 T10
- Quebec House TN16 1TD Kent 21 R12
- RAF Museum Cosford TF11 8UP Shrops 45 S12
- RAF Museum London NW9 5LL Gt Lon 21 M4
- Ramsey Abbey Gatehouse PE26 1DH Cambs 39 L3
- Reculver Towers & Roman Fort CT6 6SU Kent 13 P2
- Red House DA6 8JF Gt Lon 21 S7
- Restormel Castle PL22 0EE Cnwll 4 E8
- RHS Garden Harlow Carr HG3 1QB N York 63 R9
- RHS Garden Wisley GU23 6QB Surrey 20 J11
- Richborough Roman Fort & Amphitheatre CT13 9JW Kent 13 R3
- Richmond Castle DL10 4QW N York 69 Q12
- Roche Abbey S66 8NW Rothm 57 R9
- Rochester Castle ME1 1SW Medway 12 D2
- Rockbourne Roman Villa SP6 3PG Hants 8 G5
- Roman Baths, Bath BA1 1LZ BaNES 17 U4
- Royal Botanic Gardens, Kew TW9 3AB Gt Lon 21 L7
- Royal Observatory Greenwich SE10 8XJ Gt Lon 21 Q7
- Rufford Abbey NG22 9DF Notts 57 T14
- Rufford Old Hall L40 1SG Lancs 55 L3
- Runnymede & Ankerwycke SL4 2JJ W & M 20 G8
- Rushton Triangular Lodge NN14 1RP N Nthn 38 B4
- Rycote Chapel OX9 2PA Oxon 30 E12
- St Leonard's Tower ME19 6PE Kent 12 C4
- St Michael's Mount TR17 0HT Cnwll 2 E11
- St Paul's Cathedral EC4M 8AD Gt Lon 21 P6
- Salisbury Cathedral SP1 2EJ Wilts 8 G3
- Saltram PL7 1UH C Plym 5 N9
- Sandham Memorial Chapel RG20 9JT Hants 19 Q8
- Sandringham Estate PE35 6EH Norfk 49 U8
- Saxtead Green Post Mill IP13 9QQ Suffk 41 N8
- Scarborough Castle YO11 1HY N York 65 P2
- Science Museum SW7 2DD Gt Lon 21 N7
- Scotney Castle TN3 8JN Kent 12 C8
- Shaw's Corner AL6 9BX Herts 31 Q9
- Sheffield Park & Garden TN22 3QX E Susx 11 Q6
- Sherborne Old Castle DT9 3SA Dorset 17 R13
- Sissinghurst Castle Garden TN17 2AB Kent 12 F8
- Sizergh LA8 8AE W & F 61 T2
- Smallhythe Place TN30 7NG Kent 12 G10
- Snowshill Manor & Garden WR12 7JU Gloucs 36 E14
- Souter Lighthouse & The Leas SR6 7NH S Tyne 77 U13
- Speke Hall L24 1XD Lpool 54 K10
- Spinnaker Tower PO1 3TT C Port 9 S9
- Stokesay Castle SY7 9AH Shrops 34 K4
- Stonehenge SP4 7DE Wilts 18 H12
- Stourhead BA12 6QD Wilts 17 U10
- Stowe MK18 5EQ Bucks 30 E5
- Sulgrave Manor & Garden OX17 2SD W Nthn 37 Q11
- Sunnycroft TF1 2DR Wrekin 45 Q11
- Sutton Hoo IP12 3DJ Suffk 41 N11
- Sutton House & Breaker's Yard E9 6JQ Gt Lon 21 Q5
- Tate Britain SW1P 4RG Gt Lon 21 N7
- Tate Liverpool L3 4BB Lpool 54 H9
- Tate Modern SE1 9TG Gt Lon 21 P6
- Tattershall Castle LN4 4LR Lincs 48 K2
- Tatton Park WA16 6QN Ches E 55 R10
- The British Library NW1 2DB Gt Lon 21 N6
- The British Museum WC1B 3DG Gt Lon 21 N6
- The Deep HU1 4DP C KuH 65 P14
- The Lost Gardens of Heligan PL26 6EN Cnwll 3 P7
- The Lowry M50 3AZ Salfd 55 T7
- The National Gallery WC2N 5DN Gt Lon 21 N6
- The Tank Museum BH20 6JG Dorset 8 A11
- The Vyne RG24 9HL Hants 19 T9
- The Weir Garden HR4 7QF Herefs 34 K12
- Thornton Abbey & Gatehouse DN39 6TU N Linc 58 K3
- Thorpe Park Resort KT16 8PN Surrey 20 H9
- Tilbury Fort RM18 7NR Thurr 22 G12
- Tintagel Castle PL34 0HE Cnwll 4 C3
- Tintinhull Garden BA22 8PZ Somset 17 P13
- Totnes Castle TQ9 5NU Devon 5 U8
- Tower of London EC3N 4AB Gt Lon 21 P6
- Townend LA23 1LB W & F 67 P12
- Treasurer's House YO1 7JL York 64 E9
- Trelissick Garden TR3 6QL Cnwll 3 L9
- Trengwainton Garden TR20 8RZ Cnwll 2 C10
- Trerice TR8 4PG Cnwll 3 L5
- Tropical World Leeds LS8 2ER Leeds 63 S12
- Twycross Zoo CV9 3PX Leics 46 K12
- Ullswater 'Steamers' CA11 0US W & F 67 N9
- Upnor Castle ME2 4XG Medway 22 J13
- Uppark House & Garden GU31 5QR W Susx 10 B7
- Upton House & Gardens OX15 6HT Warwks 37 L11
- Victoria & Albert Museum SW7 2RL Gt Lon 21 N7
- Waddesdon Manor HP18 0JH Bucks 30 F9
- Wakehurst RH17 6TN W Susx 11 N4
- Wall Roman Site WS14 0AW Staffs 46 E12
- Wallington NE61 4AR Nthumb 77 L9
- Walmer Castle & Gardens CT14 7LJ Kent 13 S6
- Warkworth Castle & Hermitage NE65 0UJ Nthumb 77 Q4
- Warner Bros. Studio Tour London WD25 7LR Herts 31 N12
- Warwick Castle CV34 4QU Warwks 36 J8
- Washington Old Hall NE38 7LE Sundld 70 D1
- Waterperry Gardens OX33 1LG Oxon 30 D11
- Weeting Castle IP27 0RQ Norfk 40 C3
- Wenlock Priory TF13 6HS Shrops 45 P13
- West Midland Safari Park DY12 1LF Worcs 35 T5
- West Wycombe Park, Village & Hill HP14 3AJ Bucks 20 D4
- Westbury Court Garden GL14 1PD Gloucs 28 D5
- Westminster Abbey SW1P 3PA Gt Lon 21 N7
- Westonbirt, The National Arboretum GL8 8QS Gloucs 28 G9
- Weston Park TF11 8LE Staffs 45 T11
- Westwood Manor BA15 2AF Wilts 18 B9
- Whipsnade Zoo ZSL LU6 2LF C Beds 31 M9
- Whitby Abbey YO22 4JT N York 71 R10
- Wicksteed Park NN15 6NJ Nhants 38 C5
- Wightwick Manor & Gardens WV6 8EE Wolves 45 U14
- Wild Place Project BS10 7TP S Glos 27 V11
- Wimpole Estate SG8 0BW Cambs 39 M10
- Winchester Cathedral SO23 9LS Hants 9 P3
- Winchester City Mill SO23 0EJ Hants 9 P3
- Windermere Jetty Museum LA23 1BN W & F 67 P13
- Windsor Castle SL4 1NJ W & M 20 G7
- Winkworth Arboretum GU8 4AD Surrey 10 F2
- Woburn Safari Park MK17 9QN C Beds 31 L6
- Wollaton Hall NG8 2AE C Nott 47 P6
- Wookey Hole Caves BA5 1BA Somset 17 P7
- Woolsthorpe Manor NG33 5PD Lincs 48 D9
- Wordsworth House CA13 9RX Cumb 66 H6
- Wrest Park MK45 4HR Beds C 31 N5
- Wroxeter Roman City SY5 6PR Shrops 45 N12
- WWT Arundel Wetland Centre BN18 9PB W Susx 10 G9
- WWT Slimbridge Wetland Centre GL2 7BT Gloucs 28 D6
- Yarmouth Castle PO41 0PB IoW 9 M11
- York Minster YO1 7HH York 64 E9

SCOTLAND

- Aberdour Castle & Gardens KY3 0SL Fife 83 N1
- Alloa Tower FK10 1PP Clacks 90 C13
- Arbroath Abbey DD11 1EG Angus 91 T3
- Arduaine Garden PA34 4XQ Ag & B 87 P3
- Bachelors' Club KA5 5RB S Ayrs 81 N7
- Balmoral Castle & Estate AB35 5TB Abers 98 D5
- Balvenie Castle AB55 4DH Moray 104 C7
- Bannockburn FK7 0LJ Stirlg 89 S7
- Blackness Castle EH49 7NH Falk 83 L2
- Blair Castle & Gardens PH18 5TL P & K 97 P10
- Bothwell Castle G71 8BL S Lans 82 C7
- Branklyn Garden PH2 7BB P & K 90 H7
- Brodick Castle, Garden & Country Park KA27 8HY N Ayrs 80 E5
- Brodie Castle IV36 2TE Moray 103 Q4
- Broughton House & Garden DG6 4JX D & G 73 R9
- Burleigh Castle KY13 9GG P & K 90 H11
- Caerlaverock Castle DG1 4RU D & G 74 K12
- Cardoness Castle DG7 2EH D & G 73 P8
- Castle Campbell FK14 7PP Clacks 90 E12
- Castle Fraser, Garden & Estate AB51 7LD Abers 105 L13
- Castle Kennedy Gardens DG9 8SL D & G 72 E7
- Castle Menzies PH15 2JD P & K 90 B2
- Corgarff Castle AB36 8YP Abers 98 D2
- Craigievar Castle AB33 8JF Abers 98 K2
- Craigmillar Castle EH16 4SY C Edin 83 Q4
- Crarae Garden PA32 8YA Ag & B 87 T6
- Crathes Castle, Garden & Estate AB31 5QJ Abers 99 N4
- Crichton Castle EH37 5XA Mdloth 83 S6
- Crossraguel Abbey KA19 8HQ S Ayrs 80 K11
- Culloden IV2 5EU Highld 102 K6
- Culross KY12 8JH Fife 82 J1
- Culzean Castle & Country Park KA19 8LE S Ayrs 80 J10
- Dallas Dhu Distillery IV36 2RR Moray 103 R4
- David Livingstone Birthplace G72 9BY S Lans 82 C7
- Dirleton Castle & Gardens EH39 5ER E Loth 84 E2
- Doune Castle FK16 6EA Stirlg 89 R5
- Drum Castle, Garden & Estate AB31 5EY Abers 99 P3
- Dryburgh Abbey TD6 0RQ Border 84 F12
- Duff House AB45 3SX Abers 104 K3
- Dumbarton Castle G82 1JJ W Duns 88 J11
- Dundrennan Abbey DG6 4QH D & G 73 S10
- Dunnottar Castle AB39 2TL Abers 99 R7
- Dunstaffnage Castle & Chapel PA37 1PZ Ag & B 94 B12
- Dynamic Earth EH8 8AS C Edin 83 Q4
- Edinburgh Castle EH1 2NG C Edin 83 Q4
- Edinburgh Zoo RZSS EH12 6TS C Edin 83 P4
- Edzell Castle & Garden DD9 7UE Angus 98 K10
- Eilean Donan Castle IV40 8DX Highld 101 M6
- Elgin Cathedral IV30 1HU Moray 103 V3
- Falkirk Wheel FK1 4RS Falk 82 G2
- Falkland Palace & Garden KY15 7BU Fife 91 L10
- Fort George IV2 7TE Highld 103 L4
- Fyvie Castle AB53 8JS Abers 105 M8
- Georgian House EH2 4DR C Edin 83 P4
- Gladstone's Land EH1 2NT C Edin 83 Q4
- Glamis Castle DD8 1RJ Angus 91 N2
- Glasgow Botanic Gardens G12 0UE C Glas 89 N12
- Glasgow Cathedral G4 0QZ C Glas 89 P12
- Glasgow Science Centre G51 1EA C Glas 89 N12
- Glen Grant Distillery AB38 7BS Moray 104 B6
- Glenluce Abbey DG8 0AF D & G 72 F8
- Greenbank Garden G76 8RB E Rens 81 R1
- Haddo House AB41 7EQ Abers 105 P9
- Harmony Garden TD6 9LJ Border 84 E12
- Hermitage Castle TD9 0LU Border 75 U6
- Highland Wildlife Park RZSS PH21 1NL Highld 97 N3
- Hill House G84 9AJ Ag & B 88 G9
- Hill of Tarvit Mansion & Garden KY15 5PB Fife 91 N9
- Holmwood G44 3YG C Glas 89 N14
- House of Dun DD10 9LQ Angus 99 M12
- House of the Binns EH49 7NA W Loth 83 L3
- Huntingtower Castle PH1 3JL P & K 90 G7
- Huntly Castle AB54 4SH Abers 104 G7
- Inchmahome Priory FK8 3RA Stirlg 89 N5
- Inveresk Lodge Garden EH21 7TE E Loth 83 R4
- Inverewe IV22 2LG Highld 107 Q8
- Inverlochy Castle PH33 6SN Highld 94 G3
- Kellie Castle & Garden KY10 2RF Fife 91 R10
- Kildrummy Castle AB33 8RA Abers 104 F12
- Killiecrankie PH16 5LG P & K 97 Q11
- Leith Hall Garden & Estate AB54 4NQ Abers 104 G10
- Linlithgow Palace EH49 7AL W Loth 82 K3
- Lochleven Castle KY13 8UF P & K 90 H11
- Logan Botanic Garden DG9 9ND D & G 72 D11
- Malleny Garden EH14 7AF C Edin 83 N5
- Melrose Abbey TD6 9LG Border 84 E12
- National Museum of Scotland EH1 1JF C Edin 83 Q4
- Newark Castle PA14 5NH Inver 88 H11
- Palace of Holyroodhouse EH8 8DX C Edin 83 Q4
- Pitmedden Garden AB41 7PD Abers 105 P10
- Preston Mill & Phantassie Doocot EH40 3DS E Loth 84 F3
- Priorwood Garden TD6 9PX Border 84 E12
- Robert Smail's Printing Works EH44 6HA Border 83 R11
- Rothesay Castle PA20 0DA Ag & B 88 C13
- Royal Botanic Garden Edinburgh EH3 5LR C Edin 83 P3
- Royal Yacht Britannia EH6 6JJ C Edin 83 Q3
- St Andrews Aquarium KY16 9AS Fife 91 R8
- St Andrews Botanic Garden KY16 8RT Fife 91 R8
- Scone Palace PH2 6BD P & K 90 H6
- Scottish Seabird Centre EH39 4SS E Loth 84 F1
- Smailholm Tower TD5 7PG Border 84 G12
- Souter Johnnie's Cottage KA19 8HY S Ayrs 80 J11
- Stirling Castle FK8 1EJ Stirlg 89 S7
- Sweetheart Abbey DG2 8BU D & G 74 J12
- Tantallon Castle EH39 5PN E Loth 84 F1
- The Burrell Collection G43 1AT C Glas 89 N13
- The Hunterian Museum G12 8QQ C Glas 89 N12
- The Tenement House G3 6QN C Glas 89 N12
- Threave Castle DG7 1TJ D & G 74 D13
- Threave Garden & Estate DG7 1RX D & G 74 E13
- Tolquhon Castle AB41 7LP Abers 105 P10
- Traquair House EH44 6PW Border 83 R11
- Urquhart Castle IV63 6XJ Highld 102 F10
- Weaver's Cottage PA10 2JG Rens 88 K13
- Whithorn Priory & Museum DG8 8PY D & G 73 L11

WALES

- Aberconwy House LL32 8AY Conwy 53 N7
- Aberdulais Tin Works & Waterfall SA10 8EU Neath 26 D8
- Beaumaris Castle LL58 8AP IoA 52 K7
- Big Pit National Coal Museum NP4 9XP Torfn 27 N6
- Bodnant Garden LL28 5RE Conwy 53 P8
- Caerleon Roman Fortress & Baths NP18 1AE Newpt 27 Q9
- Caernarfon Castle LL55 2AY Gwynd 52 G10
- Caldicot Castle & Country Park NP26 4NU Mons 27 T10
- Cardiff Castle CF10 3RB Cardif 27 M12
- Castell Coch CF15 7JS Cardif 27 L11
- Chirk Castle LL14 5AF Wrexhm 44 G6
- Colby Woodland Garden SA67 8PP Pembks 25 L9
- Conwy Castle LL32 8AY Conwy 53 N7
- Criccieth Castle LL52 0DP Gwynd 42 K6
- Cyfarthfa Castle Museum CF47 8RE Myr Td 26 J6
- Dinefwr SA19 6RT Carmth 25 V6
- Dolaucothi SA19 8US Carmth 33 N12
- Erddig LL13 0YT Wrexhm 44 H4
- Ffestiniog Railway LL49 9NF Gwynd 43 M6
- Harlech Castle LL46 2YH Gwynd 43 L7
- Llanerchaeron SA48 8DG Cerdgn 32 J8
- National Showcaves Centre for Wales SA9 1GJ Powys 26 E4
- Penrhyn Castle & Garden LL57 4HT Gwynd 52 K8
- Plas Newydd House & Garden LL61 6DQ IoA 52 H9
- Plas yn Rhiw LL53 8AB Gwynd 42 D8
- Portmeirion LL48 6ER Gwynd 43 L6
- Powis Castle & Garden SY21 8RF Powys 44 F12
- Raglan Castle NP15 2BT Mons 27 S6
- St Davids Cathedral SA62 6RD Pembks 24 C5
- St Fagans National Museum of History CF5 6XB Cardif 27 L12
- Sygun Copper Mine LL55 4NE Gwynd 43 M4
- Tintern Abbey NP16 6SE Mons 27 U7
- Tudor Merchant's House SA70 7BX Pembks 24 K10
- Tŷ Mawr Wybrnant LL25 0HJ Conwy 43 Q3
- Valle Crucis Abbey LL20 8DD Denbgs 44 F5

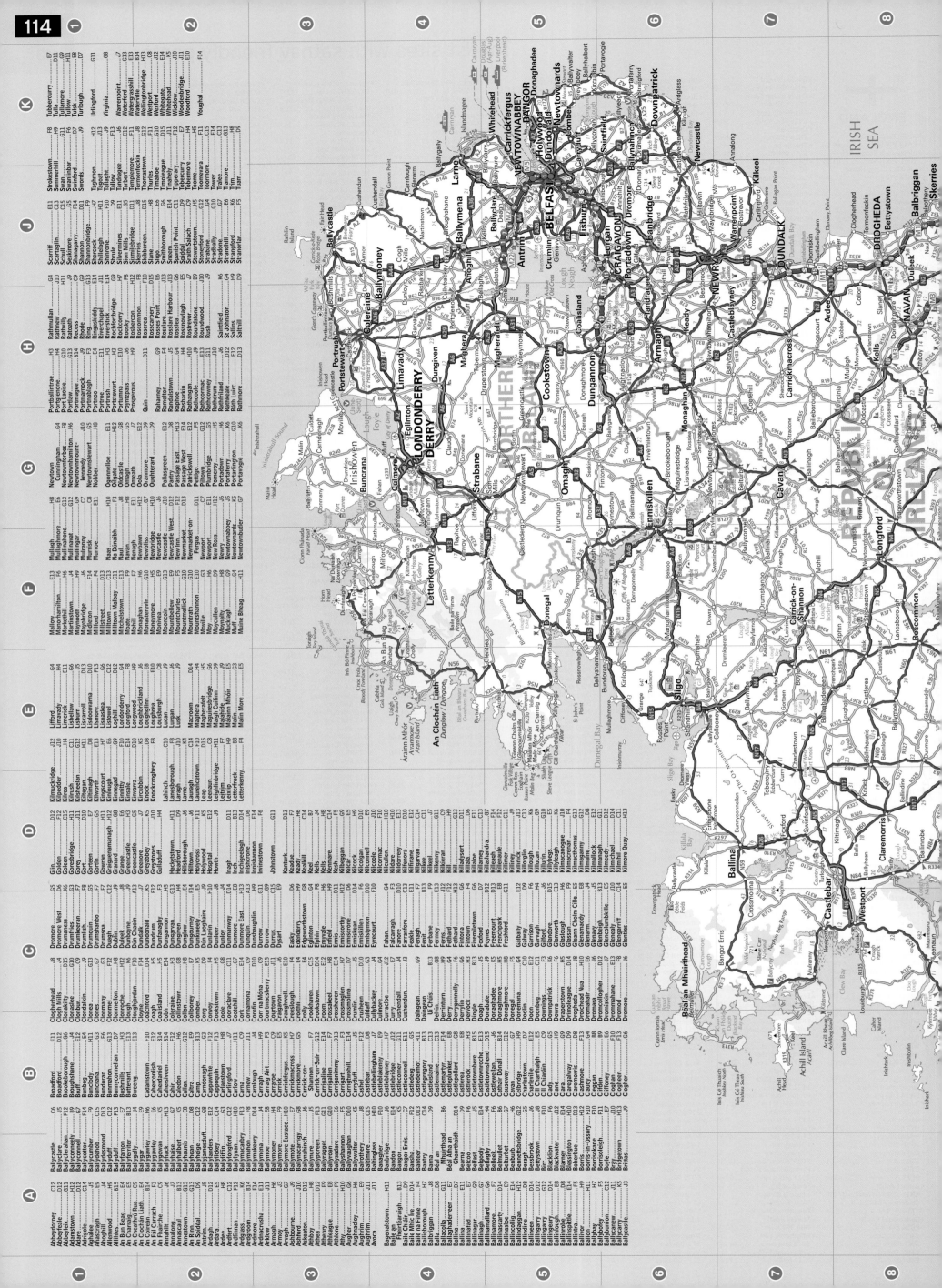

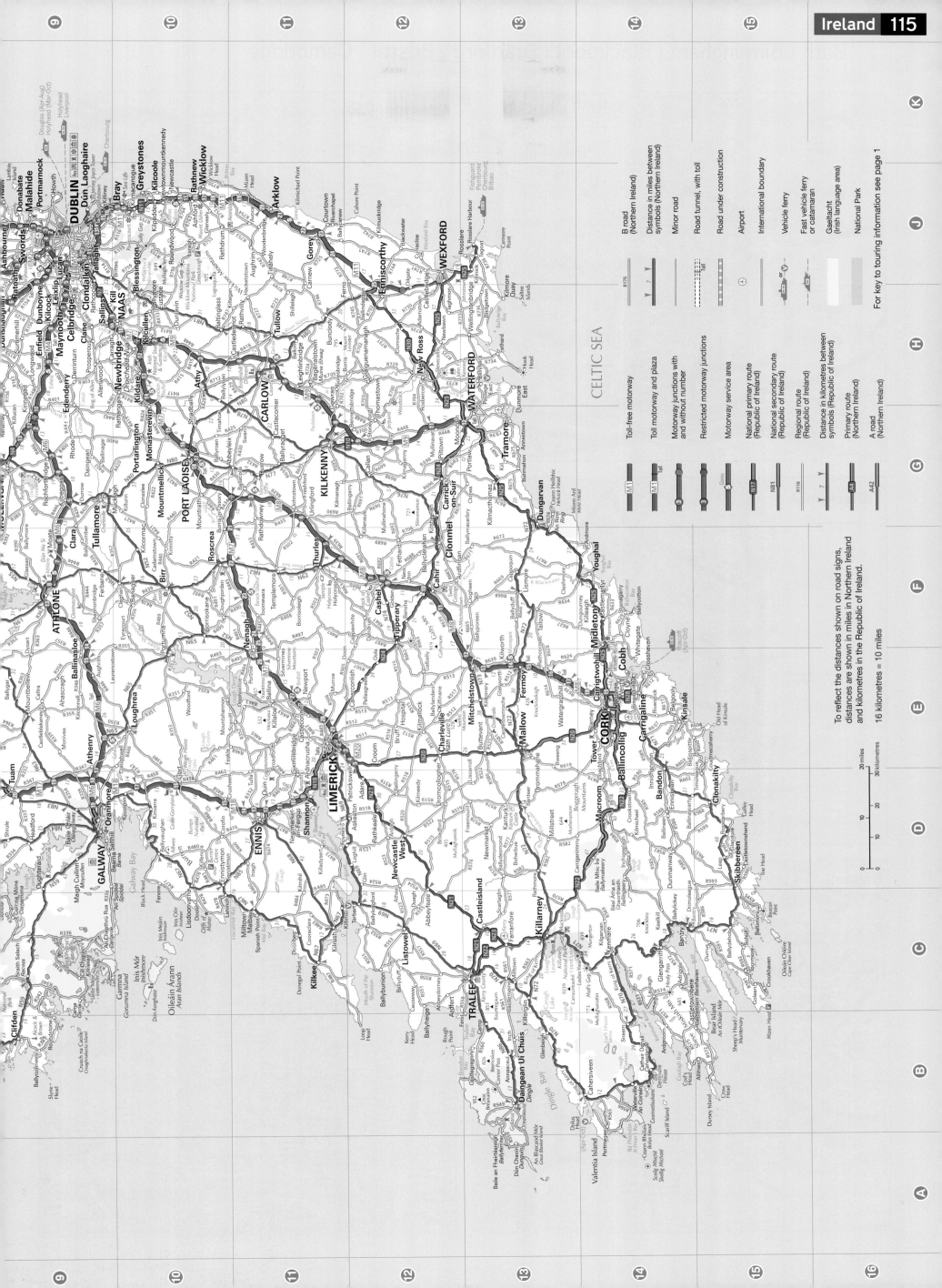

CELTIC SEA

M1		Toll-free motorway
M1 Toll		Toll motorway and plaza
		Motorway junctions with and without number
		Restricted motorway junctions
		Motorway service area
N17		National primary route (Republic of Ireland)
N81		National secondary route (Republic of Ireland)
R116		Regional route (Republic of Ireland)
7		Distance in kilometres between symbols (Republic of Ireland)
A4		Primary route (Northern Ireland)
A42		A road (Northern Ireland)

B176		B road (Northern Ireland)
7		Distance in miles between symbols (Northern Ireland)
		Minor road
		Road tunnel, with toll
		Road under construction
		Airport
		International boundary
		Vehicle ferry
		Fast vehicle ferry or catamaran
		Gaeltacht (Irish language area)
		National Park
		For key to touring information see page 1

To reflect the distances shown on road signs, distances are shown in miles in Northern Ireland and kilometres in the Republic of Ireland.

16 kilometres = 10 miles

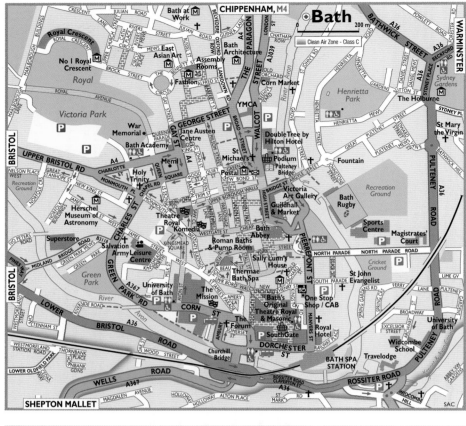

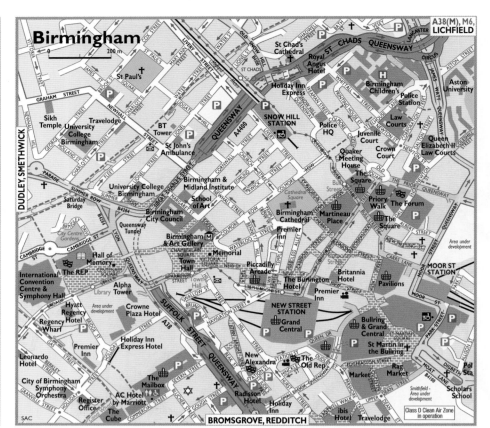

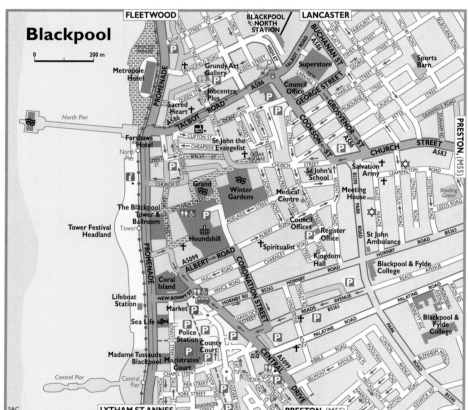

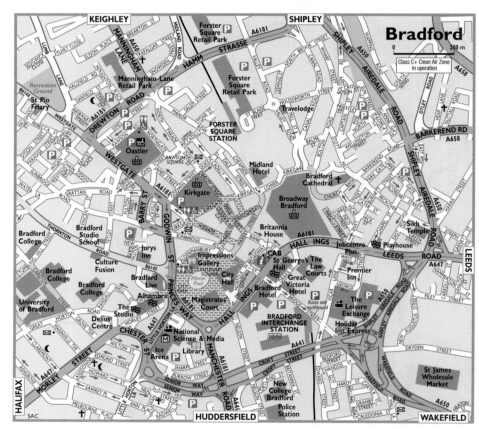

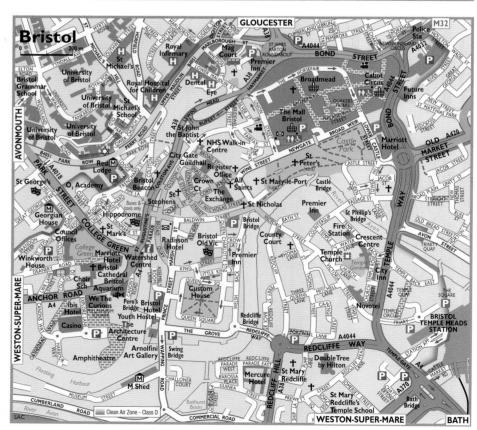

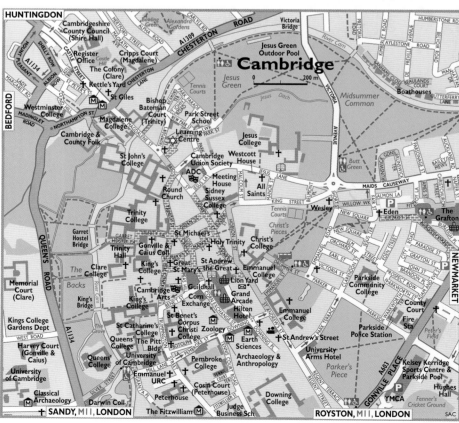

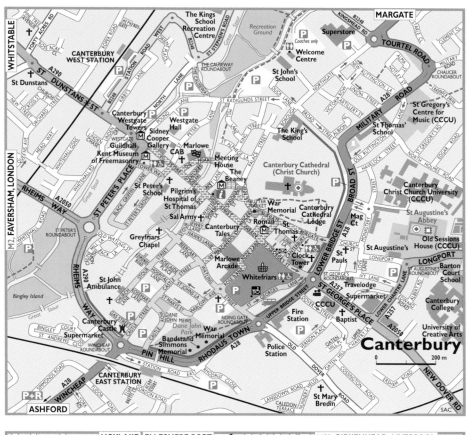

Canterbury

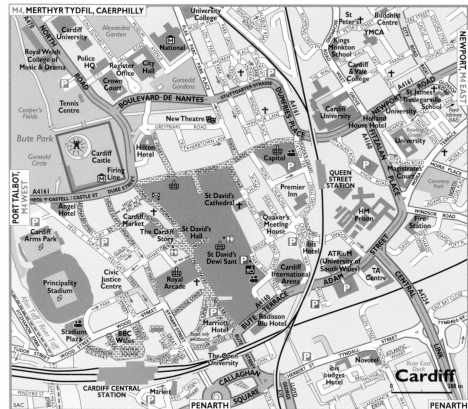

Cardiff

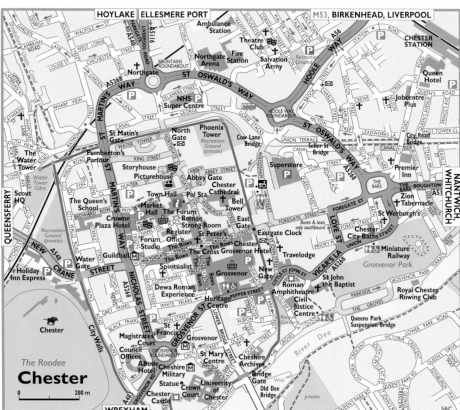

Chester

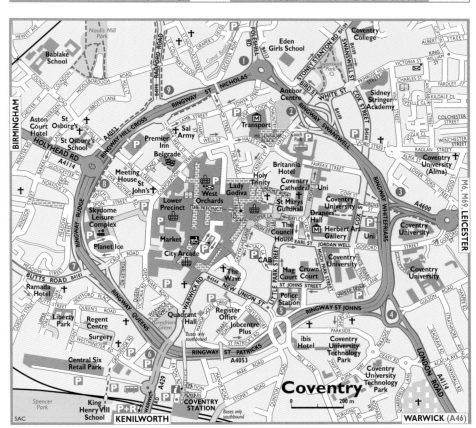

Coventry

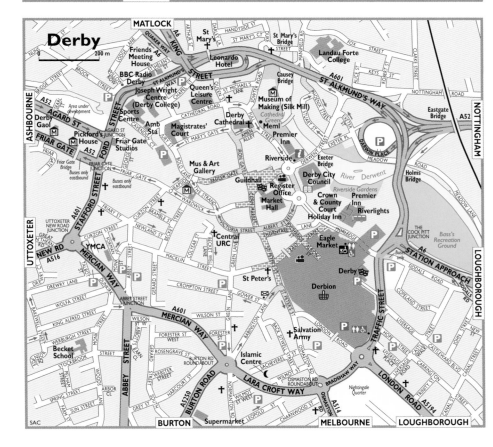

Derby

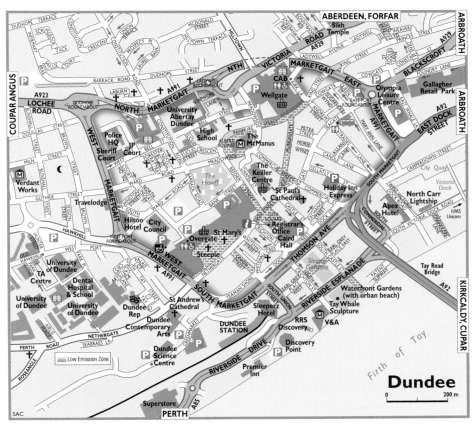

Dundee

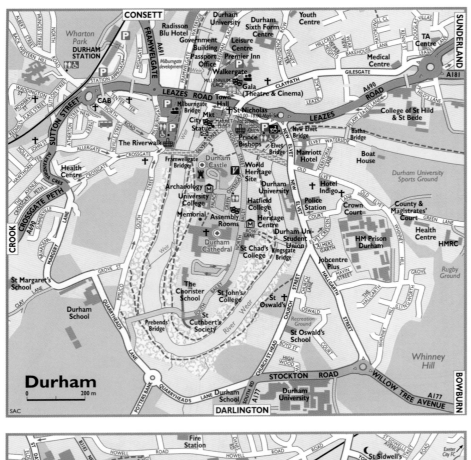

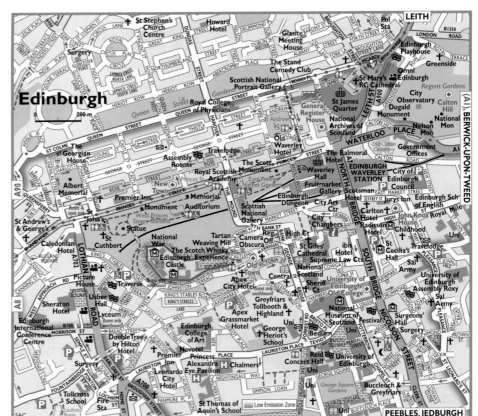

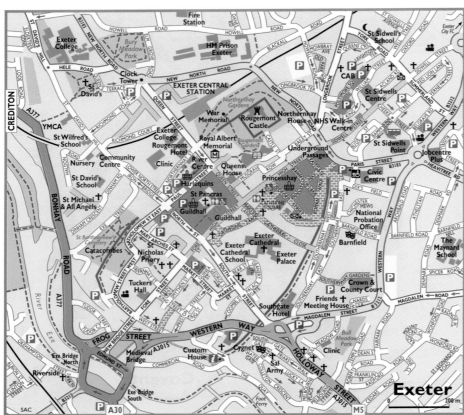

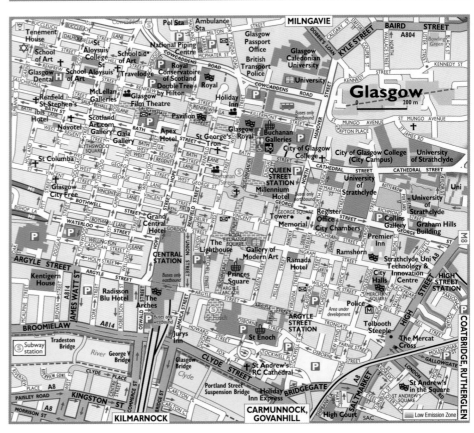

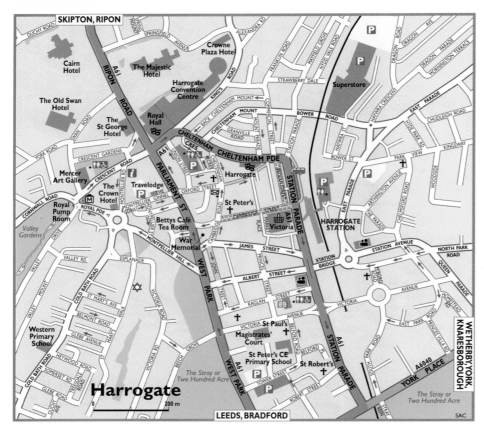

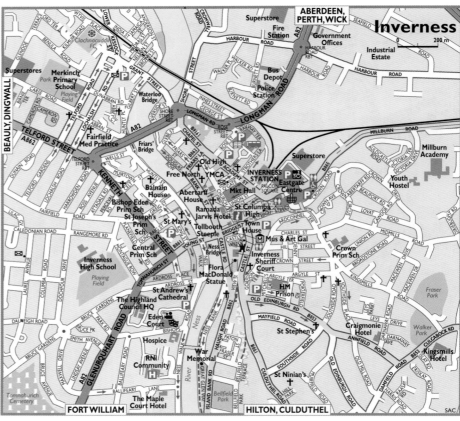

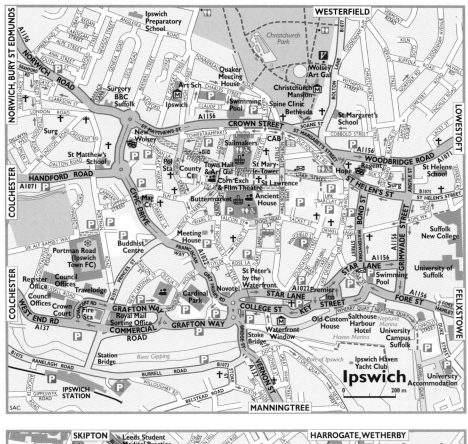

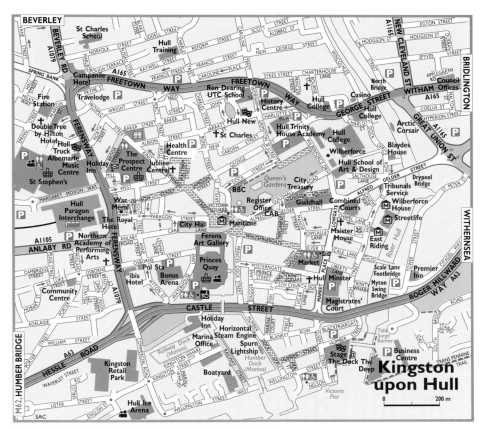

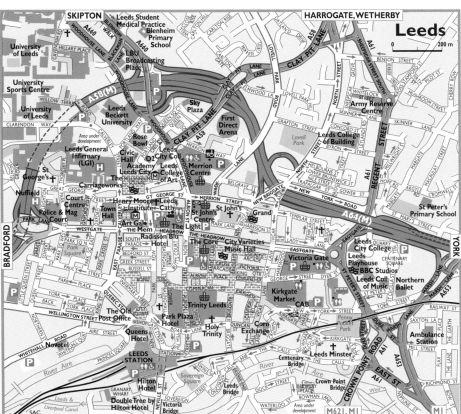

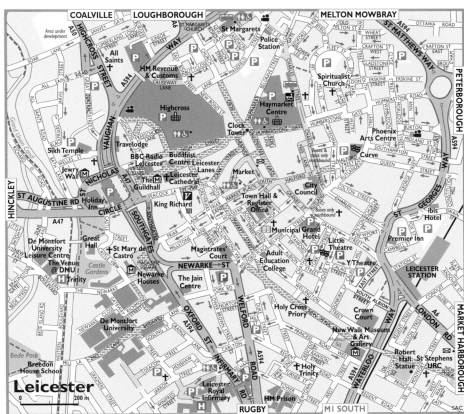

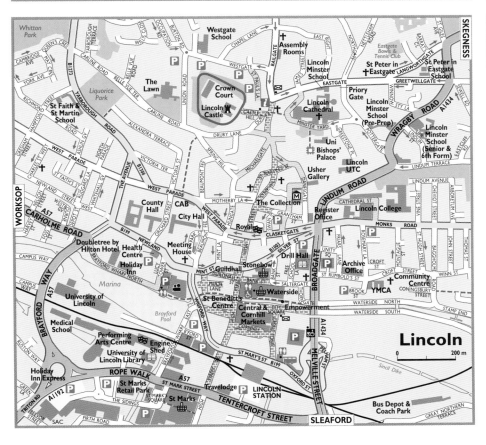

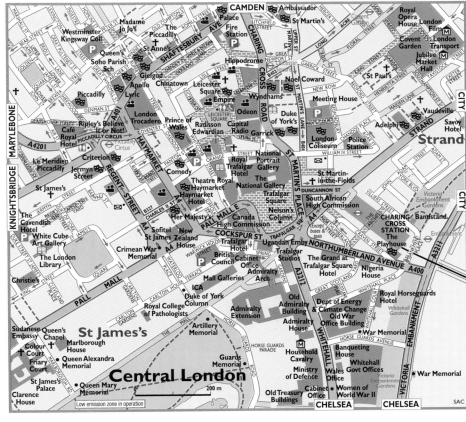

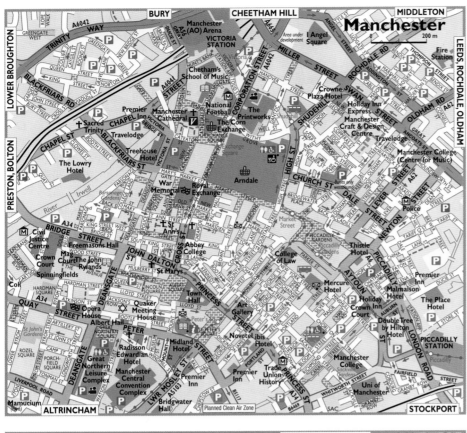

Manchester

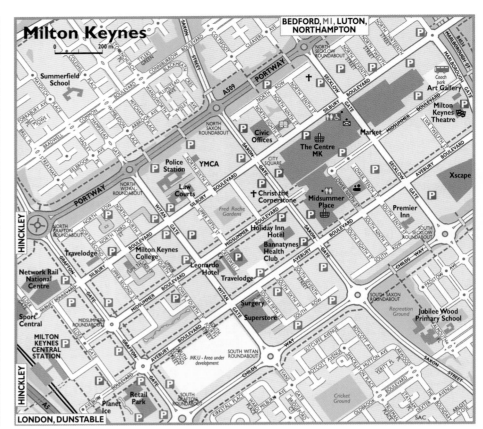

Milton Keynes

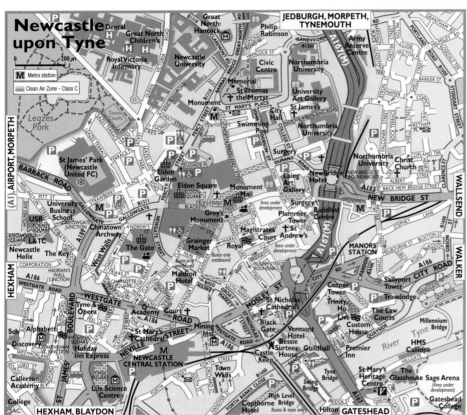

Newcastle upon Tyne

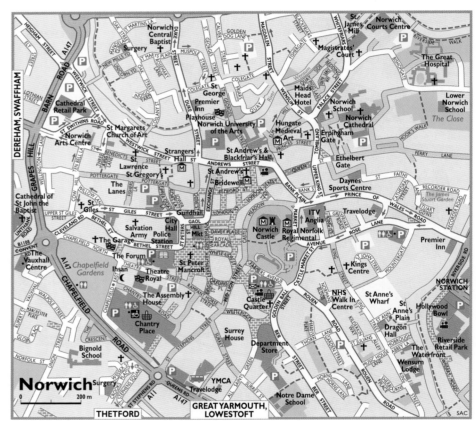

Norwich

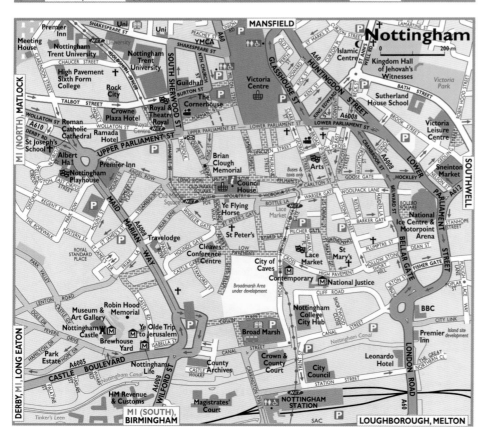

Nottingham

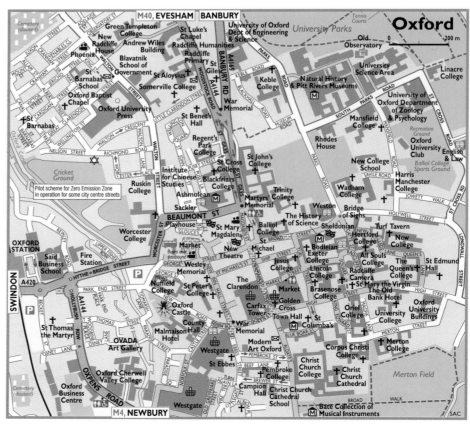

Oxford

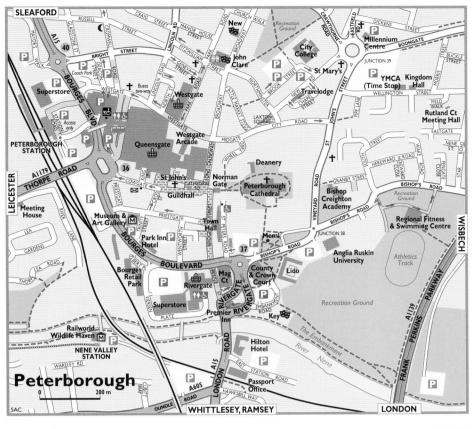

Peterborough

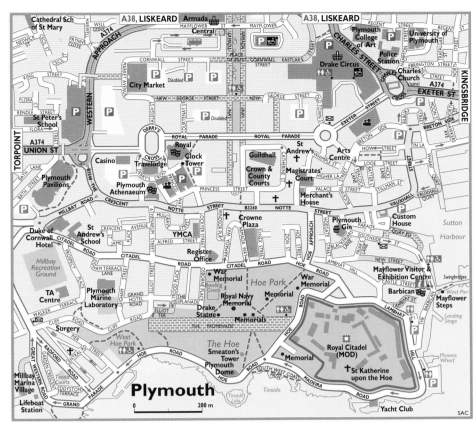

Plymouth

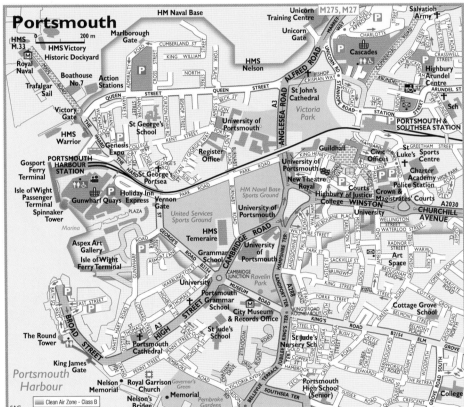

Portsmouth

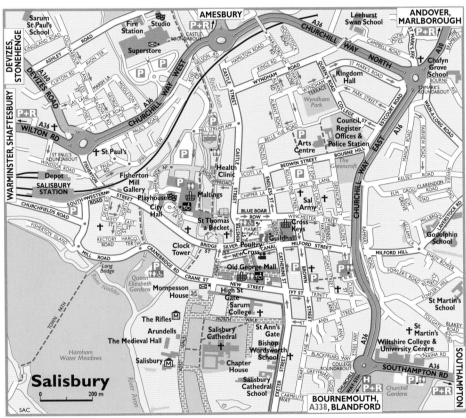

Salisbury

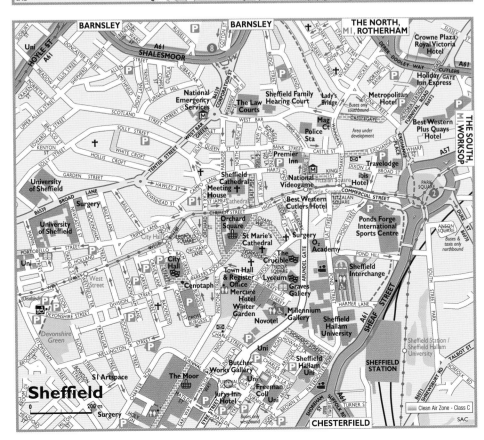

Sheffield

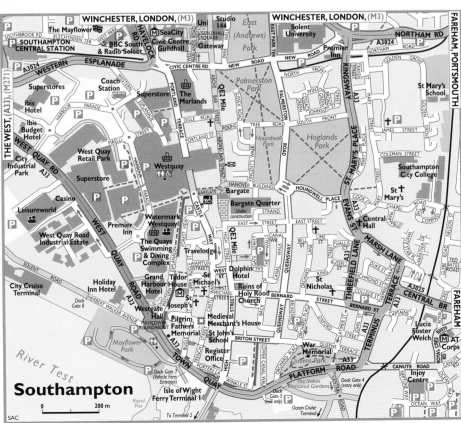

Southampton

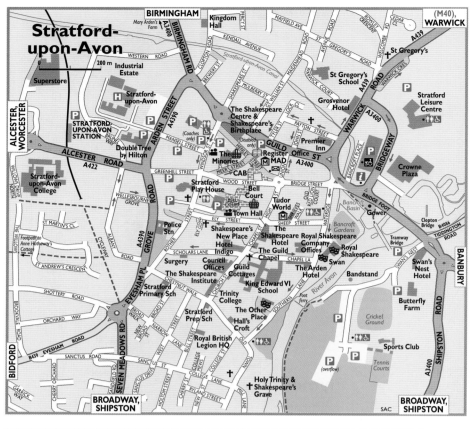

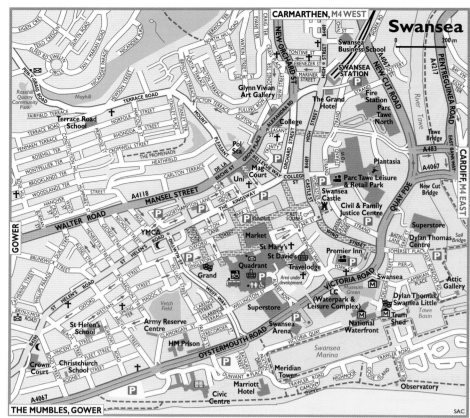

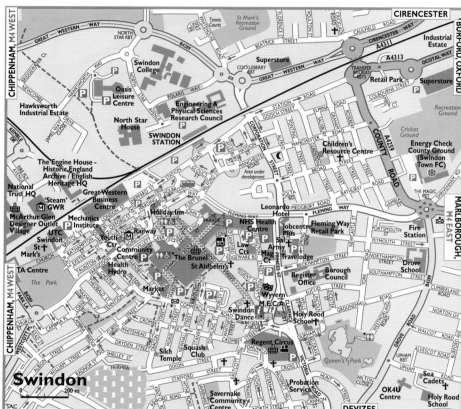

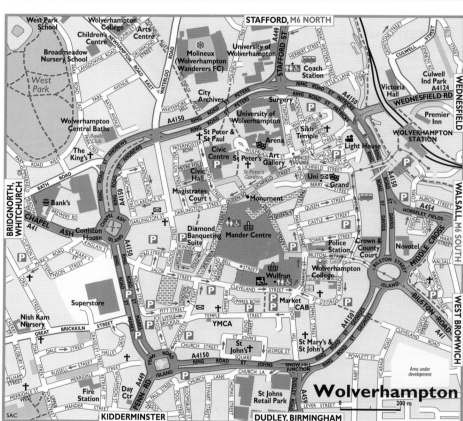

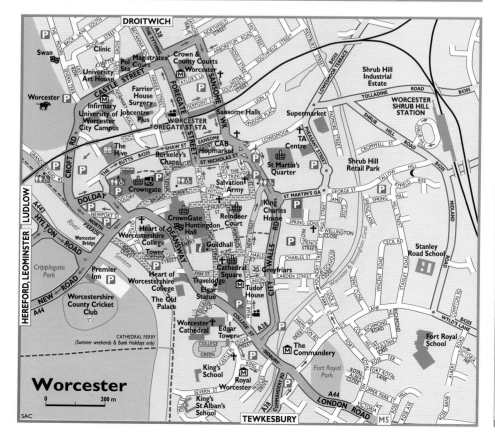

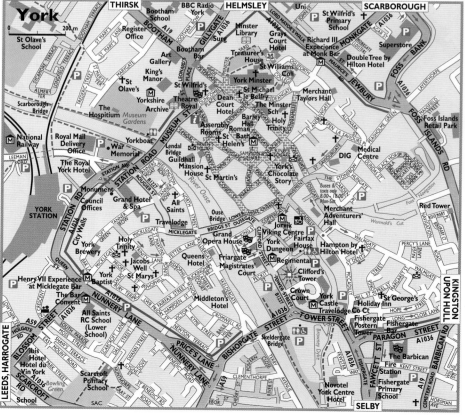

This index lists places appearing in the main map section of the atlas in alphabetical order. The reference following each name gives the atlas page number and grid reference of the square in which the place appears. The map shows counties, unitary authorities and administrative areas, together with a list of the abbreviated name forms used in the index. The top 100 places of tourist interest are indexed in red, World Heritage sites in green, motorway service areas in blue, airports in blue italic and National Parks in green italic.

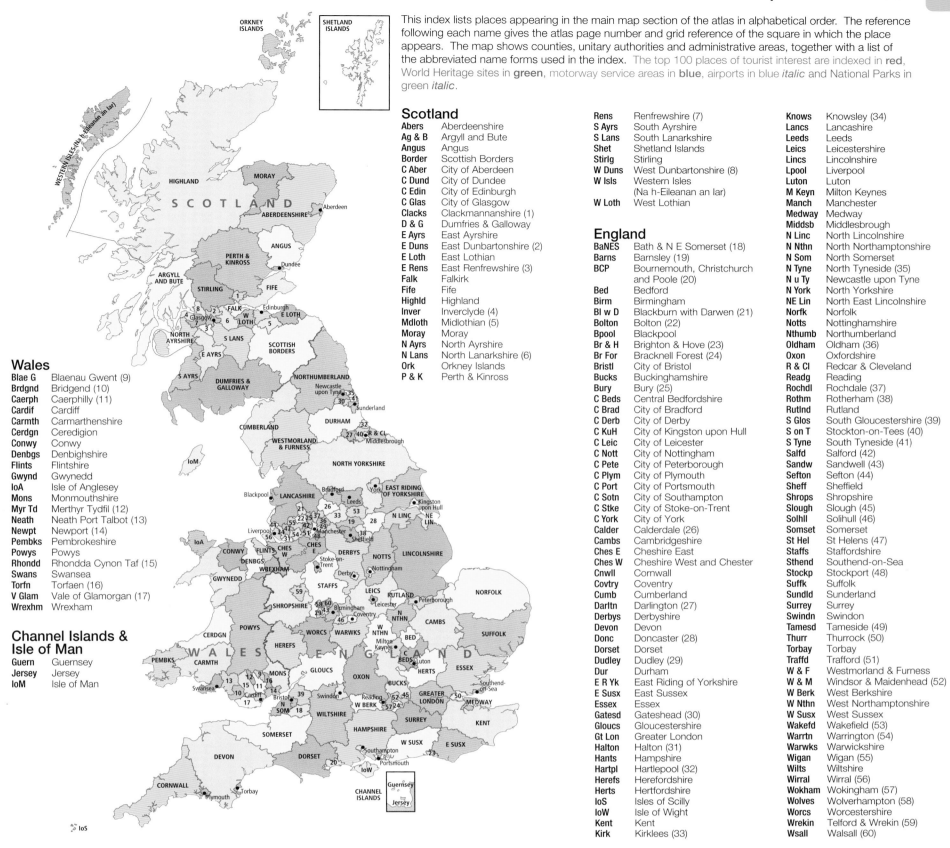

Wales

Blae G	Blaenau Gwent (9)
Brdgnd	Bridgend (10)
Caerph	Caerphilly (11)
Cardif	Cardiff
Carmth	Carmarthenshire
Cerdgn	Ceredigion
Conwy	Conwy
Denbgs	Denbighshire
Flints	Flintshire
Gwynd	Gwynedd
IoA	Isle of Anglesey
Mons	Monmouthshire
Myr Td	Merthyr Tydfil (12)
Neath	Neath Port Talbot (13)
Newpt	Newport (14)
Pembks	Pembrokeshire
Powys	Powys
Rhondd	Rhondda Cynon Taf (15)
Swans	Swansea
Torfn	Torfaen (16)
V Glam	Vale of Glamorgan (17)
Wrexhm	Wrexham

Channel Islands & Isle of Man

Guern	Guernsey
Jersey	Jersey
IoM	Isle of Man

Scotland

Abers	Aberdeenshire
Ag & B	Argyll and Bute
Angus	Angus
Border	Scottish Borders
C Aber	City of Aberdeen
C Dund	City of Dundee
C Edin	City of Edinburgh
C Glas	City of Glasgow
Clacks	Clackmannanshire (1)
D & G	Dumfries & Galloway
E Ayrs	East Ayrshire
E Duns	East Dunbartonshire (2)
E Loth	East Lothian
E Rens	East Renfrewshire (3)
Falk	Falkirk
Fife	Fife
Highld	Highland
Inver	Inverclyde (4)
Mdloth	Midlothian (5)
Moray	Moray
N Ayrs	North Ayrshire
N Lans	North Lanarkshire (6)
Ork	Orkney Islands
P & K	Perth & Kinross

Rens	Renfrewshire (7)
S Ayrs	South Ayrshire
S Lans	South Lanarkshire
Shet	Shetland Islands
Stirlg	Stirling
W Duns	West Dunbartonshire (8)
W Isls	Western Isles (Na h-Eileanan an Iar)
W Loth	West Lothian

England

BaNES	Bath & N E Somerset (18)
Barns	Barnsley (19)
BCP	Bournemouth, Christchurch and Poole (20)
Bed	Bedford
Birm	Birmingham
Bl w D	Blackburn with Darwen (21)
Bolton	Bolton (22)
Bpool	Blackpool
Br & H	Brighton & Hove (23)
Br For	Bracknell Forest (24)
Bristl	City of Bristol
Bucks	Buckinghamshire
Bury	Bury (25)
C Beds	Central Bedfordshire
C Brad	City of Bradford
C Derb	City of Derby
C KuH	City of Kingston upon Hull
C Leic	City of Leicester
C Nott	City of Nottingham
C Pete	City of Peterborough
C Plym	City of Plymouth
C Port	City of Portsmouth
C Sotn	City of Southampton
C Stke	City of Stoke-on-Trent
C York	City of York
Calder	Calderdale (26)
Cambs	Cambridgeshire
Ches E	Cheshire East
Ches W	Cheshire West and Chester
Cnwll	Cornwall
Covtry	Coventry
Cumb	Cumberland
Darltn	Darlington (27)
Derbys	Derbyshire
Devon	Devon
Donc	Doncaster (28)
Dorset	Dorset
Dudley	Dudley (29)
Dur	Durham
E R Yk	East Riding of Yorkshire
E Susx	East Sussex
Essex	Essex
Gatesd	Gateshead (30)
Gloucs	Gloucestershire
Gt Lon	Greater London
Halton	Halton (31)
Hants	Hampshire
Hartpl	Hartlepool (32)
Herefs	Herefordshire
Herts	Hertfordshire
IoS	Isles of Scilly
IoW	Isle of Wight
Kent	Kent
Kirk	Kirklees (33)

Knows	Knowsley (34)
Lancs	Lancashire
Leeds	Leeds
Leics	Leicestershire
Lincs	Lincolnshire
Lpool	Liverpool
Luton	Luton
M Keyn	Milton Keynes
Manch	Manchester
Medway	Medway
Middsb	Middlesbrough
N Linc	North Lincolnshire
N Nthn	North Northamptonshire
N Som	North Somerset
N Tyne	North Tyneside (35)
N u Ty	Newcastle upon Tyne
N York	North Yorkshire
NE Lin	North East Lincolnshire
Norfk	Norfolk
Notts	Nottinghamshire
Nthumb	Northumberland
Oldham	Oldham (36)
Oxon	Oxfordshire
R & Cl	Redcar & Cleveland
Readg	Reading
Rochdl	Rochdale (37)
Rothm	Rotherham (38)
Rutlnd	Rutland
S Glos	South Gloucestershire (39)
S on T	Stockton-on-Tees (40)
S Tyne	South Tyneside (41)
Salfd	Salford (42)
Sandw	Sandwell (43)
Sefton	Sefton (44)
Sheff	Sheffield
Shrops	Shropshire
Slough	Slough (45)
Solhll	Solihull (46)
Somset	Somerset
St Hel	St Helens (47)
Staffs	Staffordshire
Sthend	Southend-on-Sea
Stockp	Stockport (48)
Suffk	Suffolk
Sundld	Sunderland
Surrey	Surrey
Swindn	Swindon
Tamesd	Tameside (49)
Thurr	Thurrock (50)
Torbay	Torbay
Traffd	Trafford (51)
W & F	Westmorland & Furness
W & M	Windsor & Maidenhead (52)
W Berk	West Berkshire
W Nthn	West Northamptonshire
W Susx	West Sussex
Wakefd	Wakefield (53)
Warrtn	Warrington (54)
Warwks	Warwickshire
Wigan	Wigan (55)
Wilts	Wiltshire
Wirral	Wirral (56)
Wokham	Wokingham (57)
Wolves	Wolverhampton (58)
Worcs	Worcestershire
Wrekin	Telford & Wrekin (59)
Wsall	Walsall (60)

Using the National Grid

With an Ordnance Survey National Grid reference you can pinpoint anywhere in the country in this atlas. The blue grid lines which divide the main-map pages into 5km squares for ease of indexing also match the National Grid. A National Grid reference gives two letters and some figures. An example is how to find the summit of Snowdon using its 4-figure grid reference of **SH6154**.

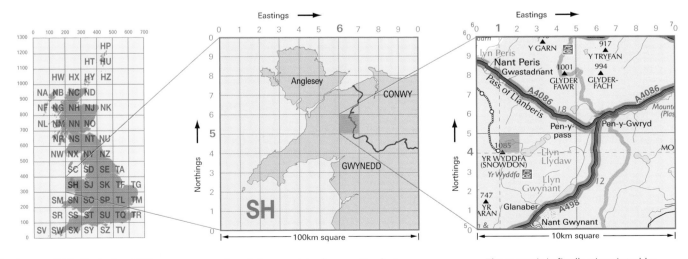

The letters **SH** indicate the 100km square of the National Grid in which Snowdon is located.

In a 4-figure grid reference the first two figures (eastings) are read along the map from left to right, the second two (northings) up the map. The figures **6** and **5**, the first and third figures of the Snowdon reference, indicate the 10km square within the **SH** square, lying above (north) and right (east) of the intersection of the vertical (easting) line **6** and horizontal (northing) line **5**.

The summit is finally pinpointed by figures **1** and **4** which locate a 1km square within the 10km square. At road atlas scales these grid lines are normally estimated by eye.

A

Abbas Combe Somset 17 T12
Abberley Worcs 35 S7
Abberley Common Worcs 35 R7
Abberton Essex 23 P4
Abberton Worcs 36 C10
Abberwick Nthumb 77 N3
Abbess Roding Essex 22 E5
Abbey Devon 6 F2
Abbeycwmhir Powys 34 C6
Abbeydale Sheff 57 M10
Abbey Dore Herefs 27 R1
Abbey Green Staffs 46 C2
Abbey Hill Somset 16 J13
Abbey Hulton C Stke 46 B4
Abbey St Bathans Border 84 K6
Abbeystead Lancs 62 B9
Abbeytown Cumb 66 J2
Abbey Village Lancs 55 P2
Abbey Wood Gt Lon 21 S7
Abbotrule Border 76 C3
Abbots Bickington Devon 14 J10
Abbots Bromley Staffs 46 E9
Abbotsbury Dorset 7 Q7
Abbot's Chair Derbys 56 F8
Abbots Deuglie P & K 90 H9
Abbotsham Devon 14 K7
Abbotskerswell Devon 5 V7
Abbots Langley Herts 31 N12
Abbotsleigh Devon 5 U11
Abbots Leigh N Som 27 U13
Abbotsley Cambs 38 K9
Abbots Morton Worcs 36 D9
Abbots Ripton Cambs 38 K5
Abbot's Salford Warwks 36 E10
Abbotstone Hants 9 R2
Abbotswood Hants 9 M4
Abbots Worthy Hants 9 P2
Abbotts Ann Hants 19 M12
Abbott Street Dorset 8 D8
Abcott Shrops 34 J5
Abdon Shrops 35 N3
Abenhall Gloucs 28 C4
Aberaeron Cerdgn 32 J8
Aberaman Rhondd 26 J7
Aberangell Gwynd 43 R11
Aber-arad Carmth 32 F12
Aberarder Highld 102 H10
Aberargie P & K 90 J8
Aberarth Cerdgn 32 J8
Aberavon Neath 26 C10
Aber-banc Cerdgn 32 G12
Aberbargoed Caerph 27 M7
Aberbeeg Blae G 27 N7
Abercanaid Myr Td 26 K7
Abercarn Caerph 27 N9
Abercastle Pembks 24 E4
Abercegir Powys 43 R13
Aberchalder Highld 96 C3
Aberchirder Abers 104 J5
Aber Clydach Powys 27 L3
Abercorn W Loth 83 L3
Abercraf Powys 26 E5
Abercregan Neath 26 E8
Abercwmboi Rhondd 26 J8
Abercych Pembks 32 D12
Abercynon Rhondd 26 K9
Aberdalgie P & K 90 G7
Aberdare Rhondd 26 J7
Aberdaron Gwynd 42 C8
Aberdeen C Aber 99 S2
Aberdeen Airport C Aber 105 P13
Aberdesach Gwynd 42 H3
Aberdour Fife 83 N1
Aberdulais Neath 26 D8
Aberdyfi Gwynd 33 M1
Aberedw Powys 34 C11
Abereiddy Pembks 24 C4
Abererch Gwynd 42 G6
Aberfan Myr Td 26 K7
Aberfeldy P & K 90 C2
Aberffraw IoA 52 E9
Aberffrwd Cerdgn 33 N5
Aberford Leeds 63 U12
Aberfoyle Stirlg 89 M5
Abergarw Brdgnd 26 G11
Abergarwed Neath 26 E7
Abergavenny Mons 27 P5
Abergele Conwy 53 R7
Aber-giar Carmth 32 K12
Abergorlech Carmth 25 U4
Abergwesyn Powys 33 S10
Abergwili Carmth 25 R6
Abergwydol Powys 43 Q13
Abergwynfi Neath 26 F8
Abergwyngregyn Gwynd 53 L8
Abergynolwyn Gwynd 43 N12
Aberhafesp Powys 34 C2
Aberhosan Powys 33 R1
Aberkenfig Brdgnd 26 F11
Aberlady E Loth 84 D3
Aberlemno Angus 98 J12
Aberllefenni Gwynd 43 Q12
Aberllynfi Powys 34 E13
Aberlour, Charlestown of Moray 104 B7
Abermagwr Cerdgn 33 N6
Aber-meurig Cerdgn 33 L9
Abermorddu Flints 44 H2
Abermule Powys 34 E2
Abernant Carmth 25 P6
Abernant Rhondd 26 J7
Abernethy P & K 90 J8
Abernyte P & K 91 L5
Aberporth Cerdgn 32 E10
Abersoch Gwynd 42 F8
Abersychan Torfn 27 P7
Aberthin V Glam 26 J13
Abertillery Blae G 27 N7
Abertridwr Caerph 27 L10
Abertridwr Powys 44 B10
Abertysswg Caerph 27 L6
Aberuthven P & K 90 E8
Aberwheeler Denbgs 54 C13
Aberyscir Powys 26 H2
Aberystwyth Cerdgn 33 L4
Abingdon-on-Thames Oxon 29 U8
Abinger Common Surrey 20 K13
Abinger Hammer Surrey 20 J13
Abington S Lans 82 H14
Abington W Nthn 37 U8
Abington Pigotts Cambs 31 T4
Abington Services S Lans 82 H14
Abingworth W Susx 10 J7
Ab Kettleby Leics 47 T9
Ab Lench Worcs 36 D10
Ablington Gloucs 29 M6
Ablington Wilts 18 J11
Abney Derbys 56 J10
Above Church Staffs 46 D3
Aboyne Abers 98 J4
Abhainn Suidhe W Isls 106 f8
Abram Wigan 55 P6
Abriachan Highld 102 G8
Abridge Essex 21 S3
Abronhill N Lans 89 S10
Abson S Glos 28 D13
Abthorpe W Nthn 37 R11
Aby Lincs 59 R11
Acaster Malbis C York 64 D10
Acaster Selby N York 64 D11
Accrington Lancs 62 F14
Acha Ag & B 92 F8
Achahoish Ag & B 87 P10
Achalader P & K 90 H2
Achaleven Ag & B 94 C12
Acha Mor W Isls 106 i6
Achanalt Highld 108 D12
Achandunie Highld 109 L10
Achany Highld 108 K4
Acharacle Highld 93 R5
Acharn Highld 93 S8
Acharn P & K 95 V10
Achavanich Highld 112 E8
Achduart Highld 107 T4
Achfary Highld 110 F9
Achgarve Highld 107 Q6
A'Chill Highld 100 b9
Achiltibuie Highld 107 T3
Achina Highld 111 Q4
Achinhoan Ag & B 79 P12
Achintee Highld 101 N3
Achintraid Highld 101 L4
Achlyness Highld 110 E6
Achmelvich Highld 110 B12
Achmore Highld 101 M5
Achmore W Isls 106 i6
Achnacarnin Highld 110 A10
Achnacarry Highld 101 T14
Achnacloich Highld 100 e9
Achnaconeran Highld 102 D12
Achnacroish Ag & B 94 B10
Achnadrish Ag & B 93 M8
Achnafauld P & K 90 C4
Achnagarron Highld 109 M10
Achnaha Highld 93 M5
Achnahaird Highld 107 T2
Achnahannet Highld 103 Q10
Achnairn Highld 108 K2
Achnalea Highld 94 B6
Achnamara Ag & B 87 P8
Achnasheen Highld 108 B13
Achnashellach Highld 101 Q2
Achnastank Moray 104 B9
Achosnich Highld 93 L5
Achranich Highld 93 S9
Achreamie Highld 112 B3
Achriabhach Highld 94 G5
Achriesgill Highld 110 F6
Achtoty Highld 111 P4
Achurch N Nthn 38 F4
Achvaich Highld 109 N6
Achvarasdal Highld 112 A4
Ackenthwaite W & F 61 U3
Ackergill Highld 112 J6
Acklam Middsb 70 G9
Acklam N York 64 H7
Ackleton Shrops 45 S14
Acklington Nthumb 77 Q5
Ackton Wakefd 57 P2
Ackworth Moor Top Wakefd 57 P3
Acle Norfk 51 R11
Acock's Green Birm 36 F4
Acol Kent 13 R2
Acomb C York 64 D9
Acomb Nthumb 76 J12
Acombe Somset 6 G2
Aconbury Herefs 35 M14
Acre Lancs 55 S2
Acrefair Wrexhm 44 G5
Acresford Derbys 46 J11
Acton Ches E 45 P3
Acton Dorset 8 D13
Acton Gt Lon 21 M6
Acton Shrops 34 H4
Acton Staffs 45 T5
Acton Suffk 40 E11
Acton Worcs 35 T7
Acton Wrexhm 44 H3
Acton Beauchamp Herefs 35 Q10
Acton Bridge Ches W 55 N11
Acton Burnell Shrops 45 M13
Acton Green Herefs 35 Q10
Acton Pigott Shrops 45 M13
Acton Round Shrops 35 P1
Acton Scott Shrops 35 L3
Acton Trussell Staffs 46 B10
Acton Turville S Glos 18 B4
Adbaston Staffs 45 S8
Adber Dorset 17 Q12
Adbolton Notts 47 Q6
Adderbury Oxon 37 N13
Adderley Shrops 45 Q6
Adderstone Nthumb 85 S12
Addiewell W Loth 82 J6
Addingham C Brad 63 M10
Addington Bucks 30 F7
Addington Gt Lon 21 Q10
Addington Kent 12 C4
Addiscombe Gt Lon 21 P9
Addlestone Surrey 20 J10
Addlestonemoor Surrey 20 J9
Addlethorpe Lincs 59 T13
Adeney Wrekin 45 Q10
Adeyfield Herts 31 N11
Adfa Powys 44 C13
Adforton Herefs 34 K6
Adisham Kent 13 P5
Adlestrop Gloucs 29 P2
Adlingfleet E R Yk 58 D2
Adlington Ches E 56 D10
Adlington Lancs 55 P4
Admaston Staffs 46 D9
Admaston Wrekin 45 P11
Admington Warwks 36 H11
Adpar Cerdgn 32 F12
Adsborough Somset 16 J11
Adscombe Somset 16 G9
Adstock Bucks 30 F7
Adstone W Nthn 37 Q10
Adswood Stockp 56 C9
Adversane W Susx 10 H6
Advie Highld 103 T9
Adwalton Leeds 63 Q14
Adwell Oxon 30 E13
Adwick le Street Donc 57 R5
Adwick upon Dearne Donc 57 Q6
Ae D & G 74 J8
Ae Bridgend D & G 74 K8
Afan Forest Park Neath 26 F8
Affetside Bury 55 S4
Affleck Abers 104 H7
Affpuddle Dorset 7 V6
Affric Lodge Highld 101 T7
Afon-wen Flints 54 D12
Afon Wen Gwynd 42 H6
Afton Devon 5 U8
Afton IoW 9 L11
Agglethorpe N York 63 M2
Aigburth Lpool 54 J9
Aike E R Yk 65 N10
Aiketgate W & F 67 Q3
Aikhead Cumb 66 K3
Aikton Cumb 67 L2
Ailby Lincs 59 R11
Ailey Herefs 34 H11
Ailsworth C Pete 48 H14
Ainderby Quernhow N York 63 S3
Ainderby Steeple N York 63 S1
Aingers Green Essex 23 R3
Ainsdale Sefton 54 H4
Ainsdale-on-Sea Sefton 54 G4
Ainstable W & F 67 R3
Ainsworth Bury 55 S4
Ainthorpe N York 71 M11
Aintree Sefton 54 J7
Ainville W Loth 83 M6
Aird Ag & B 87 P5
Aird D & G 72 D7
Aird Highld 100 e9
Aird W Isls 106 k5
Àird a' Mhulaidh W Isls 106 g7
Aird Asaig W Isls 106 g8
Aird Dhubh Highld 100 g5
Airdeny Ag & B 94 D13
Airdrie N Lans 82 E5
Airdriehill N Lans 82 E5
Airds of Kells D & G 73 R5
Àird Uig W Isls 106 f5
Airidh a bhruaich W Isls 106 h7
Airieland D & G 73 T8
Airlie Angus 98 E13
Airmyn E R Yk 58 B2
Airntully P & K 90 G4
Airor Highld 100 g9
Airth Falk 82 H1
Airton N York 62 J8
Aisby Lincs 48 F6
Aisby Lincs 58 E8
Aisgill W & F 68 G13
Aish Devon 5 R8
Aish Devon 5 U9
Aisholt Somset 16 G9
Aiskew N York 63 R2
Aislaby N York 64 H2
Aislaby N York 71 Q11
Aislaby S on T 70 F10
Aisthorpe Lincs 58 F10
Aith Shet 106 t8
Akeld Nthumb 85 P13
Akeley Bucks 30 F5
Akenham Suffk 41 L11
Albaston Cnwll 5 L6
Alberbury Shrops 44 J11
Albourne W Susx 11 M7
Albourne Green W Susx 11 M7
Albrighton Shrops 45 L10
Albrighton Shrops 45 T13
Alburgh Norfk 41 N3
Albury Herts 22 B3
Albury Oxon 30 E11
Albury Surrey 20 H13
Albury End Herts 22 B3
Albury Heath Surrey 20 J13
Alby Hill Norfk 51 L7
Alcaig Highld 102 G4
Alcaston Shrops 35 L3
Alcester Warwks 36 E9
Alciston E Susx 11 S9
Alcombe Somset 16 C7
Alcombe Wilts 18 B7
Alconbury Cambs 38 J5
Alconbury Weald Cambs 38 K5
Alconbury Weston Cambs 38 J5
Aldborough N York 63 U6
Aldborough Norfk 51 L7
Aldbourne Wilts 19 L5
Aldbrough E R Yk 65 S12
Aldbrough St John N York 69 R10
Aldbury Herts 31 L10
Aldcliffe Lancs 61 T7
Aldclune P & K 97 P11
Aldeburgh Suffk 41 S9
Aldeby Norfk 41 R2
Aldenham Herts 20 K3
Alderbury Wilts 8 H3
Aldercar Derbys 47 M4
Alderford Norfk 50 K10
Alderholt Dorset 8 G6
Alderley Gloucs 28 E9
Alderley Edge Ches E 55 T11
Aldermans Green Covtry 37 L4
Aldermaston W Berk 19 S7
Alderminster Warwks 36 H11
Alder Moor Staffs 46 H8
Aldersey Green Ches W 45 L2
Aldershot Hants 20 E12
Alderton Gloucs 36 D14
Alderton Shrops 45 L9
Alderton Suffk 41 P12
Alderton W Nthn 37 T11
Alderton Wilts 28 F11
Alderwasley Derbys 46 K3
Aldfield N York 63 R6
Aldford Ches W 44 K2
Aldgate Rutlnd 48 E13
Aldham Essex 23 M2
Aldham Suffk 40 J11
Aldingbourne W Susx 10 E9
Aldingham W & F 61 P5
Aldington Kent 13 L8
Aldington Worcs 36 E12
Aldington Corner Kent 13 L8
Aldivalloch Moray 104 D10
Aldochlay Ag & B 88 J7
Aldon Shrops 34 K5
Aldoth Cumb 66 H3
Aldreth Cambs 39 P6
Aldridge Wsall 46 E13
Aldringham Suffk 41 R8
Aldro N York 64 J7
Aldsworth Gloucs 29 N6
Aldsworth W Susx 10 B9
Aldunie Moray 104 D10
Aldwark Derbys 46 H2
Aldwark N York 64 B7
Aldwick W Susx 10 E11
Aldwincle N Nthn 38 F4
Aldworth W Berk 19 S5
Alexandria W Duns 88 J10
Aley Somset 16 G9
Alfardisworthy Devon 14 G10
Alfington Devon 6 F5
Alfold Surrey 10 G4
Alfold Bars W Susx 10 G4
Alfold Crossways Surrey 10 G3
Alford Abers 104 H12
Alford Lincs 59 S11
Alford Somset 17 R10
Alfreton Derbys 47 M2
Alfrick Worcs 35 R10
Alfrick Pound Worcs 35 R10
Alfriston E Susx 11 S10
Algarkirk Lincs 49 L6
Alhampton Somset 17 R10
Alkborough N Linc 58 E2
Alkerton Gloucs 28 E6
Alkerton Oxon 37 L12
Alkham Kent 13 Q7
Alkington Shrops 45 M6
Alkmonton Derbys 46 G6
Allaleigh Devon 5 U10
Allanaquoich Abers 97 U5
Allanbank N Lans 82 F7
Allanton Border 85 M8
Allanton N Lans 82 F7
Allanton S Lans 82 D8
Allaston Gloucs 28 B7
Allbrook Hants 9 P4
All Cannings Wilts 18 G8
Allendale Nthumb 68 H1
Allen End Warwks 36 G1
Allenheads Nthumb 68 J3
Allensford Dur 69 N2
Allen's Green Herts 22 C4
Allensmore Herefs 35 L13
Allenton C Derb 47 L7
Aller Devon 15 S7
Aller Somset 17 M11
Allerby Cumb 66 G5
Allercombe Devon 6 D6
Aller Cross Devon 15 R7
Allerford Somset 16 B7
Allerston N York 64 K3
Allerthorpe E R Yk 64 H10
Allerton C Brad 63 N13
Allerton Highld 103 L2
Allerton Lpool 54 J9
Allerton Bywater Leeds 63 U14
Allerton Mauleverer N York 63 U8
Allesley Covtry 36 K4
Allestree C Derb 46 K6
Allet Cnwll 2 K7
Allexton Leics 48 B13
Allgreave Ches E 56 E13
Allhallows Medway 22 K12
Allhallows-on-Sea Medway 22 K12
Alligin Shuas Highld 107 P13
Allimore Green Staffs 45 U10
Allington Dorset 7 N6
Allington Kent 12 E4
Allington Lincs 48 C5
Allington Wilts 18 C5
Allington Wilts 18 G8
Allington Wilts 18 K13
Allithwaite W & F 61 R4
Alloa Clacks 90 C13
Allonby Cumb 66 G4
Allostock Ches W 55 R12
Alloway S Ayrs 81 L9
Allowenshay Somset 7 L2
All Saints South Elmham Suffk 41 P4
Allscott Shrops 35 R1
Allscott Wrekin 45 P11
All Stretton Shrops 35 L1
Alltami Flints 54 G13
Alltchaorunn Highld 94 H8
Alltmawr Powys 34 C11
Alltsigh Highld 102 E12
Alltwalis Carmth 25 R4
Alltwen Neath 26 C7
Alltyblaca Cerdgn 32 K11
Allwood Green Suffk 40 H6
Almeley Herefs 34 H10
Almeley Wooton Herefs 34 H10
Almer Dorset 8 C9
Almholme Donc 57 S5
Almington Staffs 45 R7
Almodington W Susx 10 C11
Almondbank P & K 90 G6
Almondbury Kirk 56 J4
Almondsbury S Glos 28 B11
Alne N York 64 B6
Alness Highld 109 M11
Alnham Nthumb 76 K3
Alnmouth Nthumb 77 Q3
Alnwick Nthumb 77 P3
Alperton Gt Lon 21 L6
Alphamstone Essex 40 E13
Alpheton Suffk 40 E10
Alphington Devon 6 B6
Alpington Norfk 51 N13
Alport Derbys 56 K14
Alpraham Ches E 45 N2
Alresford Essex 23 Q3
Alrewas Staffs 46 G11
Alsager Ches E 45 S2
Alsagers Bank Staffs 45 S4
Alsop en le Dale Derbys 46 G3
Alston Devon 6 K4
Alston W & F 68 F3
Alstone Gloucs 36 C14
Alstone Somset 16 K7
Alstonefield Staffs 46 F2
Alston Sutton Somset 17 M6
Alswear Devon 15 R8
Alt Oldham 56 D6
Altandhu Highld 107 S2
Altarnun Cnwll 4 G4
Altass Highld 108 J4
Altcreich Ag & B 93 R11
Altgaltraig Ag & B 88 B11
Altham Lancs 62 F13
Althorne Essex 23 M8
Althorpe N Linc 58 D5
Altnabreac Station Highld 112 B7
Altnaharra Highld 111 M9
Altofts Wakefd 57 N2
Alton Derbys 57 N14
Alton Hants 19 V13
Alton Staffs 46 E5
Alton Wilts 18 J11
Alton Barnes Wilts 18 H8
Alton Pancras Dorset 7 T4
Alton Priors Wilts 18 H8
Alton Towers Staffs 46 E5
Altrincham Traffd 55 S9
Altskeith Hotel Stirlg 89 L5
Alva Clacks 90 C12
Alvanley Ches W 55 L12
Alvaston C Derb 47 L7
Alvechurch Worcs 36 D6
Alvecote Warwks 46 H13
Alvediston Wilts 8 D4
Alveley Shrops 35 S4
Alverdiscott Devon 15 M7
Alverstoke Hants 9 S9
Alverstone IoW 9 R11
Alverthorpe Wakefd 57 M2
Alverton Notts 47 U5
Alves Moray 103 T3
Alvescot Oxon 29 Q7
Alveston S Glos 28 B10
Alveston Warwks 36 H9
Alvingham Lincs 59 Q8
Alvington Gloucs 28 B7
Alwalton C Pete 38 H1
Alweston Dorset 7 S2
Alwinton Nthumb 76 J4
Alwoodley Leeds 63 R11
Alwoodley Gates Leeds 63 S11
Alyth P & K 90 K2
Am Bàgh a Tuath W Isls 106 c18
Ambergate Derbys 46 K3
Amber Hill Lincs 48 K4
Amberley Gloucs 28 G7
Amberley W Susx 10 G8
Amber Row Derbys 47 L2
Amberstone E Susx 11 T8
Amble Nthumb 77 R5
Amblecote Dudley 35 U3
Ambler Thorn C Brad 63 M14
Ambleside W & F 67 N12
Ambleston Pembks 24 H5
Ambrosden Oxon 30 D9
Amcotts N Linc 58 E4
America Cambs 39 P5
Amersham Bucks 20 G3
Amersham Common Bucks 20 G3
Amersham Old Town Bucks 20 G3
Amersham on the Hill Bucks 20 G3
Amerton Staffs 46 C8
Amesbury Wilts 18 J12
Amhuinnsuidhe W Isls 106 f8
Amington Staffs 46 H13
Amisfield D & G 74 K9
Amlwch IoA 52 F4
Ammanford Carmth 26 A5
Amotherby N York 64 G5
Ampfield Hants 9 N4
Ampleforth N York 64 D4
Ampney Crucis Gloucs 29 L7
Ampney St Mary Gloucs 29 L7
Ampney St Peter Gloucs 29 L7
Amport Hants 19 M12
Ampthill C Beds 31 M5
Ampton Suffk 40 E6
Amroth Pembks 25 L9
Amulree P & K 90 C4
Amwell Herts 31 Q10
Anaheilt Highld 93 U6
Ancaster Lincs 48 E5
Ancells Farm Hants 20 D11
Anchor Shrops 34 E3
Ancroft Nthumb 85 P9
Ancrum Border 84 G14
Ancton W Susx 10 F10
Anderby Lincs 59 T11
Anderby Creek Lincs 59 U11
Andersea Somset 16 K10
Andersfield Somset 16 H10
Anderson Dorset 8 B9
Anderton Ches W 55 P11
Anderton Cnwll 5 L10
Andover Hants 19 N11
Andover Down Hants 19 N11
Andoversford Gloucs 28 K4
Andreas IoM 60 g3
Anelog Gwynd 42 C8
Anerley Gt Lon 21 P9
Anfield Lpool 54 J8
Angarrack Cnwll 2 F9
Angarrick Cnwll 2 K9
Angelbank Shrops 35 N5
Angersleigh Somset 16 G13
Angerton Cumb 66 K1
Angle Pembks 24 E10
Anglesey IoA 52 F6
Anglesey Abbey Cambs 39 R8
Angmering W Susx 10 H10
Angram N York 64 C10
Angram N York 68 J13
Angrouse Cnwll 2 H13
Anick Nthumb 76 J12
Ankerville Highld 109 Q10
Ankle Hill Leics 47 U10
Anlaby E R Yk 65 N14
Anmer Norfk 50 B8
Anmore Hants 9 T6
Annan D & G 75 N12
Annandale Water Services D & G 75 M7
Annaside Cumb 60 K2
Annat Highld 107 Q14
Annathill N Lans 82 D4
Anna Valley Hants 19 N12
Annbank S Ayrs 81 N8
Anne Hathaway's Cottage Warwks 36 G10
Annesley Notts 47 P3
Annesley Woodhouse Notts 47 N3
Annfield Plain Dur 69 Q2
Anniesland C Glas 89 M12
Annitsford N Tyne 77 R11
Annscroft Shrops 45 L12
Ansdell Lancs 61 Q14
Ansford Somset 17 R10
Ansley Warwks 36 K2
Anslow Staffs 46 H8
Anslow Gate Staffs 46 G9
Anslow Lees Staffs 46 H9
Ansteadbrook Surrey 10 E4
Anstey Hants 10 A2
Anstey Herts 39 P14
Anstey Leics 47 Q12
Anstruther Fife 91 S11
Ansty W Susx 11 M6
Ansty Warwks 37 M4
Ansty Wilts 8 D3
Ansty Cross Dorset 7 U4
An Tairbeart W Isls 106 g8
Anthill Common Hants 9 S6
Anthonys Surrey 20 H10
Anthorn Cumb 75 N14
Antingham Norfk 51 N7
An t-Ob W Isls 106 f10
Antonine Wall 89 T10
Anton's Gowt Lincs 49 M4
Antony Cnwll 5 L10
Antrobus Ches W 55 P11
Anvil Corner Devon 14 J12
Anvil Green Kent 13 M6
Anwick Lincs 48 H3
Anwoth D & G 73 P8
Aperfield Gt Lon 21 R11
Apes Dale Worcs 36 C6
Apethorpe N Nthn 38 F1
Apeton Staffs 45 U10
Apley Lincs 58 K11
Apperknowle Derbys 57 N11
Apperley Gloucs 28 G2
Apperley Bridge C Brad 63 P12
Apperley Dene Nthumb 77 M14
Appersett N York 62 H1
Appin Ag & B 94 C9
Appleby N Linc 58 G4
Appleby-in-Westmorland W & F 68 E8
Appleby Magna Leics 46 K12
Appleby Parva Leics 46 K12
Appleby Street Herts 31 T12
Applecross Highld 100 g5
Appledore Devon 6 E2
Appledore Devon 15 L6
Appledore Kent 12 J10
Appledore Heath Kent 12 J9
Appleford Oxon 19 R2
Applegarth Town D & G 75 M9
Applehaigh Wakefd 57 N4
Applemore Hants 9 M7
Appleshaw Hants 19 M11
Applethwaite Cumb 67 L7
Appleton Halton 55 M9
Appleton Oxon 29 T7
Appleton Warrtn 55 P10
Appleton-le-Moors N York 64 G2
Appleton-le-Street N York 64 G5
Appleton Roebuck N York 64 D11
Appleton Thorn Warrtn 55 P10
Appleton Wiske N York 70 E12
Appletreehall Border 75 V2
Appletreewick N York 63 M7
Appley Somset 16 E12
Appley Bridge Lancs 55 M5
Apse Heath IoW 9 R12
Apsley End C Beds 31 P6
Apuldram W Susx 10 C10
Arabella Highld 109 Q9
Arbirlot Angus 91 T3
Arborfield Wokham 20 C9
Arborfield Cross Wokham 20 C9
Arborfield Green Wokham 20 C9
Arbourthorne Sheff 57 N9
Arbroath Angus 91 T3
Arbuthnott Abers 99 P8
Arcadia Kent 12 G8
Archddu Carmth 25 R10
Archdeacon Newton Darltn 69 S9
Archencarroch W Duns 88 K9
Archiestown Moray 104 A7
Archirondel Jersey 7 f2
Arclid Ches E 45 S1
Ardallie Abers 105 S8
Ardanaiseig Hotel Ag & B 94 F14
Ardaneaskan Highld 101 L4
Ardarroch Highld 101 L4
Ardbeg Ag & B 78 G6
Ardbeg Ag & B 88 C12
Ardbeg Ag & B 88 E9
Ardcharnich Highld 108 B7
Ardchiavaig Ag & B 86 F2
Ardchonnell Ag & B 87 T3
Ardchronie Highld 109 L7
Ardchullarie More Stirlg 89 N3
Arddarroch Ag & B 88 F7
Arddleen Powys 44 G10
Ard Dorch Highld 100 e7
Ardechive Highld 101 S13
Ardeer N Ayrs 80 K4
Ardeley Herts 31 T7
Ardelve Highld 101 M6
Arden Ag & B 88 J9
Ardens Grafton Warwks 36 F10
Ardentallen Ag & B 93 U14
Ardentinny Ag & B 88 E8
Ardentraive Ag & B 88 B11
Ardeonaig Stirlg 95 T11
Ardersier Highld 103 L5
Ardessie Highld 107 U7
Ardfern Ag & B 87 Q5
Ardfernal Ag & B 86 K11
Ardgartan Ag & B 88 G5
Ardgay Highld 108 K6
Ardgour Highld 94 E6
Ardgowan Inver 88 F11
Ardhallow Ag & B 88 E11
Ardhasig W Isls 106 g8
Ardheslaig Highld 107 N13
Ardindrean Highld 108 B7
Ardingly W Susx 11 N5
Ardington Oxon 29 T10
Ardington Wick Oxon 29 T10
Ardlamont Ag & B 87 T12
Ardleigh Essex 23 Q2
Ardleigh Heath Essex 23 P1
Ardler P & K 91 L3
Ardley Oxon 30 B7
Ardley End Essex 22 D5
Ardlui Ag & B 88 H2
Ardlussa Ag & B 87 L8
Ardmair Highld 107 V5
Ardmaleish Ag & B 88 C12
Ardminish Ag & B 79 L6
Ardmolich Highld 93 S4
Ardmore Ag & B 88 H10
Ardmore Highld 109 N7
Ardnadam Ag & B 88 E9
Ardnagrask Highld 102 F6
Ardnamurchan Highld 93 P5
Ardnarff Highld 101 M4
Ardnastang Highld 93 U6
Ardpatrick Ag & B 79 P4
Ardrishaig Ag & B 87 R8
Ardross Highld 109 L10
Ardrossan N Ayrs 80 J4
Ardsley Barns 57 N5
Ardslignish Highld 93 P6
Ardtalla Ag & B 78 H5
Ardtoe Highld 93 Q4
Arduaine Ag & B 87 P3
Ardullie Highld 102 G3
Ardvasar Highld 100 f9
Ardvorlich P & K 95 S14
Ardvourlie W Isls 106 g7
Ardwell D & G 72 E10
Ardwick Manch 56 C7
Areley Kings Worcs 35 S6
Arevegaig Highld 93 R5
Arford Hants 10 C3
Arglam E R Yk 64 H12
Argoed Caerph 27 M8
Argoed Shrops 44 H9
Argoed Mill Powys 33 U8
Argos Hill E Susx 11 T5
Argyll Forest Park Ag & B 88 F5
Aribruach W Isls 106 h7
Aridhglas Ag & B 92 J14
Arileod Ag & B 92 F8
Arinagour Ag & B 92 G7
Ariogan Ag & B 94 B13
Arisaig Highld 93 R1
Arisaig House Highld 93 R2
Arkendale N York 63 T7
Arkesden Essex 39 Q14
Arkholme Lancs 62 B5
Arkleby Cumb 66 H5
Arkleton D & G 75 S7
Arkle Town N York 69 M12
Arkley Gt Lon 21 M3
Arksey Donc 57 S5
Arkwright Town Derbys 57 P12
Arle Gloucs 28 H3
Arlecdon Cumb 66 F9
Arlescote Warwks 37 L11
Arlesey C Beds 31 Q5
Arleston Wrekin 45 Q11
Arley Ches E 55 Q10
Arlingham Gloucs 28 D5
Arlington Devon 15 P4
Arlington E Susx 11 S9
Arlington Gloucs 29 M6
Arlington Beccott Devon 15 P4
Armadale Highld 100 f9
Armadale Highld 111 R4
Armadale W Loth 82 H5
Armaside Cumb 66 J7
Armathwaite W & F 67 R3
Arminghall Norfk 51 N13
Armitage Staffs 46 E10
Armitage Bridge Kirk 56 H4
Armley Leeds 63 R13
Armscote Warwks 36 H12
Armshead Staffs 46 B4
Armston N Nthn 38 G3
Armthorpe Donc 57 T6
Arnabost Ag & B 92 G6
Arnaby Cumb 61 M3
Arncliffe N York 62 J5
Arncliffe Cote N York 62 J5
Arncroach Fife 91 R10
Arndilly House Moray 104 B6
Arne Dorset 8 D11
Arnesby Leics 37 R2
Arngask P & K 90 H9
Arnisdale Highld 101 L9
Arnish Highld 100 e5
Arniston Mdloth 83 R6
Arnol W Isls 106 i4
Arnold E R Yk 65 Q11
Arnold Notts 47 Q4
Arnprior Stirlg 89 P7
Arnside W & F 61 T4
Aros Ag & B 93 P9
Arowry Wrexhm 45 L6
Arrad Foot W & F 61 Q3
Arram E R Yk 65 N11
Arran N Ayrs 79 S8
Arrathorne N York 69 R14
Arreton IoW 9 Q11
Arrina Highld 107 M13
Arrington Cambs 39 M10
Arrochar Ag & B 88 G5
Arrow Warwks 36 E9
Arrowfield Top Worcs 36 D6
Arscott Shrops 44 K12
Artafallie Highld 102 H6
Arthington Leeds 63 R11
Arthingworth W Nthn 37 U4
Arthog Gwynd 43 M11
Arthrath Abers 105 R8
Arthursdale Leeds 63 T12
Artrochie Abers 105 S9
Arundel W Susx 10 G9
Asby Cumb 66 G8
Ascog Ag & B 88 D13
Ascot W & M 20 F9
Ascott Warwks 36 K14
Ascott Earl Oxon 29 R4
Ascott-under-Wychwood Oxon 29 R4
Asenby N York 63 T4
Asfordby Leics 47 T10
Asfordby Hill Leics 47 T10
Asgarby Lincs 48 H4
Asgarby Lincs 59 P13
Ash Devon 5 U11
Ash Devon 15 M11
Ash Dorset 8 B6
Ash Kent 12 B3
Ash Kent 13 Q4
Ash Somset 16 J12
Ash Somset 17 N12
Ash Surrey 20 F12
Ashampstead W Berk 19 S5
Ashampstead Green W Berk 19 S5
Ashbocking Suffk 41 L10
Ashbourne Derbys 46 G4
Ashbrittle Somset 16 E12
Ashburnham Place E Susx 12 C13
Ashburton Devon 5 T6
Ashbury Devon 15 M13
Ashbury Oxon 29 Q10
Ashby N Linc 58 E5
Ashby by Partney Lincs 59 R13
Ashby cum Fenby NE Lin 59 N6
Ashby de la Launde Lincs 48 G2
Ashby-de-la-Zouch Leics 47 L10
Ashby Folville Leics 47 T11
Ashby Magna Leics 37 Q2
Ashby Parva Leics 37 P3
Ashby Puerorum Lincs 59 P12
Ashby St Ledgers W Nthn 37 Q7
Ashby St Mary Norfk 51 P13
Ashchurch Gloucs 36 B14
Ashcombe Devon 6 B9
Ashcombe N Som 16 K4
Ashcott Somset 17 M9
Ashdon Essex 39 S12
Ashdown Forest E Susx 11 R4
Ashe Hants 19 R10
Asheldham Essex 23 N7
Ashen Essex 40 B12
Ashendon Bucks 30 F10
Asheridge Bucks 30 K12
Ashfield Hants 9 M5
Ashfield Herefs 28 A3
Ashfield Stirlg 89 S5
Ashfield cum Thorpe Suffk 41 M8
Ashfield Green Suffk 40 C9
Ashfield Green Suffk 41 N6
Ashfold Crossways W Susx 11 L5
Ashford Devon 5 R11
Ashford Devon 15 M5
Ashford Kent 12 K7
Ashford Surrey 20 J8
Ashford Bowdler Shrops 35 M6
Ashford Carbonell Shrops 35 M6
Ashford Hill Hants 19 S8
Ashford in the Water Derbys 56 J13
Ashgill S Lans 82 E8
Ash Green Surrey 20 F13
Ash Green Warwks 36 K4
Ashill Devon 6 E2
Ashill Norfk 50 E13
Ashill Somset 16 K13
Ashingdon Essex 23 L9
Ashington BCP 8 E9
Ashington Nthumb 77 R8
Ashington Somset 17 Q12
Ashington W Susx 10 J7
Ashkirk Border 75 U1
Ashlett Hants 9 P8
Ashleworth Gloucs 28 F2
Ashleworth Quay Gloucs 28 F2
Ashley Cambs 39 U8
Ashley Ches E 55 S10
Ashley Devon 15 Q10
Ashley Dorset 8 G8
Ashley Gloucs 28 H9
Ashley Hants 8 K9
Ashley Hants 9 M2
Ashley Kent 13 R6
Ashley N Nthn 37 U2
Ashley Staffs 45 S6
Ashley Wilts 18 B7
Ashley Green Bucks 31 L11
Ashleyhay Derbys 46 J3
Ashley Heath Dorset 8 G8
Ashley Moor Herefs 35 L7
Ash Magna Shrops 45 N6
Ashmansworth Hants 19 P9
Ashmansworthy Devon 14 H9
Ashmead Green Gloucs 28 E8
Ashmill Devon 14 J13
Ash Mill Devon 15 S8
Ashmore Dorset 8 C5
Ashmore Green W Berk 19 R7
Ashorne Warwks 36 K9
Ashover Derbys 57 M14
Ashover Hay Derbys 46 K1
Ashow Warwks 36 K6
Ash Parva Shrops 45 N6
Ashperton Herefs 35 P12
Ashprington Devon 5 U9
Ash Priors Somset 16 G11
Ashreigney Devon 15 P10
Ash Street Suffk 40 H11
Ashtead Surrey 21 L11
Ash Thomas Devon 6 D2
Ashton C Pete 48 H12
Ashton Cnwll 2 G11
Ashton Devon 5 V4
Ashton Hants 9 Q5
Ashton Herefs 35 M8
Ashton Inver 88 F10
Ashton N Nthn 38 G3
Ashton Somset 17 M7
Ashton W Nthn 37 U11
Ashton Common Wilts 18 C9
Ashton Hayes Ches W 55 M13
Ashton Hill Wilts 18 D9
Ashton-in-Makerfield Wigan 55 N7
Ashton Keynes Wilts 28 K9
Ashton-on-Ribble Lancs 61 U13
Ashton under Hill Worcs 36 C13
Ashton-under-Lyne Tamesd 56 D7
Ashton upon Mersey Traffd 55 S8
Ashton Vale Bristl 17 Q2
Ashurst Hants 9 L6
Ashurst Kent 11 S3
Ashurst Lancs 55 L5
Ashurst W Susx 10 K7
Ashurst Wood W Susx 11 Q3
Ash Vale Surrey 20 E12
Ashwater Devon 14 J13
Ashwell Herts 31 S5
Ashwell Rutlnd 48 C11
Ashwell Somset 17 L13
Ashwell End Herts 31 S4
Ashwellthorpe Norfk 50 K14
Ashwick Somset 17 R7
Ashwicken Norfk 50 B10
Ashwood Staffs 35 U3
Askam in Furness W & F 61 N4
Askern Donc 57 S4
Askerswell Dorset 7 P6
Askett Bucks 30 H11
Askham Notts 58 B12
Askham W & F 67 R8
Askham Bryan C York 64 D10
Askham Richard C York 64 C10
Asknish Ag & B 87 S7
Askrigg N York 62 J1
Askwith N York 63 P10
Aslackby Lincs 48 G7
Aslacton Norfk 41 L2
Aslockton Notts 47 T6
Asney Somset 17 N9
Aspall Suffk 41 L8
Aspatria Cumb 66 H4
Aspenden Herts 31 U7
Aspenshaw Derbys 56 F9
Asperton Lincs 49 L6
Aspley Staffs 45 T7
Aspley Guise C Beds 30 K5
Aspley Heath C Beds 30 K6
Aspley Heath Warwks 36 E6
Aspull Wigan 55 P5
Aspull Common Wigan 55 P7
Asselby E R Yk 64 G14
Asserby Lincs 59 S11
Asserby Turn Lincs 59 S11
Assington Suffk 40 F13
Assington Green Suffk 40 C10
Astbury Ches E 45 T1
Astcote W Nthn 37 S10
Asterby Lincs 59 N11
Asterley Shrops 44 J12
Asterton Shrops 34 J2
Asthall Oxon 29 Q5
Asthall Leigh Oxon 29 R5
Astle Highld 109 N6
Astley Shrops 45 M10
Astley Warwks 36 K3
Astley Wigan 55 R6
Astley Worcs 35 S7
Astley Abbots Shrops 35 R1
Astley Bridge Bolton 55 R4
Astley Cross Worcs 35 T7
Astley Green Wigan 55 R7
Aston Birm 36 E3
Aston Ches E 45 P4
Aston Ches W 55 N11
Aston Derbys 56 J10
Aston Flints 54 H13
Aston Herefs 35 L8
Aston Herts 31 S8
Aston Oxon 29 R7
Aston Rothm 57 Q9
Aston Shrops 35 T2
Aston Shrops 45 M8
Aston Staffs 45 S5
Aston Staffs 45 U9
Aston Wokham 20 C6
Aston Wrekin 45 P12
Aston Abbotts Bucks 30 H8
Aston Botterell Shrops 35 P4
Aston-by-Stone Staffs 46 B7
Aston Cantlow Warwks 36 F8
Aston Clinton Bucks 30 J10
Aston Crews Herefs 28 C3
Aston Cross Gloucs 36 B14
Aston End Herts 31 S8
Aston-Eyre Shrops 35 Q2
Aston Fields Worcs 36 C7
Aston Flamville Leics 37 N2
Aston Heath Ches W 55 N11
Aston Ingham Herefs 28 C3
Aston juxta Mondrum Ches E 45 P2
Aston le Walls W Nthn 37 N10
Aston Magna Gloucs 36 G13
Aston Munslow Shrops 35 M3
Aston-on-Carrant Gloucs 36 B14
Aston on Clun Shrops 34 J4
Aston Pigott Shrops 44 H12
Aston Rogers Shrops 44 H12
Aston Rowant Oxon 20 B3
Aston Sandford Bucks 30 G11
Aston Somerville Worcs 36 D13
Aston-sub-Edge Gloucs 36 F12
Aston Tirrold Oxon 19 S3
Aston-upon-Trent Derbys 47 M8
Aston Upthorpe Oxon 19 S3
Astrop W Nthn 30 B5
Astrope Herts 30 J10
Astwick C Beds 31 R5
Astwith Derbys 57 P14
Astwood M Keyn 38 E11
Astwood Worcs 36 B7
Astwood Bank Worcs 36 D8
Aswarby Lincs 48 G6
Aswardby Lincs 59 Q12
Atcham Shrops 45 M12
Atch Lench Worcs 36 D10
Athelhampton Dorset 7 U6
Athelington Suffk 41 M6
Athelney Somset 16 K11
Athelstaneford E Loth 84 E3
Atherfield Green IoW 9 P13
Atherington Devon 15 N8
Atherington W Susx 10 G10
Atherstone Somset 17 L13
Atherstone Warwks 46 K14
Atherstone on Stour Warwks 36 H10
Atherton Wigan 55 Q6
Atley Hill N York 69 S12
Atlow Derbys 46 H4
Attadale Highld 101 N4
Attenborough Notts 47 P7
Atterby Lincs 58 G8
Attercliffe Sheff 57 N9
Atterley Shrops 45 P14
Atterton Leics 47 L14
Attingham Park Shrops 45 M11
Attleborough Norfk 40 H1
Attleborough Warwks 37 L2
Attlebridge Norfk 50 K10
Attleton Green Suffk 40 B10
Atwick E R Yk 65 R9
Atworth Wilts 18 C7
Auberrow Herefs 35 L11
Aubourn Lincs 58 F14
Auchbreck Moray 103 V10
Auchedly Abers 105 P9
Auchenblae Abers 99 N8
Auchenbowie Stirlg 89 S8
Auchencairn D & G 73 T9
Auchencairn D & G 74 J9
Auchencairn N Ayrs 80 E7
Auchencrow Border 85 M6
Auchendinny Mdloth 83 Q6
Auchengray S Lans 82 J8
Auchenhalrig Moray 104 D3
Auchenheath S Lans 82 F10
Auchenhessnane D & G 74 F6
Auchenlochan Ag & B 87 T11
Auchenmade N Ayrs 81 M3
Auchenmalg D & G 72 G9
Auchentiber N Ayrs 81 M3
Auchindrain Ag & B 88 B5
Auchindrean Highld 108 B8
Auchininna Abers 104 K6
Auchinleck E Ayrs 81 R8
Auchinloch N Lans 89 Q11
Auchinstarry N Lans 89 R10
Auchintore Highld 94 F4
Auchiries Abers 105 T8
Auchlean Highld 97 P4
Auchlee Abers 99 R4
Auchleven Abers 104 J11
Auchlochan S Lans 82 F11
Auchlossan Abers 98 K3
Auchlyne Stirlg 95 Q13
Auchmillan E Ayrs 81 Q7
Auchmithie Angus 91 U3
Auchmuirbridge Fife 90 K11
Auchnacree Angus 98 H11
Auchnagatt Abers 105 Q7
Auchnarrow Moray 103 V11
Auchnotteroch D & G 72 B7
Auchroisk Moray 104 C5
Auchterarder P & K 90 D9
Auchteraw Highld 96 D2
Auchterblair Highld 103 P11
Auchtercairn Highld 107 P9
Auchterderran Fife 90 K12
Auchterhouse Angus 91 M4
Auchterless Abers 105 L7
Auchtermuchty Fife 90 K9
Auchterneed Highld 102 E4
Auchtertool Fife 90 K13
Auchtertyre Highld 101 L6
Auchtubh Stirlg 89 N1
Auckengill Highld 112 J4
Auckley Donc 57 T6
Audenshaw Tamesd 56 D7
Audlem Ches E 45 Q5
Audley Staffs 45 S3
Audley End Essex 39 R13
Audley End Essex 40 D13
Audley End Suffk 40 E10
Audley End House & Gardens Essex 39 R13
Audmore Staffs 45 T9
Audnam Dudley 35 U3
Aughertree Cumb 67 L5
Aughton E R Yk 64 G12
Aughton Lancs 54 J5
Aughton Lancs 62 B6
Aughton Rothm 57 Q9
Aughton Wilts 18 K9
Aughton Park Lancs 54 K5
Auldearn Highld 103 P4
Aulden Herefs 35 L10
Auldgirth D & G 74 H8
Auldhouse S Lans 81 S2
Ault a' chruinn Highld 101 N7
Aultbea Highld 107 Q7
Aultgrishin Highld 107 M7
Aultguish Inn Highld 108 F10
Ault Hucknall Derbys 57 Q13
Aultmore Moray 104 E5
Aultnagoire Highld 102 F11
Aultnamain Highld 109 M8
Aunby Lincs 48 F11
Aunk Devon 6 D4
Aunsby Lincs 48 F6
Aust S Glos 28 A10
Austendike Lincs 49 L9
Austerfield Donc 57 U8
Austerlands Oldham 56 E5
Austhorpe Leeds 63 T13
Austonley Kirk 56 H5
Austrey Warwks 46 J12
Austwick N York 62 F6
Authorpe Lincs 59 Q10
Authorpe Row Lincs 59 T12
Avebury Wilts 18 H7
Avebury Wilts 18 H7
Avebury Trusloe Wilts 18 G7
Aveley Thurr 22 E11
Avening Gloucs 28 G8
Averham Notts 47 U3
Aveton Gifford Devon 5 R11
Aviemore Highld 103 N13
Avington W Berk 19 N7
Avoch Highld 102 K4
Avon Hants 8 G9
Avonbridge Falk 82 H4
Avon Dassett Warwks 37 M10
Avonmouth Bristl 27 U12
Avonwick Devon 5 S9
Awbridge Hants 9 L4
Awkley S Glos 28 A10
Awliscombe Devon 6 F4
Awre Gloucs 28 D6
Awsworth Notts 47 N5
Axborough Worcs 35 U5
Axbridge Somset 17 M6
Axford Hants 19 T12
Axford Wilts 18 K6
Axmansford Hants 19 S8
Axminster Devon 6 J5
Axmouth Devon 6 J6
Axton Flints 54 D10
Aycliffe Dur 69 S8
Aydon Nthumb 77 L12
Aylburton Gloucs 28 B7
Ayle Nthumb 68 F3
Aylesbeare Devon 6 D6
Aylesbury Bucks 30 H10
Aylesby NE Lin 59 M5
Aylesford Kent 12 D4
Aylesham Kent 13 P5
Aylestone C Leic 47 Q13
Aylestone Park C Leic 47 Q13
Aylmerton Norfk 51 L6
Aylsham Norfk 51 L8
Aylton Herefs 35 Q13
Aylworth Gloucs 29 M3
Aymestrey Herefs 34 K7
Aynho W Nthn 30 B6
Ayot Green Herts 31 R10
Ayot St Lawrence Herts 31 Q9
Ayot St Peter Herts 31 R9
Ayr S Ayrs 81 L8
Aysgarth N York 63 L2
Ayshford Devon 16 D13
Ayside W & F 61 R3
Ayston Rutlnd 48 C13
Aythorpe Roding Essex 22 E4
Ayton Border 85 N6
Azerley N York 63 R5

B

Babbacombe Torbay 6 B11
Babbington Notts 47 N5
Babbinswood Shrops 44 H8
Babbs Green Herts 31 U9
Babcary Somset 17 Q11
Babel Carmth 33 R13
Babel Green Suffk 40 B11
Babell Flints 54 E12
Babeny Devon 5 R5
Bablock Hythe Oxon 29 T7
Babraham Cambs 39 R10
Babworth Notts 57 U10
Bachau IoA 52 F6
Bache Shrops 35 L4
Bacheldre Powys 34 F2
Bachelor's Bump E Susx 12 F13
Backaland Ork 106 u16
Backbarrow W & F 61 R3
Backe Carmth 25 N7
Backfolds Abers 105 S5
Backford Ches W 54 J12
Backford Cross Ches W 54 J12
Backies Highld 109 Q4
Back of Keppoch Highld 100 f11
Back o' th' Brook Staffs 46 E3
Back Street Suffk 40 B9
Backwell N Som 17 N3
Backworth N Tyne 77 S11
Bacon's End Solhll 36 G3
Baconsthorpe Norfk 50 K6
Bacton Herefs 27 R1
Bacton Norfk 51 P7
Bacton Suffk 40 J7
Bacton Green Suffk 40 H7
Bacup Lancs 56 C2
Badachro Highld 107 N10
Badanloch Highld 111 R10
Badbury Swindn 18 J4
Badby W Nthn 37 Q9
Badcall Highld 110 E5
Badcaul Highld 107 T6
Baddeley Edge C Stke 46 B3
Baddeley Green C Stke 46 B3
Baddesley Clinton Warwks 36 H6
Baddesley Ensor Warwks 46 J14
Baddidarrach Highld 110 B12
Baddinsgill Border 83 M8
Badenscoth Abers 104 K8
Badentarbet Highld 107 T3
Badenyon Abers 104 C12
Badersfield Norfk 51 N9
Badgall Cnwll 4 G3
Badgeney Cambs 39 P1
Badger Shrops 45 S14
Badger's Cross Cnwll 2 D10
Badgers Mount Kent 21 S10
Badgeworth Gloucs 28 H4
Badgworth Somset 17 L6
Badharlick Cnwll 4 H3
Badicaul Highld 100 g7
Badingham Suffk 41 P7
Badlesmere Kent 12 K5
Badlieu Border 75 L2
Badlipster Highld 112 F7
Badluarach Highld 107 S6
Badninish Highld 109 P6
Badrallach Highld 107 U6
Badsey Worcs 36 E12
Badshot Lea Surrey 20 E13
Badsworth Wakefd 57 Q4
Badwell Ash Suffk 40 G7
Badwell Green Suffk 40 H7
Bagber Dorset 7 U2
Bagby N York 64 B3
Bag Enderby Lincs 59 Q12
Bagendon Gloucs 28 K6
Bagginswood Shrops 35 Q4
Baggrow Cumb 66 J4
Bàgh a' Chaisteil W Isls 106 b19
Bagham Kent 13 L5
Bagillt Flints 54 F11
Baginton Warwks 36 K6
Baglan Neath 26 C9
Bagley Leeds 63 Q12
Bagley Shrops 44 K8
Bagley Somset 17 N7
Bagmore Hants 19 U12
Bagnall Staffs 46 B3
Bagnor W Berk 19 Q7
Bagshot Surrey 20 F10
Bagshot Wilts 19 M7
Bagstone S Glos 28 C10
Bagthorpe Notts 47 N3
Bagworth Leics 47 M12
Bagwyllydiart Herefs 27 S2
Baildon C Brad 63 P12
Baildon Green C Brad 63 N12
Baile Ailein W Isls 106 h6
Baile a' Mhanaich W Isls 106 c13
Baile Mòr Ag & B 92 H14
Bailey Green Hants 9 T3
Baileyhead Cumb 75 V10
Bailiff Bridge Calder 56 H1
Baillieston C Glas 82 C6
Bailrigg Lancs 61 T8
Bainbridge N York 62 J1
Bainshole Abers 104 J8
Bainton C Pete 48 G12
Bainton E R Yk 65 M9
Bainton Oxon 30 C7
Baintown Fife 91 N11
Bairnkine Border 76 D2
Baker's End Herts 31 U9
Baker Street Thurr 22 F11
Bakewell Derbys 56 K13
Bala Gwynd 43 T6
Balallan W Isls 106 h6
Balbeg Highld 102 D9
Balbeggie P & K 90 J6
Balblair Highld 102 K2
Balby Donc 57 S6
Balcary D & G 73 U10
Balchraggan Highld 102 F7
Balchrick Highld 110 D4
Balcombe W Susx 11 N4
Balcombe Lane W Susx 11 N4
Balcomie Links Fife 91 T10
Baldersby N York 63 T4
Baldersby St James N York 63 T4
Balderstone Lancs 62 C13
Balderstone Rochdl 56 D4
Balderton Notts 48 B3
Baldhu Cnwll 2 K8
Baldinnie Fife 91 P9
Baldinnies P & K 90 F8
Baldock Herts 31 R6
Baldock Services Herts 31 R5
Baldovie C Dund 91 Q5
Baldrine IoM 60 g6
Baldslow E Susx 12 F13
Baldwin IoM 60 f6
Baldwinholme Cumb 67 M2
Baldwin's Gate Staffs 45 S6
Baldwin's Hill W Susx 11 P3
Bale Norfk 50 H6
Baledgarno P & K 91 L5
Balemartine Ag & B 92 B10
Balerno C Edin 83 N5
Balfarg Fife 91 L11
Balfield Angus 98 J10
Balfour Ork 106 t18
Balfron Stirlg 89 M8
Balgaveny Abers 104 K7
Balgonar Fife 90 F13
Balgowan D & G 72 E11
Balgowan Highld 96 J5
Balgown Highld 100 c3
Balgracie D & G 72 B7
Balgray S Lans 82 G14
Balham Gt Lon 21 N8
Balhary P & K 91 L2
Balholmie P & K 90 H4
Baligill Highld 111 T3
Balintore Angus 98 D12
Balintore Highld 109 R9
Balintraid Highld 109 N10
Balivanich W Isls 106 c13
Balk N York 64 B3
Balkeerie Angus 91 M3
Balkholme E R Yk 64 H14
Ballabeg IoM 60 d8
Ballachulish Highld 94 F7
Ballafesson IoM 60 c8
Ballajora IoM 60 h4
Ballakilpheric IoM 60 c8
Ballamodha IoM 60 d8
Ballantrae S Ayrs 72 D3
Ballards Gore Essex 23 M9
Ballards Green Warwks 36 J2
Ballasalla IoM 60 d8
Ballater Abers 98 F4
Ballaugh IoM 60 e4
Ballchraggan Highld 109 P9
Ballencrieff E Loth 84 D3
Ballevullin Ag & B 92 B9
Ball Green C Stke 45 U3
Ball Haye Green Staffs 46 C2
Ball Hill Hants 19 P8

Ballianlay – Bollow 125

Ballianlay Ag & B 88 B13
Ballidon Derbys 46 H3
Balliekine N Ayrs 79 R8
Balliemore Ag & B 88 D6
Balligmorrie S Ayrs 72 G1
Ballimore Stirlg 89 M2
Ballindalloch Moray 103 U8
Ballindean P & K 91 L6
Ballingdon Suffk 40 E12
Ballinger Common Bucks 30 K12
Ballingham Herefs 28 A1
Ballingry Fife 90 J12
Ballinluig P & K 97 R13
Ballinshoe Angus 98 G13
Ballintuim P & K 97 U12
Balloch Highld 102 K6
Balloch N Lans 89 R11
Balloch P & K 89 T2
Balloch S Ayrs 81 L13
Balloch W Duns 88 J9
Balls Cross W Susx 10 F5
Balls Green E Susx 11 R3
Ball's Green Gloucs 28 G8
Ballygown Ag & B 93 L10
Ballygrant Ag & B 86 F12
Ballyhaugh Ag & B 92 F7
Balmacara Highld 100 h7
Balmaclellan D & G 73 R4
Balmae D & G 73 R11
Balmaha Stirlg 88 K7
Balmalcolm Fife 91 M10
Balmangan D & G 73 Q10
Balmedie Abers 105 R12
Balmer Heath Shrops 44 K7
Balmerino Fife 91 N7
Balmerlawn Hants 9 L8
Balmichael N Ayrs 79 S9
Balmore E Duns 89 N11
Balmuchy Highld 109 R9
Balmule Fife 90 K14
Balmullo Fife 91 P7
Balnacoil Highld 109 Q2
Balnacra Highld 101 P2
Balnacroft Abers 98 D5
Balnafoich Highld 102 J8
Balnaguard P & K 97 Q13
Balnahard Ag & B 93 M12
Balnain Highld 102 D9
Balnakeil Highld 110 H3
Balne N York 57 S3
Balquharn P & K 90 F4
Balquhidder Stirlg 89 M1
Balsall Common Solhll 36 H5
Balsall Heath Birm 36 E4
Balsall Street Solhll 36 H5
Balscote Oxon 37 L12
Balsham Cambs 39 S10
Baltasound Shet 106 w3
Balterley Staffs 45 S3
Balterley Green Staffs 45 S3
Balterley Heath Staffs 45 R3
Baltersan D & G 73 L7
Balthangie Abers 105 N5
Baltonsborough Somset 17 P10
Balvicar Ag & B 87 P2
Balvraid Highld 101 L8
Balvraid Highld 103 M9
Balwest Cnwll 2 F10
Bamber Bridge Lancs 55 N1
Bamber's Green Essex 22 E3
Bamburgh Nthumb 85 T12
Bamburgh Castle Nthumb 85 T11
Bamford Derbys 56 K10
Bamford Rochdl 56 C4
Bampton Devon 16 C12
Bampton Oxon 29 R7
Bampton W & F 67 R9
Bampton Grange W & F 67 R9
Banavie Highld 94 G3
Banbury Oxon 37 N12
Bancffosfelen Carmth 25 S8
Banchory Abers 99 M4
Banchory-Devenick Abers 99 S3
Bancycapel Carmth 25 R8
Bancyfelin Carmth 25 P7
Banc-y-ffordd Carmth 25 R3
Bandirran P & K 90 K5
Bandrake Head W & F 61 Q2
Banff Abers 104 K3
Bangor Gwynd 52 J8
Bangor-on-Dee Wrexhm 44 J4
Bangors Cnwll 14 F13
Bangor's Green Lancs 54 J5
Bangour Village W Loth 82 K4
Bangrove Suffk 40 F6
Banham Norfk 40 J3
Bank Hants 8 K7
Bankend D & G 74 K12
Bankfoot P & K 90 G4
Bankglen E Ayrs 81 R10
Bank Ground W & F 67 M13
Bankhead C Aber 105 P13
Bankhead S Lans 82 J10
Bank Newton N York 62 J9
Banknock Falk 89 S10
Banks Cumb 76 B13
Banks Lancs 54 J2
Banks Green Worcs 36 C7
Bankshill D & G 75 N9
Bank Street Worcs 35 P8
Bank Top Calder 56 H2
Bank Top Lancs 55 M5
Bannau Brycheiniog National Park 26 J3
Banningham Norfk 51 M8
Bannister Green Essex 22 G3
Bannockburn Stirlg 89 T7
Banstead Surrey 21 N11
Bantham Devon 5 R12
Banton N Lans 89 R10
Banwell N Som 17 L5
Bapchild Kent 12 H3
Bapton Wilts 18 E13
Barabhas W Isls 106 i4
Barassie S Ayrs 81 L6
Barbaraville Highld 109 N10
Barber Booth Derbys 56 H10
Barber Green W & F 61 R3
Barbieston S Ayrs 81 N9
Barbon W & F 62 C3
Barbridge Ches E 45 P2
Barbrook Devon 15 R3
Barby W Nthn 37 P6
Barcaldine Ag & B 94 D10
Barcheston Warwks 36 J13
Barclose Cumb 75 T13
Barcombe E Susx 11 Q8
Barcombe Cross E Susx 11 Q7
Barcroft C Brad 63 L12
Barden N York 69 P14
Barden Park Kent 21 U13
Bardfield End Green Essex 22 F1
Bardfield Saling Essex 22 G2
Bardney Lincs 58 K13
Bardon Leics 47 M11
Bardon Mill Nthumb 76 F13
Bardowie E Duns 89 N11
Bardown E Susx 12 C10
Bardrainney Inver 88 H11
Bardsea W & F 61 Q5
Bardsey Leeds 63 T11
Bardsey Island Gwynd 42 B9
Bardsley Oldham 56 D6
Bardwell Suffk 40 F6
Bare Lancs 61 T7
Bareppa Cnwll 2 K11
Barfad D & G 72 J6
Barford Norfk 50 K12
Barford Warwks 36 J8
Barford St John Oxon 37 M14
Barford St Martin Wilts 8 F2
Barford St Michael Oxon 37 M14
Barfrestone Kent 13 Q5
Bargate Derbys 47 L4
Bargeddie N Lans 82 C6
Bargoed Caerph 27 M8
Bargrennan D & G 72 K4
Barham Cambs 38 H5
Barham Kent 13 P5
Barham Suffk 40 K10
Bar Hill Cambs 39 N8
Barholm Lincs 48 G11
Barkby Leics 47 R12
Barkby Thorpe Leics 47 R12
Barkers Green Shrops 45 M8
Barkestone-le-Vale Leics 47 U7
Barkham Wokham 20 C9
Barking Gt Lon 21 R6
Barking Suffk 40 J10
Barking Riverside Gt Lon 21 S6
Barkingside Gt Lon 21 R5
Barking Tye Suffk 40 J10
Barkisland Calder 56 G3
Barkla Shop Cnwll 2 J6
Barkston Lincs 48 D5
Barkston Ash N York 64 B12
Barkway Herts 31 U5
Barlanark C Glas 89 Q13
Barlaston Staffs 45 U6
Barlavington W Susx 10 F7
Barlborough Derbys 57 Q11
Barlby N York 64 E13
Barlestone Leics 47 M12
Barley Herts 39 P13
Barley Lancs 62 G11
Barleycroft End Herts 22 B2
Barley Hole Rothm 57 N7
Barleythorpe Rutlnd 48 B12
Barling Essex 23 M10
Barlings Lincs 58 J12
Barlochan D & G 73 U8
Barlow Derbys 57 M12
Barlow Gatesd 77 P13
Barlow N York 64 E14
Barmby Moor E R Yk 64 H10
Barmby on the Marsh E R Yk 64 F14
Barmer Norfk 50 D7
Barming Heath Kent 12 D4
Barmollack Ag & B 79 Q7
Barmouth Gwynd 43 M10
Barmpton Darltn 70 D9
Barmston E R Yk 65 R8
Barnaby Green Suffk 41 S4
Barnacarry Ag & B 87 U7
Barnack C Pete 48 G12
Barnacle Warwks 37 L4
Barnard Castle Dur 69 N9
Barnard Gate Oxon 29 T5
Barnardiston Suffk 40 B11
Barnbarroch D & G 66 B1
Barnburgh Donc 57 Q6
Barnby Suffk 41 S3
Barnby Dun Donc 57 T5
Barnby in the Willows Notts 48 C3
Barnby Moor Notts 57 U10
Barncorkrie D & G 72 D12
Barnehurst Gt Lon 21 S7
Barnes Gt Lon 21 M7
Barnes Street Kent 12 B6
Barnet Gt Lon 21 M3
Barnetby le Wold N Linc 58 J5
Barnet Gate Gt Lon 21 M3
Barney Norfk 50 G7
Barnham Suffk 40 E5
Barnham W Susx 10 F10
Barnham Broom Norfk 50 J12
Barnhead Angus 99 M12
Barnhill C Dund 91 Q5
Barnhill Ches W 45 L3
Barnhill Moray 103 T4
Barnhills D & G 72 B5
Barningham Dur 69 N10
Barningham Suffk 40 G5
Barnoldby le Beck NE Lin 59 M6
Barnoldswick Lancs 62 H10
Barnsdale Bar Donc 57 R4
Barns Green W Susx 10 J5
Barnsley Barns 57 M5
Barnsley Gloucs 29 L7
Barnsole Kent 13 Q4
Barnstaple Devon 15 N6
Barnston Essex 22 F4
Barnston Wirral 54 G10
Barnstone Notts 47 T6
Barnt Green Worcs 36 D6
Barnton C Edin 83 N4
Barnton Ches W 55 P12
Barnwell All Saints N Nthn 38 F4
Barnwell St Andrew N Nthn 38 G4
Barnwood Gloucs 28 G4
Baron's Cross Herefs 35 L9
Baronwood W & F 67 R4
Barr S Ayrs 80 K14
Barra W Isls 106 b18
Barra Airport W Isls 106 c18
Barrachan D & G 72 K10
Barraigh W Isls 106 b18
Barrananaoil Ag & B 87 Q4
Barrapoll Ag & B 92 A10
Barras W & F 68 H10
Barrasford Nthumb 76 J11
Barregarrow IoM 60 e5
Barrets Green Ches E 45 N2
Barrhead E Rens 89 L14
Barrhill S Ayrs 72 G3
Barrington Cambs 39 N11
Barrington Somset 17 L13
Barripper Cnwll 2 G9
Barrmill N Ayrs 81 M2
Barrock Highld 112 G2
Barrow Gloucs 28 G3
Barrow Lancs 62 E12
Barrow Rutlnd 48 C10
Barrow Shrops 45 Q13
Barrow Somset 17 T10
Barrow Suffk 40 C8
Barroway Drove Norfk 49 S13
Barrow Bridge Bolton 55 Q4
Barrow Burn Nthumb 76 H3
Barrowby Lincs 48 C6
Barrow Common N Som 17 P3
Barrowden Rutlnd 48 D13
Barrowford Lancs 62 H12
Barrow Gurney N Som 17 P3
Barrow Haven N Linc 58 J2
Barrow Hill Derbys 57 P11
Barrow-in-Furness W & F 61 N6
Barrow Island W & F 61 M6
Barrow Nook Lancs 54 K6
Barrow's Green Ches E 45 Q2
Barrows Green W & F 61 U2
Barrow Street Wilts 8 A2
Barrow-upon-Humber N Linc 58 J2
Barrow upon Soar Leics 47 Q10
Barrow upon Trent Derbys 47 L8
Barrow Vale BaNES 17 R4
Barry Angus 91 R5
Barry V Glam 16 F3
Barry Island V Glam 16 F3
Barsby Leics 47 S11
Barsham Suffk 41 Q3
Barston Solhll 36 H5
Bartestree Herefs 35 N12
Barthol Chapel Abers 105 N9
Bartholomew Green Essex 22 H3
Barthomley Ches E 45 S3
Bartley Hants 9 L6
Bartley Green Birm 36 D4
Bartlow Cambs 39 S11
Barton Cambs 39 P9
Barton Ches W 44 K3
Barton Gloucs 29 L2
Barton Herefs 34 G9
Barton Lancs 54 J5
Barton Lancs 61 U12
Barton N York 69 R11
Barton Oxon 30 C11
Barton Torbay 6 B11
Barton Warwks 36 F10
Barton Bendish Norfk 50 B12
Barton End Gloucs 28 F8
Barton Green Staffs 46 G10
Barton Hartshorn Bucks 30 D6
Barton Hill N York 64 G7
Barton in Fabis Notts 47 P7
Barton in the Beans Leics 47 L12
Barton-le-Clay C Beds 31 N6
Barton-le-Street N York 64 G5
Barton-le-Willows N York 64 G7
Barton Mills Suffk 40 B6
Barton-on-Sea Hants 8 J10
Barton-on-the-Heath Warwks 36 J14
Barton St David Somset 17 P10
Barton Seagrave N Nthn 38 C5
Barton Stacey Hants 19 P12
Barton Town Devon 15 Q4
Barton Turf Norfk 51 Q9
Barton-under-Needwood Staffs 46 G10
Barton-upon-Humber N Linc 58 H2
Barton upon Irwell Salfd 55 S7
Barton Waterside N Linc 58 H2
Barugh Barns 57 M5
Barugh Green Barns 57 M5
Barvas W Isls 106 i4
Barway Cambs 39 S5
Barwell Leics 37 M1
Barwick Devon 15 N11
Barwick Herts 31 U9
Barwick Somset 7 Q2
Barwick in Elmet Leeds 63 U12
Baschurch Shrops 44 K9
Bascote Warwks 37 M8
Bascote Heath Warwks 37 L8
Base Green Suffk 40 H8
Basford Green Staffs 46 C3
Bashall Eaves Lancs 62 D11
Bashall Town Lancs 62 E11
Bashley Hants 8 J9
Basildon Essex 22 H10
Basingstoke Hants 19 T10
Baslow Derbys 57 L12
Bason Bridge Somset 16 K7
Bassaleg Newpt 27 P10
Bassendean Border 84 G9
Bassenthwaite Cumb 66 K6
Bassett C Sotn 9 N5
Bassingbourn-cum-Kneesworth Cambs 31 T4
Bassingfield Notts 47 R6
Bassingham Lincs 48 D2
Bassingthorpe Lincs 48 E8
Bassus Green Herts 31 T7
Basted Kent 12 B4
Baston Lincs 48 H11
Bastwick Norfk 51 R10
Batch Somset 16 K5
Batchworth Herts 20 J4
Batchworth Heath Herts 20 J4
Batcombe Dorset 7 R4
Batcombe Somset 17 S9
Bate Heath Ches E 55 Q11
Batford Herts 31 P9
Bath BaNES 17 T4
Bath BaNES 17 U4
Bathampton BaNES 17 U3
Bathealton Somset 16 E12
Batheaston BaNES 17 U3
Bathford BaNES 17 U3
Bathgate W Loth 82 J5
Bathley Notts 47 U2
Bathpool Cnwll 4 H6
Bathpool Somset 16 J11
Bath Side Essex 23 U1
Bathville W Loth 82 H5
Bathway Somset 17 Q6
Batley Kirk 56 K2
Batsford Gloucs 36 G14
Batson Devon 5 S13
Battersby N York 70 J11
Battersea Gt Lon 21 N7
Battisborough Cross Devon 5 P11
Battisford Suffk 40 J10
Battisford Tye Suffk 40 H10
Battle E Susx 12 E12
Battle Powys 26 J1
Battleborough Somset 16 K6
Battledown Gloucs 28 J3
Battledykes Angus 98 H12
Battlefield Shrops 45 M10
Battlesbridge Essex 22 J9
Battlesden C Beds 31 L7
Battleton Somset 16 B11
Battlies Green Suffk 40 F8
Battram Leics 47 M12
Battramsley Cross Hants 9 L9
Batt's Corner Hants 10 C2
Baughton Worcs 35 U12
Baughurst Hants 19 S8
Baulds Abers 99 L5
Baulking Oxon 29 R9
Baumber Lincs 59 M12
Baunton Gloucs 28 K7
Baveney Wood Shrops 35 Q5
Baverstock Wilts 8 E2
Bawburgh Norfk 51 L12
Bawdeswell Norfk 50 H9
Bawdrip Somset 16 K9
Bawdsey Suffk 41 P12
Bawsey Norfk 49 U9
Bawtry Donc 57 T8
Baxenden Lancs 55 S1
Baxterley Warwks 36 J1
Baxter's Green Suffk 40 C9
Bay Highld 100 b4
Bayble W Isls 106 k5
Baybridge Hants 9 Q4
Baybridge Nthumb 69 L2
Baycliff W & F 61 P5
Baydon Wilts 19 L5
Bayford Herts 31 T11
Bayford Somset 17 T11
Bayhead W Isls 106 c12
Bay Horse Lancs 61 T9
Bayley's Hill Kent 21 T12
Baylham Suffk 40 K10
Baynard's Green Oxon 30 B7
Baysdale Abbey N York 70 K11
Baysham Herefs 27 V2
Bayston Hill Shrops 45 L12
Baythorne End Essex 40 B12
Bayton Worcs 35 Q6
Bayton Common Worcs 35 R6
Bayworth Oxon 29 U7
Beach S Glos 17 T2
Beachampton Bucks 30 G5
Beachamwell Norfk 50 C12
Beachley Gloucs 27 V9
Beachy Head E Susx 11 T11
Beacon Devon 6 G3
Beacon End Essex 23 N2
Beacon Hill Kent 12 F9
Beacon Hill Notts 48 B3
Beacon Hill Surrey 10 D3
Beacon's Bottom Bucks 20 C3
Beaconsfield Bucks 20 F4
Beaconsfield Services Bucks 20 G5
Beadlam N York 64 F3
Beadlow C Beds 31 P5
Beadnell Nthumb 85 U13
Beaford Devon 15 N9
Beal N York 57 R1
Beal Nthumb 85 R10
Bealbury Cnwll 4 K7
Bealsmill Cnwll 4 K5
Beam Hill Staffs 46 H8
Beamhurst Staffs 46 E6
Beaminster Dorset 7 N4
Beamish Dur 69 R2
Beamish - The Living Museum of the North Dur 69 R2
Beamsley N York 63 M9
Bean Kent 22 E13
Beanacre Wilts 18 D7
Beanley Nthumb 77 M2
Beardon Devon 5 N4
Beardwood Bl w D 62 D14
Beare Devon 6 C4
Beare Green Surrey 10 K2
Bearley Warwks 36 G8
Bearley Cross Warwks 36 G8
Bearpark Dur 69 R4
Bearsden E Duns 89 M11
Bearsted Kent 12 F4
Bearstone Shrops 45 R6
Bearwood BCP 8 E9
Bearwood Birm 36 D3
Bearwood Herefs 34 J9
Beattock D & G 75 L5
Beauchamp Roding Essex 22 E6
Beauchief Sheff 57 M10
Beaudesert Warwks 36 G7
Beaufort Blae G 27 M5
Beaulieu Essex 22 H6
Beaulieu Hants 9 M8
Beaulieu (National Motor Museum/Palace House) Hants 9 M8
Beaulieu Road Station Hants 9 L7
Beauly Highld 102 F6
Beaumaris IoA 52 K7
Beaumaris Castle IoA 52 K7
Beaumont Cumb 75 R14
Beaumont Essex 23 S3
Beaumont Jersey 7 c3
Beaumont Hill Darltn 69 S9
Beaumont Leys C Leic 47 Q12
Beausale Warwks 36 H6
Beauworth Hants 9 R3
Beaworthy Devon 15 L13
Beazley End Essex 22 H2
Bebington Wirral 54 H10
Bebside Nthumb 77 R9
Beccles Suffk 41 R3
Becconsall Lancs 55 L2
Beckbury Shrops 45 S13
Beckenham Gt Lon 21 Q9
Beckermet Cumb 66 F11
Beckett End Norfk 50 C14
Beckfoot Cumb 61 M2
Beckfoot Cumb 66 G3
Beckfoot Cumb 66 J12
Beck Foot W & F 68 D13
Beckford Worcs 36 C13
Beckhampton Wilts 18 G7
Beck Hole N York 71 P12
Beckingham Lincs 48 C3
Beckingham Notts 58 C9
Beckington Somset 18 B10
Beckjay Shrops 34 J5
Beckley E Susx 12 G11
Beckley Hants 8 J9
Beckley Oxon 30 C10
Beck Row Suffk 39 U5
Becks C Brad 63 L10
Beck Side W & F 61 N3
Beck Side W & F 61 R3
Beckton Gt Lon 21 R6
Beckwithshaw N York 63 R9
Becontree Gt Lon 21 S5
Becquet Vincent Jersey 7 d2
Bedale N York 63 R2
Bedburn Dur 69 N6
Bedchester Dorset 8 B5
Beddau Rhondd 26 K10
Beddgelert Gwynd 43 L4
Beddingham E Susx 11 Q9
Beddington Gt Lon 21 P9
Beddington Corner Gt Lon 21 N9
Bedfield Suffk 41 M7
Bedfield Little Green Suffk 41 M7
Bedford Bed 38 F11
Bedgebury Cross Kent 12 D9
Bedgrove Bucks 30 H10
Bedham W Susx 10 G6
Bedhampton Hants 9 U7
Bedingfield Suffk 41 L7
Bedingfield Green Suffk 41 L7
Bedlam N York 63 R7
Bedlington Nthumb 77 R9
Bedlinog Myr Td 26 K7
Bedminster Bristl 17 Q2
Bedminster Down Bristl 17 Q2
Bedmond Herts 31 N12
Bednall Staffs 46 C10
Bedrule Border 76 C2
Bedstone Shrops 34 J5
Bedwas Caerph 27 M10
Bedwellty Caerph 27 M7
Bedworth Warwks 37 L3
Bedworth Woodlands Warwks 36 K3
Beeby Leics 47 S12
Beech Hants 19 U13
Beech Staffs 45 U6
Beech Hill W Berk 19 U8
Beechingstoke Wilts 18 G9
Beedon W Berk 19 Q5
Beedon Hill W Berk 19 Q5
Beeford E R Yk 65 Q9
Beeley Derbys 57 L13
Beelsby NE Lin 59 M6
Beenham W Berk 19 S7
Beenham's Heath W & M 20 D7
Beeny Cnwll 4 E2
Beer Devon 6 H7
Beer Somset 17 M10
Beercrocombe Somset 16 K12
Beer Hackett Dorset 7 R2
Beesands Devon 5 U12
Beesby Lincs 59 S10
Beeson Devon 5 U12
Beeston C Beds 38 J11
Beeston Ches W 45 M2
Beeston Leeds 63 R13
Beeston Norfk 50 F10
Beeston Notts 47 P6
Beeston Regis Norfk 51 L5
Beeswing D & G 74 G12
Beetham Somset 6 J2
Beetham W & F 61 T4
Beetley Norfk 50 G10
Began Cardif 27 N11
Begbroke Oxon 29 U5
Begdale Cambs 49 Q12
Begelly Pembks 24 K9
Beggarington Hill Leeds 57 L2
Beggar's Bush Powys 34 G8
Beguildy Powys 34 E5
Beighton Norfk 51 Q12
Beighton Sheff 57 P10
Beinn Na Faoghla W Isls 106 d13
Beith N Ayrs 81 M2
Bekesbourne Kent 13 N4
Bekesbourne Hill Kent 13 N4
Belaugh Norfk 51 N10
Belbroughton Worcs 36 B5
Belchalwell Dorset 7 U3
Belchalwell Street Dorset 7 U3
Belchamp Otten Essex 40 D12
Belchamp St Paul Essex 40 C12
Belchamp Walter Essex 40 D12
Belchford Lincs 59 N11
Belford Nthumb 85 S12
Belgrave C Leic 47 Q12
Belhaven E Loth 84 H3
Belhelvie Abers 105 Q12
Belhinnie Abers 104 F10
Bellabeg Abers 104 D13
Bellamore Herefs 34 J12
Bellanoch Ag & B 87 P7
Bellasize E R Yk 64 J14
Bellaty Angus 98 C12
Bell Bar Herts 31 S11
Bell Busk N York 62 J8
Belleau Lincs 59 R11
Bell End Worcs 36 B5
Bellerby N York 69 P14
Bellever Devon 5 R5
Belle Vue Cumb 67 N1
Belle Vue Wakefd 57 M3
Bellfield S Lans 82 F12
Bellfields Surrey 20 G12
Bell Heath Worcs 36 B5
Bell Hill Hants 9 U4
Bellingdon Bucks 30 K11
Bellingham Nthumb 76 G9
Belloch Ag & B 79 M8
Bellochantuy Ag & B 79 M9
Bell o' th' Hill Ches W 45 M4
Bellows Cross Dorset 8 F6
Bells Cross Suffk 41 L10
Bellshill N Lans 82 D6
Bellshill Nthumb 85 S12
Bellside N Lans 82 F7
Bellsquarry W Loth 83 L5
Bells Yew Green E Susx 11 U3
Belluton BaNES 17 R4
Belmaduthy Highld 102 H4
Belmesthorpe Rutlnd 48 F11
Belmont Bl w D 55 Q3
Belmont Dur 70 D4
Belmont Gt Lon 21 N10
Belmont S Ayrs 81 L9
Belmont Shet 106 v3
Belnacraig Abers 104 D12
Belowda Cnwll 3 P4
Belper Derbys 46 K4
Belper Lane End Derbys 46 K4
Belph Derbys 57 R11
Belsay Nthumb 77 M10
Belses Border 84 F13
Belsford Devon 5 T9
Belsize Herts 31 M12
Belstead Suffk 40 K12
Belstone Devon 5 Q2
Belthorn Bl w D 55 R2
Beltinge Kent 13 N2
Beltingham Nthumb 76 F13
Beltoft N Linc 58 D5
Belton Leics 47 M9
Belton Lincs 48 D6
Belton N Linc 58 C5
Belton Norfk 51 S13
Belton House Lincs 48 D6
Belton in Rutland Rutlnd 48 B13
Beltring Kent 12 C6
Belvedere Gt Lon 21 S7
Belvoir Leics 48 B7
Bembridge IoW 9 S11
Bemerton Wilts 8 G2
Bempton E R Yk 65 R5
Benacre Suffk 41 T4
Benbecula W Isls 106 d13
Benbecula Airport W Isls 106 c13
Benbuie D & G 74 D6
Benderloch Ag & B 94 C11
Benenden Kent 12 F9
Benfieldside Dur 69 N2
Benfleet Essex 22 J10
Bengate Norfk 51 P8
Bengeo Herts 31 T10
Bengeworth Worcs 36 D12
Benhall Green Suffk 41 Q8
Benhall Street Suffk 41 Q8
Benholm Abers 99 Q10
Beningbrough N York 64 C8
Benington Herts 31 S8
Benington Lincs 49 N4
Benington Sea End Lincs 49 P4
Benllech IoA 52 H6
Benmore Ag & B 88 D8
Bennacott Cnwll 4 H2
Bennan N Ayrs 80 D8
Bennet Head W & F 67 P8
Bennetland E R Yk 64 J14
Bennett End Bucks 20 C3
Ben Nevis Highld 94 H4
Benniworth Lincs 59 M10
Benover Kent 12 D6
Ben Rhydding C Brad 63 N10
Benslie N Ayrs 81 L4
Benson Oxon 19 T2
Bentfield Green Essex 22 D2
Benthall Shrops 45 Q13
Bentham Gloucs 28 H4
Benthoul C Aber 99 Q3
Bentlawnt Shrops 44 H13
Bentley Donc 57 S5
Bentley E R Yk 65 N12
Bentley Hants 10 B2
Bentley Suffk 40 K13
Bentley Warwks 36 J1
Bentley Heath Herts 21 N3
Bentley Heath Solhll 36 G5
Benton Devon 15 Q5
Bentpath D & G 75 R7
Bentwichen Devon 15 R6
Bentworth Hants 19 U12
Benvie Angus 91 M5
Benville Dorset 7 P4
Benwick Cambs 39 M2
Beoley Worcs 36 E7
Beoraidbeg Highld 100 f10
Bepton W Susx 10 D7
Berden Essex 22 C2
Berea Pembks 24 C4
Bere Alston Devon 5 L7
Bere Ferrers Devon 5 M8
Berepper Cnwll 2 H12
Bere Regis Dorset 8 A10
Bergh Apton Norfk 51 P13
Berhill Somset 17 M9
Berinsfield Oxon 30 C13
Berkeley Gloucs 28 C8
Berkeley Heath Gloucs 28 C8
Berkeley Road Gloucs 28 D7
Berkhamsted Herts 31 L11
Berkley Somset 18 B11
Berkswell Solhll 36 H5
Bermondsey Gt Lon 21 P7
Bermuda Warwks 37 L3
Bernera Highld 100 h7
Bernisdale Highld 100 d4
Berrick Prior Oxon 19 T2
Berrick Salome Oxon 19 T2
Berriedale Highld 112 D12
Berrier W & F 67 N7
Berriew Powys 44 E13
Berrington Nthumb 85 Q10
Berrington Shrops 45 M12
Berrington Worcs 35 N7
Berrington Green Worcs 35 N7
Berrow Somset 16 J6
Berrow Worcs 35 S14
Berrow Green Worcs 35 R9
Berry Brow Kirk 56 H4
Berry Cross Devon 15 L10
Berry Down Cross Devon 15 N4
Berryfield Wilts 18 D8
Berryfields Bucks 30 G9
Berry Hill Gloucs 27 V5
Berry Hill Pembks 24 J2
Berryhillock Moray 104 G3
Berryhillock Moray 104 G5
Berrynarbor Devon 15 N3
Berry Pomeroy Devon 5 U8
Berry's Green Gt Lon 21 R11
Bersham Wrexhm 44 H4
Bersted W Susx 10 E10
Bertha Park P & K 90 G6
Berthengam Flints 54 D11
Berwick E Susx 11 S9
Berwick Bassett Wilts 18 G6
Berwick Hill Nthumb 77 P10
Berwick St James Wilts 18 G13
Berwick St John Wilts 8 C4
Berwick St Leonard Wilts 8 C2
Berwick Station E Susx 11 S9
Berwick-upon-Tweed Nthumb 85 P8
Bescaby Leics 48 B8
Bescar Lancs 54 J4
Besford Shrops 45 N8
Besford Worcs 36 B12
Bessacarr Donc 57 T6
Bessels Leigh Oxon 29 U7
Besses o' th' Barn Bury 55 T5
Bessingby E R Yk 65 R6
Bessingham Norfk 51 L6
Bestbeech Hill E Susx 11 U4
Besthorpe Norfk 40 J1
Besthorpe Notts 58 D14
Bestwood Village Notts 47 Q4
Beswick E R Yk 65 N10
Betchcott Shrops 44 K14
Betchworth Surrey 21 M12
Bethania Cerdgn 33 L8
Bethania Gwynd 43 P5
Bethel Gwynd 43 U6
Bethel Gwynd 52 H9
Bethel IoA 52 E8
Bethel Powys 44 D9
Bethersden Kent 12 H7
Bethesda Gwynd 52 K9
Bethesda Gwynd 52 K9
Bethesda Pembks 24 J7
Bethlehem Carmth 26 B2
Bethnal Green Gt Lon 21 P6
Betley Staffs 45 S4
Betsham Kent 22 F13
Betteshanger Kent 13 R5
Bettiscombe Dorset 7 L4
Bettisfield Wrexhm 45 L6
Betton Shrops 45 Q6
Betton Strange Shrops 45 M12
Bettws Brdgnd 26 G10
Bettws Newpt 27 P9
Bettws Cedewain Powys 34 D1
Bettws Ifan Cerdgn 32 F11
Bettws-Newydd Mons 27 R6
Bettyhill Highld 111 Q4
Betws Carmth 26 A5
Betws Bledrws Cerdgn 33 L10
Betws Garmon Gwynd 52 H11
Betws Gwerfil Goch Denbgs 44 B4
Betws-y-Coed Conwy 53 N11
Betws-yn-Rhos Conwy 53 R8
Beulah Cerdgn 32 E11
Beulah Powys 33 T10
Bevendean Br & H 11 N9
Bevercotes Notts 57 U12
Beverley E R Yk 65 N12
Beverston Gloucs 28 G9
Bevington Gloucs 28 C8
Bewaldeth Cumb 66 K6
Bewcastle Cumb 76 B11
Bewdley Worcs 35 S5
Bewerley N York 63 P6
Bewholme E R Yk 65 R10
Bewlbridge Kent 12 C9
Bexhill-on-Sea E Susx 12 D14
Bexley Gt Lon 21 S8
Bexleyheath Gt Lon 21 S7
Bexleyhill W Susx 10 E5
Bexon Kent 12 G4
Bexwell Norfk 49 T13
Beyton Suffk 40 F8
Beyton Green Suffk 40 F8
Bhaltos W Isls 106 f5
Bhatarsaigh W Isls 106 b19
Bibstone S Glos 28 C9
Bibury Gloucs 29 M6
Bicester Oxon 30 C8
Bickenhill Solhll 36 G4
Bicker Lincs 48 K6
Bicker Bar Lincs 48 K6
Bicker Gauntlet Lincs 48 K6
Bickershaw Wigan 55 P6
Bickerstaffe Lancs 54 K6
Bickerton Ches E 45 M3
Bickerton Devon 5 U13
Bickerton N York 64 B9
Bickerton Nthumb 76 K5
Bickford Staffs 45 U11
Bickington Devon 5 U6
Bickington Devon 15 M6
Bickleigh Devon 5 N8
Bickleigh Devon 6 B3
Bickleton Devon 15 M6
Bickley Ches W 45 M4
Bickley Gt Lon 21 R9
Bickley N York 65 L1
Bickley Worcs 35 P6
Bickley Moss Ches W 45 M4
Bicknacre Essex 22 J7
Bicknoller Somset 16 F9
Bicknor Kent 12 G4
Bickton Hants 8 G6
Bicton Herefs 35 L8
Bicton Shrops 34 G4
Bicton Shrops 44 K10
Bidborough Kent 11 T2
Bidden Hants 20 B13
Biddenden Kent 12 G8
Biddenden Green Kent 12 G7
Biddenham Bed 38 F10
Biddestone Wilts 18 C6
Biddisham Somset 17 L6
Biddlesden Bucks 30 D5
Biddlestone Nthumb 76 K4
Biddulph Staffs 45 U2
Biddulph Moor Staffs 46 B2
Bideford Devon 15 L7
Bidford-on-Avon Warwks 36 F10
Bidston Wirral 54 G8
Bielby E R Yk 64 H11
Bieldside C Aber 99 R3
Bierley IoW 9 Q13
Bierton Bucks 30 H9
Big Balcraig D & G 72 K11
Bigbury Devon 5 R11
Bigbury-on-Sea Devon 5 R12
Bigby Lincs 58 J5
Biggar S Lans 82 K11
Biggar W & F 61 M6
Biggin Derbys 46 G2
Biggin Derbys 46 J4
Biggin N York 64 C13
Biggin Hill Gt Lon 21 R11
Biggleswade C Beds 31 Q4
Bigholms D & G 75 R9
Bighouse Highld 111 T4
Bighton Hants 9 S2
Biglands Cumb 67 L2
Bignall End Staffs 45 T3
Bignor W Susx 10 F8
Bigrigg Cumb 66 F10
Big Sand Highld 107 N9
Bigton Shet 106 t11
Bilborough C Nott 47 P5
Bilbrook Somset 16 D8
Bilbrook Staffs 45 U13
Bilbrough N York 64 C10
Bilbster Highld 112 G6
Bildershaw Dur 69 R8
Bildeston Suffk 40 G11
Billacott Cnwll 4 H2
Billericay Essex 22 G9
Billesdon Leics 47 T13
Billesley Warwks 36 F9
Billingborough Lincs 48 H7
Billinge St Hel 55 M6
Billingford Norfk 41 L5
Billingford Norfk 50 H9
Billingham S on T 70 G8
Billinghay Lincs 48 J3
Billingley Barns 57 P6
Billingshurst W Susx 10 H5
Billingsley Shrops 35 R4
Billington C Beds 30 K8
Billington Lancs 62 E12
Billington Staffs 45 U9
Billockby Norfk 51 R11
Billy Row Dur 69 Q5
Bilsborrow Lancs 61 U12
Bilsby Lincs 59 S11
Bilsham W Susx 10 F10
Bilsington Kent 12 K9
Bilsthorpe Notts 47 R1
Bilsthorpe Moor Notts 47 S1
Bilston Mdloth 83 Q6
Bilston Wolves 36 C1
Bilstone Leics 47 L12
Bilting Kent 13 L6
Bilton E R Yk 65 R13
Bilton N York 63 S8
Bilton Nthumb 77 Q3
Bilton Warwks 37 N6
Bilton Banks Nthumb 77 Q3
Bilton-in-Ainsty N York 64 B10
Binbrook Lincs 59 M8
Binchester Blocks Dur 69 R6
Bincombe Dorset 7 S8
Binegar Somset 17 R7
Bines Green W Susx 10 K7
Binfield Br For 20 D8
Binfield Heath Oxon 20 B7
Bingfield Nthumb 76 K11
Bingham Notts 47 T6
Bingham's Melcombe Dorset 7 U4
Bingley C Brad 63 N12
Bings Heath Shrops 45 M10
Binham Norfk 50 G6
Binley Covtry 37 L5
Binley Hants 19 P10
Binley Woods Warwks 37 L5
Binnegar Dorset 8 B11
Binniehill Falk 82 G4
Binscombe Surrey 20 G13
Binsey Oxon 29 U6
Binstead IoW 9 R10
Binsted Hants 10 B2
Binsted W Susx 10 F9
Binton Warwks 36 F10
Bintree Norfk 50 H9
Binweston Shrops 44 H13
Birch Essex 23 M4
Birch Rochdl 56 C5
Birchall Staffs 46 C3
Bircham Newton Norfk 50 C7
Bircham Tofts Norfk 50 C7
Birchanger Essex 22 D3
Birchanger Green Services Essex 22 D3
Birch Cross Staffs 46 F7
Birchencliffe Kirk 56 H3
Bircher Herefs 35 L7
Birchett's Green E Susx 12 C9
Birchfield Birm 36 E2
Birch Green Essex 23 M4
Birch Green Herts 31 S10
Birch Green Worcs 35 U11
Birchgrove Cardif 27 M12
Birchgrove Swans 26 C8
Birchgrove W Susx 11 Q5
Birch Heath Ches W 45 M1
Birch Hill Ches W 55 M12
Birchington Kent 13 R2
Birchington-on-Sea Kent 13 Q2
Birchley Heath Warwks 36 J2
Birchmoor Warwks 46 J13
Birchmoor Green C Beds 31 L6
Birchover Derbys 46 H1
Birch Services Rochdl 55 T5
Birch Vale Derbys 56 F9
Birchwood Lincs 58 F13
Birch Wood Somset 6 H2
Birchwood Warrtn 55 Q8
Bircotes Notts 57 T8
Birdbrook Essex 40 B12
Birdforth N York 64 B4
Birdham W Susx 10 C10
Birdingbury Warwks 37 M7
Birdlip Gloucs 28 H5
Birdoswald Cumb 76 C12
Birdsall N York 64 J6
Birds Edge Kirk 56 K5
Birds Green Essex 22 E6
Birdsgreen Shrops 35 S3
Birdsmoorgate Dorset 7 L4
Bird Street Suffk 40 H10
Birdwell Barns 57 M6
Birdwood Gloucs 28 D4
Birgham Border 84 K11
Birichin Highld 109 P6
Birkacre Lancs 55 N4
Birkby N York 70 D12
Birkdale Sefton 54 H4
Birkenbog Abers 104 G2
Birkenhead Wirral 54 H9
Birkenhead (Queensway) Tunnel Lpool 54 H9
Birkenhills Abers 105 L6
Birkenshaw Kirk 63 Q14
Birkhall Abers 98 E5
Birkhill Angus 91 N5
Birkhill D & G 75 P2
Birkholme Lincs 48 E9
Birkin N York 57 R1
Birks Leeds 57 L1
Birkshaw Nthumb 76 F12
Birley Herefs 35 L10
Birley Carr Sheff 57 M8
Birling Kent 12 C3
Birling Nthumb 77 Q4
Birling Gap E Susx 11 T11
Birlingham Worcs 36 B12
Birmingham Birm 36 E3
Birmingham Airport Solhll 36 G4
Birnam P & K 90 F3
Birness Abers 105 R9
Birse Abers 98 K4
Birsemore Abers 98 J4
Birstall Kirk 56 K1
Birstall Leics 47 Q12
Birstwith N York 63 Q8
Birthorpe Lincs 48 H7
Birtley Gatesd 69 S1
Birtley Herefs 34 J7
Birtley Nthumb 76 H10
Birts Street Worcs 35 S13
Bisbrooke Rutlnd 48 C14
Biscathorpe Lincs 59 M10
Biscovey Cnwll 3 R6
Bisham W & M 20 D5
Bishampton Worcs 36 C10
Bish Mill Devon 15 R7
Bishop Auckland Dur 69 R7
Bishopbridge Lincs 58 H8
Bishopbriggs E Duns 89 P11
Bishop Burton E R Yk 65 M12
Bishop Middleham Dur 70 D6
Bishopmill Moray 103 V3
Bishop Monkton N York 63 S6
Bishop Norton Lincs 58 G8
Bishopsbourne Kent 13 N5
Bishops Cannings Wilts 18 F8
Bishop's Castle Shrops 34 H3
Bishop's Caundle Dorset 7 S2
Bishop's Cleeve Gloucs 28 J2
Bishop's Frome Herefs 35 Q11
Bishops Gate Surrey 20 G8
Bishop's Green Essex 22 F4
Bishop's Green Hants 19 R8
Bishop's Hull Somset 16 H12
Bishop's Itchington Warwks 37 L9
Bishops Lydeard Somset 16 G11
Bishop's Norton Gloucs 28 F3
Bishop's Nympton Devon 15 S8
Bishop's Offley Staffs 45 S8
Bishop's Stortford Herts 22 C3
Bishop's Sutton Hants 9 S2
Bishop's Tachbrook Warwks 36 K8
Bishop's Tawton Devon 15 N7
Bishopsteignton Devon 6 B10
Bishopstoke Hants 9 P5
Bishopston Swans 25 U13
Bishopstone Bucks 30 H10
Bishopstone E Susx 11 R10
Bishopstone Herefs 34 K12
Bishopstone Kent 13 P2
Bishopstone Swindn 29 P11
Bishopstone Wilts 8 F3
Bishopstrow Wilts 18 C12
Bishop Sutton BaNES 17 Q5
Bishop's Waltham Hants 9 R5
Bishopswood Somset 6 J2
Bishop's Wood Staffs 45 T12
Bishopsworth Bristl 17 Q3
Bishop Thornton N York 63 R7
Bishopthorpe C York 64 D10
Bishopton Darltn 70 E8
Bishopton Rens 88 K11
Bishopton Warwks 36 G9
Bishop Wilton E R Yk 64 H8
Bishton Newpt 27 R10
Bishton Staffs 46 D9
Bisley Gloucs 28 H6
Bisley Surrey 20 G11
Bisley Camp Surrey 20 F11
Bispham Bpool 61 Q11
Bispham Green Lancs 55 L4
Bissoe Cnwll 2 K8
Bisterne Hants 8 G8
Bitchet Green Kent 21 U12
Bitchfield Lincs 48 E8
Bittadon Devon 15 M4
Bittaford Devon 5 R9
Bittering Norfk 50 F10
Bitterley Shrops 35 N5
Bitterne C Sotn 9 P6
Bitteswell Leics 37 P3
Bitton S Glos 17 S3
Bix Oxon 20 B6
Bixter Shet 106 t8
Blaby Leics 47 Q14
Blackadder Border 85 L8
Blackawton Devon 5 U10
Blackbeck Cumb 66 F11
Blackborough Devon 6 E3
Blackborough End Norfk 49 U10
Black Bourton Oxon 29 Q7
Blackboys E Susx 11 S6
Blackbrook Derbys 46 K4
Blackbrook St Hel 55 M7
Blackbrook Staffs 45 S6
Blackbrook Surrey 21 L13
Blackburn Abers 105 N13
Blackburn Bl w D 62 D14
Blackburn Rothm 57 N8
Blackburn W Loth 82 J5
Blackburn with Darwen Services Bl w D 55 Q2
Black Callerton N u Ty 77 P12
Black Carr Norfk 40 J1
Black Corner W Susx 11 M3
Blackcraig E Ayrs 81 S11
Black Crofts Ag & B 94 C12
Black Cross Cnwll 3 N4
Blackden Heath Ches E 55 S12
Blackdog Abers 105 R13
Black Dog Devon 15 T11
Blackdown Devon 5 N5
Blackdown Dorset 7 L4
Blackdyke Cumb 66 H2
Blacker Barns 57 M5
Blacker Hill Barns 57 N6
Blackfen Gt Lon 21 S8
Blackfield Hants 9 N8
Blackford Cumb 75 S13
Blackford P & K 90 C10
Blackford Somset 17 M7
Blackford Somset 17 S11
Blackfordby Leics 46 K10
Blackgang IoW 9 P13
Blackhall C Edin 83 P4
Blackhall Colliery Dur 70 G5
Blackhall Mill Gatesd 69 P1
Blackhall Rocks Dur 70 G5
Blackham E Susx 11 R2
Blackhaugh Border 83 T11
Blackheath Essex 23 P3
Blackheath Gt Lon 21 Q7
Blackheath Sandw 36 C3
Blackheath Suffk 41 R6
Blackheath Surrey 20 H13
Black Heddon Nthumb 77 M10
Blackhill Abers 105 T4
Blackhill Abers 105 T7
Blackhill Dur 69 N2
Blackhill of Clackriach Abers 105 Q6
Blackjack Lincs 49 L6
Blackland Wilts 18 F7
Black Lane Ends Lancs 62 J11
Blacklaw D & G 74 K4
Blackley Manch 56 C6
Blacklunans P & K 97 U11
Blackmarstone Herefs 35 M13
Blackmill Brdgnd 26 G10
Blackmoor Hants 10 B4
Black Moor Leeds 63 R12
Blackmoor N Som 17 N4
Blackmoorfoot Kirk 56 G4
Blackmoor Gate Devon 15 P4
Blackmore Essex 22 F7
Blackmore End Essex 22 H1
Blackmore End Herts 31 Q9
Black Mountains 27 P2
Blackness Falk 83 L3
Blacknest Hants 10 B2
Blacknest W & M 20 G9
Black Notley Essex 22 J3
Blacko Lancs 62 H11
Black Pill Swans 25 V12
Blackpool Bpool 61 Q12
Blackpool Devon 5 U6
Blackpool Devon 5 V11
Blackpool Gate Cumb 76 A10
Blackpool Zoo Bpool 61 Q12
Blackridge W Loth 82 G5
Blackrock Cnwll 2 H10
Blackrock Mons 27 N5
Blackrod Bolton 55 P4
Blacksboat Moray 103 U8
Blackshaw D & G 74 K12
Blackshaw Head Calder 62 K14
Blacksmith's Green Suffk 40 K7
Blacksnape Bl w D 55 R2
Blackstone W Susx 11 L7
Black Street Suffk 41 T3
Black Tar Pembks 24 G9
Blackthorn Oxon 30 D9
Blackthorpe Suffk 40 F8
Blacktoft E R Yk 58 D2
Blacktop C Aber 99 R3
Black Torrington Devon 15 L11
Blackwall Derbys 46 J4
Blackwall Tunnel Gt Lon 21 Q6
Blackwater Cnwll 2 J7
Blackwater Hants 20 D11
Blackwater IoW 9 Q11
Blackwater Somset 16 J13
Blackwaterfoot N Ayrs 79 S10
Blackwell Cumb 67 P2
Blackwell Darltn 69 S10
Blackwell Derbys 47 M2
Blackwell Derbys 56 H12
Blackwell Warwks 36 H12
Blackwell Worcs 36 C6
Blackwellsend Green Gloucs 28 E2
Blackwood Caerph 27 M8
Blackwood D & G 74 H8
Blackwood S Lans 82 E10
Blackwood Hill Staffs 46 B2
Blacon Ches W 54 J13
Bladbean Kent 13 N6
Bladnoch D & G 73 L9
Bladon Oxon 25 T5
Bladon Somset 17 M12
Blaenannerch Cerdgn 32 D11
Blaenau Ffestiniog Gwynd 43 P4
Blaenau Ffestiniog Gwynd 43 P4
Blaenavon Torfn 27 P6
Blaenavon Industrial Landscape Torfn 27 N6
Blaencwm Rhondd 26 G8
Blaen Dyryn Powys 33 T13
Blaenffos Pembks 25 L3
Blaengarw Brdgnd 26 G9
Blaengeuffordd Cerdgn 33 M4
Blaengwrach Neath 26 F6
Blaengwynfi Neath 26 F8
Blaenllechau Rhondd 26 J8
Blaenpennal Cerdgn 33 M8
Blaenplwyf Cerdgn 33 L5
Blaenporth Cerdgn 32 E11
Blaenrhondda Rhondd 26 G8
Blaenwaun Carmth 25 M5
Blaen-y-coed Carmth 25 P5
Blaen-y-cwm Blae G 27 L5
Blaenycwm Cerdgn 33 R5
Blagdon N Som 17 P5
Blagdon Somset 16 H13
Blagdon Torbay 5 V8
Blagdon Hill Somset 16 H13
Blagill W & F 68 F3
Blaguegate Lancs 55 L5
Blaich Highld 94 E3
Blain Highld 93 R5
Blaina Blae G 27 N6
Blair Atholl P & K 97 P10
Blair Drummond Stirlg 89 R6
Blairgowrie P & K 90 J2
Blairhall Fife 90 F14
Blairingone P & K 90 E12
Blairlogie Stirlg 89 T6
Blairmore Ag & B 88 E9
Blairmore Highld 110 D5
Blair's Ferry Ag & B 87 T12
Blaisdon Gloucs 28 D4
Blakebrook Worcs 35 T5
Blakedown Worcs 35 U5
Blake End Essex 22 H3
Blakeley Lane Staffs 46 C4
Blakemere Ches W 55 N12
Blakemere Herefs 34 J12
Blakemore Devon 5 T8
Blakenall Heath Wsall 46 D13
Blakeney Gloucs 28 C6
Blakeney Norfk 50 H5
Blakenhall Ches E 45 R4
Blakenhall Wolves 36 B1
Blakeshall Worcs 35 T4
Blakesley W Nthn 37 R10
Blanchland Nthumb 69 L2
Blandford Camp Dorset 8 C7
Blandford Forum Dorset 8 B7
Blandford St Mary Dorset 8 B7
Bland Hill N York 63 Q9
Blanefield Stirlg 89 M10
Blankney Lincs 48 G1
Blantyre S Lans 82 C7
Blàr a' Chaorainn Highld 94 G5
Blarghour Ag & B 87 T3
Blargie Highld 96 J5
Blarmachfoldach Highld 94 F5
Blashford Hants 8 H7
Blaston Leics 38 B1
Blatherwycke N Nthn 38 E1
Blawith W & F 61 P2
Blawquhairn D & G 73 Q3
Blaxhall Suffk 41 Q9
Blaxton Donc 57 U6
Blaydon Gatesd 77 P13
Bleadney Somset 17 N7
Bleadon N Som 16 K5
Bleak Street Somset 17 U10
Blean Kent 13 M3
Bleasby Lincs 58 K10
Bleasby Notts 47 T4
Bleasdale Lancs 62 B10
Bleatarn W & F 68 F10
Bleathwood Herefs 35 N6
Blebocraigs Fife 91 P8
Bleddfa Powys 34 F7
Bledington Gloucs 29 P3
Bledlow Bucks 30 G12
Bledlow Ridge Bucks 20 C3
Bleet Wilts 18 C9
Blegbie E Loth 84 D6
Blencarn W & F 68 D6
Blencogo Cumb 66 J3
Blendworth Hants 9 U6
Blenheim Palace Oxon 29 T4
Blennerhasset Cumb 66 J4
Bletchingdon Oxon 30 B9
Bletchingley Surrey 21 P12
Bletchley M Keyn 30 J6
Bletchley Shrops 45 P7
Bletchley Park Museum M Keyn 30 J6
Bletherston Pembks 24 J6
Bletsoe Bed 38 F9
Blewbury Oxon 19 R3
Blickling Norfk 51 L8
Blidworth Notts 47 Q2
Blidworth Bottoms Notts 47 Q3
Blindburn Nthumb 76 G3
Blindcrake Cumb 66 H6
Blindley Heath Surrey 21 Q13
Blindwells E Loth 83 T4
Blisland Cnwll 4 E6
Blissford Hants 8 H6
Bliss Gate Worcs 35 R6
Blisworth W Nthn 37 T10
Blithbury Staffs 46 E10
Blitterlees Cumb 66 H2
Blockley Gloucs 36 G14
Blofield Norfk 51 P12
Blofield Heath Norfk 51 P11
Blo Norton Norfk 40 H5
Bloomfield Border 84 F14
Blore Staffs 45 R7
Blore Staffs 46 F4
Blounce Hants 20 B13
Blounts Green Staffs 46 E7
Blowick Sefton 54 J3
Bloxham Oxon 37 M13
Bloxholm Lincs 48 G3
Bloxwich Wsall 46 C13
Bloxworth Dorset 8 B10
Blubberhouses N York 63 P8
Blue Anchor Cnwll 3 N5
Blue Anchor Somset 16 D8
Blue Bell Hill Kent 12 D3
Blue John Cavern Derbys 56 H10
Blundellsands Sefton 54 H7
Blundeston Suffk 41 T1
Blunham C Beds 38 J10
Blunsdon St Andrew Swindn 29 M10
Bluntington Worcs 35 V6
Bluntisham Cambs 39 N6
Blunts Cnwll 4 J8
Blunts Green Warwks 36 F7
Blurton C Stke 45 U5
Blyborough Lincs 58 F8
Blyford Suffk 41 R5
Blymhill Staffs 45 T11
Blymhill Lawn Staffs 45 T11
Blyth Notts 57 T9
Blyth Nthumb 77 S9
Blyth Bridge Border 83 M9
Blythburgh Suffk 41 R5
Blythe Border 84 F9
Blythe Bridge Staffs 46 C5
Blythe End Warwks 36 H2
Blythe Marsh Staffs 46 C5
Blyth Services Notts 57 T9
Blyton Lincs 58 E8
Boarhills Fife 91 S9
Boarhunt Hants 9 S7
Boarley Kent 12 E4
Boarsgreave Lancs 55 T2
Boarshead E Susx 11 S4
Boar's Head Wigan 55 N5
Boars Hill Oxon 29 U7
Boarstall Bucks 30 D10
Boasley Cross Devon 5 N2
Boath Highld 108 K10
Boat of Garten Highld 103 P12
Bobbing Kent 12 G2
Bobbington Staffs 35 T2
Bobbingworth Essex 22 D6
Bocaddon Cnwll 4 F9
Bocking Essex 22 J3
Bocking Churchstreet Essex 22 J2
Bockleton Worcs 35 N8
Boconnoc Cnwll 4 E8
Boddam Abers 105 U7
Boddam Shet 106 t12
Boddington Gloucs 28 G2
Bodedern IoA 52 D6
Bodelwyddan Denbgs 53 T7
Bodenham Herefs 35 M10
Bodenham Wilts 8 H3
Bodenham Moor Herefs 35 M10
Bodewryd IoA 52 F4
Bodfari Denbgs 54 C12
Bodffordd IoA 52 F7
Bodham Norfk 50 K5
Bodiam E Susx 12 E10
Bodicote Oxon 37 N13
Bodieve Cnwll 3 P2
Bodinnick Cnwll 4 E10
Bodle Street Green E Susx 11 V8
Bodmin Cnwll 3 R3
Bodmin Moor Cnwll 4 F5
Bodney Norfk 50 D14
Bodorgan IoA 52 E9
Bodsham Kent 13 M6
Boduan Gwynd 42 F6
Bodwen Cnwll 3 Q4
Bodymoor Heath Warwks 36 G1
Bogallan Highld 102 H5
Bogbrae Abers 105 S8
Bogend S Ayrs 81 N6
Boggs Holdings E Loth 84 C4
Boghall Mdloth 83 P5
Boghall W Loth 82 J5
Boghead S Lans 82 E10
Bogmoor Moray 104 D3
Bogmuir Abers 99 L9
Bogniebrae Abers 104 H6
Bognor Regis W Susx 10 E11
Bogroy Highld 103 P11
Bogue D & G 73 Q3
Bohetherick Cnwll 5 L7
Bohortha Cnwll 3 M10
Bohuntine Highld 96 B7
Bojewyan Cnwll 2 B10
Bokiddick Cnwll 3 R4
Bolam Dur 69 Q8
Bolam Nthumb 77 N9
Bolberry Devon 5 R13
Bold Heath St Hel 55 M9
Boldmere Birm 36 F2
Boldon Colliery S Tyne 77 S13
Boldre Hants 9 L9
Boldron Dur 69 M10
Bole Notts 58 C9
Bolehill Derbys 46 J2
Bole Hill Derbys 57 M12
Bolenowe Cnwll 2 H9
Bolham Devon 16 C13
Bolham Water Devon 6 G2
Bolingey Cnwll 2 K6
Bollington Ches E 56 D11
Bollington Cross Ches E 56 D11
Bollow Gloucs 28 D5

Bolney W Susx 11 M6
Bolnhurst Bed 38 G9
Bolnore W Susx 11 N6
Bolshan Angus 99 L13
Bolsover Derbys 57 Q12
Bolster Moor Kirk 56 G3
Bolsterstone Sheff 57 L7
Boltby N York 64 B2
Bolter End Bucks 20 C4
Bolton Bolton 55 R5
Bolton E Loth 84 E4
Bolton E R Yk 64 H9
Bolton Nthumb 77 N3
Bolton W & F 68 D8
Bolton Abbey N York 63 M9
Bolton Bridge N York 63 M9
Bolton-by-Bowland Lancs 62 F10
Boltonfellend Cumb 75 U12
Boltongate Cumb 66 K4
Bolton-le-Sands Lancs 61 T6
Bolton Low Houses Cumb 66 K4
Bolton New Houses Cumb 66 K4
Bolton-on-Swale N York 69 S13
Bolton Percy N York 64 C11
Bolton Town End Lancs 61 T6
Bolton upon Dearne Barns 57 Q6
Bolventor Cnwll 4 F5
Bomarsund Nthumb 77 R9
Bomere Heath Shrops 45 L10
Bonar Bridge Highld 109 L6
Bonawe Ag & B 94 E12
Bonby N Linc 58 H3
Boncath Pembks 25 M3
Bonchester Bridge Border 76 B3
Bonchurch IoW 9 R13
Bondleigh Devon 15 Q12
Bonds Lancs 61 T11
Bonehill Devon 5 S5
Bonehill Staffs 46 G13
Bo'ness Falk 82 K2
Boney Hay Staffs 46 D11
Bonhill W Duns 88 J10
Boningale Shrops 45 T13
Bonjedward Border 84 H14
Bonkle N Lans 82 F7
Bonnington Angus 91 S4
Bonnington Kent 13 L8
Bonnybank Fife 91 N11
Bonnybridge Falk 89 T10
Bonnykelly Abers 105 P5
Bonnyrigg Mdloth 83 R5
Bonnyton Angus 91 M4
Bonsall Derbys 46 J2
Bonshaw Tower D & G 75 P11
Bont Mons 27 R4
Bontddu Gwynd 43 N10
Bont-Dolgadfan Powys 43 S13
Bont-goch Cerdgn 33 N3
Bonthorpe Lincs 59 S12
Bontnewydd Cerdgn 33 M7
Bontnewydd Gwynd 52 G11
Bontuchel Denbgs 44 C2
Bonvilston V Glam 26 K13
Bonwm Denbgs 44 D5
Bon-y-maen Swans 26 B8
Boode Devon 15 M5
Booker Bucks 20 D4
Booley Shrops 45 N8
Boon Border 84 F9
Boon Hill Staffs 45 T3
Boorley Green Hants 9 Q6
Boosbeck R & Cl 71 L9
Boose's Green Essex 22 K1
Boot Cumb 66 J12
Booth Calder 56 F1
Boothby Graffoe Lincs 48 E2
Boothby Pagnell Lincs 48 E7
Boothferry E R Yk 58 B1
Booth Green Ches E 56 D10
Boothstown Salfd 55 R6
Boothtown Calder 56 G1
Boothville W Nthn 37 U8
Bootle Cumb 61 L2
Bootle Sefton 54 H7
Boots Green Ches W 55 S12
Boot Street Suffk 41 M11
Booze N York 69 M12
Boraston Shrops 35 P7
Bordeaux Guern 6 e2
Borden Kent 12 G3
Borden W Susx 10 C6
Border Cumb 66 J2
Bordesley Worcs 36 D7
Bordley N York 62 J6
Bordon Hants 10 B3
Boreham Essex 22 J6
Boreham Wilts 18 C12
Boreham Street E Susx 11 V8
Borehamwood Herts 21 L3
Boreland D & G 75 N7
Boreraig Highld 100 a4
Boreton Shrops 45 M12
Borgh W Isls 106 b18
Borgh W Isls 106 j3
Borgie Highld 111 P5
Borgue D & G 73 Q10
Borgue Highld 112 D11
Borley Essex 40 D12
Borley Green Essex 40 D12
Borley Green Suffk 40 G8
Borneskitaig Highld 100 c2
Borness D & G 73 Q10
Boroughbridge N York 63 T6
Borough Green Kent 12 B4
Borras Head Wrexhm 44 J3
Borrowash Derbys 47 M7
Borrowby N York 63 U2
Borrowby N York 71 N9
Borrowdale Cumb 67 L9
Borrowstoun Falk 82 J2
Borstal Medway 12 D2
Borth Cerdgn 33 M2
Borthwick Mdloth 83 S7
Borthwickbrae Border 75 T3
Borthwickshiels Border 75 T2
Borth-y-Gest Gwynd 43 L6
Borve Highld 100 d5
Borve W Isls 106 b18
Borve W Isls 106 f9
Borve W Isls 106 j3
Borwick Lancs 61 U5
Borwick Lodge W & F 67 M13
Borwick Rails Cumb 61 M4
Bosavern Cnwll 2 B10
Bosbury Herefs 35 Q12
Boscarne Cnwll 3 Q3
Boscastle Cnwll 4 D2
Boscombe BCP 8 G10
Boscombe Wilts 18 K13
Boscoppa Cnwll 3 Q6
Bosham W Susx 10 C10
Bosham Hoe W Susx 10 C10
Bosherston Pembks 24 G12
Boskednan Cnwll 2 C10
Boskenna Cnwll 2 C12
Bosley Ches E 56 D13
Bosoughan Cnwll 3 M4
Bossall N York 64 G7
Bossiney Cnwll 4 D3
Bossingham Kent 13 N6
Bossington Somset 15 U3
Bostock Green Ches W 55 Q13
Boston Lincs 49 M5
Boston Spa Leeds 63 U10
Boswarthan Cnwll 2 C10
Boswinger Cnwll 3 P8
Botallack Cnwll 2 B10
Botany Bay Gt Lon 21 N3
Botcheston Leics 47 N13
Botesdale Suffk 40 H5
Bothal Nthumb 77 Q8
Bothampstead W Berk 19 R5
Bothamsall Notts 57 U12
Bothel Cumb 66 J5
Bothenhampton Dorset 7 N6
Bothwell S Lans 82 D7
Bothwell Services (southbound) S Lans 82 D7
Botley Bucks 31 L12
Botley Hants 9 Q6
Botley Oxon 29 U6
Botolph Claydon Bucks 30 F8
Botolphs W Susx 10 K9
Botolph's Bridge Kent 13 M9
Bottesford Leics 48 B6
Bottesford N Linc 58 E5
Bottisham Cambs 39 R8
Bottomcraig Fife 91 N7
Bottom of Hutton Lancs 55 L1
Bottom o' th' Moor Bolton 55 Q4
Bottoms Calder 56 D2
Bottoms Cnwll 2 B12
Botts Green Warwks 36 H2
Botusfleming Cnwll 5 L8
Botwnnog Gwynd 42 E7
Bough Beech Kent 21 S13
Boughrood Powys 34 D13
Boughspring Gloucs 27 V8
Boughton Norfk 49 V13
Boughton Notts 57 U13
Boughton W Nthn 37 U7
Boughton Aluph Kent 12 K6
Boughton End C Beds 31 L5
Boughton Green Kent 12 E5
Boughton Lees Kent 12 K6
Boughton Malherbe Kent 12 G6
Boughton Monchelsea Kent 12 E5
Boughton Street Kent 13 L4
Boulby R & Cl 71 N9
Boulder Clough Calder 56 F2
Bouldnor IoW 9 M11
Bouldon Shrops 35 M3
Boulmer Nthumb 77 R3
Boulston Pembks 24 G8
Boultenstone Abers 104 E13
Boultham Lincs 58 G13
Boundary Staffs 46 C5
Bourn Cambs 39 M9
Bournbrook Birm 36 D4
Bourne Lincs 48 G9
Bournebridge Essex 22 D9
Bourne End Bed 38 F8
Bourne End Bucks 20 E5
Bourne End C Beds 31 L4
Bourne End Herts 31 M11
Bournemouth BCP 8 F10
Bournemouth Airport BCP 8 G9
Bournes Green Gloucs 28 H7
Bournes Green Sthend 23 M10
Bournheath Worcs 36 C6
Bournmoor Dur 70 D2
Bournstream Gloucs 28 D9
Bournville Birm 36 D4
Bourton Dorset 17 U10
Bourton N Som 17 L4
Bourton Oxon 29 P10
Bourton Shrops 35 N1
Bourton Wilts 18 F8
Bourton on Dunsmore Warwks 37 M6
Bourton-on-the-Hill Gloucs 29 N1
Bourton-on-the-Water Gloucs 29 N3
Bousd Ag & B 92 H6
Boustead Hill Cumb 75 Q14
Bouth W & F 61 Q2
Bouthwaite N York 63 N5
Bouts Worcs 36 D9
Boveney Bucks 20 F7
Boveridge Dorset 8 F6
Bovey Tracey Devon 5 U5
Bovingdon Herts 31 M12
Bovingdon Green Bucks 20 D5
Bovinger Essex 22 D6
Bovington Dorset 8 A11
Bovington Camp Dorset 8 A11
Bow Cumb 67 M1
Bow Devon 5 U9
Bow Devon 15 R12
Bow Gt Lon 21 Q6
Bow Ork 106 s20
Bowbank Dur 68 K8
Bow Brickhill M Keyn 30 K6
Bowbridge Gloucs 28 G6
Bowburn Dur 70 D5
Bowcombe IoW 9 P11
Bowd Devon 6 F6
Bowden Border 84 F12
Bowden Devon 5 U11
Bowden Hill Wilts 18 D7
Bowdon Traffd 55 S9
Bower Highld 112 F4
Bowerchalke Wilts 8 E4
Bowerhill Wilts 18 D8
Bower Hinton Somset 17 N13
Bower House Tye Suffk 40 G12
Bowermadden Highld 112 F4
Bowers Staffs 45 T6
Bowers Gifford Essex 22 J10
Bowershall Fife 90 G13
Bower's Row Leeds 63 U14
Bowes Dur 69 L10
Bowgreave Lancs 61 T11
Bowhouse D & G 74 K12
Bowithick Cnwll 4 F4
Bowker's Green Lancs 54 K6
Bowland Border 84 D10
Bowland Bridge W & F 61 S2
Bowley Herefs 35 M10
Bowley Town Herefs 35 M10
Bowlhead Green Surrey 10 E3
Bowling C Brad 63 P13
Bowling W Duns 88 K11
Bowling Bank Wrexhm 44 J4
Bowling Green Worcs 35 T10
Bowmanstead W & F 67 M13
Bowmore Ag & B 78 E4
Bowness-on-Solway Cumb 75 P13
Bowness-on-Windermere W & F 67 P13
Bow of Fife Fife 91 M9
Bowriefauld Angus 91 R2
Bowscale W & F 67 N6
Bowsden Nthumb 85 P10
Bowston W & F 67 Q13
Bow Street Cerdgn 33 M3
Bow Street Norfk 50 H14
Bowthorpe Norfk 51 L12
Box Gloucs 28 G7
Box Wilts 18 B7
Boxbush Gloucs 28 C3
Boxbush Gloucs 28 D5
Box End Bed 38 F11
Boxford Suffk 40 G12
Boxford W Berk 19 P6
Boxgrove W Susx 10 E9
Box Hill Surrey 21 L12
Boxley Kent 12 E4
Boxmoor Herts 31 M11
Box's Shop Cnwll 14 F12
Boxted Essex 23 P1
Boxted Suffk 40 D10
Boxted Cross Essex 23 P1
Boxwell Gloucs 28 F9
Boxworth Cambs 39 M8
Boyden End Suffk 40 B9
Boyden Gate Kent 13 P2
Boylestone Derbys 46 G6
Boyndie Abers 104 J3
Boyndlie Abers 105 Q3
Boynton E R Yk 65 Q6
Boysack Angus 91 T2
Boys Hill Dorset 7 S2
Boythorpe Derbys 57 N13
Boyton Cnwll 4 J2
Boyton Suffk 41 Q11
Boyton Wilts 18 E13
Boyton Cross Essex 22 F6
Boyton End Suffk 40 B12
Bozeat N Nthn 38 D9
Braaid IoM 60 e7
Brabling Green Suffk 41 N8
Brabourne Kent 13 M7
Brabourne Lees Kent 13 L7
Brabstermire Highld 112 H3
Bracadale Highld 100 c6
Braceborough Lincs 48 G11
Bracebridge Heath Lincs 58 G13
Bracebridge Low Fields Lincs 58 G13
Braceby Lincs 48 F6
Bracewell Lancs 62 H10
Brackenfield Derbys 47 L2
Brackenhirst N Lans 82 D5
Brackenthwaite Cumb 67 L3
Brackenthwaite N York 63 R9
Brackla Brdgnd 26 G12
Bracklesham W Susx 10 C11
Brackletter Highld 94 H2
Brackley W Nthn 30 C5
Brackley Hatch W Nthn 30 D4
Bracknell Br For 20 E9
Braco P & K 89 T4
Bracobrae Moray 104 G5
Bracon Ash Norfk 51 L14
Bracora Highld 100 g10
Bracorina Highld 100 g10
Bradaford Devon 4 K2
Bradbourne Derbys 46 H3
Bradbury Dur 70 D7
Bradden W Nthn 37 R11
Braddock Cnwll 4 F8
Bradeley C Stke 45 U3
Bradenham Bucks 20 D3
Bradenstoke Wilts 18 F5
Bradfield Devon 6 E3
Bradfield Essex 23 R1
Bradfield Norfk 51 N7
Bradfield Sheff 57 L8
Bradfield W Berk 19 T6
Bradfield Combust Suffk 40 E9
Bradfield Green Ches E 45 Q2
Bradfield Heath Essex 23 R1
Bradfield St Clare Suffk 40 F9
Bradfield St George Suffk 40 F9
Bradfield Southend W Berk 19 S6
Bradford C Brad 63 P13
Bradford Cnwll 4 E5
Bradford Devon 14 K11
Bradford Nthumb 77 M10
Bradford Nthumb 85 T12
Bradford Abbas Dorset 7 Q2
Bradford Leigh Wilts 18 B8
Bradford-on-Avon Wilts 18 B8
Bradford-on-Tone Somset 16 G12
Bradford Peverell Dorset 7 S6
Bradiford Devon 15 N6
Brading IoW 9 S11
Bradley Ches W 45 M4
Bradley Derbys 46 H4
Bradley Hants 19 T12
Bradley Kirk 56 J2
Bradley N York 63 L3
Bradley NE Lin 59 M5
Bradley Staffs 45 U10
Bradley Wolves 36 C1
Bradley Worcs 36 C8
Bradley Wrexhm 44 H3
Bradley Green Somset 16 J9
Bradley Green Warwks 46 J13
Bradley Green Worcs 36 C8
Bradley in the Moors Staffs 46 E5
Bradley Stoke S Glos 28 B11
Bradmore Notts 47 Q7
Bradney Somset 16 K9
Bradninch Devon 6 C4
Bradninch Devon 15 P6
Bradnop Staffs 46 D2
Bradnor Green Herefs 34 G9
Bradpole Dorset 7 N6
Bradshaw Bolton 55 R4
Bradshaw Calder 63 M14
Bradshaw Kirk 56 G4
Bradstone Devon 4 K4
Bradwall Green Ches E 55 S14
Bradwell Derbys 56 J10
Bradwell Devon 15 M4
Bradwell Essex 22 K3
Bradwell M Keyn 30 H4
Bradwell Norfk 51 T13
Bradwell-on-Sea Essex 23 P6
Bradwell Waterside Essex 23 N6
Bradworthy Devon 14 H10
Brae Highld 102 J3
Brae Shet 106 t7
Braeface Falk 89 S9
Braehead Angus 99 M13
Braehead D & G 73 L9
Braehead S Lans 82 J8
Braeintra Highld 101 M5
Braemar Abers 98 B5
Braemore Highld 108 B9
Braemore Highld 112 C11
Brae Roy Lodge Highld 96 C5
Braeside Inver 88 F11
Braes of Coul Angus 98 D12
Braes of Enzie Moray 104 D4
Braes of Ullapool Highld 108 A6
Braeswick Ork 106 v16
Braevallich Ag & B 87 T4
Braewick Shet 106 s6
Brafferton Darltn 69 S8
Brafferton N York 63 U5
Brafield-on-the-Green W Nthn 38 B9
Bragar W Isls 106 h4
Bragbury End Herts 31 S8
Braidwood S Lans 82 F9
Brailsford Derbys 46 J5
Brailsford Green Derbys 46 J5
Brain's Green Gloucs 28 C6
Braintree Essex 22 J3
Braiseworth Suffk 40 K6
Braishfield Hants 9 M3
Braiswick Essex 23 N2
Braithwaite C Brad 63 L11
Braithwaite Cumb 66 K8
Braithwell Donc 57 R8
Braken Hill Wakefd 57 P3
Bramber W Susx 10 K8
Brambridge Hants 9 P4
Bramcote Notts 47 P6
Bramcote Warwks 37 M3
Bramdean Hants 9 S3
Bramerton Norfk 51 N13
Bramfield Herts 31 S9
Bramfield Suffk 41 Q6
Bramford Suffk 40 K11
Bramhall Stockp 56 C10
Bramham Leeds 63 U11
Bramhope Leeds 63 R11
Bramley Hants 19 U9
Bramley Leeds 63 Q12
Bramley Rothm 57 Q8
Bramley Surrey 10 G2
Bramley Corner Hants 19 T9
Bramley Green Hants 19 U9
Bramley Head N York 63 N8
Bramling Kent 13 P4
Brampford Speke Devon 6 B5
Brampton Cambs 38 K6
Brampton Cumb 76 A13
Brampton Lincs 58 D11
Brampton Norfk 51 M9
Brampton Rothm 57 P6
Brampton Suffk 41 R4
Brampton W & F 68 E8
Brampton Abbotts Herefs 28 B2
Brampton Ash N Nthn 37 U3
Brampton Bryan Herefs 34 J6
Brampton-en-le-Morthen Rothm 57 Q9
Bramshall Staffs 46 E7
Bramshaw Hants 8 K5
Bramshill Hants 20 B10
Bramshott Hants 10 C4
Bramwell Somset 17 M11
Branault Highld 93 N5
Brancaster Norfk 50 C5
Brancaster Staithe Norfk 50 C5
Brancepeth Dur 69 R5
Branchill Moray 103 S5
Brand End Lincs 49 N4
Branderburgh Moray 104 A1
Brandesburton E R Yk 65 Q10
Brandeston Suffk 41 M8
Brand Green Gloucs 28 D2
Brandis Corner Devon 14 K12
Brandiston Norfk 50 K9
Brandon Dur 69 R4
Brandon Lincs 48 D4
Brandon Nthumb 77 L2
Brandon Suffk 40 C3
Brandon Warwks 37 M5
Brandon Bank Norfk 39 T3
Brandon Creek Norfk 39 T2
Brandon Parva Norfk 50 J12
Brandsby N York 64 D5
Brandy Wharf Lincs 58 H7
Brane Cnwll 2 C11
Bran End Essex 22 G2
Branksome BCP 8 E10
Branksome Park BCP 8 F10
Bransbury Hants 19 P12
Bransby Lincs 58 E11
Branscombe Devon 6 G7
Bransford Worcs 35 S10
Bransgore Hants 8 H9
Bransholme C KuH 65 Q13
Bransley Shrops 35 Q5
Branson's Cross Worcs 36 E6
Branston Leics 48 B8
Branston Lincs 58 H13
Branston Staffs 46 H9
Branston Booths Lincs 58 J13
Branstone IoW 9 R12
Brant Broughton Lincs 48 D3
Brantham Suffk 40 K14
Branthwaite Cumb 66 G8
Branthwaite Cumb 67 L5
Brantingham E R Yk 65 L14
Branton Donc 57 T6
Branton Nthumb 77 L2
Branton Green N York 63 U7
Branxton Nthumb 85 M11
Brassey Green Ches W 45 M1
Brasside Dur 69 S3
Brassington Derbys 46 H3
Brasted Kent 21 S11
Brasted Chart Kent 21 S12
Brathens Abers 99 M4
Bratoft Lincs 59 S14
Brattleby Lincs 58 F10
Bratton Somset 16 B7
Bratton Wilts 18 D10
Bratton Wrekin 45 P11
Bratton Clovelly Devon 5 M2
Bratton Fleming Devon 15 P5
Bratton Seymour Somset 17 S11
Braughing Herts 31 U7
Braughing Friars Herts 22 B3
Braunston Rutlnd 48 B12
Braunston W Nthn 37 P7
Braunstone Town Leics 47 Q13
Braunton Devon 15 L5
Brawby N York 64 G4
Brawl Highld 111 S3
Braworth N York 70 H11
Bray W & M 20 F7
Braybrooke N Nthn 37 U4
Braydon Wilts 29 L10
Braydon Brook Wilts 28 J9
Braydon Side Wilts 28 K10
Brayford Devon 15 Q6
Bray's Hill E Susx 12 C13
Bray Shop Cnwll 4 J6
Braystones Cumb 66 F11
Braythorn N York 63 Q10
Brayton N York 64 E13
Braywick W & M 20 E7
Braywoodside W & M 20 E7
Brazacott Cnwll 4 H2
Breach Kent 12 F2
Breach Kent 13 N6
Breachwood Green Herts 31 Q8
Breacleit W Isls 106 g5
Breaclete W Isls 106 g5
Breaden Heath Shrops 44 K6
Breadsall Derbys 47 L6
Breadstone Gloucs 28 D7
Breage Cnwll 2 G11
Breakachy Highld 102 E7
Breakish Highld 100 f7
Brealangwell Lodge Highld 108 J6
Bream Gloucs 28 B6
Breamore Hants 8 H5
Brean Somset 16 J5
Breanais W Isls 106 e6
Brearley Calder 56 F1
Brearton N York 63 S7
Breascleit W Isls 106 h5
Breasclete W Isls 106 h5
Breaston Derbys 47 N7
Brechfa Carmth 25 T4
Brechin Angus 99 L11
Breckles Norfk 40 G2
Brecon Powys 26 J2
Brecon Beacons National Park 26 J3
Bredbury Stockp 56 D8
Brede E Susx 12 F12
Bredenbury Herefs 35 P9
Bredfield Suffk 41 N10
Bredgar Kent 12 G3
Bredhurst Kent 12 E3
Bredon Worcs 36 B13
Bredon's Hardwick Worcs 36 B13
Bredon's Norton Worcs 36 B13
Bredward Herefs 34 G10
Bredwardine Herefs 34 H12
Breedon on the Hill Leics 47 M9
Breich W Loth 82 J6
Breightmet Bolton 55 R5
Breighton E R Yk 64 G13
Breinton Herefs 35 L13
Bremhill Wilts 18 E6
Bremridge Devon 15 Q7
Brenchley Kent 12 C7
Brendon Devon 14 J11
Brendon Devon 15 S3
Brendon Hill Somset 16 D10
Brenfield Ag & B 87 Q9
Brenish W Isls 106 e6
Brenkley N u Ty 77 Q10
Brent Cross Gt Lon 21 M5
Brent Eleigh Suffk 40 F11
Brentford Gt Lon 21 L7
Brentingby Leics 47 U10
Brent Knoll Somset 16 K6
Brent Mill Devon 5 R9
Brent Pelham Herts 22 B1
Brentwood Essex 22 E9
Brenzett Kent 12 K10
Brenzett Green Kent 12 K10
Brereton Staffs 46 E10
Brereton Green Ches E 55 S14
Brereton Heath Ches E 55 T13
Brereton Hill Staffs 46 E10
Bressay Shet 106 v9
Bressingham Norfk 40 J4
Bressingham Common Norfk 40 J4
Bretby Derbys 46 J9
Bretford Warwks 37 M5
Bretforton Worcs 36 E12
Bretherton Lancs 55 L2
Brettabister Shet 106 u8
Brettenham Norfk 40 F4
Brettenham Suffk 40 G10
Bretton C Pete 48 J13
Bretton Derbys 56 K11
Bretton Flints 54 J14
Brewers End Essex 22 E3
Brewer Street Surrey 21 P12
Brewood Staffs 45 U12
Briantspuddle Dorset 7 V6
Brick End Essex 22 E2
Brickendon Herts 31 T11
Bricket Wood Herts 31 P12
Brick Houses Sheff 57 M10
Brickkiln Green Essex 22 H1
Bricklehampton Worcs 36 C12
Bride IoM 60 g2
Bridekirk Cumb 66 H6
Bridell Pembks 32 C12
Bridestowe Devon 5 N3
Brideswell Abers 104 H8
Bridford Devon 5 U3
Bridge Kent 13 N5
Bridge End Cumb 61 M3
Bridge End Cumb 67 N3
Bridge End Devon 5 R11
Bridge End Dur 69 M5
Bridge End Essex 22 G1
Bridge End Lincs 48 H6
Bridgefoot Angus 91 N4
Bridgefoot Cumb 66 G7
Bridge Green Essex 39 Q13
Bridgehampton Somset 17 Q12
Bridge Hewick N York 63 S5
Bridgehill Dur 69 N2
Bridgehouse Gate N York 63 P6
Bridgemary Hants 9 R8
Bridgemere Ches E 45 R4
Bridgend Abers 104 G8
Bridgend Ag & B 78 E3
Bridgend Ag & B 79 P8
Bridgend Ag & B 87 R7
Bridgend Angus 98 J10
Bridgend Brdgnd 26 G12
Bridgend Cerdgn 32 C11
Bridgend D & G 75 L4
Bridgend Devon 5 P11
Bridgend Fife 91 N9
Bridgend Moray 104 D9
Bridgend P & K 90 H7
Bridgend W & F 67 P10
Bridgend W Loth 82 K3
Bridgend of Lintrathen Angus 98 D13
Bridge of Alford Abers 104 H12
Bridge of Allan Stirlg 89 S6
Bridge of Avon Moray 103 U12
Bridge of Avon Moray 103 U8
Bridge of Balgie P & K 95 R9
Bridge of Brewlands Angus 98 B11
Bridge of Brown Highld 103 T11
Bridge of Cally P & K 97 U13
Bridge of Canny Abers 99 M4
Bridge of Craigisla Angus 98 D13
Bridge of Dee D & G 74 D14
Bridge of Don C Aber 99 S2
Bridge of Dun Angus 99 M12
Bridge of Dye Abers 99 M6
Bridge of Earn P & K 90 H8
Bridge of Ericht P & K 95 Q7
Bridge of Feugh Abers 99 N4
Bridge of Gairn Abers 98 F4
Bridge of Gaur P & K 95 Q7
Bridge of Marnoch Abers 104 H5
Bridge of Muchalls Abers 99 R5
Bridge of Orchy Ag & B 94 K11
Bridge of Tilt P & K 97 P10
Bridge of Tynet Moray 104 D3
Bridge of Walls Shet 106 s8
Bridge of Weir Rens 88 J12
Bridge Reeve Devon 15 Q10
Bridgerule Devon 14 G12
Bridges Shrops 34 J1
Bridge Sollers Herefs 34 K12
Bridge Street Suffk 40 E11
Bridgetown Cnwll 4 J3
Bridgetown Somset 16 B10
Bridge Trafford Ches W 55 L12
Bridge Yate S Glos 28 C13
Bridgham Norfk 40 G3
Bridgnorth Shrops 35 R2
Bridgwater Somset 16 J9
Bridgwater Services Somset 16 K10
Bridlington E R Yk 65 R6
Bridport Dorset 7 N6
Bridstow Herefs 28 A3
Brierfield Lancs 62 G12
Brierley Barns 57 P4
Brierley Gloucs 28 B4
Brierley Herefs 35 L9
Brierley Hill Dudley 36 B3
Brierlow Bar Derbys 56 G13
Brierton Hartpl 70 G6
Briery Cumb 67 L8
Brigg N Linc 58 H5
Briggate Norfk 51 P8
Briggswath N York 71 Q11
Brigham Cumb 66 G6
Brigham Cumb 67 L8
Brigham E R Yk 65 P9
Brighouse Calder 56 H2
Brighstone IoW 9 N12
Brightgate Derbys 46 J2
Brighthampton Oxon 29 S7
Brightholmlee Sheff 57 L7
Brightley Devon 15 P13
Brightling E Susx 12 C11
Brightlingsea Essex 23 Q4
Brighton Br & H 11 N10
Brighton Cnwll 3 N6
Brighton City Airport W Susx 10 K9
Brighton le Sands Sefton 54 H7
Brightons Falk 82 H3
Brightwalton W Berk 19 P5
Brightwalton Green W Berk 19 P5
Brightwalton Holt W Berk 19 P5
Brightwell Suffk 41 N12
Brightwell Baldwin Oxon 30 E13
Brightwell-cum-Sotwell Oxon 19 S2
Brightwell Upperton Oxon 19 U2
Brignall Dur 69 N10
Brig o'Turk Stirlg 89 M4
Brigsley NE Lin 59 N6
Brigsteer W & F 61 T2
Brigstock N Nthn 38 D3
Brill Bucks 30 E10
Brill Cnwll 2 J11
Brilley Herefs 34 G11
Brimfield Herefs 35 M7
Brimfield Cross Herefs 35 M7
Brimington Derbys 57 P12
Brimley Devon 5 U5
Brimpsfield Gloucs 28 H5
Brimpton W Berk 19 S8
Brimpton Common W Berk 19 S8
Brimscombe Gloucs 28 G7
Brimstage Wirral 54 H10
Brincliffe Sheff 57 M10
Brind E R Yk 64 G13
Brindham Somset 17 P9
Brindister Shet 106 s8
Brindle Lancs 55 N2
Brindley Ches E 45 N3
Brineton Staffs 45 T11
Bringhurst Leics 38 B2
Bringsty Common Herefs 35 R9
Brington Cambs 38 G5
Brinian Ork 106 t17
Briningham Norfk 50 H7
Brinkely Notts 47 T3
Brinkhill Lincs 59 Q12
Brinkley Cambs 39 T10
Brinklow Warwks 37 M5
Brinkworth Wilts 28 K11
Brinscall Lancs 55 P2
Brinscombe Somset 17 M6
Brinsea N Som 17 M4
Brinsley Notts 47 N4
Brinsop Herefs 34 K12
Brinsworth Rothm 57 P9
Brinton Norfk 50 H6
Brisco Cumb 67 P2
Brisley Norfk 50 F9
Brislington Bristl 17 R2
Brissenden Green Kent 12 H8
Bristol Bristl 28 A13
Bristol Airport N Som 17 P3
Briston Norfk 50 J7
Brisworthy Devon 5 P7
Britannia Lancs 56 C2
Britford Wilts 8 H3
Brithdir Caerph 27 L7
Brithdir Gwynd 43 Q10
British Legion Village Kent 12 D4
Briton Ferry Neath 26 C9
Britwell Salome Oxon 19 U2
Brixham Torbay 6 B13
Brixton Devon 5 P10
Brixton Gt Lon 21 P7
Brixton Deverill Wilts 18 C13
Brixworth W Nthn 37 T6
Brize Norton Oxon 29 Q6
Brize Norton Airport Oxon 29 Q6
Broad Alley Worcs 35 U7
Broad Blunsdon Swindn 29 M9
Broadbottom Tamesd 56 E8
Broadbridge W Susx 10 C9
Broadbridge Heath W Susx 10 J4
Broad Campden Gloucs 36 G13
Broad Carr Calder 56 G3
Broad Chalke Wilts 8 E3
Broad Clough Lancs 56 C2
Broadclyst Devon 6 C5
Broadfield Inver 88 H11
Broadfield Pembks 24 K10
Broadford Highld 100 f7
Broad Ford Kent 12 D8
Broadford Bridge W Susx 10 H6
Broadgairhill Border 75 P3
Broadgrass Green Suffk 40 G8
Broad Green Cambs 39 U8
Broad Green Essex 23 L3
Broad Green Worcs 35 S9
Broad Green Worcs 36 C6
Broadhaugh Border 85 M7
Broad Haven Pembks 24 E8
Broadheath Traffd 55 S9
Broadhembury Devon 6 F4
Broadhempston Devon 5 U7
Broad Hill Cambs 39 S5
Broad Hinton Wilts 18 H5
Broadholme Lincs 58 E12
Broadland Row E Susx 12 F12
Broadlay Carmth 25 Q9
Broad Layings Hants 19 P8
Broadley Essex 22 B6
Broadley Lancs 56 C3
Broadley Moray 104 D3
Broadley Common Essex 22 B6
Broad Marston Worcs 36 F11
Broadmayne Dorset 7 T7
Broad Meadow Staffs 45 T4
Broadmere Hants 19 T11
Broadmoor Gloucs 28 B4
Broadmoor Pembks 24 J9
Broadnymett Devon 15 R12
Broad Oak Carmth 25 U6
Broad Oak Cumb 66 H14
Broadoak Dorset 7 M5
Broad Oak E Susx 11 U6
Broad Oak E Susx 12 F12
Broadoak Gloucs 28 C5
Broad Oak Hants 20 C12
Broad Oak Herefs 27 T3
Broad Oak Kent 13 N3
Broad Oak St Hel 55 M7
Broadoak Wrexhm 44 J2
Broad Road Suffk 41 N5
Broadsands Torbay 6 A13
Broad's Green Essex 22 G5
Broadstairs Kent 13 S2
Broadstone BCP 8 E9
Broadstone Mons 27 U7
Broadstone Shrops 35 M3
Broad Street E Susx 12 G12
Broad Street Essex 22 E4
Broad Street Kent 12 F4
Broad Street Kent 13 M7
Broad Street Medway 22 J13
Broad Street Wilts 18 H9
Broad Street Green Essex 23 L6
Broad Town Wilts 18 G5
Broadwas Worcs 35 S9
Broadwater Herts 31 R8
Broadwater W Susx 10 J10
Broadwaters Worcs 35 T5
Broadway Carmth 25 N8
Broadway Carmth 25 Q9
Broadway Pembks 24 E8
Broadway Somset 16 K13
Broadway Suffk 41 Q5
Broadway Worcs 36 E13
Broadwell Gloucs 28 A5
Broadwell Gloucs 29 P2
Broadwell Oxon 29 Q7
Broadwell Warwks 37 N7
Broadwey Dorset 7 S8
Broadwindsor Dorset 7 M4
Broadwood Kelly Devon 15 P11
Broadwoodwidger Devon 5 L3
Brobury Herefs 34 H12
Brochel Highld 100 e5
Brochroy Ag & B 94 E12
Brock Lancs 61 U11
Brockamin Worcs 35 S10
Brockbridge Hants 9 S5
Brockdish Norfk 41 M5
Brockencote Worcs 35 U6
Brockenhurst Hants 9 L8
Brocketsbrae S Lans 82 F11
Brockford Green Suffk 40 K7
Brockford Street Suffk 40 K7
Brockhall W Nthn 37 R8
Brockhall Village Lancs 62 E12
Brockham Surrey 21 L13
Brockhampton Gloucs 28 H2
Brockhampton Gloucs 28 K3
Brockhampton Hants 9 U7
Brockhampton Herefs 28 A1
Brockhampton Green Dorset 7 T3
Brockholes Kirk 56 J4
Brockhurst Derbys 57 M14
Brockhurst Warwks 37 N4
Brocklebank Cumb 67 M4
Brocklesby Lincs 58 K4
Brockley N Som 17 N3
Brockley Suffk 40 D6
Brockley Green Suffk 40 B11
Brockley Green Suffk 40 D10
Brockleymoor W & F 67 Q5
Brockmoor Dudley 36 B3
Brockscombe Devon 15 L13
Brock's Green Hants 19 R8
Brockton Shrops 34 H3
Brockton Shrops 35 N2
Brockton Shrops 44 H13
Brockton Shrops 45 R13
Brockton Staffs 45 T7
Brockweir Gloucs 27 U7
Brockwood Park Hants 9 S3
Brockworth Gloucs 28 G4
Brocton Cnwll 3 Q3
Brocton Staffs 46 C10
Brodick N Ayrs 80 E5
Brodie Moray 103 Q4
Brodsworth Donc 57 R5
Brogaig Highld 100 d3
Brogborough C Beds 31 L5
Brokenborough Wilts 28 H10
Broken Cross Ches E 56 C12
Broken Cross Ches W 55 Q12
Brokerswood Wilts 18 B10
Bromborough Wirral 54 J10
Brome Suffk 40 K5
Brome Street Suffk 41 L5
Bromeswell Suffk 41 P10
Bromfield Cumb 66 J3
Bromfield Shrops 35 L5
Bromham Bed 38 F10
Bromham Wilts 18 E7
Bromley Barns 57 M7
Bromley Dudley 36 B3
Bromley Gt Lon 21 R9
Bromley Shrops 35 R1
Bromley Common Gt Lon 21 R9
Bromley Cross Bolton 55 R4
Bromley Cross Essex 23 Q2
Bromley Green Kent 12 J8
Bromlow Shrops 44 H13
Brompton Medway 12 E2
Brompton N York 70 E13
Brompton-by-Sawdon N York 65 L3
Brompton-on-Swale N York 69 R13
Brompton Ralph Somset 16 E10
Brompton Regis Somset 16 C10
Bromsash Herefs 28 C3
Bromsberrow Gloucs 35 R14
Bromsberrow Heath Gloucs 35 R14
Bromsgrove Worcs 36 C6
Bromstead Heath Staffs 45 S10
Bromyard Herefs 35 Q10
Bromyard Downs Herefs 35 Q9
Bronaber Gwynd 43 P7
Bronant Cerdgn 33 M7
Broncroft Shrops 35 M3
Brongest Cerdgn 32 F11
Bronington Wrexhm 45 L6
Bronllys Powys 34 D14
Bronwydd Carmth 25 R6
Bronydd Powys 34 F11
Bronygarth Shrops 44 G6
Brook Carmth 25 N9
Brook Hants 8 K6
Brook Hants 9 L3
Brook IoW 9 M12
Brook Kent 13 L7
Brook Surrey 10 E3
Brook Surrey 20 J13
Brooke Norfk 51 N14
Brooke Rutlnd 48 B12
Brookenby Lincs 59 M7
Brook End Bed 38 G8
Brook End C Beds 38 J11
Brook End Cambs 38 G6
Brook End M Keyn 30 K4
Brookfield Rens 88 K13
Brookhampton Oxon 30 D13
Brookhampton Somset 17 R11
Brook Hill Hants 8 K6
Brookhouse Denbgs 54 C13
Brookhouse Lancs 61 U7
Brookhouse Rothm 57 R9
Brookhouse Green Ches E 45 T1
Brookhouses Derbys 56 F9
Brookland Kent 12 J10
Brooklands Traffd 55 S8
Brookmans Park Herts 31 R12
Brooks Powys 44 D14
Brooksby Leics 47 S10
Brooks End Kent 13 Q2
Brooks Green W Susx 10 J6
Brook Street Essex 22 E9
Brook Street Kent 12 H9
Brook Street Suffk 40 D11
Brook Street W Susx 11 N5
Brookthorpe Gloucs 28 F5
Brookville Norfk 40 B1
Brookwood Surrey 20 G11
Broom C Beds 31 Q4
Broom Rothm 57 P8
Broom Warwks 36 E10
Broombank Worcs 35 Q6
Broome Norfk 41 Q2
Broome Shrops 34 K4
Broome Worcs 36 B5
Broomedge Warrtn 55 R9
Broome Park Nthumb 77 N3
Broomer's Corner W Susx 10 J6
Broomershill W Susx 10 H7
Broomfield Essex 22 H5
Broomfield Kent 12 F5
Broomfield Kent 13 N2
Broomfield Somset 16 H10
Broomfields Shrops 44 K10
Broomfleet E R Yk 58 E1
Broom Green Norfk 50 G9
Broomhall W & M 20 G9
Broomhaugh Nthumb 77 L13
Broom Hill Barns 57 P6
Broom Hill Dorset 8 E8
Broom Hill Notts 47 P4
Broomhill Nthumb 77 Q5
Broom Hill Worcs 36 B5
Broomhill Green Ches E 45 P4
Broomley Nthumb 77 L13
Broompark Dur 69 R4
Broom's Green Gloucs 35 R14
Broomsthorpe Norfk 50 D8
Broom Street Kent 12 K3
Brora Highld 109 S4
Broseley Shrops 45 Q13
Brotherhouse Bar Lincs 49 L11
Brotherlee Dur 68 K5
Brothertoft Lincs 49 L4
Brotherton N York 57 Q1
Brotton R & Cl 71 L9
Broubster Highld 112 B5
Brough Derbys 56 J10
Brough E R Yk 58 F1
Brough Highld 112 F2
Brough Notts 48 B2
Brough Shet 106 v7
Brough W & F 68 G10
Broughall Shrops 45 N5
Brough Lodge Shet 106 v4
Brough Sowerby W & F 68 G10
Broughton Border 83 M11
Broughton Bucks 30 H10
Broughton Cambs 39 L5
Broughton Flints 54 H14
Broughton Hants 9 L2
Broughton Lancs 61 U13
Broughton M Keyn 30 J5
Broughton N Linc 58 G5
Broughton N Nthn 38 B5
Broughton N York 62 J9
Broughton N York 64 H5
Broughton Oxon 37 M13
Broughton Salfd 55 T6
Broughton Staffs 45 S7
Broughton V Glam 16 B2
Broughton Astley Leics 37 P2
Broughton Beck W & F 61 P3
Broughton Gifford Wilts 18 C8
Broughton Green Worcs 36 C8
Broughton Hackett Worcs 36 B10
Broughton-in-Furness W & F 61 N2
Broughton Mains D & G 73 M10
Broughton Mills W & F 61 N1
Broughton Moor Cumb 66 G6
Broughton Poggs Oxon 29 P7
Broughton Tower W & F 61 N2
Broughty Ferry C Dund 91 Q5
Brough with St Giles N York 69 R13
Brow End W & F 61 P5
Brownber W & F 68 F11
Brown Candover Hants 19 S13
Brown Edge Lancs 54 J4
Brown Edge Staffs 46 B3
Brown Heath Ches W 55 L14
Brownheath Shrops 45 L8
Brownhill Abers 105 P7
Brownhills Fife 91 R8
Brownhills Wsall 46 D12
Brownieside Nthumb 85 T14
Browninghill Green Hants 19 S8
Brown Knowl Ches W 45 L3
Brown Lees Staffs 45 U2
Brownlow Heath Ches E 45 T1
Brownrigg Cumb 66 F8
Brownrigg Cumb 66 J2
Brownsea Island Dorset 8 E11
Brown's Green Birm 36 E2
Brownsham Devon 14 G7
Browns Hill Gloucs 28 G7
Brownsover Warwks 37 P5
Brownston Devon 5 R10
Brown Street Suffk 40 J8
Browston Green Norfk 51 S13
Broxa N York 65 L1
Broxbourne Herts 31 U11
Broxburn E Loth 84 H3
Broxburn W Loth 83 L4
Broxfield Nthumb 77 Q2
Broxted Essex 22 E2
Broxton Ches W 45 L3
Broyle Side E Susx 11 R8
Bruan Highld 112 H9
Bruar P & K 97 N10
Bruchag Ag & B 88 D14
Bruera Ches W 44 K1
Bruern Abbey Oxon 29 Q3
Bruichladdich Ag & B 78 D3
Bruisyard Suffk 41 P7
Bruisyard Street Suffk 41 P7
Brumby N Linc 58 E5
Brund Staffs 46 F1
Brundall Norfk 51 P12
Brundish Suffk 41 N7
Brundish Street Suffk 41 N6
Brunery Highld 93 S4
Brunnion Cnwll 2 E9
Brunslow Shrops 34 J4
Brunswick Village N u Ty 77 Q11
Bruntcliffe Leeds 57 L1
Brunthwaite C Brad 63 M10
Bruntingthorpe Leics 37 R3
Brunton Fife 91 M7
Brunton Nthumb 85 U14
Brunton Wilts 18 K9
Brushford Devon 15 Q11
Brushford Somset 16 B11
Bruton Somset 17 S9
Bryan's Green Worcs 35 U7
Bryanston Dorset 8 B7
Bryant's Bottom Bucks 20 E3
Brydekirk D & G 75 N11
Bryher IoS 2 b2
Brymbo Wrexhm 44 G3
Brympton Somset 17 P13
Bryn Carmth 25 T10
Bryn Ches W 55 P12
Bryn Neath 26 E9
Bryn Shrops 34 G3
Bryn Wigan 55 N6
Brynamman Carmth 26 C5
Brynberian Pembks 24 K3
Brynbryddan Neath 26 D9
Bryn Bwbach Gwynd 43 M6
Bryncae Rhondd 26 H11
Bryncethin Brdgnd 26 G11
Bryncir Gwynd 42 J5
Bryn-côch Neath 26 C8
Bryncroes Gwynd 42 D7
Bryncrug Gwynd 43 M13
Bryn Du IoA 52 D8
Bryn-Eden Gwynd 43 P8
Bryneglwys Denbgs 44 D4
Bryneglwys & Abergynolwyn Slate Landscape Gwynd 43 N12
Brynfields Wrexhm 44 H5
Brynford Flints 54 E12
Bryn Gates Wigan 55 N6
Bryn Golau Rhondd 26 J10
Bryngwran IoA 52 E7
Bryngwyn Mons 27 R6
Bryngwyn Powys 34 E11
Bryn-Henllan Pembks 24 H3
Brynhoffnant Cerdgn 32 F10
Bryning Lancs 61 S14
Brynithel Blae G 27 N7
Brynmawr Blae G 27 M5
Bryn-mawr Gwynd 42 D7
Brynmenyn Brdgnd 26 G11
Brynmill Swans 26 A9
Brynna Rhondd 26 H11
Brynnau Gwynion Rhondd 26 H11
Bryn-penarth Powys 44 D13
Bryn Pydew Conwy 53 P7
Brynrefail Gwynd 52 J10
Brynrefail IoA 52 G5
Brynsadler Rhondd 26 J11
Bryn Saith Marchog Denbgs 44 C3
Brynsiencyn IoA 52 G9
Brynteg IoA 52 G6
Bryn-y-bal Flints 54 G14
Bryn-y-Maen Conwy 53 P7
Bryn-yr-Eos Wrexhm 44 G5
Bualintur Highld 100 d7
Buarth-draw Flints 54 E11
Bubbenhall Warwks 37 L6
Bubwith E R Yk 64 G12
Buccleuch Border 75 R3
Buchanan Smithy Stirlg 89 L8
Buchanhaven Abers 105 U6
Buchanty P & K 90 D6
Buchany Stirlg 89 R5
Buchlyvie Stirlg 89 N7
Buckabank Cumb 67 N3
Buckden Cambs 38 J7
Buckden N York 62 J4
Buckenham Norfk 51 Q12
Buckerell Devon 6 F4
Buckfast Devon 5 S7
Buckfastleigh Devon 5 S7
Buckhaven Fife 91 N12
Buckholt Mons 27 U4
Buckhorn Devon 14 J13
Buckhorn Weston Dorset 17 U12
Buckhurst Hill Essex 21 R4
Buckie Moray 104 E2
Buckingham Bucks 30 E6
Buckland Bucks 30 J10
Buckland Devon 5 R12
Buckland Gloucs 36 E13
Buckland Hants 9 L9
Buckland Herts 31 U6
Buckland Kent 13 R7
Buckland Oxon 29 R8
Buckland Surrey 21 M12
Buckland Brewer Devon 14 K8
Buckland Common Bucks 30 K11
Buckland Dinham Somset 17 U6
Buckland Filleigh Devon 15 L11
Buckland in the Moor Devon 5 S6
Buckland Monachorum Devon 5 M7
Buckland Newton Dorset 7 S3
Buckland Ripers Dorset 7 S8
Buckland St Mary Somset 6 J2
Buckland-Tout-Saints Devon 5 T11
Bucklebury W Berk 19 S6
Bucklers Hard Hants 9 N8
Bucklesham Suffk 41 M12
Buckley Flints 54 G14
Buckley Green Warwks 36 G7
Bucklow Hill Ches E 55 R10
Buckminster Leics 48 C9
Bucknall C Stke 46 B4
Bucknall Lincs 59 L13
Bucknell Oxon 30 C7
Bucknell Shrops 34 J6
Buckpool Moray 104 E2
Bucksburn C Aber 99 R2
Buck's Cross Devon 14 J8
Bucks Green W Susx 10 H4
Buckshaw Village Lancs 55 N2
Bucks Hill Herts 31 N12
Bucks Horn Oak Hants 10 C2
Buck's Mills Devon 14 J8
Buckton E R Yk 65 R5
Buckton Herefs 34 J6
Buckton Nthumb 85 R11
Buckworth Cambs 38 H5
Budby Notts 57 T13
Buddileigh Staffs 45 R4
Bude Cnwll 14 F11
Budge's Shop Cnwll 4 J9
Budlake Devon 6 C4
Budle Nthumb 85 T11
Budleigh Salterton Devon 6 E8
Budlett's Common E Susx 11 R6
Budock Water Cnwll 2 K10
Buerton Ches E 45 Q5
Bugbrooke W Nthn 37 S9
Bugford Devon 5 U10
Buglawton Ches E 56 C14
Bugle Cnwll 3 Q5
Bugley Dorset 17 U12
Bugthorpe E R Yk 64 H8
Buildwas Shrops 45 P13
Builth Road Powys 34 B10
Builth Wells Powys 34 B10
Bulbourne Herts 30 K10
Bulbridge Wilts 8 F2
Bulby Lincs 48 G8
Bulcote Notts 47 S5
Bulford Wilts 18 J12
Bulford Camp Wilts 18 J12
Bulkeley Ches E 45 M3
Bulkington Warwks 37 L3
Bulkington Wilts 18 D9
Bulkworthy Devon 14 J10
Bullamoor N York 70 E14
Bull Bay IoA 52 F4
Bullbridge Derbys 47 L3
Bullbrook Br For 20 E9
Bullen's Green Herts 31 R11
Bulley Gloucs 28 E4
Bullgill Cumb 66 G5
Bullingham Herefs 35 M13
Bullinghope Herefs 35 M13
Bullington Hants 19 Q12
Bullington Lincs 58 J11
Bullockstone Kent 13 N2
Bull's Green Herts 31 S9
Bull's Green Norfk 41 R2
Bulmer Essex 40 D12
Bulmer N York 64 F6
Bulmer Tye Essex 40 D13
Bulphan Thurr 22 F10
Bulstone Devon 6 G7
Bulstrode Herts 31 M12
Bulverhythe E Susx 12 E14
Bulwark Abers 105 Q6
Bulwell C Nott 47 P5
Bulwick N Nthn 38 E2
Bumble's Green Essex 22 B6
Bunacaimb Highld 100 f11
Bunarkaig Highld 101 T14
Bunbury Ches E 45 N2
Bunbury Heath Ches E 45 N2
Bunchrew Highld 102 H6
Buncton W Susx 10 J8
Bundalloch Highld 101 M6
Bunessan Ag & B 86 F1
Bungay Suffk 41 P3
Bunker's Hill Lincs 49 L3
Bunnahabhain Ag & B 86 G11
Bunny Notts 47 Q8
Buntait Highld 102 D9
Buntingford Herts 31 U7
Bunwell Norfk 40 K2
Bunwell Hill Norfk 40 K2
Bupton Derbys 46 H6
Burbage Derbys 56 F12
Burbage Leics 37 M2
Burbage Wilts 18 K8
Burcher Herefs 34 H8
Burchett's Green W & M 20 D6
Burcombe Wilts 8 F2
Burcot Oxon 30 C13
Burcot Worcs 36 C6
Burcote Shrops 35 R1
Burcott Bucks 30 H9
Burcott Bucks 30 J8
Burdale N York 64 K7
Bures Essex 40 F14
Burford Oxon 29 Q5
Burford Shrops 35 N7
Burg Ag & B 92 K9
Burgate Suffk 40 J5
Burgates Hants 10 B5
Burge End Herts 31 P6
Burgess Hill W Susx 11 N7
Burgh Suffk 41 M10
Burgh by Sands Cumb 75 R14
Burgh Castle Norfk 51 S12
Burghclere Hants 19 Q8
Burghead Moray 103 T2
Burghfield W Berk 19 U7
Burghfield Common W Berk 19 U7
Burgh Heath Surrey 21 M11
Burgh Hill E Susx 12 D10
Burghill Herefs 35 L12
Burgh Island Devon 5 Q12
Burgh le Marsh Lincs 59 T13
Burgh next Aylsham Norfk 51 M8
Burgh on Bain Lincs 59 M9
Burgh St Margaret Norfk 51 R11
Burgh St Peter Norfk 41 S2
Burghwallis Donc 57 R4
Burham Kent 12 D3
Buriton Hants 9 U5
Burland Ches E 45 P3
Burlawn Cnwll 3 P2
Burleigh Gloucs 28 G7
Burlescombe Devon 16 E13
Burleston Dorset 7 U6
Burlestone Devon 5 U11
Burley Hants 8 J8
Burley Rutlnd 48 C11
Burley Shrops 35 L4
Burleydam Ches E 45 P5
Burley Gate Herefs 35 N11
Burley in Wharfedale C Brad 63 P10
Burley Lawn Hants 8 J8
Burley Street Hants 8 J8
Burley Wood Head C Brad 63 P11
Burlingham Green Norfk 51 Q11
Burlingjobb Powys 34 G9
Burlington Shrops 45 S11
Burlton Shrops 45 L8
Burmarsh Kent 13 M9
Burmington Warwks 36 J13
Burn N York 64 D14
Burnage Manch 56 C8
Burnaston Derbys 46 J7
Burnbanks W & F 67 R9
Burnbrae N Lans 82 G7
Burn Bridge N York 63 R9
Burnby E R Yk 64 J10
Burn Cross Sheff 57 M7
Burndell W Susx 10 F10
Burnden Bolton 55 R5
Burnedge Rochdl 56 D4
Burneside W & F 67 R13
Burneston N York 63 S3
Burnett BaNES 17 S3
Burnfoot Border 75 T3
Burnfoot Border 75 V2
Burnfoot D & G 74 J7
Burnfoot D & G 75 R8
Burnfoot D & G 75 S6
Burnfoot P & K 90 E11
Burnham Bucks 20 F6
Burnham N Linc 58 J3
Burnham Deepdale Norfk 50 D5
Burnham Green Herts 31 S9
Burnham Market Norfk 50 D5
Burnham Norton Norfk 50 D5
Burnham-on-Crouch Essex 23 M8
Burnham-on-Sea Somset 16 K7
Burnham Overy Norfk 50 D5
Burnham Overy Staithe Norfk 50 D5
Burnham Thorpe Norfk 50 E5
Burnhead D & G 74 G6
Burnhervie Abers 105 L12
Burnhill Green Staffs 45 S13
Burnhope Dur 69 Q3
Burnhouse N Ayrs 81 M2
Burniston N York 71 T14
Burnley Lancs 62 G13
Burnmouth Border 85 P6
Burn Naze Lancs 61 Q11
Burn of Cambus Stirlg 89 R5
Burnopfield Dur 69 Q1
Burnrigg Cumb 67 Q1
Burnsall N York 63 L7
Burnside Angus 98 G12
Burnside Angus 98 J13
Burnside Fife 90 J10
Burnside Moray 103 U2
Burnside of Duntrune Angus 91 P5
Burntcommon Surrey 20 H12
Burntheath Derbys 46 H7
Burnt Heath Essex 23 Q2
Burnt Hill W Berk 19 S6
Burnthouse Cnwll 2 K9
Burnt Houses Dur 69 P8
Burntisland Fife 83 P1
Burnt Oak E Susx 11 S5
Burnton E Ayrs 81 P11
Burntwood Flints 54 G14
Burntwood Staffs 46 E12
Burntwood Green Staffs 46 E12
Burnt Yates N York 63 R7
Burnworthy Somset 16 G13
Burpham Surrey 20 H12
Burpham W Susx 10 G9
Burradon N Tyne 77 R11
Burradon Nthumb 76 K4
Burrafirth Shet 106 w2
Burras Cnwll 2 H10
Burraton Cnwll 5 L7
Burravoe Shet 106 v5
Burray Village Ork 106 t20
Burrells W & F 68 E9
Burrelton P & K 90 K4
Burridge Devon 6 K3
Burridge Devon 15 N5
Burridge Hants 9 Q6
Burrill N York 63 Q2
Burringham N Linc 58 D5
Burrington Devon 15 P9
Burrington Herefs 34 K6
Burrington N Som 17 N5
Burrough End Cambs 39 T9
Burrough Green Cambs 39 T9
Burrough on the Hill Leics 47 U11
Burrow Lancs 62 C5
Burrow Somset 16 B8
Burrow Bridge Somset 17 L10
Burrowhill Surrey 20 G10
Burrows Cross Surrey 20 J13
Burry Swans 25 S12
Burry Green Swans 25 S12

Burry Port Carmth 25 R10
Burscough Lancs 54 K4
Burscough Bridge Lancs 54 K4
Bursea E R Yk 64 J13
Burshill E R Yk 65 P10
Bursledon Hants 9 P7
Burslem C Stke 45 U4
Burstall Suffk 40 J12
Burstock Dorset 7 M4
Burston Norfk 40 K6
Burston Staffs 46 B7
Burstow Surrey 11 N2
Burstwick E R Yk 65 S14
Burtersett N York 62 H2
Burtholme Cumb 76 A13
Burthorpe Green Suffk 40 U8
Burthwaite Cumb 67 P3
Burthy Cnwll 3 N5
Burtle Somset 17 L8
Burtle Hill Somset 17 L8
Burtoft Lincs 49 L6
Burton BCP 8 H10
Burton Ches W 54 H12
Burton Ches W 55 M14
Burton Dorset 7 S6
Burton Nthumb 85 T12
Burton Pembks 24 G8
Burton Somset 7 P2
Burton Somset 16 G8
Burton Wilts 17 V10
Burton Wilts 18 B5
Burton Agnes E R Yk 65 Q7
Burton Bradstock Dorset 7 N7
Burton-by-Lincoln Lincs 58 F12
Burton Coggles Lincs 48 E9
Burton Dassett Warwks 37 L10
Burton End Essex 22 D3
Burton End Suffk 39 U11
Burton Fleming E R Yk 65 P5
Burton Green Warwks 36 J5
Burton Green Wrexhm 44 H2
Burton Hastings Warwks 37 M3
Burton Hill Wilts 28 H10
Burton-in-Kendal W & F 61 U4
  Services W & F 61 U4
Burton in Lonsdale N York 62 D5
Burton Joyce Notts 47 R5
Burton Latimer Nhts 38 D6
Burton Lazars Leics 47 U10
Burton Leonard N York 63 S7
Burton on the Wolds Leics 47 S9
Burton Overy Leics 47 S14
Burton Pedwardine Lincs 48 H5
Burton Pidsea E R Yk 65 S13
Burton Salmon N York 57 Q1
Burton's Green Essex 22 K2
Burton upon Stather N Linc 58 E3
Burton upon Trent Staffs 46 H9
Burton Waters Lincs 58 F12
Burtonwood Warrtn 55 N8
Burtonwood Services Warrtn 55 N8
Burwardsley Ches W 45 M2
Burwarton Shrops 35 P3
Burwash E Susx 12 C11
Burwash Common E Susx 11 U6
Burwash Weald E Susx 11 U6
Burwell Cambs 39 S7
Burwell Lincs 59 Q11
Burwen IoA 52 F4
Burwick Ork 106 t21
Bury Bury 55 T4
Bury Cambs 39 L4
Bury Somset 16 B11
Bury W Susx 10 G8
Bury End C Beds 31 P5
Bury Green Herts 22 C3
Bury St Edmunds Suffk 40 H7
Burythorpe N York 64 H7
Busby E Rens 89 R1
Busby Stoop N York 63 T3
Buscot Oxon 29 P8
Bush Abers 99 P10
Bush Cnwll 14 F11
Bush Bank Herefs 35 L10
Bushbury Wolves 46 B13
Bushby Leics 47 S13
Bushey Herts 20 K3
Bushey Heath Herts 20 K4
Bush Green Norfk 41 L3
Bush Green Suffk 40 F9
Bush Hill Park Gt Lon 21 P3
Bushley Worcs 35 U13
Bushley Green Worcs 35 U14
Bushmead Bed 38 J8
Bushmoor Shrops 34 K3
Bushton Wilts 18 G5
Bushy Common Norfk 50 F11
Busk Cumb 68 E7
Buslingthorpe Lincs 58 J9
Bussage Gloucs 28 G7
Bussex Somset 17 L9
Butcher's Cross E Susx 11 T5
Butcombe N Som 17 P4
Bute Ag & B 88 B12
Butleigh Somset 17 P9
Butleigh Wootton Somset 17 P9
Butler's Cross Bucks 30 H11
Butler's Hill Notts 47 P4
Butlers Marston Warwks 36 K10
Butley Suffk 41 R10
Butley High Corner Suffk 41 Q11
Buttercrambe N York 64 G8
Butterdean Border 84 K6
Butterknowle Dur 69 P7
Butterleigh Devon 6 B3
Butterley Derbys 47 M3
Buttermere Cumb 66 J9
Buttermere Wilts 19 M8
Buttershaw C Brad 63 N13
Butterstone P & K 90 G2
Butterton Staffs 45 T5
Butterton Staffs 46 D2
Butterwick Dur 70 E6
Butterwick Lincs 49 N4
Butterwick N York 64 G4
Butterwick N York 65 M5
Butt Green Ches E 45 Q3
Buttington Powys 44 F12
Buttonbridge Shrops 35 S5
Buttonoak Shrops 35 S5
Buttsash Hants 9 N7
Buttsbear Cross Cnwll 14 G12
Butt's Green Essex 22 J7
Buxhall Suffk 40 H9
Buxhall Fen Street Suffk 40 H9
Buxted E Susx 11 R5
Buxton Derbys 56 F12
Buxton Norfk 51 M9
Buxton Heath Norfk 50 K9
Bwlch Powys 27 M3
Bwlchgwyn Wrexhm 44 G3
Bwlchllan Cerdgn 33 L9
Bwlchnewydd Carmth 25 Q6
Bwlchtocyn Gwynd 42 F8
Bwlch-y-cibau Powys 44 E10
Bwlch-y-Ddar Powys 44 E8
Bwlch-y-ffrid Powys 34 B2
Bwlch-y-groes Pembks 25 M4
Bwlchymyrdd Swans 25 U11
Bwlch-y-sarnau Powys 34 B6
Byermoor Gatesd 69 Q1
Byers Green Dur 69 R6
Byfield Nhts 37 P10
Byfleet Surrey 20 J10
Byford Herefs 34 J12
Bygrave Herts 31 S5
Byker N u Ty 77 R13
Byland Abbey N York 64 C4
Bylaugh Norfk 50 H10
Byley Ches W 55 R13
Bynea Carmth 25 T11
Byram N York 57 Q1
Byrness Nthumb 76 F5
Bystock Devon 6 E8
Bythorn Cambs 38 G5
Byton Herefs 34 J8
Bywell Nthumb 77 L13
Byworth W Susx 10 F6

C

Cabbacott Devon 14 K8
Cabourne Lincs 58 K6
Cabrach Ag & B 78 H3
Cabrach Moray 104 D10
Cabus Lancs 61 T10
Cackle Street E Susx 11 R5
Cackle Street E Susx 12 C12
Cackle Street E Susx 12 F12
Cadbury Devon 6 B3
Cadbury Barton Devon 15 Q9
Cadbury World Birm 36 Q4
Cadder E Duns 89 P11
Caddington C Beds 31 N9
Caddonfoot Border 84 C11
Cade Devon 57 N6
Cadeby Donc 57 R6
Cadeby Leics 47 M13
Cadeleigh Devon 6 B3
Cade Street E Susx 11 U6
Cadgwith Cnwll 2 J14
Cadham Fife 91 L11
Cadishead Salfd 55 R8
Cadle Swans 25 V11
Cadley Lancs 61 U13
Cadley Wilts 18 K10
Cadley Wilts 18 K7
Cadmore End Bucks 20 C4
Cadnam Hants 9 L6
Cadney N Linc 58 H6
Cadole Flints 54 F14
Cadoxton V Glam 16 F3
Cadoxton Juxta-Neath Neath 26 D8
Cadwst Derbys 44 B6
Caeathro Gwynd 52 H10
Caehopkin Powys 26 E5
Caenby Lincs 58 G9
Caerau Brdgnd 26 F9
Caerau Cardif 27 L12
Cae'r-bont Powys 26 E5
Cae'r bryn Carmth 25 U8
Caerdeon Gwynd 43 N10
Caer Farchell Pembks 24 C5
Caergeiliog IoA 52 D7
Caergwrle Flints 44 H2
Caerhowel Powys 44 F14
Caerhun Conwy 53 N8
Caerlanrig Border 75 S5
Caerleon Newpt 27 Q10
Caerloggas Cnwll 43 Q9
Caernarfon Gwynd 52 G10
Caernarfon Castle Gwynd 52 G10
Caerphilly Caerph 27 M10
Caersws Powys 34 B2
Caerwedros Cerdgn 32 G9
Caerwent Mons 27 T9
Caerwys Flints 54 D12
Caerynwch Gwynd 43 Q10
Caggle Street Mons 27 R4
Caim IoA 52 K6
Caio Carmth 33 N13
Cairinis W Isls 106 d12
Cairnbaan Ag & B 87 Q7
Cairnbulg Abers 105 T2
Cairncross Border 85 M6
Cairncurran Inver 88 H11
Cairndow Ag & B 88 E3
Cairngorms National Park 97 T3
Cairnie Abers 104 F7
Cairn Lodge Services S Lans 82 G12
Cairnorrie Abers 105 P7
Cairnryan D & G 72 D6
Cairnty Moray 104 C5
Caister-on-Sea Norfk 51 T11
Caistor Lincs 58 K6
Caistor St Edmund Norfk 51 M13
Caistron Nthumb 76 K6
Cakebole Worcs 35 U6
Cake Street Norfk 40 J2
Calais Street Suffk 40 G13
Calanais W Isls 106 h5
Calbourne IoW 9 N11
Calceby Lincs 59 Q11
Calcoed Flints 54 E12
Calcot Gloucs 29 L5
Calcot W Berk 19 U6
Calcot Row W Berk 19 U6
Calcots Moray 104 B3
Calcott Kent 13 N3
Calcutt N York 63 S8
Calcutt Wilts 18 H8
Calcutts Wrekin 29 M9
Caldback Cumb 67 N2
Caldbeck Cumb 67 N4
Caldbergh N York 63 L2
Caldecote Cambs 38 J4
Caldecote Cambs 39 M9
Caldecote Herts 31 R5
Caldecote N Nthn 38 C10
Caldecote Rutlnd 38 E2
Caldecote M Keyn 30 J5
Caldecott Nhts 38 E7
Caldecott Oxon 29 U8
Caldecott Rutlnd 38 C2
Calder Cumb 66 F11
Calderbank N Lans 82 E6
Calder Bridge Cumb 66 F11
Calderbrook Rochdl 56 D3
Caldercruix N Lans 82 F5
Calder Grove Wakefd 57 M3
Caldermill S Lans 81 T4
Caldermore Rochdl 56 D3
Calder Vale Lancs 61 U11
Calderwood S Lans 81 T1
Caldey Island Pembks 24 K11
Caldicot Mons 27 T10
Caldwell N York 69 Q10
Caldwell Derbys 46 H10
Caldy Wirral 54 F9
Calenick Cnwll 3 L8
Calf of Man IoM 60 b9
Calford Green Suffk 40 B11
Calfsound Ork 106 u16
Calgary Ag & B 92 K8
Califer Moray 103 Q4
California Falk 82 H3
California Norfk 51 T10
California Cross Devon 5 S10
Calke Derbys 47 L9
Calke Abbey Derbys 47 L9
Callakille Highld 107 L13
Callaly Nthumb 89 P4
Callanish W Isls 106 h5
Callaughton Shrops 45 P13
Callerton N u Ty 77 P12
Callestick Cnwll 3 L6
Calligarry Highld 100 f9
Callington Cnwll 4 K6
Callingwood Staffs 46 G9
Callow Herefs 35 L14
Callow End Worcs 35 T11
Callow Hill Wilts 28 K4
Callow Hill Worcs 35 K11
Callow Hill Worcs 36 B6
Callows Grave Worcs 35 N7
Calmore Hants 9 L6
Calmsden Gloucs 28 K6
Calne Wilts 18 E6
Calow Derbys 57 P12
Calshot Hants 9 P8
Calstock Cnwll 5 L7
Calstone Wellington Wilts 18 F7
Calthorpe Norfk 51 L7
Calthorpe Street Norfk 51 R7
Calthwaite W & F 67 Q4
Calton N York 62 J9
Calton Staffs 46 F3
Calveley Ches E 45 N2
Calver Derbys 56 K12
Calver Hill Herefs 34 J11
Calverleigh Devon 6 B2
Calverley Leeds 63 Q12
Calvert Bucks 30 E7
Calverton M Keyn 30 G5
Calverton Notts 47 R4
Calvine P & K 97 P11
Calvo Cumb 66 H2
Calzeat Border 83 M11
Cam Gloucs 28 D8
Camasachoirce Highld 93 T6
Camasine Highld 93 T6
Camas Luinie Highld 101 N6
Camastianavaig Highld 100 d6
Camault Muir Highld 102 F7
Camber E Susx 12 H12
Camberley Surrey 20 E10
Camberwell Gt Lon 21 P7
Camblesforth N York 57 S13
Cambo Nthumb 77 L9
Cambois Nthumb 77 S9
Camborne Cnwll 2 G8
Camborne & Redruth Mining District Cnwll 2 G8
Cambourne Cambs 39 M9
Cambridge Cambs 39 P9
Cambridge Gloucs 28 D7
Cambridge Airport Cambs 39 Q9
Cambus Clacks 90 C13
Cambusavie Highld 109 P5
Cambusbarron Stirlg 89 S7
Cambuskenneth Stirlg 90 B13
Cambuslang S Lans 89 Q13
Cambus o' May Abers 98 J4
Cambuswallace S Lans 82 K11
Camden Town Gt Lon 21 N6
Cameley BaNES 17 R5
Camelford Cnwll 4 E4
Camelon Falk 82 H2
Camelot Theme Park Lancs 55 M2
Camer's Green Worcs 35 R13
Camerory Highld 103 R9
Cample D & G 74 G7
Campmuir P & K 90 K4
Camps W Loth 83 L5
Campsall Donc 57 R4
Campsea Ash Suffk 41 P9
Camps End Cambs 39 T12
Campton C Beds 31 P5
Camptown Border 76 D3
Camrose Pembks 24 F6
Camserney P & K 90 E14
Camusnagaul Highld 94 F4
Camusnagaul Highld 107 U5
Camusteel Highld 100 g5
Camusterrach Highld 100 g5
Canada Hants 8 K4
Canal Foot W & F 61 Q4
Canaston Bridge Pembks 24 J7
Candacraig Abers 98 E4
Candlesby Lincs 59 S13
Candle Street Suffk 40 H6
Candover Green Shrops 45 M12
Candy Mill Border 83 L10
Cane End Oxon 19 U5
Canewdon Essex 23 M9
Canford Bottom Dorset 8 E8
Canford Cliffs BCP 8 E11
Canford Heath BCP 8 E10
Canford Magna BCP 8 E9
Canhams Green Suffk 40 J7
Canisbay Highld 112 H2
Canklow Rothm 57 P8
Canley Covtry 36 K5
Canna Highld 100 b9
Cann Common Dorset 8 B4
Cannich Highld 102 D9
Cannington Somset 16 J9
Canning Town Gt Lon 21 R6
Cannock Staffs 46 C11
Cannock Chase Staffs 46 C10
Cannock Wood Staffs 46 D11
Cannon Bridge Herefs 34 K12
Canon Frome Herefs 35 P12
Canon Pyon Herefs 35 L11
Canons Ashby W Nthn 37 Q10
Canonstown Cnwll 2 F9
Canterbury Kent 13 M4
Canterbury Cathedral Kent 13 N4
Cantley Norfk 51 Q13
Cantlop Shrops 45 M12
Canton Cardif 27 M12
Cantraywood Highld 103 L6
Cantsfield Lancs 62 C5
Canvey Island Essex 22 J11
Canwick Lincs 58 G13
Canworthy Water Cnwll 4 G2
Caol Highld 94 G3
Caolas Scalpaigh W Isls 106 h9
Caoles Ag & B 92 D9
Caonich Highld 101 R13
Capel Kent 12 B7
Capel Surrey 10 K2
Capel Bangor Cerdgn 33 N4
Capel Betws Lleucu Cerdgn 33 M9
Capel Coch IoA 52 G6
Capel Curig Conwy 53 M11
Capel Cynon Cerdgn 32 G11
Capel Dewi Carmth 25 S6
Capel Dewi Cerdgn 32 J12
Capel-Dewi Cerdgn 33 M4
Capel Garmon Conwy 53 N11
Capel Green Suffk 41 P11
Capel Gwyn Carmth 25 S6
Capel Gwyn IoA 52 D7
Capel Gwynfe Carmth 26 C3
Capel Hendre Carmth 25 U8
Capel Isaac Carmth 25 U5
Capel Iwan Carmth 25 N3
Capel-le-Ferne Kent 13 Q8
Capelles Guern 6 d2
Capel Llanilltern Cardif 27 M14
Capel Mawr IoA 52 F8
Capel Parc IoA 52 F5
Capel St Andrew Suffk 41 Q11
Capel St Mary Suffk 40 J13
Capel Seion Cerdgn 33 M5
Capel Trisant Cerdgn 33 P5
Capeluchaf Gwynd 42 H4
Capelulo Conwy 53 M7
Capel-y-ffin Powys 27 N1
Capel-y-graig Gwynd 52 H9
Capenhurst Ches W 54 J12
Capernwray Lancs 61 U5
Cape Wrath Highld 110 F1
Capheaton Nthumb 77 L9
Caplaw E Rens 88 D5
Capon's Green Suffk 41 N7
Cappercleuch Border 83 P14
Capstone Medway 12 E2
Capton Devon 5 U10
Capton W & F 90 G3
Caradon Mining District Cnwll 4 H6
Caradon Town Cnwll 4 H6
Carbeth Stirlg 89 N10
Carbis Cnwll 3 Q5
Carbis Bay Cnwll 2 E9
Carbost Highld 100 c6
Carbost Highld 100 d5
Carbrook Sheff 57 N9
Carbrooke Norfk 50 G13
Carburton Notts 57 T12
Carclaze Cnwll 3 Q6
Car Colston Notts 47 T5
Carcroft Donc 57 R4
Cardenden Fife 91 K12
Cardeston Shrops 44 J11
Cardewlees Cumb 67 N2
Cardhu Moray 104 B7
Cardiff Cardif 27 M12
Cardiff Airport V Glam 16 E3
Cardiff Gate Services Cardif 27 N11
Cardiff West Services Cardif 26 K12
Cardigan Cerdgn 32 C11
Cardinal's Green Cambs 39 T11
Cardington Bed 38 G11
Cardington Shrops 45 M13
Cardinham Cnwll 4 F7
Cardrain D & G 72 E13
Cardrona Border 83 R11
Cardross Ag & B 88 H10
Cardryne D & G 72 D13
Cardurnock Cumb 75 N14
Careby Lincs 48 F10
Careston Angus 98 J11
Carew Pembks 24 H10
Carew Cheriton Pembks 24 H10
Carew Newton Pembks 24 H10
Carey Herefs 35 N13
Carfin N Lans 82 E7
Carfraemill Border 84 D8
Cargate Green Norfk 51 Q11
Cargenbridge D & G 74 J11
Cargill P & K 90 J4
Cargo Cumb 75 S14
Cargreen Cnwll 5 L8
Cargurrel Cnwll 3 M9
Carham Nthumb 85 M12
Carhampton Somset 16 D8
Carharrack Cnwll 2 J8
Carie P & K 95 V8
Carinish W Isls 106 d12
Carisbrooke IoW 9 P11
Cark W & F 61 R4
Carkeel Cnwll 5 L8
Càrlabhagh W Isls 106 h4
Carland Cross Cnwll 3 M6
Carlbury N York 69 R9
Carlby Lincs 48 G11
Carlcroft Nthumb 76 G3
Carlton Notts 47 R5
Carlton S on T 70 D8
Carlton Suffk 41 Q8
Carlton Colville Suffk 41 T3
Carlton Curlieu Leics 37 S1
Carlton Green Cambs 39 T10
Carlton Husthwaite N York 64 B4
Carlton-in-Cleveland N York 70 H12
Carlton in Lindrick Notts 57 S10
Carlton-le-Moorland Lincs 48 D2
Carlton Miniott N York 63 T3
Carlton-on-Trent Notts 58 C14
Carlton Scroop Lincs 48 D4
Carluke S Lans 82 F8
Carlyon Bay Cnwll 3 R6
Carmacoup S Lans 82 G12
Carmarthen Carmth 25 R6
Carmel Carmth 25 U7
Carmel Flints 54 E11
Carmel Gwynd 52 G12
Carmel Green Ag & B 82 H11
Carmunnock C Glas 89 Q13
Carmyle C Glas 89 P13
Carmyllie Angus 91 R3
Carnaby E R Yk 65 Q6
Carnbee Fife 91 R10
Carnbo P & K 90 G11
Carn Brea Cnwll 2 H8
Carnbrogie Abers 105 P10
Candu Highld 101 M6
Carnduff S Lans 81 T2
Carne Cnwll 2 J10
Carne Cnwll 3 N10
Carnell E Ayrs 81 P6
Carnewas Cnwll 3 M3
Carnforth Lancs 61 T5
Carn-gorm Highld 101 N7
Carnhedryn Pembks 24 D5
Carnhell Green Cnwll 2 G9
Carnie Abers 99 Q2
Carnkie Cnwll 2 H9
Carnkie Cnwll 2 H8
Carnkief Cnwll 2 K6
Carno Powys 33 U1
Carnock Fife 90 F14
Carnon Downs Cnwll 2 K8
Carnousie Abers 104 K5
Carnoustie Angus 91 S5
Carnsmerry Cnwll 3 Q5
Carnwath S Lans 82 J9
Carnyorth Cnwll 2 B10
Carol Green Solhll 36 J5
Carperby N York 63 L2
Carpalla Cnwll 3 P6
Carr Rothm 57 R8
Carradale Ag & B 79 Q8
Carradale Village Ag & B 79 P8
Carrbridge Highld 103 P10
Carr Gate Wakefd 57 M2
Carrhouse N Linc 58 C5
Carrick Ag & B 88 B6
Carrick Castle Ag & B 88 F6
Carriden Falk 82 K2
Carrington Mdloth 83 R6
Carrington Lincs 49 N2
Carrington Traffd 55 R8
Carrog Denbgs 44 D5
Carron Falk 82 H2
Carron Moray 104 B8
Carronbridge D & G 74 G6
Carron Bridge Stirlg 89 R9
Carronshore Falk 82 H2
Carrow Hill Mons 27 S9
Carr Shield Nthumb 68 H3
Carruth House Inver 88 H12
Carrutherstown D & G 75 M11
Carr Vale Derbys 57 Q13
Carrville Dur 70 D4
Carsaig Ag & B 86 J1
Carseriggan D & G 72 J6
Carsethorn D & G 74 J14
Carshalton Gt Lon 21 N10
Carsington Derbys 46 J3
Carskey Ag & B 79 M15
Carsluith D & G 73 N8
Carsphairn D & G 73 R3
Carstairs S Lans 82 H9
Carstairs Junction S Lans 82 J9
Carswell Marsh Oxon 29 R8
Carter's Clay Hants 9 L4
Carters Green Essex 22 D5
Carterton Oxon 29 Q6
Carterway Heads Nthumb 69 M2
Carthew Cnwll 3 Q5
Carthorpe N York 63 S3
Cartington Nthumb 77 L5
Cartland S Lans 82 G10
Cartledge Derbys 57 M11
Cartmel W & F 61 R4
Cartmel Fell W & F 61 R2
Carway Carmth 25 S9
Carwinley Cumb 75 T11
Cashe's Green Gloucs 28 F6
Cashmoor Dorset 8 D6
Cassington Oxon 29 U5
Cassop Dur 70 D5
Castallack Cnwll 2 C11
Castel Guern 6 d3
Castel-y-bwch Torfn 27 P9
Casterton W & F 62 C4
Castle Cnwll 3 Q9
Castle Acre Norfk 50 D11
Castle Ashby W Nthn 38 C9
Castlebay W Isls 106 b19
Castle Bolton N York 63 L1
Castle Bromwich Solhll 36 F3
Castle Bytham Lincs 48 F10
Castlebythe Pembks 24 H5
Castle Caereinion Powys 44 E12
Castle Camps Cambs 39 T12
Castle Carrock Cumb 67 R1
Castlecary Falk 89 S10
Castle Cary Somset 17 R10
Castle Combe Wilts 18 B5
Castlecraig Highld 109 R11
Castle Donington Leics 47 M8
Castle Douglas D & G 74 E13
Castle Eaton Swindn 29 M8
Castle Eden Dur 70 F5
Castle End C Pete 48 H14
Castleford Wakefd 57 P1
Castle Frome Herefs 35 Q11
Castle Gate Cnwll 2 D10
Castle Green Cumb 61 U2
Castle Green Surrey 20 G10
Castle Gresley Derbys 46 J10
Castle Hedingham Essex 40 C13
Castlehill Border 83 N11
Castle Hill Kent 12 C7
Castle Hill Suffk 40 K12
Castlehill W Duns 88 J10
Castle Howard N York 64 G5
Castle Kennedy D & G 72 E8
Castle Lachlan Ag & B 87 U6
Castlemartin Pembks 24 E11
Castlemilk C Glas 89 Q14
Castle Morris Pembks 24 F4
Castlemorton Common Worcs 35 S13
Castle O'er D & G 75 R8
Castle Rising Norfk 49 U9
Castleside Dur 69 N3
Castle Stuart Highld 102 K6
Castlethorpe M Keyn 30 H4
Castlethorpe N Linc 58 F5
Castleton Ag & B 87 Q9
Castleton Derbys 56 J10
Castleton N York 71 L11
Castleton Newpt 27 P11
Castleton Rochdl 56 C4
Castletown Ches W 45 L2
Castletown Dorset 7 S10
Castletown Highld 112 E3
Castletown IoM 60 d9
Castletown Sundld 77 T14
Castletown ToM 60 d9
Castley N York 63 R11
Caston Norfk 40 G1
Castor C Pete 48 H14
Caswell Bay Swans 25 U13
Catacol N Ayrs 79 S6
Catbrook Mons 27 U7
Catchall Cnwll 2 C11
Catchem's Corner Solhll 36 J5
Catchgate Dur 69 Q2
Catcliffe Rothm 57 P9
Catcomb Wilts 18 E5
Catcott Somset 17 L9
Caterham Surrey 21 P11
Catfield Norfk 51 Q9
Catfirth Shet 106 u8
Catford Gt Lon 21 Q8
Catforth Lancs 61 T12
Cathcart C Glas 89 N13
Cathedine Powys 27 L2
Catherine-de-Barnes Solhll 36 G4
Catherine Slack C Brad 63 M14
Catherington Hants 9 T6
Catherston Leweston Dorset 7 L6
Catherton Shrops 35 Q5
Catisfield Hants 9 R7
Catlodge Highld 96 J5
Catlow Lancs 62 H12
Catlowdy Cumb 75 U10
Catmere End Essex 39 R13
Catmore W Berk 19 Q4
Caton Devon 5 T6
Caton Lancs 61 U7
Caton Green Lancs 62 B6
Cator Court Devon 5 R4
Catrine E Ayrs 81 R7
Cat's Ash Newpt 27 R9
Catsfield E Susx 12 D13
Catsfield Stream E Susx 12 D13
Catsgore Somset 17 P11
Catsham Somset 17 Q10
Catshill Worcs 36 B6
Cattadale Ag & B 79 M13
Cattal N York 63 U9
Cattawade Suffk 40 K14
Catterall Lancs 61 T11
Catteralslane Shrops 45 N5
Catterick N York 69 R13
Catterick Bridge N York 69 R13
Catterick Garrison N York 69 Q13
Catterlen Cumb 67 Q6
Catterline Abers 99 R8
Catterton N York 64 C10
Catteshall Surrey 10 F2
Catthorpe Leics 37 Q5
Cattistock Dorset 7 Q5
Catton N York 63 U4
Catton Nthumb 76 G14
Catwick E R Yk 65 R11
Catworth Cambs 38 G6
Caudle Green Gloucs 28 H5
Caulcott C Beds 31 N4
Caulcott Oxon 30 B8
Cauldhame Stirlg 89 P7
Cauldmill Border 76 B2
Cauldon Staffs 46 E4
Cauldon Lowe Staffs 46 E4
Caulkerbush D & G 66 E1
Caulside D & G 75 T9
Caundle Marsh Dorset 7 S2
Caunsall Worcs 35 U4
Caunton Notts 47 U1
Causeway Hants 9 V4
Causeway End D & G 73 L7
Causeway End Essex 22 G4
Causewayend S Lans 82 K11
Causeway End W & F 61 U3
Causewayhead Cumb 66 H2
Causewayhead Stirlg 89 S7
Causey Park Bridge Nthumb 77 P7
Cavendish Suffk 40 D11
Cavenham Suffk 40 C6
Caversfield Oxon 30 C7
Caversham Readg 20 B8
Caverswall Staffs 46 C5
Caverton Mill Border 84 J13
Cavil E R Yk 64 F13
Cawdor Highld 103 M5
Cawkwell Lincs 59 N11
Cawood N York 64 D12
Cawsand Cnwll 5 L10
Cawston Norfk 50 K9
Cawston Warwks 37 N6
Cawthorne Barns 57 L5
Cawthorpe Lincs 48 G9
Caxton Cambs 39 M9
Caxton End Cambs 39 M9
Caxton Gibbet Cambs 39 L8
Caynham Shrops 35 N6
Caythorpe Lincs 48 D4
Caythorpe Notts 47 S4
Cayton N York 65 P3
Ceann a Bhaigh W Isls 106 c12
Ceannacroc Lodge Highld 101 U9
Cearsiadar W Isls 106 j6
Ceciliford Mons 27 U7
Cefn Newpt 27 Q10
Cefn Berain Conwy 53 S9
Cefn-brith Conwy 53 T11
Cefn-bryn-brain Carmth 26 C5
Cefn Byrle Powys 26 F5
Cefn Canel Powys 44 F8
Cefn-coed-y-cymmer Myr Td 26 J6
Cefn Cribwr Brdgnd 26 F11
Cefn Cross Brdgnd 26 F11
Cefn-ddwysarn Gwynd 43 U6
Cefn-Einion Shrops 34 G3
Cefneithin Carmth 25 U8
Cefngorwydd Powys 33 T11
Cefn-mawr Wrexhm 44 G5
Cefn-y-bedd Flints 44 H2
Cefn-y-pant Carmth 25 L5
Ceint IoA 52 G7
Cellan Cerdgn 33 M11
Cellardyke Fife 91 S11
Cellarhead Staffs 46 C4
Celleron W & F 67 R7
Celynen Caerph 27 P7
Cemaes IoA 52 E4
Cemmaes Powys 43 R12
Cemmaes Road Powys 43 R12
Cenarth Carmth 25 N3
Cerbyd Pembks 24 D5
Ceres Fife 91 P9
Cerne Abbas Dorset 7 R4
Cerney Wick Gloucs 28 K8
Cerrigceinwen IoA 52 F8
Cerrigydrudion Conwy 43 U3
Ceunant Gwynd 52 H10
Chaceley Gloucs 35 U14
Chacewater Cnwll 2 K8
Chackmore Bucks 30 E5
Chacombe W Nthn 37 N12
Chadbury Worcs 36 D11
Chadderton Oldham 56 D6
Chadderton Fold Oldham 56 C5
Chaddesden C Derb 47 L6
Chaddesley Corbett Worcs 35 U5
Chaddlehanger Devon 5 M5
Chaddleworth W Berk 19 Q5
Chadlington Oxon 29 R3
Chadshunt Warwks 37 L10
Chadwell Leics 47 U9
Chadwell Shrops 45 S11
Chadwell End Bed 38 G7
Chadwell Heath Gt Lon 21 S5
Chadwell St Mary Thurr 22 F12
Chadwick Worcs 35 T7
Chadwick End Solhll 36 H5
Chadwick Green St Hel 55 M7
Chaffcombe Somset 7 K2
Chafford Hundred Thurr 22 F12
Chagford Devon 5 S3
Chailey E Susx 11 P7
Chainbridge Cambs 49 Q13
Chainhurst Kent 12 D6
Chalbury Dorset 8 E7
Chalbury Common Dorset 8 E7
Chaldon Surrey 21 P11
Chaldon Herring Dorset 7 U8
Chale IoW 9 N13
Chale Green IoW 9 N13
Chalfont Common Bucks 20 H4
Chalfont St Giles Bucks 20 H4
Chalfont St Peter Bucks 20 H4
Chalford Gloucs 28 G7
Chalford Wilts 18 B10
Chalford Oxon 30 D12
Chalgrave C Beds 31 M7
Chalgrove Oxon 19 U2
Chalk Kent 22 G13
Chalkhouse Green Oxon 20 B7
Chalkway Somset 7 L3
Chalkwell Kent 12 G3
Challaborough Devon 5 R11
Challacombe Devon 15 Q4
Challock Kent 12 K5
Chalmington Dorset 7 Q4
Chalton C Beds 31 N8
Chalton C Beds 31 P4
Chalton Hants 9 U5
Chalvey Slough 20 G7
Chalvington E Susx 11 S8
Chambers Green Kent 12 J6
Chandler's Cross Herts 20 J3
Chandlers Cross Worcs 35 S13
Chandler's Ford Hants 9 N4
Channel's End Bed 38 H9
Channel Tunnel Terminal Kent 13 N8
Chantry Somset 17 T7
Chantry Suffk 40 K12
Chapel Fife 91 L13
Chapel Allerton Leeds 63 S12
Chapel Allerton Somset 17 M7
Chapel Amble Cnwll 3 P1
Chapel Brampton W Nthn 37 T7
Chapelbridge Cambs 39 L2
Chapel Chorlton Staffs 45 U6
Chapel Cross E Susx 11 U6
Chapel End Bed 38 H9
Chapel End C Beds 31 N4
Chapel End Cambs 38 K5
Chapel End Warwks 36 K2
Chapel-en-le-Frith Derbys 56 G10
Chapelgate Lincs 49 P9
Chapel Green Warwks 36 J3
Chapel Green Warwks 37 N8
Chapel Haddlesey N York 57 S2
Chapel Hill Abers 105 T8
Chapel Hill Lincs 48 K2
Chapel Hill Mons 27 U7
Chapel Hill N York 63 S11
Chapelhope Border 75 Q2
Chapelknowe D & G 75 R11
Chapel Lawn Shrops 34 H5
Chapel-le-Dale N York 62 F4
Chapel Leigh Somset 16 F11
Chapel Milton Derbys 56 G10
Chapel of Garioch Abers 105 L11
Chapel Rossan D & G 72 E10
Chapel Row E Susx 11 U8
Chapel Row W Berk 19 S7
Chapel Row Essex 22 J7
Chapels W & F 61 N3
Chapel St Leonards Lincs 59 U12
Chapel Stile W & F 67 L12
Chapelton Abers 99 R5
Chapelton Angus 91 S3
Chapelton Devon 15 N7
Chapelton S Lans 81 T2
Chapeltown Bl w D 55 R4
Chapeltown Moray 104 A12
Chapeltown Sheff 57 N8
Chapmanslade Wilts 18 B11
Chapmans Well Devon 4 K2
Chapmore End Herts 31 U10
Chappel Essex 23 L2
Charaton Cnwll 4 J7
Chard Somset 7 L3
Chard Junction Somset 7 L3
Chardleigh Green Somset 6 K2
Chardstock Devon 6 K3
Charfield S Glos 28 D9
Chargrove Gloucs 28 H4
Charing Kent 12 J6
Charing Heath Kent 12 H6
Charing Hill Kent 12 K5
Charingworth Gloucs 36 H13
Charlbury Oxon 29 S4
Charlcombe BaNES 17 T3
Charlcutt Wilts 18 E5
Charlecote Warwks 36 J9
Charlemont Sandw 36 D2
Charles Devon 15 Q6
Charles Tye Suffk 40 H10
Charleshill Surrey 10 E2
Charleston Angus 91 L2
Charlestown C Aber 99 S3
Charlestown C Brad 63 P13
Charlestown Calder 56 E1
Charlestown Cnwll 3 R6
Charlestown Derbys 56 F8
Charlestown Dorset 7 S9
Charlestown Fife 90 E14
Charlestown Highld 102 K5
Charlestown Highld 107 P7
Charlestown Salfd 55 T6
Charlestown of Aberlour Moray 104 B7
Charles Wood Cnwll 2 J8
Charlesworth Derbys 56 F8
Charlinch Somset 16 H9
Charlottetown Fife 91 L9
Charlton Gt Lon 21 R7
Charlton Hants 19 N11
Charlton Herts 31 Q7
Charlton Nthumb 76 H9
Charlton Oxon 29 U9
Charlton Somset 17 R6
Charlton Somset 17 S7
Charlton Somset 17 T9
Charlton Surrey 20 K9
Charlton W Susx 10 D7
Charlton Wilts 8 D3
Charlton Wilts 18 K8
Charlton Wilts 28 H10
Charlton Worcs 35 V4
Charlton Worcs 36 D11
Charlton Wrekin 45 M11
Charlton Abbots Gloucs 28 K3
Charlton Adam Somset 17 P11
Charlton All Saints Wilts 8 H3
Charlton Down Dorset 7 R5
Charlton Hill Shrops 45 N12
Charlton Horethorne Somset 17 S12
Charlton Kings Gloucs 28 J3
Charlton Mackrell Somset 17 P11
Charlton Marshall Dorset 8 C8
Charlton Musgrove Somset 17 T11
Charlton-on-Otmoor Oxon 30 C9
Charlton on the Hill Dorset 8 B8
Charlton St Peter Wilts 18 H9
Charlwood Hants 9 U3
Charlwood Surrey 11 L2
Charminster Dorset 7 R6
Charmouth Dorset 7 L6
Charndon Bucks 30 D8
Charnes Staffs 45 S7
Charney Bassett Oxon 29 S8
Charnock Green Lancs 55 N2
Charnock Richard Lancs 55 N3
Charsfield Suffk 41 N9
Chart Corner Kent 12 E5
Charter Alley Hants 19 S9
Charterhouse Somset 17 N5
Charterville Allotments Oxon 29 R5
Chartham Kent 13 M5
Chartham Hatch Kent 13 M5
Chart Hill Kent 12 E6
Chartridge Bucks 30 K12
Chart Sutton Kent 12 F6
Charvil Wokham 20 C7
Charwelton W Nthn 37 P9
Chase Cross Gt Lon 22 D9
Chase Terrace Staffs 46 D12
Chasetown Staffs 46 D12
Chastleton Oxon 29 Q2
Chasty Devon 14 J12
Chatburn Lancs 62 F11
Chatcull Staffs 45 S7
Chatham Caerph 27 M9
Chatham Medway 12 E2
Chatham Green Essex 22 H4
Chathill Nthumb 85 T13
Chatley Worcs 35 U8
Chattenden Medway 22 H13
Chatter End Essex 22 C2
Chatteris Cambs 39 N3
Chatterton Lancs 55 S3
Chattisham Suffk 40 J12
Chatto Border 84 K14
Chatton Nthumb 85 R13
Chaul End C Beds 31 N8
Chavel Shrops 44 K11
Chavey Down Br For 20 E9
Chawleigh Devon 15 R10
Chawley Oxon 29 U7
Chawston Bed 38 J9
Chawton Hants 9 V2
Chaxhill Gloucs 28 D5
Chazey Heath Oxon 19 U5
Cheadle Staffs 46 D5
Cheadle Stockp 56 C9
Cheadle Heath Stockp 56 C9
Cheadle Hulme Stockp 56 C9
Cheam Gt Lon 21 M10
Cheapside W & F 20 G9
Chearsley Bucks 30 F10
Chebsey Staffs 45 U8
Checkendon Oxon 19 U4
Checkley Ches E 45 R4
Checkley Herefs 35 N13
Checkley Staffs 46 D6
Checkley Green Ches E 45 R4
Chedburgh Suffk 40 C9
Cheddar Somset 17 M6
Cheddington Bucks 30 K9
Cheddleton Staffs 46 C3
Cheddleton Heath Staffs 46 C3
Cheddon Fitzpaine Somset 16 H11
Chedglow Wilts 28 H9
Chedgrave Norfk 51 Q14
Chedington Dorset 7 N3
Chediston Suffk 41 Q5
Chedworth Gloucs 29 L5
Chedzoy Somset 16 K9
Cheeseman's Green Kent 12 K8
Cheetham Hill Manch 55 T6
Cheldon Devon 15 R10
Chelford Ches E 55 T12
Chellaston C Derb 47 L7
Chellington Bed 38 E9
Chelmarsh Shrops 35 R3
Chelmondiston Suffk 41 M13
Chelmorton Derbys 56 H13
Chelmsford Essex 22 H6
Chelmsley Wood Solhll 36 G3
Chelsea Gt Lon 21 N7
Chelsfield Gt Lon 21 S10
Chelsham Surrey 21 Q11
Chelston Somset 16 G12
Chelsworth Suffk 40 G11
Cheltenham Gloucs 28 J3
Chelveston N Nthn 38 E7
Chelvey N Som 17 N3
Chelwood BaNES 17 R4
Chelwood Common E Susx 11 Q5
Chelwood Gate E Susx 11 Q4
Chelworth Wilts 28 J9
Chelworth Lower Green Wilts 29 L9
Chelworth Upper Green Wilts 29 L9
Cheney Longville Shrops 34 K4
Chenies Bucks 20 H3
Chepstow Mons 27 U8
Chequerbent Bolton 55 Q5
Chequers Corner Norfk 49 Q12
Cherhill Wilts 18 F6
Cherington Gloucs 28 H8
Cherington Warwks 36 J13
Cheriton Devon 15 S3
Cheriton Hants 9 S3
Cheriton Kent 13 P8
Cheriton Pembks 24 G11
Cheriton Swans 25 R12
Cheriton Bishop Devon 5 S2
Cheriton Fitzpaine Devon 15 U11
Cherrington Wrekin 45 Q10
Cherry Burton E R Yk 65 M11
Cherry Hinton Cambs 39 Q9
Cherry Orchard Worcs 35 U10
Cherry Willingham Lincs 58 H12
Chertsey Surrey 20 H9
Cherwell Valley Services Oxon 30 B7
Cheselbourne Dorset 7 U5
Chesham Bucks 31 L12
Chesham Bury 55 T4
Chesham Bois Bucks 20 H3
Chesham End Bucks 31 U12
Cheshunt Herts 31 U12
Chesil Beach Dorset 7 Q9
Chesley Kent 12 G3
Cheslyn Hay Staffs 46 B12
Chessetts Wood Warwks 36 G6
Chessington Gt Lon 21 L10
Chessington World of Adventures Gt Lon 21 L10
Chester Ches W 54 K13
Chesterblade Somset 17 S8
Chesterfield Derbys 57 N12
Chesterfield Staffs 46 F12
Chester-le-Street Dur 69 S2
Chester Moor Dur 69 S3
Chesters Border 84 G13
Chesters Border 84 G14
Chester Services Ches W 55 L12
Chesterton Cambs 38 H1
Chesterton Cambs 39 Q8
Chesterton Gloucs 28 J7
Chesterton Oxon 30 C8
Chesterton Shrops 45 S14
Chesterton Staffs 45 U4
Chesterton Green Warwks 37 L9
Chesterwood Nthumb 76 H13
Chestfield Kent 13 M2
Chestnut Street Kent 12 G3
Cheston Devon 5 R9
Cheswardine Shrops 45 R8
Cheswick Nthumb 85 R10
Cheswick Green Solhll 36 G5
Chetnole Dorset 7 R3
Chettiscombe Devon 16 C13
Chettisham Cambs 39 R3
Chettle Dorset 8 C6
Chetton Shrops 35 Q2
Chetwode Bucks 30 D7
Chetwynd Wrekin 45 S9
Chetwynd Aston Wrekin 45 S10
Cheveley Cambs 39 U8
Chevening Kent 21 S11
Cheverton IoW 9 P12
Chevington Suffk 40 C9
Chevithorne Devon 16 C13
Chew Magna BaNES 17 Q4
Chew Moor Bolton 55 Q5
Chew Stoke BaNES 17 P4
Chewton Keynsham BaNES 17 R3
Chewton Mendip Somset 17 Q6
Chichacott Devon 15 P12
Chicheley M Keyn 38 D11
Chichester W Susx 10 C9
Chickerell Dorset 7 R8
Chickering Suffk 41 M5
Chicklade Wilts 8 C2
Chickward Herefs 34 G10
Chicksands C Beds 31 P4
Chidden Hants 9 T5
Chiddingfold Surrey 10 F3
Chiddingly E Susx 11 S7
Chiddingstone Kent 21 S13
Chiddingstone Causeway Kent 21 T13
Chiddingstone Hoath Kent 11 R2
Chideock Dorset 7 M6
Chidham W Susx 10 B9
Chidswell Kirk 57 L2
Chieveley Services W Berk 19 Q6
Chignall St James Essex 22 G6
Chignall Smealy Essex 22 G5
Chigwell Essex 21 R4
Chigwell Row Essex 21 S4
Chilbolton Hants 19 N12
Chilbolton Down Hants 19 P12
Chilcomb Hants 9 Q3
Chilcombe Dorset 7 P6
Chilcompton Somset 17 R6
Chilcote Leics 46 J11
Childer Thornton Ches W 54 J11
Child Okeford Dorset 8 B6
Childrey Oxon 29 R9
Child's Ercall Shrops 45 Q9
Childswickham Worcs 36 E13
Childwall Lpool 54 K9
Childwick Bury Herts 31 P10
Chilfrome Dorset 7 P5
Chilgrove W Susx 10 C8
Chilham Kent 13 L5
Chilhampton Wilts 8 F2
Chilla Devon 14 K12
Chillaton Devon 5 L4
Chillenden Kent 13 Q5
Chillerton IoW 9 P12
Chillesford Suffk 41 R11
Chillingham Nthumb 85 R13
Chillington Devon 5 T12
Chillington Somset 7 M2
Chilmark Wilts 8 D2
Chilmington Green Kent 12 K7
Chilson Oxon 29 R4
Chilsworthy Cnwll 5 L6
Chilsworthy Devon 14 J12
Chiltern Green C Beds 31 P9
Chiltern Hills 20 D5
Chilthorne Domer Somset 17 P13
Chilton Bucks 30 E10
Chilton Devon 15 U11
Chilton Dur 69 S6
Chilton Oxon 19 Q3
Chilton Suffk 40 E11
Chilton Candover Hants 19 S13
Chilton Cantelo Somset 17 Q12
Chilton Foliat Wilts 19 M6
Chilton Polden Somset 17 L9
Chilton Street Suffk 40 C11
Chilton Trinity Somset 16 J9
Chilwell Notts 47 P6
Chilworth Hants 9 N5
Chilworth Surrey 10 G1
Chimney Oxon 29 R7
Chineham Hants 19 U9
Chingford Gt Lon 21 Q4
Chinley Derbys 56 F10
Chinnor Oxon 30 F12
Chipchase Castle Nthumb 76 J11
Chipnall Shrops 45 R7
Chippenham Cambs 39 U7
Chippenham Wilts 18 D6
Chipperfield Herts 31 M12
Chipping Herts 31 U6
Chipping Lancs 62 C11
Chipping Campden Gloucs 36 G13
Chipping Hill Essex 23 K4
Chipping Norton Oxon 29 R2
Chipping Ongar Essex 22 E7
Chipping Sodbury S Glos 28 D11
Chipping Warden W Nthn 37 N11
Chipshop Devon 5 L5
Chipstable Somset 16 E11
Chipstead Kent 21 T11
Chipstead Surrey 21 N11
Chirbury Shrops 44 G14
Chirk Wrexhm 44 G6
Chirnside Border 85 M7
Chirnsidebridge Border 85 M7
Chirton Wilts 18 G9
Chisbury Wilts 19 L7
Chiselborough Somset 7 N2
Chiseldon Swindn 18 J5
Chiselhampton Oxon 19 U1
Chisholme Border 75 U3
Chislehurst Gt Lon 21 R8
Chislet Kent 13 P3
Chiswell Green Herts 31 P12
Chiswick Gt Lon 21 M7
Chiswick End Cambs 39 N11
Chisworth Derbys 56 F8
Chitcombe E Susx 12 F11
Chithurst W Susx 10 C6
Chittering Cambs 39 Q7
Chitterne Wilts 18 E12
Chittlehamholt Devon 15 Q8
Chittlehampton Devon 15 P7
Chittoe Wilts 18 E7
Chivelstone Devon 5 T13
Chiverton Cross Cnwll 2 J7
Chlenry D & G 72 E7
Chobham Surrey 20 G10
Cholderton Wilts 18 K12
Cholesbury Bucks 30 K11
Chollerford Nthumb 76 J11
Chollerton Nthumb 76 J11
Cholmondeston Ches E 45 Q2
Cholsey Oxon 19 S3
Cholstrey Herefs 35 L9
Chop Gate N York 70 J13
Choppington Nthumb 77 R9
Chopwell Gatesd 77 N14
Chorley Ches E 45 N3
Chorley Lancs 55 N3
Chorley Shrops 35 Q4
Chorley Staffs 46 E11
Chorleywood Herts 20 H3
Chorleywood West Herts 20 H3
Chorlton Ches E 45 R3
Chorlton-cum-Hardy Manch 55 T8
Chorlton Lane Ches W 45 L4
Choulton Shrops 34 J3
Chowley Ches W 45 L2
Chrishall Essex 39 P13
Chrisswell Inver 88 F11
Christchurch BCP 8 H10
Christchurch Cambs 49 Q14
Christchurch Gloucs 27 V5
Christchurch Newpt 27 Q10
Christian Malford Wilts 18 D5
Christmas Common Oxon 20 B3
Christmas Pie Surrey 20 F12
Christon N Som 17 L5
Christon Bank Nthumb 85 U13
Christow Devon 5 U3
Christ's Hospital W Susx 10 K5
Chuck Hatch E Susx 11 R4
Chudleigh Devon 5 V4
Chudleigh Knighton Devon 5 V5
Chulmleigh Devon 15 Q9
Chunal Derbys 56 F8
Church Lancs 62 E14
Churcham Gloucs 28 E4
Church Aston Wrekin 45 R10
Church Brampton W Nthn 37 T7
Church Brough W & F 68 G10
Church Broughton Derbys 46 H7
Church Cove Cnwll 2 J14
Church Crookham Hants 20 D12
Churchdown Gloucs 28 G4
Church Eaton Staffs 45 T10
Church End Bed 38 E11
Church End Bed 38 G10
Church End Bucks 30 F11
Church End C Beds 31 L5
Church End C Beds 31 M6
Church End C Beds 31 N4
Church End Cambs 39 L4
Church End Cambs 39 N2
Church End Cambs 49 M14
Church End Essex 22 F2
Church End Essex 22 G3
Church End Essex 40 B14
Church End Gt Lon 21 M5
Church End Hants 19 U9
Church End Herts 31 Q9
Church End Herts 31 S9
Church End Herts 31 T11
Church End Lincs 48 K6
Church End Lincs 49 N8
Church End Warwks 36 H2
Church End Warwks 36 J2
Church Enstone Oxon 29 S2
Church Fenton N York 64 C12
Churchfield Sandw 36 D2
Churchgate Herts 31 U12
Churchgate Street Essex 22 C5
Church Green Devon 6 G5
Church Gresley Derbys 46 J11
Church Hanborough Oxon 29 T5
Church Hill Ches W 55 P13
Church Hill Staffs 46 C11
Church Houses N York 71 L13
Churchill Devon 6 J4
Churchill Devon 15 M4
Churchill N Som 17 M5
Churchill Oxon 29 Q3
Churchill Worcs 35 T5
Churchill Worcs 36 C10
Churchinford Somset 6 H2
Church Knowle Dorset 8 D12
Church Laneham Notts 58 D11
Church Langton Leics 37 T2
Church Lawford Warwks 37 N6
Church Lawton Ches E 45 T3
Church Leigh Staffs 46 D7
Church Lench Worcs 36 D10
Church Mayfield Staffs 46 F4
Church Minshull Ches E 45 Q1
Church Norton W Susx 10 D11
Church Preen Shrops 45 N13
Church Pulverbatch Shrops 44 K13
Churchstanton Somset 6 H2
Churchstoke Powys 34 G2
Churchstow Devon 5 S11
Church Stowe W Nthn 37 R9
Church Street Essex 40 C12
Church Street Kent 22 H13
Church Stretton Shrops 45 L14
Churchthorpe Lincs 59 Q7
Churchtown BCP 8 G9
Churchtown Cnwll 4 E3
Churchtown Derbys 57 L13
Churchtown Devon 15 Q4
Churchtown IoM 60 g4
Churchtown Lancs 61 T11
Churchtown Sefton 54 J3
Church Town Surrey 21 Q12
Church Village Rhondd 26 K11
Church Warsop Notts 57 S13
Church Wilne Derbys 47 M7
Churnsike Lodge Nthumb 76 F11
Churston Ferrers Torbay 6 B13
Churt Surrey 10 D3
Churton Ches W 45 L2
Churwell Leeds 63 R14
Chute Cadley Wilts 19 L9
Chweffordd Conwy 53 R8
Chyandour Cnwll 2 D10
Chyanvounder Cnwll 2 H11
Chyeowling Cnwll 2 K9
Chyvarloe Cnwll 2 H11
Cil Powys 44 E8
Cilan Uchaf Gwynd 42 E8
Cilcain Flints 54 E13
Cilcennin Cerdgn 33 L8
Cilcewydd Powys 44 F13
Cilfor Gwynd 43 L5
Cilfrew Neath 26 D7
Cilfynydd Rhondd 26 K9
Cilgerran Pembks 32 C12
Cilgwyn Carmth 26 C2
Cilgwyn Gwynd 52 G12
Cilgwyn Pembks 24 J4
Ciliau-Aeron Cerdgn 32 K9
Cilmaengwyn Neath 26 C6
Cilmery Powys 33 U10
Cilrhedyn Pembks 25 M3
Cilsan Carmth 25 U6

Ciltalgarth Gwynd....43 S5
Cilycwm Carmth....33 Q13
Cimla Neath....26 D8
Cinderford Gloucs....28 C5
Cinder Hill Wolves....36 A2
Cippenham Slough....20 G6
Cirencester Gloucs....28 E7
Ciladilla N York....69 K13
City Gt Lon....21 P6
City V Glam....26 H12
City Airport Gt Lon....21 R6
City Dulas IoA....52 G5
Clachaig Ag & B....92 F7
Clachaig Ag & B....88 D9
Clachaig Inn Highld....94 G2
Clachan Ag & B....79 P4
Clachan Ag & B....87 P2
Clachan Ag & B....88 C5
Clachan Ag & B....94 B10
Clachan Highld....100 e6
Clachan-a-Luib W Isls....106 d12
Clachan Mor Ag & B....92 C6
Clachan na Luib W Isls....106 d12
Clachan of Campsie
E Duns....89 P10
Clachan-Seil Ag & B....87 P2
Clachnaharry Highld....102 H6
Clachtoll Highld....110 A10
Clacket Lane Services
Surrey....21 R12
Clackmannan Clacks....90 D13
Clackmannanshire
Bridge Fife....90 D14
Clacton-on-Sea Essex....23 S4
Cladich Ag & B....88 C1
Cladswell Worcs....36 E9
Claggan Highld....93 S9
Claigan Highld....100 b4
Clandown BaNES....17 S5
Clanfield Hants....9 T5
Clanfield Oxon....29 Q7
Clannaborough Devon....15 R12
Clanville Hants....19 M11
Clanville Somset....17 R10
Claonaig Ag & B....79 Q8
Clapgate Dorset....8 E8
Clapgate Herts....22 B3
Clapham Bed....38 F10
Clapham Devon....6 A7
Clapham Gt Lon....21 N7
Clapham Lancs....62 E6
Clapham N York....62 E6
Clapham W Susx....10 H9
Clapham Green Bed....38 F10
Clap Hill Kent....13 L8
Clappersgate W & F....67 N12
Clapton Somset....7 M3
Clapton Somset....17 R6
Clapton-in-Gordano
N Som....27 T13
Clapton-on-the-Hill
Gloucs....29 N4
Clapworthy Devon....15 Q8
Clarach Cerdgn....33 M4
Claravale Gatesd....77 N13
Clarbeston Pembks....24 H6
Clarbeston Road Pembks....24 H6
Clarborough Notts....58 B10
Clare Suffk....40 C11
Clarebrand D & G....74 E12
Clarencefield D & G....75 L12
Clarewood Nthumb....77 L11
Clarilaw Border....76 A2
Clark's Green Surrey....10 K3
Clarkston E Rens....89 N14
Clashmore Highld....109 N7
Clashmore Highld....110 A10
Clashnessie Highld....110 B10
Clashnoir Moray....104 A11
Clatt Abers....104 G10
Clatter Powys....33 U2
Clatterford End Essex....22 F5
Clatworthy Somset....16 E10
Claughton Lancs....61 U11
Claughton Lancs....62 B6
Claughton Wirral....54 H9
Clavershay Somset....16 J10
Claverdon Warwks....36 G7
Claverham N Som....17 N3
Clavering Essex....22 C1
Claverley Shrops....35 S2
Claverton BaNES....17 U4
Claverton Down BaNES....17 U4
Clawdd-coch V Glam....26 K12
Clawdd-newydd Denbgs....44 C3
Clawthorpe W & F....61 U4
Clawton Devon....14 J13
Claxby Lincs....58 K8
Claxby Lincs....59 Q12
Claxton N York....64 F8
Claxton Norfk....51 P13
Claybrooke Magna Leics....37 N3
Clay Common Suffk....41 S4
Clay Coton W Nhn....37 Q5
Clay Cross Derbys....57 N14
Claydon Oxon....37 M11
Clay End Herts....31 T8
Claygate D & G....75 S10
Claygate Kent....12 D7
Claygate Surrey....21 L10
Claygate Cross Kent....12 B4
Clayhall Gt Lon....21 R4
Clayhanger Devon....16 D12
Clayhanger Wsall....46 D13
Clayhidon Devon....16 F13
Clayhill E Susx....12 F11
Clayhill Hants....9 L7
Clayhithe Cambs....39 R8
Clayock Highld....112 E5
Claypit Hill Cambs....39 N10
Claypits Gloucs....28 E6
Claypole Lincs....48 B4
Claythorpe Lincs....59 R11
Clayton C Brad....63 N12
Clayton Donc....57 Q5
Clayton W Susx....11 M8
Clayton Green Lancs....55 P1
Clayton-le-Moors Lancs....62 F13
Clayton-le-Woods Lancs....55 N1
Clayton West Kirk....57 L4
Clayworth Notts....58 B9
Cleadale Highld....100 d10
Cleadon S Tyne....77 T13
Cleadon Park S Tyne....77 T13
Clearbrook Devon....5 N6
Clearwell Gloucs....27 V6
Cleasby N York....69 S10
Cleat Ork....106 t21
Cleatlam Dur....69 P9
Cleator Cumb....66 F10
Cleator Moor Cumb....66 F9
Cleckheaton Kirk....63 N1
Cleedownton Shrops....35 N4
Cleehill Shrops....35 N5
Cleekhimin N Lans....82 E7
Clee St Margaret Shrops....35 N4
Cleestanton Shrops....35 N5
Cleethorpes NE Lin....59 P5
Cleeton St Mary Shrops....35 P5
Cleeve N Som....17 N3
Cleeve Oxon....19 T4
Cleeve Hill Gloucs....28 H2
Cleeve Prior Worcs....36 F11
Cleghornie E Loth....84 F2
Clehonger Herefs....35 K13
Cleish P & K....90 G12
Cleland N Lans....82 F7
Clement's End C Beds....31 M10
Clement Street Kent....22 D13
Clenamacrie Ag & B....94 C13
Clench Common Wilts....18 H8
Clenchwarton Norfk....49 S9
Clenerty Abers....105 M3
Clent Worcs....36 B5
Cleobury Mortimer Shrops....35 P5
Cleobury North Shrops....35 P3
Cleongart Ag & B....79 M9
Clephanton Highld....103 M5
Clerkhill D & G....75 U6
Cleuch-head D & G....74 F5
Clevancy Wilts....18 G5
Clevedon N Som....17 M3
Cleveley Oxon....29 S2
Cleveleys Lancs....61 Q11
Cleverton Wilts....28 J10
Clewer Somset....17 M6
Cley next the Sea Norfk....50 H5
Cliburn W & F....67 S8
Cliddesden Hants....19 T11
Cliff Warwks....46 H14
Cliffe Lancs....62 G13
Cliffe Medway....22 H12
Cliffe N York....57 F13
Cliffe N York....69 R9
Cliff End E Susx....12 G13
Cliffe Woods Medway....22 H13
Clifford Herefs....34 F11
Clifford Leeds....63 U11
Clifford Chambers Warwks....36 G10
Clifford's Mesne Gloucs....28 D3
Cliffsend Kent....13 R2
Clifton Bristl....27 V13
Clifton C Beds....31 Q5
Clifton C Nott....47 P7
Clifton C York....64 D9
Clifton Calder....56 J2
Clifton Derbys....46 G5
Clifton Devon....15 N4
Clifton Donc....57 R7
Clifton Lancs....61 T13
Clifton N York....63 M10
Clifton Nthumb....77 Q9
Clifton Oxon....29 U1
Clifton Salfd....55 S6
Clifton Worcs....35 T11
Clifton Campville Staffs....46 J11
Clifton Hampden Oxon....30 B13
Clifton Reynes M Keyn....38 D10
Clifton upon Dunsmore
Warwks....37 P5
Clifton upon Teme Worcs....35 R8
Cliftonville Kent....13 S1
Climping W Susx....10 F10
Clink Somset....17 U7
Clint N York....63 R8
Clinterty C Aber....105 N13
Clint Green Norfk....50 H11
Clintmains Border....84 G12
Clipiau Gwynd....43 R11
Clippesby Norfk....51 R11
Clipsham Rutlnd....48 E11
Clipston Nhants....37 U4
Clipston Notts....47 R7
Clipstone C Beds....30 K7
Clipstone Notts....57 R13
Clitheroe Lancs....62 E11
Clive Shrops....45 M9
Cliveden Bucks....20 F5
Clixby Lincs....58 J6
Cloatley Wilts....28 J9
Cloccaenog Denbgs....44 C3
Clochan Moray....104 D3
Clock Face St Hel....55 M7
Cloddiau Powys....44 F12
Clodock Herefs....27 Q2
Cloford Somset....17 T8
Clola Abers....105 S7
Clophill C Beds....31 N5
Clopton Nhants....38 G4
Clopton Suffk....41 M10
Clopton Corner Suffk....41 M10
Clopton Green Suffk....40 C9
Clos du Valle Guern....6 e1
Closeburn D & G....74 H7
Closeburnmill D & G....74 H7
Closeclark IoM....60 d7
Closworth Somset....7 Q2
Clothall Herts....31 S6
Clothall Common Herts....31 S6
Clotton Ches W....55 M14
Cloudesley Bush Warwks....37 N3
Clouds Herefs....35 N13
Clough Oldham....56 D5
Clough Foot Calder....56 D2
Clough Head Calder....56 H2
Cloughton N York....71 T14
Cloughton Newlands
N York....71 T13
Clousta Shet....106 t8
Clova Angus....98 E9
Clovelly Devon....14 H8
Clovenfords Border....84 D11
Clovenstone Abers....105 L13
Clow Bridge Lancs....62 G14
Clowne Derbys....57 Q11
Clows Top Worcs....35 R6
Cluanie Inn Highld....101 R9
Cluanie Lodge Highld....101 R9
Clubworthy Cnwll....4 H2
Clugston D & G....72 K8
Clun Shrops....34 H4
Clunas Highld....103 N6
Clunbury Shrops....34 J4
Clunderwen Carmth....24 J7
Clune Highld....103 L10
Clunes Highld....101 T14
Clungunford Shrops....34 J5
Clunton Shrops....34 H4
Clutton BaNES....17 R5
Clutton Ches W....45 L3
Clutton Hill BaNES....17 R5
Clwt-y-bont Gwynd....52 J10
Clydach Mons....27 P5
Clydach Swans....26 B7
Clydach Vale Rhondd....26 H9
Clydebank W Duns....89 L11
Clyffe Pypard Wilts....18 G5
Clynder Ag & B....88 G9
Clyne Neath....26 E7
Clynnog Fawr Gwynd....42 H4
Clyro Powys....34 F12
Clyst Honiton Devon....6 C6
Clyst Hydon Devon....6 D4
Clyst St George Devon....6 C7
Clyst St Lawrence Devon....6 D4
Clyst St Mary Devon....6 C6
Cnoc W Isls....106 j5
Cnwch Coch Cerdgn....33 N6
Coad's Green Cnwll....4 H5
Coal Aston Derbys....57 N11
Coalbrookdale Wrekin....45 Q12
Coalburn S Lans....82 F12
Coalburns Gatesd....77 N13
Coalcleugh Nthumb....68 H3
Coaley Gloucs....28 E7
Coalmoor Wrekin....45 Q12
Coalpit Heath S Glos....28 C12
Coal Pool Wsall....46 D14
Coalport Wrekin....45 Q13
Coalsnaughton Clacks....90 D12
Coal Street Suffk....41 M6
Coaltown of Balgonie Fife....91 L11
Coaltown of Wemyss Fife....91 M12
Coalville Leics....47 M11
Coalway Gloucs....27 V5
Coanwood Nthumb....76 D14
Coat Somset....17 M11
Coatbridge N Lans....82 D5
Coatdyke N Lans....82 D5
Coate Swindn....29 N11
Coate Wilts....18 F8
Coates Cambs....39 M1
Coates Gloucs....28 H7
Coates Lincs....58 F10
Coates Notts....58 D10
Coates W Susx....10 F7
Coatham R & Cl....70 J7
Coatham Mundeville
Darltn....69 S8
Cobbaton Devon....15 P7
Coberley Gloucs....28 J4
Cobhall Common Herefs....35 L13
Cobham Kent....12 C2
Cobham Surrey....20 K10
Cobham Services Surrey....20 K11
Coblers Green Essex....22 G4
Cobley Dorset....8 E4
Cobnash Herefs....35 L8
Cobridge C Stke....45 U4
Coburby Abers....105 Q2
Cock Alley Derbys....57 P12
Cockayne N York....70 K13
Cockayne Hatley C Beds....39 L11
Cock Bank Wrexhm....44 J4
Cock Bevington Warwks....36 E9
Cock Bridge Abers....98 B2
Cockburnspath Border....84 K4
Cock Clarks Essex....23 L7
Cockenzie and Port
Seton E Loth....83 U4
Cocker Bar Lancs....55 M2
Cocker Brook Lancs....55 S1
Cockerham Lancs....61 T10
Cockermouth Cumb....66 H6
Cockernhel Herts....31 P9
Cockersdale Leeds....63 Q14
Cockett Swans....26 A9
Cockfield Dur....69 P8
Cockfield Suffk....40 F10
Cockfosters Gt Lon....21 N3
Cock Green Essex....22 G4
Cockhill Somset....17 R10
Cocking W Susx....10 D7
Cocking Causeway W Susx....10 D7
Cockington Torbay....6 A12
Cocklake Somset....17 M7
Cockley Beck W & F....66 K12
Cockley Cley Norfk....50 B13
Cock Marling E Susx....12 G12
Cockpole Green Wokham....20 C6
Cocks Cnwll....2 J6
Cockshutford Shrops....35 N4
Cockshutt Shrops....44 K8
Cock Street Kent....12 E5
Cockthorpe Norfk....50 G5
Cockwells Cnwll....2 E10
Cockwood Devon....6 C8
Cockwood Somset....16 H8
Cockyard Derbys....56 F11
Cockyard Herefs....27 T1
Coddenham Suffk....40 K10
Coddington Ches W....45 L2
Coddington Herefs....35 R12
Coddington Notts....48 B3
Codford St Mary Wilts....18 E13
Codford St Peter Wilts....18 E13
Codicote Herts....31 R9
Codmore Hill W Susx....10 H6
Codnor Derbys....47 M4
Codrington S Glos....28 D12
Codsall Staffs....45 U13
Codsall Wood Staffs....45 T13
Coed Darcy Neath....26 C8
Coedely Rhondd....26 H6
Coed Hirwaun Neath....26 E11
Coedkernew Newpt....27 P11
Coed Morgan Mons....27 R5
Coedpoeth Wrexhm....44 F3
Coedway Powys....44 H11
Coed-y-Bryn Cerdgn....32 G11
Coed-y-caerau Newpt....27 R9
Coed-y-paen Mons....27 Q8
Coed-y-parc Gwynd....52 K9
Coed-yr-ynys Powys....27 M3
Coed Ystumgwern Gwynd....43 L9
Coelbren Powys....26 F5
Coffinswell Devon....6 A11
Cofton Devon....6 C8
Cofton Hackett Worcs....36 D6
Cogan V Glam....16 G2
Cogenhoe W Nthn....38 B8
Cogges Oxon....29 S6
Coggeshall Essex....23 L3
Coggin's Mill E Susx....11 S5
Coignafearn Highld....102 K12
Coilacriech Abers....98 E4
Coilantogle Stirlg....89 M4
Coillore Highld....100 c6
Col W Isls....106 j5
Colaboll Highld....108 J2
Colan Cnwll....3 M4
Colaton Raleigh Devon....6 E7
Colbost Highld....100 b5
Colburn N York....69 Q13
Colby Cumb....68 D8
Colby IoM....60 d7
Colby Norfk....51 M7
Colby W & F....68 K8
Colchester Essex....23 N2
Colchester Zoo Essex....23 L3
Cold Ash W Berk....19 R7
Cold Ashby W Nhn....37 S5
Cold Ashton S Glos....28 E13
Cold Aston Gloucs....29 N4
Coldbackie Highld....111 N5
Coldbeck W & F....68 F12
Cold Blow Pembks....24 K8
Cold Brayfield M Keyn....38 D10
Coldean Br & H....11 N9
Coldeast Devon....5 U6
Colden Calder....56 G14
Colden Common Hants....9 P4
Coldfair Green Suffk....41 R8
Coldham Cambs....49 P13
Cold Hanworth Lincs....58 H10
Coldharbour Cnwll....2 J8
Coldharbour Devon....6 E2
Coldharbour Gloucs....27 V7
Cold Harbour Herts....31 N9
Cold Harbour Oxon....19 T5
Coldharbour Surrey....10 J2
Cold Hatton Wrekin....45 P9
Cold Hatton Heath Wrekin....45 P9
Cold Hesledon Dur....70 F3
Cold Hiendley Wakefd....57 N4
Cold Higham W Nhn....37 S10
Coldingham Border....85 N5
Cold Kirby N York....64 C2
Coldmeece Staffs....45 U7
Cold Newton Leics....47 T12
Cold Northcott Cnwll....4 G3
Cold Norton Essex....23 L7
Cold Overton Leics....48 B11
Coldred Kent....13 Q6
Coldridge Devon....15 Q11
Coldstream Border....85 L11
Coldwaltham W Susx....10 G7
Coldwell Herefs....34 K13
Coldwells Abers....105 R8
Cole Somset....17 S10
Colebatch Shrops....34 H3
Colebrook Devon....6 D4
Colebrook C Plym....5 N9
Colebrooke Devon....6 D3
Coleby Lincs....48 E1
Coleby N Linc....58 E3
Coleford Devon....15 S12
Coleford Gloucs....27 V6
Coleford Somset....17 S8
Coleford Water Somset....16 F10
Colegate End Norfk....41 L3
Cole Green Essex....22 H4
Cole Green Herts....31 S10
Cole Henley Hants....19 Q10
Colehill Dorset....8 E8
Coleman Green Herts....31 Q10
Coleman's Hatch E Susx....11 R4
Colemere Shrops....44 K7
Colemore Hants....9 U2
Colemore Green Shrops....35 R14
Colenden P & K....90 H6
Coleorton Leics....47 M10
Colerne Wilts....18 B6
Colesbourne Gloucs....28 J5
Coles Cross Dorset....7 L4
Colesden Bed....38 H9
Coles Green Suffk....40 K12
Coleshill Bucks....20 G3
Coleshill Oxon....29 Q9
Coleshill Warwks....36 H3
Colestocks Devon....6 E4
Coley BaNES....17 Q5
Colgate W Susx....11 L4
Colinsburgh Fife....91 R11
Colinton C Edin....83 P5
Colintraive Ag & B....88 B11
Colkirk Norfk....50 F9
Coll Ag & B....92 G7
Coll W Isls....106 j5
Collafirth Shet....106 u6
Collafirth Shet....106 u5
Collaton Devon....5 S13
Collaton St Mary Torbay....5 V9
College of Roseisle Moray....103 T2
College Town Br For....20 E10
Collessie Fife....91 L9
Colleton Mills Devon....15 Q9
Collier's End Herts....31 U8
Collier's Green Kent....12 E8
Collier Street Kent....12 D6
Colliery Row Sundld....70 D3
Collieston Abers....105 S10
Collin D & G....75 L10
Collingbourne Ducis Wilts....18 K10
Collingbourne Kingston
Wilts....18 K9
Collingham Leeds....63 S11
Collingham Notts....48 B1
Collington Herefs....35 P8
Collingtree W Nhn....37 U9
Collins Green Warrtn....55 N8
Collins Green Worcs....35 R9
Colliston Angus....91 T2
Colliton Devon....6 E4
Collyweston N Nthn....48 E13
Colmonell S Ayrs....80 G12
Colmworth Bed....38 H9
Colnabaichin Abers....98 B2
Colnbrook Slough....20 H7
Colne Cambs....39 M6
Colne Lancs....62 H11
Colne Bridge Kirk....56 J3
Colne Edge Lancs....62 H11
Colne Engaine Essex....23 L1
Colney Norfk....51 L12
Colney Heath Herts....31 R11
Colney Street Herts....31 P12
Coln Rogers Gloucs....29 L6
Coln St Aldwyns Gloucs....29 M7
Coln St Dennis Gloucs....29 L5
Colonsay Ag & B....86 F6
Colonsay Airport Ag & B....86 F7
Colpy Abers....104 J8
Colquhar Border....83 R10
Colquite Cnwll....3 R2
Colscott Devon....14 J9
Colsterdale N York....63 M2
Colsterworth Lincs....48 E9
Colston Bassett Notts....47 S7
Coltfield Moray....103 T3
Colt Hill Hants....20 C12
Colthouse Cumb....67 N13
Coltishall Norfk....51 N10
Coltness N Lans....82 F7
Colton Cumb....61 P1
Colton Leeds....63 U13
Colton N York....64 C11
Colton Norfk....50 K12
Colton Staffs....46 E9
Colt's Hill Kent....12 B7

Cruden Bay Abers 105 T8
Crudgington Wrekin 45 P10
Crudie Abers 105 M4
Crudwell Wilts 28 J9
Cruft Devon 15 M13
Crûg Powys 34 E6
Crugmeer Cnwll 3 N1
Crugybar Carmth 33 N13
Crug-y-byddar Powys 34 E4
Crumlin Caerph 27 N8
Crumplehorn Cnwll 4 G10
Crumpsall Manch 55 T6
Crundale Kent 13 L6
Crundale Pembks 24 G7
Crunwere Pembks 25 L8
Cruwys Morchard Devon 15 U10
Crux Easton Hants 19 P9
Cruxton Dorset 7 R5
Crwbin Carmth 25 S8
Cryers Hill Bucks 20 E3
Crymych Pembks 25 L4
Crynant Neath 26 D7
Crystal Palace Gt Lon 21 P8
Cuaig Highld 107 M13
Cuan Ag & B 87 P3
Cubbington Warwks 36 K7
Cubert Cnwll 2 K5
Cubley Barns 56 K6
Cublington Bucks 30 H8
Cublington Herefs 34 K13
Cuckfield W Susx 11 N5
Cucklington Somset 17 U11
Cuckney Notts 57 S12
Cuckoo Bridge Lincs 48 K9
Cuckoo's Corner Hants 10 A2
Cuckoo's Nest Ches W 44 J1
Cuddesdon Oxon 30 C12
Cuddington Bucks 30 F10
Cuddington Ches W 55 N12
Cuddington Heath Ches W 45 L4
Cuddy Hill Lancs 61 T12
Cudham Gt Lon 21 R11
Cudliptown Devon 5 N5
Cudnell BCP 8 F9
Cudworth Barns 57 N5
Cudworth Somset 7 L2
Cuerdley Cross Warrtn 55 M9
Cufaude Hants 19 U9
Cuffley Herts 31 T12
Cuil Highld 94 D7
Culbokie Highld 102 H4
Culbone Somset 15 T3
Culburnie Highld 102 E7
Culcabock Highld 102 J7
Culcharry Highld 103 N5
Culcheth Warrtn 55 Q8
Culdrain Abers 104 G9
Culduie Highld 100 g5
Culford Suffk 40 D6
Culgaith W & F 68 D7
Culham Oxon 30 B13
Culkein Highld 110 A10
Culkein Drumbeg Highld 110 C10
Culkerton Gloucs 28 H8
Cullen Moray 104 G2
Cullercoats N Tyne 77 T11
Cullerlie Abers 99 P3
Cullicudden Highld 102 H3
Cullingworth C Brad 63 M12
Cuillin Hills Highld 100 d7
Cullipool Ag & B 87 N3
Cullivoe Shet 106 v3
Culloden Highld 102 K6
Cullompton Devon 6 D3
Cullompton Services Devon 6 D3
Culm Davy Devon 16 F13
Culmington Shrops 35 L4
Culmstock Devon 6 F2
Culnacraig Highld 107 U4
Culnaightrie D & G 73 T9
Culnaknock Highld 100 e3
Culpho Suffk 41 M11
Culrain Highld 108 K6
Culross Fife 82 J1
Culroy S Ayrs 81 L10
Culsalmond Abers 104 K9
Culscadden D & G 73 M10
Culshabbin D & G 72 J9
Culswick Shet 106 s9
Cultercullen Abers 105 Q11
Cults C Aber 99 R3
Culverstone Green Kent 12 B3
Culverthorpe Lincs 48 F5
Culworth W Nthn 37 P11
Culzean Castle & Country Park S Ayrs 80 J10
Cumbernauld N Lans 89 S11
Cumbernauld Village N Lans 89 S10
Cumberworth Lincs 59 T12
Cumdivock Cumb 67 M3
Cuminestown Abers 105 N5
Cumledge Border 84 K7
Cummersdale Cumb 67 N2
Cummertrees D & G 75 M12
Cummingston Moray 103 T2
Cumnock E Ayrs 81 R8
Cumnor Oxon 29 U7
Cumrew Cumb 67 S2
Cumrue D & G 75 L8
Cumwhinton Cumb 67 Q2
Cumwhitton Cumb 67 R2
Cundall N York 63 U5
Cunninghamhead N Ayrs 81 M4
Cunningsburgh Shet 106 u10
Cupar Fife 91 N9
Cupar Muir Fife 91 N9
Curbar Derbys 57 L12
Curbridge Hants 9 Q6
Curbridge Oxon 29 R6
Curdridge Hants 9 Q6
Curdworth Warwks 36 G2
Curland Somset 16 J13
Curridge W Berk 19 Q6
Currie C Edin 83 N5
Curry Mallet Somset 16 K12
Curry Rivel Somset 17 L11
Curteis Corner Kent 12 G8
Curtisden Green Kent 12 D7
Curtisknowle Devon 5 S10
Cury Cnwll 2 H12
Cushnie Abers 104 G13
Cushuish Somset 16 G10
Cusop Herefs 34 F12
Cusworth Donc 57 R6
Cutcloy D & G 73 M13
Cutcombe Somset 16 B9
Cutgate Rochdl 56 C4
Cuthill Highld 109 P7
Cutiau Gwynd 43 M10
Cutler's Green Essex 22 E1
Cutmadoc Cnwll 3 R4
Cutmere Cnwll 4 J8
Cutnall Green Worcs 35 U7
Cutsdean Gloucs 29 L1
Cutthorpe Derbys 57 M12
Cuttivett Cnwll 4 K8
Cuxham Oxon 30 E13
Cuxton Medway 12 D2
Cuxwold Lincs 59 L6
Cwm Blae G 27 M6
Cwm Denbgs 54 C11
Cwmafan Neath 26 D9
Cwmaman Rhondd 26 J8
Cwmann Carmth 33 L11
Cwmavon Torfn 27 P6
Cwmbach Carmth 25 N5
Cwmbach Carmth 25 S10
Cwmbach Powys 34 E14
Cwmbach Rhondd 26 J7
Cwmbach Llechrhyd Powys 34 B10
Cwmbelan Powys 33 T4
Cwmbran Torfn 27 P9
Cwmbrwyno Cerdgn 33 P4
Cwm Capel Carmth 25 S10
Cwmcarn Caerph 27 N9
Cwmcarvan Mons 27 T6
Cwm-celyn Blae G 27 N6
Cwm-Cewydd Gwynd 43 S11
Cwm-cou Cerdgn 32 E12
Cwm Crawnon Powys 27 L4
Cwmdare Rhondd 26 H7
Cwmdu Carmth 26 A1
Cwmdu Powys 27 M3
Cwmdu Swans 26 A9
Cwmduad Carmth 25 Q4
Cwm Dulais Swans 25 V10
Cwmdwr Carmth 33 P14
Cwmfelin Brdgnd 26 F10
Cwmfelin Myr Td 26 K7
Cwmfelin Boeth Carmth 25 L7
Cwmfelinfach Caerph 27 M9
Cwmfelin Mynach Carmth 25 M6
Cwmffrwd Carmth 25 R7
Cwmgiedd Powys 26 D5
Cwmgorse Carmth 26 C5
Cwm Gwaun Pembks 24 H4
Cwmgwili Carmth 25 U8
Cwmgwrach Neath 26 F7
Cwmhiraeth Carmth 25 P3
Cwmifor Carmth 26 B2
Cwm Irfon Powys 33 S11
Cwmisfael Carmth 25 S7
Cwm Llinau Powys 43 R12
Cwmllynfell Neath 26 C5
Cwmmawr Carmth 25 T8
Cwm Morgan Carmth 25 N4
Cwmparc Rhondd 26 G8
Cwmpengraig Carmth 25 Q3
Cwm Penmachno Conwy 43 Q4
Cwmpennar Rhondd 26 J7
Cwmrhos Powys 27 M3
Cwmrhydyceirw Swans 26 B8
Cwmsychbant Cerdgn 32 J11
Cwmtillery Blae G 27 N6
Cwm-twrch Isaf Powys 26 D5
Cwm-twrch Uchaf Powys 26 D5
Cwm-y-glo Carmth 25 U8
Cwm-y-glo Gwynd 52 J10
Cwmyoy Mons 27 P3
Cwmystwyth Cerdgn 33 Q6
Cwrt Gwynd 43 N14
Cwrtnewydd Cerdgn 32 J11
Cwrt-y-gollen Powys 27 N4
Cyfarthfa Castle Museum Myr Td 26 J6
Cyffylliog Denbgs 44 C2
Cyfronydd Powys 44 D12
Cylibebyll Neath 26 C7
Cymau Flints 44 G2
Cymmer Neath 26 F8
Cymmer Rhondd 26 J9
Cyncoed Cardif 27 M11
Cynghordy Carmth 33 R12
Cynheidre Carmth 25 S9
Cynonville Neath 26 E8
Cynwyd Denbgs 44 C5
Cynwyl Elfed Carmth 25 Q5

D

Daccombe Devon 6 B11
Dacre N York 63 P7
Dacre W & F 67 Q7
Dacre Banks N York 63 P7
Daddry Shield Dur 68 J5
Dadford Bucks 30 E5
Dadlington Leics 47 M14
Dafen Carmth 25 T10
Daffy Green Norfk 50 G12
Dagenham Gt Lon 22 D11
Daglingworth Gloucs 28 J6
Dagnall Bucks 31 L9
Dagworth Suffk 40 H8
Dail bho Dheas W Isls 106 j2
Dailly S Ayrs 80 K12
Dainton Devon 5 V7
Dairsie Fife 91 P8
Daisy Hill Bolton 55 Q6
Daisy Hill Leeds 63 R14
Dalabrog W Isls 106 c16
Dalavich Ag & B 87 T3
Dalbeattie D & G 74 F13
Dalbury Derbys 46 J7
Dalby IoM 60 c7
Dalby Lincs 59 R13
Dalby N York 64 E5
Dalcapon P & K 97 R13
Dalchalm Highld 109 S3
Dalchreichart Highld 102 A13
Dalchruin P & K 89 R2
Dalcrue P & K 90 F6
Dalderby Lincs 59 N13
Daldith Devon 6 D8
Dale Pembks 24 D9
Dale W & F 67 R4
Dale Abbey Derbys 47 M6
Dale Bottom Cumb 67 L8
Dale End Derbys 46 H1
Dale End N York 62 K10
Dale Hill E Susx 12 D9
Dalehouse N York 71 N9
Dalelia Highld 93 S5
Dalgarven N Ayrs 80 K3
Dalgety Bay Fife 83 N2
Dalgig E Ayrs 81 R10
Dalginross P & K 89 S1
Dalguise P & K 90 E2
Dalhalvaig Highld 111 T6
Dalham Suffk 40 B8
Daliburgh W Isls 106 c16
Dalkeith Mdloth 83 R5
Dallas Moray 103 T5
Dallinghoo Suffk 41 N9
Dallington E Susx 11 V7
Dallington W Nthn 37 T8
Dallow N York 63 P5
Dalmally Ag & B 94 H13
Dalmary Stirlg 89 M6
Dalmellington E Ayrs 81 P11
Dalmeny C Edin 83 M3
Dalmore Highld 109 M11
Dalmuir W Duns 89 L11
Dalnabreck Highld 93 S5
Dalnacardoch P & K 97 L9
Dalnahaitnach Highld 103 N12
Dalnaspidal P & K 96 J9
Dalnawillan Lodge Highld 112 B8
Dalness Highld 94 H8
Dalqueich P & K 90 G11
Dalquhairn S Ayrs 81 L13
Dalreavoch Highld 109 P3
Dalry N Ayrs 80 K3
Dalrymple E Ayrs 81 M10
Dalserf S Lans 82 E8
Dalsmeran Ag & B 79 L13
Dalston Cumb 67 N2
Dalston Gt Lon 21 P6
Dalswinton D & G 74 H8
Dalton D & G 75 N11
Dalton Lancs 55 L5
Dalton N York 63 U4
Dalton N York 69 P11
Dalton Nthumb 77 N11
Dalton Rothm 57 Q8
Dalton-in-Furness W & F 61 N5
Dalton-le-Dale Dur 70 F3
Dalton Magna Rothm 57 Q8
Dalton-on-Tees N York 69 S11
Dalton Parva Rothm 57 Q8
Dalton Piercy Hartpl 70 G6
Dalveich Stirlg 95 S14
Dalwhinnie Highld 96 J7
Dalwood Devon 6 H4
Damask Green Herts 31 S7
Damerham Hants 8 G5
Damgate Norfk 51 R12
Dam Green Norfk 40 H3
Damnaglaur D & G 72 E12
Danaway Kent 12 G3
Danbury Essex 22 J6
Danby N York 71 M11
Danby Bottom N York 71 L12
Danby Wiske N York 70 D13
Dandaleith Moray 104 B6
Danderhall Mdloth 83 R5
Danebridge Ches E 56 E13
Dane End Herts 31 T8
Danegate E Susx 11 T4
Danehill E Susx 11 Q5
Dane Hills C Leic 47 Q13
Danemoor Green Norfk 50 J12
Danesford Shrops 35 R2
Danesmoor Derbys 57 P14
Dane Street Kent 13 L5
Daniel's Water Kent 12 J7
Danshillock Abers 105 L4
Danskine E Loth 84 F5
Danthorpe E R Yk 65 T13
Danzey Green Warwks 36 F7
Dapple Heath Staffs 46 D8
Darby Green Hants 20 D10
Darcy Lever Bolton 55 R5
Dardy Powys 27 N4
Darenth Kent 22 E13
Daresbury Halton 55 N10
Darfield Barns 57 P6
Darfoulds Notts 57 S11
Dargate Kent 13 L3
Dargavel Rens 88 K11
Darite Cnwll 4 H7
Darland Medway 12 E2
Darland Wrexhm 44 J2
Darlaston Wsall 36 C1
Darlaston Green Wsall 36 C1
Darley N York 63 Q8
Darley Abbey C Derb 47 L6
Darley Bridge Derbys 46 J1
Darley Dale Derbys 57 L14
Darley Green Solhll 36 G6
Darleyhall Herts 31 P8
Darley Head N York 63 P7
Darlingscott Warwks 36 H12
Darlington Darltn 69 S10
Darliston Shrops 45 N7
Darlton Notts 58 C12
Darnford Staffs 46 F12
Darnick Border 84 E12
Darowen Powys 43 R13
Darra Abers 105 L6
Darracott Devon 14 F9
Darracott Devon 15 L5
Darras Hall Nthumb 77 P11
Darrington Wakefd 57 Q3
Darsham Suffk 41 R7
Darshill Somset 17 R8
Dartford Kent 22 D13
Dartford Crossing Kent 22 E12
Dartington Devon 5 T8
Dartmeet Devon 5 R6
Dartmoor National Park Devon 5 R5
Dartmouth Devon 5 V10
Darton Barns 57 M4
Darvel E Ayrs 81 R5
Darwell Hole E Susx 12 C12
Darwen Bl w D 55 Q2
Datchet W & M 20 G7
Datchworth Herts 31 S9
Datchworth Green Herts 31 S9
Daubhill Bolton 55 R5
Daugh of Kinermony Moray 104 A7
Dauntsey Wilts 18 E4
Dava Highld 103 R8
Davenham Ches W 55 Q12
Davenport Stockp 56 D9
Davenport Green Ches E 55 T11
Davenport Green Traffd 55 T9
Daventry W Nthn 37 Q8
Davidson's Mains C Edin 83 P3
Davidstow Cnwll 4 E4
David Street Kent 12 B3
Davington D & G 75 P5
Davington Kent 12 K3
Daviot Abers 105 L10
Daviot Highld 102 K8
Daviot House Highld 102 K7
Davis's Town E Susx 11 S7
Davoch of Grange Moray 104 F5
Davyhulme Traffd 55 S7
Daw End Wsall 46 D13
Dawesgreen Surrey 21 M13
Dawley Wrekin 45 Q12
Dawlish Devon 6 C9
Dawlish Warren Devon 6 C9
Dawn Conwy 53 Q8
Daws Green Somset 16 G12
Daws Heath Essex 22 K10
Daw's House Cnwll 4 J4
Dawsmere Lincs 49 P7
Daybrook Notts 47 Q4
Day Green Ches E 45 S2
Dayhills Staffs 46 C7
Dayhouse Bank Worcs 36 C5
Daylesford Gloucs 29 P2
Ddol Flints 54 D12
Ddol-Cownwy Powys 44 B10
Deal Kent 13 S5
Dean Cumb 66 G7
Dean Devon 5 S8
Dean Devon 15 P3
Dean Devon 15 R3
Dean Dorset 8 D5
Dean Hants 9 N2
Dean Hants 9 R5
Dean Lancs 56 C1
Dean Oxon 29 R3
Dean Somset 17 S8
Dean Bottom Kent 21 U9
Deanburnhaugh Border 75 S3
Deancombe Devon 5 S8
Dean Court Oxon 29 U6
Deane Bolton 55 Q5
Deane Hants 19 R10
Dean End Dorset 8 D5
Dean Head Barns 57 L6
Deanhead Kirk 56 F3
Deanland Dorset 8 D5
Deanlane End W Susx 9 U6
Dean Prior Devon 5 S8
Deanraw Nthumb 76 G13
Dean Row Ches E 56 C10
Deans W Loth 82 K5
Deanscales Cumb 66 G7
Deanshanger W Nthn 30 G5
Deanshaugh Moray 104 D5
Deanston Stirlg 89 R5
Dean Street Kent 12 D5
Dearham Cumb 66 G5
Dearnley Rochdl 56 D3
Debach Suffk 41 M10
Debden Essex 22 C8
Debden Essex 39 S14
Debden Green Essex 22 E1
Debenham Suffk 41 L8
Deblin's Green Worcs 35 T11
Dechmont W Loth 82 K4
Deddington Oxon 29 U1
Dedham Essex 40 J14
Dedham Heath Essex 23 Q1
Dedworth W & M 20 F7
Deene N Nthn 38 D2
Deenethorpe N Nthn 38 E2
Deepcar Sheff 57 L7
Deepcut Surrey 20 F11
Deepdale W & F 62 D3
Deepdale N York 62 H4
Deepdale N York 62 E3
Deeping Gate C Pete 48 H12
Deeping St James Lincs 48 J12
Deeping St Nicholas Lincs 48 K10
Deerhurst Gloucs 28 G1
Deerhurst Walton Gloucs 28 G2
Deerton Street Kent 12 J3
Deeside Industrial Park Flints 54 H12
Defford Worcs 36 B12
Defynnog Powys 26 G2
Deganwy Conwy 53 N7
Degnish Ag & B 87 P3
Deighton C York 64 E11
Deighton N York 70 E12
Deiniolen Gwynd 52 J10
Delabole Cnwll 4 D4
Delamere Ches W 55 N13
Delamere Park Ches W 55 P12
Delfrigs Abers 105 R11
Delley Devon 15 M8
Delliefure Highld 103 S9
Dell Quay W Susx 10 C10
Delly End Oxon 29 S5
Delnabo Moray 103 U12
Delny Highld 109 N10
Delph Oldham 56 E5
Delves Dur 69 P3
Delvin End Essex 40 C13
Dembleby Lincs 48 F6
Demelza Cnwll 3 P4
Denaby Donc 57 Q7
Denaby Main Donc 57 Q7
Denbies Surrey 20 K12
Denbigh Denbgs 54 C13
Denbrae Fife 91 N8
Denbury Devon 5 U7
Denby Derbys 47 L4
Denby Bottles Derbys 47 L4
Denby Dale Kirk 56 K5
Denchworth Oxon 29 S9
Dendron W & F 61 N5
Denel End C Beds 31 M5
Denfield P & K 90 E8
Denford N Nthn 38 E5
Dengie Essex 23 N7
Denham Bucks 20 H5
Denham Suffk 40 C8
Denham Suffk 41 L6
Denham End Suffk 40 C8
Denham Green Bucks 20 H5
Denham Green Suffk 41 L6
Denhead Abers 105 R5
Denhead Fife 91 Q9
Denhead of Gray C Dund 91 M5
Denholm Border 76 B2
Denholme C Brad 63 M13
Denholme Clough C Brad 63 M13
Denio Gwynd 42 G6
Denmead Hants 9 T6
Denmore C Aber 105 Q13
Denne Park W Susx 10 K5
Dennington Suffk 41 N7
Denny Falk 89 T9
Dennyloanhead Falk 89 T9
Den of Lindores Fife 91 L8
Denshaw Oldham 56 E4
Denside of Durris Abers 99 Q4
Densole Kent 13 P7
Denston Suffk 40 C10
Denstone Staffs 46 F5
Denstroude Kent 13 L3
Dent W & F 62 E2
Denton Cambs 38 J3
Denton Darltn 69 R9
Denton E Susx 11 R10
Denton Kent 13 P6
Denton Kent 22 G13
Denton Lincs 48 C7
Denton N York 63 N10
Denton N Nthn 38 B9
Denton Norfk 41 N3
Denton Oxon 30 C12
Denton Tamesd 56 D7
Denton W Nthn 38 B9
Denver Norfk 49 T13
Denwick Nthumb 77 Q3
Deopham Norfk 50 H13
Deopham Green Norfk 40 H1
Depden Suffk 40 C9
Depden Green Suffk 40 C9
Deptford Gt Lon 21 Q7
Deptford Wilts 18 F13
Derby C Derb 47 L6
Derbyhaven IoM 60 d9
Derculich P & K 97 P13
Dereham Norfk 50 G11
Deri Caerph 27 L7
Derril Devon 14 H12
Derringstone Kent 13 P6
Derrington Staffs 45 U9
Derriton Devon 14 H12
Derry Hill Wilts 18 E6
Derrythorpe N Linc 58 D5
Dersingham Norfk 49 U7
Dervaig Ag & B 93 L8
Derwen Denbgs 44 C3
Derwenlas Powys 43 P14
Derwent Valley Mills Derbys 46 K2
Derwent Water Cumb 67 L8
Derwydd Carmth 26 A4
Desborough N Nthn 38 B4
Desford Leics 47 N13
Detchant Nthumb 85 R11
Detling Kent 12 E4
Deuxhill Shrops 35 Q3
Devauden Mons 27 T8
Devil's Bridge Cerdgn 33 P5
Devitts Green Warwks 36 J2
Devizes Wilts 18 F8
Devonport C Plym 5 M10
Devonside Clacks 90 D12
Devoran Cnwll 2 K9
Devoran & Perran Cnwll 2 K9
Dewarton Mdloth 83 S6
Dewlish Dorset 7 U5
Dewsbury Kirk 56 K2
Dewsbury Moor Kirk 56 K2
Deytheur Powys 44 F10
Dial N Som 17 P3
Dial Green W Susx 10 E5
Dial Post W Susx 10 K7
Dibberford Dorset 7 N4
Dibden Hants 9 N7
Dibden Purlieu Hants 9 N7
Dickens Heath Solhll 36 F5
Dickleburgh Norfk 41 L4
Didbrook Gloucs 29 L1
Didcot Oxon 19 R2
Diddington Cambs 38 J7
Diddlebury Shrops 35 M3
Didley Herefs 35 L14
Didling W Susx 10 C7
Didmarton Gloucs 28 F10
Didsbury Manch 55 T8
Didworthy Devon 5 R8
Digby Lincs 48 G3
Digg Highld 100 d3
Diggle Oldham 56 F5
Digmoor Lancs 55 L5
Digswell Herts 31 R9
Digswell Water Herts 31 S10
Dihewyd Cerdgn 32 J9
Dilham Norfk 51 P8
Dilhorne Staffs 46 C5
Dill Hall Lancs 62 F14
Dillington Cambs 38 H7
Dilston Nthumb 76 K13
Dilton Wilts 18 C11
Dilton Marsh Wilts 18 B11
Dilwyn Herefs 34 K10
Dimple Bolton 55 R3
Dimple Derbys 46 J1
Dinas Carmth 25 N4
Dinas Cnwll 3 N2
Dinas Gwynd 42 E6
Dinas Gwynd 52 G11
Dinas Rhondd 26 J9
Dinas Cross Pembks 24 H3
Dinas Dinlle Gwynd 52 F11
Dinas-Mawddwy Gwynd 43 S10
Dinas Powys V Glam 16 G2
Dinder Somset 17 Q8
Dinedor Herefs 35 M13
Dingestow Mons 27 T5
Dingle Lpool 54 J9
Dingleden Kent 12 F9
Dingley N Nthn 37 U3
Dingwall Highld 102 F4
Dinmael Conwy 44 B5
Dinnet Abers 98 H4
Dinnington N u Ty 77 Q11
Dinnington Rothm 57 R9
Dinnington Somset 7 M2
Dinorwig Gwynd 52 J10
Dinorwig Slate Landscape Gwynd 52 J10
Dinton Bucks 30 G10
Dinton Wilts 8 E2
Dinwoodie D & G 75 M7
Dinworthy Devon 14 H9
Dipford Somset 16 H12
Dipley Hants 20 B11
Dippen Ag & B 79 Q8
Dippenhall Surrey 20 D13
Dippermill Devon 14 K11
Dippertown Devon 5 L4
Dippin N Ayrs 80 E8
Dipple Moray 104 C4
Dipple S Ayrs 80 J12
Diptford Devon 5 S9
Dipton Dur 69 Q2
Diptonmill Nthumb 76 J13
Dirleton E Loth 84 E2
Dirt Pot Nthumb 68 J3
Discoed Powys 34 G8
Diseworth Leics 47 N9
Dishforth N York 63 T5
Disley Ches E 56 E10
Diss Norfk 40 K4
Disserth Powys 34 B9
Distington Cumb 66 F8
Ditchampton Wilts 8 F2
Ditcheat Somset 17 R9
Ditchingham Norfk 41 P2
Ditchling E Susx 11 N7
Ditherington Shrops 45 M11
Ditteridge Wilts 18 B7
Dittisham Devon 5 V9
Ditton Kent 12 D4
Ditton Green Cambs 39 U9
Ditton Priors Shrops 35 P3
Dixton Gloucs 28 J1
Dixton Mons 27 U5
Dizzard Cnwll 14 E13
Dobcross Oldham 56 E5
Dobwalls Cnwll 4 G7
Doccombe Devon 5 T3
Dochgarroch Highld 102 H7
Dockenfield Surrey 10 C2
Docker Lancs 62 B5
Docking Norfk 50 C6
Docklow Herefs 35 N9
Dockray Cumb 67 L2
Dockray W & F 67 N8
Dodbrooke Devon 5 S12
Doddinghurst Essex 22 E8
Doddington Cambs 39 P2
Doddington Kent 12 H4
Doddington Lincs 58 F12
Doddington Nthumb 85 P12
Doddington Shrops 35 P5
Doddiscombsleigh Devon 5 V3
Dodd's Green Ches E 45 P5
Doddshill Norfk 49 U8
Doddy Cross Cnwll 4 J8
Dodford W Nthn 37 R8
Dodford Worcs 36 B6
Dodington S Glos 28 E11
Dodington Somset 16 G8
Dodleston Ches W 44 J1
Dodscott Devon 15 M9
Dodside E Rens 81 Q2
Dod's Leigh Staffs 46 D7
Dodworth Barns 57 M5
Dodworth Bottom Barns 57 M6
Dodworth Green Barns 57 M6
Doe Bank Birm 46 F14
Doe Lea Derbys 57 Q13
Dogdyke Lincs 48 K2
Dogley Lane Kirk 56 J4
Dogmersfield Hants 20 C12
Dogridge Wilts 29 L10
Dogsthorpe C Pete 48 J13
Dog Village Devon 6 C5
Dolanog Powys 44 C11
Dolau Powys 34 D7
Dolaucothi Carmth 33 N12
Dolbenmaen Gwynd 42 K5
Doley Staffs 45 R7
Dolfach Powys 33 U4
Dolfor Powys 34 D3
Dol-för Powys 43 R12
Dolgarrog Conwy 53 N9
Dolgellau Gwynd 43 P10
Dolgoch Gwynd 43 N13
Dol-gran Carmth 25 R4
Doll Highld 109 R4
Dollar Clacks 90 E12
Dollarfield Clacks 90 E12
Dolley Green Powys 34 G7
Dollwen Cerdgn 33 N4
Dolphin Flints 54 E12
Dolphinholme Lancs 61 U9
Dolphinton S Lans 83 M9
Dolton Devon 15 N10
Dolwen Conwy 53 Q8
Dolwyddelan Conwy 43 P3
Dolybont Cerdgn 33 M3
Dolyhir Powys 34 F9
Domgay Powys 44 G10
Donaldson's Lodge Nthumb 85 M10
Doncaster Donc 57 S6
Doncaster Carr Donc 57 S6
Doncaster North Services Donc 57 U4
Donhead St Andrew Wilts 8 C4
Donhead St Mary Wilts 8 C4
Donibristle Fife 90 J14
Doniford Somset 16 E8
Donington Lincs 48 K6
Donington on Bain Lincs 59 M10
Donington Park Services Leics 47 N8
Donington Southing Lincs 48 K7
Donisthorpe Leics 46 K11
Donkey Street Kent 13 M9
Donkey Town Surrey 20 F10
Donnington Gloucs 29 N2
Donnington Herefs 35 R14
Donnington Shrops 45 N12
Donnington W Berk 19 Q7
Donnington W Susx 10 D10
Donnington Wrekin 45 R11
Donnington Wood Wrekin 45 R11
Donyatt Somset 6 K2
Doomsday Green W Susx 10 K5
Doonfoot S Ayrs 81 L9
Dora's Green Hants 20 D13
Dorback Lodge Highld 103 S12
Dorchester Dorset 7 S6
Dorchester-on-Thames Oxon 19 S2
Dordon Warwks 46 J13
Dore Sheff 57 M10
Dores Highld 102 G9
Dorking Surrey 21 L13
Dorking Tye Suffk 40 F13
Dormansland Surrey 11 Q2
Dormans Park Surrey 11 P2
Dormington Herefs 35 N12
Dormston Worcs 36 C9
Dorn Gloucs 29 P1
Dorney Bucks 20 F7
Dorney Reach Bucks 20 F7
Dornie Highld 101 M6
Dornoch Highld 109 P7
Dornock D & G 75 P12
Dorrery Highld 112 C6
Dorridge Solhll 36 G6
Dorrington Lincs 48 G3
Dorrington Shrops 45 L13
Dorrington Shrops 45 R5
Dorsington Warwks 36 F11
Dorstone Herefs 34 H12
Dorton Bucks 30 E10
Dosthill Staffs 46 H14
Dothan IoA 52 E8
Dottery Dorset 7 N5
Doublebois Cnwll 4 F8
Doughton Gloucs 28 G9
Douglas IoM 60 f7
Douglas S Lans 82 F12
Douglas and Angus C Dund 91 P5
Douglas Pier Ag & B 88 E6
Douglastown Angus 91 P2
Douglas Water S Lans 82 G11
Douglas West S Lans 82 F12
Doulting Somset 17 R8
Dounby Ork 106 r17
Doune Highld 108 G4
Doune Stirlg 89 R5
Dounepark S Ayrs 80 H13
Dounie Highld 108 K6
Dousland Devon 5 N7
Dovaston Shrops 44 J9
Dove Dale Derbys 46 F3
Dove Green Notts 47 N3
Dove Holes Derbys 56 G11
Dovenby Cumb 66 G6
Dover Kent 13 R7
Dover Wigan 55 P6
Dover Castle Kent 13 R7
Dovercourt Essex 23 T1
Doverdale Worcs 35 U7
Doveridge Derbys 46 F7
Doversgreen Surrey 21 N13
Dowally P & K 90 F2
Dowbridge Lancs 61 S13
Dowdeswell Gloucs 28 K4
Dowlais Myr Td 26 K6
Dowland Devon 15 N10
Dowlish Ford Somset 7 L2
Dowlish Wake Somset 7 L2
Down Ampney Gloucs 29 L8
Downderry Cnwll 4 J10
Downe Gt Lon 21 R10
Downend Gloucs 28 F8
Downend IoW 9 Q11
Downend S Glos 28 C12
Downend W Berk 19 Q5
Downfield C Dund 91 N5
Downgate Cnwll 4 H6
Downgate Cnwll 4 K6
Downham Essex 22 H8
Downham Gt Lon 21 Q8
Downham Lancs 62 F11
Downham Market Norfk 49 T13
Down Hatherley Gloucs 28 G3
Downhead Somset 17 P11
Downhead Somset 17 S7
Downhill Cnwll 3 M3
Downhill P & K 90 G6
Downholland Cross Lancs 54 J5
Downholme N York 69 P13
Downicarey Devon 4 K2
Downies Abers 99 S5
Downing Flints 54 E11
Downley Bucks 20 D3
Down St Mary Devon 15 R12
Downside Somset 17 R6
Downside Somset 17 R8
Downside Surrey 20 K11
Down Thomas Devon 5 N10
Downton Hants 8 K10
Downton Wilts 8 H4
Dowsby Lincs 48 H8
Dowsdale Lincs 49 L11
Doxey Staffs 45 U9
Doxford Nthumb 85 T14
Doynton S Glos 17 T2
Draethen Caerph 27 N10
Draffan S Lans 82 E9
Dragonby N Linc 58 F4
Dragons Green W Susx 10 J6
Drakeholes Notts 58 B8
Drakelow Worcs 35 T4
Drakemyre N Ayrs 80 K2
Drakes Broughton Worcs 36 B11
Drakewalls Cnwll 5 L6
Draughton N York 63 L9
Draughton W Nthn 37 U5
Drax N York 57 U1
Drax Hales N York 57 U1
Draycote Warwks 37 M6
Draycot Foliat Swindn 18 J5
Draycott Derbys 47 M7
Draycott Gloucs 36 G13
Draycott Shrops 35 T2
Draycott Somset 17 N6
Draycott Somset 17 Q12
Draycott Worcs 35 U11
Draycott in the Clay Staffs 46 G8
Draycott in the Moors Staffs 46 C5
Drayford Devon 15 S10
Drayton C Port 9 T8
Drayton Leics 38 B2
Drayton Lincs 48 K6
Drayton Norfk 51 L11
Drayton Oxon 29 U9
Drayton Oxon 37 M12
Drayton Somset 17 M12
Drayton Somset 17 N13
Drayton Worcs 36 B5
Drayton Bassett Staffs 46 G13
Drayton Beauchamp Bucks 30 K10
Drayton Manor Resort Staffs 46 G13
Drayton Parslow Bucks 30 H7
Drayton St Leonard Oxon 30 C13
Drebley N York 63 M8
Dreemskerry IoM 60 h4
Dreen Hill Pembks 24 F8
Drefach Carmth 25 Q3
Drefach Carmth 25 T8
Drefach Cerdgn 32 J11
Drefelin Carmth 25 Q3
Dreghorn N Ayrs 81 M5
Drellingore Kent 13 P7
Drem E Loth 84 E3
Dresden C Stke 46 B5
Drewsteignton Devon 5 S2
Driby Lincs 59 Q12
Driffield E R Yk 65 N8
Driffield Gloucs 29 L8
Driffield Cross Roads Gloucs 29 L8
Drift Cnwll 2 C11
Drigg Cumb 66 G13
Drighlington Leeds 63 Q14
Drimnin Highld 93 P8
Drimpton Dorset 7 M4
Drimsallie Highld 94 D3
Dringhouses C York 64 D10
Drinkstone Suffk 40 G8
Drinkstone Green Suffk 40 G8
Drive End Dorset 7 Q3
Driver's End Herts 31 R8
Drointon Staffs 46 D8
Droitwich Spa Worcs 35 U8
Dron P & K 90 H8
Dronfield Derbys 57 N11
Dronfield Woodhouse Derbys 57 M11
Drongan E Ayrs 81 N9
Dronley Angus 91 M4
Droop Dorset 7 U3
Dropping Well Rothm 57 N8
Droxford Hants 9 S5
Droylsden Tamesd 56 D7
Druid Denbgs 44 B5
Druidston Pembks 24 E7
Druimarbin Highld 94 F4
Druimavuic Ag & B 94 E9
Druimdrishaig Ag & B 87 N11
Druimindarroch Highld 93 R2
Drum Ag & B 87 S10
Drum P & K 90 F11
Drumalbin S Lans 82 H11
Drumbeg Highld 110 C10
Drumblade Abers 104 H7
Drumbreddon D & G 72 D11
Drumbuie Highld 100 g6
Drumburgh Cumb 75 Q14
Drumburn D & G 66 C2
Drumburn D & G 74 J13
Drumchapel C Glas 89 M11
Drumchastle P & K 95 T7
Drumclog S Lans 81 S5
Drumeldrie Fife 91 P11
Drumelzier Border 83 M12
Drumfearn Highld 100 f8
Drumfrennie Abers 99 N4
Drumgley Angus 98 G13
Drumguish Highld 97 M4
Drumin Moray 103 U9
Drumjohn D & G 81 Q13
Drumlamford S Ayrs 72 H4
Drumlasie Abers 99 L2
Drumleaning Cumb 67 L2
Drumlemble Ag & B 79 M12
Drumlithie Abers 99 P7
Drummoddie D & G 72 K10
Drummore D & G 72 E12
Drummuir Moray 104 D7
Drumnadrochit Highld 102 F9
Drumnagorrach Moray 104 G5
Drumoak Abers 99 P4
Drumpark D & G 74 G10
Drumrunie Highld 108 B3
Drumshang S Ayrs 80 K10
Drumuie Highld 100 d5
Drumuillie Highld 103 P11
Drumvaich Stirlg 89 Q5
Drunzie P & K 90 H10
Druridge Nthumb 77 R6
Drury Flints 54 G14
Drws-y-coed Gwynd 52 H12
Drybeck W & F 68 E9
Drybridge Moray 104 E3
Drybridge N Ayrs 81 M5
Drybrook Gloucs 28 B4
Dryburgh Border 84 F12
Dry Doddington Lincs 48 C4
Dry Drayton Cambs 39 N8
Dryhill Kent 21 S12
Drymen Stirlg 89 L8
Drymuir Abers 105 Q6
Drynoch Highld 100 d6
Dry Sandford Oxon 29 U7
Dryslwyn Carmth 25 U6
Dry Street Essex 22 G10
Dryton Shrops 45 N12
Dubford Abers 105 M3
Dublin Suffk 41 L7
Duchally Highld 110 H13
Duck End Bed 31 N4
Duck End Cambs 38 K8
Duck End Essex 22 G2
Duck End Essex 39 U14
Duckend Green Essex 22 H3
Duckington Ches W 45 L3
Ducklington Oxon 29 S6
Duck's Cross Bed 38 H9
Duddenhoe End Essex 39 Q13
Duddingston C Edin 83 Q4
Duddington N Nthn 48 E13
Duddlestone Somset 16 H12
Duddleswell E Susx 11 R5
Duddlewick Shrops 35 Q4
Duddo Nthumb 85 N10
Duddon Ches W 55 M14
Duddon Bridge Cumb 61 M2
Duddon Common Ches W 55 M13
Dudleston Shrops 44 H6
Dudleston Heath Shrops 44 J6
Dudley Dudley 36 B2
Dudley N Tyne 77 R11
Dudley Hill C Brad 63 P13
Dudley Port Sandw 36 C2
Dudnill Shrops 35 P6
Dudsbury Dorset 8 F9
Dudswell Herts 31 L11
Duffield Derbys 46 K5
Duffryn Neath 26 E8
Dufftown Moray 104 C7
Duffus Moray 103 U3
Dufton W & F 68 E7
Duggleby N York 64 K6
Duirinish Highld 100 h6
Duisdalemore Highld 100 g8
Duisky Highld 94 E4
Dukestown Blae G 27 L5
Duke Street Suffk 40 J12
Dukinfield Tamesd 56 D7
Dulas IoA 52 G5
Dulcote Somset 17 Q8
Dulford Devon 6 E3
Dull P & K 90 B2
Dullatur N Lans 89 R10
Dullingham Cambs 39 T9
Dullingham Ley Cambs 39 T9
Dulnain Bridge Highld 103 Q11
Duloe Bed 38 J8
Duloe Cnwll 4 G9
Dulsie Bridge Highld 103 P7
Dulverton Somset 16 B11
Dulwich Gt Lon 21 P8
Dumbarton W Duns 88 J10
Dumbleton Gloucs 36 D13
Dumfries D & G 74 J10
Dumgoyne Stirlg 89 M9
Dummer Hants 19 S11
Dumpton Kent 13 S2
Dun Angus 99 M12
Dunalastair P & K 95 U7
Dunan Ag & B 88 E11
Dunan Highld 100 e7
Dunan P & K 95 P7
Dunaverty Ag & B 79 M14
Dunball Somset 16 K8
Dunbar E Loth 84 H3
Dunbeath Highld 112 E11
Dunbeg Ag & B 94 B12
Dunblane Stirlg 89 S5
Dunbog Fife 91 L8
Dunbridge Hants 9 L3
Duncanston Highld 102 G4
Duncanstone Abers 104 H10
Dunchideock Devon 6 A7
Dunchurch Warwks 37 N6
Duncote W Nthn 37 S10
Duncow D & G 74 J9
Duncrievie P & K 90 H11
Duncton W Susx 10 F7
Dundee C Dund 91 P5
Dundee Airport C Dund 91 N6
Dundon Somset 17 M10
Dundonald S Ayrs 81 M6
Dundonnell Highld 107 U7
Dundraw Cumb 66 K3
Dundreggan Highld 102 B13
Dundrennan D & G 73 S10
Dundry N Som 17 Q3
Dunecht Abers 99 P2
Dunfermline Fife 83 L1
Dunfield Gloucs 29 M8
Dunford Bridge Barns 56 J6
Dungate Kent 12 J4
Dungavel S Lans 81 S5
Dunge Wilts 18 C10
Dungeness Kent 13 L12
Dungworth Sheff 57 L9
Dunham Massey Traffd 55 R9
Dunham-on-the-Hill Ches W 55 L12
Dunham-on-Trent Notts 58 D12
Dunhampstead Worcs 36 B8
Dunhampton Worcs 35 T7
Dunham Town Traffd 55 R9
Dunham Woodhouses Traffd 55 R9
Dunholme Lincs 58 H11
Dunino Fife 91 R9
Dunipace Falk 89 T9
Dunkeld P & K 90 F3
Dunkerton BaNES 17 T5
Dunkeswell Devon 6 F3
Dunkeswick N York 63 S10
Dunkirk Ches W 54 J12
Dunkirk Kent 13 L4
Dunkirk S Glos 28 E10
Dunkirk Wilts 18 E8
Dunk's Green Kent 12 B5
Dunlappie Angus 98 K10
Dunley Hants 19 Q10
Dunley Worcs 35 S7
Dunlop E Ayrs 81 N3
Dunmaglass Highld 102 G11
Dunmere Cnwll 3 Q3
Dunmore Falk 90 C14
Dunnet Highld 112 F2
Dunnichen Angus 91 R2
Dunning P & K 90 F9
Dunnington C York 64 F9
Dunnington E R Yk 65 R9
Dunnington Warwks 36 E10
Dunnockshaw Lancs 62 G14
Dunn Street Kent 12 E3
Dunoon Ag & B 88 E10
Dunphail Moray 103 R6
Dunragit D & G 72 F8
Duns Border 84 K8
Dunsa Derbys 56 K12
Dunsby Lincs 48 H8
Dunscar Bolton 55 R4
Dunscore D & G 74 G9
Dunscroft Donc 57 T5
Dunsdale R & Cl 70 K9
Dunsden Green Oxon 20 B7
Dunsdon Devon 14 H11
Dunsfold Surrey 10 G3
Dunsford Devon 5 U3
Dunshalt Fife 91 L9
Dunshillock Abers 105 R6
Dunsill Notts 47 N1
Dunsley N York 71 Q10
Dunsley Staffs 35 U4
Dunsmore Bucks 30 J11
Dunsop Bridge Lancs 62 D10
Dunstable C Beds 31 M8
Dunstall Staffs 46 G9
Dunstall Common Worcs 35 U12
Dunstall Green Suffk 40 B8
Dunstan Nthumb 77 Q2
Dunstan Steads Nthumb 77 Q1
Dunster Somset 16 C8
Duns Tew Oxon 29 U2
Dunston Gatesd 77 Q13
Dunston Lincs 58 J14
Dunston Norfk 51 M13
Dunston Staffs 46 B10
Dunstone Devon 5 P10
Dunstone Devon 5 S5
Dunston Heath Staffs 46 B10
Dunsville Donc 57 T5
Dunswell E R Yk 65 P12
Dunsyre S Lans 83 L9
Dunterton Devon 4 K5
Dunthrop Oxon 29 S2
Duntisbourne Abbots Gloucs 28 J6
Duntisbourne Leer Gloucs 28 J6
Duntisbourne Rouse Gloucs 28 J6
Duntish Dorset 7 S3
Duntocher W Duns 89 L11
Dunton Bucks 30 H8
Dunton C Beds 31 R4
Dunton Norfk 50 E7
Dunton Bassett Leics 37 P2
Dunton Green Kent 21 T11
Dunton Wayletts Essex 22 G9
Duntulm Highld 100 d2
Dunure S Ayrs 80 K9
Dunvant Swans 25 U12
Dunvegan Highld 100 b5
Dunwich Suffk 41 S6
Dunwood Staffs 46 B2
Durdar Cumb 67 P2
Durgan Cnwll 2 K11
Durgates E Susx 12 B9
Durham Dur 69 S4
Durham Cathedral Dur 69 S4
Durham Services Dur 70 D5
Durisdeer D & G 74 G5
Durisdeermill D & G 74 G5
Durkar Wakefd 57 M3
Durleigh Somset 16 J9
Durley Hants 9 Q5
Durley Wilts 18 K8
Durley Street Hants 9 Q5
Durlock Kent 13 Q4
Durlock Kent 13 R3
Durlow Common Herefs 35 P13
Durn Rochdl 56 D3
Durness Highld 110 J3
Durno Abers 105 L10
Duror Highld 94 D7
Durran Ag & B 87 T4
Durrington W Susx 10 J9
Durrington Wilts 18 J12
Dursley Gloucs 28 E8
Dursley Cross Gloucs 28 C3
Durston Somset 16 J11
Durweston Dorset 8 B7
Duston W Nthn 37 U8
Duthil Highld 103 P11
Dutlas Powys 34 F5
Duton Hill Essex 22 F2
Dutson Cnwll 4 J3
Dutton Ches W 55 N11
Duxford Cambs 39 Q11
Duxford Oxon 29 S8
Duxford IWM Cambs 39 Q11
Dwygyfylchi Conwy 53 M7
Dwyran IoA 52 F10
Dyce C Aber 105 P13
Dyer's End Essex 40 B13
Dyfatty Carmth 25 S10
Dyffrydan Gwynd 43 N11
Dyffryn Brdgnd 26 F9
Dyffryn Myr Td 26 K7
Dyffryn V Glam 16 E2
Dyffryn Ardudwy Gwynd 43 L9
Dyffryn Castell Cerdgn 33 Q4
Dyffryn Cellwen Neath 26 F5
Dyke Lincs 48 H8
Dyke Moray 103 Q4
Dykehead Angus 98 C13
Dykehead Angus 98 F12
Dykehead N Lans 82 G7
Dykehead Stirlg 89 N7
Dykelands Abers 99 N10
Dykends Angus 98 C12
Dykeside Abers 105 L7
Dykes of Gray C Dund 91 M5
Dylife Powys 33 S2
Dymchurch Kent 13 M10
Dymock Gloucs 35 R14
Dynamic Earth C Edin 83 Q4
Dyrham S Glos 28 D12
Dysart Fife 91 M13
Dyserth Denbgs 54 C11

E

Eachway Worcs 36 C5
Eachwick Nthumb 77 N11
Eagland Hill Lancs 61 S10
Eagle Lincs 58 E13
Eagle Barnsdale Lincs 58 E13
Eagle Moor Lincs 58 E13
Eaglescliffe S on T 70 F9
Eaglesfield Cumb 66 G7
Eaglesfield D & G 75 P11
Eaglesham E Rens 81 R2
Eagley Bolton 55 R4
Eairy IoM 60 d7
Eakring Notts 47 S1
Ealand N Linc 58 C4
Ealing Gt Lon 21 L6
Eals Nthumb 76 E14
Eamont Bridge W & F 67 R7
Earby Lancs 62 J10
Earcroft Bl w D 55 Q2
Eardington Shrops 35 R2
Eardisland Herefs 34 K9
Eardisley Herefs 34 H11
Eardiston Shrops 44 J8
Eardiston Worcs 35 Q7
Earith Cambs 39 N6
Earle Nthumb 85 P13
Earlestown St Hel 55 N7
Earley Wokham 20 B8
Earlham Norfk 51 L12
Earlish Highld 100 c3
Earls Barton N Nthn 38 C8
Earls Colne Essex 23 L2
Earls Common Worcs 36 C9
Earl's Croome Worcs 35 U12
Earlsditton Shrops 35 P5
Earlsdon Covtry 36 K5
Earl's Down E Susx 11 U7
Earlsferry Fife 91 Q11
Earlsfield Gt Lon 21 N8
Earlsford Abers 105 N9
Earl's Green Suffk 40 H7
Earlsheaton Kirk 56 K2
Earl Shilton Leics 47 N14
Earl Soham Suffk 41 M8
Earl Sterndale Derbys 56 G13
Earlston Border 84 F11
Earlston E Ayrs 81 N5
Earl Stonham Suffk 40 K9
Earlswood Surrey 21 N13
Earlswood Warwks 36 F6
Earlswood Common Mons 27 T9
Earnley W Susx 10 C11
Earnshaw Bridge Lancs 55 M2
Earsdon N Tyne 77 S11
Earsdon Nthumb 77 P7
Earsham Norfk 41 P3
Earswick C York 64 E8
Eartham W Susx 10 E9
Earthcott S Glos 28 C10
Easby N York 70 J11
Easdale Ag & B 87 N2
Easebourne W Susx 10 D6
Easenhall Warwks 37 N5
Eashing Surrey 10 E2
Easington Bucks 30 E10
Easington Dur 70 F4
Easington E R Yk 59 Q3
Easington Nthumb 85 S12
Easington Oxon 30 E13
Easington R & Cl 71 M9
Easington Colliery Dur 70 F4
Easington Lane Sundld 70 E3
Easingwold N York 64 C6
Easole Street Kent 13 Q5
Eassie and Nevay Angus 91 M3
East Aberthaw V Glam 16 D3
East Allington Devon 5 T11
East Anstey Devon 15 U7
East Anton Hants 19 N11
East Appleton N York 69 R13
East Ardsley Leeds 57 M1
East Ashey IoW 9 R11
East Ashling W Susx 10 C9
East Aston Hants 19 P11
East Ayton N York 65 M2
East Balsdon Cnwll 14 G13
East Bank Blae G 27 N6
East Barkwith Lincs 59 L10
East Barming Kent 12 D5
East Barnby N York 71 P10
East Barnet Gt Lon 21 N3
East Barns E Loth 84 J3
East Barsham Norfk 50 F7
East Beckham Norfk 51 L6
East Bedfont Gt Lon 20 J8
East Bergholt Suffk 40 J14
East Bierley Kirk 63 P14
East Bilney Norfk 50 G10
East Blatchington E Susx 11 R10
East Bloxworth Dorset 8 B10
East Boldon S Tyne 77 T13
East Boldre Hants 9 M8
East Bolton Nthumb 77 N2
Eastbourne Darltn 70 D10
Eastbourne E Susx 11 U11
East Bower Somset 16 K9
East Bradenham Norfk 50 F12
East Brent Somset 16 K6
Eastbridge Suffk 41 S7
East Bridgford Notts 47 S5
East Briscoe Dur 69 L9
Eastbrook V Glam 16 G2
East Buckland Devon 15 Q6
East Budleigh Devon 6 E8
Eastburn C Brad 63 L11
Eastburn E R Yk 65 M8
East Burnham Bucks 20 G6
East Burton Dorset 8 A11
Eastbury W Berk 19 M5
East Butsfield Dur 69 P3
East Butterwick N Linc 58 D5
Eastby N York 63 L9
East Calder W Loth 83 L5
East Carleton Norfk 51 L13
East Carlton Leeds 63 Q11
East Carlton N Nthn 38 B3
East Chaldon Dorset 7 U8
East Challow Oxon 29 S10
East Charleton Devon 5 T12
East Chelborough Dorset 7 Q3
East Chiltington E Susx 11 P7
East Chinnock Somset 7 N2
East Chisenbury Wilts 18 H10
East Cholderton Hants 19 L11
Eastchurch Kent 23 N13
East Clandon Surrey 20 J12
East Claydon Bucks 30 F7
East Clevedon N Som 17 M2
East Coker Somset 7 P2
Eastcombe Gloucs 28 G7
Eastcombe Somset 16 G10
East Compton Somset 17 R8
East Cornworthy Devon 5 V10
Eastcote Gt Lon 20 K5
Eastcote Solhll 36 G5
Eastcote W Nthn 37 S10
Eastcott Cnwll 14 G9
Eastcott Wilts 18 F9
East Cottingwith E R Yk 64 G11
Eastcourt Wilts 18 K8
Eastcourt Wilts 28 J9
East Cowes IoW 9 Q9
East Cowick E R Yk 57 U2
East Cowton N York 70 D12
East Cramlington Nthumb 77 R10
East Cranmore Somset 17 S8
East Creech Dorset 8 C12
East Curthwaite Cumb 67 M3
East Dean E Susx 11 T11
East Dean Gloucs 28 C3
East Dean Hants 8 K3
East Dean W Susx 10 E8
Eastdown Devon 5 U11
East Down Devon 15 P4
East Drayton Notts 58 C11
East Dulwich Gt Lon 21 P7
East Dundry N Som 17 Q3
East Ella C KuH 65 P14
East End Bed 38 H9
East End C Beds 31 L4
East End E R Yk 59 N1
East End E R Yk 65 R13
East End Essex 22 B5
East End Essex 23 M9
East End Hants 9 M9
East End Hants 19 P8
East End Herts 22 C2
East End Kent 12 F8
East End Kent 23 N13
East End M Keyn 30 K4
East End Oxon 29 S5
East End Somset 17 S7
East End Suffk 40 K13
Easter Balmoral Abers 98 D5
Easter Compton S Glos 27 V11
Easter Dalziel Highld 103 L5
Eastergate W Susx 10 E9
Easterhouse C Glas 89 Q12
Easter Howgate Mdloth 83 P6
Easter Kinkell Highld 102 G4
Easter Moniack Highld 102 F7
Eastern Green Covtry 36 J5
Easter Ord Abers 99 Q3
Easter Pitkierie Fife 91 S10
Easter Skeld Shet 106 t9
Easter Softlaw Border 84 K12
Easterton Wilts 18 F10
Eastertown Somset 16 K6
East Everleigh Wilts 18 K10
East Farleigh Kent 12 D5
East Farndon W Nthn 37 T3
East Ferry Lincs 58 D7
Eastfield N Lans 82 G6
Eastfield N York 65 N3
East Firsby Lincs 58 H9
East Fortune E Loth 84 E3
East Garforth Leeds 63 U13
East Garston W Berk 19 N5
Eastgate Dur 69 L5
Eastgate Lincs 48 H10
Eastgate Norfk 50 K9
East Ginge Oxon 29 T10
East Goscote Leics 47 R11
East Grafton Wilts 18 L8
East Green Suffk 41 R8
East Grimstead Wilts 8 J3
East Grinstead W Susx 11 P3
East Guldeford E Susx 12 H11
East Haddon W Nthn 37 S7
East Hagbourne Oxon 19 R3
East Halton N Linc 58 K3
East Ham Gt Lon 21 R6
Eastham Wirral 54 J10
Eastham Ferry Wirral 54 J10
Easthampton Herefs 34 K8
East Hanney Oxon 29 T9
East Hanningfield Essex 22 J7
East Hardwick Wakefd 57 Q3
East Harling Norfk 40 G3
East Harlsey N York 70 F13
East Harnham Wilts 8 G3
East Harptree BaNES 17 Q5
East Hartford Nthumb 77 R10
East Harting W Susx 10 B7
East Hatch Wilts 8 C3
East Hatley Cambs 39 L10
Easthaugh Norfk 50 K10
East Hauxwell N York 69 Q14
East Haven Angus 91 S4
Eastheath Wokham 20 D9
East Heckington Lincs 48 J5

Foxt – Gwalchmai 131

Foxt Staffs 46 D4
Foxton Cambs 39 P11
Foxton Dur 70 E8
Foxton Leics 37 T3
Foxton N York 70 F13
Foxup N York 62 H4
Foxwist Green Ches W 55 P13
Foxwood Shrops 35 P5
Foy Herefs 28 A2
Foyers Highld 102 E11
Foynesfield Highld 103 N5
Fraddam Cnwll 2 F10
Fraddon Cnwll 3 N5
Fradley Staffs 46 G11
Fradswell Staffs 46 C7
Fraisthorpe E R Yk 65 R7
Framfield E Susx 11 R6
Framingham Earl Norfk 51 N13
Framingham Pigot Norfk 51 N13
Framlingham Suffk 41 N8
Frampton Dorset 7 R5
Frampton Lincs 49 M6
Frampton Cotterell S Glos 28 C11
Frampton Mansell Gloucs 28 H7
Frampton-on-Severn Gloucs 28 D6
Frampton West End Lincs 49 M5
Framsden Suffk 41 L9
Framwellgate Moor Dur 69 S4
Franche Worcs 35 T5
Frandley Ches W 55 P11
Frankaborough Devon 4 K2
Frankby Wirral 54 F9
Frankfort Norfk 51 P9
Franklands Gate Herefs 35 M11
Frankley Worcs 36 C4
Frankley Services Worcs 36 C4
Franksbridge Powys 34 D9
Frankton Warwks 37 M6
Frant E Susx 11 T3
Fraserburgh Abers 105 R2
Frating Essex 23 Q3
Frating Green Essex 23 Q3
Fratton C Port 9 T8
Freathy Cnwll 4 K10
Freckenham Suffk 39 U6
Freckleton Lancs 61 S14
Freebirch Derbys 57 M12
Freeby Leics 48 B9
Freefolk Hants 19 Q11
Freehay Staffs 46 D5
Freeland Oxon 29 T5
Freethorpe Norfk 51 R12
Freethorpe Common Norfk 51 R13
Freiston Lincs 49 N5
Fremington Devon 15 M6
Fremington N York 69 M13
Frenchay S Glos 28 B12
Frenchbeer Devon 5 R3
French Street Kent 21 S12
Frenich P & K 97 N12
Frensham Surrey 10 C2
Freshfield Sefton 54 G5
Freshford Wilts 17 U4
Freshwater IoW 9 L11
Freshwater Bay IoW 9 L11
Freshwater East Pembks 24 H11
Fressingfield Suffk 41 N5
Freston Suffk 41 L13
Freswick Highld 112 J3
Fretherne Gloucs 28 D5
Frettenham Norfk 51 M10
Freuchie Fife 91 L10
Freystrop Pembks 24 G8
Friar Park Sandw 36 D2
Friar's Gate E Susx 11 R4
Friars' Hill N York 64 G2
Friar Waddon Dorset 7 R7
Friday Bridge Cambs 49 Q13
Friday Street Suffk 41 M9
Friday Street Suffk 41 P10
Friday Street Suffk 41 Q8
Friday Street Surrey 20 K13
Fridaythorpe E R Yk 64 K8
Friden Derbys 46 G1
Friendly Calder 56 G2
Friern Barnet Gt Lon 21 N4
Friesthorpe Lincs 58 J10
Frieston Lincs 48 D4
Frieth Bucks 20 C4
Friezeland Notts 47 N3
Frilford Oxon 29 T8
Frilsham W Berk 19 R6
Frimley Surrey 20 E11
Frimley Green Surrey 20 E11
Frindsbury Medway 12 D2
Fring Norfk 50 B7
Fringford Oxon 30 D7
Frinsted Kent 12 G4
Frinton-on-Sea Essex 23 T3
Friockheim Angus 91 S2
Friog Gwynd 43 M11
Frisby on the Wreake Leics 47 S10
Friskney Lincs 49 Q2
Friskney Eaudike Lincs 49 Q2
Friston E Susx 11 T11
Friston Suffk 41 R8
Fritchley Derbys 47 L3
Fritham Hants 8 J6
Frith Bank Lincs 49 M4
Frith Common Worcs 35 Q7
Frithelstock Devon 15 L9
Frithelstock Stone Devon 15 L9
Frithend Hants 10 C3
Frithsden Herts 31 M11
Frithville Lincs 49 M3
Frittenden Kent 12 F7
Frittiscombe Devon 5 U12
Fritton Norfk 41 M2
Fritton Norfk 51 S13
Fritwell Oxon 30 B7
Frizinghall C Brad 63 N12
Frizington Cumb 66 F9
Frocester Gloucs 28 E7
Frodesley Shrops 45 M13
Frodsham Ches W 55 M11
Frogden Border 84 K13
Frog End Cambs 39 N11
Frog End Cambs 39 R9
Froggatt Derbys 56 K11
Froghall Staffs 46 D4
Frogham Hants 8 H6
Frogham Kent 13 Q5
Frogmore Devon 5 T12
Frognall Lincs 48 J11
Frogpool Cnwll 2 K8
Frog Pool Worcs 35 T7
Frogwell Cnwll 4 J7
Frolesworth Leics 37 P2
Frome Somset 17 U7
Frome St Quintin Dorset 7 Q4
Fromes Hill Herefs 35 Q11
Fron Gwynd 42 G6
Fron Gwynd 52 H12
Fron Powys 44 E14
Fron Powys 44 F13
Froncysyllte Wrexhm 44 G5
Fron-goch Gwynd 43 T6
Fron Isaf Wrexhm 44 G5
Frostenden Suffk 41 S4
Frosterley Dur 69 M5
Froxfield C Beds 31 L6
Froxfield Wilts 19 L7
Froxfield Green Hants 9 U3
Fryern Hill Hants 9 N4
Fryerning Essex 22 F7
Fryton N York 64 F5
Fuinary Highld 93 Q9
Fulbeck Lincs 48 D3
Fulbourn Cambs 39 R9
Fulbrook Oxon 29 Q5
Fulflood Hants 9 P2
Fulford C York 64 E10
Fulford Somset 16 H11
Fulford Staffs 46 C6
Fulham Gt Lon 21 N7
Fulking W Susx 11 L8
Fullaford Devon 15 Q5
Fullarton N Ayrs 81 L5
Fuller's End Essex 22 D2
Fuller's Moor Ches W 45 L3
Fuller Street Essex 22 H4
Fuller Street Kent 21 U11
Fullerton Hants 19 N13
Fulletby Lincs 59 N12
Fullready Warwks 36 J11
Full Sutton E R Yk 64 G8
Fullwood E Ayrs 81 N2
Fulmer Bucks 20 G5
Fulmodeston Norfk 50 G7
Fulnetby Lincs 58 J11
Fulney Lincs 49 L9
Fulstone Kirk 56 J5
Fulstow Lincs 59 P7
Fulwell Oxon 29 S3
Fulwell Sundld 77 T14
Fulwood Lancs 61 U13
Fulwood Notts 47 N2
Fulwood Sheff 57 M9
Fulwood Somset 16 H12
Fundenhall Norfk 41 L1
Funtington W Susx 10 C9
Funtley Hants 9 R7
Funtullich P & K 95 V13
Furley Devon 6 J4
Furnace Ag & B 87 U5
Furnace Carmth 25 T10
Furnace Cerdgn 33 N1
Furnace End Warwks 36 H2
Furner's Green E Susx 11 Q5
Furness Vale Derbys 56 F10
Furneux Pelham Herts 22 B2
Further Quarter Kent 12 G8
Furtho W Nthn 30 G4
Furzehill Devon 15 R3
Furzehill Dorset 8 E8
Furzehills Lincs 59 N12
Furzeley Corner Hants 9 T6
Furze Platt W & M 20 E6
Furzley Hants 8 K5
Fyfett Somset 6 H2
Fyfield Essex 22 E6
Fyfield Hants 19 L11
Fyfield Oxon 29 T8
Fyfield Wilts 18 H7
Fyfield Wilts 18 J8
Fyfield Bavant Wilts 8 E3
Fylingthorpe N York 71 R12
Fyning W Susx 10 C6
Fyvie Abers 105 M8

G

Gabroc Hill E Ayrs 81 P2
Gaddesby Leics 47 S11
Gaddesden Row Herts 31 N10
Gadfa IoA 52 G5
Gadgirth S Ayrs 81 N8
Gadlas Shrops 44 J6
Gaer Powys 27 M3
Gaerllwyd Mons 27 S8
Gaerwen IoA 52 G8
Gagingwell Oxon 29 T2
Gailes N Ayrs 81 L5
Gailey Staffs 46 B11
Gainford Dur 69 Q9
Gainsborough Lincs 58 D9
Gainsborough Suffk 41 L12
Gainsford End Essex 40 B13
Gairloch Highld 107 P9
Gairlochy Highld 94 H2
Gairneybridge P & K 90 H12
Gaisgill W & F 68 D11
Gaitsgill Cumb 67 N3
Galashiels Border 84 D11
Galgate Lancs 61 T8
Galhampton Somset 17 R11
Gallanachbeg Ag & B 93 U13
Gallanachmore Ag & B 93 U13
Gallantry Bank Ches E 45 M3
Gallatown Fife 91 L13
Galley Common Warwks 36 K2
Galleywood Essex 22 H7
Gallovie Highld 96 H6
Galloway Forest Park 73 L2
Gallowfauld Angus 91 P3
Gallowhill P & K 90 J4
Gallows Green Essex 23 M2
Gallows Green Worcs 36 B8
Gallowstree Common Oxon 19 U4
Galltair Highld 100 h7
Gallt-y-foel Gwynd 52 J10
Gallypot Street E Susx 11 R3
Galmisdale Highld 93 M2
Galmpton Devon 5 R12
Galmpton Torbay 6 A13
Galphay N York 63 R5
Galston E Ayrs 81 Q5
Gamballs Green Staffs 56 F13
Gamblesby W & F 68 D5
Gambles Green Essex 22 J5
Gamelsby Cumb 67 L2
Gamesley Derbys 56 F8
Gamlingay Cambs 38 K10
Gamlingay Cinques Cambs 38 K10
Gamlingay Great Heath Cambs 38 K10
Gammersgill N York 63 M3
Gamrie Abers 105 M3
Gamston Notts 47 Q6
Gamston Notts 58 B11
Ganarew Herefs 27 U4
Ganavan Bay Ag & B 94 B12
Gang Cnwll 4 J7
Ganllwyd Gwynd 43 P9
Gannachy Angus 98 K9
Ganstead E R Yk 65 Q13
Ganthorpe N York 64 F5
Ganton N York 65 M4
Ganwick Corner Herts 21 N3
Gappah Devon 5 V5
Garbity Moray 104 C5
Garboldisham Norfk 40 H4
Garbole Highld 103 L11
Garchory Abers 104 C13
Garden City Flints 54 H13
Gardeners Green Wokham 20 D9
Gardenstown Abers 105 N3
Garden Village Sheff 57 L7
Garderhouse Shet 106 t9
Gardham E R Yk 65 M11
Gare Hill Somset 17 U8
Garelochhead Ag & B 88 F7
Garford Oxon 29 T8
Garforth Leeds 63 U13
Gargrave N York 62 J9
Gargunnock Stirlg 89 R7
Garlic Street Norfk 41 M4
Garlieston D & G 73 M10
Garlinge Kent 13 R2
Garlinge Green Kent 13 M5
Garlogie Abers 99 P2
Garmond Abers 105 N5
Garmouth Moray 104 C3
Garmston Shrops 45 P12
Garnant Carmth 26 B5
Garndolbenmaen Gwynd 42 J5
Garnett Bridge W & F 67 R13
Garnfadryn Gwynd 42 E7
Garnlydan Blae G 27 M5
Garnswllt Swans 26 A6
Garn-yr-erw Torfn 27 N6
Garrabost W Isls 106 k5
Garrallan E Ayrs 81 Q9
Garras Cnwll 2 J12
Garreg Gwynd 43 M5
Garrigill W & F 68 F4
Garriston N York 69 Q14
Garroch D & G 73 P3
Garrochtrie D & G 72 E12
Garrochty Ag & B 80 F2
Garros Highld 100 d3
Garsdale W & F 62 E2
Garsdale Head W & F 62 F1
Garsdon Wilts 28 J10
Garshall Green Staffs 46 C7
Garsington Oxon 30 C12
Garstang Lancs 61 T10
Garston Herts 31 P12
Garston Lpool 54 K10
Garswood St Hel 55 N7
Gartachossan Ag & B 78 E3
Gartcosh N Lans 82 C5
Garth Brdgnd 26 F9
Garth Mons 27 Q9
Garth Powys 33 U11
Garth Powys 34 G6
Garth Wrexhm 44 G5
Garthamlock C Glas 89 Q12
Garthbrengy Powys 34 B14
Gartheli Cerdgn 33 L9
Garthmyl Powys 44 E14
Garthorpe Leics 48 B9
Garthorpe N Linc 58 D3
Garth Row W & F 67 R13
Garths W & F 61 U2
Gartly Abers 104 G9
Gartmore Stirlg 89 M6
Gartness N Lans 82 E6
Gartness Stirlg 89 M8
Gartocharn W Duns 88 K8
Garton E R Yk 65 T12
Garton-on-the-Wolds E R Yk 65 M8
Gartymore Highld 109 U2
Garva Bridge Highld 96 G5
Garvald Border 83 M9
Garvald E Loth 84 F4
Garvan Highld 94 D3
Garvard Ag & B 86 F7
Garve Highld 102 C3
Garvellachs Ag & B 87 M3
Garvestone Norfk 50 H12
Garvock Inver 88 G11
Garway Herefs 27 T3
Garway Common Herefs 27 T3
Garway Hill Herefs 27 S2
Garynahine W Isls 106 h5
Garyvard W Isls 106 i7
Gasper Wilts 17 U10
Gastard Wilts 18 C7
Gasthorpe Norfk 40 G4
Gaston Green Essex 22 C4
Gatcombe IoW 9 P11
Gateacre Lpool 54 K9
Gatebeck W & F 61 U2
Gate Burton Lincs 58 D10
Gateford Notts 57 S10
Gateforth N York 64 D14
Gatehead E Ayrs 81 M5
Gate Helmsley N York 64 F8
Gatehouse Nthumb 76 F8
Gatehouse of Fleet D & G 73 P8
Gateley Norfk 50 G9
Gatenby N York 63 S2
Gatesgarth Cumb 66 J9
Gateshaw Border 76 F1
Gateshead Gatesd 77 R13
Gates Heath Ches W 45 L1
Gateside Angus 91 P3
Gateside E Rens 89 L14
Gateside Fife 90 J10
Gateside N Ayrs 81 M2
Gateslack D & G 74 G5
Gathurst Wigan 55 M5
Gatley Stockp 55 T9
Gatton Surrey 21 N12
Gattonside Border 84 E11
Gatwick Airport W Susx 11 M2
Gaufron Powys 33 U7
Gaulby Leics 47 S13
Gauldry Fife 91 N7
Gauldswell P & K 98 C13
Gaulkthorn Lancs 55 S1
Gaultree Norfk 49 Q12
Gaunton's Bank Ches E 45 N4
Gaunt's Common Dorset 8 E7
Gaunt's End Essex 22 E2
Gautby Lincs 59 L12
Gavinton Border 84 K8
Gawber Barns 57 M5
Gawcott Bucks 30 E6
Gawsworth Ches E 56 C13
Gawthorpe Wakefd 57 L2
Gawthrop W & F 62 D2
Gawthwaite W & F 61 P3
Gay Bowers Essex 22 J7
Gaydon Warwks 37 L10
Gayhurst M Keyn 38 B11
Gayle N York 62 H2
Gayles N York 69 P11
Gay Street W Susx 10 H6
Gayton Norfk 50 B10
Gayton Staffs 46 C8
Gayton W Nthn 37 T10
Gayton Wirral 54 G10
Gayton le Marsh Lincs 59 R10
Gayton Thorpe Norfk 50 B10
Gaywood Norfk 49 T9
Gazeley Suffk 40 B8
Gear Cnwll 2 J12
Gearraidh Bhaird W Isls 106 i7
Gearraidh na h-Aibhne W Isls 106 h5
Geary Highld 100 b3
Gedding Suffk 40 F9
Geddington N Nthn 38 C4
Gedling Notts 47 R5
Gedney Lincs 49 P9
Gedney Broadgate Lincs 49 P9
Gedney Drove End Lincs 49 Q8
Gedney Dyke Lincs 49 P8
Gedney Hill Lincs 49 M11
Gee Cross Tamesd 56 E8
Geeston Rutlnd 48 E13
Geirinis W Isls 106 c14
Geldeston Norfk 41 Q2
Gelli Rhondd 26 H9
Gelli Torfn 27 P9
Gellideg Myr Td 26 J6
Gellifor Denbgs 44 D1
Gelligaer Caerph 27 L8
Gelligroes Caerph 27 M9
Gelligron Neath 26 C7
Gellilydan Gwynd 43 N6
Gellinudd Neath 26 C7
Gelly Pembks 24 J7
Gellyburn P & K 90 G4
Gellywen Carmth 25 N6
Gelston D & G 74 E14
Gelston Lincs 48 D4
Gembling E R Yk 65 Q8
Gentleshaw Staffs 46 E11
Georgefield D & G 75 Q7
George Green Bucks 20 G6
Georgeham Devon 15 L5
Georgemas Junction Station Highld 112 E5
George Nympton Devon 15 R8
Georgetown Blae G 27 M6
Georgia Cnwll 2 D9
Georth Ork 106 s17
Gerinish W Isls 106 c14
Gerlan Gwynd 52 K9
Germansweek Devon 5 L2
Germoe Cnwll 2 F11
Gerrans Cnwll 3 M9
Gerrards Cross Bucks 20 H5
Gerrick R & Cl 71 M10
Gestingthorpe Essex 40 D13
Gethsemane Pembks 24 J2
Geuffordd Powys 44 F11
Gib Hill Ches W 55 P11
Gibraltar Lincs 49 S2
Gibsmere Notts 47 T4
Giddeahall Wilts 18 C6
Giddy Green Dorset 8 A11
Gidea Park Gt Lon 22 D9
Gidleigh Devon 5 R3
Giffnock E Rens 89 N14
Gifford E Loth 84 E5
Giffordtown Fife 91 L9
Giggleswick N York 62 G7
Gigha Ag & B 79 L6
Gilberdyke E R Yk 64 J14
Gilbert's End Worcs 35 T12
Gilbert Street Hants 9 S2
Gilchriston E Loth 84 D5
Gilcrux Cumb 66 H5
Gildersome Leeds 63 Q14
Gildingwells Rothm 57 S9
Gilesgate Moor Dur 69 S4
Gileston V Glam 16 D3
Gilfach Caerph 27 M8
Gilfach Goch Brdgnd 26 H9
Gilfachrheda Cerdgn 32 H9
Gilgarran Cumb 66 F8
Gill W & F 67 P7
Gillamoor N York 64 F2
Gillan Cnwll 2 K11
Gillen Highld 100 b4
Gillesbie D & G 75 N7
Gilling East N York 64 E4
Gillingham Dorset 17 V11
Gillingham Medway 12 E2
Gillingham Norfk 41 R2
Gilling West N York 69 Q11
Gillock Highld 112 F5
Gillow Heath Staffs 45 U2
Gills Highld 112 H2
Gill's Green Kent 12 E9
Gilmanscleuch Border 75 R1
Gilmerton C Edin 83 Q5
Gilmerton P & K 90 C7
Gilmonby Dur 69 L10
Gilmorton Leics 37 Q3
Gilsland Nthumb 76 C12
Gilson Warwks 36 G3
Gilstead C Brad 63 N12
Gilston Border 84 C7
Gilston Herts 22 B5
Gilston Park Herts 22 B5
Giltbrook Notts 47 N4
Gilwern Mons 27 N5
Gimingham Norfk 51 N6
Ginclough Ches E 56 E11
Gingers Green E Susx 11 U8
Gipping Suffk 40 J8
Gipsey Bridge Lincs 49 L4
Girdle Toll N Ayrs 81 L4
Girlington C Brad 63 N13
Girlsta Shet 106 u8
Girsby N York 70 E11
Girtford C Beds 38 J11
Girthon D & G 73 Q9
Girton Cambs 39 P8
Girton Notts 58 D13
Girvan S Ayrs 80 H13
Gisburn Lancs 62 G10
Gisleham Suffk 41 T3
Gislingham Suffk 40 J6
Gissing Norfk 40 K3
Gittisham Devon 6 F5
Givons Grove Surrey 21 L12
Gladestry Powys 34 F9
Gladsmuir E Loth 84 D4
Glais Swans 26 C7
Glaisdale N York 71 N11
Glamis Angus 91 N2
Glanaber Gwynd 43 M3
Glanaman Carmth 26 B5
Glandford Norfk 50 H5
Glan-Duar Carmth 32 K12
Glandwr Pembks 25 L5
Glan-Dwyfach Gwynd 42 J5
Glandy Cross Carmth 24 K5
Glandyfi Cerdgn 33 N1
Glangrwyney Powys 27 N4
Glanllynfi Brdgnd 26 F9
Glanmule Powys 34 E2
Glanrhyd Pembks 32 B12
Glan-rhyd Powys 26 D6
Glanton Nthumb 77 M3
Glanton Pike Nthumb 77 M3
Glanvilles Wootton Dorset 7 S3
Glan-y-don Flints 54 E11
Glan-y-llyn Cardif 27 L11
Glan-y-nant Powys 33 T4
Glan-yr-afon Gwynd 43 T5
Glan-yr-afon Gwynd 44 B5
Glan-yr-afon IoA 52 K6
Glan-yr-afon Swans 26 A6
Glan-y-wern Gwynd 43 M7
Glapthorn N Nthn 38 F2
Glapwell Derbys 57 Q13
Glasbury Powys 34 E13
Glascoed Denbgs 53 S8
Glascoed Mons 27 Q7
Glascote Staffs 46 H13
Glascwm Powys 34 E10
Glasfryn Conwy 43 T3
Glasgow C Glas 89 N12
Glasgow Airport Rens 89 L12
Glasgow Prestwick Airport S Ayrs 81 M7
Glasgow Science Centre C Glas 89 N12
Glasinfryn Gwynd 52 J9
Glasnacardoch Bay Highld 100 f10
Glasnakille Highld 100 e8
Glasphein Highld 100 a5
Glaspwll Powys 43 P14
Glassenbury Kent 12 E8
Glassford S Lans 82 D9
Glasshoughton Wakefd 57 P2
Glasshouse Gloucs 28 D3
Glasshouse Hill Gloucs 28 D3
Glasshouses N York 63 P7
Glasslaw Abers 105 P4
Glasson Cumb 75 Q13
Glassonby W & F 67 S5
Glasson Dock Lancs 61 S8
Glasterlaw Angus 98 K13
Glaston Rutlnd 48 C13
Glastonbury Somset 17 P9
Glatton Cambs 38 J3
Glazebrook Warrtn 55 Q8
Glazebury Warrtn 55 Q7
Glazeley Shrops 35 R3
Gleadless Sheff 57 N10
Gleadsmoss Ches E 55 T13
Gleaston W & F 61 P5
Glebe Highld 102 F12
Gledhow Leeds 63 S12
Gledpark D & G 73 Q9
Gledrid Shrops 44 H6
Glemsford Suffk 40 D11
Glen Achulish Highld 94 F7
Glenallachie Moray 104 B7
Glenancross Highld 100 f10
Glenaros House Ag & B 93 P10
Glen Auldyn IoM 60 g4
Glenbarr Ag & B 79 M8
Glenbarry Abers 104 H5
Glenbeg Highld 93 P6
Glenbervie Abers 99 P7
Glenboig N Lans 82 D5
Glenborrodale Highld 93 Q6
Glenbranter Ag & B 88 D6
Glenbreck Border 75 L1
Glenbrittle Highld 100 d7
Glenbuck E Ayrs 82 D13
Glencally Angus 98 F11
Glencaple D & G 74 J12
Glencarse P & K 90 J7
Glencoe Highld 94 G7
Glencothe Border 83 L13
Glencraig Fife 90 J13
Glencrosh D & G 74 E8
Glendale Highld 100 a5
Glendaruel Ag & B 87 T9
Glendevon P & K 90 E11
Glendoe Lodge Highld 96 E2
Glendoick P & K 90 K7
Glenduckie Fife 91 L8
Glenegedale Ag & B 78 E5
Glenelg Highld 100 h8
Glenerney Moray 103 R6
Glenfarg P & K 90 H9
Glenfield Leics 47 P12
Glenfinnan Highld 94 C2
Glenfintaig Lodge Highld 94 J1
Glenfoot P & K 90 J8
Glenfyne Lodge Ag & B 88 F2
Glengarnock N Ayrs 81 L2
Glengolly Highld 112 D3
Glengorm Castle Ag & B 93 L7
Glengrasco Highld 100 d5
Glenholm Border 83 M12
Glenhoul D & G 73 Q2
Glenkin Ag & B 88 D9
Glenkindie Abers 104 E13
Glenlivet Moray 103 U10
Glenlochar D & G 74 D13
Glenlomond P & K 90 J11
Glenluce D & G 72 F8
Glenmassen Ag & B 88 D8
Glenmavis N Lans 82 E5
Glen Maye IoM 60 c7
Glen Mona IoM 60 h5
Glenmore Highld 100 d5
Glenmore Lodge Highld 97 R2
Glen Nevis House Highld 94 G4
Glenochil Clacks 90 C12
Glen Parva Leics 47 Q14
Glenquiech Angus 98 G11
Glenralloch Ag & B 87 R12
Glenridding W & F 67 N9
Glenrothes Fife 91 L11
Glenshero Lodge Highld 96 H5
Glenstriven Ag & B 88 C10
Glentham Lincs 58 H8
Glentrool D & G 72 K4
Glen Trool Lodge D & G 73 L3
Glentruim Highld 96 K5
Glentworth Lincs 58 F9
Glenuig Highld 93 R3
Glenvarragill Highld 100 d6
Glen Vine IoM 60 e7
Glenwhilly D & G 72 F5
Glespin S Lans 82 F13
Glewstone Herefs 27 V3
Glinton C Pete 48 J12
Glooston Leics 37 U1
Glossop Derbys 56 F8
Gloster Hill Nthumb 77 R5
Gloucester Gloucs 28 F4
Gloucester Services Gloucs 28 F5
Gloucestershire Airport Gloucs 28 G3
Glusburn N York 63 L10
Glutt Lodge Highld 112 B9
Gluvian Cnwll 3 N4
Glympton Oxon 29 T3
Glynarthen Cerdgn 32 F11
Glyn Ceiriog Wrexhm 44 F6
Glyncoch Rhondd 26 K9
Glyncorrwg Neath 26 F8
Glynde E Susx 11 R9
Glyndebourne E Susx 11 R8
Glyndyfrdwy Denbgs 44 D5
Glynneath Neath 26 F6
Glynogwr Brdgnd 26 H10
Glyntaff Rhondd 26 K10
Glyntawe Powys 26 E4
Glynteg Carmth 25 Q3
Gnosall Staffs 45 T9
Gnosall Heath Staffs 45 T9
Goadby Leics 47 U14
Goadby Marwood Leics 47 U8
Goatacre Wilts 18 F5
Goatham Green E Susx 12 F11
Goathill Dorset 17 S13
Goathland N York 71 P12
Goathurst Somset 16 J10
Goathurst Common Kent 21 S12
Goat Lees Kent 12 K6
Gobowen Shrops 44 H7
Godalming Surrey 10 F2
Goddard's Corner Suffk 41 N7
Goddard's Green Kent 12 F9
Goddards Green W Susx 11 M6
Godden Green Kent 21 U11
Godford Cross Devon 6 F4
Godington Oxon 30 D7
Godley Tamesd 56 E7
Godmanchester Cambs 38 K6
Godmanstone Dorset 7 S5
Godmersham Kent 13 L5
Godney Somset 17 N8
Godolphin Cross Cnwll 2 G10
Godre'r-graig Neath 26 D6
Godshill Hants 8 H5
Godshill IoW 9 Q12
Godstone Staffs 46 D7
Godstone Surrey 21 Q12
Godsworthy Devon 5 N5
Godwinscroft Hants 8 H9
Goetre Mons 27 Q6
Goff's Oak Herts 31 T12
Gogar C Edin 83 N4
Goginan Cerdgn 33 N4
Golan Gwynd 42 K5
Golant Cnwll 4 E10
Golberdon Cnwll 4 J6
Golborne Wigan 55 P7
Golcar Kirk 56 G3
Goldcliff Newpt 27 R11
Golden Cross E Susx 11 S8
Golden Green Kent 12 B6
Golden Grove Carmth 25 U7
Goldenhill C Stke 45 U3
Golden Hill Pembks 24 G10
Golden Pot Hants 19 V12
Golden Valley Derbys 47 M3
Golders Green Gt Lon 21 M5
Goldfinch Bottom W Berk 19 R8
Goldhanger Essex 23 M6
Gold Hill Cambs 39 R2
Gold Hill Dorset 8 A6
Golding Shrops 45 M13
Goldington Bed 38 G10
Goldsborough N York 63 T8
Goldsborough N York 71 P10
Goldsithney Cnwll 2 E10
Goldstone Kent 13 Q3
Goldstone Shrops 45 R8
Goldthorpe Barns 57 Q6
Goldworthy Devon 14 J8
Golford Kent 12 E8
Golford Green Kent 12 E8
Gollanfield Highld 103 M5
Gollinglith Foot N York 63 P3
Golly Wrexhm 44 H2
Golsoncott Somset 16 D9
Golspie Highld 109 Q4
Gomeldon Wilts 18 J13
Gomersal Kirk 56 K1
Gomshall Surrey 20 J13
Gonalston Notts 47 S4
Gonerby Hill Foot Lincs 48 D6
Gonerby Moor Lincs 48 C6
Gonfirth Shet 106 t7
Goodameavy Devon 5 N8
Good Easter Essex 22 F5
Gooderstone Norfk 50 C13
Goodleigh Devon 15 P6
Goodmanham E R Yk 64 K11
Goodmayes Gt Lon 21 S5
Goodnestone Kent 12 K3
Goodnestone Kent 13 Q5
Goodrich Herefs 27 V4
Goodrington Torbay 6 A13
Goodshaw Lancs 55 T1
Goodshaw Fold Lancs 55 T1
Goodstone Devon 5 T6
Goodwick Pembks 24 F3
Goodwood W Susx 10 D9
Goodworth Clatford Hants 19 N12
Goodyers End Warwks 36 K3
Goole E R Yk 58 B2
Goole Fields E R Yk 58 C2
Goom's Hill Worcs 36 D10
Goonbell Cnwll 2 J7
Goonhavern Cnwll 2 K6
Goonvrea Cnwll 2 J7
Goosecruives Abers 99 P7
Gooseford Devon 5 R2
Goose Green Essex 23 R2
Goose Green Kent 12 B5
Goose Green Kent 12 F8
Goose Green S Glos 28 C13
Goose Green W Susx 10 J7
Goose Green Wigan 55 N6
Gooseham Cnwll 14 F9
Gooseham Mill Cnwll 14 F9
Goosehill Green Worcs 36 B8
Goose Pool Herefs 35 L13
Goosey Oxon 29 S9
Goosnargh Lancs 62 B12
Goostrey Ches E 55 S12
Gordano Services N Som 27 U12
Gorddinog Conwy 53 L8
Gordon Border 84 G10
Gordon Arms Hotel Border 83 R13
Gordonstown Abers 104 H4
Gordonstown Abers 105 L8
Gore Powys 34 G9
Gorebridge Mdloth 83 R6
Gorefield Cambs 49 P11
Gore Pit Essex 23 L4
Gores Wilts 18 H9
Gore Street Kent 13 Q2
Gorey Jersey 7 f3
Goring Oxon 19 T4
Goring-by-Sea W Susx 10 J10
Goring Heath Oxon 19 U5
Gorleston-on-Sea Norfk 51 T13
Gorrachie Abers 105 L4
Gorran Churchtown Cnwll 3 P8
Gorran Haven Cnwll 3 Q8
Gorran High Lanes Cnwll 3 P8
Gorrig Cerdgn 32 H12
Gors Cerdgn 33 M5
Gorsedd Flints 54 E11
Gorseddau Slate Landscape Gwynd 43 L5
Gorse Hill Swindn 29 N10
Gorseinon Swans 25 U11
Gorseybank Derbys 46 J3
Gorsgoch Cerdgn 32 J10
Gorslas Carmth 25 U8
Gorsley Gloucs 28 C2
Gorsley Common Herefs 28 C2
Gorstage Ches W 55 P12
Gorstan Highld 102 C3
Gorstella Ches W 44 J1
Gorsten Ag & B 93 S12
Gorst Hill Worcs 35 R6
Gorsty Hill Staffs 46 F8
Gorthleck Highld 102 F11
Gorton Manch 56 C7
Gosbeck Suffk 41 L9
Gosberton Lincs 48 K7
Gosberton Clough Lincs 48 J8
Gosfield Essex 22 J2
Gosford Devon 6 F5
Gosford Oxon 29 U5
Gosforth Cumb 66 G12
Gosforth N u Ty 77 Q12
Gosling Street Somset 17 P10
Gosmore Herts 31 Q7
Gospel End Staffs 35 U2
Gospel Green W Susx 10 E4
Gosport Hants 9 S9
Gossard's Green C Beds 31 L4
Gossington Gloucs 28 D7
Goswick Nthumb 85 R10
Gotham Notts 47 P7
Gotherington Gloucs 28 J2
Gotton Somset 16 H11
Goudhurst Kent 12 D8
Goulceby Lincs 59 N11
Gourdas Abers 105 M7
Gourdie C Dund 91 N5
Gourdon Abers 99 Q9
Gourock Inver 88 F10
Govan C Glas 89 M12
Goveton Devon 5 T11
Govilon Mons 27 P5
Gowdall E R Yk 57 T2
Gower Highld 102 F4
Gower Swans 25 T12
Gowerton Swans 25 U11
Gowkhall Fife 90 G14
Gowthorpe E R Yk 64 H9
Goxhill E R Yk 65 R11
Goxhill N Linc 58 K2
Goytre Neath 26 D10
Grabhair W Isls 106 i7
Graby Lincs 48 G8
Grade Cnwll 2 J14
Gradeley Green Ches E 45 N3
Graffham W Susx 10 E7
Grafham Cambs 38 J7
Grafham Surrey 10 G2
Grafton Herefs 35 L13
Grafton Oxon 29 Q7
Grafton Shrops 44 K10
Grafton Worcs 35 N8
Grafton Worcs 36 C13
Grafton Flyford Worcs 36 C9
Grafton Regis W Nthn 37 U11
Grafton Underwood N Nthn 38 D4
Grafty Green Kent 12 G6
Graianrhyd Denbgs 44 F2
Graig Conwy 53 P8
Graig Denbgs 54 C12
Graigfechan Denbgs 44 D3
Grain Medway 23 L12
Grains Bar Oldham 56 E5
Grainsby Lincs 59 N7
Grainthorpe Lincs 59 Q7
Grampound Cnwll 3 N7
Grampound Road Cnwll 3 N6
Gramsdal W Isls 106 d13
Gramsdale W Isls 106 d13
Granborough Bucks 30 G7
Granby Notts 47 U6
Grandborough Warwks 37 N7
Grand Chemins Jersey 7 e3
Grandes Rocques Guern 6 d2
Grandtully P & K 97 Q13
Grange Cumb 67 L9
Grange Medway 12 E2
Grange P & K 91 L6
Grange Wirral 54 F9
Grange Crossroads Moray 104 F5
Grange Hall Moray 103 S3
Grangehall S Lans 82 J10
Grange Hill Essex 21 R4
Grangemill Derbys 46 H2
Grange Moor Kirk 56 K3
Grangemouth Falk 82 H2
Grange of Lindores Fife 91 L8
Grange-over-Sands W & F 61 S4
Grangepans Falk 82 K2
Grange Park W Nthn 37 U9
Grangetown R & Cl 70 H8
Grangetown Sundld 70 F2
Grange Villa Dur 69 R2
Gransmoor E R Yk 65 Q8
Gransmore Green Essex 22 G3
Granston Pembks 24 E4
Grantchester Cambs 39 P9
Grantham Lincs 48 D6
Granton C Edin 83 P3
Grantown-on-Spey Highld 103 R10
Grantsfield Herefs 35 M8
Grantshouse Border 85 L5
Grappenhall Warrtn 55 P9
Grasby Lincs 58 J6
Grasmere W & F 67 M11
Grasscroft Oldham 56 E6
Grassendale Lpool 54 J9
Grassgarth Cumb 67 M4
Grass Green Essex 40 B13
Grassington N York 63 L7
Grassmoor Derbys 57 P13
Grassthorpe Notts 58 C13
Grateley Hants 19 L12
Gratwich Staffs 46 D7
Graveley Cambs 39 L8
Graveley Herts 31 R7
Gravelly Hill Birm 36 F2
Gravelsbank Shrops 44 H13
Graveney Kent 13 L3
Gravesend Kent 22 G13
Gravir W Isls 106 i7
Grayingham Lincs 58 F7
Grayrigg W & F 67 S13
Grays Thurr 22 F12
Grayshott Hants 10 D3
Grayson Green Cumb 66 E7
Grayswood Surrey 10 E4
Graythorpe Hartpl 70 H7
Grazeley Wokham 19 U7
Greasbrough Rothm 57 P7
Greasby Wirral 54 G9
Greasley Notts 47 N4
Great Abington Cambs 39 R11
Great Addington N Nthn 38 E5
Great Alne Warwks 36 F9
Great Altcar Lancs 54 H5
Great Amwell Herts 31 U10
Great Asby W & F 68 E10
Great Ashfield Suffk 40 G7
Great Ayton N York 70 J10
Great Baddow Essex 22 H7
Great Badminton S Glos 28 F11
Great Bardfield Essex 22 G1
Great Barford Bed 38 H10
Great Barr Sandw 36 D1
Great Barrington Gloucs 29 P5
Great Barrow Ches W 55 L13
Great Barton Suffk 40 E7
Great Barugh N York 64 G4
Great Bavington Nthumb 76 K9
Great Bealings Suffk 41 M11
Great Bedwyn Wilts 19 L8
Great Bentley Essex 23 R3
Great Billing W Nthn 38 B8
Great Bircham Norfk 50 C7
Great Blakenham Suffk 40 K10
Great Blencow W & F 67 Q6
Great Bolas Wrekin 45 P9
Great Bookham Surrey 20 K12
Great Bosullow Cnwll 2 C10
Great Bourton Oxon 37 N11
Great Bowden Leics 37 T3
Great Bradley Suffk 39 U10
Great Braxted Essex 23 L5
Great Bricett Suffk 40 H10
Great Brickhill Bucks 30 K6
Great Bridge Sandw 36 C2
Great Bridgeford Staffs 45 U8
Great Brington W Nthn 37 S7
Great Bromley Essex 23 Q2
Great Broughton Cumb 66 G6
Great Broughton N York 70 H11
Great Budworth Ches W 55 Q11
Great Burdon Darltn 70 D9
Great Burstead Essex 22 G9
Great Busby N York 70 H11
Great Canfield Essex 22 E4
Great Carlton Lincs 59 R9
Great Casterton Rutlnd 48 F12
Great Chalfield Wilts 18 C8
Great Chart Kent 12 J7
Great Chatwell Staffs 45 S11
Great Chell C Stke 45 U3
Great Chesterford Essex 39 R12
Great Cheverell Wilts 18 E10
Great Chishill Cambs 39 P13
Great Clacton Essex 23 S4
Great Cliff Wakefd 57 M3
Great Clifton Cumb 66 F7
Great Coates NE Lin 59 M5
Great Comberton Worcs 36 C12
Great Comp Kent 12 B4
Great Corby Cumb 67 Q2
Great Cornard Suffk 40 E12
Great Cowden E R Yk 65 S11
Great Coxwell Oxon 29 Q9
Great Cransley N Nthn 38 B5
Great Cressingham Norfk 50 E13
Great Crosthwaite Cumb 67 L8
Great Cubley Derbys 46 G6
Great Cumbrae Island N Ayrs 80 H1
Great Dalby Leics 47 T11
Great Denham Bed 38 F11
Great Doddington N Nthn 38 C8
Great Doward Herefs 27 U4
Great Dunham Norfk 50 E11
Great Dunmow Essex 22 F3
Great Durnford Wilts 18 H13
Great Easton Essex 22 F2
Great Easton Leics 38 B2
Great Eccleston Lancs 61 S11
Great Edstone N York 64 G3
Great Ellingham Norfk 40 H1
Great Elm Somset 17 T7
Great Everdon W Nthn 37 Q9
Great Eversden Cambs 39 N10
Great Fencote N York 69 S14
Greatfield Wilts 29 L10
Great Finborough Suffk 40 H9
Greatford Lincs 48 G11
Great Fransham Norfk 50 E11
Great Gaddesden Herts 31 M10
Greatgate Staffs 46 E6
Great Gidding Cambs 38 H4
Great Givendale E R Yk 64 J9
Great Glemham Suffk 41 P8
Great Glen Leics 47 S14
Great Gonerby Lincs 48 C6
Great Gransden Cambs 39 L9
Great Green Cambs 31 S4
Great Green Norfk 41 N3
Great Green Suffk 40 F7
Great Green Suffk 40 F9
Great Habton N York 64 H4
Great Hale Lincs 48 H5
Great Hallingbury Essex 22 D4
Greatham Hants 10 B4
Greatham Hartpl 70 G7
Greatham W Susx 10 G7
Great Hampden Bucks 30 H12
Great Harrowden N Nthn 38 C6
Great Harwood Lancs 62 E13
Great Haseley Oxon 30 D12
Great Hatfield E R Yk 65 R11
Great Haywood Staffs 46 C9
Great Heck N York 57 S2
Great Henny Essex 40 E13
Great Hinton Wilts 18 D9
Great Hockham Norfk 40 G2
Great Holland Essex 23 T4
Great Hollands Br For 20 E9
Great Horkesley Essex 23 N1
Great Hormead Herts 22 B2
Great Horton C Brad 63 N13
Great Horwood Bucks 30 G6
Great Houghton Barns 57 P5
Great Houghton W Nthn 37 U9
Great Hucklow Derbys 56 J11
Great Kelk E R Yk 65 Q8
Great Kimble Bucks 30 H11
Great Kingshill Bucks 20 E3
Great Langdale W & F 67 L11
Great Langton N York 69 S13
Great Leighs Essex 22 H4
Great Limber Lincs 58 K5
Great Linford M Keyn 30 J4
Great Livermere Suffk 40 E6
Great Longstone Derbys 56 K12
Great Lumley Dur 69 S3
Great Lyth Shrops 45 L12
Great Malvern Worcs 35 S11
Great Maplestead Essex 40 D14
Great Marton Bpool 61 Q12
Great Massingham Norfk 50 C9
Great Melton Norfk 50 K12
Great Meols Wirral 54 F8
Great Milton Oxon 30 D12
Great Missenden Bucks 30 J12
Great Mitton Lancs 62 E12
Great Mongeham Kent 13 S5
Great Moulton Norfk 41 L2
Great Munden Herts 31 U8
Great Musgrave W & F 68 G10
Great Ness Shrops 44 J10
Great Notley Essex 22 H3
Great Oak Mons 27 R5
Great Oakley Essex 23 S2
Great Oakley N Nthn 38 C3
Great Offley Herts 31 P7
Great Ormside W & F 68 F9
Great Orton Cumb 67 M2
Great Ouseburn N York 63 U7
Great Oxendon W Nthn 37 T4
Great Oxney Green Essex 22 G6
Great Palgrave Norfk 50 D11
Great Parndon Essex 22 B6
Great Pattenden Kent 12 D7
Great Paxton Cambs 38 K8
Great Plumpton Lancs 61 R13
Great Plumstead Norfk 51 P11
Great Ponton Lincs 48 D7
Great Potheridge Devon 15 M10
Great Preston Leeds 63 U14
Great Purston W Nthn 30 B5
Great Raveley Cambs 39 L4
Great Rissington Gloucs 29 N4
Great Rollright Oxon 29 R1
Great Ryburgh Norfk 50 G8
Great Ryle Nthumb 77 L3
Great Ryton Shrops 45 L13
Great Saling Essex 22 G2
Great Salkeld W & F 67 S5
Great Sampford Essex 39 T13
Great Saredon Staffs 46 C12
Great Saughall Ches W 54 J13
Great Saxham Suffk 40 C8
Great Shefford W Berk 19 N5
Great Shelford Cambs 39 Q10
Great Smeaton N York 70 D12
Great Snoring Norfk 50 F7
Great Somerford Wilts 28 J11
Great Soudley Shrops 45 R8
Great Stainton Darltn 70 D8
Great Stambridge Essex 23 L9
Great Staughton Cambs 38 H8
Great Steeping Lincs 59 R14
Great Stonar Kent 13 R4
Greatstone-on-Sea Kent 13 L11
Great Strickland W & F 67 S8
Great Stukeley Cambs 38 K6
Great Sturton Lincs 59 M11
Great Sutton Ches W 54 J11
Great Sutton Shrops 35 M4
Great Swinburne Nthumb 76 J10
Great Tew Oxon 29 T2
Great Tey Essex 23 L2
Great Thurlow Suffk 39 U10
Great Torrington Devon 15 L9
Great Tosson Nthumb 77 L5
Great Totham Essex 23 L5
Great Totham Essex 23 L5
Great Tows Lincs 59 M8
Great Urswick W & F 61 P5
Great Wakering Essex 23 M10
Great Waldingfield Suffk 40 F12
Great Walsingham Norfk 50 F6
Great Waltham Essex 22 G5
Great Warford Ches E 55 T11
Great Warley Essex 22 E9
Great Washbourne Gloucs 36 C14
Great Weeke Devon 5 S3
Great Welnetham Suffk 40 E9
Great Wenham Suffk 40 J13
Great Whittington Nthumb 77 L11
Great Wigborough Essex 23 N4
Great Wilbraham Cambs 39 S9
Great Wilne Derbys 47 M7
Great Wishford Wilts 18 G13
Great Witchingham Norfk 50 K9
Great Witcombe Gloucs 28 H5
Great Witley Worcs 35 S7
Great Wolford Warwks 36 J14
Greatworth W Nthn 30 C4
Great Wratting Suffk 39 U11
Great Wymondley Herts 31 R7
Great Wyrley Staffs 46 C12
Great Wytheford Shrops 45 N10
Great Yarmouth Norfk 51 T12
Great Yeldham Essex 40 C13
Grebby Lincs 59 R13
Greeba IoM 60 e6
Green Denbgs 54 C13
Green Bank W & F 61 R3
Greenbottom Cnwll 2 K7
Greenburn W Loth 82 H6
Greencroft Hall Dur 69 Q3
Green Cross Surrey 10 D3
Green Down Somset 17 Q6
Green End Bed 38 F11
Green End Bed 38 G8
Green End Bed 38 H10
Green End Bed 38 H8
Green End Cambs 38 J4
Green End Cambs 38 K6
Green End Cambs 39 N9
Green End Cambs 39 Q7
Green End Cambs 39 Q8
Green End Herts 31 S6
Green End Herts 31 T6
Green End Herts 31 T8
Greenend Oxon 29 R3
Green End Warwks 36 J3
Greenfield Ag & B 88 F7
Greenfield C Beds 31 N6
Greenfield Flints 54 E11
Greenfield Highld 101 U11
Greenfield Oldham 56 E6
Greenfield Oxon 20 B4
Greenford Gt Lon 20 K6
Greengairs N Lans 82 E4
Greengates C Brad 63 P12
Greengill Cumb 66 H5
Greenhalgh Lancs 61 S12
Greenham Somset 16 E12
Greenham W Berk 19 Q7
Green Hammerton N York 64 B8
Greenhaugh Nthumb 76 F8
Green Head Cumb 67 N3
Greenhead Nthumb 76 D12
Green Heath Staffs 46 C11
Greenheys Salfd 55 R6
Greenhill D & G 75 M10
Greenhill Falk 89 T10
Greenhill Herefs 35 R11
Greenhill Kent 13 N2
Greenhill Leics 47 M11
Greenhill S Lans 82 H12
Green Hill Wilts 29 L10
Greenhillocks Derbys 47 M4
Greenhills S Lans 81 S2
Greenhithe Kent 22 E12
Greenholm E Ayrs 81 Q5
Greenholme W & F 67 S11
Greenhouse Border 84 F14
Greenhow Hill N York 63 N7
Greenland Highld 112 F3
Greenland Sheff 57 N9
Greenlands Bucks 20 C5
Green Lane Devon 5 T5
Green Lane Worcs 36 E8
Greenlaw Border 84 J9
Greenlea D & G 74 K10
Greenloaning P & K 89 T4
Green Moor Barns 57 L7
Greenmount Bury 55 S4
Green Oak E R Yk 64 J14
Greenock Inver 88 G10
Greenodd W & F 61 Q3
Green Ore Somset 17 Q6
Green Park Readg 20 B8
Green Quarter W & F 67 Q12
Greensgate Norfk 50 K10
Greenshields S Lans 82 K10
Greenside Gatesd 77 N13
Greenside Kirk 56 J3
Greens Norton W Nthn 37 S11
Greenstead Green Essex 22 K2
Greensted Essex 22 D7
Green Street E Susx 12 E13
Green Street Gloucs 28 G4
Green Street Herts 21 L3
Green Street Herts 22 C3
Green Street Worcs 35 U11
Green Street Green Gt Lon 21 S10
Green Street Green Kent 22 E13
Greenstreet Green Suffk 40 H11
Green Tye Herts 22 B4
Greenway Gloucs 35 R14
Greenway Somset 16 K12
Greenway V Glam 26 K13
Greenway Worcs 35 R6
Greenwich Gt Lon 21 Q7
Greenwich Maritime Gt Lon 21 Q7
Greet Gloucs 28 K1
Greete Shrops 35 N6
Greetham Lincs 59 P12
Greetham Rutlnd 48 D11
Greetland Calder 56 G2
Gregson Lane Lancs 55 N1
Greinton Somset 17 M9
Grenaby IoM 60 d8
Grendon N Nthn 38 C8
Grendon Warwks 46 J14
Grendon Green Herefs 35 N9
Grendon Underwood Bucks 30 E8
Grenofen Devon 5 M6
Grenoside Sheff 57 M8
Greosabhagh W Isls 106 g9
Gresford Wrexhm 44 H3
Gresham Norfk 51 L6
Greshornish Highld 100 c4
Gressenhall Norfk 50 G10
Gressenhall Green Norfk 50 G10
Gressingham Lancs 62 B6
Gresty Green Ches E 45 R3
Greta Bridge Dur 69 N10
Gretna D & G 75 R12
Gretna Green D & G 75 R12
Gretna Services D & G 75 R12
Gretton Gloucs 28 K1
Gretton N Nthn 38 C2
Gretton Shrops 35 M1
Grewelthorpe N York 63 Q4
Grey Friars Suffk 41 S6
Greygarth N York 63 P5
Grey Green N Linc 58 C5
Greylake Somset 17 L10
Greylees Lincs 48 F5
Greyrigg D & G 75 L8
Greys Green Oxon 20 B6
Greysouthen Cumb 66 G7
Greystoke W & F 67 P6
Greystone Angus 91 R3
Greywell Hants 20 B12
Gribb Dorset 7 L4
Gribthorpe E R Yk 64 H12
Griff Warwks 37 L3
Griffithstown Torfn 27 P8
Griffydam Leics 47 M10
Griggs Green Hants 10 C4
Grimeford Village Lancs 55 P4
Grimesthorpe Sheff 57 N9
Grimethorpe Barns 57 P5
Grimister Shet 106 u4
Grimley Worcs 35 T8
Grimmet S Ayrs 81 L10
Grimoldby Lincs 59 Q9
Grimpo Shrops 44 J8
Grimsargh Lancs 62 B13
Grimsby NE Lin 59 N4
Grimscote W Nthn 37 S10
Grimscott Cnwll 14 G11
Grimshader W Isls 106 j6
Grimshaw Bl w D 55 R2
Grimshaw Green Lancs 55 L4
Grimsthorpe Lincs 48 F9
Grimston E R Yk 65 T12
Grimston Leics 47 S9
Grimston Norfk 50 B9
Grimstone Dorset 7 R6
Grimstone End Suffk 40 F7
Grinacombe Moor Devon 5 L2
Grindale E R Yk 65 Q5
Grindle Shrops 45 S13
Grindleford Derbys 56 K11
Grindleton Lancs 62 F10
Grindley Brook Shrops 45 M5
Grindlow Derbys 56 J11
Grindon Nthumb 85 N10
Grindon S on T 70 E7
Grindon Staffs 46 E3
Grindon Hill Nthumb 76 G12
Grindonrigg Nthumb 85 N10
Gringley on the Hill Notts 58 B8
Grinsdale Cumb 75 S14
Grinshill Shrops 45 M9
Grinton N York 69 M13
Griomsiadar W Isls 106 j6
Grishipoll Ag & B 92 F7
Grisling Common E Susx 11 Q6
Gristhorpe N York 65 P3
Griston Norfk 50 F14
Gritley Ork 106 u19
Grittenham Wilts 28 K11
Grittleton Wilts 18 C4
Grizebeck W & F 61 N3
Grizedale W & F 67 M14
Groby Leics 47 P12
Groes Conwy 53 T10
Groes-faen Rhondd 26 K11
Groesffordd Gwynd 42 E6
Groesffordd Powys 26 K2
Groesffordd Marli Denbgs 53 T8
Groeslon Gwynd 52 G11
Groeslon Gwynd 52 H10
Groes-lwyd Powys 44 F11
Groes-Wen Caerph 27 L10
Grogarry W Isls 106 c15
Grogport Ag & B 79 Q7
Groigearraidh W Isls 106 c15
Gromford Suffk 41 Q9
Gronant Flints 54 C10
Groombridge E Susx 11 S3
Grosebay W Isls 106 g9
Grosmont Mons 27 S3
Grosmont N York 71 P11
Groton Suffk 40 G12
Grotton Oldham 56 E6
Grouville Jersey 7 e3
Grove Bucks 30 K8
Grove Dorset 7 S10
Grove Kent 13 P3
Grove Notts 58 B11
Grove Oxon 29 T9
Grove Pembks 24 G10
Grove Green Kent 12 E4
Grovenhurst Kent 12 D7
Grove Park Gt Lon 21 R8
Grovesend S Glos 28 C10
Grovesend Swans 25 U10
Grubb Street Kent 21 U9
Gruinard Highld 107 R7
Gruinart Ag & B 86 D12
Grula Highld 100 c7
Gruline Ag & B 93 N10
Grumbla Cnwll 2 C11
Grundisburgh Suffk 41 M10
Gruting Shet 106 s9
Grutness Shet 106 u12
Gualachulain Highld 94 G9
Guanockgate Lincs 49 N11
Guardbridge Fife 91 Q8
Guarlford Worcs 35 T11
Guay P & K 90 F2
Guernsey Guern 6 d3
Guernsey Airport Guern 6 c3
Guestling Green E Susx 12 G13
Guestling Thorn E Susx 12 G12
Guestwick Norfk 50 J8
Guide Bridge Tamesd 56 D7
Guide Post Nthumb 77 R8
Guilden Morden Cambs 31 S4
Guilden Sutton Ches W 54 K13
Guildford Surrey 20 G13
Guildstead Kent 12 F3
Guildtown P & K 90 H5
Guilsborough W Nthn 37 S6
Guilsfield Powys 44 F11
Guilton Kent 13 Q4
Guiltreehill S Ayrs 81 M10
Guineaford Devon 15 N5
Guisborough R & Cl 70 K9
Guiseley Leeds 63 P11
Guist Norfk 50 H8
Guiting Power Gloucs 29 L3
Gullane E Loth 84 D2
Gulling Green Suffk 40 D9
Gulval Cnwll 2 D10
Gulworthy Devon 5 M6
Gumfreston Pembks 24 K10
Gumley Leics 37 S3
Gummow's Shop Cnwll 3 M5
Gunby E R Yk 64 G12
Gunby Lincs 48 D9
Gundleton Hants 9 S2
Gun Green Kent 12 E9
Gun Hill E Susx 11 T8
Gun Hill Warwks 36 J3
Gunn Devon 15 P6
Gunnerside N York 69 L13
Gunnerton Nthumb 76 J11
Gunness N Linc 58 D4
Gunnislake Cnwll 5 L6
Gunnista Shet 106 v9
Gunthorpe C Pete 48 J13
Gunthorpe N Linc 58 D7
Gunthorpe Norfk 50 H7
Gunthorpe Notts 47 S5
Gunton Suffk 41 T1
Gunwalloe Cnwll 2 H12
Gupworthy Somset 16 C10
Gurnard IoW 9 P9
Gurnett Ches E 56 D12
Gurney Slade Somset 17 R7
Gurnos Powys 26 D6
Gushmere Kent 12 K4
Gussage All Saints Dorset 8 E6
Gussage St Andrew Dorset 8 D6
Gussage St Michael Dorset 8 D6
Guston Kent 13 R7
Gutcher Shet 106 v4
Guthrie Angus 98 K13
Guyhirn Cambs 49 P13
Guyhirn Gull Cambs 49 N13
Guy's Marsh Dorset 8 A4
Guyzance Nthumb 77 Q5
Gwaenysgor Flints 54 C10
Gwalchmai IoA 52 E7

Gwastadnant Gwynd 52 K11
Gwaun-Cae-Gurwen Carmth 26 B5
Gwbert on Sea Cerdgn 32 C10
Gwealavellan Cnwll 2 G8
Gweek Cnwll 2 J11
Gwehelog Mons 27 R7
Gwenddwr Powys 34 C12
Gwennap Cnwll 2 J8
Gwennap Mining District Cnwll 2 K8
Gwenter Cnwll 2 J13
Gwernaffield Flints 54 F13
Gwernesney Mons 27 S7
Gwernogle Carmth 25 T4
Gwernymynydd Flints 44 F1
Gwersyllt Wrexhm 44 H3
Gwespyr Flints 54 D10
Gwindra Cnwll 3 P6
Gwinear Cnwll 2 F9
Gwithian Cnwll 2 F8
Gwredog IoA 52 F5
Gwrhay Caerph 27 M8
Gwyddelwern Denbgs 44 C4
Gwyddgrug Carmth 25 S3
Gwynfryn Wrexhm 44 G3
Gwystre Powys 34 C7
Gwytherin Conwy 53 Q10
Gyfelia Wrexhm 44 H4
Gyrn Goch Gwynd 42 H4

H

Habberley Shrops 44 J13
Habberley Worcs 35 T5
Habergham Lancs 62 G13
Habertoft Lincs 59 T13
Habin W Susx 10 C6
Habrough NE Lin 58 K4
Hacconby Lincs 48 H8
Haceby Lincs 48 F6
Hacheston Suffk 41 P9
Hackbridge Gt Lon 21 N9
Hackenthorpe Sheff 57 P10
Hackford Norfk 50 J13
Hackforth N York 69 R14
Hack Green Ches E 45 P4
Hackland Ork 106 s17
Hackleton W Nthn 38 B9
Hacklinge Kent 13 R5
Hackman's Gate Worcs 35 U5
Hackness N York 65 M1
Hackness Somset 16 K7
Hackney Gt Lon 21 P6
Hackthorn Lincs 58 G10
Hackthorpe W & F 67 R8
Hacton Gt Lon 22 E10
Hadden Border 84 K11
Haddenham Bucks 30 F11
Haddenham Cambs 39 Q5
Haddington E Loth 84 E4
Haddington Lincs 58 F14
Haddiscoe Norfk 41 R1
Haddon Cambs 38 H2
Hade Edge Kirk 56 H6
Hadfield Derbys 56 F7
Hadham Cross Herts 22 B4
Hadham Ford Herts 22 B3
Hadleigh Essex 22 K10
Hadleigh Suffk 40 H12
Hadleigh Heath Suffk 40 G12
Hadley Worcs 35 U8
Hadley Wrekin 45 Q11
Hadley End Staffs 46 F9
Hadley Wood Gt Lon 21 N3
Hadlow Kent 12 B5
Hadlow Down E Susx 11 S6
Hadnall Shrops 45 M9
Hadrian's Wall 76 K12
Hadstock Essex 39 S12
Hadston Nthumb 77 R5
Hadzor Worcs 36 B8
Haffenden Quarter Kent 12 G7
Hafodunos Conwy 53 Q9
Hafod-y-bwch Wrexhm 44 H4
Hafod-y-coed Blae G 27 N7
Hafodyrynys Caerph 27 N8
Haggate Lancs 62 H12
Haggbeck Cumb 75 U11
Haggersta Shet 106 t9
Haggerston Nthumb 85 Q10
Haggington Hill Devon 15 N3
Haggs Falk 89 S10
Hagley Herefs 35 N12
Hagley Worcs 36 B4
Hagmore Green Suffk 40 G13
Hagnaby Lincs 59 P14
Hagnaby Lincs 59 S11
Hagworthingham Lincs 59 P13
Haigh Wigan 55 P5
Haighton Green Lancs 62 B13
Haile Cumb 66 F11
Hailes Gloucs 28 K1
Hailey Herts 31 U10
Hailey Oxon 19 T3
Hailey Oxon 29 S5
Hailsham E Susx 11 T9
Hail Weston Cambs 38 J8
Hainault Gt Lon 21 S4
Haine Kent 13 S2
Hainford Norfk 51 M10
Hainton Lincs 59 L10
Hainworth C Brad 63 M12
Haisthorpe E R Yk 65 Q7
Hakin Pembks 24 E9
Halam Notts 47 S3
Halbeath Fife 90 H14
Halberton Devon 6 D2
Halcro Highld 112 F4
Hale Halton 55 L10
Hale Hants 8 H5
Hale Somset 17 T11
Hale Surrey 20 D13
Hale Traffd 55 S9
Hale W & F 61 U4
Hale Bank Halton 55 L10
Hale Barns Traffd 55 S9
Hale Green E Susx 11 T8
Hale Nook Lancs 61 R11
Hales Norfk 41 Q1
Hales Staffs 45 R7
Halesgate Lincs 49 M8
Hales Green Derbys 46 G5
Halesowen Dudley 36 C4
Hales Place Kent 13 M4
Hale Street Kent 12 C6
Halesville Essex 23 M9
Halesworth Suffk 41 Q5
Halewood Knows 55 L9
Halford Devon 5 U6
Halford Shrops 34 K4
Halford Warwks 36 J11
Halfpenny W & F 61 U2
Halfpenny Green Staffs 35 T2
Halfpenny Houses N York 63 Q3
Halfway Carmth 26 A1
Halfway Carmth 33 R14
Halfway Sheff 57 P10
Halfway W Berk 19 P7
Halfway Bridge W Susx 10 E6
Halfway House Shrops 44 H11
Halfway Houses Kent 23 M13
Halifax Calder 56 G1
Halket E Ayrs 81 N2
Halkirk Highld 112 D5
Halkyn Flints 54 F12
Hall E Rens 81 N2
Hallam Fields Derbys 47 N6
Halland E Susx 11 R7
Hallaton Leics 37 U1
Hallatrow BaNES 17 R5
Hallbankgate Cumb 76 B14
Hallbeck W & F 62 C2
Hall Cliffe Wakefd 57 L3
Hall Cross Lancs 61 S13
Hall Dunnerdale W & F 66 K13
Hallen S Glos 27 V11
Hall End Bed 38 F11
Hall End C Beds 31 N5
Hallfield Gate Derbys 47 L2
Hallgarth Dur 70 D4
Hallglen Falk 82 G3
Hall Green Birm 36 F4
Hallin Highld 100 b4
Halling Medway 12 D3
Hallington Lincs 59 P9
Hallington Nthumb 76 K10
Halliwell Bolton 55 Q4
Halloughton Notts 47 S3
Hallow Worcs 35 T9
Hallow Heath Worcs 35 T9
Hallsands Devon 5 U13
Hall's Green Essex 22 B6
Hall's Green Herts 31 S7
Hallthwaites Cumb 61 M2
Hallworthy Cnwll 4 F3
Hallyne Border 83 N10
Halmer End Staffs 45 S4
Halmond's Frome Herefs 35 Q11
Halmore Gloucs 28 D7
Halnaker W Susx 10 E9
Halsall Lancs 54 J4
Halse Somset 16 F11
Halse W Nthn 30 C4
Halsetown Cnwll 2 E9
Halsham E R Yk 59 N1
Halsinger Devon 15 M5
Halstead Essex 22 K1
Halstead Kent 21 S10
Halstead Leics 47 U12
Halstock Dorset 7 P3
Halsway Somset 16 F9
Haltcliff Bridge W & F 67 N5
Haltham Lincs 59 M14
Haltoft End Lincs 49 N4
Halton Bucks 30 J11
Halton Halton 55 M10
Halton Lancs 61 U7
Halton Leeds 63 T13
Halton Nthumb 76 K12
Halton Wrexhm 44 H6
Halton East N York 63 L9
Halton Fenside Lincs 59 R14
Halton Gill N York 62 H4
Halton Green Lancs 61 U6
Halton Holegate Lincs 59 R13
Halton Lea Gate Nthumb 76 C14
Halton Quay Cnwll 5 L7
Halton Shields Nthumb 77 L12
Halton West N York 62 G9
Haltwhistle Nthumb 76 E13
Halvana Cnwll 4 G5
Halvergate Norfk 51 R12
Halwell Devon 5 T10
Halwill Devon 14 K13
Halwill Junction Devon 14 K12
Ham Devon 6 H4
Ham Gloucs 28 C8
Ham Gloucs 28 J3
Ham Gt Lon 21 L8
Ham Kent 13 R5
Ham Somset 16 J11
Ham Somset 17 S7
Ham Wilts 19 M8
Hambleden Bucks 20 C5
Hambledon Hants 9 S6
Hambledon Surrey 10 F3
Hamble-le-Rice Hants 9 P7
Hambleton Lancs 61 R11
Hambleton N York 64 D13
Hambleton Moss Side Lancs 61 R11
Hambridge Somset 17 L12
Hambrook S Glos 28 B12
Hambrook W Susx 10 B9
Ham Common Dorset 17 V11
Hameringham Lincs 59 P13
Hamerton Cambs 38 H5
Ham Green Herefs 35 S12
Ham Green Kent 12 F2
Ham Green Kent 12 G10
Ham Green N Som 27 U12
Ham Green Worcs 36 D8
Ham Hill Kent 12 C3
Hamilton S Lans 82 D7
Hamilton Services (northbound) S Lans 82 D7
Hamlet Dorset 7 Q3
Hammer W Susx 10 D4
Hammerpot W Susx 10 H9
Hammersmith Gt Lon 21 M7
Hammer Vale Hants 10 D4
Hammerwich Staffs 46 E12
Hammerwood E Susx 11 Q3
Hammond Street Herts 31 T12
Hammoon Dorset 7 V2
Hamnavoe Shet 106 t10
Hampden Park E Susx 11 U10
Hamperden End Essex 22 E1
Hampnett Gloucs 29 L4
Hampole Donc 57 R4
Hampreston Dorset 8 F9
Hampsfield W & F 61 S3
Hampson Green Lancs 61 T9
Hampstead Gt Lon 21 N5
Hampstead Norreys W Berk 19 R5
Hampsthwaite N York 63 R8
Hampton Devon 6 J5
Hampton Gt Lon 20 K9
Hampton Kent 13 N2
Hampton Shrops 35 R3
Hampton Swindn 29 N9
Hampton Worcs 36 D12
Hampton Bishop Herefs 35 N13
Hampton Court Palace Gt Lon 21 L9
Hampton Fields Gloucs 28 G8
Hampton Green Ches W 45 M4
Hampton Hargate C Pete 38 J2
Hampton Heath Ches W 45 M4
Hampton-in-Arden Solhll 36 H4
Hampton Loade Shrops 35 R3
Hampton Lovett Worcs 35 U7
Hampton Lucy Warwks 36 J9
Hampton Magna Warwks 36 J7
Hampton on the Hill Warwks 36 J8
Hampton Park Wilts 8 H2
Hampton Poyle Oxon 30 B9
Hampton Vale C Pete 38 J2
Hampton Wick Gt Lon 21 L9
Hamptworth Wilts 8 J5
Hamrow Norfk 50 F9
Hamsey E Susx 11 Q8
Hamsey Green Surrey 21 Q11
Hamstall Ridware Staffs 46 F10
Hamstead Birm 36 E2
Hamstead IoW 9 N10
Hamstead Marshall W Berk 19 P7
Hamsterley Dur 69 P1
Hamsterley Dur 69 P6
Hamsterley Mill Dur 69 P1
Hamstreet Kent 12 K9
Ham Street Somset 17 Q10
Hamwood N Som 17 L5
Hamworthy BCP 8 D10
Hanbury Staffs 46 G8
Hanbury Worcs 36 C8
Hanby Lincs 48 F7
Hanchet End Suffk 39 T11
Hanchurch Staffs 45 T5
Handa Island Highld 110 C7
Handale R & Cl 71 M9
Hand and Pen Devon 6 D5
Handbridge Ches W 54 K13
Handcross W Susx 11 M5
Handforth Ches E 56 C10
Hand Green Ches W 45 M1
Handley Ches W 45 L2
Handley Derbys 47 L1
Handley Green Essex 22 G7
Handsacre Staffs 46 E10
Handsworth Birm 36 D3
Handsworth Sheff 57 P9
Handy Cross Bucks 20 E4
Hanford C Stke 45 U5
Hanford Dorset 8 A6
Hanging Heaton Kirk 57 L2
Hanging Houghton W Nthn 37 U6
Hanging Langford Wilts 18 F13
Hangleton Br & H 11 M9
Hangleton W Susx 10 H10
Hanham S Glos 17 R2
Hankelow Ches E 45 Q4
Hankerton Wilts 28 J9
Hankham E Susx 11 U9
Hanley C Stke 45 U4
Hanley Broadheath Worcs 35 Q7
Hanley Castle Worcs 35 T12
Hanley Child Worcs 35 Q7
Hanley Swan Worcs 35 T12
Hanley William Worcs 35 Q7
Hanlith N York 62 H7
Hanmer Wrexhm 45 L6
Hannaford Devon 15 P7
Hannah Lincs 59 S11
Hannington Hants 19 R9
Hannington Swindn 29 N9
Hannington W Nthn 38 B6
Hannington Wick Swindn 29 N8
Hanscombe End C Beds 31 P6
Hanslope M Keyn 38 B11
Hanthorpe Lincs 48 G9
Hanwell Gt Lon 21 L7
Hanwell Oxon 37 M12
Hanwood Shrops 44 K12
Hanworth Gt Lon 20 K8
Hanworth Norfk 51 L6
Happendon S Lans 82 G12
Happisburgh Norfk 51 Q7
Happisburgh Common Norfk 51 Q8
Hapsford Ches W 55 L12
Hapton Lancs 62 F13
Hapton Norfk 41 L1
Harberton Devon 5 T9
Harbertonford Devon 5 T9
Harbledown Kent 13 M4
Harborne Birm 36 D4
Harborough Magna Warwks 37 N5
Harbottle Nthumb 76 J5
Harbourneford Devon 5 S8
Harbours Hill Worcs 36 C7
Harbridge Hants 8 G6
Harbridge Green Hants 8 G6
Harburn W Loth 82 K6
Harbury Warwks 37 L9
Harby Leics 47 T7
Harby Notts 58 E12
Harcombe Devon 6 A8
Harcombe Devon 6 G6
Harcombe Bottom Devon 6 K5
Harden C Brad 63 M12
Harden Wsall 46 D13
Hardendale W & F 67 S10
Hardenhuish Wilts 18 D6
Hardgate Abers 99 P3
Hardgate D & G 74 F12
Hardgate N York 63 R7
Hardgate W Duns 89 M11
Hardham W Susx 10 G7
Hardhorn Lancs 61 R12
Hardingham Norfk 50 H13
Hardingstone W Nthn 37 U9
Hardington Somset 17 T6
Hardington Mandeville Somset 7 P2
Hardington Marsh Somset 7 P3
Hardington Moor Somset 7 P2
Hardisworthy Devon 14 F8
Hardley Hants 9 N8
Hardley Street Norfk 51 Q13
Hardmead M Keyn 38 D11
Hardraw N York 62 H1
Hardsough Lancs 55 S2
Hardstoft Derbys 57 P14
Hardway Hants 9 S8
Hardway Somset 17 T10
Hardwick Bucks 30 H9
Hardwick Cambs 39 N9
Hardwick Derbys 57 Q14
Hardwick N Nthn 38 B7
Hardwick Norfk 41 M3
Hardwick Oxon 29 S6
Hardwick Oxon 30 C7
Hardwick Rothm 57 Q9
Hardwick Wsall 46 E14
Hardwicke Gloucs 28 E5
Hardwicke Gloucs 28 H2
Hardwick Village Notts 57 T11
Hardy's Green Essex 23 M3
Harebeating E Susx 11 T8
Hareby Lincs 59 P13
Hare Croft C Brad 63 M12
Harefield Gt Lon 20 J4
Hare Green Essex 23 R2
Hare Hatch Wokham 20 D7
Harehill Derbys 46 G6
Harehills Leeds 63 S13
Harehope Nthumb 77 M1
Harelaw Border 84 E14
Harelaw D & G 75 T10
Harelaw Dur 69 Q2
Hareplain Kent 12 F8
Haresceugh W & F 68 D4
Harescombe Gloucs 28 F5
Haresfield Gloucs 28 F5
Harestock Hants 9 P2
Hare Street Essex 22 B6
Hare Street Essex 22 D7
Hare Street Herts 31 U7
Harewood Leeds 63 S10
Harewood End Herefs 27 U2
Harford Devon 5 Q9
Hargate Norfk 40 K2
Hargatewall Derbys 56 H11
Hargrave Ches W 45 L1
Hargrave N Nthn 38 F6
Hargrave Suffk 40 C9
Harker Cumb 75 S13
Harkstead Suffk 41 L14
Harlaston Staffs 46 H11
Harlaxton Lincs 48 C7
Harlech Gwynd 43 L7
Harlech Castle Gwynd 43 L7
Harlescott Shrops 45 L10
Harlesden Gt Lon 21 M6
Harlesthorpe Derbys 57 Q11
Harleston Devon 5 T11
Harleston Norfk 41 M4
Harleston Suffk 40 H8
Harlestone W Nthn 37 T8
Harle Syke Lancs 62 H12
Harley Rothm 57 N7
Harley Shrops 45 N13
Harling Road Norfk 40 G3
Harlington C Beds 31 M6
Harlington Donc 57 Q6
Harlington Gt Lon 20 J7
Harlosh Highld 100 b5
Harlow Essex 22 B5
Harlow Hill Nthumb 77 M12
Harlthorpe E R Yk 64 G12
Harlton Cambs 39 N10
Harlyn Cnwll 3 M1
Harman's Cross Dorset 8 D12
Harmby N York 63 N2
Harmer Green Herts 31 S9
Harmer Hill Shrops 45 L9
Harmondsworth Gt Lon 20 J7
Harmston Lincs 48 E1
Harnage Shrops 45 N13
Harnham Nthumb 77 M9
Harnhill Gloucs 29 L7
Harold Hill Gt Lon 22 D9
Haroldston West Pembks 24 E7
Haroldswick Shet 106 w2
Harold Wood Gt Lon 22 E9
Harome N York 64 E3
Harpenden Herts 31 P10
Harpford Devon 6 E6
Harpham E R Yk 65 P7
Harpley Norfk 50 C8
Harpley Worcs 35 Q8
Harpole W Nthn 37 S8
Harpsdale Highld 112 D5
Harpsden Oxon 20 C6
Harpswell Lincs 58 F9
Harpurhey Manch 56 C6
Harpur Hill Derbys 56 G12
Harraby Cumb 67 P2
Harracott Devon 15 N7
Harrapool Highld 100 f7
Harras Cumb 66 E9
Harrietfield P & K 90 E6
Harrietsham Kent 12 G5
Harringay Gt Lon 21 P5
Harrington Cumb 66 E7
Harrington Lincs 59 Q12
Harrington N Nthn 37 U4
Harringworth N Nthn 38 D1
Harris W Isls 106 f9
Harriseahead Staffs 45 U2
Harriston Cumb 66 J4
Harrogate N York 63 S8
Harrold Bed 38 D9
Harrop Dale Oldham 56 F5
Harrow Gt Lon 21 L5
Harrowbarrow Cnwll 5 L6
Harrowden Bed 38 G11
Harrowgate Village Darltn 69 S9
Harrow Green Suffk 40 E10
Harrow Hill Gloucs 28 C4
Harrow on the Hill Gt Lon 21 L5
Harrow Weald Gt Lon 21 L4
Harston Cambs 39 P10
Harston Leics 48 B7
Harswell E R Yk 64 J11
Hart Hartpl 70 G5
Hartburn Nthumb 77 M8
Hartburn S on T 70 F9
Hartest Suffk 40 D10
Hartfield E Susx 11 R3
Hartford Cambs 39 L6
Hartford Ches W 55 P12
Hartford Somset 16 C11
Hartfordbridge Hants 20 C11
Hartford End Essex 22 G4
Hartforth N York 69 Q11
Hartgrove Dorset 8 A5
Harthill Ches W 45 L2
Harthill N Lans 82 H6
Harthill Rothm 57 Q10
Harthope D & G 74 K3
Hartington Derbys 46 F1
Hartington Nthumb 77 L8
Hartland Devon 14 G8
Hartland Quay Devon 14 F8
Hartlebury Worcs 35 T6
Hartlepool Hartpl 70 H6
Hartley Kent 12 B2
Hartley Kent 12 E9
Hartley Nthumb 77 S10
Hartley W & F 68 G11
Hartley Green Kent 12 B2
Hartley Green Staffs 46 C8
Hartley Wespall Hants 19 U9
Hartley Wintney Hants 20 C11
Hartlip Kent 12 F3
Hartoft End N York 71 M14
Harton N York 64 G7
Harton S Tyne 77 T12
Harton Shrops 35 L3
Hartpury Gloucs 28 E3
Hartshead Kirk 56 J2
Hartshead Moor Services Calder 56 J2
Hartshead Moor Top Kirk 56 J1
Hartshill C Stke 45 U4
Hartshill Warwks 36 K2
Hartshorne Derbys 46 K9
Hartside Nthumb 76 K2
Hartsop W & F 67 P10
Hart Station Hartpl 70 G5
Hartswell Somset 16 E11
Hartwell W Nthn 37 U10
Hartwith N York 63 Q7
Hartwood N Lans 82 F7
Hartwoodmyres Border 84 C14
Harvel Kent 12 C3
Harvington Worcs 35 U6
Harvington Worcs 36 E11
Harwell Notts 57 U8
Harwell Oxon 29 U10
Harwich Essex 23 U1
Harwood Bolton 55 R4
Harwood Dur 68 H6
Harwood Nthumb 77 L7
Harwood Dale N York 71 S13
Harwood Lee Bolton 55 R4
Harworth Notts 57 T8
Hasbury Dudley 36 C4
Hascombe Surrey 10 G3
Haselbech W Nthn 37 T5
Haselbury Plucknett Somset 7 N2
Haseley Warwks 36 H7
Haseley Green Warwks 36 H7
Haseley Knob Warwks 36 H6
Haselor Warwks 36 F9
Hasfield Gloucs 28 F2
Hasguard Pembks 24 E9
Hasholme E R Yk 64 J13
Haskayne Lancs 54 J5
Hasketon Suffk 41 M10
Hasland Derbys 57 N13
Haslemere Surrey 10 E4
Haslingden Lancs 55 S2
Haslingfield Cambs 39 P10
Haslington Ches E 45 R2
Hassall Ches E 45 S2
Hassall Green Ches E 45 S2
Hassell Street Kent 13 L6
Hassingham Norfk 51 Q12
Hassness Cumb 66 J9
Hassocks W Susx 11 N7
Hassop Derbys 56 K12
Haste Hill Surrey 10 E4
Haster Highld 112 H6
Hasthorpe Lincs 59 S13
Hastingleigh Kent 13 L6
Hastings E Susx 12 F14
Hastings Somset 16 K13
Hastingwood Essex 22 C6
Hastoe Herts 30 K11
Haswell Dur 70 E4
Haswell Plough Dur 70 E4
Hatch C Beds 38 J11
Hatch Beauchamp Somset 16 K12
Hatch End Bed 38 G8
Hatch End Gt Lon 20 K4
Hatchet Gate Hants 9 M8
Hatching Green Herts 31 P10
Hatchmere Ches W 55 N12
Hatch Warren Hants 19 T11
Hatcliffe NE Lin 59 M6
Hatfield Donc 57 U5
Hatfield Herefs 35 N9
Hatfield Herts 31 R11
Hatfield Worcs 35 U10
Hatfield Broad Oak Essex 22 D4
Hatfield Heath Essex 22 D4
Hatfield Peverel Essex 22 J5
Hatfield Woodhouse Donc 57 U5
Hatford Oxon 29 R9
Hatherden Hants 19 M10
Hatherleigh Devon 15 M12
Hathern Leics 47 P9
Hatherop Gloucs 29 N6
Hathersage Derbys 56 K10
Hathersage Booths Derbys 56 K10
Hatherton Ches E 45 Q4
Hatherton Staffs 46 C11
Hatley St George Cambs 39 L10
Hatt Cnwll 4 K8
Hattersley Tamesd 56 E8
Hattingley Hants 19 T13
Hatton Abers 105 T8
Hatton Angus 91 Q3
Hatton Derbys 46 H7
Hatton Gt Lon 20 J7
Hatton Lincs 59 L11
Hatton Shrops 35 L2
Hatton Warrtn 55 N10
Hatton Warwks 36 H7
Hatton Heath Ches W 45 L1
Hatton of Fintray Abers 105 N12
Hatton Park Warwks 36 J7
Haugh E Ayrs 81 P7
Haugh Lincs 59 R11
Haugh Rochdl 56 D4
Haugham Lincs 59 P10
Haughhead E Duns 89 P10
Haugh Head Nthumb 85 Q13
Haughley Suffk 40 H8
Haughley Green Suffk 40 H8
Haugh of Glass Moray 104 E8
Haugh of Urr D & G 74 F12
Haughs of Kinnaird Angus 99 L12
Haughton Ches E 45 N2
Haughton Notts 57 U12
Haughton Powys 44 H10
Haughton Shrops 35 Q1
Haughton Shrops 44 J8
Haughton Shrops 45 N10
Haughton Shrops 45 R12
Haughton Staffs 45 U9
Haughton Green Tamesd 56 D8
Haughton le Skerne Darltn 70 D9
Haultwick Herts 31 T8
Haunton Staffs 46 H11
Hautes Croix Jersey 7 d1
Hauxton Cambs 39 P10
Havannah Ches E 56 C14
Havant Hants 9 U7
Haven Herefs 34 K10
Haven Bank Lincs 48 K3
Haven Side E R Yk 65 R14
Havenstreet IoW 9 R10
Havercroft Wakefd 57 N4
Haverfordwest Pembks 24 G7
Haverhill Suffk 39 U11
Haverigg Cumb 61 M4
Havering-atte-Bower Gt Lon 22 D9
Havering's Grove Essex 22 G9
Haversham M Keyn 30 H4
Haverthwaite W & F 61 Q3
Haverton Hill S on T 70 G8
Havyatt N Som 17 N4
Havyatt Somset 17 P9
Hawarden Flints 54 H13
Hawbridge Worcs 36 B11
Hawbush Green Essex 22 J3
Hawcoat W & F 61 N5
Hawen Cerdgn 32 F11
Hawes N York 62 H2
Hawe's Green Norfk 51 M14
Hawford Worcs 35 T8
Hawick Border 75 V3
Hawkchurch Devon 6 K4
Hawkedon Suffk 40 C10
Hawkenbury Kent 12 F6
Hawkeridge Wilts 18 C10
Hawkerland Devon 6 E7
Hawker's Cove Cnwll 3 N1
Hawkesbury S Glos 28 E10
Hawkesbury Warwks 37 L4
Hawkesbury Upton S Glos 28 E10
Hawkes End Covtry 36 J4
Hawk Green Stockp 56 E9
Hawkhead Rens 89 M13
Hawkhill Nthumb 77 Q3
Hawkhurst Kent 12 E9
Hawkhurst Common E Susx 11 S7
Hawkinge Kent 13 P8
Hawkley Hants 9 U3
Hawkley Wigan 55 N6
Hawkridge Somset 15 U6
Hawksdale Cumb 67 N3
Hawkshaw Bury 55 S3
Hawkshead W & F 67 N13
Hawkshead Hill W & F 67 M13
Hawksland S Lans 82 F11
Hawkspur Green Essex 22 G1
Hawkstone Shrops 45 N7
Hawkswick N York 62 K5
Hawksworth Leeds 63 P11
Hawksworth Notts 47 U5
Hawkwell Essex 23 L9
Hawkwell Nthumb 77 M11
Hawley Hants 20 E11
Hawley Kent 22 D13
Hawling Gloucs 29 L3
Hawnby N York 64 C2
Haworth C Brad 63 L12
Hawridge Bucks 30 K11
Hawstead Suffk 40 E9
Hawstead Green Suffk 40 E9
Hawthorn Dur 70 F3
Hawthorn Hants 9 T2
Hawthorn Rhondd 26 K10
Hawthorn Hill Br For 20 E8
Hawthorn Hill Lincs 48 K2
Hawthorpe Lincs 48 F8
Hawton Notts 47 U3
Haxby C York 64 E8
Haxby Gates C York 64 E8
Haxey N Linc 58 C7
Haxey Carr N Linc 58 C6
Haxted Surrey 21 R13
Haxton Wilts 18 H11
Hay Cnwll 3 P2
Hay Cnwll 3 P6
Haydock St Hel 55 N7
Haydon BaNES 17 S6
Haydon Dorset 17 S13
Haydon Somset 16 J12
Haydon Bridge Nthumb 76 G13
Haydon Wick Swindn 29 M10
Haye Cnwll 4 K6
Hayes Gt Lon 20 J6
Hayes Gt Lon 21 R9
Hayes End Gt Lon 20 J6
Hayfield Ag & B 94 F14
Hayfield Derbys 56 F9
Hayfield Green Donc 57 U7
Haygate Wrekin 45 P11
Hay Green Norfk 49 R10
Hayhillock Angus 91 R3
Hayle Cnwll 2 F9
Hayle Port Cnwll 2 F9
Hayley Green Dudley 36 C4
Hayling Island Hants 9 U8
Haymoor Green Ches E 45 Q3
Hayne Devon 5 T3
Hayne Devon 16 C13
Haynes C Beds 31 N4
Haynes Church End C Beds 31 N4
Haynes West End C Beds 31 N4
Hay-on-Wye Powys 34 F12
Hayscastle Pembks 24 E5
Hayscastle Cross Pembks 24 F5
Hay Street Herts 31 U7
Hayton Cumb 66 H4
Hayton Cumb 75 V14
Hayton E R Yk 64 J10
Hayton Notts 58 B10
Hayton's Bent Shrops 35 M4
Haytor Vale Devon 5 T5
Haytown Devon 14 J10
Haywards Heath W Susx 11 N6
Haywood Donc 57 S4
Haywood Herefs 35 L14
Haywood Oaks Notts 47 R2
Hazards Green E Susx 12 C13
Hazelbank S Lans 82 F9
Hazelbury Bryan Dorset 7 T3
Hazeleigh Essex 22 K7
Hazeley Hants 20 B11
Hazelford Notts 47 T4
Hazel Grove Stockp 56 D9
Hazelhurst Tamesd 56 E6
Hazelslade Staffs 46 D11
Hazel Street Kent 12 C8
Hazel Stub Suffk 39 U12
Hazelton Walls Fife 91 M7
Hazelwood Derbys 46 K4
Hazlemere Bucks 20 E3
Hazlerigg N u Ty 77 Q11
Hazles Staffs 46 D4
Hazleton Gloucs 29 L4
Heacham Norfk 49 U6
Headbourne Worthy Hants 9 P2
Headbrook Herefs 34 G9
Headcorn Kent 12 F7
Headingley Leeds 63 R12
Headington Oxon 30 B11
Headlam Dur 69 Q9
Headlesscross N Lans 82 H7
Headless Cross Worcs 36 D7
Headley Hants 10 C3
Headley Hants 19 R8
Headley Surrey 21 M12
Headley Down Hants 10 C3
Headley Heath Worcs 36 E5
Headon Devon 14 J12
Headon Notts 58 B11
Heads Nook Cumb 67 R2
Heage Derbys 47 L3
Healaugh N York 64 C10
Healaugh N York 69 M13
Heald Green Stockp 55 T9
Heale Devon 15 P3
Heale Somset 16 H12
Heale Somset 17 L11
Healey N York 63 P3
Healey Nthumb 77 L14
Healey Rochdl 56 C3
Healey Wakefd 57 L3
Healeyfield Dur 69 N3
Healing NE Lin 59 M4
Heamoor Cnwll 2 D10
Heanor Derbys 47 M4
Heanton Punchardon Devon 15 M5
Heapham Lincs 58 E9
Hearn Hants 10 C3
Heart of Scotland Services N Lans 82 H6
Hearts Delight Kent 12 G3
Heasley Mill Devon 15 R6
Heaste Highld 100 f8
Heath Derbys 57 P13
Heath Wakefd 57 N2
Heath and Reach C Beds 30 K7
Heath Common W Susx 10 J7
Heathcote Derbys 46 F1
Heathcote Shrops 45 Q8
Heath End Bucks 20 E3
Heath End Hants 19 P8
Heath End Leics 47 L9
Heath End Warwks 36 H8
Heather Leics 47 L11
Heathfield Cambs 39 Q11
Heathfield Devon 5 U5
Heathfield E Susx 11 T6
Heathfield N York 63 N6
Heathfield Somset 16 G11
Heathfield Village Oxon 30 B9
Heath Green Worcs 36 E6
Heath Hall D & G 74 J10
Heath Hayes & Wimblebury Staffs 46 D11
Heath Hill Shrops 45 S11
Heath House Somset 17 M7
Heathrow Airport Gt Lon 20 J7
Heathstock Devon 6 H4
Heathton Shrops 35 T2
Heath Town Wolves 46 B14
Heathwaite N York 70 G12
Heatley Staffs 46 E8
Heatley Warrtn 55 R9
Heaton Bolton 55 Q5
Heaton C Brad 63 N12
Heaton Lancs 61 S7
Heaton N u Ty 77 R12
Heaton Staffs 56 E14
Heaton Chapel Stockp 56 C8
Heaton Mersey Stockp 56 C8
Heaton Norris Stockp 56 C8
Heaton's Bridge Lancs 54 K4
Heaverham Kent 21 U11
Heaviley Stockp 56 D9
Heavitree Devon 6 B6
Hebburn S Tyne 77 S13
Hebden N York 63 L7
Hebden Bridge Calder 56 E1
Hebden Green Ches W 55 P13
Hebing End Herts 31 T8
Hebron Carmth 25 L5
Hebron IoA 52 G6
Hebron Nthumb 77 P8
Heckfield Hants 20 B10
Heckfield Green Suffk 41 L5
Heckfordbridge Essex 23 M3
Heckington Lincs 48 H5
Heckmondwike Kirk 56 K2
Heddington Wilts 18 E7
Heddon-on-the-Wall Nthumb 77 N12
Hedenham Norfk 41 P2
Hedge End Hants 9 P6
Hedgerley Bucks 20 G5
Hedgerley Green Bucks 20 G5
Hedging Somset 16 K11
Hedley on the Hill Nthumb 77 M14
Hednesford Staffs 46 C11
Hedon E R Yk 65 R14
Hedsor Bucks 20 F5
Heeley Sheff 57 N10
Hegdon Hill Herefs 35 N10
Heglibister Shet 106 t8
Heighington Darltn 69 R8
Heighington Lincs 58 H13
Heightington Worcs 35 S6
Heiton Border 84 J12
Hele Devon 5 S6
Hele Devon 6 C4
Hele Devon 15 M3
Hele Somset 16 G12
Helebridge Cnwll 14 F12
Hele Lane Devon 15 S10
Helensburgh Ag & B 88 G9
Helenton S Ayrs 81 M6
Helford Cnwll 2 K11
Helford Passage Cnwll 2 K11
Helhoughton Norfk 50 E8
Helions Bumpstead Essex 39 U12
Hellaby Rothm 57 R8
Helland Cnwll 3 R2
Hellandbridge Cnwll 3 R2
Hell Corner W Berk 19 N8
Hellescott Cnwll 4 H3
Hellesdon Norfk 51 M11
Hellesveor Cnwll 2 E8
Hellidon W Nthn 37 P9
Hellifield N York 62 H8
Hellingly E Susx 11 T8
Hellington Norfk 51 P13
Helm Nthumb 77 P6
Helmdon W Nthn 30 C4
Helme Kirk 56 G4
Helmingham Suffk 41 L9
Helmington Row Dur 69 Q5
Helmsdale Highld 112 B13
Helmshore Lancs 55 S2
Helmsley N York 64 E3
Helperby N York 63 U6
Helperthorpe N York 65 M5
Helpringham Lincs 48 H5
Helpston C Pete 48 H12
Helsby Ches W 55 L11
Helsey Lincs 59 T12
Helston Cnwll 2 H11
Helstone Cnwll 4 D4
Helton W & F 67 R8
Helwith N York 69 N12
Helwith Bridge N York 62 G6
Hemblington Norfk 51 P11
Hembridge Somset 17 Q9
Hemel Hempstead Herts 31 N11
Hemerdon Devon 5 P9
Hemingbrough N York 64 F13
Hemingby Lincs 59 M12
Hemingfield Barns 57 N6
Hemingford Abbots Cambs 39 L6
Hemingford Grey Cambs 39 L6
Hemingstone Suffk 40 K10
Hemington Leics 47 N8
Hemington N Nthn 38 G3
Hemington Somset 17 T6
Hemley Suffk 41 N12
Hemlington Middsb 70 H10
Hempholme E R Yk 65 P9
Hempnall Norfk 41 M2
Hempnall Green Norfk 41 M2
Hempriggs Moray 103 T3
Hempstead Essex 39 T13
Hempstead Medway 12 E3
Hempstead Norfk 50 K6
Hempstead Norfk 51 R8
Hempsted Gloucs 28 F4
Hempton Norfk 50 F8
Hempton Oxon 29 T1
Hemsby Norfk 51 S10
Hemswell Lincs 58 F8
Hemswell Cliff Lincs 58 F9
Hemsworth Wakefd 57 P4
Hemyock Devon 6 F2
Henbury Bristl 27 V12
Henbury Ches E 56 C12
Hendham Devon 5 S10
Hendomen Powys 44 F14
Hendon Gt Lon 21 M5
Hendon Sundld 70 F1
Hendra Cnwll 2 J9
Hendra Cnwll 3 Q1
Hendre Brdgnd 26 G11
Hendre Flints 54 E13
Hendredenny Caerph 27 L10
Hendy Carmth 25 U10
Heneglwys IoA 52 F7
Henfield W Susx 11 L7
Henford Devon 4 K2
Henfynyw Cerdgn 32 J8
Henghurst Kent 12 J8
Hengoed Caerph 27 M9
Hengoed Powys 34 F10
Hengoed Shrops 44 G7
Hengrave Suffk 40 D7
Henham Essex 22 D2
Heniarth Powys 44 D12
Henlade Somset 16 J12
Henley Dorset 7 S4
Henley Gloucs 28 H4
Henley Shrops 35 L3
Henley Shrops 35 M5
Henley Somset 17 M10
Henley Suffk 41 L10
Henley W Susx 10 D5
Henley Green Covtry 37 L4
Henley-in-Arden Warwks 36 G7
Henley-on-Thames Oxon 20 C6
Henley Park Surrey 20 F12
Henley's Down E Susx 12 D13
Henley Street Kent 12 C2
Henllan Cerdgn 32 G12
Henllan Denbgs 53 T9
Henllan Amgoed Carmth 25 L7
Henllys Torfn 27 P9
Henlow C Beds 31 Q5
Henlow Camp C Beds 31 Q5
Hennock Devon 5 U4
Henny Street Essex 40 E13
Henryd Conwy 53 N8
Henry's Moat (Castell Hendre) Pembks 24 H5
Hensall N York 57 S2
Henshaw Nthumb 76 F13
Hensingham Cumb 66 E9
Henstead Suffk 41 S3
Hensting Hants 9 P4
Henstridge Somset 17 T13
Henstridge Ash Somset 17 T12
Henstridge Marsh Somset 17 T12
Henton Oxon 30 G12
Henton Somset 17 N7
Henwick Worcs 35 T9
Henwood Cnwll 4 H6
Henwood Oxon 29 U7
Heolgerrig Myr Td 26 J6
Heol-las Swans 26 B8
Heol Senni Powys 26 G3
Heol-y-Cyw Brdgnd 26 G11
Hepburn Nthumb 85 R14
Hepple Nthumb 76 K5
Hepscott Nthumb 77 Q9
Heptonstall Calder 62 K14
Hepworth Kirk 56 J5
Hepworth Suffk 40 G6
Herbrandston Pembks 24 E9
Hereford Herefs 35 M13
Hereson Kent 13 S2
Heribusta Highld 100 c2
Heriot Border 83 T8
Hermiston C Edin 83 N4
Hermitage Border 75 V6
Hermitage Dorset 7 S3
Hermitage W Berk 19 R6
Hermitage W Susx 10 B9
Hermit Hill Barns 57 M6
Hermon Carmth 25 Q4
Hermon IoA 52 E9
Hermon Pembks 25 M4
Herne Kent 13 N2
Herne Bay Kent 13 N2
Herne Common Kent 13 N2
Herne Hill Gt Lon 21 P8
Herne Pound Kent 12 C5
Herner Devon 15 N7
Hernhill Kent 13 L3
Herodsfoot Cnwll 4 G8
Heronden Kent 13 Q5
Herongate Essex 22 F9
Heronsford S Ayrs 72 E3
Heronsgate Herts 20 H4
Herriard Hants 19 U11
Herringfleet Suffk 51 S14
Herring's Green Bed 31 N4
Herringswell Suffk 40 B6
Herringthorpe Rothm 57 P8
Herrington Sundld 70 E2
Hersden Kent 13 P3
Hersham Cnwll 14 G11
Hersham Surrey 20 K10
Herstmonceux E Susx 11 U8
Herston Dorset 8 E13
Herston Ork 106 t20
Hertford Herts 31 T10
Hertford Heath Herts 31 U10
Hertingfordbury Herts 31 T10
Hesketh Bank Lancs 54 K2
Hesketh Lane Lancs 62 C11
Hesket Newmarket Cumb 67 M5
Heskin Green Lancs 55 M3
Hesleden Dur 70 F5
Hesleden N York 62 H5
Hesley Donc 57 T8
Hesleyside Nthumb 76 G9
Heslington C York 64 E9
Hessay C York 64 C9
Hessenford Cnwll 4 J9
Hessett Suffk 40 F8
Hessle E R Yk 58 H1
Hessle Wakefd 57 P3
Hest Bank Lancs 61 T6
Hestley Green Suffk 41 L7
Heston Gt Lon 20 K7
Heston Services Gt Lon 20 K7
Hestwall Ork 106 r18
Heswall Wirral 54 G10
Hethe Oxon 30 C7
Hethersett Norfk 50 K13
Hethersgill Cumb 75 U12
Hetherside Cumb 75 T12
Hetherson Green Ches W 45 M3
Hethpool Nthumb 85 M13
Hett Dur 69 S5
Hetton N York 62 K8
Hetton-le-Hole Sundld 70 E3
Hetton Steads Nthumb 85 Q11
Heugh Nthumb 77 M11
Heughhead Abers 104 D13
Heugh Head Border 85 M6
Heveningham Suffk 41 P6
Hever Kent 21 S13
Heversham W & F 61 T3
Hevingham Norfk 51 L9
Hewas Water Cnwll 3 P7
Hewelsfield Gloucs 27 V7
Hewenden C Brad 63 M12
Hewish N Som 17 M4
Hewish Somset 7 M3
Hewood Dorset 7 L4
Hexham Nthumb 76 J13
Hextable Kent 22 D13
Hexthorpe Donc 57 S6
Hexton Herts 31 P6
Hexworthy Cnwll 4 K4
Hexworthy Devon 5 R6
Hey Lancs 62 H11
Heybridge Essex 22 F8
Heybridge Essex 23 L6
Heybridge Basin Essex 23 L6
Heybrook Bay Devon 5 M11
Heydon Cambs 39 P13
Heydon Norfk 50 K8
Heydour Lincs 48 F6
Hey Houses Lancs 61 Q14
Heylipoll Ag & B 92 B10
Heylor Shet 106 s5
Heyrod Tamesd 56 E7
Heysham Lancs 61 S7
Heyshaw N York 63 P7
Heyshott W Susx 10 D7
Heyside Oldham 56 D5
Heytesbury Wilts 18 D12
Heythrop Oxon 29 S2
Heywood Rochdl 56 C4
Heywood Wilts 18 C10
Hibaldstow N Linc 58 G6
Hickleton Donc 57 Q5
Hickling Norfk 51 R9
Hickling Notts 47 S8
Hickling Green Norfk 51 R9
Hickling Heath Norfk 51 R9
Hickling Pastures Notts 47 S8
Hickmans Green Kent 13 L4
Hicks Forstal Kent 13 N3
Hickstead W Susx 11 M6
Hidcote Bartrim Gloucs 36 G12
Hidcote Boyce Gloucs 36 G12
High Ackworth Wakefd 57 P3
Higham Barns 57 M5
Higham Derbys 47 L2
Higham Kent 12 B6
Higham Kent 22 H13
Higham Lancs 62 G12
Higham Suffk 40 B7
Higham Suffk 40 H13
Higham Dykes Nthumb 77 N10
Higham Ferrers N Nthn 38 E7
Higham Gobion C Beds 31 P6
Higham Hill Gt Lon 21 Q4
Higham on the Hill Leics 37 L1
Highampton Devon 15 L12
Highams Park Gt Lon 21 Q4
High Angerton Nthumb 77 M8
High Ardwell D & G 72 D10
High Auldgirth D & G 74 H8
High Bankhill W & F 67 S4
High Barnet Gt Lon 21 N3
High Beach Essex 21 R3
High Bentham N York 62 D6
High Bewaldeth Cumb 66 K6
High Bickington Devon 15 P8
High Biggins W & F 62 C4
High Birkwith N York 62 G4
High Blantyre S Lans 82 C7
High Bonnybridge Falk 89 T10
High Borrans W & F 67 P12
High Bradley N York 63 L10
High Bray Devon 15 Q6
Highbridge Hants 9 P4
Highbridge Somset 16 K7
Highbrook W Susx 11 P4
High Brooms Kent 11 T2
High Bullen Devon 15 M8
Highburton Kirk 56 J4
Highbury Gt Lon 21 P5
Highbury Somset 17 S7
High Buston Nthumb 77 Q4
High Callerton Nthumb 77 P11
High Casterton W & F 62 C4
High Catton E R Yk 64 G9
Highclere Hants 19 P9
Highcliffe BCP 8 J10
High Close Dur 69 Q9
High Cogges Oxon 29 S6
High Common Norfk 50 G12
High Coniscliffe Darltn 69 R9
High Crosby Cumb 75 U14
High Cross Cnwll 2 J11
High Cross E Ayrs 81 N3
High Cross Hants 9 U3
High Cross Herts 31 U9
Highcross Lancs 61 Q12
High Cross W Susx 11 L7
High Cross Warwks 36 H7
High Drummore D & G 72 E12
High Dubmire Sundld 70 D3
High Easter Essex 22 F5
High Eggborough N York 57 S2
High Ellington N York 63 P3
Higher Alham Somset 17 S8
Higher Ansty Dorset 7 U4
Higher Ballam Lancs 61 R13
Higher Bartle Lancs 61 U13
Higher Berry End C Beds 31 L6
Higher Bockhampton Dorset 7 T6
Higher Brixham Torbay 6 B14
Higher Burrowton Devon 6 D5
Higher Burwardsley Ches W 45 M2
High Ercall Wrekin 45 N10
Higher Chillington Somset 7 L2
Higher Clovelly Devon 14 H8
Highercombe Somset 16 B10
Higher Coombe Dorset 7 P6
Higher Disley Ches E 56 E10
Higher Folds Wigan 55 Q6
Higherford Lancs 62 H11
Higher Gabwell Devon 6 B11
Higher Halstock Leigh Dorset 7 P3
Higher Harpers Lancs 62 G12
Higher Heysham Lancs 61 S7
Higher Hurdsfield Ches E 56 D12
Higher Irlam Salfd 55 R7
Higher Kingcombe Dorset 7 P5
Higher Kinnerton Flints 44 H1
Higher Marston Ches W 55 Q11
Higher Muddiford Devon 15 N5
Higher Nyland Dorset 17 T12
Higher Ogden Rochdl 56 E4
Higher Pentire Cnwll 2 H11
Higher Penwortham Lancs 61 U14
Higher Prestacott Devon 14 J13
Higher Studfold N York 62 G5
Higher Town Cnwll 3 L8
Higher Town Cnwll 3 Q4
Higher Town IoS 2 c1
Higher Tregantle Cnwll 5 L10
Higher Walton Lancs 55 N1
Higher Walton Warrtn 55 N9
Higher Wambrook Somset 6 J3
Higher Waterston Dorset 7 T5
Higher Whatcombe Dorset 8 A8
Higher Wheelton Lancs 55 P2
Higher Whitley Ches W 55 P10
Higher Wincham Ches W 55 Q11
Higher Wraxhall Dorset 7 Q4
Higher Wych Ches W 45 L5
High Etherley Dur 69 Q7
High Ferry Lincs 49 N4
Highfield E R Yk 64 G12
Highfield Gatesd 77 N14
Highfield N Ayrs 81 L2
Highfields Donc 57 R5
Highfields Caldecote Cambs 39 N9
High Flats Kirk 56 K5
High Garrett Essex 22 J2
Highgate E Susx 11 Q4
Highgate Gt Lon 21 N5
Highgate Kent 12 E9
Highgate Lincs 49 P4
High Grange Dur 69 Q6
High Grantley N York 63 Q6
High Green Kirk 56 K4
High Green Norfk 41 L3
High Green Norfk 50 K12
High Green Sheff 57 M7
High Green Shrops 35 R4
High Green Suffk 40 E8
High Green W & F 67 P12
High Green Worcs 35 U11
Highgreen Manor Nthumb 76 G7
High Halden Kent 12 G8
High Halstow Medway 22 J12
High Ham Somset 17 M10
High Harrington Cumb 66 F7
High Harrogate N York 63 S8
High Haswell Dur 70 E4
High Hatton Shrops 45 P9
High Hauxley Nthumb 77 R5
High Hawsker N York 71 R11
High Hesket W & F 67 Q4
High Hoyland Barns 57 L5
High Hunsley E R Yk 65 M12
High Hurstwood E Susx 11 R5
High Hutton N York 64 H6
High Ireby Cumb 66 K5
High Kelling Norfk 50 K5
High Kilburn N York 64 C4
High Killerby N York 65 P3
High Knipe W & F 67 R9
High Lands Dur 69 P7
Highlane Ches E 56 C13
Highlane Derbys 57 P10
High Lane Stockp 56 E9
High Lanes Cnwll 2 F9
High Laver Essex 22 D6
Highlaws Cumb 66 H3
Highleadon Gloucs 28 E3
High Legh Ches E 55 R10
Highleigh W Susx 10 C11
High Leven S on T 70 G10
Highley Shrops 35 R4
High Littleton BaNES 17 R5
High Lorton Cumb 66 J7
High Marishes N York 64 J4
High Marnham Notts 58 D12
High Melton Donc 57 R6
High Mickley Nthumb 77 M13
Highmoor Cumb 67 L3
Highmoor Oxon 20 B6
Highmoor Cross Oxon 20 B6
Highmoor Hill Mons 27 T10
High Moorsley Sundld 70 D3
Highnam Gloucs 28 E3
High Newport Sundld 70 E2
High Newton W & F 61 S3
High Newton-by-the-Sea Nthumb 85 U13
High Nibthwaite W & F 61 P2
High Offley Staffs 45 S8
High Ongar Essex 22 E7
High Onn Staffs 45 T10
High Park Corner Essex 23 P3
High Pennyvenie E Ayrs 81 P11
High Pittington Dur 70 D4
High Post Wilts 18 J13
Highridge N Som 17 Q3
High Roding Essex 22 F4
High Row Cumb 67 N5
High Row W & F 67 N8
High Salter Lancs 62 C7
High Salvington W Susx 10 J9
High Scales Cumb 66 J3
High Seaton Cumb 66 F6
High Shaw N York 62 H1
High Side Cumb 66 K6
High Spen Gatesd 77 N14
Highstead Kent 13 P2
Highsted Kent 12 H3
High Stoop Dur 69 P4
High Street Cnwll 3 P6
High Street Kent 12 D9
Highstreet Kent 13 L3
High Street Suffk 41 R6
High Street Suffk 41 R9
Highstreet Green Essex 40 C14
Highstreet Green Surrey 10 F3
Hightae D & G 75 L10
Highter's Heath Birm 36 E5
High Throston Hartpl 70 G6
Hightown Ches E 45 U1
Hightown Hants 8 H8
Hightown Sefton 54 H6
High Town Staffs 46 C11
Hightown Green Suffk 40 G9
High Toynton Lincs 59 N13
High Trewhitt Nthumb 77 L4
High Urpeth Dur 69 R2
High Valleyfield Fife 82 K1
High Warden Nthumb 76 J12
Highway Herefs 35 L11
Highway Wilts 18 F6
Highweek Devon 5 U6
High Westwood Dur 69 P1
Highwood Essex 22 F7
Highwood Staffs 46 E7
Highwood W Susx 10 K4
Highwood Hill Gt Lon 21 M4
Highwoods Essex 23 P2
High Woolaston Gloucs 28 A8
High Worsall N York 70 E11
Highworth Swindn 29 P9
High Wray W & F 67 N13
High Wych Herts 22 C5
High Wycombe Bucks 20 E4
Hilborough Norfk 50 D13
Hilcote Derbys 47 N2
Hilcott Wilts 18 H9
Hildenborough Kent 21 U13
Hilden Park Kent 21 U13
Hildersham Cambs 39 R11
Hilderstone Staffs 46 C7
Hilderthorpe E R Yk 65 R6
Hilfield Dorset 7 R3
Hilgay Norfk 49 T14
Hill S Glos 28 B8
Hill Warwks 37 N7
Hillam N York 64 C14
Hillbeck W & F 68 G9
Hillborough Kent 13 P2
Hill Brow Hants 10 B5
Hillbutts Dorset 8 D8
Hill Chorlton Staffs 45 S6
Hillclifflane Derbys 46 J4
Hill Common Norfk 51 R9
Hill Common Somset 16 F11
Hill Deverill Wilts 18 C12
Hilldyke Lincs 49 M4
Hill End Dur 69 M5
Hillend Fife 83 M2
Hill End Fife 90 F12
Hill End Gloucs 36 B13
Hillend Mdloth 83 Q5
Hillend N Lans 82 F5
Hillend Swans 25 R12
Hillersland Gloucs 27 V5
Hillerton Devon 15 R13
Hillesden Bucks 30 E7
Hillesley Gloucs 28 E10
Hillfarrance Somset 16 G12
Hill Green Kent 12 F3
Hillgrove W Susx 10 E5
Hillhampton Herefs 35 N11
Hillhead Abers 104 H8
Hillhead Devon 6 B14
Hill Head Hants 9 Q8
Hillhead S Lans 82 J10
Hillhead of Cocklaw Abers 105 T7
Hilliard's Cross Staffs 46 G11
Hilliclay Highld 112 E4
Hillingdon Gt Lon 20 J6
Hillington C Glas 89 M13
Hillington Norfk 50 B8
Hillis Corner IoW 9 P10
Hillmorton Warwks 37 P6
Hillock Vale Lancs 62 F14
Hill of Beath Fife 90 J13
Hill of Fearn Highld 109 Q9
Hillowton D & G 74 E13
Hillpool Worcs 35 U5
Hillpound Hants 9 R5
Hill Ridware Staffs 46 E10
Hillside Abers 99 S4
Hillside Angus 99 N11
Hillside Devon 5 S8
Hill Side Kirk 56 J3
Hill Side Worcs 35 S8
Hills Town Derbys 57 Q13
Hillstreet Hants 9 L5
Hillswick Shet 106 s6
Hill Top Dur 69 L8
Hill Top Hants 9 N8
Hill Top Kirk 56 G4
Hill Top Rothm 57 N8
Hill Top Sandw 36 C2
Hill Top Wakefd 57 M3
Hillwell Shet 106 t12
Hilmarton Wilts 18 F5
Hilperton Wilts 18 C9
Hilperton Marsh Wilts 18 C9
Hilsea C Port 9 T8
Hilston E R Yk 65 T13
Hiltingbury Hants 9 N4
Hilton Border 85 M8
Hilton Cambs 39 L7
Hilton Derbys 46 H7
Hilton Dorset 7 U4
Hilton Dur 69 Q8
Hilton S on T 70 G10
Hilton Shrops 35 S1
Hilton W & F 68 F8
Hilton of Cadboll Highld 109 R9
Hilton Park Services Staffs 46 C13
Himbleton Worcs 36 B9
Himley Staffs 35 U2
Hincaster W & F 61 U3
Hinchley Wood Surrey 21 L9
Hinckley Leics 37 M2
Hinderclay Suffk 40 H5
Hinderwell N York 71 N9
Hindford Shrops 44 H7
Hindhead Surrey 10 D3

Hindhead Tunnel Surrey 10 D3
Hindle Fold Lancs 62 E13
Hindley Nthumb 77 L14
Hindley Wigan 55 P6
Hindley Green Wigan 55 P6
Hindlip Worcs 35 U9
Hindolveston Norfk 50 H8
Hindon Wilts 8 C2
Hindringham Norfk 50 G6
Hingham Norfk 50 H13
Hinksford Staffs 35 U3
Hinstock Shrops 45 Q8
Hintlesham Suffk 40 J12
Hinton Gloucs 28 C7
Hinton Hants 8 J9
Hinton Herefs 34 H13
Hinton S Glos 28 D12
Hinton Shrops 35 Q4
Hinton Shrops 44 K12
Hinton W Nthn 37 P10
Hinton Admiral Hants 8 J9
Hinton Ampner Hants 9 S3
Hinton Blewett BaNES 17 Q5
Hinton Charterhouse BaNES 17 U5
Hinton Cross Worcs 36 D12
Hinton-in-the-Hedges W Nthn 30 C5
Hinton Marsh Hants 9 R3
Hinton Martell Dorset 8 E7
Hinton on the Green Worcs 36 D12
Hinton Parva Swindn 29 P11
Hinton St George Somset 7 M2
Hinton St Mary Dorset 17 U13
Hinton Waldrist Oxon 29 S8
Hints Shrops 35 P6
Hints Staffs 46 G13
Hinwick Bed 38 D8
Hinxhill Kent 12 K7
Hinxton Cambs 39 Q11
Hinxworth Herts 31 R4
Hipperholme Calder 56 H1
Hipsburn Nthumb 77 Q3
Hipswell N York 69 Q13
Hirn Abers 99 N3
Hirnant Powys 44 B9
Hirst Nthumb 77 R8
Hirst Courtney N York 57 T2
Hirwaen Denbgs 44 D1
Hirwaun Rhondd 26 H6
Hiscott Devon 15 M7
Histon Cambs 39 P8
Hitcham Suffk 40 G10
Hitcham Causeway Suffk 40 G10
Hitcham Street Suffk 40 G10
Hitchin Herts 31 Q7
Hither Green Gt Lon 21 Q8
Hittisleigh Devon 15 R13
Hive E R Yk 64 J13
Hixon Staffs 46 D8
Hoaden Kent 13 Q4
Hoar Cross Staffs 46 F9
Hoarwithy Herefs 27 U2
Hoath Kent 13 P3
Hoathly Kent 12 C8
Hobarris Shrops 34 H5
Hobbles Green Suffk 40 B10
Hobbs Cross Essex 21 S3
Hobbs Cross Essex 22 C5
Hobkirk Border 76 B3
Hobland Hall Norfk 51 T13
Hobsick Notts 47 N4
Hobson Dur 69 Q1
Hoby Leics 47 S10
Hoccombe Somset 16 F11
Hockering Norfk 50 J11
Hockerton Notts 47 T2
Hockley Ches E 56 D10
Hockley Covtry 36 J5
Hockley Essex 22 K9
Hockley Staffs 46 H13
Hockley Heath Solhll 36 G6
Hockliffe C Beds 31 L7
Hockwold cum Wilton Norfk 40 B3
Hockworthy Devon 16 D13
Hoddesdon Herts 31 U11
Hoddlesden Bl w D 55 R2
Hoddom Cross D & G 75 N11
Hoddom Mains D & G 75 N11
Hodgehill Ches E 55 T13
Hodgeston Pembks 24 H11
Hodnet Shrops 45 P8
Hodsock Notts 57 T9
Hodsoll Street Kent 12 B3
Hodson Swindn 18 J4
Hodthorpe Derbys 57 R11
Hoe Hants 9 R5
Hoe Norfk 50 G10
Hoe Benham W Berk 19 P7
Hoe Gate Hants 9 S6
Hoff W & F 68 E9
Hogben's Hill Kent 12 K4
Hoggards Green Suffk 40 E9
Hoggeston Bucks 30 H8
Hoggrill's End Warwks 36 H2
Hog Hill E Susx 12 G12
Hoghton Lancs 55 P1
Hoghton Bottoms Lancs 55 P1
Hognaston Derbys 46 H3
Hogsthorpe Lincs 59 T12
Holbeach Lincs 49 N9
Holbeach Bank Lincs 49 N8
Holbeach Clough Lincs 49 N8
Holbeach Drove Lincs 49 M11
Holbeach Hurn Lincs 49 N8
Holbeach St Johns Lincs 49 N10
Holbeach St Mark's Lincs 49 N7
Holbeach St Matthew Lincs 49 P7
Holbeck Notts 57 R12
Holbeck Woodhouse Notts 57 R12
Holberrow Green Worcs 36 D9
Holbeton Devon 5 Q10
Holborn Gt Lon 21 P6
Holborough Kent 12 C3
Holbrook Derbys 47 L5
Holbrook Sheff 57 P10
Holbrook Suffk 41 L13
Holbrook Moor Derbys 47 L4
Holbrooks Covtry 36 K4
Holburn Nthumb 85 Q11
Holbury Hants 9 N8
Holcombe Devon 6 C10
Holcombe Somset 17 S7
Holcombe Rogus Devon 16 E13
Holcot W Nthn 37 U7
Holden Lancs 62 F10
Holdenby W Nthn 37 S7
Holden Gate Calder 56 C2
Holder's Green Essex 22 F2
Holdgate Shrops 35 N3
Holdingham Lincs 48 G4
Holditch Dorset 6 K4
Holdsworth Calder 63 M14
Holehouse Derbys 56 F8
Hole-in-the-Wall Herefs 28 B2
Holemoor Devon 14 K11
Hole Street W Susx 10 J8
Holford Somset 16 G8
Holgate C York 64 D9
Holker W & F 61 R4
Holkham Norfk 50 E5
Hollacombe Devon 14 J12
Holland Fen Lincs 48 K4
Holland Lees Lancs 55 M5
Holland-on-Sea Essex 23 S4
Hollandstoun Ork 106 w14
Hollee D & G 75 Q12
Hollesley Suffk 41 Q12
Hollicombe Torbay 6 A12
Hollingbourne Kent 12 F4
Hollingbury Br & H 11 N9
Hollingdon Bucks 30 J7
Hollingrove E Susx 12 C11
Hollingthorpe Leeds 63 T13
Hollington Derbys 46 H6
Hollington Staffs 46 E6
Hollingworth Tamesd 56 F7
Hollins Bury 55 T5
Hollins Derbys 57 M12
Hollins Staffs 46 C4
Hollinsclough Staffs 56 G13
Hollins End Sheff 57 N10
Hollins Green Warrtn 55 Q8
Hollins Lane Lancs 61 T9
Hollinswood Wrekin 45 R12
Hollinwood Shrops 45 M6
Hollocombe Devon 15 P10
Holloway Derbys 46 K2
Holloway Gt Lon 21 P5
Holloway Wilts 8 B2
Hollowell W Nthn 37 S6
Hollowmoor Heath Ches W 55 L13
Hollows D & G 75 S10
Hollybush Caerph 27 M7
Hollybush E Ayrs 81 M9
Hollybush Herefs 35 S13
Holly End Norfk 49 Q12
Holly Green Worcs 35 U12
Hollyhurst Ches E 45 N5
Hollym E R Yk 59 P1
Hollywater Hants 10 C4
Hollywood Worcs 36 E5
Holmbridge Kirk 56 H5
Holmbury St Mary Surrey 10 J2
Holmbush Cnwll 3 Q6
Holmcroft Staffs 46 B9
Holme Cambs 38 J3
Holme Kirk 56 H5
Holme N Linc 58 F5
Holme N York 63 T3
Holme Notts 48 B2
Holme W & F 61 U4
Holme Chapel Lancs 62 H14
Holme Green N York 64 D11
Holme Hale Norfk 50 E12
Holme Lacy Herefs 35 N13
Holme Marsh Herefs 34 H10
Holme next the Sea Norfk 50 B5
Holme on the Wolds E R Yk 65 M10
Holme Pierrepont Notts 47 R6
Holmer Herefs 35 M12
Holmer Green Bucks 20 F3
Holme St Cuthbert Cumb 66 H3
Holmes Chapel Ches E 55 S13
Holmesfield Derbys 57 M11
Holmes Hill E Susx 11 S8
Holmeswood Lancs 54 K3
Holmethorpe Surrey 21 N12
Holme upon Spalding Moor E R Yk 64 J12
Holmewood Derbys 57 P13
Holmfield Calder 63 M14
Holmfirth Kirk 56 H5
Holmgate Derbys 57 N14
Holmhead E Ayrs 81 R8
Holmpton E R Yk 59 Q2
Holmrook Cumb 66 G13
Holmshurst E Susx 12 B10
Holmside Dur 69 R3
Holmwrangle Cumb 67 R3
Holne Devon 5 S7
Holnest Dorset 7 S3
Holnicote Somset 16 B7
Holsworthy Devon 14 H12
Holsworthy Beacon Devon 14 J11
Holt Dorset 8 E8
Holt Norfk 50 J6
Holt Wilts 18 C8
Holt Worcs 35 T8
Holt Wrexhm 44 K3
Holtby C York 64 F9
Holt End Worcs 36 E7
Holt Fleet Worcs 35 T8
Holt Green Lancs 54 J5
Holt Heath Dorset 8 F8
Holt Heath Worcs 35 T8
Holton Oxon 30 D11
Holton Somset 17 S11
Holton Suffk 41 R5
Holton cum Beckering Lincs 58 K10
Holton Heath Dorset 8 C10
Holton Hill E Susx 12 C10
Holton le Clay Lincs 59 N6
Holton le Moor Lincs 58 J7
Holton St Mary Suffk 40 J13
Holt Street Kent 13 Q5
Holtye E Susx 11 R3
Holway Flints 54 E11
Holwell Dorset 7 S2
Holwell Herts 31 Q6
Holwell Leics 47 T9
Holwell Oxon 29 P6
Holwick Dur 68 K7
Holworth Dorset 7 U8
Holybourne Hants 10 A2
Holy Cross Worcs 36 B5
Holyfield Essex 31 U12
Holyhead IoA 52 B6
Holy Island IoA 52 C6
Holy Island Nthumb 85 S10
Holy Island Nthumb 85 S10
Holymoorside Derbys 57 M13
Holyport W & M 20 E7
Holystone Nthumb 76 K5
Holytown N Lans 82 E6
Holywell C Beds 31 M9
Holywell Cambs 39 M6
Holywell Cnwll 2 K5
Holywell Dorset 7 Q4
Holywell Flints 54 E11
Holywell Nthumb 77 S11
Holywell Warwks 36 H7
Holywell Green Calder 56 G3
Holywell Lake Somset 16 F12
Holywell Row Suffk 40 B5
Holywood D & G 74 H9
Holywood Village D & G 74 J10
Homer Shrops 45 P13
Homer Green Sefton 54 H6
Homersfield Suffk 41 N3
Homescales W & F 62 B2
Hom Green Herefs 28 A3
Homington Wilts 8 G3
Honeyborough Pembks 24 F9
Honeybourne Worcs 36 F12
Honeychurch Devon 15 P12
Honey Hill Kent 13 M3
Honeystreet Wilts 18 H8
Honey Tye Suffk 40 G13
Honiley Warwks 36 H6
Honing Norfk 51 P8
Honingham Norfk 50 K11
Honington Lincs 48 D5
Honington Suffk 40 F6
Honington Warwks 36 J12
Honiton Devon 6 G4
Honley Kirk 56 H4
Honnington Wrekin 45 R10
Hoo Kent 13 Q3
Hoobrook Worcs 35 T6
Hood Green Barns 57 M6
Hood Hill Rothm 57 N7
Hooe C Plym 5 N10
Hooe E Susx 12 C13
Hoo End Herts 31 Q8
Hoo Green Ches E 55 R10
Hoohill Bpool 61 Q12
Hook Cambs 39 P2
Hook Devon 6 K3
Hook E R Yk 58 C1
Hook Gt Lon 21 L10
Hook Hants 9 Q7
Hook Hants 20 B12
Hook Pembks 24 G8
Hook Wilts 29 L11
Hook-a-Gate Shrops 45 L12
Hook Bank Worcs 35 T12
Hooke Dorset 7 P4
Hook End Essex 22 E7
Hookgate Staffs 45 R6
Hook Green Kent 12 C8
Hook Green Kent 22 F13
Hook Norton Oxon 37 L14
Hook Street Gloucs 28 C8
Hook Street Wilts 29 L11
Hookway Devon 15 U13
Hookwood Surrey 11 M2
Hooley Surrey 21 N11
Hooley Bridge Rochdl 56 C4
Hoo Meavy Devon 5 N7
Hoo St Werburgh Medway 22 J13
Hooton Ches W 54 J11
Hooton Levitt Rothm 57 R8
Hooton Pagnell Donc 57 Q5
Hooton Roberts Rothm 57 Q7
Hopcrofts Holt Oxon 29 U2
Hope Derbys 56 J10
Hope Devon 5 R12
Hope Flints 44 H2
Hope Powys 44 G12
Hope Shrops 44 H13
Hope Staffs 46 F3
Hope Bagot Shrops 35 N6
Hope Bowdler Shrops 35 L2
Hope End Green Essex 22 E3
Hopehouse Border 75 Q2
Hopeman Moray 103 T2
Hope Mansell Herefs 28 B4
Hopesay Shrops 34 J4
Hopetown Wakefd 57 N2
Hope under Dinmore Herefs 35 M10
Hopgrove C York 64 E9
Hopperton N York 63 U8
Hop Pole Lincs 48 J11
Hopsford Warwks 37 M4
Hopstone Shrops 35 S2
Hopton Derbys 46 J3
Hopton Shrops 44 J9
Hopton Staffs 46 B8
Hopton Suffk 40 G5
Hopton Cangeford Shrops 35 M4
Hopton Castle Shrops 34 J5
Hoptonheath Shrops 34 J5
Hopton on Sea Norfk 51 T14
Hopton Wafers Shrops 35 P5
Hopwas Staffs 46 G13
Hopwood Rochdl 56 C5
Hopwood Worcs 36 D5
Hopwood Park Services Worcs 36 D6
Horam E Susx 11 T7
Horbling Lincs 48 H6
Horbury Wakefd 57 L3
Horcott Gloucs 29 N7
Horden Dur 70 F4
Horderley Shrops 34 K3
Hordle Hants 8 K9
Hordley Shrops 44 J7
Horeb Carmth 25 S9
Horeb Cerdgn 32 G12
Horfield Bristl 28 A12
Horham Suffk 41 M6
Horkesley Heath Essex 23 N2
Horkstow N Linc 58 G3
Horley Oxon 37 M12
Horley Surrey 11 M2
Hornblotton Green Somset 17 Q10
Hornby Lancs 62 B6
Hornby N York 69 R14
Hornby N York 70 E11
Horncastle Lincs 59 N13
Hornchurch Gt Lon 22 D10
Horncliffe Nthumb 85 N9
Horndean Border 85 N9
Horndean Hants 9 U6
Horndon Devon 5 N4
Horndon on the Hill Thurr 22 G11
Horne Surrey 11 N2
Horner Somset 16 B7
Horne Row Essex 22 J7
Horners Green Suffk 40 G12
Horney Common E Susx 11 R5
Horn Hill Bucks 20 H4
Horning Norfk 51 P10
Horninghold Leics 38 B1
Horninglow Staffs 46 H8
Horningsea Cambs 39 Q8
Horningsham Wilts 18 B12
Horningtoft Norfk 50 F9
Horningtops Cnwll 4 H8
Hornsbury Somset 6 K2
Hornsby Cumb 67 R2
Hornsbygate Cumb 67 R2
Horns Cross Devon 14 J8
Horns Cross E Susx 12 F11
Hornsea E R Yk 65 R10
Hornsey Gt Lon 21 P5
Horn's Green Gt Lon 21 S11
Horn Street Kent 13 N8
Hornton Oxon 37 L11
Horpit Swindn 29 P11
Horrabridge Devon 5 N7
Horringer Suffk 40 D8
Horringford IoW 9 Q11
Horrocks Fold Bolton 55 R4
Horrocksford Lancs 62 F11
Horsacott Devon 15 M6
Horsebridge Devon 5 L5
Horsebridge E Susx 11 T8
Horsebridge Hants 9 L2
Horsebridge Shrops 44 J12
Horsebridge Staffs 46 C3
Horsebrook Staffs 45 U11
Horsecastle N Som 17 M3
Horsedown Cnwll 2 G10
Horsehay Wrekin 45 Q12
Horseheath Cambs 39 T11
Horsehouse N York 63 L3
Horsell Surrey 20 G11
Horseman's Green Wrexhm 44 K5
Horsenden Bucks 30 G12
Horsey Norfk 51 S9
Horsey Somset 16 K9
Horsey Corner Norfk 51 S9
Horsford Norfk 51 L10
Horsforth Leeds 63 Q12
Horsham W Susx 10 K4
Horsham Worcs 35 R9
Horsham St Faith Norfk 51 M10
Horsington Lincs 59 L13
Horsington Somset 17 T12
Horsley Derbys 47 L5
Horsley Gloucs 28 F8
Horsley Nthumb 76 G6
Horsley Nthumb 77 M12
Horsley Cross Essex 23 R2
Horsleycross Street Essex 23 R2
Horsley-Gate Derbys 57 M11
Horsleyhill Border 76 A2
Horsley's Green Bucks 20 C4
Horsley Woodhouse Derbys 47 L5
Horsmonden Kent 12 D7
Horspath Oxon 30 C11
Horstead Norfk 51 N10
Horsted Keynes W Susx 11 P5
Horton Bucks 30 K9
Horton Dorset 8 E7
Horton Lancs 62 H9
Horton S Glos 28 E11
Horton Shrops 45 L8
Horton Somset 6 K2
Horton Staffs 46 B2
Horton Surrey 21 L10
Horton Swans 25 S13
Horton W & M 20 H7
Horton W Nthn 38 B10
Horton Wilts 18 F8
Horton Wrekin 45 Q11
Horton Cross Somset 16 K13
Horton-cum-Studley Oxon 30 C10
Horton Green Ches W 45 L4
Horton Heath Hants 9 P5
Horton-in-Ribblesdale N York 62 G5
Horton Kirby Kent 21 U9
Horwich Bolton 55 P4
Horwich End Derbys 56 F10
Horwood Devon 15 M7
Hoscar Lancs 55 L4
Hoscote Border 75 S3
Hose Leics 47 T8
Hosey Hill Kent 21 S12
Hosh P & K 90 C7
Hoswick Shet 106 u11
Hotham E R Yk 64 K13
Hothfield Kent 12 J7
Hoton Leics 47 Q9
Hott Nthumb 76 F8
Hough Ches E 45 R3
Hough Ches E 56 C11
Hougham Lincs 48 C5
Hough End Leeds 63 Q13
Hough Green Halton 55 L9
Hough-on-the-Hill Lincs 48 D4
Houghton Cambs 39 L6
Houghton Cumb 75 T14
Houghton Hants 9 L2
Houghton Nthumb 77 N12
Houghton Pembks 24 G9
Houghton W Susx 10 G8
Houghton Conquest C Beds 31 M4
Houghton Gate Dur 70 D2
Houghton Green E Susx 12 H11
Houghton Green Warrtn 55 P8
Houghton le Side Darltn 69 R8
Houghton-le-Spring Sundld 70 D3
Houghton on the Hill Leics 47 S13
Houghton Regis C Beds 31 M8
Houghton St Giles Norfk 50 F6
Houlton Warwks 37 Q6
Hound Green Hants 20 B11
Houndslow Border 84 G9
Houndsmoor Somset 16 F11
Houndwood Border 85 L6
Hounslow Gt Lon 20 K7
Househill Highld 103 N4
Houses Hill Kirk 56 J3
Housieside Abers 105 P10
Houston Rens 88 K12
Houstry Highld 112 E10
Houton Ork 106 s19
Hove Br & H 11 M10
Hove Edge Calder 56 H2
Hoveringham Notts 47 S4
Hoveton Norfk 51 P10
Hovingham N York 64 F4
Howbrook Barns 57 M7
How Caple Herefs 28 B1
Howden E R Yk 64 G14
Howden-le-Wear Dur 69 Q6
Howe Highld 112 H4
Howe IoM 60 b9
Howe N York 63 T3
Howe Norfk 51 N14
Howe Bridge Wigan 55 Q6
Howe Green Essex 22 H7
Howegreen Essex 22 K7
Howell Lincs 48 H4
How End C Beds 31 M4
Howe of Teuchar Abers 105 M6
Howes D & G 75 N12
Howe Street Essex 22 G5
Howe Street Essex 39 U14
Howey Powys 34 C9
Howgate Cumb 66 E8
Howgate Mdloth 83 P7
Howgill Lancs 62 G10
Howick Nthumb 77 R2
Howle Wrekin 45 Q9
Howle Hill Herefs 28 B3
Howlett End Essex 39 S14
Howley Somset 6 J3
How Mill Cumb 67 R1
Howmore W Isls 106 c15
Hownam Border 76 F2
Howrigg Cumb 67 M3
Howsham N Linc 58 H6
Howsham N York 64 G7
Howtel Nthumb 85 M12
Howt Green Kent 12 G2
Howton Herefs 27 S2
Howtown W & F 67 P9
How Wood Herts 31 P12
Howwood Rens 88 J13
Hoxa Ork 106 t20
Hoxne Suffk 41 L5
Hoy Ork 106 r20
Hoylake Wirral 54 F9
Hoyland Barns 57 N6
Hoyland Common Barns 57 N6
Hoylandswaine Barns 57 L6
Hoyle W Susx 10 E7
Hoyle Mill Barns 57 N5
Hubberholme N York 62 J4
Hubberston Pembks 24 E9
Hubbert's Bridge Lincs 49 L5
Huby N York 63 R10
Huby N York 64 D6
Huccaby Devon 5 R6
Hucclecote Gloucs 28 G4
Hucking Kent 12 F4
Hucknall Notts 47 P4
Huddersfield Kirk 56 H3
Huddington Worcs 36 B9
Hudnall Herts 31 M10
Hudswell N York 69 P12
Huggate E R Yk 64 K8
Hugglescote Leics 47 M11
Hughenden Valley Bucks 20 E3
Hughley Shrops 45 N14
Hugh Town IoS 2 c2
Huish Devon 15 M10
Huish Wilts 18 H8
Huish Champflower Somset 16 E11
Huish Episcopi Somset 17 M11
Hùisinis W Isls 106 e7
Huisinish W Isls 106 e7
Hulcote C Beds 30 K5
Hulcote W Nthn 37 T11
Hulcott Bucks 30 J9
Hulham Devon 6 D8
Hulland Derbys 46 H4
Hulland Ward Derbys 46 J4
Hullavington Wilts 18 C4
Hull Bridge E R Yk 65 P11
Hullbridge Essex 22 K8
Hull, Kingston upon C KuH 65 P14
Hulme Manch 55 T7
Hulme Staffs 46 B4
Hulme Warrtn 55 P8
Hulme End Staffs 46 F2
Hulme Walfield Ches E 55 T13
Hulse Heath Ches E 55 R10
Hulton Lane Ends Bolton 55 Q5
Hulverstone IoW 9 M12
Hulver Street Norfk 50 F11
Hulver Street Suffk 41 S3
Humber Devon 6 A9
Humber Herefs 35 M9
Humber Bridge N Linc 58 H2
Humberside Airport N Linc 58 J4
Humberston NE Lin 59 P5
Humberstone C Leic 47 R12
Humberton N York 63 U6
Humbie E Loth 84 D6
Humbleton E R Yk 65 S13
Humbleton Nthumb 85 P13
Humby Lincs 48 F7
Hume Border 84 J10
Humshaugh Nthumb 76 J11
Huna Highld 112 J2
Huncoat Lancs 62 F13
Huncote Leics 47 P14
Hundalee Border 76 C2
Hundall Derbys 57 N11
Hunderthwaite Dur 69 L8
Hundleby Lincs 59 Q13
Hundle Houses Lincs 48 K3
Hundleton Pembks 24 G10
Hundon Suffk 40 B11
Hundred End Lancs 54 K2
Hundred House Powys 34 D10
Hungarton Leics 47 S12
Hungerford Hants 8 H6
Hungerford Somset 16 D8
Hungerford W Berk 19 M7
Hungerford Newtown W Berk 19 N6
Hunger Hill Bolton 55 Q5
Hunger Hill Lancs 55 M4
Hungerstone Herefs 34 K13
Hungerton Lincs 48 C8
Hungryhatton Shrops 45 Q8
Hunmanby N York 65 P4
Hunningham Warwks 37 L7
Hunnington Worcs 36 C4
Hunsbury Hill W Nthn 37 T9
Hunsdon Herts 22 B5
Hunsdonbury Herts 22 B5
Hunsingore N York 63 U9
Hunslet Leeds 63 S13
Hunsonby W & F 67 S5
Hunstanton Norfk 49 U5
Hunstanworth Dur 68 K3
Hunsterson Ches E 45 Q4
Hunston Suffk 40 G7
Hunston W Susx 10 D10
Hunston Green Suffk 40 G7
Hunstrete BaNES 17 R4
Hunsworth Kirk 56 J1
Hunt End Worcs 36 D8
Hunter's Inn Devon 15 Q3
Hunter's Quay Ag & B 88 E10
Huntham Somset 16 K11
Hunthill Lodge Angus 98 H9
Huntingdon Cambs 38 K6
Huntingfield Suffk 41 P6
Huntingford Dorset 17 V11
Huntington C York 64 E8
Huntington Ches W 54 K14
Huntington E Loth 84 D4
Huntington Herefs 34 G10
Huntington Herefs 35 L12
Huntington Staffs 46 C11
Huntingtowerfield P & K 90 G6
Huntley Gloucs 28 D4
Huntly Abers 104 G8
Hunton Hants 19 Q12
Hunton Kent 12 D6
Hunton N York 63 P1
Hunton Bridge Herts 31 N12
Hunt's Corner Norfk 40 J3
Huntscott Somset 16 B8
Hunt's Cross Lpool 54 K9
Hunts Green Bucks 30 J12
Hunts Green Warwks 36 G1
Huntsham Devon 16 D12
Huntshaw Devon 15 M8
Huntshaw Cross Devon 15 M8
Huntspill Somset 16 K7
Huntstile Somset 16 J10
Huntworth Somset 16 K10
Hunwick Dur 69 Q6
Hunworth Norfk 50 J6
Hurcott Somset 17 L13
Hurdcott Wilts 8 H2
Hurdsfield Ches E 56 D12
Hurley W & M 20 D6
Hurley Warwks 36 H1
Hurley Bottom W & M 20 D6
Hurley Common Warwks 36 H1
Hurlford E Ayrs 81 P5
Hurlston Green Lancs 54 J4
Hurn BCP 8 G9
Hurn's End Lincs 49 P4
Hursley Hants 9 N3
Hurst Dorset 7 U6
Hurst N York 69 M12
Hurst Somset 17 N13
Hurst Wokham 20 C8
Hurstbourne Priors Hants 19 P11
Hurstbourne Tarrant Hants 19 N10
Hurst Green E Susx 12 D10
Hurst Green Essex 23 Q4
Hurst Green Lancs 62 D12
Hurst Green Surrey 21 R12
Hurst Hill Dudley 36 B2
Hurstley Herefs 34 J11
Hurstpierpoint W Susx 11 M7
Hurst Wickham W Susx 11 M7
Hurstwood Lancs 62 H13
Hurtiso Ork 106 u19
Hurtmore Surrey 20 F13
Hurworth Burn Dur 70 F6
Hurworth-on-Tees Darltn 70 D11
Hurworth Place Darltn 69 S11
Hury Dur 69 L9
Husbands Bosworth Leics 37 R4
Husborne Crawley C Beds 31 L5
Husthwaite N York 64 C5
Hutcherleigh Devon 5 T10
Hut Green N York 57 S2
Huthwaite Notts 47 N2
Huttoft Lincs 59 T11
Hutton Border 85 N8
Hutton E R Yk 65 N9
Hutton Essex 22 F8
Hutton Lancs 55 L1
Hutton N Som 17 L5
Hutton W & F 67 P7
Hutton Bonville N York 70 D12
Hutton Buscel N York 65 M3
Hutton Conyers N York 63 S5
Hutton Cranswick E R Yk 65 N9
Hutton End W & F 67 Q5
Hutton Hang N York 63 P2
Hutton Henry Dur 70 F5
Hutton-le-Hole N York 64 G1
Hutton Lowcross R & Cl 70 J10
Hutton Magna Dur 69 P10
Hutton Mulgrave N York 71 P11
Hutton Roof W & F 62 B4
Hutton Roof W & F 67 N6
Hutton Rudby N York 70 G11
Hutton Sessay N York 64 B4
Hutton Wandesley N York 64 C9
Huxham Devon 6 B5
Huxham Green Somset 17 Q9
Huxley Ches W 45 M1
Huyton Knows 54 K8
Hycemoor Cumb 60 K2
Hyde Gloucs 28 G7
Hyde Hants 8 H6
Hyde Tamesd 56 D8
Hyde Heath Bucks 30 K12
Hyde Lea Staffs 46 B10
Hydestile Surrey 10 F2
Hykeham Moor Lincs 58 F13
Hylands Estate Essex 22 G7
Hyndford Bridge S Lans 82 H10
Hynish Ag & B 92 B11
Hyssington Powys 34 H2
Hystfield Gloucs 28 C8
Hythe Essex 23 P2
Hythe Hants 9 N7
Hythe Kent 13 N9
Hythe Somset 17 M6
Hythe End W & M 20 H8
Hyton Cumb 60 K2

I

Ibberton Dorset 7 U3
Ible Derbys 46 H2
Ibsley Hants 8 H7
Ibstock Leics 47 M12
Ibstone Bucks 20 C4
Ibthorpe Hants 19 N10
Iburndale N York 71 Q11
Ibworth Hants 19 S10
Icelton N Som 17 L3
Ichrachan Ag & B 94 E12
Ickburgh Norfk 40 D1
Ickenham Gt Lon 20 J5
Ickford Bucks 30 D11
Ickham Kent 13 P4
Ickleford Herts 31 Q6
Icklesham E Susx 12 G12
Ickleton Cambs 39 Q12
Icklingham Suffk 40 C6
Ickornshaw N York 62 K11
Ickwell Green C Beds 38 J11
Icomb Gloucs 29 P3
Idbury Oxon 29 P4
Iddesleigh Devon 15 N11
Ide Devon 6 A6
Ideford Devon 6 A9
Ide Hill Kent 21 S12
Iden E Susx 12 H11
Iden Green Kent 12 D8
Iden Green Kent 12 F9
Idle C Brad 63 P12
Idless Cnwll 3 L7
Idlicote Warwks 36 J12
Idmiston Wilts 18 J13
Idole Carmth 25 R7
Idridgehay Derbys 46 J4
Idrigill Highld 100 c3
Idstone Oxon 29 Q11
Iffley Oxon 30 B12
Ifield W Susx 11 M3
Ifold W Susx 10 G4
Iford BCP 8 G10
Iford E Susx 11 Q9
Ifton Mons 27 T10
Ifton Heath Shrops 44 H6
Ightfield Shrops 45 N6
Ightham Kent 21 U11
Iken Suffk 41 R9
Ilam Staffs 46 F3
Ilchester Somset 17 P12
Ilderton Nthumb 77 L1
Ilford Gt Lon 21 R5
Ilford Somset 17 L13
Ilfracombe Devon 15 M3
Ilkeston Derbys 47 N5
Ilketshall St Andrew Suffk 41 Q3
Ilketshall St John Suffk 41 Q3
Ilketshall St Lawrence Suffk 41 Q4
Ilketshall St Margaret Suffk 41 P3
Ilkley C Brad 63 N10
Illand Cnwll 4 H5
Illey Dudley 36 C4
Illidge Green Ches E 55 S14
Illingworth Calder 63 M14
Illogan Cnwll 2 H8
Illston on the Hill Leics 47 T14
Ilmer Bucks 30 G11
Ilmington Warwks 36 H12
Ilminster Somset 7 L2
Ilsington Devon 5 T5
Ilsington Dorset 7 U6
Ilston Swans 25 U12
Ilton N York 63 P4
Ilton Somset 17 L13
Imachar N Ayrs 79 R7
Immingham NE Lin 59 L4
Immingham Dock NE Lin 59 L3
Impington Cambs 39 P8
Ince Ches W 55 L11
Ince Blundell Sefton 54 H6
Ince-in-Makerfield Wigan 55 N6
Inchbae Lodge Highld 108 G11
Inchbare Angus 99 L10
Inchberry Moray 104 C4
Incheril Highld 107 T12
Inchinnan Rens 89 L12
Inchlaggan Highld 101 T11
Inchmichael P & K 90 K6
Inchmore Highld 102 G6
Inchnadamph Highld 110 F12
Inchture P & K 91 L6
Inchyra P & K 90 J7
Indian Queens Cnwll 3 N5
Ingatestone Essex 22 F8
Ingbirchworth Barns 56 K5
Ingerthorpe N York 63 R6
Ingestre Staffs 46 C9
Ingham Lincs 58 F10
Ingham Norfk 51 Q8
Ingham Suffk 40 E6
Ingham Corner Norfk 51 Q8
Ingleborough Norfk 49 Q10
Ingleby Derbys 46 K8
Ingleby Arncliffe N York 70 F12
Ingleby Barwick S on T 70 F10
Ingleby Cross N York 70 G12
Ingleby Greenhow N York 70 J11
Ingleigh Green Devon 15 P11
Inglesbatch BaNES 17 T4
Inglesham Swindn 29 P8
Ingleston D & G 74 J12
Ingleton Dur 69 Q8
Ingleton N York 62 D5
Inglewhite Lancs 61 U12
Ingmanthorpe N York 63 U9
Ingoe Nthumb 77 L11
Ingol Lancs 61 U13
Ingoldisthorpe Norfk 49 U7
Ingoldmells Lincs 59 U13
Ingoldsby Lincs 48 F8
Ingram Nthumb 77 L2
Ingrave Essex 22 F9
Ingrow C Brad 63 M12
Ings W & F 67 P13
Ingst S Glos 28 A10
Ingthorpe Rutlnd 48 E12
Ingworth Norfk 51 L8
Inkberrow Worcs 36 D9
Inkerman Dur 69 P5
Inkersall Green Derbys 57 P12
Inkhorn Abers 105 Q8
Inkpen W Berk 19 N8
Inkstack Highld 112 G2
Inmarsh Wilts 18 D8
Innellan Ag & B 88 E11
Innerleithen Border 83 R11
Innerleven Fife 91 N11
Innermessan D & G 72 D7
Innerwick E Loth 84 J4
Innesmill Moray 104 B3
Innsworth Gloucs 28 G3
Insch Abers 104 J10
Insh Highld 97 N3
Inshes Highld 102 J7
Inskip Lancs 61 T12
Inskip Moss Side Lancs 61 T12
Instow Devon 15 L6
Insworke Cnwll 5 L10
Intake Sheff 57 N10
Inver Abers 98 C5
Inver Highld 109 R8
Inver P & K 90 F3
Inverailort Highld 93 T2
Inveralligin Highld 107 P13
Inverallochy Abers 105 S2
Inveran Highld 108 K5
Inveraray Ag & B 88 C4
Inverarish Highld 100 e6
Inverarity Angus 91 Q3
Inverarnan Stirlg 88 H2
Inverarnie Highld 102 J9
Inverasdale Highld 107 P8
Inverbeg Ag & B 88 H6
Inverbervie Abers 99 Q9
Inverboyndie Abers 104 K3
Invercreran Lodge Ag & B 94 E9
Inverdruie Highld 103 N13
Inveresk E Loth 83 R4
Inveresragan Ag & B 94 D11
Inverey Abers 97 T6
Inverfarigaig Highld 102 F11
Inverfolla Ag & B 94 D10
Invergarry Highld 96 C3
Invergeldie P & K 95 U13
Invergloy Highld 101 U14
Invergordon Highld 109 N11
Invergowrie P & K 91 M5
Inverguseran Highld 100 g9
Inverhadden P & K 95 T7
Inverie Highld 100 g9
Inverinan Ag & B 87 T2
Inverinate Highld 101 N7
Inverkeilor Angus 91 U2
Inverkeithing Fife 83 M2
Inverkeithny Abers 104 J6
Inverkip Inver 88 F11
Inverkirkaig Highld 110 B13
Inverlael Highld 108 B7
Inverlair Highld 96 C8
Inverliever Lodge Ag & B 87 R4
Inverlochy Ag & B 94 H13
Invermark Angus 98 G7
Invermoriston Highld 102 D12
Invernaver Highld 111 Q4
Inverneill Ag & B 87 Q9
Inverness Highld 102 J6
Inverness Airport Highld 103 L5
Invernettie Abers 105 U7
Invernoaden Ag & B 88 D6
Inveroran Hotel Ag & B 94 K10
Inverquharity Angus 98 G12
Inverquhomery Abers 105 S6
Inverroy Highld 96 B7
Inversanda Highld 94 C7
Invershiel Highld 101 N8
Invershin Highld 108 K5
Invershore Highld 112 F9
Inversnaid Hotel Stirlg 88 H4
Inverugie Abers 105 T6
Inveruglas Ag & B 88 H4
Inveruglass Highld 97 N3
Inverurie Abers 105 M11
Inwardleigh Devon 15 N13
Inworth Essex 23 L4
Iochdar W Isls 106 c14
Iona Ag & B 92 H13
Iping W Susx 10 D6
iPort Logistics Park Donc 57 T7
Ipplepen Devon 5 U7
Ipsden Oxon 19 T3
Ipstones Staffs 46 D4
Ipswich Suffk 41 L12
Irby Wirral 54 G10
Irby in the Marsh Lincs 59 S14
Irby upon Humber NE Lin 59 L6
Irchester N Nthn 38 D7
Ireby Cumb 66 K5
Ireby Lancs 62 D4
Ireland C Beds 31 P4
Ireleth W & F 61 N4
Ireshopeburn Dur 68 J5
Ireton Wood Derbys 46 J4
Irlam Salfd 55 R8
Irnham Lincs 48 F8
Iron Acton S Glos 28 C11
Iron Bridge Cambs 49 Q14
Ironbridge Wrekin 45 Q13
Ironbridge Gorge Wrekin 45 Q13
Iron Cross Warwks 36 E10
Ironmacannie D & G 73 R4
Irons Bottom Surrey 21 M13
Ironville Derbys 47 M3
Irstead Norfk 51 Q9
Irthington Cumb 75 U13
Irthlingborough N Nthn 38 D6
Irton N York 65 N3
Irvine N Ayrs 81 L5
Isauld Highld 112 A3
Isbister Shet 106 t4
Isbister Shet 106 v7
Isfield E Susx 11 Q7
Isham N Nthn 38 C6
Isington Hants 10 B2
Islandpool Worcs 35 U4
Islay Ag & B 78 F4
Islay Airport Ag & B 78 E5
Isle Abbotts Somset 17 L12
Isle Brewers Somset 17 L12
Isleham Cambs 39 T6
Isle of Dogs Gt Lon 21 Q7
Isle of Grain Medway 23 L12
Isle of Lewis W Isls 106 i5
Isle of Man IoM 60 f5
Isle of Man Ronaldsway Airport IoM 60 d9
Isle of Mull Ag & B 93 Q11
Isle of Purbeck Dorset 8 E12
Isle of Sheppey Kent 12 J2
Isle of Skye Highld 100 d6
Isle of Thanet Kent 13 R2
Isle of Walney W & F 61 M6
Isle of Whithorn D & G 73 M12
Isle of Wight IoW 9 Q11
Isleornsay Highld 100 g8
Isles of Scilly IoS 2 c2
Isles of Scilly St Mary's Airport IoS 2 c2
Islesteps D & G 74 J11
Islet Village Guern 6 e2
Isleworth Gt Lon 21 L7
Isley Walton Leics 47 M9
Islibhig W Isls 106 f6
Islington Gt Lon 21 P6
Islip N Nthn 38 E5
Islip Oxon 30 B10
Islivig W Isls 106 f6
Isombridge Wrekin 45 P11
Istead Rise Kent 22 F13
Itchen Abbas Hants 9 Q2
Itchen Stoke Hants 9 R2
Itchingfield W Susx 10 J5
Itchington S Glos 28 C10
Itteringham Norfk 50 K7
Itton Devon 15 Q13
Itton Mons 27 T8
Itton Common Mons 27 T8
Ivegill W & F 67 P4
Ivelet N York 68 K13
Iver Bucks 20 H6
Iver Heath Bucks 20 H6
Iveston Dur 69 P2
Ivinghoe Bucks 30 K9
Ivinghoe Aston Bucks 31 L9
Ivington Herefs 35 L9
Ivington Green Herefs 35 L9
Ivybridge Devon 5 Q9
Ivychurch Kent 12 K10
Ivy Cross Dorset 8 B4
Ivy Hatch Kent 21 U12
Ivy Todd Norfk 50 E12
Iwade Kent 12 H2
Iwerne Courtney Dorset 8 B6
Iwerne Minster Dorset 8 B6
Ixworth Suffk 40 F6
Ixworth Thorpe Suffk 40 F6

J

Jack Green Lancs 55 N1
Jack Hill N York 63 P9
Jack-in-the-Green Devon 6 D5
Jack's Bush Hants 19 L13
Jacksdale Notts 47 M3
Jackson Bridge Kirk 56 J5
Jackton S Lans 81 R2
Jacobstow Cnwll 14 E13
Jacobstowe Devon 15 N12
Jacobs Well Surrey 20 G12
Jameston Pembks 24 J11
Jamestown Highld 102 E4
Jamestown W Duns 88 J9
Janetstown Highld 112 E10
Jardine Hall D & G 75 M8
Jarrow S Tyne 77 S13
Jarvis Brook E Susx 11 S5
Jasper's Green Essex 22 H2
Jawcraig Falk 89 T10
Jaywick Essex 23 S5
Jealott's Hill Br For 20 E8
Jeater Houses N York 70 F14
Jedburgh Border 76 C1
Jeffreyston Pembks 24 J9
Jemimaville Highld 102 K2
Jerbourg Guern 6 e4
Jersey Jersey 7 d2
Jersey Airport Jersey 7 b2
Jersey Marine Neath 26 C9
Jerusalem Lincs 58 F12
Jesmond N u Ty 77 R12
Jevington E Susx 11 T10
Jingle Street Mons 27 T5
Jockey End Herts 31 M10
Jodrell Bank Ches E 55 S12
Jodrell Bank Ches E 55 S12
Johnby W & F 67 P6
John Lennon Airport Lpool 54 K10
John o' Groats Highld 112 J2
Johns Cross E Susx 12 D11
Johnshaven Abers 99 P10
Johnson Street Norfk 51 Q10
Johnston Pembks 24 F8
Johnstone D & G 75 P5
Johnstone Rens 88 K13
Johnstonebridge D & G 75 M7
Johnstown Carmth 25 Q7
Johnstown Wrexhm 44 H4
Joppa C Edin 83 R4
Joppa Cerdgn 33 L7
Joppa S Ayrs 81 N9
Jordans Bucks 20 G4
Jordanston Pembks 24 F4
Jordanthorpe Sheff 57 N10
Joyden's Wood Kent 22 D13
Jubilee Corner Kent 12 F6
Jump Barns 57 N6
Jumper's Town E Susx 11 R4
Juniper Nthumb 76 J14
Juniper Green C Edin 83 N5
Jura Ag & B 86 J9
Jurassic Coast Devon 6 K7
Jurby IoM 60 f3
Jurston Devon 5 R4

K

Kaber W & F 68 G10
Kaimend S Lans 82 J9
Kames Ag & B 87 T11
Kames E Ayrs 82 C13
Kea Cnwll 3 L8
Keadby N Linc 58 D4
Keal Cotes Lincs 49 N1
Kearby Town End N York 63 S10
Kearsley Bolton 55 S6
Kearsley Nthumb 77 L10
Kearsney Kent 13 Q7
Kearstwick W & F 62 C4
Kearton N York 69 L13
Keasden N York 62 E6
Keaton Devon 5 Q10
Keckwick Halton 55 N10
Keddington Lincs 59 P9
Keddington Corner Lincs 59 Q9
Kedington Suffk 40 B11
Kedleston Derbys 46 K5
Keelby Lincs 59 L4
Keele Staffs 45 T4
Keele Services Staffs 45 T5
Keele University Staffs 45 T4
Keeley Green Bed 38 F11
Keelham C Brad 63 M13
Keeres Green Essex 22 E5
Keeston Pembks 24 F7
Keevil Wilts 18 D9
Kegworth Leics 47 N8
Kehelland Cnwll 2 G8
Keig Abers 104 J12
Keighley C Brad 63 M11
Keilarsbrae Clacks 90 C13
Keillour P & K 90 E6
Keiloch Abers 98 B5
Keils Ag & B 86 J12
Keinton Mandeville Somset 17 P10
Keir Mill D & G 74 G7
Keirsleywell Row Nthumb 68 G2
Keisby Lincs 48 F8
Keisley W & F 68 F8
Keiss Highld 112 H4
Keith Moray 104 E5
Keithick P & K 90 K4
Keithock Angus 99 L11
Keithtown Highld 102 F4
Kelbrook Lancs 62 J11
Kelby Lincs 48 F5
Keld N York 68 J12
Keld W & F 67 S10
Keld Head N York 64 H3
Keldholme N York 64 G2
Kelfield N Linc 58 D6
Kelfield N York 64 D12
Kelham Notts 47 U2
Kelhead D & G 75 M12
Kellacott Devon 5 L3
Kellamergh Lancs 61 S14
Kellas Angus 91 Q4
Kellas Moray 103 U5
Kellaton Devon 5 U13
Kelleth W & F 68 E11
Kelling Norfk 50 J5
Kellingley N York 57 R2
Kellington N York 57 S2
Kelloe Dur 70 D5
Kelloholm D & G 74 D3
Kells Cumb 66 E9
Kelly Devon 4 K4
Kelly Bray Cnwll 4 K6
Kelmarsh W Nthn 37 T5
Kelmscott Oxon 29 P8
Kelsale Suffk 41 Q7
Kelsall Ches W 55 M13
Kelshall Herts 31 T5
Kelsick Cumb 66 J2
Kelso Border 84 J12
Kelstedge Derbys 57 M14
Kelstern Lincs 59 M9
Kelsterton Flints 54 G12
Kelston BaNES 17 T3
Keltneyburn P & K 95 V9
Kelton D & G 74 J11
Kelty Fife 90 H13
Kelvedon Essex 23 L4
Kelvedon Hatch Essex 22 E8
Kelvinhead N Lans 89 S10
Kelynack Cnwll 2 B11
Kemacott Devon 15 Q3
Kemback Fife 91 P9
Kemberton Shrops 45 R13
Kemble Gloucs 28 J8
Kemble Wick Gloucs 28 J8
Kemerton Worcs 36 C13
Kemeys Commander Mons 27 Q7
Kemnay Abers 105 L12
Kempe's Corner Kent 12 K6
Kempley Gloucs 28 C2
Kempley Green Gloucs 28 C2
Kempsey Worcs 35 T11
Kempsford Gloucs 29 N8
Kemps Green Warwks 36 F6
Kempshott Hants 19 T10
Kempston Bed 38 F11
Kempston Hardwick Bed 31 M4
Kempton Shrops 34 J4
Kemp Town Br & H 11 N10
Kemsing Kent 21 U11
Kemsley Kent 12 H2
Kemsley Street Kent 12 F3
Kenardington Kent 12 J9
Kenchester Herefs 34 K12
Kencot Oxon 29 Q7
Kendal W & F 67 R14
Kenderchurch Herefs 27 S2
Kendleshire S Glos 28 C12
Kenfig Brdgnd 26 E11
Kenfig Hill Brdgnd 26 E11
Kenilworth Warwks 36 J6
Kenley Gt Lon 21 P10
Kenley Shrops 45 N13
Kenmore Highld 107 N13
Kenmore P & K 95 V9
Kenn Devon 6 B7
Kenn N Som 17 M3
Kennacraig Ag & B 79 Q3
Kennall Vale Cnwll 2 J9
Kennards House Cnwll 4 H4
Kenneggy Cnwll 2 F11
Kennerleigh Devon 15 T11
Kennet Clacks 90 D13
Kennethmont Abers 104 G10
Kennett Cambs 39 U7
Kennford Devon 6 B7
Kenninghall Norfk 40 H3
Kennington Kent 12 K6
Kennington Oxon 30 B12
Kennington Lees Kent 12 K6
Kennoway Fife 91 N11
Kenny Somset 16 K13
Kenny Hill Suffk 39 U5
Kennythorpe N York 64 H6
Kenovay Ag & B 92 B9
Kensaleyre Highld 100 d4
Kensington Gt Lon 21 N7
Kensington Palace Gt Lon 21 N6
Kensworth Common C Beds 31 M9
Kentallen Highld 94 E7
Kentchurch Herefs 27 S2
Kentford Suffk 40 B7
Kent Green Ches E 45 T2
Kentisbeare Devon 6 E3
Kentisbury Devon 15 P4
Kentisbury Ford Devon 15 P4
Kentish Town Gt Lon 21 N6
Kentmere W & F 67 Q12
Kenton Devon 6 C8
Kenton Gt Lon 21 L5
Kenton N u Ty 77 Q12
Kenton Suffk 41 L7
Kenton Bankfoot N u Ty 77 Q12
Kentra Highld 93 R5
Kents Bank W & F 61 R4
Kentsboro Hants 19 M13
Kent's Green Gloucs 28 D3
Kent's Oak Hants 9 L4
Kent Street E Susx 12 E12
Kent Street Kent 12 C5
Kenwick Shrops 44 K7
Kenwyn Cnwll 3 L7
Kenyon Warrtn 55 P7
Keoldale Highld 110 H3
Keppoch Highld 101 M7
Kepwick N York 64 B1
Keresley Covtry 36 K4
Kermincham Ches E 55 T13
Kernborough Devon 5 T12
Kerne Bridge Herefs 28 A4
Kerrera Ag & B 93 U13
Kerridge Ches E 56 D11
Kerridge-end Ches E 56 D11
Kerris Cnwll 2 C11
Kerry Powys 34 D2
Kerrycroy Ag & B 88 D13
Kersall Notts 47 T1
Kersbrook Devon 6 E8
Kerscott Devon 15 P7
Kersey Suffk 40 H12
Kersey Tye Suffk 40 G12
Kersey Upland Suffk 40 G12
Kershader W Isls 106 i7
Kershopefoot Cumb 75 U9
Kersoe Worcs 36 C12
Kerswell Devon 6 E3
Kerswell Green Worcs 35 U11
Kerthen Wood Cnwll 2 F10
Kesgrave Suffk 41 M11
Kessingland Suffk 41 T3
Kessingland Beach Suffk 41 T3
Kestle Cnwll 3 P7
Kestle Mill Cnwll 3 L5
Keston Gt Lon 21 R10
Keswick Cumb 67 L8
Keswick Norfk 51 M13
Ketsby Lincs 59 Q11
Kettering N Nthn 38 C5
Ketteringham Norfk 51 L13
Kettins P & K 90 K4
Kettlebaston Suffk 40 G10
Kettlebridge Fife 91 M10
Kettlebrook Staffs 46 H13
Kettleburgh Suffk 41 N8
Kettle Green Herts 22 B4
Kettleholm D & G 75 M10
Kettleness N York 71 P9
Kettleshulme Ches E 56 E11
Kettlesing N York 63 Q8
Kettlesing Bottom N York 63 Q8
Kettlestone Norfk 50 G7
Kettlethorpe Lincs 58 D11
Kettletoft Ork 106 v16
Kettlewell N York 62 K5
Ketton Rutlnd 48 E13
Kew Gt Lon 21 L7
Kew Royal Botanic Gardens Gt Lon 21 L7
Kewstoke N Som 16 K4
Kexbrough Barns 57 M5
Kexby C York 64 G9
Kexby Lincs 58 E9
Key Green Ches E 56 C14
Key Green N York 71 P12
Keyham Leics 47 S12
Keyhaven Hants 9 L10
Keyingham E R Yk 59 M1
Keymer W Susx 11 N7
Keynsham BaNES 17 S3
Keysoe Bed 38 G8
Keysoe Row Bed 38 G8
Keyston Cambs 38 F5
Key Street Kent 12 G3
Keyworth Notts 47 R7
Kibbear Somset 16 H12
Kibblesworth Gatesd 69 R1
Kibworth Beauchamp Leics 37 S2
Kibworth Harcourt Leics 37 S2
Kidbrooke Gt Lon 21 R7
Kidburngill Cumb 66 G8
Kiddemore Green Staffs 45 U12
Kidderminster Worcs 35 T5
Kiddington Oxon 29 T3
Kidd's Moor Norfk 50 K13
Kidlington Oxon 29 U5
Kidmore End Oxon 19 U5
Kidsdale D & G 73 L12
Kidsgrove Staffs 45 T3
Kidstones N York 62 K3
Kidwelly Carmth 25 R9
Kiel Crofts Ag & B 94 C11
Kielder Nthumb 76 C7
Kielder Forest 76 C8
Kiells Ag & B 86 G12
Kilbarchan Rens 88 K13
Kilbeg Highld 100 f9
Kilberry Ag & B 79 N3
Kilbirnie N Ayrs 81 L2
Kilbride Ag & B 87 N10
Kilbride Ag & B 88 B12
Kilbuiack Moray 103 S3
Kilburn Derbys 47 L4
Kilburn Gt Lon 21 M6
Kilburn N York 64 C4
Kilby Leics 37 R1
Kilchamaig Ag & B 79 Q3
Kilchattan Ag & B 80 G2
Kilchattan Ag & B 86 F6
Kilcheran Ag & B 93 U11
Kilchoan Highld 93 M6
Kilchoman Ag & B 78 C3
Kilchrenan Ag & B 94 E14
Kilconquhar Fife 91 Q11
Kilcot Gloucs 28 C2
Kilcoy Highld 102 G5
Kilcreggan Ag & B 88 F9
Kildale N York 70 K11
Kildalloig Ag & B 79 P12
Kildary Highld 109 P10
Kildavaig Ag & B 87 T12
Kildavanan Ag & B 88 B12
Kildonan Highld 111 U12
Kildonan N Ayrs 80 E8
Kildonan Lodge Highld 111 U12
Kildonnan Highld 93 M1
Kildrochet House D & G 72 D8
Kildrummy Abers 104 F12
Kildwick N York 63 L10
Kilfinan Ag & B 87 S10
Kilfinnan Highld 96 B4
Kilford Denbgs 54 C13
Kilgetty Pembks 24 K9
Kilgrammie S Ayrs 80 K12
Kilgwrrwg Common Mons 27 T8
Kilham E R Yk 65 P7
Kilham Nthumb 85 M12
Kilkenneth Ag & B 92 A10
Kilkenzie Ag & B 79 M11
Kilkerran Ag & B 79 N12
Kilkhampton Cnwll 14 G10
Killamarsh Derbys 57 Q10
Killay Swans 25 V12
Killearn Stirlg 89 M8
Killen Highld 102 J4
Killerby Darltn 69 Q9
Killerton Devon 6 C4
Killichonan P & K 95 Q7
Killiechonate Highld 94 J2
Killiechronan Ag & B 93 N10
Killiecrankie P & K 97 Q11
Killilan Highld 101 N5
Killimster Highld 112 H5
Killin Stirlg 95 R12
Killinghall N York 63 R8
Killington Devon 15 Q3
Killington W & F 62 C2
Killington Lake Services W & F 62 B1
Killingworth N Tyne 77 R11
Killiow Cnwll 3 L8
Killochyett Border 84 D9
Kilmacolm Inver 88 J11
Kilmahog Stirlg 89 P4
Kilmahumaig Ag & B 87 P7
Kilmaluag Highld 100 d2
Kilmany Fife 91 N7
Kilmarnock E Ayrs 81 N5
Kilmartin Ag & B 87 Q6
Kilmaurs E Ayrs 81 N4
Kilmelford Ag & B 87 R3
Kilmersdon Somset 17 S6
Kilmeston Hants 9 R3
Kilmichael Ag & B 79 M11
Kilmichael Glassary Ag & B 87 R7
Kilmichael of Inverlussa Ag & B 87 P8
Kilmington Devon 6 J5

Kilmington Wilts ...17 U9
Kilmington Common Wilts ...17 U9
Kilmington Street Wilts ...17 U9
Kilmorack Highld ...102 E7
Kilmore Ag & B ...94 B13
Kilmore Highld ...100 f9
Kilmory Ag & B ...87 N11
Kilmory Highld ...93 N5
Kilmory N Ayrs ...80 D8
Kilmuir Highld ...100 b5
Kilmuir Highld ...102 J8
Kilmuir Highld ...102 q4
Kilmuir Highld ...109 P10
Kilmun Ag & B ...88 E9
Kilncadzow S Lans ...82 G9
Kilndown Kent ...12 D8
Kiln Green Wokham ...20 D7
Kilnhill Cumb ...66 K6
Kilnhurst Rothm ...57 Q7
Kilninver Ag & B ...87 Q3
Kiln Pit Hill Nthumb ...69 M11
Kilnsea E R Yk ...59 R3
Kilnsey N York ...64 D1
Kilnwick E R Yk ...65 M10
Kilnwick Percy E R Yk ...65 K11
Kilnwood Vale W Susx ...11 L4
Kiloran Ag & B ...86 F6
Kilpatrick N Ayrs ...79 S10
Kilpeck Herefs ...27 S1
Kilpin E R Yk ...58 C1
Kilpin Pike E R Yk ...58 C1
Kilrenny Fife ...91 S11
Kilsby Nhants ...37 Q6
Kilspindie P & K ...90 K6
Kilsyth N Lans ...89 R10
Kiltarlity Highld ...102 F7
Kilton R & Cl ...71 M9
Kilvaxter Highld ...100 c3
Kilve Somset ...16 F8
Kilvington Notts ...48 B4
Kilwinning N Ayrs ...80 J4
Kimberley Norfk ...50 J13
Kimberley Notts ...47 N5
Kimberworth Rothm ...57 P8
Kimblesworth Dur ...69 S3
Kimble Wick Bucks ...30 H11
Kimbolton Cambs ...38 H7
Kimbolton Herefs ...35 M8
Kimcote Leics ...37 Q3
Kimmeridge Dorset ...8 C13
Kimmerston Nthumb ...85 P11
Kimpton Hants ...19 L11
Kimpton Herts ...31 Q9
Kimworthy Devon ...14 H10
Kinbrace Highld ...111 T10
Kinbuck Stirlg ...89 S4
Kincaple Fife ...91 P8
Kincardine Highld ...109 L7
Kincardine Fife ...90 D14
Kincardine Bridge Fife ...82 H1
Kincardine O'Neil Abers ...98 K4
Kinclaven P & K ...90 J4
Kincorth C Aber ...99 S3
Kincorth House Moray ...103 R3
Kincraig Highld ...97 N3
Kincraigie P & K ...90 D2
Kindallachan P & K ...90 D2
Kinerarach Ag & B ...79 M5
Kineton Gloucs ...29 L2
Kineton Warwks ...36 K10
Kinfauns P & K ...90 J7
Kingarth Ag & B ...88 D11
Kingcausie Abers ...99 R4
Kingcoed Mons ...27 S6
Kingerby Lincs ...58 J8
Kingford Devon ...14 G11
Kingham Oxon ...29 Q3
Kinghorn Fife ...83 Q1
Kinglassie Fife ...91 M11
Kingoodie P & K ...91 M6
King's Acre Herefs ...35 L12
Kingsand Cnwll ...5 L10
Kingsbarns Fife ...91 S9
Kingsbridge Devon ...5 S12
Kingsbridge Somset ...16 D9
Kingsbridge Swans ...25 U11
King's Bromley Staffs ...46 F10
Kingsbrook Bucks ...30 H10
Kingsbury Gt Lon ...21 L5
Kingsbury Warwks ...36 H1
Kingsbury Episcopi Somset ...17 M12
King's Caple Herefs ...27 V2
Kingsclere Hants ...19 R9
King's Cliffe N Nhan ...38 F1
Kings Clipstone Notts ...57 T14
Kingscote Gloucs ...28 F8
Kingscott Devon ...15 M9
King's Coughton Warwks ...36 E9
Kingscross N Ayrs ...80 E7
Kingsdon Somset ...17 P11
Kingsdown Kent ...13 S6
Kingsdown Swindn ...29 N10
Kingsdown Wilts ...18 B7
Kingseat Abers ...105 Q12
Kingseat Fife ...90 H13
Kingsey Bucks ...30 F11
Kingsfold W Susx ...10 K3
Kingsford C Aber ...99 R2
Kingsford E Ayrs ...81 N3
Kingsford Worcs ...35 T4
Kingsgate Kent ...13 S1
King's Green Gloucs ...35 S14
Kingshall Street Suffk ...40 F8
Kingsheanton Devon ...15 N5
King's Heath Birm ...36 E4
Kings Hill Kent ...12 C4
King's Hill Wsall ...36 C14
Kingsholm Hotel Highld ...94 K8
Kingshurst Solhll ...36 G4
Kingside Hill Cumb ...66 J2
Kingskerswell Devon ...6 A11
Kingskettle Fife ...91 M10
Kingsland Herefs ...35 L8
Kingsland IoA ...52 C6
Kings Langley Herts ...31 N12
Kingsley Ches W ...55 N12
Kingsley Hants ...10 B3
Kingsley Staffs ...46 D4
Kingsley Green W Susx ...10 D4
Kingsley Holt Staffs ...46 D4
Kingsley Park Nhants ...37 U8
Kingslow Shrops ...45 S14
King's Lynn Norfk ...49 T9
Kings Meaburn W & F ...68 D8
Kingsmead Hants ...9 Q6
King's Mills Guern ...6 c3
King's Moss St Hel ...55 L6
Kingsmuir Angus ...91 Q3
Kingsmuir Fife ...91 R9
Kings Muir Border ...83 Q11
Kings Newnham Warwks ...37 N5
King's Newton Derbys ...47 L9
Kingsnorth Kent ...12 K8
King's Norton Birm ...36 E5
King's Norton Leics ...47 S13
Kings Nympton Devon ...15 Q9
King's Pyon Herefs ...34 K10
Kings Ripton Cambs ...39 L5
King's Somborne Hants ...9 M2
King's Stag Dorset ...7 S2
King's Stanley Gloucs ...28 F7
King's Sutton Oxon ...37 N13
Kingstanding Birm ...36 E1
Kingsteignton Devon ...5 V6
Kingsthorne Herefs ...103 P8
King's Stanley Derbys ...56 Q12
Kingsthorpe N York ...27 T1
Kingsthorpe W Nthn ...37 U7
Kingston Cambs ...39 M9
Kingston Cnwll ...4 K5
Kingston Devon ...5 Q11
Kingston Devon ...6 E7
Kingston Dorset ...7 U3
Kingston Dorset ...8 D13
Kingston E Loth ...84 E2
Kingston Hants ...8 H8
Kingston IoW ...9 P12
Kingston Kent ...13 N5
Kingston W Susx ...10 H10
Kingston Bagpuize Oxon ...29 U8
Kingston Blount Oxon ...20 B3
Kingston by Sea W Susx ...11 L9
Kingston Deverill Wilts ...18 B13
Kingstone Herefs ...35 L13
Kingstone Somset ...7 L2
Kingstone Staffs ...46 D8
Kingston Lacy Dorset ...8 D8
Kingston Lisle Oxon ...29 S10
Kingston near Lewes E Susx ...11 P9
Kingston on Soar Notts ...47 P8
Kingston on Spey Moray ...104 C2
Kingston Russell Dorset ...7 Q6
Kingston St Mary Somset ...16 H11
Kingston Seymour N Som ...17 M3

Kingston Stert Oxon ...30 F12
Kingston upon Hull C KuH ...65 P14
Kingston upon Thames Gt Lon ...21 L9
Kingstown Cumb ...75 S14
Kingswear Devon ...6 A14
Kingswells C Aber ...99 R2
Kingsweston Bristl ...27 U12
Kingswinford Dudley ...35 U3
Kingswood Bucks ...30 E9
Kingswood Gloucs ...28 D9
Kingswood Kent ...12 F5
Kingswood Powys ...44 F13
Kingswood S Glos ...28 B13
Kingswood Somset ...16 F9
Kingswood Surrey ...21 M11
Kingswood Warwks ...36 G6
Kingswood Brook Warwks ...36 G6
Kingswood Common Herefs ...34 G10
Kirk Sandall Donc ...57 T5
Kirksanton Cumb ...61 L3
Kirk Smeaton N York ...57 R3
Kirkstall Leeds ...63 R12
Kirkstile Abers ...104 G8
Kirkstile D & G ...75 T9
Kirkstone Pass Inn W & F ...67 P11
Kirkstyle Highld ...112 H2
Kirkthorpe Wakefd ...57 N2
Kirkton Abers ...104 J10
Kirkton D & G ...74 J9
Kirkton Fife ...91 N6
Kirkton Highld ...101 L6
Kirkton Highld ...101 N3
Kirkton P & K ...90 E8
Kirkton Manor Border ...83 P11
Kirkton of Airlie Angus ...98 E13
Kirkton of Auchterhouse Angus ...91 M4
Kirkton of Barevan Highld ...103 M6
Kirkton of Monikie Angus ...91 R4
Kirkton of Rayne Abers ...104 K9
Kirkton of Skene Abers ...99 Q2
Kirkton of Tealing Angus ...91 N4
Kirkton of Tough Abers ...104 J13
Kirktown Abers ...105 R2
Kirktown Abers ...105 T3
Kirktown of Alvah Abers ...104 K3
Kirktown of Bourtie Abers ...105 N11
Kirktown of Deskford Moray ...104 G3
Kirktown of Fetteresso Abers ...99 R6
Kirktown of Mortlach Moray ...104 C8
Kirktown of Slains Abers ...105 S10
Kirkurd Border ...83 M10
Kirkwall Ork ...106 t18
Kirkwall Airport Ork ...106 t19
Kirkwhelpington Nthumb ...76 J9
Kirmington N Linc ...58 K4
Kirmond le Mire Lincs ...58 K9
Kirn Ag & B ...88 E10
Kirriemuir Angus ...98 F13
Kirstead Green Norfk ...41 N1
Kirtlebridge D & G ...75 P11
Kirtling Cambs ...39 U9
Kirtling Green Cambs ...39 U9
Kirtlington Oxon ...29 U4
Kirtomy Highld ...111 Q4
Kirton Lincs ...49 M6
Kirton Notts ...57 U13
Kirton Suffk ...41 M12
Kirton End Lincs ...49 L5
Kirtonhill W Duns ...88 K10
Kirton Holme Lincs ...49 L5
Kirton in Lindsey N Linc ...58 F7
Kirwaugh D & G ...73 L8
Kishorn Highld ...101 L4
Kislingbury W Nthn ...37 S9
Kitebrook Warwks ...29 P1
Kite Green Warwks ...36 G7
Kites Hardwick Warwks ...37 N7
Kitleigh Cnwll ...14 F13
Kitt Green Wigan ...55 M5
Kittisford Somset ...16 E12
Kittle Swans ...25 U12
Kitt's Green Birm ...36 G3
Kittybrewster C Aber ...99 S2
Kitwood Hants ...9 U2
Kivernoll Herefs ...27 T1
Kiveton Park Rothm ...57 Q10
Knaith Lincs ...58 D10
Knaith Park Lincs ...58 D10
Knap Corner Dorset ...17 V12
Knaphill Surrey ...20 G11
Knapp Somset ...16 K11
Knapp Hill Hants ...9 N4
Knapthorpe Notts ...47 T2
Knapton N York ...64 J6
Knapton N York ...64 K4
Knapton Norfk ...51 P7
Knapton Green Herefs ...34 K10
Knapwell Cambs ...39 M8
Knaresborough N York ...63 T8
Knarsdale Nthumb ...68 F3
Knaven Abers ...105 P7
Knayton N York ...64 B3
Knebworth Herts ...31 S8
Knedlington E R Yk ...64 G14
Kneesall Notts ...57 U14
Kneesworth Cambs ...39 P11
Kneeton Notts ...47 T4
Knelston Swans ...25 S13
Knenhall Staffs ...46 B6
Knettishall Suffk ...40 G5
Knightacott Devon ...15 Q5
Knightcote Warwks ...37 M10
Knightley Staffs ...45 T9
Knightley Dale Staffs ...45 T9
Knighton BCP ...8 F9
Knighton C Leic ...47 R13
Knighton Devon ...5 N11
Knighton Dorset ...7 T2
Knighton Powys ...34 G6
Knighton Somset ...16 G8
Knighton Staffs ...45 R5
Knighton Staffs ...45 S7
Knighton Wilts ...19 L6
Knighton on Teme Worcs ...35 P7
Knightsbridge Gloucs ...28 G2
Knightsmill Cnwll ...4 D4
Knightwick Worcs ...35 R9
Knill Herefs ...34 G8
Knipoch Ag & B ...93 U14
Knipton Leics ...48 B7
Knitsley Dur ...69 P3
Kniveton Derbys ...46 H3
Knock Cumb ...68 E7
Knock Highld ...100 f9
Knock Moray ...104 G5
Knock W Isls ...106 j5
Knockally Highld ...112 D11
Knockan Highld ...108 C2
Knockando Moray ...103 U7
Knockbain Highld ...102 H5
Knockbain Highld ...102 G6
Knockdee Highld ...112 E4
Knockdown Wilts ...28 F11
Knockeen S Ayrs ...81 L13
Knockenkelly N Ayrs ...80 E7
Knockentiber E Ayrs ...81 N5
Knockhall Kent ...22 E13
Knockholt Kent ...21 S11
Knockholt Pound Kent ...21 S11
Knockin Shrops ...44 H9
Knockinlaw E Ayrs ...81 N5
Knocknain D & G ...72 B7
Knockrome Ag & B ...86 K11
Knocksharry IoM ...60 d5
Knocksheen D & G ...73 P3
Knockvennie Smithy D & G ...74 D14
Knodishall Suffk ...41 R8
Knodishall Common Suffk ...41 R8
Knole Park S Glos ...28 A11
Knolls Green Ches E ...55 T11
Knook Wilts ...18 D12
Knossington Leics ...48 B12
Knott End-on-Sea Lancs ...61 R10
Knotting Bed ...38 F8
Knotting Green Bed ...38 F8
Knottingley Wakefd ...57 R2
Knotty Ash Lpool ...54 K8
Knotty Green Bucks ...20 F4
Knowbury Shrops ...35 N5

Kirkley Suffk ...41 T2
Kirklington N York ...63 S3
Kirklington Notts ...47 S2
Kirklinton Cumb ...75 T12
Kirkliston C Edin ...83 M4
Kirkmabreck D & G ...73 P7
Kirkmaiden D & G ...72 E12
Kirk Merrington Dur ...69 S6
Kirkmichael IoM ...60 e4
Kirkmichael P & K ...97 T12
Kirkmichael S Ayrs ...81 L11
Kirkmuirhill S Lans ...82 E10
Kirknewton Nthumb ...85 N12
Kirknewton W Loth ...83 M5
Kirkney Abers ...104 G9
Kirk of Shotts N Lans ...82 F6
Kirkoswald Cumb ...67 S4
Kirkoswald S Ayrs ...80 J11
Kirkpatrick D & G ...74 H7
Kirkpatrick Durham D & G ...74 E11
Kirkpatrick-Fleming D & G ...75 Q11
Kirkstead Lincs ...59 L14
Krumlin Calder ...56 G3
Kuggar Cnwll ...2 J13
Kyleakin Highld ...100 g7
Kyle of Lochalsh Highld ...100 g7
Kylerhea Highld ...100 g7
Kylesku Highld ...110 D10
Kylesmorar Highld ...100 h10
Kyles Scalpay W Isls ...106 h9
Kylestrome Highld ...110 D10
Kynaston Herefs ...35 P13
Kynaston Shrops ...44 H9
Kynnersley Wrekin ...45 Q10
Kyre Park Worcs ...35 P8
Kyrewood Worcs ...35 N7
Kyrle Somset ...16 E12

L

La Bellieuse Guern ...6 d3
Lacasaigh W Isls ...106 i6
Lacasdal W Isls ...106 j5
Laceby NE Lin ...59 M5
Lacey Green Bucks ...30 H12
Lach Dennis Ches W ...55 R12
Lackenby R & Cl ...70 J9
Lackford Suffk ...40 C6
Lackford Green Suffk ...40 C6
Lacock Wilts ...18 D7
Ladbroke Warwks ...37 M9
Ladderedge Staffs ...46 C3
Laddingford Kent ...12 C6
Lade Bank Lincs ...49 N3
Ladock Cnwll ...3 M6
Lady Ork ...106 v15
Ladybank Fife ...91 M10
Ladycross Cnwll ...4 J3
Lady Hall W & F ...61 M2
Ladykirk Border ...85 M9
Ladyridge Herefs ...28 A1
Lady's Green Suffk ...40 B9
Ladywood Birm ...36 E3
Ladywood Worcs ...35 U8
La Fontenelle Guern ...6 e1
La Fosse Guern ...6 d4
Lag D & G ...74 G8
Lagavulin Ag & B ...78 E5
Lagg N Ayrs ...80 D8
Laggan Highld ...96 B4
Laggan Highld ...96 J5
Lagganlia Highld ...97 P3
Lagness W Susx ...10 D10
La Greve Guern ...6 e2
La Grève de Lecq Jersey ...7 b1
La Hougue Bie Jersey ...7 e3
La Houguette Guern ...6 c3
Laid Highld ...110 J5
Laide Highld ...107 R6
Laig Highld ...100 d11
Laigh Clunch C Ayrs ...81 P3
Laigh Fenwick C Ayrs ...81 P4
Laigh Glenmuir S Ayrs ...81 S8
Laighstonehall S Lans ...82 D8
Laindon Essex ...22 F10
Lairg Highld ...108 K5
Lairigmor Highld ...94 G3
Laisterdyke C Brad ...63 P13
Laithes W & F ...67 Q6
Lake Devon ...15 N6
Lake IoW ...9 R12
Lake Wilts ...18 H13
Lake District National Park Cumb ...66 K10
Lakenham Norfk ...51 M12
Lakenheath Suffk ...40 B4
Laker's Green Surrey ...10 G3
Lakes End Norfk ...39 R1
Lakeside W & F ...61 R2
Laleham Surrey ...20 J9
Laleston Brdgnd ...26 F12
Lamanva Cnwll ...2 K10
Lamarsh Essex ...40 E14
Lamas Norfk ...51 M9
Lambden Border ...84 J10
Lamberhurst Kent ...12 C8
Lamberhurst Down Kent ...12 C8
Lamberton Border ...85 P7
Lambeth Gt Lon ...21 P7
Lambfair Green Suffk ...40 B10
Lambley Notts ...47 R4
Lambley Nthumb ...76 D14
Lambourn W Berk ...19 M5
Lambourne End Essex ...21 S4
Lambourn Woodlands W Berk ...19 M5
Lamb Roe Lancs ...62 E12
Lambs Green W Susx ...11 L3
Lambston Pembks ...24 F7
Lamellion Cnwll ...4 G8
Lamerton Devon ...5 M5
Lamesley Gatesd ...77 R14
Lamington S Lans ...82 J11
Lamlash N Ayrs ...80 E6
Lamonby Cumb ...67 N4
Lamorick Cnwll ...3 Q4
Lamorna Cnwll ...2 C11
Lamorran Cnwll ...3 M8
Lampen Cnwll ...4 G6
Lampeter Cerdgn ...33 L11
Lampeter Velfrey Pembks ...25 L8
Lamphey Pembks ...24 H10
Lamplugh Cumb ...66 G8
Lamport W Nthn ...37 U6
Lamyatt Somset ...17 S9
Lana Devon ...14 H11
Lana Devon ...14 H13
Lanark S Lans ...82 G10
Lancaster Lancs ...61 T7
Lancaut Gloucs ...27 U8
Lanchester Dur ...69 Q3
Lancing W Susx ...10 K10
L'Ancresse Guern ...6 e1
Landbeach Cambs ...39 Q8
Landcross Devon ...15 L8
Landerberry Abers ...99 P3
Landewednack Cnwll ...2 J14
Landford Wilts ...8 K4
Land-hallow Highld ...112 E9
Landimore Swans ...25 S12
Landkey Devon ...15 N6
Landore Swans ...26 A8
Landrake Cnwll ...4 K8
Landscove Devon ...5 T7
Land's End Cnwll ...2 B12
Land's End Airport Cnwll ...2 B12
Landshipping Pembks ...24 H8
Landue Cnwll ...4 K4
Landulph Cnwll ...5 L8
Landwade Suffk ...39 U7
Landywood Staffs ...46 C13
Lane Cnwll ...3 L4
Laneast Cnwll ...4 G4
Lane Bottom Lancs ...62 H12
Lane End Bucks ...20 D4
Lane End Cnwll ...3 R2
Lane End Hants ...9 R3
Lane End Kent ...22 E13
Lane End Lancs ...62 H11
Lane End W & F ...66 J12
Lane End Wilts ...18 B11
Lane Ends Derbys ...46 H7
Lane Ends Lancs ...62 H13
Lane Ends N York ...62 K11
Lane Green Staffs ...45 U12
Laneham Notts ...58 D11
Lanehead Dur ...68 J5
Lane Head Dur ...69 P9
Lane Head Wigan ...55 P7
Lanehead Nthumb ...76 E9

Knowe D & G ...72 J5
Knowehead D & G ...73 Q1
Knoweside S Ayrs ...80 J10
Knowes of Elrick Abers ...104 J5
Knowl Hill W & M ...20 D7
Knowle Bristl ...17 R2
Knowle Devon ...6 D8
Knowle Devon ...15 L5
Knowle Devon ...15 S12
Knowle Shrops ...35 N6
Knowle Solhll ...36 G5
Knowle Somset ...16 C8
Knowle Cross Devon ...6 D6
Knowlefield Cumb ...75 T14
Knowle Green Lancs ...62 C13
Knowle Hill Surrey ...20 G9
Knowle St Giles Somset ...6 K2
Knowle Village Hants ...9 R7
Knowle Wood Calder ...56 D2
Knowl Green Essex ...40 C12
Knowl Hill W & M ...20 D7
Knowlton Dorset ...8 E7
Knowlton Kent ...13 Q5
Knowsley Knows ...54 K7
Knowsley Safari Knows ...55 L8
Knowstone Devon ...15 U8
Knox Bridge Kent ...12 F7
Knoydart Highld ...100 h9
Knuckles Powys ...34 G6
Knutsford Ches E ...55 S11
Knutsford Services Ches E ...55 S11
Knutton Staffs ...45 T4
Krumlin Calder ...56 G3

Knowle D & G ...72 J5

Lane Head Wigan ...55 P7
Lane Head Wsall ...46 C13
Lane Side Lancs ...55 S2
Laneshaw Bridge Lancs ...62 J11
Lane Side Lancs ...55 S2
Langaford Devon ...14 K13
Langailge Highld ...93 S5
Langaller Somset ...16 J11
Langar Notts ...47 T7
Langbank Rens ...88 J11
Langbar N York ...63 M9
Langbaurgh N York ...70 J10
Langcliffe N York ...62 G7
Langdale End N York ...71 N13
Langdon Cnwll ...4 J3
Langdon Beck Dur ...68 J6
Langdon Hills Essex ...22 G10
Langdown Hants ...9 N7
Langdyke Fife ...91 M11
Langenhoe Essex ...23 P4
Langford C Beds ...31 Q4
Langford Devon ...6 C4
Langford Essex ...22 K6
Langford N Som ...17 M4
Langford Notts ...48 B2
Langford Oxon ...29 P7
Langford Budville Somset ...16 F12
Langham Dorset ...17 U11
Langham Essex ...23 P1
Langham Norfk ...50 H5
Langham Rutlnd ...48 B11
Langham Suffk ...40 G7
Langho Lancs ...62 E13
Langholm D & G ...75 S9
Langland Swans ...25 V13
Langlee Border ...84 F12
Langley Ches E ...56 D12
Langley Derbys ...47 M4
Langley Gloucs ...28 K3
Langley Hants ...9 N8
Langley Herts ...31 R8
Langley Kent ...12 F5
Langley Nthumb ...76 G13
Langley Oxon ...29 Q5
Langley Rochdl ...56 C5
Langley Slough ...20 H7
Langley Somset ...16 E11
Langley W Susx ...10 C5
Langley Warwks ...36 G8
Langley Burrell Wilts ...18 D5
Langley Castle Nthumb ...76 G13
Langley Common Derbys ...46 J6
Langley Green Derbys ...46 J6
Langley Green Essex ...23 M3
Langley Green Warwks ...36 G8
Langley Heath Kent ...12 F5
Langley Lower Green Essex ...39 P14
Langley Marsh Somset ...16 E11
Langley Mill Derbys ...47 M4
Langley Moor Dur ...69 S4
Langley Park Dur ...69 R3
Langley Street Norfk ...51 Q13
Langley Upper Green Essex ...39 P14
Langney E Susx ...11 U10
Langold Notts ...57 S9
Langore Cnwll ...4 H4
Langport Somset ...17 M11
Langrick Lincs ...49 L4
Langridge BaNES ...17 T3
Langridgeford Devon ...15 N8
Langrigg Cumb ...66 K3
Langrish Hants ...9 U3
Langsett Barns ...56 K6
Langside P & K ...89 R3
Langstone Hants ...9 U8
Langstone Newpt ...27 R10
Langthorne N York ...63 R1
Langthorpe N York ...63 T6
Langthwaite N York ...69 M12
Langtoft E R Yk ...65 N6
Langtoft Lincs ...48 H11
Langton Dur ...69 Q9
Langton Lincs ...59 L12
Langton Lincs ...59 M13
Langton by Wragby Lincs ...58 K11
Langton Green Kent ...11 S3
Langton Green Suffk ...40 K6
Langton Herring Dorset ...7 R8
Langton Long Blandford Dorset ...8 C7
Langton Matravers Dorset ...8 E13
Langtree Devon ...15 L10
Langtree Week Devon ...15 L10
Langwathby Cumb ...67 S6
Langwell Highld ...108 J1
Langwell House Highld ...112 D12
Langwith Derbys ...57 R12
Langwith Junction Derbys ...57 R13
Langworth Lincs ...58 J11
Lanhydrock Cnwll ...3 R3
Lanivet Cnwll ...3 R3
Lanjeth Cnwll ...3 P5
Lank Cnwll ...4 C5
Lanlivery Cnwll ...3 R5
Lanner Cnwll ...2 J9
Lanreath Cnwll ...4 F9
Lansallos Cnwll ...4 F10
Lanteglos Cnwll ...4 C4
Lanteglos Highway Cnwll ...4 F10
Lanton Border ...76 F1
Lanton Nthumb ...85 N12
La Passee Guern ...6 d2
Lapford Devon ...15 R11
Laphroaig Ag & B ...78 E6
Lapley Staffs ...45 U11
La Pulente Jersey ...7 a3
Lapworth Warwks ...36 G6
Larachbeg Highld ...93 R9
Larbert Falk ...82 G2
Larbreck Lancs ...61 S11
Largie Abers ...104 J9
Largiemore Ag & B ...87 S8
Largoward Fife ...91 Q10
Largs N Ayrs ...88 H14
Largymore N Ayrs ...80 E8
Larkbeare Devon ...6 E5
Larkfield Inver ...88 F11
Larkfield Kent ...12 D4
Larkhall S Lans ...82 E9
Larkhill Wilts ...18 H12
Larling Norfk ...40 G3
La Rocque Jersey ...7 e4
La Rousaillerie Guern ...6 d2
Lartington Dur ...69 N9
Lasborough Gloucs ...28 F8
Lasham Hants ...19 U12
Lashbrook Devon ...14 K11
Lashbrook Devon ...14 K11
Lashenden Kent ...12 F7
Lask Edge Staffs ...46 B2
Lassodie Fife ...90 H12
Lasswade Mdloth ...83 R5
Lastingham N York ...71 L13
Latcham Somset ...17 M7
Latchford Herts ...31 U8
Latchford Oxon ...30 E12
Latchingdon Essex ...23 L7
Latchley Cnwll ...5 L6
Lately Common Warrtn ...55 Q8
Lathbury M Keyn ...38 C11
Latheron Highld ...112 E9
Latheronwheel Highld ...112 E9
Lathones Fife ...91 Q9
Latimer Bucks ...20 H3
Latteridge S Glos ...28 C10
Lattiford Somset ...17 S11
Latton Wilts ...29 L8
Lauder Border ...84 F9
Laugharne Carmth ...25 Q8
Laughterton Lincs ...58 D11
Laughton E Susx ...11 S8
Laughton Leics ...37 R3
Laughton Lincs ...48 D7
Laughton Lincs ...58 E6
Laughton-en-le-Morthen Rothm ...57 R9
Launcells Cnwll ...14 F11
Launcells Cross Cnwll ...14 G11
Launceston Cnwll ...4 J4
Launton Oxon ...30 D8
Laurencekirk Abers ...99 N9
Laurieston D & G ...73 R7
Laurieston Falk ...82 H3
Lavendon M Keyn ...38 D10
Lavenham Suffk ...40 F11
Laverhay D & G ...75 N6
Lavernock V Glam ...16 G3
Laversdale Cumb ...75 U13
Laverstock Wilts ...8 H2
Laverstoke Hants ...19 R11
Laverton Gloucs ...36 E14
Laverton N York ...63 Q5
Laverton Somset ...17 U5
La Villette Guern ...6 d4
Law S Lans ...82 G9
Lawers P & K ...95 T11
Lawford Essex ...23 Q1
Lawford Somset ...16 F9
Law Hill S Lans ...82 F9
Lawhitton Cnwll ...4 K4
Lawkland N York ...62 F6
Lawkland Green N York ...62 F6
Lawley Wrekin ...45 Q12
Lawnhead Staffs ...45 T8
Lawrence Weston Bristl ...27 V12
Lawrenny Pembks ...24 H9
Lawshall Suffk ...40 E10
Lawshall Green Suffk ...40 E10
Laxay W Isls ...106 i6
Laxdale W Isls ...106 j5
Laxey IoM ...60 g6
Laxfield Suffk ...41 N6
Laxford Bridge Highld ...110 F7
Laxo Shet ...106 u7
Laxton E R Yk ...58 C1
Laxton Nhants ...38 E1
Laxton Notts ...57 U13
Layer Breton Essex ...23 M4
Layer-de-la-Haye Essex ...23 N4
Layer Marney Essex ...23 M4
Layham Suffk ...40 H12
Laymore Dorset ...7 L4
Laytham E R Yk ...64 G12
Layter's Green Bucks ...20 G4
Laytham E R Yk ...64 G12
Laythes Cumb ...66 K2
Lazenby R & Cl ...70 J9
Lazonby Cumb ...67 S5
Lea Derbys ...46 K2
Lea Herefs ...28 B2
Lea Lincs ...58 D10
Lea Shrops ...34 J3
Lea Shrops ...44 K14
Lea Wilts ...28 J10
Leachkin Highld ...102 H7
Leadburn Border ...83 P7
Leadenham Lincs ...48 D3
Leaden Roding Essex ...22 E5
Leadgate Cumb ...68 G2
Leadgate Dur ...69 P2
Leadgate Nthumb ...69 P2
Leadhills S Lans ...74 H2
Leadingcross Green Kent ...12 G5
Leafield Oxon ...29 R5
Leagrave Luton ...31 N8
Leahead Ches W ...55 Q12
Lea Heath Staffs ...46 D8
Leake N York ...63 U1
Leake Common Side Lincs ...49 N3
Lealholm N York ...71 N11
Lealholm Side N York ...71 N11
Lealt Highld ...100 e3
Lea Marston Warwks ...36 H2
Leamington Hastings Warwks ...37 M7
Leamington Spa Warwks ...36 K8
Leamside Dur ...70 D3
Leap Cross E Susx ...11 T8
Learney Abers ...99 L3
Leasgill W & F ...61 T3
Leasingham Lincs ...48 G4
Leasingthorne Dur ...69 S6
Leatherhead Surrey ...21 L11
Leathley N York ...63 Q10
Leaton Shrops ...45 L10
Leaton Wrekin ...45 Q11
Lea Town Lancs ...61 T13
Leaveland Kent ...12 K5
Leavenheath Suffk ...40 F13
Leavening N York ...64 H6
Leaves Green Gt Lon ...21 R10
Lea Yeat W & F ...62 F2
Lebberston N York ...65 P3
Le Bigard Guern ...6 c4
Le Bourg Guern ...6 e4
Le Bourg Jersey ...7 f4
Lechlade on Thames Gloucs ...29 P8
Lecht Gruinart Ag & B ...86 D12
Leck Lancs ...62 C4
Leckbuie P & K ...95 U10
Leckford Hants ...19 N13
Leckfurin Highld ...111 Q5
Leckgruinart Ag & B ...86 D12
Leckhampstead Bucks ...30 F5
Leckhampstead W Berk ...19 P5
Leckhampstead Thicket W Berk ...19 P5
Leckhampton Gloucs ...28 H4
Leckmelm Highld ...108 B6
Leckwith V Glam ...27 M13
Leconfield E R Yk ...65 N11
Ledaig Ag & B ...94 C11
Ledburn Bucks ...30 K8
Ledbury Herefs ...35 R13
Ledgemoor Herefs ...34 K10
Ledicot Herefs ...34 K9
Ledmore Highld ...108 D2
Lednagullin Highld ...111 Q5
Ledsham Ches W ...54 J11
Ledsham Leeds ...57 Q1
Ledston Leeds ...57 Q1
Ledston Luck Leeds ...63 U13
Ledwell Oxon ...29 U3
Lee Ag & B ...93 L10
Lee Devon ...14 K4
Lee Hants ...9 M5
Lee Shrops ...44 K7
Leebotwood Shrops ...45 L14
Lee Brockhurst Shrops ...45 M8
Leece Cumb ...61 N6
Lee Chapel Essex ...22 G10
Lee Clump Bucks ...30 K12
Lee Common Bucks ...30 K12
Leeds Kent ...12 F5
Leeds Leeds ...63 R13
Leeds Bradford Airport Leeds ...63 Q11
Leeds Castle Kent ...12 F5
Leeds Skelton Lake Services Leeds ...57 T13
Leedstown Cnwll ...2 F10
Lee Green Ches E ...45 Q1
Leegomery Wrekin ...45 Q11
Lee Mill Devon ...5 P9
Leeming C Brad ...63 L13
Leeming N York ...63 R2
Leeming Bar N York ...63 R2
Leeming Bar Rest Area N York ...63 R2
Lee Moor Devon ...5 P8
Lee-on-the-Solent Hants ...9 R8
Lees C Brad ...63 L13
Lees Derbys ...46 J6
Lees Oldham ...56 E6
Lees Green Derbys ...46 H6
Leesthorpe Leics ...47 U11
Lee Street Surrey ...11 M2
Leeswood Flints ...44 G1
Leetown P & K ...90 K7
Leftwich Ches W ...55 Q12
Legar Powys ...27 N4
Legbourne Lincs ...59 Q10
Legburthwaite Cumb ...67 M9
Legerwood Border ...84 F10
Legoland W & M ...20 G8
Legsby Lincs ...58 J9
Le Haguais Jersey ...7 e4
Leicester C Leic ...47 Q13
Leicester Forest East Leics ...47 P13
Leicester Forest East Services Leics ...47 P13
Leigh Dorset ...7 R2
Leigh Gloucs ...28 G3
Leigh Kent ...21 T13
Leigh Shrops ...44 J12
Leigh Surrey ...11 M2
Leigh Wigan ...55 P6
Leigh Wilts ...28 K9
Leigh Worcs ...35 S10
Leigh Beck Essex ...23 L11
Leigh Common Somset ...17 S11
Leigh Delamere Wilts ...18 C5
Leigh Delamere Services Wilts ...18 C5
Leigh Green Kent ...12 J9
Leigh Knoweglass S Lans ...81 R2
Leighland Chapel Somset ...16 D9
Leigh-on-Sea Sthend ...22 K11
Leigh Park Dorset ...8 F9
Leigh Sinton Worcs ...35 S10
Leighswood Wsall ...46 D13
Leighterton Gloucs ...28 F9
Leighton Powys ...44 F12
Leighton Shrops ...45 P12
Leighton Somset ...17 T7
Leighton Bromswold Cambs ...38 H5
Leighton Buzzard C Beds ...30 K7
Leigh upon Mendip Somset ...17 S6
Leigh Woods N Som ...27 V13
Leinthall Earls Herefs ...34 K7
Leinthall Starkes Herefs ...34 K7
Leintwardine Herefs ...34 J6
Leire Leics ...37 P3
Leiston Suffk ...41 R8
Leith C Edin ...83 Q3
Leitholm Border ...84 K10
Lelant Cnwll ...2 E9
Lelley E R Yk ...65 S13
Lem Hill Worcs ...35 R5
Lemmington Hall Nthumb ...77 P3
Lempitlaw Border ...84 K12
Lemreway W Isls ...106 i7
Lemsford Herts ...31 R10
Lenchwick Worcs ...36 D11
Lendalfoot S Ayrs ...72 E1
Lendrick Stirlg ...89 N4
Lendrum Terrace Abers ...105 U7
Lenham Kent ...12 G5
Lenham Heath Kent ...12 H6
Lenie Highld ...102 F10
Lennel Border ...85 L10
Lennox Plunton D & G ...73 R8
Lennoxtown E Duns ...89 P10
Lenton C Nott ...47 Q6
Lenton Lincs ...48 F7
Lenwade Norfk ...50 K10
Leny Highld ...108 E8
Lenzie E Duns ...89 Q11
Leochel-Cushnie Abers ...104 H13
Leomansley Staffs ...46 F12
Leominster Herefs ...35 L9
Leonard Stanley Gloucs ...28 F7
Leoville Jersey ...7 a2
Lepe Hants ...9 N9
Lephin Highld ...100 a5
Leppington N York ...64 H7
Lepton Kirk ...56 K3
Lerags Ag & B ...94 B13
L'Erée Guern ...6 c3
Lerryn Cnwll ...4 E9
Lerwick Shet ...106 u9
Lesbury Nthumb ...77 Q3
Les Arquêts Guern ...6 c3
Les Hubits Guern ...6 e4
Leslie Abers ...104 H11
Leslie Fife ...91 L11
Lesmahagow S Lans ...82 F11
Les Murchez Guern ...6 d4
Les Nicolles Guern ...6 d4
Les Quartiers Guern ...6 e2
Les Quennevais Jersey ...7 b3
Les Sages Guern ...6 c4
Lessingham Norfk ...51 Q8
Lessonhall Cumb ...66 K2
Lesnewth Cnwll ...4 E3
Les Villets Guern ...6 c4
Lestowder Cnwll ...2 K12
Leswalt D & G ...72 C7
L'Etacq Jersey ...7 a2
Letchmore Heath Herts ...31 P13
Letchworth Garden City Herts ...31 R6
Letcombe Bassett Oxon ...29 S10
Letcombe Regis Oxon ...29 S10
Letham Angus ...91 R3
Letham Border ...76 F4
Letham Falk ...82 H2
Letham Fife ...91 M9
Letham Grange Angus ...91 T2
Lethenty Abers ...104 K7
Lethenty Abers ...105 M7
Letheringham Suffk ...41 M9
Letheringsett Norfk ...50 J6
Lettaford Devon ...5 S4
Lettaford Devon ...5 S4
Letterewe Highld ...107 R9
Letterfearn Highld ...101 M7
Letterfinlay Lodge Hotel Highld ...96 B4
Lettermorar Highld ...100 h11
Letters Highld ...108 B7
Lettershaw S Lans ...74 H2
Letterston Pembks ...24 G5
Lettoch Highld ...103 R12
Lettoch Highld ...103 T10
Letton Herefs ...34 J12
Letton Herefs ...34 J6
Letty Green Herts ...31 S10
Letwell Rothm ...57 S9
Leuchars Fife ...91 P7
Leumrabhagh W Isls ...106 i7
Leurbost W Isls ...106 i6
Levalsa Meor Cnwll ...3 Q7
Levan Inver ...88 E11
Levaneap Shet ...106 u7
Levedale Staffs ...45 U11
Leven E R Yk ...65 Q11
Leven Fife ...91 N11
Levencorroch N Ayrs ...80 E8
Levens W & F ...61 T2
Levens Green Herts ...31 U8
Levenshulme Manch ...56 C8
Levenwick Shet ...106 u10
Leverburgh W Isls ...106 f10
Leverington Cambs ...49 P11
Leverstock Green Herts ...31 N12
Leverton Lincs ...49 N4
Leverton Highgate Lincs ...49 N4
Le Villocq Guern ...6 d3
Levington Suffk ...41 M13
Levisham N York ...71 M13
Lew Oxon ...29 R6
Lewannick Cnwll ...4 H5
Lewcombe Dorset ...7 Q3
Lewdown Devon ...5 L3
Lewes E Susx ...11 Q8
Leweston Pembks ...24 F6
Lewisham Gt Lon ...21 Q7
Lewiston Highld ...102 F10
Lewistown Brdgnd ...26 G9
Lewknor Oxon ...20 B3
Leworthy Devon ...14 H12
Leworthy Devon ...15 Q5
Lewson Street Kent ...12 J3
Lewth Lancs ...61 T12
Lewtrenchard Devon ...5 L3
Lexden Essex ...23 N3
Lexworthy Somset ...16 H9
Leybourne Kent ...12 C4
Leyburn N York ...69 P14
Leycett Staffs ...45 S4
Leyhill Bucks ...30 K12
Leyland Lancs ...55 M2
Leylodge Abers ...105 M13
Leys Abers ...105 S5
Leys P & K ...91 L5
Leysdown-on-Sea Kent ...23 P13
Leysmill Angus ...91 T2
Leys of Cossans Angus ...91 N2
Leysters Herefs ...35 N8
Leyton Gt Lon ...21 Q5
Leytonstone Gt Lon ...21 R5
Lezant Cnwll ...4 J5
Lezerea Cnwll ...2 H10
Lezayre IoM ...60 f3
Lhanbryde Moray ...104 B3
Libanus Powys ...26 H3
Libberton S Lans ...82 J10
Libbery Worcs ...36 C9
Liberton C Edin ...83 Q4
Lichfield Staffs ...46 F12
Lickey Worcs ...36 C6
Lickey End Worcs ...36 C6
Lickey Rock Worcs ...36 C6
Lickfold W Susx ...10 E5
Liddaton Green Devon ...5 L4
Liddesdale Highld ...93 S6
Liddington Swindn ...29 P10
Lidgate Suffk ...40 B9
Lidget Donc ...57 T6
Lidgett Notts ...57 S13
Lidham Hill E Susx ...12 F12
Lidlington C Beds ...31 L5
Lidsey W Susx ...10 E10
Lidsing Kent ...12 E3
Liff Angus ...91 M5
Lifton Devon ...4 K3
Liftondown Devon ...4 K3
Lighthorne Warwks ...36 K10
Lighthorne Heath Warwks ...36 K10
Lightwater Surrey ...20 G10
Lightwater Valley Family Adventure Park N York ...63 R4
Lightwood C Stke ...46 B5
Lightwood Green Ches E ...45 P5
Lightwood Green Wrexhm ...44 J4
Lilbourne Nhants ...37 Q5
Lilburn Tower Nthumb ...85 Q14
Lilleshall Wrekin ...45 R10
Lilley Herts ...31 P7
Lilley W Berk ...19 P6
Lilliesleaf Border ...84 E14
Lillingstone Dayrell Bucks ...30 F5
Lillingstone Lovell Bucks ...30 F4
Lillington Dorset ...17 R13
Lilliput BCP ...8 E10
Lilstock Somset ...16 G8
Lilyhurst Shrops ...45 R11
Limbrick Lancs ...55 P3
Limbury Luton ...31 N7
Limebrook Herefs ...34 J7
Limefield Bury ...55 T4
Limekilnburn S Lans ...82 D8
Limekilns Fife ...83 L2
Limerigg Falk ...82 G4
Limerstone IoW ...9 N12
Limestone Brae Nthumb ...68 G3
Lime Street Worcs ...35 T14
Limington Somset ...17 P12
Limmerhaugh E Ayrs ...81 S7
Limpenhoe Norfk ...51 Q13
Limpley Stoke Wilts ...17 U4
Limpsfield Surrey ...21 R12
Limpsfield Chart Surrey ...21 R12
Linby Notts ...47 P3
Linchmere W Susx ...10 D4
Lincluden D & G ...74 J10
Lincoln Lincs ...58 F12
Lincomb Worcs ...35 T7
Lincombe Devon ...5 S12
Lincombe Devon ...15 L3
Lindale W & F ...61 T3
Lindal in Furness W & F ...61 N4
Lindean Border ...84 E12
Lindfield W Susx ...11 N5
Lindford Hants ...10 C3
Lindley N York ...63 Q10
Lindores Fife ...91 L8
Lindow End Ches E ...55 T11
Lindridge Worcs ...35 Q7
Lindsell Essex ...22 F2
Lindsey Suffk ...40 G12
Lindsey Tye Suffk ...40 G11
Liney Somset ...17 L9
Linford Hants ...8 H7
Linford Thurr ...22 G12
Lingbob C Brad ...63 M12
Lingdale R & Cl ...71 L9
Lingen Herefs ...34 J7
Lingfield Surrey ...11 P2
Lingfield Common Surrey ...11 P2
Lingwood Norfk ...51 Q12
Linicro Highld ...100 c3
Linkend Worcs ...35 T14
Linkenholt Hants ...19 M9
Linkhill Kent ...12 F10
Linkinhorne Cnwll ...4 J6
Linktown Fife ...91 M13
Linley Shrops ...34 J1
Linley Green Herefs ...35 Q10
Linleygreen Shrops ...45 Q14
Linlithgow W Loth ...82 K3
Linshiels Nthumb ...76 J5
Linsidemore Highld ...108 J5
Linslade C Beds ...30 K7
Linstead Parva Suffk ...41 P5
Linstock Cumb ...75 U14
Linthurst Worcs ...36 C6
Linthwaite Kirk ...56 H4
Lintlaw Border ...85 M8
Lintmill Moray ...104 G2
Linton Border ...76 K1
Linton Cambs ...39 S11
Linton Derbys ...46 J10
Linton Herefs ...28 B2
Linton Kent ...12 D6
Linton Leeds ...63 U10
Linton N York ...62 K6
Linton Nthumb ...77 R7
Linton Hill Herefs ...28 B2
Linton-on-Ouse N York ...64 B7
Linwood Hants ...8 H7
Linwood Lincs ...58 K9
Linwood Rens ...88 K13
Lionacleit W Isls ...106 c14
Lional W Isls ...106 k2
Lions Green E Susx ...11 T7
Liphook Hants ...10 C4
Liscard Wirral ...54 H8
Liscombe Somset ...15 U6
Liskeard Cnwll ...4 G8
Lismore Ag & B ...93 D10
Liss Hants ...10 B5
Lissett E R Yk ...65 Q9
Liss Forest Hants ...10 B5
Lissington Lincs ...58 K10
Liston Essex ...40 E12
Lisvane Cardif ...27 M11
Liswerry Newpt ...27 R11
Litcham Norfk ...50 E10
Litchborough W Nthn ...37 R10
Litchfield Hants ...19 R9
Litherland Sefton ...54 H7
Litlington Cambs ...39 N11
Litlington E Susx ...11 S10
Little Abington Cambs ...39 R11
Little Addington N Nhan ...38 E6
Little Airies D & G ...73 L8
Little Almshoe Herts ...31 R7
Little Alne Warwks ...36 F8
Little Altcar Sefton ...54 H5
Little Amwell Herts ...31 T10
Little Asby W & F ...68 E11
Little Aston Staffs ...46 E13
Little Atherfield IoW ...9 P13
Little Ayton N York ...70 J10
Little Baddow Essex ...22 H6
Little Badminton S Glos ...28 F11
Little Bampton Cumb ...67 L1
Little Bardfield Essex ...22 G1
Little Barford Bed ...38 J9
Little Barningham Norfk ...50 K7
Little Barrington Gloucs ...29 P5
Little Barrow Ches W ...54 K12
Little Barugh N York ...64 H4
Little Bavington Nthumb ...76 K10
Little Bealings Suffk ...41 M11
Littlebeck N York ...71 Q11
Little Bedwyn Wilts ...19 L7
Little Bentley Essex ...23 R3
Little Berkhamsted Herts ...31 S11
Little Billing N Nhan ...38 B8
Little Billington C Beds ...30 K8
Little Birch Herefs ...27 U1
Little Bispham Bpool ...61 Q11
Little Blakenham Suffk ...40 K11
Little Blencow W & F ...67 Q6
Little Bloxwich Wsall ...46 D13
Little Bognor W Susx ...10 G6
Little Bolehill Derbys ...46 J3
Little Bollington Ches E ...55 R9
Little Bookham Surrey ...20 K11
Littleborough Devon ...15 U11
Littleborough Notts ...58 D9
Littleborough Rochdl ...56 D4
Littlebourne Kent ...13 N4
Little Bourton Oxon ...37 N12
Little Bowden Leics ...37 U3
Little Bradley Suffk ...39 U10
Little Braxted Essex ...22 K5
Little Brechin Angus ...98 K11
Littlebredy Dorset ...7 P7
Little Brickhill M Keyn ...30 K6
Little Bridgeford Staffs ...45 U8
Little Brington W Nthn ...37 S8
Little Bromley Essex ...23 Q2
Little Broughton Cumb ...66 G5
Little Budworth Ches W ...55 N13
Little Burstead Essex ...22 F9
Little Bytham Lincs ...48 F10
Little Canfield Essex ...22 E3
Little Carlton Lincs ...59 R9
Little Carlton Notts ...47 U2
Little Casterton Rutlnd ...48 F12
Little Catwick E R Yk ...65 Q11
Little Catworth Cambs ...38 H6
Little Cawthorpe Lincs ...59 R10
Little Chalfont Bucks ...20 G3
Little Chart Kent ...12 H6
Little Chesterford Essex ...39 R12
Little Cheverell Wilts ...18 E10
Little Chishill Cambs ...39 Q13
Little Clacton Essex ...23 S4
Little Clanfield Oxon ...29 Q7
Little Clifton Cumb ...66 G7
Little Coates NE Lin ...59 M5
Little Comberton Worcs ...36 C12
Little Common E Susx ...12 D14
Little Compton Warwks ...29 Q2
Little Corby Cumb ...67 Q1
Little Cornard Suffk ...40 E13
Littlecott Wilts ...18 H9
Little Cowarne Herefs ...35 N10
Little Coxwell Oxon ...29 Q9
Little Crakehall N York ...63 R1
Little Cransley W Nthn ...38 B5
Little Crawley M Keyn ...38 D11
Little Creaton W Nthn ...37 T6
Little Cressingham Norfk ...50 E13
Little Crosby Sefton ...54 H6
Little Crosthwaite Cumb ...66 K7
Little Cubley Derbys ...46 G6
Little Dalby Leics ...47 U11
Littledean Gloucs ...28 C5
Little Dewchurch Herefs ...27 U1
Little Doward Herefs ...27 U4
Littledown Hants ...19 L9
Little Downham Cambs ...39 R4
Little Driffield E R Yk ...65 N8
Little Dunham Norfk ...50 F11

Little Dunkeld P & K 90 F3
Little Dunmow Essex 22 G3
Little Durnford Wilts 8 G2
Little Easton Essex 22 F3
Little Eaton Derbys 47 L5
Little Ellingham Norfk 50 H14
Little Elm Somset 17 T7
Little Everdon W Nthn 37 Q9
Little Eversden Cambs 39 N10
Little Faringdon Oxon 29 P7
Little Fencote N York 64 S14
Little Fenton N York 64 C12
Littleferry Highld 109 Q5
Little Fransham Norfk 50 F11
Little Gaddesden Herts 31 L10
Little Garway Herefs 27 S3
Little Gidding Cambs 38 H4
Little Glemham Suffk 41 P9
Little Gorsley Herefs 28 C3
Little Gransden Cambs 39 L9
Little Green Somset 17 T7
Little Green Notts 47 U5
Little Grimsby Lincs 59 P8
Little Gringley Notts 58 B10
Little Habton N York 64 G4
Little Hadham Herts 22 B3
Little Hale Lincs 48 H5
Little Hallam Derbys 47 N5
Little Hallingbury Essex 22 D4
Littleham Devon 6
Littleham Devon 14 K8
Little Hampden Bucks 30 J12
Littlehampton W Susx 10 G10
Little Hanford Dorset 8 A6
Little Harrowden N Nthn 38 B6
Little Haseley Oxon 30 D12
Little Hatfield E R Yk 65 R11
Little Hautbois Norfk 51 N9
Little Haven Pembks 24 E8
Littlehaven W Susx 10 K4
Little Hay Staffs 46 F13
Little Hayfield Derbys 56 F9
Little Haywood Staffs 46 D9
Little Heath Staffs 45 U10
Little Heath W Berk 19 U6
Littlehempston Devon 5 U8
Little Hereford Herefs 35 N7
Little Horkesley Essex 23 N1
Little Hormead Herts 22 B2
Little Horsted E Susx 11 R7
Little Horton C Brad 63 P13
Little Horton Wilts 18 F8
Little Horwood Bucks 30 G6
Little Houghton Barns 57 Q5
Littlehoughton Nthumb 77 Q2
Little Houghton W Nthn 38 B9
Little Hucklow Derbys 56 J11
Little Hulton Salfd 55 R6
Little Hungerford W Berk 19 R6
Little Hutton N York 64 B4
Little Irchester N Nthn 38 D7
Little Kelk E R Yk 65 P8
Little Keyford Somset 17 T8
Little Kimble Bucks 30 H11
Little Kineton Warwks 36 K10
Little Kingshill Bucks 20 E3
Little Knox D & G 74 F13
Little Langdale W & F 67 M12
Little Langford Wilts 18 F13
Little Laver Essex 22 D6
Little Leigh Ches W 55 P12
Little Leighs Essex 22 H4
Little Lever Bolton 55 S5
Little Linford M Keyn 30 H4
Little Load Somset 17 N12
Little London Bucks 30 D10
Little London E Susx 11 S8
Little London Essex 22 D1
Little London Gloucs 28 C4
Little London Hants 19 Q10
Little London Hants 19 T9
Little London Leeds 63 Q12
Little London Lincs 48 K9
Little London Lincs 49 N8
Little London Lincs 49 P9
Little London Norfk 49 S8
Little London Norfk 50 H8
Little London Powys 34 B3
Little Longstone Derbys 56 J12
Little Madeley Staffs 45 S4
Little Malvern Worcs 35 S12
Little Maplestead Essex 40 D13
Little Marcle Herefs 35 Q13
Little Marland Devon 15 M10
Little Marlow Bucks 20 E5
Little Massingham Norfk 50 C9
Little Melton Norfk 51 L12
Littlemill Abers 98 E4
Littlemill Highld 103 P5
Little Mill Mons 27 Q7
Little Milton Oxon 30 D12
Little Missenden Bucks 20 F3
Little Mongeham Kent 13 R5
Littlemoor Derbys 57 N14
Little Moor Somset 16 K10
Littlemore Oxon 30 B12
Little Musgrave W & F 68 G10
Little Ness Shrops 44 K10
Little Neston Ches W 54 G11
Little Newcastle Pembks 24 G5
Little Newsham Dur 69 P9
Little Norton Somset 17 N13
Little Oakley Essex 23 T1
Little Oakley N Nthn 38 C3
Little Odell Bed 38 D9
Little Offley Herts 31 P7
Little Ormside W & F 68 F9
Little Orton Cumb 67 N1
Little Ouse Cambs 39 T3
Little Ouseburn N York 63 U7
Littleover C Derb 47 L6
Little Oxendon Nthn 37 T4
Little Packington Warwks 36 H4
Little Pattenden Kent 12 D6
Little Paxton Cambs 38 J8
Little Petherick Cnwll 3 N2
Little Plumpton Lancs 61 R13
Little Plumstead Norfk 51 P11
Little Ponton Lincs 48 D7
Littleport Cambs 39 S3
Littleport Bridge Cambs 39 S4
Little Posbrook Hants 9 Q8
Little Potheridge Devon 15 M10
Little Preston Leeds 63 T13
Little Preston N Nthn 37 Q10
Littler Ches W 55 P13
Little Raveley Cambs 39 L5
Little Reedness E R Yk 58 D2
Little Ribston N York 63 T9
Little Rissington Gloucs 29 N4
Little Rollright Oxon 29 Q1
Little Rowsley Derbys 56 K13
Little Ryburgh Norfk 50 G8
Little Ryle Nthumb 77 L3
Little Ryton Shrops 45 L13
Little Salkeld W & F 67 S6
Little Sampford Essex 22 G1
Little Sandhurst Br For 20 D10
Little Saredon Staffs 46 B12
Little Saughall Ches W 54 H13
Little Scatwell Highld 102 C4
Little Shelford Cambs 39 Q10
Little Shrewley Warwks 36 H7
Little Silver Devon 6 B3
Little Singleton Lancs 61 R12
Little Skipwith N York 64 F11
Little Smeaton N York 57 S3
Little Snoring Norfk 50 G7
Little Sodbury S Glos 28 E11
Little Sodbury End S Glos 28 E11
Little Somborne Hants 9 M2
Little Somerford Wilts 28 J10
Little Soudley Shrops 45 R8
Little Stainforth N York 62 G6
Little Stainton Darltn 70 D8
Little Stanion N Nthn 38 C3
Little Stanney Ches W 54 J12
Little Staughton Bed 38 H8
Little Steeping Lincs 59 R14
Little Stoke Staffs 45 U6
Littlestone-on-Sea Kent 13 L11
Little Stonham Suffk 40 K8
Little Stretton Leics 47 T13
Little Stretton Shrops 34 K2
Little Strickland W & F 68 D9
Little Stukeley Cambs 38 K6
Little Sugnall Staffs 45 T7
Little Sutton Ches W 54 J11
Little Sutton Shrops 35 M4
Little Swinburne Nthumb 76 J10
Little Sypland D & G 73 S9
Little Tew Oxon 29 S2
Little Tey Essex 23 L3
Little Thetford Cambs 39 R5
Little Thirkleby N York 64 B4
Little Thornage Norfk 50 J6
Little Thornton Lancs 61 R11
Little Thorpe Dur 70 F4
Littlethorpe Leics 37 P1
Littlethorpe N York 63 S6
Little Thurlow Suffk 39 U10
Little Thurlow Green Suffk 39 U10
Little Thurrock Thurr 22 F12

Littleton BaNES 17 Q3
Littleton Ches W 54 K13
Littleton D & G 73 Q8
Littleton Dorset 8 B8
Littleton Hants 9 P2
Littleton Somset 17 N10
Littleton Surrey 20 J9
Littleton Drew Wilts 18 B4
Littleton of Airlie Angus 98 E13
Littleton-on-Severn S Glos 28 A10
Littleton Panell Wilts 18 E9
Little Torrington Devon 15 L9
Little Totham Essex 23 L5
Little Town Cumb 66 K9
Littletown Dur 70 D4
Little Town Lancs 62 D12
Little Town Warrtn 55 P8
Little Twycross Leics 46 K12
Little Urswick W & F 61 P5
Little Wakering Essex 23 L10
Little Walden Essex 39 R12
Little Waldingfield Suffk 40 F11
Little Walsingham Norfk 50 F6
Little Waltham Essex 22 H5
Little Warley Essex 22 F9
Little Washbourne Gloucs 36 C14
Little Weighton E R Yk 65 M13
Little Weldon N Nthn 38 C3
Little Welnetham Suffk 40 E9
Little Welton Lincs 59 P9
Little Wenham Suffk 40 J13
Little Wenlock Wrekin 45 P12
Little Weston Somset 17 R11
Little Whitefield IoW 9 R11
Little Whittingham Green Suffk 41 N5
Little Whittington Nthumb 76 K12
Littlewick Green W & F 20 D7
Little Wilbraham Cambs 39 R9
Littlewindsor Dorset 7 M4
Little Witcombe Gloucs 28 H4
Little Witley Worcs 35 S8
Little Wittenham Oxon 19 S2
Little Wolford Warwks 36 J14
Littleworth Bucks 30 J9
Littleworth Oxon 29 R8
Littleworth Staffs 46 C11
Littleworth Staffs 46 D10
Little Worth W Susx 10 K6
Littleworth Worcs 35 U10
Littleworth Worcs 36 C8
Littleworth Common Bucks 20 F6
Little Wratting Suffk 39 U11
Little Wymington Bed 38 D8
Little Wymondley Herts 31 R7
Little Wyrley Staffs 46 D12
Little Wytheford Shrops 45 N10
Little Yeldham Essex 40 C13
Litton Derbys 56 J12
Litton N York 62 J5
Litton Somset 17 Q5
Litton Cheney Dorset 7 P6
Liurbost W Isls 106 i6
Liverpool Lpool 54 H8
Liversedge Kirk 56 K1
Liverton Devon 5 U6
Liverton R & Cl 71 M9
Liverton Mines R & Cl 71 M9
Liverton Street Kent 12 G6
Livingston W Loth 83 K5
Livingston Village W Loth 82 K5
Lixwm Flints 54 E12
Lizard Cnwll 2 J14
Llaingoch IoA 52 B6
Llaithddu Powys 34 B3
Llan Powys 43 S13
Llanaber Gwynd 43 M10
Llanaelhaearn Gwynd 42 G5
Llanafan Cerdgn 33 N6
Llanafan-Fawr Powys 33 U9
Llanallgo IoA 52 H5
Llanarmon Gwynd 42 H5
Llanarmon Dyffryn Ceiriog Wrexhm 44 E7
Llanarmon-yn-Ial Denbgs 44 E2
Llanarth Cerdgn 32 H9
Llanarth Mons 27 R5
Llanarthne Carmth 25 T6
Llanasa Flints 54 D10
Llanbabo IoA 52 E5
Llanbadarn Fawr Cerdgn 33 M4
Llanbadarn Fynydd Powys 34 C5
Llanbadarn-y-garreg Powys 34 D11
Llanbadoc Mons 27 R8
Llanbadrig IoA 52 E3
Llanbeder Newpt 27 R9
Llanbedr Gwynd 43 L8
Llanbedr Powys 27 N3
Llanbedr Powys 34 E13
Llanbedr-Dyffryn-Clwyd Denbgs 44 D2
Llanbedrgoch IoA 52 H6
Llanbedrog Gwynd 42 F7
Llanbedr-y-cennin Conwy 53 N10
Llanberis Gwynd 52 J10
Llanbethery V Glam 16 D3
Llanbister Powys 34 D6
Llanblethian V Glam 16 C2
Llanboidy Carmth 25 M6
Llanbradach Caerph 27 L8
Llanbrynmair Powys 43 S13
Llancadle V Glam 16 D3
Llancarfan V Glam 16 D2
Llancayo Mons 27 R7
Llancloudy Herefs 27 T3
Llancynfelyn Cerdgn 33 M2
Llandaff Cardif 27 M12
Llandanwg Gwynd 43 L8
Llandarcy Neath 26 C8
Llandawke Carmth 25 L7
Llanddaniel Fab IoA 52 G8
Llanddarog Carmth 25 T7
Llanddeiniol Cerdgn 33 L6
Llanddeiniolen Gwynd 52 H9
Llandderfel Gwynd 43 U6
Llanddeusant Carmth 26 E3
Llanddeusant IoA 52 D5
Llanddew Powys 34 D13
Llanddewi Swans 25 S13
Llanddewi Brefi Cerdgn 33 N9
Llanddewi'r Cwm Powys 34 B11
Llanddewi Rhydderch Mons 27 R5
Llanddewi Velfrey Pembks 24 K7
Llanddewi Ystradenni Powys 34 D7
Llanddoged Conwy 53 P10
Llanddona IoA 52 H7
Llanddowror Carmth 25 L8
Llanddulas Conwy 53 R7
Llanddwywe Gwynd 43 L9
Llanddyfnan IoA 52 G6
Llandecwyn Gwynd 43 M7
Llandefaelog-Tre'r-Graig Powys 27 M1
Llandefalle Powys 34 D13
Llandegfan IoA 52 J8
Llandegla Denbgs 44 E3
Llandegley Powys 34 D8
Llandegveth Mons 27 Q8
Llandegwning Gwynd 42 E7
Llandeilo Carmth 26 A3
Llandeilo Graban Powys 34 C12
Llandeilo'r Fan Powys 33 S13
Llandeloy Pembks 24 E5
Llandenny Mons 27 S7
Llandevaud Newpt 27 S9
Llandevenny Newpt 27 S10
Llandinabo Herefs 27 U2
Llandinam Powys 34 B3
Llandissilio Pembks 24 K6
Llandogo Mons 27 U6
Llandough V Glam 16 C2
Llandough V Glam 16 K2
Llandovery Carmth 33 Q14
Llandow V Glam 16 B2
Llandre Carmth 33 N13
Llandre Cerdgn 33 M3
Llandre Isaf Pembks 24 K5
Llandrillo Denbgs 44 C6
Llandrindod Wells Powys 34 C8
Llandrinio Powys 44 G10
Llandudno Conwy 53 N6
Llandudno Junction Conwy 53 N7
Llandulas Powys 33 T11
Llandwrog Gwynd 52 G11
Llandybie Carmth 25 U7
Llandyfaelog Carmth 25 R8
Llandyfan Carmth 26 A5
Llandyfriog Cerdgn 32 G12
Llandyfrydog IoA 52 F5
Llandygai Gwynd 52 J8
Llandygwydd Cerdgn 32 E12
Llandynan Denbgs 44 E4
Llandyrnog Denbgs 54 C13
Llandyssil Powys 34 E1
Llandysul Cerdgn 32 H12

Llanedeyrn Cardif 27 N11
Llanedi Carmth 25 U9
Llaneglwys Powys 34 C13
Llanegryn Gwynd 43 M12
Llanegwad Carmth 25 T6
Llaneilian IoA 52 G4
Llanelian-yn-Rhôs Conwy 53 Q7
Llanelidan Denbgs 44 D3
Llanelieu Powys 34 E14
Llanellen Mons 27 Q5
Llanelli Carmth 25 T10
Llanelltyd Gwynd 43 P10
Llanelly Mons 27 N5
Llanelly Hill Mons 27 N5
Llanelwedd Powys 34 B10
Llanenddwyn Gwynd 43 L9
Llanengan Gwynd 42 E8
Llanerch Powys 34 H2
Llanerchymedd IoA 52 F6
Llanerfyl Powys 44 B12
Llanfabon Caerph 27 L7
Llanfachraeth IoA 52 D6
Llanfachreth Gwynd 43 P9
Llanfaelog IoA 52 D7
Llanfaelrhys Gwynd 42 D8
Llanfaenor Mons 27 S4
Llanfaes IoA 52 K7
Llanfaes Powys 26 K2
Llanfaethlu IoA 52 D5
Llanfaglan Gwynd 52 F10
Llanfair Gwynd 43 L8
Llanfair Caereinion Powys 44 D12
Llanfair Clydogau Cerdgn 33 M10
Llanfair Dyffryn Clwyd Denbgs 44 D2
Llanfairfechan Conwy 53 L8
Llanfair Kilgeddin Mons 27 R6
Llanfair-Nant-Gwyn Pembks 25 L3
Llanfairpwllgwyngyll IoA 52 H8
Llanfair Talhaiarn Conwy 53 R9
Llanfair Waterdine Shrops 34 F5
Llanfairynghornwy IoA 52 D3
Llanfair-yn-Neubwll IoA 52 D7
Llanfallteg Carmth 25 L6
Llanfallteg West Carmth 24 K7
Llanfarian Cerdgn 33 L5
Llanfechain Powys 44 E9
Llanfechell IoA 52 E3
Llanfendigaid Gwynd 43 L12
Llanferres Denbgs 44 E1
Llan Ffestiniog Gwynd 43 P5
Llanfflewyn IoA 52 E4
Llanfigael IoA 52 D6
Llanfihangel-ar-arth Carmth 25 Q4
Llanfihangel Glyn Myfyr Conwy 43 U4
Llanfihangel Nant Bran Powys 33 T14
Llanfihangel-nant-Melan Powys 34 E9
Llanfihangel Rhydithon Powys
Llanfihangel Rogiet Mons 27 T10
Llanfihangel Tal-y-llyn Powys 27 L2
Llanfihangel-uwch-Gwili Carmth 25 S5
Llanfihangel-y-Creuddyn Cerdgn 33 N5
Llanfihangel-yng-Ngwynfa Powys 44 C10
Llanfihangel yn Nhowyn IoA 52 D7
Llanfihangel-y-pennant Gwynd 42 J3
Llanfihangel-y-pennant Gwynd 43 N12
Llanfihangel-y-traethau Gwynd 43 L7
Llanfilo Powys 34 D14
Llanfoist Mons 27 P5
Llanfor Gwynd 43 T7
Llanfrechfa Torfn 27 Q9
Llanfrothen Gwynd 43 M5
Llanfrynach Powys 26 K2
Llanfwrog Denbgs 44 D2
Llanfwrog IoA 52 D5
Llanfyllin Powys 44 D10
Llanfynydd Carmth 25 U5
Llanfynydd Flints 44 F2
Llanfyrnach Pembks 25 M4
Llangadfan Powys 44 B11
Llangadog Carmth 26 D2
Llangadwaladr IoA 52 E8
Llangadwaladr Powys 44 E7
Llangaffo IoA 52 F8
Llangain Carmth 25 R7
Llangammarch Wells Powys 33 T11
Llangan V Glam 26 H12
Llangarron Herefs 27 U3
Llangasty-Talyllyn Powys 27 L2
Llangathen Carmth 25 U6
Llangattock Powys 27 N4
Llangattock Lingoed Mons 27 R3
Llangattock-Vibon-Avel Mons 27 T4
Llangedwyn Powys 44 E9
Llangefni IoA 52 G7
Llangeinor Brdgnd 26 G10
Llangeitho Cerdgn 33 M9
Llangeler Carmth 25 P3
Llangelynin Gwynd 43 L12
Llangendeirne Carmth 25 R8
Llangennech Carmth 25 U9
Llangennith Swans 25 R12
Llangenny Powys 27 N4
Llangernyw Conwy 53 Q9
Llangeview Mons 27 R7
Llangian Gwynd 42 E8
Llanglydwen Carmth 25 L5
Llangoed IoA 52 K7
Llangoedmor Cerdgn 32 D12
Llangollen Denbgs 44 F5
Llangolman Pembks 24 K5
Llangorse Powys 27 L2
Llangorwen Cerdgn 33 M4
Llangovan Mons 27 T6
Llangower Gwynd 43 T7
Llangrannog Cerdgn 32 F10
Llangristiolus IoA 52 F8
Llangrove Herefs 27 U4
Llangunllo Powys 34 F6
Llangunnor Carmth 25 R6
Llangurig Powys 33 U5
Llangwm Conwy 43 T4
Llangwm Mons 27 S7
Llangwm Pembks 24 G8
Llangwm-isaf Mons 27 S7
Llangwnnadl Gwynd 42 D7
Llangwyfan Denbgs 54 C13
Llangwyllog IoA 52 F6
Llangwyryfon Cerdgn 33 L6
Llangybi Cerdgn 33 M9
Llangybi Gwynd 42 H4
Llangybi Mons 27 R8
Llangyfelach Swans 25 U11
Llangynhafal Denbgs 54 D14
Llangynidr Powys 27 M4
Llangyniew Powys 44 C11
Llangynin Carmth 25 M7
Llangynllo Cerdgn 32 G12
Llangynog Carmth 25 P7
Llangynog Powys 44 B8
Llangynwyd Brdgnd 26 F10
Llanhamlach Powys 26 K2
Llanharan Rhondd 26 J11
Llanharry Rhondd 26 J11
Llanhennock Mons 27 R8
Llanhilleth Blae G 27 N6
Llanidan IoA 52 G8
Llanidloes Powys 33 U4
Llaniestyn Gwynd 42 E7
Llanigon Powys 34 F13
Llanilar Cerdgn 33 M6
Llanilid Rhondd 26 H11
Llanina Cerdgn 32 H9
Llanishen Cardif 27 M11
Llanishen Mons 27 T7
Llanllechid Gwynd 52 K9
Llanlleonfel Powys 33 T10
Llanllugan Powys 44 C13
Llanllwch Carmth 25 Q7
Llanllwchaiarn Powys 34 D2
Llanllwni Carmth 25 R3
Llanllyfni Gwynd 42 H3
Llanmadoc Swans 25 R11
Llanmaes V Glam 16 C3
Llanmartin Newpt 27 R10
Llanmerewig Powys 34 E2
Llanmihangel V Glam 16 C2
Llanmiloe Carmth 25 L8
Llanmorlais Swans 25 S12
Llannefydd Conwy 53 S8
Llannon Carmth 25 U8
Llannor Gwynd 42 G6
Llanon Cerdgn 32 K8
Llanover Mons 27 R6
Llanpumsaint Carmth 25 R5
Llanreithan Pembks 24 E5
Llanrhaeadr Denbgs 53 U11
Llanrhaeadr-ym-Mochnant Powys 44 D8
Llanrhian Pembks 24 E4
Llanrhidian Swans 25 S12

Llanrhos Conwy 53 N6
Llanrhychwyn Conwy 53 N10
Llanrhyddlad IoA 52 D5
Llanrhystud Cerdgn 32 K7
Llanrothal Herefs 27 T4
Llanrug Gwynd 52 H10
Llanrumney Cardif 27 N11
Llanrwst Conwy 53 P10
Llansadurnen Carmth 25 M8
Llansadwrn Carmth 26 B1
Llansadwrn IoA 52 J7
Llansaint Carmth 25 Q9
Llansamlet Swans 26 B8
Llansanffraid Glan Conwy Conwy 53 P7
Llansannan Conwy 53 R9
Llansannor V Glam 16 C2
Llansantffraed Powys 27 L3
Llansantffraed-Cwmdeuddwr Powys 33 U7
Llansantffraed-in-Elvel Powys 34 C10
Llansantffraid Cerdgn 32 K7
Llansantffraid-ym-Mechain Powys 44 F9
Llansawel Carmth 25 V3
Llansilin Powys 44 F8
Llansoy Mons 27 S7
Llanspyddid Powys 26 J2
Llanstadwell Pembks 24 F10
Llansteffan Carmth 25 Q8
Llanstephan Powys 34 D12
Llantarnam Torfn 27 Q8
Llanteg Pembks 25 L8
Llanthewy Skirrid Mons 27 Q4
Llanthony Mons 27 P3
Llantilio-Crossenny Mons 27 R5
Llantilio Pertholey Mons 27 Q4
Llantood Pembks 32 C12
Llantrisant IoA 52 E6
Llantrisant Mons 27 R8
Llantrisant Rhondd 26 K11
Llantrithyd V Glam 16 D2
Llantwit Fardre Rhondd 26 K10
Llantwit Major V Glam 16 C3
Llantysilio Denbgs 44 E5
Llanuwchllyn Gwynd 43 S7
Llanvaches Newpt 27 S9
Llanvair Discoed Mons 27 S9
Llanvapley Mons 27 R5
Llanvetherine Mons 27 R4
Llanveynoe Herefs 27 Q1
Llanvihangel Crucorney Mons 27 Q3
Llanvihangel Gobion Mons 27 Q6
Llanvihangel-Ystern-Llewern Mons 27 S5
Llanwarne Herefs 27 U2
Llanwddyn Powys 43 U10
Llanwenarth Mons 27 P5
Llanwenog Cerdgn 32 J11
Llanwern Newpt 27 R10
Llanwinio Carmth 25 N5
Llanwnda Gwynd 52 G11
Llanwnda Pembks 24 F3
Llanwnnen Cerdgn 32 K11
Llanwnog Powys 34 B2
Llanwonno Rhondd 26 J8
Llanwrda Carmth 26 C1
Llanwrin Powys 43 Q13
Llanwrthwl Powys 33 U8
Llanwrtyd Powys 33 S11
Llanwrtyd Wells Powys 33 S11
Llanwyddelan Powys 44 C13
Llanyblodwel Shrops 44 F9
Llanybri Carmth 25 P8
Llanybydder Carmth 32 K12
Llanycefn Pembks 24 J6
Llanychaer Pembks 24 G4
Llanycil Gwynd 43 T7
Llanymawddwy Gwynd 43 S10
Llanymynech Powys 44 G9
Llanynghenedl IoA 52 D6
Llanynys Denbgs 54 D14
Llan-y-pwll Wrexhm 44 J3
Llanyre Powys 34 B8
Llanystumdwy Gwynd 42 J6
Llanywern Powys 27 L2
Llawhaden Pembks 24 H7
Llawnt Shrops 44 F7
Llawryglyn Powys 33 U3
Llay Wrexhm 44 J2
Llechcynfarwy IoA 52 E6
Llechfaen Powys 26 K2
Llechrhyd Caerph 27 L5
Llechryd Cerdgn 32 D12
Llechylched IoA 52 D7
Lledrod Cerdgn 33 M6
Llidiardau Gwynd 43 R5
Llidiart-y-parc Denbgs 44 D5
Llithfaen Gwynd 42 G5
Lloc Flints 54 D11
Llong Flints 44 G1
Llowes Powys 34 E12
Llundain-fach Cerdgn 33 L9
Llwydcoed Rhondd 26 H6
Llwydiarth Powys 44 B10
Llwyn Denbgs 44 C14
Llwyncelyn Cerdgn 32 J9
Llwyndafydd Cerdgn 32 G9
Llwynderw Powys 44 F12
Llwyn-drain Pembks 25 N4
Llwyn-du Mons 27 P4
Llwyngwril Gwynd 43 L12
Llwynhendy Carmth 25 U10
Llwynmawr Wrexhm 44 F6
Llwyn-on Mer Td 26 K5
Llwyn-y-brain Carmth 25 L7
Llwyn-y-groes Cerdgn 33 L9
Llwynypia Rhondd 26 H8
Llynclys Shrops 44 G9
Llynfaes IoA 52 F7
Llŷn Peninsula Gwynd 42 F7
Llyn-y-pandy Flints 54 F13
Llysfaen Conwy 53 Q7
Llyswen Powys 34 D13
Llysworney V Glam 16 C2
Llys-y-frân Pembks 24 H6
Llywel Powys 26 F1
Load Brook Sheff 57 L9
Loan Falk 82 J3
Loanend Nthumb 85 P8
Loanhead Mdloth 83 Q5
Loaningfoot D & G 66 E1
Loans S Ayrs 81 L6
Lobb Devon 15 L5
Lobhillcross Devon 5 M3
Lochailort Highld 93 R10
Lochaline Highld 93 Q9
Lochans D & G 72 C9
Locharbriggs D & G 74 J9
Lochavich Ag & B 87 Q2
Lochawe Ag & B 88 C1
Loch Baghasdail W Isls 106 c17
Lochboisdale W Isls 106 c17
Lochbuie Ag & B 93 R12
Lochcarron Highld 101 M4
Lochdon Ag & B 93 S12
Lochdonhead Ag & B 93 S12
Lochead Ag & B 79 P7
Lochearnhead Stirlg 95 N14
Lochee C Dund 91 N5
Loch Eil Highld 94 F3
Locheilside Station Highld 93 U3
Lochend Highld 102 G8
Locheport W Isls 106 d12
Loch Euphort W Isls 106 d12
Lochfoot D & G 74 H11
Lochgair Ag & B 87 T7
Lochgarthside Highld 102 F11
Lochgelly Fife 90 K13
Lochgilphead Ag & B 87 T8
Lochgoilhead Ag & B 88 F5
Loch Head D & G 72 K11
Lochieheads Fife 91 L9
Lochill Moray 104 B2
Lochindorb Lodge Highld 103 Q9
Lochinver Highld 110 B11
Loch Lomond and The Trossachs National Park 88 K3
Loch Loyal Lodge Highld 111 N7
Lochluichart Highld 102 B3
Lochmaben D & G 75 L9
Lochmaddy W Isls 106 e12
Loch nam Madadh W Isls 106 e12
Loch Ness Highld 102 F10
Lochore Fife 90 K12
Lochportain W Isls 106 e11
Lochranza N Ayrs 79 S9
Lochside Abers 99 N11
Lochside D & G 74 J10
Lochside Highld 103 N6
Lochside Highld 109 T5
Lochslin Highld 109 R9
Lochton S Ayrs 72 F4
Lochty Angus 98 H11
Lochty Fife 91 R10
Lochuisge Highld 93 T6
Lochwinnoch Rens 88 J13
Lochwood D & G 75 L7
Lockengate Cnwll 3 Q4
Lockerbie D & G 75 M9
Lockeridge Wilts 18 H7

Lockerley Hants 9 L3
Locking N Som 17 L5
Locking Stumps Warrtn 55 P8
Lockington E R Yk 65 M10
Lockington Leics 47 N8
Lockleywood Shrops 45 Q8
Locksgreen IoW 9 P10
Locks Heath Hants 9 Q7
Lockton N York 64 J2
Loddington Leics 47 U13
Loddington N Nthn 38 B5
Loddiswell Devon 5 S11
Loddon Norfk 51 Q14
Lode Cambs 39 R8
Lode Heath Solhll 36 G4
Loders Dorset 7 N5
Lodsworth W Susx 10 E6
Lofthouse Leeds 57 M1
Lofthouse N York 63 N5
Lofthouse Gate Wakefd 57 M2
Loftus R & Cl 71 M8
Logan E Ayrs 81 R8
Loganlea W Loth 82 H6
Loggerheads Staffs 45 R6
Logie Angus 99 M11
Logie Fife 91 P7
Logie Moray 103 R5
Logie Coldstone Abers 98 G3
Logie Newton Abers 104 K8
Logie Pert Angus 99 M11
Logierait P & K 97 R13
Logierieve Abers 105 Q10
Login Carmth 25 L6
Lolworth Cambs 39 N8
Lonbain Highld 100 f5
Londesborough E R Yk 64 K10
London Gt Lon 21 P6
London Apprentice Cnwll 3 Q6
London Ashford Airport Kent 13 L13
London Beach Kent 12 G8
London City Airport Gt Lon 21 R6
London Colney Herts 31 Q12
Londonderry N York 63 S2
London Gateway Services Gt Lon 21 S5
London Gatwick Airport W Susx 11 M2
London Heathrow Airport Gt Lon 20 J7
London Luton Airport Luton 31 P8
London Oxford Airport Oxon 29 U4
London Southend Airport Essex 23 L10
London Stansted Airport Essex 22 E3
Londonthorpe Lincs 48 E6
London Zoo ZSL Gt Lon 21 N6
Londubh Highld 107 Q8
Lonemore Highld 107 P8
Long Ashton N Som 17 P2
Long Bank Worcs 35 S6
Long Bennington Lincs 48 B5
Longbenton N Tyne 77 R12
Longborough Gloucs 29 N2
Long Bredy Dorset 7 P6
Longbridge Birm 36 D5
Longbridge Warwks 36 K8
Longbridge Deverill Wilts 18 C12
Long Buckby W Nthn 37 R7
Long Buckby Wharf W Nthn 37 R7
Longburgh Cumb 75 S14
Longburton Dorset 7 S2
Long Cause Devon 5 T8
Long Clawson Leics 47 T8
Longcliffe Derbys 46 H2
Long Common Hants 9 Q5
Long Compton Staffs 45 T9
Long Compton Warwks 36 J14
Longcot Oxon 29 Q9
Long Crendon Bucks 30 D11
Long Crichel Dorset 8 D6
Longcroft Cumb 75 Q14
Longcross Surrey 20 G9
Longden Shrops 44 K12
Long Ditton Surrey 21 K9
Longdon Staffs 46 D11
Longdon Worcs 35 U13
Longdon Green Staffs 46 E11
Longdon Heath Worcs 35 T13
Longdon upon Tern Wrekin 45 P10
Longdown Devon 5 V2
Longdowns Cnwll 2 J10
Long Drax N York 64 F14
Long Duckmanton Derbys 57 P12
Long Eaton Derbys 47 N7
Longfield Kent 12 B2
Longfield Hill Kent 12 C2
Longford Covtry 37 L4
Longford Derbys 46 H6
Longford Gloucs 28 F4
Longford Gt Lon 20 J7
Longford Kent 21 T11
Longford Shrops 45 P7
Longford Wrekin 45 R9
Longforgan P & K 91 L6
Longformacus Border 84 H9
Longframlington Nthumb 77 P5
Long Green Ches W 54 J11
Long Green Worcs 35 T13
Longham Dorset 8 F9
Longham Norfk 50 F10
Long Hanborough Oxon 29 U5
Longhaven Abers 105 U8
Long Hedges Lincs 49 N4
Longhirst Nthumb 77 Q9
Longhope Gloucs 28 C4
Longhope Ork 106 r20
Longhorsley Nthumb 77 P8
Longhoughton Nthumb 77 Q2
Long Itchington Warwks 37 M8
Longlands Cumb 67 L5
Longlane Derbys 46 H6
Longlane W Berk 19 Q6
Long Lawford Warwks 37 N5
Longleat Safari & Adventure Park Wilts 18 B12
Longlevens Gloucs 28 F4
Longley Calder 56 G3
Longley Green Worcs 35 R10
Longmanhill Abers 105 L3
Long Marston Herts 30 J10
Long Marston N York 64 C9
Long Marston Warwks 36 G11
Long Marton W & F 68 E7
Long Melford Suffk 40 E11
Longmoor Camp Hants 10 B4
Longmorn Moray 104 B4
Long Newnton Gloucs 28 H8
Longnewton Border 84 F13
Long Newton E Loth 84 E5
Longnewton S on T 70 E8
Longney Gloucs 28 E5
Longniddry E Loth 84 D3
Longnor Shrops 44 K12
Longnor Staffs 56 G14
Longparish Hants 19 Q11
Long Preston N York 62 G8
Longridge Lancs 62 C12
Longridge Staffs 46 B10
Longridge W Loth 82 H6
Longriggend N Lans 82 G4
Long Riston E R Yk 65 R11
Longrock Cnwll 2 D10
Longsdon Staffs 46 B2
Longshaw Wigan 55 N6
Longside Abers 105 T6
Long Sight Oldham 56 D5
Longslow Shrops 45 P6
Longstanton Cambs 39 N8
Longstock Hants 19 N12
Longstone Pembks 24 K8
Longstowe Cambs 39 M10
Long Stratton Norfk 41 L2
Long Street M Keyn 30 G4
Long Sutton Hants 20 B13
Long Sutton Lincs 49 P9
Long Sutton Somset 17 N11
Longthorpe C Pete 38 J1
Long Thurlow Suffk 40 J7
Longthwaite Cumb 67 P8
Longton Lancs 55 L1
Longton C Stke 46 B5
Longtown Cumb 75 T12
Longtown Herefs 27 Q2
Longville in the Dale Shrops 35 M1
Long Waste Wrekin 45 P10
Long Whatton Leics 47 N9
Longwick Bucks 30 F12
Long Wittenham Oxon 19 S2
Longwitton Nthumb 77 M8
Longwood D & G 74 H11
Longworth Oxon 29 S8
Longyester E Loth 84 E5

Lôn-las Swans 26 C8
Lonmay Abers 105 S4
Lonmore Highld 100 b5
Loose Kent 12 E5
Loosebeare Devon 15 R11
Loosegate Lincs 49 M8
Loosley Row Bucks 30 H12
Lootcherbrae Abers 104 J5
Lopcombe Corner Wilts 19 L13
Lopen Somset 7 N2
Loppington Shrops 45 L8
Lorbottle Nthumb 77 L5
Lordington W Susx 10 B9
Lords Wood Medway 12 E3
Lornty P & K 90 H2
Loscoe Derbys 47 M4
Loscombe Dorset 7 N5
Losgaintir W Isls 106 f9
Lossiemouth Moray 104 A1
Lostford Shrops 45 P7
Lostock Gralam Ches W 55 Q12
Lostock Green Ches W 55 Q12
Lostock Hall Lancs 55 M1
Lostock Hall Fold Bolton 55 R5
Lostock Junction Bolton 55 Q5
Lostwithiel Cnwll 3 R5
Lothbeg Highld 109 S2
Lothersdale N York 62 K10
Lothmore Highld 109 T2
Loudwater Bucks 20 F4
Loughborough Leics 47 P10
Loughor Swans 25 U11
Loughton Essex 21 R3
Loughton M Keyn 30 H5
Loughton Shrops 35 P4
Lound Lincs 48 G11
Lound Notts 57 U10
Lound Suffk 51 T14
Lounston Devon 5 T5
Louth Lincs 59 Q9
Lovedean Hants 9 T6
Lover Wilts 8 K4
Loversall Donc 57 S7
Loves Green Essex 22 F6
Lovesome Hill N York 70 D13
Loveston Pembks 24 H9
Lovington Somset 17 Q10
Low Ackworth Wakefd 57 Q3
Low Angerton Nthumb 77 M9
Lowbands Gloucs 28 E1
Low Barbeth D & G 72 C6
Low Barlings Lincs 58 J12
Low Bell End N York 71 N14
Low Bentham N York 62 C6
Low Biggins W & F 62 C4
Low Borrowbridge W & F 68 D12
Low Bradfield Sheff 57 L8
Low Bradley N York 62 K10
Low Braithwaite W & F 67 P4
Low Burnham N Linc 58 C5
Low Buston Nthumb 77 Q4
Lowca Cumb 66 E8
Low Catton E R Yk 64 G9
Low Coniscliffe Darltn 69 S10
Low Crosby Cumb 75 U14
Low Dinsdale Darltn 70 D10
Lowe Shrops 45 L7
Low Ellington N York 63 Q3
Lower Aisholt Somset 16 H9
Lower Ansty Dorset 7 U4
Lower Apperley Gloucs 28 G2
Lower Arboll Highld 109 R9
Lower Arncott Oxon 30 D9
Lower Ashton Devon 5 U3
Lower Assendon Oxon 20 B6
Lower Badcall Highld 110 D6
Lower Ballam Lancs 61 R13
Lower Bartle Lancs 61 T13
Lower Basildon W Berk 19 U5
Lower Bearwood Herefs 34 K9
Lower Beeding W Susx 11 L5
Lower Benefield N Nthn 38 E3
Lower Bentley Worcs 36 C7
Lower Bentham N York
Lower Beobridge Shrops 35 S2
Lower Birchwood Derbys 47 M3
Lower Boddington W Nthn 37 N10
Lower Boscaswell Cnwll 2 B11
Lower Bourne Surrey 10 C2
Lower Brailes Warwks 36 K13
Lower Breakish Highld 100 f7
Lower Bredbury Stockp 56 D8
Lower Broadheath Worcs 35 T9
Lower Buckenhill Herefs 35 N13
Lower Bullingham Herefs 35 M13
Lower Bullington Hants 19 Q12
Lower Burgate Hants 8 H5
Lower Burrowton Devon 6 D5
Lower Burton Herefs 34 K10
Lower Caldecote C Beds 38 J11
Lower Cam Gloucs 28 D7
Lower Canada N Som 17 L4
Lower Catesby W Nthn 37 P9
Lower Chapel Powys 34 B13
Lower Chicksgrove Wilts 8 D3
Lower Chute Wilts 19 L10
Lower Clapton Gt Lon 21 P6
Lower Clent Worcs 36 B5
Lower Common Hants 20 B10
Lower Creedy Devon 15 T12
Lower Crossings Derbys 56 F9
Lower Cumberworth Kirk 56 K5
Lower Darwen Bl w D 55 Q1
Lower Dean Bed 38 G7
Lower Denby Kirk 56 K5
Lower Diabaig Highld 107 P13
Lower Dicker E Susx 11 T8
Lower Dinchope Shrops 34 K4
Lower Down Shrops 34 H4
Lower Dunsforth N York 63 U7
Lower Egleton Herefs 35 P12
Lower Elkstone Staffs 46 D2
Lower Ellastone Staffs 46 F5
Lower End Bucks 30 C8
Lower End M Keyn 30 K7
Lower Everleigh Wilts 18 J10
Lower Exbury Hants 9 P9
Lower Eythorne Kent 13 Q6
Lower Failand N Som 27 U13
Lower Farringdon Hants 19 V13
Lower Feltham Gt Lon 20 K8
Lower Fittleworth W Susx 10 G6
Lower Foxdale IoM 60 d7
Lower Frankton Shrops 44 H7
Lower Freystrop Pembks 24 G8
Lower Froyle Hants 19 V13
Lower Gabwell Devon 6 B11
Lower Gledfield Highld 108 K6
Lower Godney Somset 17 N8
Lower Gornal Dudley 36 B2
Lower Gravenhurst C Beds 31 Q5
Lower Green Herts 31 U6
Lower Green Herts 39 M14
Lower Green Kent 11 T3
Lower Green Kent 12 B7
Lower Green Norfk 50 G6
Lower Green Staffs 46 B12
Lower Green Suffk 40 D7
Lower Halstock Leigh Dorset 7 P3
Lower Halstow Kent 12 F2
Lower Hamworthy BCP 8 D10
Lower Hardres Kent 13 N5
Lower Hardwick Herefs 34 K10
Lower Hartlip Kent 12 F3
Lower Hartshay Derbys 47 L3
Lower Hartwell Bucks 30 G10
Lower Hawthwaite Cumb 61 N2
Lower Haysden Kent 21 U13
Lower Hayton Shrops 35 M4
Lower Hergest Herefs 34 G10
Lower Heyford Oxon 29 U3
Lower Heysham Lancs 61 S8
Lower Higham Kent 22 H13
Lower Holbrook Suffk 40 K14
Lower Hordley Shrops 44 J8
Lower Horncroft W Susx 10 G6
Lower Horsebridge E Susx 11 T8
Lower Houses Kirk 56 J4
Lower Howsell Worcs 35 S11
Lower Irlam Salfd 55 R7
Lower Kilburn Derbys 47 L5
Lower Kilcott Gloucs 28 E9
Lower Killeyan Ag & B 78 C6
Lower Kingcombe Dorset 7 P4
Lower Kingswood Surrey 21 M12
Lower Kinnerton Ches W 54 H14
Lower Langford N Som 17 N4
Lower Largo Fife 91 Q11
Lower Leigh Staffs 46 D6
Lower Lemington Gloucs 36 H14
Lower Loxhore Devon 15 P5
Lower Lovacott Devon 15 N7
Lower Lydbrook Gloucs 28 A4

Lower Lye Herefs 34 K7
Lower Machen Newpt 27 N10
Lower Maes-coed Herefs 27 Q1
Lower Mannington Dorset 8 F8
Lower Marston Somset 17 U8
Lower Meend Gloucs 27 U6
Lower Merridge Somset 16 H10
Lower Middleton Cheney W Nthn 30 B4
Lower Milton Somset 17 P8
Lower Moor Worcs 36 C11
Lower Morton S Glos 28 B9
Lower Nazeing Essex 31 U11
Lower Norton Warwks 36 H8
Lower Nyland Dorset 17 U12
Lower Oddington Gloucs 29 N2
Lower Ollach Highld 100 e6
Lower Penarth V Glam 16 G3
Lower Penn Staffs 35 U1
Lower Pennington Hants 9 L9
Lower Penwortham Lancs 55 L1
Lower Peover Ches E 55 R12
Lower Place Rochdl 56 D4
Lower Pollicott Bucks 30 F10
Lower Quinton Warwks 36 G11
Lower Rainham Medway 12 F2
Lower Raydon Suffk 40 H13
Lower Roadwater Somset 16 D9
Lower Salter Lancs 62 C7
Lower Seagry Wilts 18 E4
Lower Shelton C Beds 31 L4
Lower Sheering Essex 22 C5
Lower Shiplake Oxon 20 C7
Lower Shuckburgh Warwks 37 N8
Lower Slaughter Gloucs 29 M3
Lower Soothill Kirk 57 L2
Lower Soudley Gloucs 28 C6
Lower Standen Kent 13 P7
Lower Stanton St Quintin Wilts 18 D4
Lower Stoke Medway 22 K13
Lower Stondon C Beds 31 Q5
Lower Stonnall Staffs 46 E13
Lower Stow Bedon Norfk 40 F1
Lower Street E Susx 12 D13
Lower Street Norfk 51 N6
Lower Street Suffk 40 K10
Lower Stretton Warrtn 55 P10
Lower Stroud Dorset 7 N4
Lower Sundon C Beds 31 N7
Lower Swanwick Hants 9 P7
Lower Swell Gloucs 29 N3
Lower Tadmarton Oxon 37 M13
Lower Tale Devon 6 E4
Lower Tasburgh Norfk 41 L1
Lower Tean Staffs 46 D6
Lower Thurlton Norfk 51 R14
Lower Town Cnwll 2 H11
Lower Town Devon 5 S6
Lower Town Herefs 35 P12
Lower Town Pembks 24 G3
Lower Trebullett Cnwll 4 J6
Lower Treluswell Cnwll 2 K9
Lower Tregantle Cnwll 4 K9
Lower Tysoe Warwks 36 K11
Lower Ufford Suffk 41 N10
Lower Upcott Devon 5 V3
Lower Upham Hants 9 Q5
Lower Upnor Medway 22 J13
Lower Vexford Somset 16 F9
Lower Walton Warrtn 55 P9
Lower Waterston Dorset 7 T5
Lower Weare Somset 17 M6
Lower Weedon W Nthn 37 Q9
Lower Welson Herefs 34 G10
Lower Westmancote Worcs 36 B13
Lower Whatcombe Dorset 8 B8
Lower Whatley Somset 17 T7
Lower Whitley Ches W 55 P11
Lower Wick Gloucs 28 D8
Lower Wick Worcs 35 T10
Lower Wield Hants 19 T12
Lower Willingdon E Susx 11 T10
Lower Withington Ches E 55 T13
Lower Woodend Bucks 20 D5
Lower Woodford Wilts 8 G2
Lower Wraxall Dorset 7 Q4
Lower Wyche Worcs 35 S12
Lower Wyke C Brad 63 P14

Ludgershall Wilts 19 L10
Ludgershall Bucks 30 D9
Ludgvan Cnwll 2 D10
Ludham Norfk 51 Q10
Ludlow Shrops 35 M5
Ludney Somset 7 L2
Ludwell Wilts 8 C4
Ludworth Dur 70 E4
Luffenhall Herts 31 S7
Luffincott Devon 4 J2
Luffness E Loth 84 D2
Lugar E Ayrs 81 R7
Luggate Burn E Loth 84 G4
Lugg Green Herefs 34 K8
Luggiebank N Lans 89 S11
Lugton E Ayrs 81 N2
Lugwardine Herefs 35 M12
Luib Highld 100 e7
Luing Ag & B 87 P4
Lulham Herefs 34 K12
Lullington Derbys 46 J11
Lullington E Susx 11 S10
Lullington Somset 17 U6
Lulsgate Bottom N Som 17 P3
Lumb Calder 56 F2
Lumb Lancs 55 T2
Lumby N York 64 B13
Lumloch E Duns 89 P11
Lumphanan Abers 98 K2
Lumphinnans Fife 90 J13
Lumsden Abers 104 F11
Lunan Angus 98 H13
Lunanhead Angus 98 H13
Luncarty P & K 90 F6
Lund E R Yk 65 M10
Lund N York 64 F13
Lundie Angus 91 L4
Lundie Stirlg 89 M5
Lundin Links Fife 91 Q11
Lundin Mill Fife 91 Q11
Lunna Shet 106 u7
Lunsford Kent 12 D4
Lunsford's Cross E Susx 12 D13
Lunt Sefton 54 H6
Luntley Herefs 34 J9
Luppitt Devon 6 G4
Lupridge Devon 5 S10
Lupset Wakefd 57 M3
Lupton W & F 62 B3
Lurgashall W Susx 10 E5
Lurley Devon 16 C13
Luscombe Devon 5 T9
Luss Ag & B 88 H6
Lussagiven Ag & B 87 L8
Lusta Highld 100 b4
Lustleigh Devon 5 T4
Luston Herefs 35 L8
Luthermuir Abers 99 M10
Luthrie Fife 91 M8
Lutley Dudley 36 B4
Luton Devon 6 B9
Luton Devon 6 E4
Luton Luton 31 P8
Luton Medway 12 E3
Luton Airport Luton 31 P8
Lutterworth Leics 37 P4
Lutton Devon 5 P8
Lutton Devon 5 Q10
Lutton Lincs 49 P9
Lutton N Nthn 38 H3
Luxborough Somset 16 C9
Luxley Gloucs 28 C3
Luxulyan Cnwll 3 Q5
Luzley Tamesd 56 E7
Lybster Highld 112 F9
Lydbury North Shrops 34 H3
Lydcott Devon 15 Q5
Lydd Kent 13 L11
Lydd Airport Kent 13 L11
Lydden Kent 13 Q6
Lydden Kent 13 S3
Lyddington Rutlnd 38 B1
Lyde Green Hants 20 B10
Lydeard St Lawrence Somset 16 F10
Lydford Devon 5 N4
Lydford on Fosse Somset 17 Q10
Lydgate Calder 56 E2
Lydgate Rochdl 56 E5
Lydham Shrops 34 H2
Lydiard Green Wilts 29 L10
Lydiard Millicent Wilts 29 L10
Lydiard Tregoze Swindn 29 M11
Lydiate Sefton 54 J6
Lydiate Ash Worcs 36 C6
Lydlinch Dorset 7 T2
Lydstep Pembks 24 J10
Lye Dudley 36 B4
Lye Cross N Som 17 N4
Lye Green Bucks 30 K12
Lye Green E Susx 11 T4
Lye Green Warwks 36 G7
Lye Head Worcs 35 S6
Lye's Green Wilts 18 B11
Lyford Oxon 29 S8
Lymbridge Green Kent 13 M7
Lyme Regis Dorset 6 K6
Lyminge Kent 13 N7
Lymington Hants 9 L9
Lyminster W Susx 10 G10
Lymm Warrtn 55 Q9
Lymore Hants 8 K10
Lympne Kent 13 M8
Lympsham Somset 16 K6
Lympstone Devon 6 C7
Lynbridge Devon 15 R3
Lynch Somset 15 U3
Lynch Green Norfk 51 L12
Lyndhurst Hants 9 L7
Lyndon Rutlnd 48 D13
Lyne Border 83 P11
Lyne Surrey 20 H9
Lyne Down Herefs 35 Q14
Lyneal Shrops 44 K7
Lyneham Oxon 29 Q4
Lyneham Wilts 18 F5
Lyneholmeford Cumb 76 B12
Lynemore Highld 103 R10
Lynemouth Nthumb 77 S8
Lyne of Skene Abers 105 M13
Lynesack Dur 69 N7
Lyness Ork 106 r20
Lyng Norfk 50 J10
Lyng Somset 16 K11
Lyngate Norfk 51 N7
Lynmouth Devon 15 R3
Lynn of Shenval Moray 103 U10
Lynsted Kent 12 H3
Lynstone Cnwll 14 F11
Lynton Devon 15 R3
Lyon's Gate Dorset 7 S3
Lyonshall Herefs 34 H10
Lytchett Matravers Dorset 8 C9
Lytchett Minster Dorset 8 C10
Lyth Highld 112 G4
Lytham Lancs 61 R14
Lytham St Annes Lancs 61 Q14
Lythbank Shrops 45 L12
Lythe N York 71 P10
Lythmore Highld 112 C3

M

Maaruig W Isls 106 h8
Mabe Burnthouse Cnwll 2 K10
Mablethorpe Lincs 59 T10
Macclesfield Ches E 56 D12
Macclesfield Forest Ches E 56 E12
Macduff Abers 105 L3
Macharioch Ag & B 79 Q14
Machan S Lans 82 E8
Machen Caerph 27 N10
Machrie N Ayrs 79 R8
Machrihanish Ag & B 79 L13
Machrins Ag & B 86 F7
Machynlleth Powys 43 P13
Machynys Carmth 25 T10
Mackworth Derbys 46 K6
Macmerry E Loth 84 D4
Madderty P & K 90 D7
Maddington Wilts 18 G12
Maddiston Falk 82 H3
Madehurst W Susx 10 F8
Madeley Staffs 45 S4
Madeley Wrekin 45 Q13
Madeley Heath Staffs 45 S4
Madeley Park Wood Staffs 45 S5
Madford Devon 6 F3
Madingley Cambs 39 N8
Madley Herefs 34 K13
Madresfield Worcs 35 T11
Madron Cnwll 2 C10
Maenaddwyn IoA 52 G5

Maenan Conwy 53 N9
Maenclochog Pembks 24 J5
Maendy V Glam 26 J12
Maenporth Cnwll 2 K11
Maentwrog Gwynd 43 N5
Maen-y-groes Cerdgn 32 G9
Maer Cnwll 14 F11
Maer Staffs 45 S6
Maerdy Carmth 26 B2
Maerdy Conwy 44 B5
Maerdy Rhondd 26 H8
Maesbrook Shrops 44 H9
Maesbury Shrops 44 H8
Maesbury Marsh Shrops 44 H8
Maes-glas Newpt 27 P10
Maesgwynne Carmth 25 M6
Maeshafn Denbgs 44 F1
Maesllyn Cerdgn 32 G12
Maesmynis Powys 34 B11
Maesmynis Powys 34 B11
Maesteg Brdgnd 26 F9
Maesybont Carmth 25 U7
Maesycwmmer Caerph 27 M9
Magdalen Laver Essex 22 D6
Maggieknockater Moray 104 C6
Maggots End Essex 22 C2
Magham Down E Susx 11 U8
Maghull Sefton 54 J6
Magna Park Leics 37 P4
Magor Mons 27 S10
Magor Services Mons 27 S10
Maidenbower W Susx 11 M3
Maiden Bradley Wilts 18 B13
Maidencombe Torbay 6 B11
Maidenhayne Devon 6 J5
Maiden Head N Som 17 Q3
Maidenhead W & M 20 E6
Maiden Law Dur 69 Q3
Maiden Newton Dorset 7 Q5
Maidens S Ayrs 80 J11
Maiden's Green Br For 20 F8
Maidenwell Lincs 59 P11
Maiden Wells Pembks 24 G11
Maidford W Nthn 37 R10
Maids Moreton Bucks 30 F5
Maidstone Kent 12 E4
Maidstone Services Kent 12 F4
Maidwell W Nthn 37 T5
Mail Shet 106 u9
Maindee Newpt 27 Q10
Mainland Ork 106 t19
Mainland Shet 106 u8
Mainsforth Dur 70 D6
Mains of Balhall Angus 98 J11
Mains of Balnakettle Abers 99 L9
Mains of Dalvey Highld 103 T9
Mains of Haulkerton Abers 99 N9
Mains of Lesmoir Abers 104 F10
Mains of Melgunds Angus 98 J12
Mainsriddle D & G 66 D1
Mainstone Shrops 34 G3
Maisemore Gloucs 28 F3
Major's Green Worcs 36 F5
Makeney Derbys 47 L5
Malborough Devon 5 S13
Malcoff Derbys 56 G10
Malden Rushett Gt Lon 21 L10
Maldon Essex 22 L6
Malham N York 62 J7
Maligar Highld 100 d3
Mallaig Highld 100 f10
Mallaigvaig Highld 100 f10
Malleny Mills C Edin 83 N5
Mallows Green Essex 22 C2
Malltraeth IoA 52 F9
Mallwyd Gwynd 43 S11
Malmesbury Wilts 28 H10
Malmsmead Devon 15 S3
Malpas Ches W 45 L4
Malpas Cnwll 3 L8
Malpas Newpt 27 Q9
Malshanger Hants 19 S10
Malswick Gloucs 28 D3
Maltby Lincs 59 P10
Maltby Rothm 57 R8
Maltby S on T 70 G10
Maltby le Marsh Lincs 59 S10
Malting Green Essex 23 N3
Maltman's Hill Kent 12 H7
Malton N York 64 H5
Malvern Worcs 35 S11
Malvern Hills 35 S12
Malvern Link Worcs 35 S11
Malvern Wells Worcs 35 S12
Mamble Worcs 35 Q6
Mamhilad Mons 27 Q7
Manaccan Cnwll 2 K12
Manafon Powys 44 D13
Mànais W Isls 106 g10
Manaton Devon 5 T4
Manby Lincs 59 Q9
Mancetter Warwks 36 K1
Manchester Manch 55 T7
Manchester Airport Manch 55 T10
Mancot Flints 54 H13
Mandally Highld 96 B3
Manea Cambs 39 Q3
Maney Birm 36 F1
Manfield N York 69 R10
Mangersta W Isls 106 f5
Mangerton Dorset 7 N5
Mangotsfield S Glos 28 C12
Mangrove Green Herts 31 P8
Mangurstadh W Isls 106 f5
Manhay Cnwll 2 H10
Manish W Isls 106 g10
Mankinholes Calder 56 E2
Manley Ches W 55 M12
Manmoel Caerph 27 M7
Mannal Ag & B 92 B10
Manningford Bohune Wilts 18 H9
Manningford Bruce Wilts 18 H9
Manningham C Brad 63 N12
Mannings Heath W Susx 11 L5
Mannington Dorset 8 F7
Manningtree Essex 23 R1
Mannofield C Aber 99 S3
Manorbier Pembks 24 J11
Manorbier Newton Pembks 24 H10
Manordeilo Carmth 26 B2
Manorhill Border 84 H12
Manorowen Pembks 24 F3
Manor Park Gt Lon 21 R5
Mansell Gamage Herefs 34 J12
Mansell Lacy Herefs 34 K11
Mansergh W & F 62 C3
Mansfield E Ayrs 81 S10
Mansfield Notts 47 P1
Mansfield Woodhouse Notts 57 R14
Mansriggs W & F 61 P3
Manston Dorset 17 V13
Manston Kent 13 R2
Manston Leeds 63 T13
Manswood Dorset 8 D7
Manthorpe Lincs 48 D6
Manthorpe Lincs 48 G10
Manton N Linc 58 F6
Manton Notts 57 T11
Manton Rutlnd 48 C13
Manton Wilts 18 J7
Manuden Essex 22 C2
Manwood Green Essex 22 D5
Maperton Somset 17 S11
Maplebeck Notts 47 T1
Maple Cross Herts 20 H4
Mapledurham Oxon 19 U5
Mapledurwell Hants 19 U10
Maplehurst W Susx 10 K6
Maplescombe Kent 21 U10
Mapleton Derbys 46 G4
Mapleton Kent 21 S13
Mapperley Derbys 47 M5
Mapperley Park C Nott 47 Q5
Mapperton Dorset 7 P5
Mappleborough Green Warwks 36 E7
Mappleton E R Yk 65 S11
Mapplewell Barns 57 M4
Mappowder Dorset 7 T3
Màraig W Isls 106 h8
Marazanvose Cnwll 2 K6
Marazion Cnwll 2 E10
Marbhig W Isls 106 j7
Marbury Ches E 45 N4
March Cambs 39 P1
March S Lans 74 J3
Marcham Oxon 29 U8
Marchamley Shrops 45 N8
Marchamley Wood Shrops 45 N7
Marchington Staffs 46 F7
Marchington Woodlands Staffs 46 F8
Marchwiel Wrexhm 44 J4
Marchwood Hants 9 M6
Marcross V Glam 16 B3
Marden Herefs 35 M11
Marden Kent 12 D7
Marden Wilts 18 G9
Marden Ash Essex 22 E7
Marden Beech Kent 12 D7
Marden's Hill E Susx 11 S4
Marden Thorn Kent 12 E7
Mardlebury Herts 31 S9
Mardy Mons 27 Q4
Marefield Leics 47 T12
Mareham le Fen Lincs 49 L1
Mareham on the Hill Lincs 59 N13
Marehay Derbys 47 L4
Marehill W Susx 10 H7
Maresfield E Susx 11 R6
Marfleet C KuH 65 Q14
Marford Wrexhm 44 J2
Margam Neath 26 D10
Margaret Marsh Dorset 17 V13
Margaret Roding Essex 22 E5
Margaretting Essex 22 G7
Margaretting Tye Essex 22 G7
Margate Kent 13 S1
Margnaheglish N Ayrs 80 E6
Margrie D & G 73 P9
Margrove Park R & Cl 71 L9
Marham Norfk 50 B12
Marhamchurch Cnwll 14 F12
Marham Park Suffk 40 D7
Marholm C Pete 48 H13
Marian-glas IoA 52 H6
Mariansleigh Devon 15 R8
Marine Town Kent 23 M13
Marionburgh Abers 99 N2
Marishader Highld 100 d3
Maristow Devon 5 M8
Marjoriebanks D & G 75 L9
Mark Somset 17 L7
Markbeech Kent 11 R2
Markby Lincs 59 S11
Mark Causeway Somset 17 L7
Mark Cross E Susx 11 T4
Markeaton C Derb 46 K6
Market Bosworth Leics 47 M13
Market Deeping Lincs 48 H11
Market Drayton Shrops 45 Q7
Market Harborough Leics 37 T3
Market Lavington Wilts 18 F10
Market Overton Rutlnd 48 C10
Market Rasen Lincs 58 K9
Market Stainton Lincs 59 M11
Market Warsop Notts 57 S13
Market Weighton E R Yk 64 K11
Market Weston Suffk 40 G5
Markfield Leics 47 N12
Markham Caerph 27 M7
Markham Moor Notts 58 B12
Markinch Fife 91 L11
Markington N York 63 R6
Markle E Loth 84 F3
Marksbury BaNES 17 S4
Mark's Corner IoW 9 P10
Marks Tey Essex 23 M3
Markwell Cnwll 4 K9
Markyate Herts 31 N9
Marlborough Wilts 18 J7
Marlbrook Herefs 35 M10
Marlbrook Worcs 36 C6
Marlcliff Warwks 36 E10
Marldon Devon 5 V8
Marle Green E Susx 11 T7
Marlesford Suffk 41 P9
Marley Kent 13 N5
Marley Kent 13 R5
Marley Green Ches E 45 N4
Marley Hill Gatesd 77 Q14
Marlingford Norfk 50 K12
Marloes Pembks 24 C9
Marlow Bucks 20 D5
Marlow Herefs 34 K5
Marlow Bottom Bucks 20 D5
Marlpit Hill Kent 21 R13
Marlpits E Susx 11 R5
Marlpits E Susx 12 D13
Marlpool Derbys 47 M4
Marnhull Dorset 17 U13
Marple Stockp 56 E9
Marple Bridge Stockp 56 E9
Marr Donc 57 R5
Marrick N York 69 N13
Marros Carmth 25 M9
Marsden Kirk 56 F4
Marsden S Tyne 77 T13
Marsden Height Lancs 62 H12
Marsett N York 62 J2
Marsh Bucks 30 H11
Marsh C Brad 63 L12
Marsh Devon 6 J2
Marshall's Heath Herts 31 Q10
Marshalswick Herts 31 Q11
Marsham Norfk 51 L9
Marsh Baldon Oxon 30 C13
Marsh Benham W Berk 19 P7
Marshborough Kent 13 R4
Marshbrook Shrops 34 K3
Marshchapel Lincs 59 Q7
Marsh Farm Luton 31 N7
Marshfield Newpt 27 P11
Marshfield S Glos 28 E13
Marshgate Cnwll 4 F2
Marsh Gibbon Bucks 30 D8
Marsh Green Devon 6 D6
Marsh Green Kent 11 Q2
Marsh Green Wrekin 45 P11
Marshland St James Norfk 49 R12
Marsh Lane Derbys 57 P11
Marsh Lane Gloucs 28 A6
Marshside Sefton 54 J3
Marsh Street Somset 16 C8
Marshwood Dorset 7 L5
Marske N York 69 P12
Marske-by-the-Sea R & Cl 70 K8
Marsland Green Wigan 55 Q7
Marston Ches W 55 Q11
Marston Herefs 34 J9
Marston Lincs 48 C5
Marston Oxon 30 B11
Marston Staffs 45 T11
Marston Staffs 46 B8
Marston Warwks 36 H2
Marston Wilts 18 E9
Marston Green Solhll 36 G3
Marston Jabbet Warwks 37 L3
Marston Magna Somset 17 Q12
Marston Meysey Wilts 29 M8
Marston Montgomery Derbys 46 F6
Marston Moretaine C Beds 31 L4
Marston on Dove Derbys 46 H8
Marston St Lawrence W Nthn 30 B4
Marston Stannett Herefs 35 N9
Marston Trussell W Nthn 37 S3
Marstow Herefs 27 V4
Marsworth Bucks 30 K10
Marten Wilts 19 L8
Marthall Ches E 55 S11
Martham Norfk 51 S10
Martin Hants 8 F5
Martin Kent 13 R6
Martin Lincs 48 H2
Martin Lincs 59 M13
Martindale W & F 67 P9
Martin Dales Lincs 48 J1
Martin Drove End Hants 8 F4
Martinhoe Devon 15 Q3
Martin Hussingtree Worcs 35 U8
Martinscroft Warrtn 55 Q9
Martinstown Dorset 7 R7
Martlesham Suffk 41 M11
Martlesham Heath Suffk 41 M11
Martletwy Pembks 24 H8
Martley Worcs 35 S8
Martock Somset 17 N13
Marton Ches E 56 C13
Marton Ches W 55 P13
Marton E R Yk 65 R12
Marton E R Yk 65 S6
Marton Lincs 58 D10
Marton Middsb 70 H9
Marton N York 64 G3
Marton Shrops 44 G13
Marton W & F 61 N4
Marton Warwks 37 M7
Marton-cum-Grafton N York 63 U7
Marton-le-Moor N York 63 T5
Martyr's Green Surrey 20 J11
Martyr Worthy Hants 9 Q2
Marvig W Isls 106 j7
Marwell Zoo Hants 9 Q4
Marwick Ork 106 r17
Marwood Devon 15 M5
Marybank Highld 102 E5
Maryburgh Highld 102 F4
Marygold Border 85 L7
Maryhill C Glas 89 N12
Marykirk Abers 99 M10
Maryland Mons 27 U6
Marylebone Gt Lon 21 N6
Marylebone Wigan 55 N5
Marypark Moray 103 U8
Maryport Cumb 66 F5
Maryport D & G 72 E13
Marystow Devon 5 L4
Mary Tavy Devon 5 N5
Maryton Angus 98 F13
Maryton Angus 99 M12
Marywell Abers 98 K4
Marywell Abers 99 S4
Marywell Angus 91 U3
Masham N York 63 Q3
Mashbury Essex 22 G5
Masongill N York 62 D4
Mastin Moor Derbys 57 Q11
Matching Essex 22 D5
Matching Green Essex 22 D5
Matching Tye Essex 22 D5
Matfen Nthumb 77 L11
Matfield Kent 12 C7
Mathern Mons 27 U9
Mathon Herefs 35 R11
Mathry Pembks 24 E4
Matlask Norfk 51 L7
Matlock Derbys 46 K2
Matlock Bank Derbys 46 K1
Matlock Bath Derbys 46 J2
Matlock Dale Derbys 46 J2
Matson Gloucs 28 G4
Matterdale End W & F 67 N8
Mattersey Notts 57 U9
Mattersey Thorpe Notts 57 U9
Mattingley Hants 20 B11
Mattishall Norfk 50 J11
Mattishall Burgh Norfk 50 J11
Mauchline E Ayrs 81 P7
Maud Abers 105 Q6
Maufant Jersey 7 e2
Maugersbury Gloucs 29 P2
Maughold IoM 60 h4
Mauld Highld 102 D8
Maulden C Beds 31 N5
Maulds Meaburn W & F 68 D9
Maunby N York 63 T2
Maund Bryan Herefs 35 N10
Maundown Somset 16 E11
Mautby Norfk 51 S11
Mavesyn Ridware Staffs 46 E10
Mavis Enderby Lincs 59 Q13
Mawbray Cumb 66 G3
Mawdesley Lancs 55 L4
Mawdlam Brdgnd 26 E11
Mawgan Cnwll 2 J11
Mawgan Porth Cnwll 3 M3
Maw Green Ches E 45 R2
Mawla Cnwll 2 J7
Mawnan Cnwll 2 K11
Mawnan Smith Cnwll 2 K11
Mawsley W Nthn 38 B5
Mawthorpe Lincs 59 S12
Maxey C Pete 48 H12
Maxstoke Warwks 36 H3
Maxted Street Kent 13 M7
Maxton Border 84 G12
Maxton Kent 13 R7
Maxwelltown D & G 74 J10
Maxworthy Cnwll 4 H2
Mayals Swans 25 V13
May Bank Staffs 45 U4
Maybole S Ayrs 80 K11
Maybury Surrey 20 H11
Mayes Green Surrey 10 J3
Mayfield E Susx 11 T5
Mayfield Mdloth 83 S5
Mayfield Staffs 46 G4
Mayford Surrey 20 G11
May Hill Gloucs 28 D3
Mayland Essex 23 M7
Maylandsea Essex 23 M7
Maynard's Green E Susx 11 T7
Maypole Birm 36 E5
Maypole Kent 13 P3
Maypole Mons 27 T4
Maypole Green Norfk 41 R1
Maypole Green Suffk 40 F9
Maypole Green Suffk 41 N7
May's Green Oxon 20 B6
May's Green Surrey 20 J11
Mead Devon 14 F9
Meadgate BaNES 17 S5
Meadle Bucks 30 H11
Meadowfield Dur 69 R5
Meadowtown Shrops 44 H13
Meadwell Devon 5 L4
Meaford Staffs 45 U6
Mealabost W Isls 106 j5
Meal Bank W & F 67 R13
Mealrigg Cumb 66 H3
Mealsgate Cumb 66 K4
Meanwood Leeds 63 R12
Mearbeck N York 62 G7
Meare Somset 17 N8
Meare Green Somset 16 J12
Meare Green Somset 16 K11
Mearns E Rens 81 Q1
Mears Ashby N Nthn 38 B7
Measham Leics 46 K11
Meath Green Surrey 11 M2
Meathop W & F 61 S3
Meaux E R Yk 65 P12
Meavaig W Isls 106 f5
Meavy Devon 5 N7
Medbourne Leics 38 B2
Medburn Nthumb 77 N11
Meddon Devon 14 G9
Meden Vale Notts 57 S13
Medlam Lincs 49 M2
Medlar Lancs 61 S12
Medmenham Bucks 20 D6
Medomsley Dur 69 P2
Medstead Hants 19 U13
Medway Services Medway 12 F3
Meerbrook Staffs 46 C1
Meer Common Herefs 34 J10
Meesden Herts 22 B1
Meeson Wrekin 45 P9
Meeth Devon 15 M11
Meeting Green Suffk 40 B9
Meeting House Hill Norfk 51 P8
Meidrim Carmth 25 N6
Meifod Powys 44 E11
Meigle P & K 91 L3
Meikle Carco D & G 74 E3
Meikle Earnock S Lans 82 D8
Meikle Ferry Highld 109 N7
Meikle Kilmory Ag & B 88 C13
Meikle Obney P & K 90 F4
Meikleour P & K 90 J4
Meikle Wartle Abers 105 L9
Meinciau Carmth 25 S8
Meir C Stke 46 B5
Meir Heath Staffs 46 B5
Melbost W Isls 106 j5
Melbourn Cambs 31 U4
Melbourne Derbys 47 L8
Melbourne E R Yk 64 H11
Melbourne Essex 22 G6
Melbur Cnwll 3 N6
Melbury Devon 14 J9
Melbury Abbas Dorset 8 B4
Melbury Bubb Dorset 7 Q3
Melbury Osmond Dorset 7 Q3
Melbury Sampford Dorset 7 Q3
Melchbourne Bed 38 F7
Melcombe Bingham Dorset 7 U4
Meldon Devon 5 P2
Meldon Nthumb 77 N9
Meldon Park Nthumb 77 N8
Meldreth Cambs 39 N11
Meldrum Stirlg 89 R6
Melfort Ag & B 87 Q3
Meliden Denbgs 54 C10
Melinau Pembks 25 L8
Melin-byrhedyn Powys 43 R14
Melincourt Neath 26 E7
Melin-y-coed Conwy 53 P10
Melin-y-ddol Powys 44 C12
Melin-y-wîg Denbgs 44 B4
Melkinthorpe W & F 67 S7
Melkridge Nthumb 76 E13
Melksham Wilts 18 D8
Mellangoose Cnwll 2 H11
Mell Green W Berk 19 Q5
Mellguards W & F 67 P3
Melling Lancs 62 B5
Melling Sefton 54 J6
Melling Mount Sefton 54 K6
Mellis Suffk 40 J6
Mellon Charles Highld 107 P6
Mellon Udrigle Highld 107 Q5
Mellor Lancs 62 D13
Mellor Stockp 56 E9
Mellor Brook Lancs 62 C13
Mells Somset 17 T7
Mells Suffk 41 R5
Melmerby N York 63 M2
Melmerby N York 63 S4
Melmerby W & F 68 D5
Melness Highld 111 M4
Melon Green Suffk 40 D9
Melplash Dorset 7 N5
Melrose Border 84 E12
Melsetter Ork 106 r21
Melsonby N York 69 Q11
Meltham Kirk 56 H4
Meltham Mills Kirk 56 H4
Melton E R Yk 58 G1
Melton Suffk 41 N10
Meltonby E R Yk 64 H9
Melton Constable Norfk 50 H7
Melton Mowbray Leics 47 U10
Melton Ross N Linc 58 J4
Melvaig Highld 107 M7
Melverley Shrops 44 H10
Melverley Green Shrops 44 H10
Melvich Highld 111 T4
Membury Devon 6 J4
Membury Services W Berk 19 M5
Memsie Abers 105 R3
Memus Angus 98 G12
Menabilly Cnwll 3 R6
Menagissey Cnwll 2 J7
Menai Bridge IoA 52 J8
Mendham Suffk 41 N4
Mendip Hills 17 P6
Mendlesham Suffk 40 K7
Mendlesham Green Suffk 40 J8
Menheniot Cnwll 4 H8
Menithwood Worcs 35 R7
Menna Cnwll 3 N6
Mennock D & G 74 F4
Menston C Brad 63 P11
Menstrie Clacks 90 C12
Menthorpe N York 64 G13
Mentmore Bucks 30 K9
Meoble Highld 100 g11
Meole Brace Shrops 45 L11
Meonstoke Hants 9 S5
Meon Vale Warwks 36 G11
Meopham Kent 12 B2
Meopham Green Kent 12 B2
Meopham Station Kent 12 B2
Mepal Cambs 39 P4
Meppershall C Beds 31 P5
Merbach Herefs 34 H11
Mere Ches E 55 R10
Mere Wilts 17 V10
Mere Brow Lancs 54 K3
Mereclough Lancs 62 H13
Mere Green Birm 46 F14
Mere Green Worcs 36 C8
Mere Heath Ches W 55 Q12
Meresborough Medway 12 F3
Mereworth Kent 12 C5
Meriden Solhll 36 H4
Merkadale Highld 100 c6
Merley BCP 8 E9
Merlin's Bridge Pembks 24 F8
Merrington Shrops 45 L9
Merrion Pembks 24 F11
Merriott Somset 7 M2
Merrivale Devon 5 N5
Merrow Surrey 20 H12
Merry Field Hill Dorset 8 E8
Merry Hill Herts 20 K4
Merryhill Wolves 35 U1
Merry Lees Leics 47 N12
Merrymeet Cnwll 4 H7
Mersea Island Essex 23 P4
Mersey Gateway Bridge Halton 55 M10
Mersham Kent 13 L7
Merstham Surrey 21 N12
Merston W Susx 10 D10
Merstone IoW 9 Q11
Merther Cnwll 3 M8
Merthyr Carmth 25 Q6
Merthyr Cynog Powys 33 U13
Merthyr Dyfan V Glam 16 F3
Merthyr Mawr Brdgnd 26 F12
Merthyr Tydfil Myr Td 26 J6
Merthyr Vale Myr Td 26 K8
Merton Devon 15 M10
Merton Gt Lon 21 N8
Merton Norfk 50 F14
Merton Oxon 30 C9
Meshaw Devon 15 S9
Messing Essex 23 L4
Messingham N Linc 58 E6
Metal Bridge Dur 69 S6
Metfield Suffk 41 N4
Metherell Cnwll 5 L7
Metheringham Lincs 48 G1
Methil Fife 91 N12
Methilhill Fife 91 N11
Methley Leeds 57 N1
Methley Junction Leeds 57 N1
Methlick Abers 105 P8
Methven P & K 90 F6
Methwold Norfk 40 B2
Methwold Hythe Norfk 40 B2
Mettingham Suffk 41 Q3
Metton Norfk 51 M6
Mevagissey Cnwll 3 Q8
Mexborough Donc 57 Q6
Mey Highld 112 G2
Meysey Hampton Gloucs 29 M7
Miabhaig W Isls 106 f5
Michaelchurch Herefs 27 U2
Michaelchurch Escley Herefs 34 H14
Michaelchurch-on-Arrow Powys 34 F10
Michaelstone-y-Fedw Newpt 27 N11
Michaelston-le-Pit V Glam 27 M13
Michaelstow Cnwll 4 D5
Michaelwood Services Gloucs 28 D8
Michelcombe Devon 5 R7
Micheldever Hants 19 R13
Micheldever Station Hants 19 R12
Michelmersh Hants 9 L3
Mickfield Suffk 40 K8
Micklebring Donc 57 R8
Mickleby N York 71 P10
Micklefield Leeds 63 U13
Micklefield Green Herts 20 H3
Mickleham Surrey 21 L12
Mickleover C Derb 46 K7
Micklethwaite C Brad 63 N11
Micklethwaite Cumb 67 L2
Mickleton Dur 69 L8
Mickleton Gloucs 36 G12
Mickletown Leeds 57 P1
Mickle Trafford Ches W 54 K13
Mickley Derbys 57 M11
Mickley N York 63 R4
Mickley Green Suffk 40 D9
Mickley Square Nthumb 77 M13
Mid Ardlaw Abers 105 Q3
Midbea Ork 106 t15
Mid Beltie Abers 99 L3
Mid Bockhampton BCP 8 H9
Mid Calder W Loth 83 L5
Mid Clyth Highld 112 G9
Mid Culbeuchly Abers 104 K3
Middle Assendon Oxon 20 B5
Middle Aston Oxon 29 U2
Middle Barton Oxon 29 T2
Middlebie D & G 75 P10
Middlebridge P & K 97 P10
Middle Chinnock Somset 7 N2
Middle Claydon Bucks 30 F7
Middlecliffe Barns 57 P5
Middlecott Devon 5 S3
Middlecroft Derbys 57 P12
Middle Duntisbourne Gloucs 28 J6
Middleham N York 63 N2
Middle Handley Derbys 57 P11
Middle Harling Norfk 40 G3
Middlehill Cnwll 4 H7
Middlehill Wilts 18 B7
Middlehope Shrops 35 L3
Middle Kames Ag & B 87 S8
Middle Littleton Worcs 36 E11
Middle Madeley Staffs 45 S4
Middle Maes-coed Herefs 34 H14
Middlemarsh Dorset 7 S3
Middle Mayfield Staffs 46 F5
Middle Mill Pembks 24 D5
Middlemoor Devon 5 M6
Middle Quarter Kent 12 G8
Middle Rasen Lincs 58 J9
Middle Rocombe Devon 6 B11
Middle Salter Lancs 62 C7
Middlesbrough Middsb 70 G9
Middlesceugh W & F 67 P4
Middleshaw W & F 62 B2
Middlesmoor N York 63 M5
Middle Stoford Somset 16 G12
Middle Stoke Medway 22 K12
Middlestone Dur 69 S6
Middlestone Moor Dur 69 R6
Middle Stoughton Somset 17 M7
Middlestown Wakefd 57 L3
Middle Street Gloucs 28 E7
Middle Taphouse Cnwll 4 F8
Middlethird Border 84 H10
Middleton Ag & B 92 A10
Middleton Derbys 46 J2
Middleton Derbys 56 J14
Middleton Essex 40 E13
Middleton Hants 19 P12
Middleton Herefs 35 M7
Middleton Lancs 61 S8
Middleton Leeds 63 S14
Middleton N Nthn 38 B3
Middleton N York 63 N10
Middleton N York 64 H2
Middleton Norfk 49 U10
Middleton Nthumb 77 M9
Middleton Nthumb 85 S11
Middleton P & K 90 H10
Middleton Rochdl 56 C5
Middleton Shrops 35 M5
Middleton Shrops 44 H8
Middleton Suffk 41 R7
Middleton Swans 25 R13
Middleton W & F 62 C2
Middleton Warwks 46 G14
Middleton Cheney W Nthn 37 N12
Middleton Green Staffs 46 C6
Middleton Hall Nthumb 85 P13
Middleton-in-Teesdale Dur 68 K7
Middleton Moor Suffk 41 R7
Middleton One Row Darltn 70 E10
Middleton-on-Leven N York 70 G11
Middleton-on-Sea W Susx 10 F10
Middleton on the Hill Herefs 35 M8
Middleton on the Wolds E R Yk 65 L10
Middleton Park C Aber 105 Q13
Middleton Priors Shrops 35 P2
Middleton Quernhow N York 63 S4
Middleton St George Darltn 70 D10
Middleton Scriven Shrops 35 Q3
Middleton Stoney Oxon 30 B8
Middleton Tyas N York 69 R11
Middletown Cumb 66 E11
Middle Town IoS 2 b3
Middletown N Som 17 N2
Middletown Powys 44 H11
Middle Tysoe Warwks 36 K12
Middle Wallop Hants 19 L13
Middlewich Ches E 55 R13
Middle Winterslow Wilts 8 J2
Middlewood Cnwll 4 H5
Middlewood Herefs 34 G12
Middle Woodford Wilts 18 H13
Middlewood Green Suffk 40 J8
Middle Yard Gloucs 28 F7
Middlezoy Somset 17 L10
Middridge Dur 69 R7
Midford BaNES 17 U4
Midge Hall Lancs 55 M2
Midgeholme Cumb 76 C14
Midgham W Berk 19 S7
Midgley Calder 56 F1
Midgley Wakefd 57 L4
Mid Holmwood Surrey 21 L13
Midhopestones Sheff 56 K7
Midhurst W Susx 10 D6
Mid Lavant W Susx 10 D9
Midlem Border 84 E13
Mid Mains Highld 102 D8
Midney Somset 17 N11
Midpark Ag & B 87 U14
Midsomer Norton BaNES 17 S6
Midtown Highld 111 M4
Midville Lincs 49 N2
Midway Ches E 56 D10
Mid Yell Shet 106 v4
Migdale Highld 109 L6
Migvie Abers 98 G2
Milborne Port Somset 17 S13
Milborne St Andrew Dorset 7 V5
Milborne Wick Somset 17 S12
Milbourne Nthumb 77 N10
Milbourne Wilts 28 J10
Milburn W & F 68 E7
Milbury Heath S Glos 28 C9
Milby N York 63 U6
Milcombe Oxon 37 M14
Milden Suffk 40 G11
Mildenhall Suffk 40 B6
Mildenhall Wilts 18 K7
Milebrook Powys 34 H6
Milebush Kent 12 E6
Mile Elm Wilts 18 E7
Mile End Gloucs 28 A5
Mile End Suffk 41 P3
Mileham Norfk 50 F10
Mile Oak Br & H 11 L9
Mile Oak Kent 12 C7
Mile Oak Staffs 46 G13
Miles Green Staffs 45 S4
Miles Hope Herefs 35 N8
Milesmark Fife 90 G14
Miles Platting Manch 56 C7
Mile Town Kent 23 M13
Milfield Nthumb 85 N12
Milford Derbys 47 L4
Milford Devon 14 F8
Milford Powys 34 C2
Milford Staffs 46 C9
Milford Surrey 10 E2
Milford Haven Pembks 24 F9
Milford on Sea Hants 8 K10
Milkwall Gloucs 28 A6
Millais Jersey 7 a1
Milland W Susx 10 C5
Milland Marsh W Susx 10 C5
Mill Bank Calder 56 F2
Millbeck Cumb 67 L7
Millbreck Abers 105 S7
Millbridge Surrey 10 C2
Millbrook C Beds 31 M5
Millbrook C Sotn 9 M6
Millbrook Cnwll 5 L10
Millbrook Jersey 7 c3
Millbrook Tamesd 56 E7
Mill Brow Stockp 56 E9
Millbuie Abers 99 P2
Millbuie Highld 102 G5
Millcombe Devon 5 U11
Mill Common Norfk 51 P13
Mill Common Suffk 41 R4
Millcorner E Susx 12 F11
Millcraig Highld 109 M10
Mill Cross Devon 5 S8
Milldale Staffs 46 F3
Mill End Bucks 20 C5
Millend Gloucs 28 D8
Mill End Herts 31 T6
Millerhill Mdloth 83 R5
Miller's Dale Derbys 56 H12
Millers Green Derbys 46 J3
Miller's Green Essex 22 E6
Millerston C Glas 89 P12
Millgate Lancs 56 C3
Mill Green Cambs 39 T11
Mill Green Essex 22 F7
Mill Green Herts 31 R10
Mill Green Lincs 48 K9
Mill Green Norfk 40 K4
Millgreen Shrops 45 Q8
Mill Green Staffs 46 E13
Mill Green Staffs 46 E9
Mill Green Suffk 40 G12
Mill Green Suffk 40 G9
Mill Green Suffk 40 K8
Mill Green Suffk 41 P8
Millhalf Herefs 34 G11
Millhayes Devon 6 H4
Millhead Lancs 61 T5
Millheugh S Lans 82 D8
Mill Hill E Susx 11 U9
Mill Hill Gt Lon 21 M4
Millhouse Ag & B 87 T11
Millhouse W & F 67 N5
Millhousebridge D & G 75 M8
Millhouse Green Barns 56 K6
Millhouses Barns 57 P6
Millhouses Sheff 57 M10
Milliken Park Rens 88 K13
Millin Cross Pembks 24 G8
Millington E R Yk 64 J9
Mill Lane Hants 20 C12
Millmeece Staffs 45 T7
Millness W & F 61 U3
Mill of Drummond P & K 89 T2
Mill of Haldane W Duns 88 J9
Millom Cumb 61 M3
Millook Cnwll 14 E13
Millpool Cnwll 2 F10
Millpool Cnwll 4 E6
Millport N Ayrs 80 H2
Mill Side W & F 61 S3
Mill Street Kent 12 C4
Mill Street Norfk 50 J10
Mill Street Suffk 40 J6
Millthorpe Derbys 57 M11
Millthrop W & F 62 D1
Milltimber C Aber 99 R3
Milltown Abers 98 D2
Milltown Abers 104 F12
Milltown Cnwll 4 E9
Milltown D & G 75 R10
Milltown Derbys 47 L1
Milltown Devon 15 N5
Milltown Highld 100 g5
Milltown of Auchindoun Moray 104 D7
Milltown of Campfield Abers 99 M3
Milltown of Edinvillie Moray 104 B7
Milltown of Rothiemay Moray 104 G6
Milnathort P & K 90 H11
Milngavie E Duns 89 N11
Milnrow Rochdl 56 D4
Milnthorpe W & F 61 T3
Milnthorpe Wakefd 57 M3
Milovaig Highld 100 a5
Milson Shrops 35 P6
Milstead Kent 12 H4
Milston Wilts 18 J11
Milthorpe Lincs 48 H7
Milthorpe W Nthn 37 Q11
Milton C Stke 46 B3
Milton Cambs 39 Q8
Milton Cumb 76 B13
Milton D & G 72 G9
Milton D & G 74 F11
Milton Derbys 46 K8
Milton Highld 102 E9
Milton Highld 102 G6
Milton Highld 109 P10
Milton Highld 112 H6
Milton Inver 88 J12
Milton Kent 22 G13
Milton Moray 103 U12
Milton Moray 104 G3
Milton N Som 16 K4
Milton Newpt 27 R10
Milton Notts 58 B12
Milton Oxon 29 U9
Milton Oxon 37 N13
Milton P & K 97 T11
Milton Pembks 24 H10
Milton Somset 17 N12
Milton Stirlg 89 M5
Milton W Duns 88 K11
Milton Abbas Dorset 7 V4
Milton Abbot Devon 5 L5
Milton Bridge Mdloth 83 Q6
Milton Bryan C Beds 31 L6
Milton Clevedon Somset 17 S9
Milton Combe Devon 5 M7
Milton Common Oxon 30 E12
Milton Damerel Devon 14 J10
Milton End Gloucs 28 D5
Milton End Gloucs 29 M7
Milton Ernest Bed 38 F9
Milton Green Ches W 45 L2
Milton Heights Oxon 29 U9
Milton Hill Oxon 29 U9
Milton Keynes M Keyn 30 J5
Milton Lilbourne Wilts 18 J8
Milton Malsor W Nthn 37 T9
Milton Morenish P & K 95 S11
Milton of Auchinhove Abers 98 K3
Milton of Balgonie Fife 91 M11
Milton of Buchanan Stirlg 88 K7
Milton of Campsie E Duns 89 Q10
Milton of Finavon Angus 98 H12
Milton of Leys Highld 102 J7
Milton of Murtle C Aber 99 R3
Milton on Stour Dorset 17 U11
Milton Regis Kent 12 H3
Milton Street E Susx 11 S10
Milton-under-Wychwood Oxon 29 Q4
Milverton Somset 16 F11
Milverton Warwks 36 K7
Milwich Staffs 46 C7
Milwr Flints 54 E12
Minard Ag & B 87 T6
Minchington Dorset 8 D6
Minchinhampton Gloucs 28 G7
Mindenhurst Surrey 20 F11
Mindrum Nthumb 85 L12
Minehead Somset 16 C7
Minera Wrexhm 44 G3
Minety Wilts 28 K9
Minffordd Gwynd 43 L6
Mingarrypark Highld 93 R5
Miningsby Lincs 59 P14
Minions Cnwll 4 H6
Minishant S Ayrs 81 L10
Minllyn Gwynd 43 S11
Minnigaff D & G 73 L6
Minnonie Abers 105 M3
Minshull Vernon Ches E 45 Q1
Minskip N York 63 T7
Minstead Hants 8 K6
Minsted W Susx 10 D6
Minster Kent 13 R3
Minsterley Shrops 44 J12
Minster Lovell Oxon 29 R5
Minster-on-Sea Kent 23 N13
Minsterworth Gloucs 28 E4
Minterne Magna Dorset 7 S4
Minterne Parva Dorset 7 S4
Minting Lincs 59 L12
Mintlaw Abers 105 R6
Minto Border 76 B1
Minton Shrops 34 K2
Minwear Pembks 24 H8
Minworth Birm 36 G2
Mirehouse Cumb 66 E9
Mireland Highld 112 H4
Mirfield Kirk 56 K3
Miserden Gloucs 28 H6
Miskin Rhondd 26 J11
Miskin Rhondd 26 J8
Misson Notts 57 U8
Misterton Leics 37 Q4
Misterton Notts 58 C8
Misterton Somset 7 N3
Mistley Essex 23 R1
Mistley Heath Essex 23 R1
Mitcham Gt Lon 21 N9
Mitcheldean Gloucs 28 C4
Mitchell Cnwll 3 M6
Mitchellslacks D & G 74 J6
Mitchel Troy Mons 27 T5
Mitford Nthumb 77 P8
Mithian Cnwll 2 J6
Mitton Staffs 45 U10
Mixbury Oxon 30 D6
Mixenden Calder 63 M14
Moats Tye Suffk 40 H9
Mobberley Ches E 55 S11
Mobberley Staffs 46 D5
Moccas Herefs 34 J12
Mochdre Conwy 53 P7
Mochdre Powys 34 C3
Mochrum D & G 72 J10
Mockbeggar Hants 8 H7
Mockbeggar Kent 12 D6
Mockerkin Cumb 66 G8
Modbury Devon 5 R10
Moddershall Staffs 46 B6
Moelfre IoA 52 H5
Moelfre Powys 44 E8
Moel Tryfan Gwynd 52 H11
Moffat D & G 75 L4
Mogador Surrey 21 M12
Moggerhanger C Beds 38 H11
Moira Leics 46 K10
Molash Kent 12 K5
Mol-chlach Highld 100 d8
Mold Flints 54 F14
Moldgreen Kirk 56 J3
Molehill Green Essex 22 E3
Molehill Green Essex 22 H3
Molescroft E R Yk 65 N11
Molesden Nthumb 77 N9
Molesworth Cambs 38 G5
Moll Highld 100 e6
Molland Devon 15 T7
Mollington Ches W 54 J12
Mollington Oxon 37 M11
Mollinsburn N Lans 82 D4
Monachty Cerdgn 32 K8
Mondynes Abers 99 P8
Monewden Suffk 41 M9
Moneydie P & K 90 G6
Moneyrow Green W & M 20 E7
Moniaive D & G 74 E7
Monifieth Angus 91 Q5
Monikie Angus 91 Q4
Monimail Fife 91 L9
Monington Pembks 32 B12
Monk Bretton Barns 57 N5
Monken Hadley Gt Lon 21 M3
Monk Fryston N York 64 C14
Monkhide Herefs 35 P12
Monkhill Cumb 75 R14
Monkhopton Shrops 35 P2
Monkland Herefs 35 L9
Monkleigh Devon 15 L8
Monknash V Glam 16 B2
Monkokehampton Devon 15 N11
Monkseaton N Tyne 77 S11
Monks Eleigh Suffk 40 G11
Monk's Gate W Susx 11 L5
Monks Heath Ches E 55 T12
Monk Sherborne Hants 19 T9
Monks Horton Kent 13 M7
Monksilver Somset 16 E9
Monks Kirby Warwks 37 N4
Monk Soham Suffk 41 M7
Monkspath Solhll 36 F5
Monks Risborough Bucks 30 H12
Monksthorpe Lincs 59 R13
Monk Street Essex 22 F2
Monkswood Mons 27 Q7
Monkton Devon 6 G4
Monkton Kent 13 Q3
Monkton S Ayrs 81 M7
Monkton S Tyne 77 S13
Monkton V Glam 16 B2
Monkton Combe BaNES 17 U4
Monkton Deverill Wilts 18 C13
Monkton Farleigh Wilts 18 B7
Monkton Heathfield Somset 16 J11
Monkton Up Wimborne Dorset 8 E6
Monkton Wyld Dorset 6 K5
Monkwearmouth Sundld 77 T14
Monkwood Hants 9 T2
Monmore Green Wolves 46 B14
Monmouth Mons 27 U5
Monnington on Wye Herefs 34 J12
Monreith D & G 72 K11
Montacute Somset 17 N13
Montcliffe Bolton 55 Q4
Montford Shrops 44 K11
Montford Bridge Shrops 44 K10
Montgarrie Abers 104 H12
Montgomery Powys 34 F1
Monton Salfd 55 S7
Montrose Angus 99 N12
Mont Saint Guern 6 c3
Monxton Hants 19 M12
Monyash Derbys 56 J13
Monymusk Abers 104 K12
Monzie P & K 90 C6
Moodiesburn N Lans 82 C4
Moonzie Fife 91 M8
Moor Allerton Leeds 63 S12
Moorbath Dorset 7 M5
Moorby Lincs 59 N14
Moorcot Herefs 34 J9
Moor Crichel Dorset 8 D7
Moordown BCP 8 F10
Moore Halton 55 N10
Moor End C Beds 31 L8
Moor End Calder 63 M14
Moor End Devon 15 Q11
Moorend Gloucs 28 D7
Moor End Lancs 61 R11
Moor End N York 64 E12
Moorends Donc 57 U3
Moorgreen Hants 9 P5
Moor Green Herts 31 T7
Moorgreen Notts 47 N4
Moorhall Derbys 57 M12
Moorhampton Herefs 34 J11
Moorhead C Brad 63 N12
Moor Head Leeds 63 Q14
Moorhouse Cumb 67 L2
Moorhouse Cumb 67 M1
Moorhouse Donc 57 Q4
Moorhouse Notts 58 C13
Moorhouse Bank Surrey 21 R12
Moorland Somset 16 K10
Moorlinch Somset 17 L9
Moor Monkton N York 64 C8
Moor Row Cumb 66 F10
Moor Row Cumb 66 K3
Moorsholm R & Cl 71 L10
Moorside Dorset 17 U13
Moorside Dur 69 N3
Moor Side Lancs 61 S13
Moor Side Lancs 61 T12
Moorside Leeds 63 Q12
Moor Side Lincs 49 L2
Moorside Oldham 56 D5
Moorstock Kent 13 M8
Moor Street Medway 12 F2
Moorswater Cnwll 4 G8
Moorthorpe Wakefd 57 Q4
Moortown Devon 5 N6
Moortown Hants 8 H8
Moortown IoW 9 N12
Moortown Leeds 63 R12
Moortown Lincs 58 J7
Moortown Wrekin 45 P10
Morangie Highld 109 P8
Morar Highld 100 f10
Morborne Cambs 38 H2
Morchard Bishop Devon 15 S11
Morchard Road Devon 15 S11
Morcombelake Dorset 7 M6
Morcott Rutlnd 48 D13
Morda Shrops 44 G8
Morden Dorset 8 C9
Morden Gt Lon 21 N9
Mordiford Herefs 35 N13
Mordon Dur 70 D7
More Shrops 34 H2
Morebath Devon 16 C11
Morebattle Border 84 K14
Morecambe Lancs 61 S7
Moredon Swindn 29 M10
Morefield Highld 107 V5
Morehall Kent 13 P8
Moreleigh Devon 5 T10
Morenish P & K 95 S11
Moresby Parks Cumb 66 E9
Morestead Hants 9 Q3
Moreton Dorset 7 V7
Moreton Essex 22 D6
Moreton Herefs 35 M8
Moreton Oxon 30 E12
Moreton Staffs 45 S10
Moreton Staffs 46 F8
Moreton Wirral 54 G9
Moreton Corbet Shrops 45 N9
Moreton Hall Suffk 40 E8
Moretonhampstead Devon 5 T3
Moreton-in-Marsh Gloucs 29 P1
Moreton Jeffries Herefs 35 P11
Moretonmill Shrops 45 N9
Moreton Morrell Warwks 36 K9
Moreton on Lugg Herefs 35 M11
Moreton Paddox Warwks 36 K10
Moreton Pinkney W Nthn 37 Q11
Moreton Say Shrops 45 P7
Moreton Valence Gloucs 28 E6
Morfa Cerdgn 32 F10
Morfa Bychan Gwynd 42 K6
Morfa Dinlle Gwynd 52 F11
Morfa Glas Neath 26 F6
Morfa Nefyn Gwynd 42 E5
Morganstown Cardif 27 L11
Morgan's Vale Wilts 8 H4
Morham E Loth 84 F4
Moriah Cerdgn 33 M5
Morland W & F 68 D8
Morley Ches E 55 T10
Morley Derbys 47 L5
Morley Dur 69 P7
Morley Leeds 57 L1
Morley Green Ches E 55 T10
Morley St Botolph Norfk 50 J14
Mornick Cnwll 4 J6
Morningside C Edin 83 P4
Morningside N Lans 82 F7
Morningthorpe Norfk 41 M2
Morpeth Nthumb 77 P8
Morphie Abers 99 N11
Morrey Staffs 46 F10
Morridge Side Staffs 46 D3
Morriston Swans 26 B8
Morston Norfk 50 H5
Mortehoe Devon 15 L3
Morthen Rothm 57 Q9
Mortimer W Berk 19 U8
Mortimer Common W Berk 19 U7
Mortimer's Cross Herefs 34 K8
Mortimer West End Hants 19 T8
Mortlake Gt Lon 21 M7
Morton Cumb 67 N2
Morton Derbys 47 M1
Morton IoW 9 S11
Morton Lincs 48 G9
Morton Lincs 58 D8
Morton Lincs 58 E14
Morton Notts 47 T3
Morton Shrops 44 G9
Morton W & F 67 Q5
Morton-on-Swale N York 63 S1
Morton on the Hill Norfk 50 K10
Morton Tinmouth Dur 69 Q8
Morvah Cnwll 2 C9
Morval Cnwll 4 H9
Morvich Highld 101 P7
Morville Shrops 35 Q2
Morville Heath Shrops 35 Q2
Morwenstow Cnwll 14 F9
Mosborough Sheff 57 P10
Moscow E Ayrs 81 P4
Mose Shrops 35 S2
Mosedale W & F 67 N6
Moseley Birm 36 E4
Moseley Wolves 46 B14
Moseley Worcs 35 T9
Moses Gate Bolton 55 R5
Moss Ag & B 92 B10
Moss Donc 57 S4
Moss Wrexhm 44 H3
Mossat Abers 104 F12
Mossbank Shet 106 u6
Moss Bank St Hel 55 M7
Mossbay Cumb 66 E7
Mossblown S Ayrs 81 N8
Mossbrow Traffd 55 R9
Mossburnford Border 76 D2
Mossdale D & G 73 R5
Mossdale E Ayrs 81 P12
Moss Edge Lancs 61 S11
Moss End Ches E 55 Q11
Mossend N Lans 82 D6
Mosser Mains Cumb 66 H7
Mossley Ches E 45 U1
Mossley Tamesd 56 E6
Mosspaul Inn Border 75 S6
Moss Side Cumb 66 J2
Moss-side Highld 103 N4
Moss Side Lancs 61 R13
Moss Side Sefton 54 J6
Mosstodloch Moray 104 C4
Mossyard D & G 73 N9
Mossy Lea Lancs 55 M4
Mosterton Dorset 7 N3
Moston Manch 56 C6
Moston Shrops 45 N8
Moston Green Ches E 45 R1
Mostyn Flints 54 E10
Motcombe Dorset 8 B3
Mothecombe Devon 5 Q11
Motherby W & F 67 P7
Motherwell N Lans 82 D7
Motspur Park Gt Lon 21 M9
Mottingham Gt Lon 21 R8
Mottisfont Hants 9 L3
Mottisfont Hants 9 L3
Mottistone IoW 9 N12
Mottram in Longdendale Tamesd 56 E7
Mottram St Andrew Ches E 56 C11
Mouilpied Guern 6 d3
Mouldsworth Ches W 55 M12
Moulin P & K 97 Q12
Moulsecoomb Br & H 11 N9
Moulsford Oxon 19 S4
Moulsoe M Keyn 30 K4
Moultavie Highld 109 L10
Moulton Ches W 55 Q13
Moulton Lincs 49 M9
Moulton N York 69 R12
Moulton Suffk 39 U8
Moulton V Glam 16 E3
Moulton W Nthn 37 U7
Moulton Chapel Lincs 49 L10
Moulton St Mary Norfk 51 Q12
Moulton Seas End Lincs 49 M8
Mount Cnwll 2 K5
Mount Cnwll 4 E7
Mount Kirk 56 G3
Mountain C Brad 63 M13
Mountain Ash Rhondd 26 J8
Mountain Cross Border 83 N9
Mountain Street Kent 13 L5
Mount Ambrose Cnwll 2 J8
Mount Bures Essex 40 F14
Mountfield E Susx 12 D11
Mountgerald Highld 102 G3
Mount Hawke Cnwll 2 J7
Mount Hermon Cnwll 2 H13
Mountjoy Cnwll 3 M4
Mount Lothian Mdloth 83 Q7
Mountnessing Essex 22 F8
Mounton Mons 27 U9
Mount Pleasant Ches E 45 T2
Mount Pleasant Derbys 46 J10
Mount Pleasant Derbys 46 K4
Mount Pleasant Dur 69 S6
Mount Pleasant E R Yk 65 T12
Mount Pleasant E Susx 11 Q7
Mount Pleasant Norfk 40 G2
Mount Pleasant Suffk 40 B11
Mount Pleasant Sundld 70 D2
Mount Pleasant Worcs 36 D8
Mountsorrel Leics 47 Q11
Mount Sorrel Wilts 8 E4
Mount Tabor Calder 56 G1
Mousehole Cnwll 2 D11
Mouswald D & G 75 L11
Mowbray W Susx 10 K4
Mow Cop Ches E 45 U2
Mowhaugh Border 76 G1
Mowmacre Hill C Leic 47 Q12
Mowsley Leics 37 R3
Moy Highld 96 E7
Moy Highld 103 L9
Moyle Highld 101 M8
Moylegrove Pembks 32 B12
Muasdale Ag & B 79 M7
Muchalls Abers 99 S5
Much Birch Herefs 27 U1
Much Cowarne Herefs 35 P11
Much Dewchurch Herefs 27 T1
Muchelney Somset 17 M12
Muchelney Ham Somset 17 M12
Much Hadham Herts 22 B4
Much Hoole Lancs 55 L2
Much Hoole Town Lancs 55 L2
Muchlarnick Cnwll 4 G9
Much Marcle Herefs 35 Q14
Much Wenlock Shrops 45 P14
Muck Highld 93 L3
Mucking Thurr 22 G11
Muckleburgh Military Collection Norfk 50 K5
Muckleford Dorset 7 R6
Mucklestone Staffs 45 R6
Muckley Shrops 35 P1
Muckton Lincs 59 Q10
Muddiford Devon 15 N5
Muddles Green E Susx 11 S8
Mudeford BCP 8 H10
Mudford Somset 17 Q13
Mudford Sock Somset 17 Q13
Mudgley Somset 17 N7
Mud Row Kent 23 P13
Mugdock Stirlg 89 N10
Mugeary Highld 100 d6
Mugginton Derbys 46 J5
Muggintonlane End Derbys 46 J5
Muggleswick Dur 69 M3
Muirden Abers 105 L5
Muirdrum Angus 91 S4
Muiresk Abers 104 K6
Muirhead Angus 91 M5
Muirhead Fife 91 L10
Muirhead N Lans 82 C5
Muirhouses Falk 82 K2
Muirkirk E Ayrs 82 C13
Muirmill Stirlg 89 R9
Muir of Fowlis Abers 104 H13
Muir of Miltonduff Moray 103 U4
Muir of Ord Highld 102 F5
Muirshearlich Highld 94 G2
Muirtack Abers 105 R8
Muirton P & K 90 D9
Muirton Mains Highld 102 E5
Muirton of Ardblair P & K 90 J3
Muker N York 68 K13
Mulbarton Norfk 51 L13
Mulben Moray 104 D5
Mulfra Cnwll 2 D10
Mull Ag & B 93 Q12
Mullacott Cross Devon 15 M4
Mullardoch Highld 101 U5
Mullion Cnwll 2 H13
Mullion Cove Cnwll 2 H13
Mumby Lincs 59 T12
Munderfield Row Herefs 35 P10
Munderfield Stocks Herefs 35 Q10
Mundesley Norfk 51 P6
Mundford Norfk 40 D2
Mundham Norfk 51 P14
Mundon Essex 23 L7
Mundy Bois Kent 12 H6
Mungrisdale W & F 67 N6
Munlochy Highld 102 H5
Munnoch N Ayrs 80 K3
Munsley Herefs 35 Q12
Munslow Shrops 35 M3
Murchington Devon 5 R3
Murcot Worcs 36 E12
Murcott Oxon 30 C9
Murcott Wilts 28 J9
Murkle Highld 112 E3
Murlaggan Highld 101 Q13
Murrell Green Hants 20 B11
Murroes Angus 91 Q4
Murrow Cambs 49 N12
Mursley Bucks 30 H7
Murston Kent 12 H3
Murthill Angus 98 H12
Murthly P & K 90 H4
Murton C York 64 E9
Murton Dur 70 E3
Murton N Tyne 77 S11
Murton Nthumb 85 P9
Murton Swans 25 U13
Murton W & F 68 F8
Musbury Devon 6 J6
Muscoates N York 64 F4
Musselburgh E Loth 83 R4
Muston Leics 48 B6
Muston N York 65 P4
Mustow Green Worcs 35 U6
Muswell Hill Gt Lon 21 N5
Mutehill D & G 73 R10
Mutford Suffk 41 S3
Muthill P & K 90 C8
Mutterton Devon 6 D3
Muxton Wrekin 45 R11
Mybster Highld 112 E6
Myddfai Carmth 26 D1
Myddle Shrops 45 L9
Mydroilyn Cerdgn 32 J9
Myerscough Lancs 61 T12
Myland Essex 23 N2
Mylor Cnwll 3 L9
Mylor Bridge Cnwll 3 L9
Mynachlog ddu Pembks 24 K4
Myndd-llan Flints 54 E12
Myndtown Shrops 34 J3
Mynydd Bach Cerdgn 33 P5
Mynydd-bach Mons 27 T9
Mynydd-Bach Swans 26 B8
Mynyddgarreg Carmth 25 R9
Mynydd Isa Flints 54 G14
Mynydd Llandygai Gwynd 52 K9

Mynydd Mechell IoA 52 E4
Mynytho Gwynd 42 F7
Myrebird Abers 99 N4
Myredykes Border 76 B6
Mytchett Surrey 20 E11
Mytholm Calder 56 E1
Mytholmroyd Calder 56 F1
Mythop Lancs 61 R13
Myton-on-Swale N York 63 U6

N

Naast Highld 107 P8
Nab's Head Lancs 62 C14
Na Buirgh W Isls 106 f9
Naburn C York 64 D10
Naccolt Kent 13 L7
Nackington Kent 13 N5
Nacton Suffk 41 M12
Nafferton E R Yk 65 P8
Nag's Head Gloucs 28 G8
Nailbridge Gloucs 28 B4
Nailsbourne Somset 16 H11
Nailsea N Som 17 N2
Nailstone Leics 47 M12
Nailsworth Gloucs 28 F8
Nairn Highld 103 N4
Nalderswood Surrey 21 M13
Nancegollan Cnwll 2 G10
Nancledra Cnwll 2 D9
Nanhoron Gwynd 42 E7
Nannerch Flints 54 E13
Nanpantan Leics 47 P10
Nanpean Cnwll 3 P5
Nanquidno Cnwll 2 B11
Nanstallon Cnwll 3 Q3
Nant-ddu Powys 26 J5
Nanternis Cerdgn 32 G9
Nantgaredig Carmth 25 S6
Nantgarw Rhondd 27 L10
Nant-glas Powys 33 U7
Nantglyn Denbgs 53 T10
Nantgwyn Powys 33 U5
Nant Gwynant Gwynd 43 M3
Nantlle Gwynd 52 H12
Nantlle Valley Slate Landscape Gwynd 52 H12
Nantmawr Shrops 44 G9
Nantmel Powys 34 B7
Nantmor Gwynd 43 M4
Nant Peris Gwynd 52 K11
Nantwich Ches E 45 Q3
Nant-y-Bwch Blae G 27 L5
Nantycaws Carmth 25 S7
Nant-y-derry Mons 27 Q6
Nant-y-ffin Carmth 25 U4
Nantyffyllon Brdgnd 26 F9
Nantyglo Blae G 27 M5
Nant-y-gollen Shrops 44 F8
Nant-y-moel Brdgnd 26 G9
Nant-y-pandy Conwy 53 L8
Naphill Bucks 20 D3
Napleton Worcs 35 U11
Nappa N York 62 H9
Napsbury Park Herts 31 Q12
Napton on the Hill Warwks 37 N8
Narberth Pembks 24 K8
Narborough Leics 37 P1
Narborough Norfk 50 B11
Narkurs Cnwll 4 J9
Nasareth Gwynd 42 J4
Naseby W Nthn 37 S5
Nash Bucks 30 G6
Nash Gt Lon 21 R10
Nash Herefs 34 H8
Nash Newpt 27 Q11
Nash Shrops 35 P6
Nash End Worcs 35 S4
Nashes Green Hants 19 U11
Nash Lee Bucks 30 H11
Nash Street Kent 12 B2
Nassington N Nthn 38 G1
Nastend Gloucs 28 E6
Nasty Herts 31 U8
Nateby Lancs 61 T11
Nateby W & F 68 G11
National Memorial Arboretum Staffs 46 G11
National Space Centre C Leic 47 Q12
Natland W & F 61 U2
Naughton Suffk 40 H11
Naunton Gloucs 29 M3
Naunton Worcs 35 U13
Naunton Beauchamp Worcs 36 C10
Navenby Lincs 48 E2
Navestock Essex 22 D8
Navestock Side Essex 22 E8
Navidale Highld 112 B13
Navity Highld 103 L3
Nawton N York 64 F3
Nayland Suffk 40 G14
Nazeing Essex 22 B6
Nazeing Gate Essex 22 B6
Neacroft Hants 8 H9
Neal's Green Warwks 36 K4
Neap Shet 106 v8
Near Cotton Staffs 46 E4
Near Sawrey W & F 67 N13
Neasden Gt Lon 21 M5
Neasham Darltn 70 D10
Neat Enstone Oxon 29 S3
Neath Neath 26 D8
Neatham Hants 10 A2
Neatishead Norfk 51 P9
Nebo Cerdgn 32 K7
Nebo Conwy 53 P11
Nebo Gwynd 42 J3
Nebo IoA 52 G4
Necton Norfk 50 E12
Nedd Highld 110 C10
Nedderton Nthumb 77 Q9
Nedging Suffk 40 G11
Nedging Tye Suffk 40 H11
Needham Norfk 41 M4
Needham Market Suffk 40 J9
Needham Street Suffk 40 B7
Needingworth Cambs 39 M6
Neen Savage Shrops 35 Q5
Neen Sollars Shrops 35 Q6
Neenton Shrops 35 P3
Nefyn Gwynd 42 F5
Neilston E Rens 81 P1
Nelson Caerph 27 L8
Nelson Lancs 62 H12
Nemphlar S Lans 82 G10
Nempnett Thrubwell BaNES 17 P4
Nenthall W & F 68 G3
Nenthead W & F 68 G4
Nenthorn Border 84 H11
Neopardy Devon 15 S13
Nep Town W Susx 11 L7
Nerabus Ag & B 78 C4
Nercwys Flints 44 F1
Nerston S Lans 81 S1
Nesbit Nthumb 85 P12
Nesfield N York 63 M10
Ness Ches W 54 H11
Nesscliffe Shrops 44 J10
Neston Ches W 54 G11
Neston Wilts 18 C7
Netchwood Shrops 35 P2
Nether Abington S Lans 82 H14
Nether Alderley Ches E 55 T11
Netheravon Wilts 18 H11
Nether Blainslie Border 84 E10
Netherbrae Abers 105 M4
Nether Broughton Leics 47 S8
Netherburn S Lans 82 E9
Netherbury Dorset 7 N5
Netherby Cumb 75 S11
Netherby N York 63 S10
Nether Cerne Dorset 7 S5
Nethercleuch D & G 75 M8
Nether Compton Dorset 17 Q13
Nethercote Warwks 37 P8
Nethercott Devon 14 J13
Nethercott Devon 15 L5
Nether Crimond Abers 105 N11
Nether Dallachy Moray 104 D3
Netherend Gloucs 28 A7
Nether Exe Devon 6 B4
Netherfield E Susx 12 D12
Netherfield Leics 47 Q10
Netherfield Notts 47 R5
Nether Fingland S Lans 74 H3
Nethergate N Linc 58 C7
Nethergate Norfk 50 J8
Netherhampton Wilts 8 G3
Nether Handley Derbys 57 P11
Nether Handwick Angus 91 N3
Nether Haugh Rothm 57 P7
Netherhay Dorset 7 M3
Nether Headon Notts 58 B11
Nether Heage Derbys 47 L3
Nether Heyford W Nthn 37 S9
Nether Kellet Lancs 61 U6
Nether Kinmundy Abers 105 T7
Netherland Green Staffs 46 F7
Nether Langwith Notts 57 R12
Netherley Abers 99 R5
Netherley Lpool 54 K9
Nethermill D & G 74 K8
Nethermuir Abers 105 Q7
Netherne-on-the-Hill Surrey 21 N11
Netheroyd Hill Kirk 56 H3
Nether Padley Derbys 56 K11
Nether Poppleton C York 64 D9
Nether Row Cumb 67 M5
Netherseal Derbys 46 J11
Nether Silton N York 64 B1
Nether Skyborry Shrops 34 G6
Nether Stowey Somset 16 G9
Nether Street Essex 22 E5
Netherstreet Wilts 18 E8
Netherthird E Ayrs 81 R9
Netherthong Kirk 56 H5
Netherthorpe Derbys 57 P12
Netherton Angus 98 J12
Netherton Devon 6 A10
Netherton Dudley 36 B3
Netherton Hants 19 N9
Netherton Herefs 27 U2
Netherton Kirk 56 H4
Netherton N Lans 82 E8
Netherton Nthumb 76 K4
Netherton Oxon 29 T8
Netherton P & K 97 U13
Netherton Sefton 54 J7
Netherton Shrops 35 R4
Netherton Stirlg 89 N10
Netherton Wakefd 57 L3
Netherton Worcs 36 C12
Nethertown Cumb 66 E11
Nethertown Highld 112 J1
Nethertown Lancs 62 E12
Nethertown Staffs 46 F10
Netherurd Border 83 M10
Nether Wallop Hants 19 M13
Nether Wasdale Cumb 66 H12
Nether Welton Cumb 67 N3
Nether Westcote Gloucs 29 P3
Nether Whitacre Warwks 36 H2
Nether Whitecleuch S Lans 74 F2
Nether Winchendon Bucks 30 F10
Netherwitton Nthumb 77 M7
Nethy Bridge Highld 103 R11
Netley Hants 9 P7
Netley Marsh Hants 9 L6
Nettlebed Oxon 19 U3
Nettlebridge Somset 17 R7
Nettlecombe Dorset 7 P5
Nettlecombe IoW 9 Q13
Nettleden Herts 31 M10
Nettleham Lincs 58 H11
Nettlestead Kent 12 C5
Nettlestead Green Kent 12 C5
Nettlestone IoW 9 S10
Nettlesworth Dur 69 S3
Nettleton Lincs 58 K6
Nettleton Wilts 18 B5
Nettleton Shrub Wilts 18 B5
Netton Devon 5 P11
Netton Wilts 18 H13
Neuadd Carmth 26 C3
Neuadd-ddu Powys 33 T5
Nevendon Essex 22 J9
Nevern Pembks 32 A12
Nevill Holt Leics 38 B2
New Abbey D & G 74 J12
New Aberdour Abers 105 P3
New Addington Gt Lon 21 Q10
Newall Leeds 63 P10
New Alresford Hants 9 R2
New Alyth P & K 90 K2
Newark C Pete 48 K13
Newark Ork 106 w15
Newark-on-Trent Notts 47 U3
New Arley Warwks 36 J3
New Arram E R Yk 65 N11
Newarthill N Lans 82 E7
New Ash Green Kent 12 B2
New Balderton Notts 48 B3
New Barn Kent 12 B2
Newbarn Kent 13 N7
New Barnet Gt Lon 21 N3
New Barnetby N Linc 58 J4
New Barton N Nthn 38 C8
Newbattle Mdloth 83 R5
New Bewick Nthumb 77 M1
Newbie D & G 75 N12
Newbiggin Cumb 66 G14
Newbiggin Dur 68 K7
Newbiggin Dur 69 P3
Newbiggin N York 62 K1
Newbiggin N York 63 L2
Newbiggin W & F 61 P6
Newbiggin W & F 67 Q7
Newbiggin W & F 67 S3
Newbiggin W & F 68 D7
Newbiggin-by-the-Sea Nthumb 77 S8
Newbigging Angus 91 L3
Newbigging Angus 91 P4
Newbigging Angus 91 Q4
Newbigging S Lans 82 K9
Newbiggin-on-Lune W & F 68 F12
New Bilton Warwks 37 N5
Newbold Derbys 57 N12
Newbold Leics 47 M10
Newbold on Avon Warwks 37 N5
Newbold on Stour Warwks 36 H11
Newbold Pacey Warwks 36 J9
Newbold Revel Warwks 37 N4
Newbold Verdon Leics 47 M13
New Bolingbroke Lincs 49 M2
Newborough C Pete 48 K12
Newborough IoA 52 F9
Newborough Staffs 46 F8
Newbottle Sundld 70 D2
Newbottle W Nthn 30 B5
New Boultham Lincs 58 G12
Newbourne Suffk 41 N12
New Bradwell M Keyn 30 H4
New Brampton Derbys 57 N12
New Brancepeth Dur 69 R4
Newbridge C Edin 83 M4
Newbridge Caerph 27 N8
Newbridge Cerdgn 32 K9
Newbridge Cnwll 2 C10
Newbridge Cnwll 2 K8
Newbridge D & G 74 H10
Newbridge Hants 8 K5
Newbridge IoW 9 N11
New Bridge N York 64 J2
Newbridge Oxon 29 T7
Newbridge Wrexhm 44 G5
Newbridge Green Worcs 35 T13
Newbridge-on-Usk Mons 27 R9
Newbridge-on-Wye Powys 34 B9
New Brighton Flints 54 G13
New Brighton Wirral 54 H8
New Brinsley Notts 47 N3
Newbrough Nthumb 76 H12
New Broughton Wrexhm 44 H3
New Buckenham Norfk 40 J2
Newbuildings Devon 15 S12
Newburgh Abers 105 R10
Newburgh Abers 105 R4
Newburgh Fife 90 K8
Newburgh Lancs 55 L4
Newburn N u Ty 77 P12
New Bury Bolton 55 R6
Newbury Somset 17 S7
Newbury W Berk 19 Q7
Newbury Wilts 18 B12
Newbury Park Gt Lon 21 R5
Newby Lancs 62 G10
Newby N York 62 E6
Newby N York 65 N2
Newby N York 70 H10
Newby W & F 67 S8
Newby Bridge W & F 61 R2
Newby Cross Cumb 67 N2
Newby East Cumb 75 U14
Newby Head W & F 67 S8
New Byth Abers 105 N5
Newby West Cumb 67 N2
Newby Wiske N York 63 T2
Newcastle Mons 27 S4
Newcastle Shrops 34 G4
Newcastle Airport Nthumb 77 P11
Newcastle Emlyn Carmth 32 F12
Newcastle Great Park N u Ty 77 Q11
Newcastleton Border 75 U8
Newcastle-under-Lyme Staffs 45 T4
Newcastle upon Tyne N u Ty 77 Q13
Newchapel Pembks 25 M3
Newchapel Staffs 45 U3
Newchapel Surrey 11 P2
Newchurch Blae G 27 M5
Newchurch Herefs 34 J10
Newchurch IoW 9 R11
Newchurch Kent 13 L9
Newchurch Mons 27 T8
Newchurch Powys 34 F10
Newchurch Staffs 46 F9
Newchurch in Pendle Lancs 62 G12
New Costessey Norfk 51 L11
New Cowper Cumb 66 H3
Newcraighall C Edin 83 R4
New Crofton Wakefd 57 N3
New Cross Cerdgn 33 M5
New Cross Gt Lon 21 Q7
New Cross Somset 17 M13
New Cumnock E Ayrs 81 S10
New Cut E Susx 12 F12
New Deer Abers 105 P6
New Delaval Nthumb 77 R10
New Delph Oldham 56 E5
New Denham Bucks 20 H6
Newdigate Surrey 10 K2
New Duston W Nthn 37 T8
New Earswick C York 64 E8
New Eastwood Notts 47 N4
New Edlington Donc 57 R7
New Elgin Moray 103 V3
New Ellerby E R Yk 65 R12
Newell Green Br For 20 E8
New Eltham Gt Lon 21 R8
New End Worcs 36 E8
Newenden Kent 12 F10
New England C Pete 48 J13
New England Essex 40 B12
Newent Gloucs 28 D2
New Farnley Leeds 63 R13
New Ferry Wirral 54 H9
Newfield Dur 69 R2
Newfield Dur 69 R6
Newfield Highld 109 P9
New Fletton C Pete 48 J14
New Forest National Park 8 K7
Newfound Hants 19 S10
New Fryston Wakefd 57 Q1
Newgale Pembks 24 E6
New Galloway D & G 73 Q4
Newgate Norfk 50 H5
Newgate Street Herts 31 T11
New Gilston Fife 91 P10
New Grimsby IoS 2 b1
Newhall Ches E 45 P4
Newhall Derbys 46 J9
Newham Nthumb 85 T13
New Hartley Nthumb 77 S10
Newhaven C Edin 83 Q3
Newhaven Derbys 46 G1
Newhaven E Susx 11 Q10
New Haw Surrey 20 J10
New Hedges Pembks 24 K10
New Herrington Sundld 70 D2
Newhey Rochdl 56 D4
New Holkham Norfk 50 E6
New Holland N Linc 58 J2
Newholm N York 71 Q10
New Houghton Derbys 57 Q13
New Houghton Norfk 50 C8
Newhouse N Lans 82 E6
New Houses N York 62 G5
New Hutton W & F 62 B1
New Hythe Kent 12 D4
Newick E Susx 11 Q6
Newingreen Kent 13 M8
Newington Kent 12 G3
Newington Kent 13 N8
Newington Oxon 30 D13
Newington Shrops 34 K4
Newington Bagpath Gloucs 28 F9
New Inn Carmth 25 S3
New Inn Pembks 24 J4
New Inn Torfn 27 Q8
New Invention Shrops 34 G5
New Lanark S Lans 82 G10
New Lanark Village S Lans 82 G10
Newland C KuH 65 P13
Newland E R Yk 64 J14
Newland Gloucs 27 V6
Newland N York 57 U2
Newland Oxon 29 S6
Newland Somset 15 T5
Newland W & F 61 Q4
Newland Worcs 35 S11
Newlandrig Mdloth 83 S6
Newlands Border 75 V7
Newlands Nthumb 69 N1
Newlands W & F 67 M5
Newlands of Dundurcas Moray 104 B5
New Lane Lancs 54 K4
New Lane End Warrtn 55 P8
New Langholm D & G 75 S9
New Leake Lincs 49 P2
New Leeds Abers 105 R5
New Lodge Barns 57 N5
New Longton Lancs 55 M1
New Luce D & G 72 F7
Newlyn Cnwll 2 D11
Newmachar Abers 105 P12
Newmains N Lans 82 F7
New Malden Gt Lon 21 M9
Newman's End Essex 22 D5
Newman's Green Suffk 40 E12
Newmarket Suffk 39 T8
Newmarket W Isls 106 j5
New Marske R & Cl 70 K8
New Marston Oxon 30 B11
New Marton Shrops 44 H7
New Mill Abers 99 P7
Newmill Border 75 U3
New Mill Cnwll 2 D10
New Mill Herts 30 K10
New Mill Kirk 56 J5
Newmill Moray 104 E5
Newmillerdam Wakefd 57 M3
Newmill of Inshewan Angus 98 G11
Newmills C Edin 83 N5
New Mills Cnwll 3 M6
New Mills Derbys 56 F9
Newmills Fife 82 K1
Newmills Mons 27 U6
New Mills Powys 44 C13
Newmiln P & K 90 H5
Newmilns E Ayrs 81 Q5
New Milton Hants 8 J9
New Mistley Essex 23 R1
New Moat Pembks 24 J5
Newnes Shrops 44 J7
Newney Green Essex 22 G6
Newnham Hants 20 B12
Newnham Herts 31 R5
Newnham Kent 12 J4
Newnham W Nthn 37 Q9
Newnham Bridge Worcs 35 P7
Newnham on Severn Gloucs 28 C5
New Ollerton Notts 57 U13
New Oscott Birm 36 E2
New Passage S Glos 27 U10
New Pitsligo Abers 105 P4
New Polzeath Cnwll 4 A5
Newport Cnwll 4 J3
Newport Dorset 8 B9
Newport E R Yk 64 K13
Newport Essex 39 R14
Newport Gloucs 28 D8
Newport Highld 112 D12
Newport IoW 9 Q11
Newport Newpt 27 Q10
Newport Norfk 51 T10
Newport Pembks 24 J3
Newport Wrekin 45 R10
Newport-on-Tay Fife 91 P6
Newport Pagnell M Keyn 30 J4
Newport Pagnell Services M Keyn 30 J4
Newpound Common W Susx 10 H5
New Prestwick S Ayrs 81 L8
New Quay Cerdgn 32 G9
Newquay Cnwll 3 L4
New Quay Essex 23 P3
Newquay Zoo Cnwll 3 L4
New Rackheath Norfk 51 N11
New Radnor Powys 34 F8
New Rent W & F 67 Q5
New Ridley Nthumb 77 M14
New Road Side N York 62 K11
New Romney Kent 13 L11
New Rossington Donc 57 T7
New Row Cerdgn 33 P6
New Row Lancs 62 C12
New Sauchie Clacks 90 C13
Newsbank Ches E 55 T13
Newseat Abers 105 L9
Newsham Lancs 61 U12
Newsham N York 63 T3
Newsham N York 69 P10
Newsham Nthumb 77 S10
New Sharlston Wakefd 57 N3
Newsholme E R Yk 64 G14
Newsholme Lancs 62 G9
New Shoreston Nthumb 85 T12
New Silksworth Sundld 70 E2
New Skelton R & Cl 71 L9
Newsome Kirk 56 J4
New Somerby Lincs 48 D6
New Springs Wigan 55 N5
Newstead Border 84 F12
Newstead Notts 47 P3
Newstead Nthumb 85 T13
New Stevenston N Lans 82 E7
New Street Herefs 34 H9
New Swanage Dorset 8 E12
New Swannington Leics 47 M10
Newthorpe N York 64 B13
Newthorpe Notts 47 N4
New Thundersley Essex 22 J10
Newtimber W Susx 11 M8
Newtoft Lincs 58 H9
Newton Ag & B 88 B6
Newton Border 76 C1
Newton Brdgnd 26 E12
Newton C Beds 31 R4
Newton Cambs 39 P11
Newton Cambs 49 P11
Newton Cardif 27 N12
Newton Ches W 45 M2
Newton Ches W 54 K13
Newton Ches W 55 M11
Newton Derbys 47 M2
Newton Herefs 34 H14
Newton Herefs 34 J7
Newton Herefs 35 M10
Newton Highld 102 G5
Newton Highld 102 K6
Newton Highld 103 L2
Newton Highld 112 H7
Newton Lancs 61 Q12
Newton Lancs 62 B5
Newton Lincs 48 F6
Newton Moray 103 U3
Newton Moray 104 C3
Newton N Nthn 38 C4
Newton N York 64 K5
Newton Norfk 50 D10
Newton Notts 47 S5
Newton Nthumb 76 J4
Newton Nthumb 77 L13
Newton S Lans 82 H12
Newton S Lans 89 Q13
Newton Sandw 36 D2
Newton Shrops 44 K7
Newton Somset 16 F9
Newton Staffs 46 D8
Newton Suffk 40 F12
Newton W & F 61 N5
Newton W Loth 83 L3
Newton Warwks 37 P5
Newton Wilts 8 J4
Newton Abbot Devon 5 V6
Newton Arlosh Cumb 66 K1
Newton Aycliffe Dur 69 S8
Newton Bewley Hartpl 70 G7
Newton Blossomville M Keyn 38 D10
Newton Bromswold N Nthn 38 E7
Newton Burgoland Leics 47 L12
Newton by Toft Lincs 58 H9
Newton Ferrers Devon 5 P11
Newton Ferry W Isls 106 d11
Newton Flotman Norfk 51 M14
Newtongrange Mdloth 83 R6
Newton Green Mons 27 U9
Newton Harcourt Leics 37 R1
Newton Heath Manch 56 C6
Newtonhill Abers 99 S5
Newton Hill Wakefd 57 M2
Newton-in-Bowland Lancs 62 D9
Newton Kyme N York 64 B11
Newton-le-Willows N York 63 Q2
Newton-le-Willows St Hel 55 N7
Newtonloan Mdloth 83 R6
Newton Longville Bucks 30 H6
Newton Mearns E Rens 81 Q1
Newtonmill Angus 99 L11
Newtonmore Highld 97 L4
Newton Morrell N York 69 R11
Newton Mountain Pembks 24 G9
Newton Mulgrave N York 71 N9
Newton of Balcanquhal P & K 90 J9
Newton of Balcormo Fife 91 R11
Newton of Belltrees Rens 88 J14
Newton-on-Ayr S Ayrs 81 L8
Newton-on-Ouse N York 64 C8
Newton-on-Rawcliffe N York 64 J1
Newton on the Hill Shrops 45 L9
Newton-on-the-Moor Nthumb 77 P4
Newton on Trent Lincs 58 D12
Newton Poppleford Devon 6 E7
Newton Purcell Oxon 30 D6
Newton Regis Warwks 46 J12
Newton Reigny W & F 67 Q6
Newton St Cyres Devon 15 U13
Newton St Faith Norfk 51 M10
Newton St Loe BaNES 17 T4
Newton St Petrock Devon 14 K10
Newton Solney Derbys 46 J8
Newton Stacey Hants 19 P12
Newton Stewart D & G 73 L6
Newton Tony Wilts 18 K12
Newton Tracey Devon 15 M7
Newton under Roseberry R & Cl 70 J10
Newton Underwood Nthumb 77 N8
Newton upon Derwent E R Yk 64 G10
Newton Valence Hants 9 U2
Newton Village Mdloth 83 R5
Newton Wamphray D & G 75 M7
Newton with Scales Lancs 61 T13
Newtown BCP 8 E10
Newtown Blae G 27 M6
Newtown Ches W 55 M11
Newtown Cnwll 2 F11
Newtown Cnwll 4 H5
Newtown Cumb 66 H3
Newtown Cumb 75 S13
Newtown Cumb 75 V13
Newtown D & G 74 E3
Newtown Derbys 56 E10
Newtown Devon 6 E5
Newtown Devon 15 S7
Newtown Dorset 7 N4
New Town Dorset 8 D5
New Town Dorset 8 D5
New Town Dorset 8 D7
New Town E Susx 11 R6
Newtown Gloucs 28 C7
Newtown Hants 8 K6
Newtown Hants 9 S6
Newtown Hants 19 Q8
Newtown Herefs 35 L9
Newtown Herefs 35 M14
Newtown Herefs 35 P11
Newtown Highld 96 D3
Newtown IoW 9 N10
Newtown Nthumb 77 L5
Newtown Nthumb 85 P12
Newtown Nthumb 85 Q13
Newtown Powys 34 D2
Newtown Rhondd 26 K8
Newtown Shrops 44 K9
Newtown Shrops 45 L7
Newtown Somset 6 J2
Newtown Staffs 46 B1
Newtown Staffs 46 C13
Newtown W & F 67 R8
Newtown Wigan 55 N6
Newtown Wilts 8 C3
Newtown Wilts 19 L8
Newtown Worcs 35 U9
Newtown Worcs 36 B5
Newtown-in-St Martin Cnwll 2 J12
Newtown Linford Leics 47 P12
Newtown St Boswells Border 84 F12
Newtown Unthank Leics 47 N13
New Tredegar Caerph 27 L7
New Trows S Lans 82 F11
New Tupton Derbys 57 N13
Newtyle Angus 91 L3
New Walsoken Cambs 49 Q12
New Waltham NE Lin 59 N6
New Whittington Derbys 57 N11
New Winton E Loth 84 C4
New Yatt Oxon 29 S5
Newyears Green Gt Lon 20 J5
Newyork Ag & B 87 T3
New York Lincs 48 K2
New York N Tyne 77 S11
New York N York 63 P7
New Zealand Wilts 18 F5
Nextend Herefs 34 H9
Neyland Pembks 24 G9
Niarbyl IoM 60 c7
Nibley Gloucs 28 C6
Nibley S Glos 28 C11
Nibley Green Gloucs 28 D8
Nicholashayne Devon 16 F13
Nicholaston Swans 25 T13
Nickies Hill Cumb 76 A12
Nidd N York 63 S7
Nigg C Aber 99 S3
Nigg Highld 109 Q10
Nigg Ferry Highld 109 P11
Nimlet BaNES 17 T2
Ninebanks Nthumb 68 G2
Nine Elms Swindn 29 M10
Nine Wells Pembks 24 C6
Ninfield E Susx 12 D13
Ningwood IoW 9 M11
Nisbet Border 84 H13
Nisbet Hill Border 84 K8
Niton IoW 9 Q13
Nitshill C Glas 89 M13
Noah's Ark Kent 21 U11
Noak Bridge Essex 22 G9
Noak Hill Gt Lon 22 D9
Noblethorpe Barns 57 L5
Nobold Shrops 45 L11
Nobottle W Nthn 37 S8
Nocton Lincs 58 J14
Nogdam End Norfk 51 Q13
Noke Oxon 30 B10
Nolton Pembks 24 E7
Nolton Haven Pembks 24 E7
No Man's Heath Ches W 45 M4
No Man's Heath Warwks 46 J12
No Man's Land Cnwll 4 H9
Nomansland Devon 15 T10
Nomansland Wilts 8 K5
Noneley Shrops 45 L8
Nonington Kent 13 Q5
Nook Cumb 75 U10
Nook W & F 61 U3
Norbiton Gt Lon 21 L9
Norbreck Bpool 61 Q11
Norbridge Herefs 35 R12
Norbury Ches E 45 N4
Norbury Derbys 46 F5
Norbury Gt Lon 21 P9
Norbury Shrops 34 J2
Norbury Staffs 45 S9
Norbury Common Ches E 45 N4
Norbury Junction Staffs 45 S9
Norchard Worcs 35 T7
Norcott Brook Ches W 55 P10
Norcross Lancs 61 Q11
Nordelph Norfk 49 S13
Norden Rochdl 56 C4
Nordley Shrops 35 Q1
Norfolk Broads Norfk 51 S12
Norham Nthumb 85 N9
Norland Calder 56 G2
Norley Ches W 55 N12
Norleywood Hants 9 M9
Norlington E Susx 11 Q8
Normanby Lincs 58 G9
Normanby N Linc 58 E3
Normanby N York 64 G3
Normanby R & Cl 70 H9
Normanby le Wold Lincs 58 K7
Norman Cross Cambs 38 J2
Normandy Surrey 20 F12
Normans Bay E Susx 11 V9
Norman's Green Devon 6 E4
Normanton C Derb 46 K7
Normanton Leics 48 B5
Normanton Notts 47 T3
Normanton Rutlnd 48 D12
Normanton Wakefd 57 N2
Normanton Wilts 18 H12
Normanton le Heath Leics 47 L11
Normanton on Cliffe Lincs 48 D4
Normanton on Soar Notts 47 P9
Normanton on the Wolds Notts 47 R7
Normanton on Trent Notts 58 C13
Normoss Lancs 61 Q12
Norney Surrey 10 E2
Norrington Common Wilts 18 C8
Norris Green Cnwll 5 L7
Norris Green Lpool 54 J8
Norris Hill Leics 46 K10
Norristhorpe Kirk 56 K2
Northacre Norfk 50 G14
Northall Bucks 31 L8
Northallerton N York 70 E14
Northall Green Norfk 50 G11
Northam C Sotn 9 N6
Northam Devon 15 L7
Northampton W Nthn 37 U8
Northampton Worcs 35 T7
Northampton Services W Nthn 37 T9
North Anston Rothm 57 R10
North Ascot Br For 20 F9
North Aston Oxon 29 U2
Northaw Herts 31 S12
Northay Somset 6 J2
North Baddesley Hants 9 M4
North Ballachulish Highld 94 F6
North Barrow Somset 17 R11
North Barsham Norfk 50 F6
Northbay W Isls 106 c18
North Benfleet Essex 22 J10
North Berwick E Loth 84 E1
North Bitchburn Dur 69 Q6
North Blyth Nthumb 77 S9
North Boarhunt Hants 9 S6
North Bockhampton BCP 8 H9
Northborough C Pete 48 J12
Northbourne Kent 13 R5
North Bovey Devon 5 S4
North Bradley Wilts 18 C9
North Brentor Devon 5 M4
North Brewham Somset 17 T9
North Bridge Surrey 10 F3
Northbridge Street E Susx 12 D11
Northbrook Hants 19 R13
Northbrook Oxon 29 U3
North Brook End Cambs 31 S4
North Buckland Devon 15 L4
North Burlingham Norfk 51 Q12
North Cadbury Somset 17 R11
North Carlton Lincs 58 F11
North Carlton Notts 57 S10
North Cave E R Yk 64 K13
North Cerney Gloucs 28 K6
North Chailey E Susx 11 P6
Northchapel W Susx 10 F5
North Charford Hants 8 H5
North Charlton Nthumb 85 T14
North Cheam Gt Lon 21 M9
North Cheriton Somset 17 S11
North Chideock Dorset 7 M6
Northchurch Herts 31 L11
North Cliffe E R Yk 64 K12
North Clifton Notts 58 D12
North Close Dur 69 S6
North Cockerington Lincs 59 Q8
North Connel Ag & B 94 C12
North Cornelly Brdgnd 26 E11
North Corner Cnwll 2 K13
North Cotes Lincs 59 P6
Northcott Devon 4 J2
Northcott Devon 6 E2
Northcott Devon 6 F3
North Country Cnwll 2 H8
Northcourt Oxon 29 U8
North Cove Suffk 41 S3
North Cowton N York 69 S12
North Crawley M Keyn 30 K4
North Cray Gt Lon 21 S8
North Creake Norfk 50 E6
North Curry Somset 16 K11
North Dalton E R Yk 65 L9
North Deighton N York 63 T9
Northdown Kent 13 S1
North Downs 12 H4
North Duffield N York 64 F12
Northedge Derbys 57 N13
North Elham Kent 13 N7
North Elkington Lincs 59 N8
North Elmham Norfk 50 G9
North Elmsall Wakefd 57 Q4
Northend Bucks 20 B4
North End C Port 9 T8
North End Cumb 75 R14
North End Dorset 8 A3
North End E R Yk 65 R11
North End E R Yk 65 T13
North End Essex 22 G4
North End Hants 8 G5
North End Hants 9 R3
North End Leics 47 Q10
North End Lincs 48 K5
North End Lincs 58 H7
North End Lincs 59 P6
North End Lincs 59 R9
North End N Linc 58 K2
North End N Nthn 38 E7
North End N Som 17 M3
North End Norfk 40 G2
North End Nthumb 77 N5
North End Sefton 54 H6
North End W Susx 10 F10
North End W Susx 10 J9
Northend Warwks 37 L10
Northenden Manch 55 T9
Northend Woods Bucks 20 F5
North Erradale Highld 107 M8
North Evington C Leic 47 R13
North Fambridge Essex 23 L8
North Featherstone Wakefd 57 P2
North Ferriby E R Yk 58 G1
Northfield Birm 36 D5
Northfield C Aber 99 S2
Northfield E R Yk 58 H1
Northfields Lincs 48 F12
Northfleet Kent 22 F13
North Frodingham E R Yk 65 Q9
Northgate Lincs 48 J8
North Gorley Hants 8 H6
North Green Norfk 41 M3
North Green Suffk 41 P8
North Green Suffk 41 Q7
North Greetwell Lincs 58 H12
North Grimston N York 64 J6
North Halling Medway 12 D2
North Hayling Hants 9 U8
North Hazelrigg Nthumb 85 R12
North Heasley Devon 15 R6
North Heath W Susx 10 H6
North Hele Devon 16 D12
North Hill Cnwll 4 H5
North Hillingdon Gt Lon 20 J6
North Hinksey Village Oxon 29 U6
North Holmwood Surrey 21 L13
North Huish Devon 5 S9
North Hykeham Lincs 58 F13
Northiam E Susx 12 F11
Northill C Beds 38 H11
Northington Gloucs 28 D6
Northington Hants 19 S13
North Kelsey Lincs 58 H6
North Kessock Highld 102 J6
North Killingholme N Linc 58 K3
North Kilvington N York 63 U2
North Kilworth Leics 37 R4
North Kingston Hants 8 H8
North Kyme Lincs 48 J3
North Lancing W Susx 10 K9
North Landing E R Yk 65 S5
Northlands Lincs 49 M3
Northleach Gloucs 29 M5
North Lee Bucks 30 H11
North Lees N York 63 R5
Northleigh Devon 6 G5
Northleigh Devon 15 P6
North Leigh Kent 13 M6
North Leigh Oxon 29 S5
North Leverton with Habblesthorpe Notts 58 C10
Northlew Devon 15 M13
North Littleton Worcs 36 E11
Northload Bridge Somset 17 N9
North Lopham Norfk 40 H4
North Luffenham Rutlnd 48 D13
North Marden W Susx 10 C7
North Marston Bucks 30 G8
North Middleton Mdloth 83 S7
North Middleton Nthumb 85 P14
North Millbrex Abers 105 N7
North Milmain D & G 72 D9
North Molton Devon 15 R7
Northmoor Oxon 29 T7
North Moreton Oxon 19 S3
Northmuir Angus 98 F12
North Mundham W Susx 10 D10
North Muskham Notts 47 U2
North Newbald E R Yk 65 L12
North Newington Oxon 37 M12
North Newnton Wilts 18 H9
North Newton Somset 16 K10
Northney Hants 9 U8
North Nibley Gloucs 28 D8
North Oakley Hants 19 R10
North Ockendon Gt Lon 22 E10
Northolt Gt Lon 20 K6
Northolt Airport Gt Lon 20 J5
Northop Flints 54 F13
Northop Hall Flints 54 G13
North Ormesby Middsb 70 H9
North Ormsby Lincs 59 N8
Northorpe Kirk 56 K2
Northorpe Lincs 48 G10
Northorpe Lincs 48 K6
Northorpe Lincs 58 E7
North Otterington N York 63 T2
Northover Somset 17 N9
Northover Somset 17 P12
North Owersby Lincs 58 J8
Northowram Calder 56 H1
North Perrott Somset 7 N3
North Petherton Somset 16 J10
North Petherwin Cnwll 4 H3
North Pickenham Norfk 50 E12
North Piddle Worcs 36 C10
North Poorton Dorset 7 P5
Northport Dorset 8 C11
North Poulner Hants 8 H7
North Queensferry Fife 83 M2
North Radworthy Devon 15 S6
North Rauceby Lincs 48 F4
Northrepps Norfk 51 M6
North Reston Lincs 59 Q10
North Rigton N York 63 R10
North Ripley Hants 8 H9
North Rode Ches E 56 C13
North Roe Shet 106 t5
North Ronaldsay Ork 106 w14
North Ronaldsay Airport Ork 106 w14
North Row Cumb 66 K6
North Runcton Norfk 49 T10
North Scale W & F 61 M6
North Scarle Lincs 58 D13
North Seaton Nthumb 77 R8
North Seaton Colliery Nthumb 77 R8
North Shian Ag & B 94 C10
North Shields N Tyne 77 T12
North Shoebury Sthend 23 M10
North Shore Bpool 61 Q12
North Side C Pete 49 L14
North Side Cumb 66 E7
North Skelton R & Cl 71 L9
North Somercotes Lincs 59 R7
North Stainley N York 63 R4
North Stainmore W & F 68 H9
North Stifford Thurr 22 F11
North Stoke BaNES 17 T3
North Stoke Oxon 19 T3
North Stoke W Susx 10 G8
Northstowe Cambs 39 P7
North Street Cambs 39 S7
North Street Hants 8 H5
North Street Hants 9 S2
North Street Kent 12 K4
North Street Medway 22 K13
North Street W Berk 19 T6
North Sunderland Nthumb 85 U12
North Tamerton Cnwll 14 H13
North Tawton Devon 15 Q12
North Third Stirlg 89 S8
North Thoresby Lincs 59 N7
North Togston Nthumb 77 Q5
North Tolsta W Isls 106 k4
Northton W Isls 106 e10
North Town Devon 15 M11
North Town Somset 17 Q8
North Town W & M 20 E6
North Tuddenham Norfk 50 H11
North Uist W Isls 106 c11
Northumberland National Park Nthumb 76 F9
North Walbottle N u Ty 77 P12
North Walsham Norfk 51 N7
North Waltham Hants 19 S11
North Warnborough Hants 20 B12
Northway Somset 16 F11
North Weald Bassett Essex 22 C7
North Wheatley Notts 58 C9
North Whilborough Devon 5 V7
Northwich Ches W 55 Q12
North Wick BaNES 17 Q3
Northwick S Glos 27 V10
Northwick Somset 17 L7
Northwick Worcs 35 T9
North Widcombe BaNES 17 Q5
North Willingham Lincs 59 L9
North Wingfield Derbys 57 P13
North Witham Lincs 48 D9
Northwold Norfk 40 C1
Northwood C Stke 45 U4
Northwood Derbys 57 L14
Northwood Gt Lon 20 J4
Northwood IoW 9 P10
Northwood Shrops 45 L7
Northwood Worcs 35 S5
Northwood Green Gloucs 28 D4
North Wootton Dorset 7 S2
North Wootton Norfk 49 T9
North Wootton Somset 17 Q8
North Wraxall Wilts 18 B5
North Wroughton Swindn 18 H4
North York Moors National Park 71 M12
Norton Donc 57 R3
Norton E Susx 11 R10
Norton Gloucs 28 G3
Norton Halton 55 N10
Norton Hants 19 Q12
Norton Herts 31 R6
Norton IoW 9 L11
Norton Mons 27 S3
Norton N Som 16 K4
Norton Notts 57 S12
Norton Powys 34 H7
Norton S on T 70 F8
Norton Sheff 57 N10
Norton Shrops 35 L4
Norton Shrops 35 P4
Norton Shrops 45 N12
Norton Shrops 45 R13
Norton Suffk 40 G7
Norton Swans 25 V13
Norton W Nthn 37 Q8
Norton W Susx 10 E9
Norton Wilts 28 G11
Norton Worcs 35 U10
Norton Worcs 36 D11
Norton Bavant Wilts 18 D12
Norton Bridge Staffs 45 U7
Norton Canes Staffs 46 D12
Norton Canes Services Staffs 46 D12
Norton Canon Herefs 34 J11
Norton Corner Norfk 50 J8
Norton Disney Lincs 48 C2
Norton Ferris Wilts 17 U9
Norton Fitzwarren Somset 16 G11
Norton Green IoW 9 L11
Norton Hawkfield BaNES 17 Q4
Norton Heath Essex 22 F7
Norton in Hales Shrops 45 R6
Norton-Juxta-Twycross Leics 46 K12
Norton-le-Clay N York 63 U5
Norton-le-Moors C Stke 45 U3
Norton Lindsey Warwks 36 H8
Norton Little Green Suffk 40 G7
Norton Malreward BaNES 17 R4
Norton Mandeville Essex 22 E7
Norton-on-Derwent N York 64 H5
Norton St Philip Somset 17 U5
Norton Subcourse Norfk 51 R14
Norton sub Hamdon Somset 17 N13
Norton Wood Herefs 34 J11
Norwell Notts 47 U1
Norwell Woodhouse Notts 58 B14
Norwich Norfk 51 M12
Norwich Airport Norfk 51 M11
Norwick Shet 106 w2
Norwood Clacks 90 C13
Norwood Derbys 57 Q10
Norwood Kent 13 L9
Norwood End Essex 22 E6
Norwood Green Calder 56 H1
Norwood Green Gt Lon 20 K7
Norwood Hill Surrey 11 L2
Norwoodside Cambs 49 P14
Noseley Leics 47 T14
Noss Mayo Devon 5 P11
Nosterfield N York 63 R3
Nosterfield End Cambs 39 T12
Nostie Highld 101 M6
Notgrove Gloucs 29 M3
Nottage Brdgnd 26 E12
Notter Cnwll 4 K8
Nottingham C Nott 47 Q6
Nottington Dorset 7 S8
Notton Wakefd 57 M4
Notton Wilts 18 D7
Nounsley Essex 22 J5
Noutard's Green Worcs 35 T7
Nowton Suffk 40 E8
Nox Shrops 44 K11
Nuffield Oxon 19 U3
Nunburnholme E R Yk 64 J10
Nuncargate Notts 47 P3
Nunclose W & F 67 Q3
Nuneaton Warwks 37 L2
Nuneham Courtenay Oxon 30 C13
Nunhead Gt Lon 21 P7
Nunkeeling E R Yk 65 Q10
Nun Monkton N York 64 C8
Nunney Somset 17 T7
Nunney Catch Somset 17 T8
Nunnington Herefs 35 N12
Nunnington N York 64 F4
Nunsthorpe NE Lin 59 N5
Nunthorpe C York 64 E9
Nunthorpe Middsb 70 H10
Nunthorpe Village Middsb 70 H10
Nunton Wilts 8 H3
Nunwick N York 63 S5
Nunwick Nthumb 76 H11
Nupdown S Glos 28 B8
Nup End Bucks 30 J9
Nupend Gloucs 28 E6
Nuptown Br For 20 E8
Nursling Hants 9 M5
Nursted Hants 10 B6
Nursteed Wilts 18 F8
Nurton Staffs 45 T14
Nutbourne W Susx 10 B9
Nutbourne W Susx 10 H7
Nutfield Surrey 21 P12
Nuthall Notts 47 P5
Nuthampstead Herts 39 P14
Nuthurst W Susx 10 K5
Nutley E Susx 11 Q5
Nutley Hants 19 T12
Nuttall Bury 55 S3
Nutwell Donc 57 T6
Nybster Highld 112 J4
Nyetimber W Susx 10 D11
Nyewood W Susx 10 C6
Nymans W Susx 11 M5
Nymet Rowland Devon 15 R11
Nymet Tracey Devon 15 R12
Nympsfield Gloucs 28 F7
Nynehead Somset 16 F12
Nythe Somset 17 M10
Nyton W Susx 10 E9

O

Oadby Leics 47 R13
Oad Street Kent 12 G3
Oakall Green Worcs 35 T8
Oakamoor Staffs 46 D5
Oakbank W Loth 83 L5
Oak Cross Devon 15 M13
Oakdale Caerph 27 M8
Oake Somset 16 G11
Oaken Staffs 45 U13
Oakenclough Lancs 61 U10
Oakengates Wrekin 45 R11
Oakenholt Flints 54 G12
Oakenshaw Dur 69 Q5
Oakenshaw Kirk 63 P14
Oakerthorpe Derbys 47 L3
Oakford Cerdgn 32 J9
Oakford Devon 16 B12
Oakfordbridge Devon 16 B12
Oakgrove Ches E 56 D13
Oakham Rutlnd 48 C12
Oakhanger Ches E 45 S3
Oakhanger Hants 10 B3
Oakhill Somset 17 R7
Oakhurst Kent 21 U12
Oakington Cambs 39 P8
Oaklands Herts 31 R9
Oaklands Powys 34 B10
Oakle Street Gloucs 28 E4
Oakley BCP 8 E9
Oakley Bed 38 F10
Oakley Bucks 30 D10
Oakley Fife 90 F14
Oakley Hants 19 S10
Oakley Oxon 30 G12
Oakley Suffk 41 L5
Oakley Green W & M 20 F7
Oakley Park Powys 33 U3
Oakridge Lynch Gloucs 28 H7
Oaks Lancs 62 D13
Oaks Shrops 44 K13
Oaksey Wilts 28 J9
Oaks Green Derbys 46 G7
Oakshaw Ford Cumb 75 V10
Oakshott Hants 9 U3
Oakthorpe Leics 46 K11
Oak Tree Darltn 70 E10
Oakwood C Derb 47 L6
Oakwood Nthumb 76 J12
Oakworth C Brad 63 L12
Oare Kent 12 K3
Oare Somset 15 S3
Oare Wilts 18 J8
Oasby Lincs 48 F6
Oath Somset 17 L11
Oathlaw Angus 98 H12
Oatlands Park Surrey 20 J9
Oban Ag & B 94 B13
Oban Airport Ag & B 94 C11
Obley Shrops 34 H5
Obney P & K 90 F4
Oborne Dorset 17 S13
Obthorpe Lincs 48 G11
Occold Suffk 41 L6
Occumster Highld 112 G9
Ochiltree E Ayrs 81 Q8
Ockbrook Derbys 47 M6
Ocker Hill Sandw 36 C2
Ockeridge Worcs 35 S8
Ockham Surrey 20 J11
Ockle Highld 93 P4
Ockley Surrey 10 J2
Ocle Pychard Herefs 35 N11
Octon E R Yk 65 N6
Odcombe Somset 17 P13
Odd Down BaNES 17 T4
Oddendale W & F 67 S10
Oddingley Worcs 36 B9
Oddington Oxon 30 C9
Odell Bed 38 E9
Odham Devon 15 L12
Odiham Hants 20 B12
Odsal C Brad 63 P14
Odsey Cambs 31 S5
Odstock Wilts 8 G3
Odstone Leics 47 L12
Offchurch Warwks 37 L7
Offenham Worcs 36 E11
Offerton Stockp 56 D9
Offerton Sundld 70 D1
Offham E Susx 11 Q8
Offham Kent 12 C4
Offham W Susx 10 G9
Offleymarsh Staffs 45 S8
Offord Cluny Cambs 38 K7
Offord D'Arcy Cambs 38 K7
Offton Suffk 40 J11
Offwell Devon 6 G5
Ogbourne Maizey Wilts 18 J6
Ogbourne St Andrew Wilts 18 J6
Ogbourne St George Wilts 18 K6
Ogden Calder 63 M13
Ogle Nthumb 77 N10
Oglet Lpool 54 K10
Ogmore V Glam 26 F12
Ogmore-by-Sea V Glam 26 F12
Ogmore Vale Brdgnd 26 G9
Ogwen Bank Gwynd 52 K9
Okeford Fitzpaine Dorset 7 V2
Okehampton Devon 15 N13
Oker Side Derbys 46 J1
Okewood Hill Surrey 10 J3
Olchard Devon 6 A9
Old W Nthn 37 U6
Old Aberdeen C Aber 99 S2
Old Alresford Hants 9 R2
Oldany Highld 110 B10
Old Arley Warwks 36 J2
Old Auchenbrack D & G 74 E6
Old Basford C Nott 47 Q5
Old Basing Hants 19 U10
Old Beetley Norfk 50 G10
Oldberrow Warwks 36 F7
Old Bewick Nthumb 77 M1
Old Bolingbroke Lincs 59 Q13
Old Boxted Essex 40 G14
Old Bramhope Leeds 63 Q11
Old Brampton Derbys 57 M12
Old Bridge of Urr D & G 74 E12
Old Buckenham Norfk 40 J2
Old Burghclere Hants 19 Q9
Oldbury Kent 21 U11
Oldbury Sandw 36 C3
Oldbury Shrops 35 R2
Oldbury Warwks 36 K2
Oldbury Naite S Glos 28 B9
Oldbury-on-Severn S Glos 28 B9
Oldbury on the Hill Gloucs 28 F10
Old Byland N York 64 D2
Old Cantley Donc 57 T6
Old Cassop Dur 70 D5
Oldcastle Mons 27 Q3
Oldcastle Heath Ches W 45 L4
Old Catton Norfk 51 M11
Old Churchstoke Powys 34 G2
Old Clee NE Lin 59 N5
Old Cleeve Somset 16 D8
Old Colwyn Conwy 53 Q7
Oldcotes Notts 57 S9
Old Coulsdon Gt Lon 21 P11
Old Dailly S Ayrs 80 J13
Old Dalby Leics 47 S9
Old Dam Derbys 56 H11
Old Deer Abers 105 R6
Old Ditch Somset 17 P7
Old Edlington Donc 57 R7
Old Eldon Dur 69 R7
Old Ellerby E R Yk 65 R12
Old Felixstowe Suffk 41 P13
Oldfield C Brad 63 L12
Oldfield Worcs 35 T8
Old Fletton C Pete 38 J1
Oldford Somset 17 U6
Old Forge Herefs 27 V4
Old Furnace Herefs 27 T3
Old Glossop Derbys 56 F8
Old Goole E R Yk 58 B2
Old Grimsby IoS 2 b1
Old Hall Green Herts 31 U8
Oldhall Green Suffk 40 E9
Old Hall Street Norfk 51 P7
Oldham Oldham 56 D6
Oldhamstocks E Loth 84 J4
Old Harlow Essex 22 C5
Old Heath Essex 23 P3
Old Hunstanton Norfk 49 U5
Old Hurst Cambs 39 M5
Old Hutton W & F 62 B2
Old Inns Services N Lans 89 S10
Old Kea Cnwll 3 L8
Old Kilpatrick W Duns 89 L11
Old Knebworth Herts 31 R8
Old Lakenham Norfk 51 M12
Oldland S Glos 17 S2
Old Langho Lancs 62 E12
Old Laxey IoM 60 g6
Old Leake Lincs 49 P3
Old Malton N York 64 H5
Oldmeldrum Abers 105 N10
Oldmill Cnwll 4 K6
Old Milverton Warwks 36 J7
Oldmixon N Som 16 K5
Old Newton Suffk 40 J8
Old Oxted Surrey 21 Q12
Old Philpstoun W Loth 83 L3
Old Portlethen Abers 99 S4
Old Quarrington Dur 70 D5
Old Radford C Nott 47 Q5
Old Radnor Powys 34 G9
Old Rayne Abers 104 K10
Old Romney Kent 12 K11
Old Shoreham W Susx 11 L9
Oldshoremore Highld 110 E5
Old Soar Kent 12 B5
Old Sodbury S Glos 28 E11
Old Somerby Lincs 48 E7
Oldstead N York 64 C3
Old Stratford W Nthn 30 G4
Old Struan P & K 97 N10
Old Swarland Nthumb 77 P5
Old Swinford Dudley 36 B4
Old Tebay W & F 68 D11
Old Thirsk N York 63 U3
Old Town Calder 63 L14
Old Town E Susx 11 T11
Old Town IoS 2 c2
Old Town W & F 62 B3
Old Town W & F 67 Q4
Old Trafford Traffd 55 T7
Old Tupton Derbys 57 N13
Oldwall Cumb 75 U13
Oldwalls Swans 25 S12
Old Warden C Beds 31 P4
Oldways End Somset 15 U8
Old Weston Cambs 38 G5
Old Wick Highld 112 J7
Old Windsor W & M 20 G8
Old Wives Lees Kent 13 L5
Old Woking Surrey 20 H11
Old Wolverton M Keyn 30 H4
Old Woodhall Lincs 59 M13
Old Woods Shrops 45 L9
Olgrinmore Highld 112 C6
Olive Green Staffs 46 F10
Oliver's Battery Hants 9 P3
Ollaberry Shet 106 t5
Ollach Highld 100 e6
Ollerton Ches E 55 S11
Ollerton Notts 57 U13
Ollerton Shrops 45 P8
Olmarch Cerdgn 33 M9
Olmstead Green Cambs 39 T12
Olney M Keyn 38 C10
Olrig House Highld 112 E3
Olton Solhll 36 F4
Olveston S Glos 28 B10
Ombersley Worcs 35 T8
Ompton Notts 57 U13
Once Brewed Nthumb 76 E12
Onchan IoM 60 f7
Onecote Staffs 46 D2
Onehouse Suffk 40 H9
Onen Mons 27 S5
Ongar Street Herefs 34 J7
Onibury Shrops 35 L5
Onich Highld 94 E6
Onllwyn Neath 26 E5
Onneley Staffs 45 S5
Onslow Green Essex 22 G4
Onslow Village Surrey 20 G13
Onston Ches W 55 N12
Openwoodgate Derbys 47 L4
Opinan Highld 107 M10
Orbliston Moray 104 C4
Orbost Highld 100 b5
Orby Lincs 59 S13
Orchard Portman Somset 16 H12
Orcheston Wilts 18 G11
Orcop Herefs 27 T2
Orcop Hill Herefs 27 T2
Ord Abers 104 J4
Ordhead Abers 104 K13
Ordie Abers 98 H3
Ordiequish Moray 104 C4
Ordley Nthumb 76 J14
Ordsall Notts 58 B11
Ore E Susx 12 F13
Oreleton Common Herefs 35 L7
Oreton Shrops 35 Q4

Orford Suffk 41 R10
Orford Warrtn 55 P8
Organford Dorset 8 C10
Orgreave Staffs 46 F10
Orkney Islands Ork 106 t19
Orkney Neolithic Ork 106 s18
Orlestone Kent 12 K9
Orleton Herefs 35 L7
Orleton Worcs 35 R7
Orlingbury N Nthn 38 C6
Ormathwaite Cumb 67 L7
Ormesby R & Cl 70 H9
Ormesby St Margaret Norfk 51 S11
Ormesby St Michael Norfk 51 S11
Ormiscaig Highld 107 Q6
Ormiston E Loth 83 T5
Ormsaigmore Highld 93 M6
Ormsary Ag & B 87 N11
Ormskirk Lancs 54 K5
Ornsby Hill Dur 69 Q3
Oronsay Ag & B 86 F8
Orphir Ork 106 s19
Orpington Gt Lon 21 S9
Orrell Sefton 54 H7
Orrell Wigan 55 M6
Orrell Post Wigan 55 M5
Orrisdale IoM 60 e4
Orroland D & G 73 T10
Orsett Thurr 22 F11
Orsett Heath Thurr 22 F11
Orslow Staffs 45 T10
Orston Notts 47 U5
Orthwaite Cumb 67 L6
Ortner Lancs 61 U9
Orton N Nthn 38 B5
Orton Staffs 35 U1
Orton W & F 68 D11
Orton Longueville C Pete 38 J1
Orton-on-the-Hill Leics 46 K13
Orton Rigg Cumb 67 M2
Orton Waterville C Pete 38 J1
Orwell Cambs 39 N10
Osbaldeston Lancs 62 C13
Osbaldeston Green Lancs 62 C13
Osbaldwick C York 64 E9
Osbaston Leics 47 M13
Osbaston Mons 27 U5
Osbaston Shrops 44 H9
Osborne IoW 9 Q10
Osborne IoW 9 Q10
Osbournby Lincs 48 G6
Oscroft Ches W 55 M13
Ose Highld 100 c5
Osgathorpe Leics 47 M10
Osgodby Lincs 58 J8
Osgodby N York 64 E13
Osgodby N York 65 P3
Oskaig Highld 100 e6
Oskamull Ag & B 93 M10
Osmaston Derbys 46 G5
Osmington Dorset 7 T8
Osmington Mills Dorset 7 T8
Osmondthorpe Leeds 63 S13
Osmotherley N York 70 G13
Osney Oxon 29 U6
Ospringe Kent 12 K3
Ossett Wakefd 57 L2
Ossington Notts 58 C14
Ostend Essex 23 M8
Osterley Gt Lon 21 L7
Oswaldkirk N York 64 E4
Oswaldtwistle Lancs 55 R1
Oswestry Shrops 44 G8
Otairnis W Isls 106 e11
Otford Kent 21 T11
Otham Kent 12 E5
Otham Hole Kent 12 F5
Othery Somset 17 L10
Otley Leeds 63 Q10
Otley Suffk 41 M9
Otley Green Suffk 41 M9
Otterbourne Hants 9 P4
Otterburn N York 62 H8
Otterburn Nthumb 76 H7
Otter Ferry Ag & B 87 S9
Otterham Cnwll 4 F2
Otterhampton Somset 16 H8
Otterham Quay Kent 12 F2
Otterham Station Cnwll 4 F3
Otternish W Isls 106 e11
Ottershaw Surrey 20 H10
Otterswick Shet 106 v5
Otterton Devon 6 E7
Otterwood Hants 9 N8
Ottery St Mary Devon 6 F5
Ottinge Kent 13 N7
Ottringham E R Yk 59 N2
Oughterby Cumb 67 L1
Oughtershaw N York 62 H3
Oughterside Cumb 66 H4
Oughtibridge Sheff 57 M8
Oughtrington Warrtn 55 Q9
Oulston N York 64 C5
Oulton Cumb 66 K2
Oulton Leeds 63 T14
Oulton Norfk 50 K8
Oulton Staffs 45 S9
Oulton Staffs 46 B6
Oulton Suffk 41 T2
Oulton Broad Suffk 41 T2
Oulton Street Norfk 51 L8
Oundle N Nthn 38 F3
Ounsdale Staffs 35 U2
Ousby W & F 68 D6
Ousden Suffk 40 B9
Ousefleet E R Yk 58 D2
Ouston Dur 69 S2
Outchester Nthumb 85 S12
Out Elmstead Kent 13 P5
Outgate W & F 67 N13
Outhgill W & F 68 G12
Outhill Warwks 36 F7
Outlands Staffs 45 S7
Outlane Kirk 56 G3
Out Newton E R Yk 59 Q2
Out Rawcliffe Lancs 61 S11
Out Skerries Shet 106 w6
Outwell Norfk 49 R13
Outwick Hants 8 G5
Outwood Surrey 21 P13
Outwood Wakefd 57 M2
Outwood Gate Bury 55 S5
Outwoods Leics 47 M10
Outwoods Staffs 45 S10
Ouzlewell Green Leeds 57 M1
Ovenden Calder 56 G1
Over Cambs 39 N6
Over Ches W 55 P13
Over Gloucs 28 F4
Over S Glos 28 A11
Over Burrows Derbys 46 J6
Overbury Worcs 36 C13
Overcombe Dorset 7 S8
Over Compton Dorset 17 Q13
Over End Cambs 38 G2
Overgreen Derbys 57 M12
Over Green Warwks 36 G2
Over Haddon Derbys 56 K13
Over Hulton Bolton 55 Q6
Over Kellet Lancs 61 U6
Over Kiddington Oxon 29 T3
Overleigh Somset 17 N9
Overley Staffs 46 G10
Over Monnow Mons 27 U5
Over Norton Oxon 29 R2
Over Peover Ches E 55 S12
Overpool Ches W 54 J11
Overscaig Highld 110 J12
Overseal Derbys 46 J10
Over Silton N York 70 F14
Oversland Kent 13 L4
Oversley Green Warwks 36 E9
Overstone W Nthn 37 U7
Over Stowey Somset 16 G9
Overstrand Norfk 51 M5
Over Stratton Somset 17 M13
Overstreet Wilts 18 G13
Over Tabley Ches E 55 R11
Overthorpe W Nthn 37 N12
Overton C Aber 105 P13
Overton Ches W 55 M11
Overton Hants 19 R11
Overton Lancs 61 S8
Overton N York 64 D8
Overton Shrops 35 M6
Overton Swans 25 S13
Overton Wakefd 57 L3
Overton Wrexhm 44 J5
Overton Bridge Wrexhm 44 J5
Overton Green Ches E 45 T1
Overtown Lancs 62 C4
Overtown Lancs 62 H14
Overtown N Lans 82 F8
Overtown Swindn 18 J5
Overtown Wakefd 57 N3
Over Wallop Hants 19 L13
Over Whitacre Warwks 36 J2
Over Woodhouse Derbys 57 Q12
Over Worton Oxon 29 T2
Overy Oxon 19 S2
Oving Bucks 30 G8
Oving W Susx 10 E10
Ovingdean Br & H 11 P10
Ovingham Nthumb 77 M13
Ovington Dur 69 P10
Ovington Essex 40 C12
Ovington Hants 9 R2
Ovington Norfk 50 F13
Ovington Nthumb 77 M13
Ower Hants 9 L5
Ower Hants 9 P8
Owermoigne Dorset 7 U7
Owlbury Shrops 34 H2
Owlerton Sheff 57 M9
Owlpen Gloucs 28 E8
Owl's Green Suffk 41 N7
Owlsmoor Br For 20 D10
Owlswick Bucks 30 G11
Owmby Lincs 58 H9
Owmby Lincs 58 J6
Owslebury Hants 9 Q4
Owston Donc 57 S4
Owston Leics 47 U12
Owston Ferry N Linc 58 D6
Owstwick E R Yk 65 T13
Owthorne E R Yk 65 U14
Owthorpe Notts 47 S7
Owton Manor Hartpl 70 G7
Oxborough Norfk 50 B13
Oxbridge Dorset 7 N5
Oxcombe Lincs 59 P11
Oxcroft Derbys 57 Q12
Oxen End Essex 22 G2
Oxenholme W & F 61 U2
Oxenhope C Brad 63 L13
Oxen Park W & F 61 Q2
Oxenpill Somset 17 M8
Oxenton Gloucs 28 J1
Oxenwood Wilts 19 M9
Oxford Oxon 30 B11
Oxford Airport Oxon 29 U4
Oxford Services Oxon 30 D12
Oxgangs C Edin 83 P5
Oxhey Herts 20 K3
Oxhill Dur 69 Q2
Oxhill Warwks 36 K11
Oxley Wolves 46 B13
Oxley Green Essex 23 M5
Oxley's Green E Susx 12 C11
Oxlode Cambs 39 Q3
Oxnam Border 76 D2
Oxnead Norfk 51 M9
Oxshott Surrey 20 K10
Oxshott Heath Surrey 20 K10
Oxspring Barns 57 L6
Oxted Surrey 21 Q12
Oxton Border 84 D8
Oxton N York 64 C11
Oxton Notts 47 R3
Oxton Wirral 54 H9
Oxwich Swans 25 S13
Oxwich Green Swans 25 S13
Oxwick Norfk 50 F8
Oykel Bridge Highld 108 F4
Oyne Abers 104 K10
Oystermouth Swans 25 V13
Ozleworth Gloucs 28 E9

P

Pabail W Isls 106 k5
Packers Hill Dorset 7 T2
Packington Leics 47 L11
Packmoor C Stke 45 U3
Packmores Warwks 36 J7
Padanaram Angus 98 G13
Padbury Bucks 30 F6
Paddington Gt Lon 21 N6
Paddington Warrtn 55 P9
Paddlesworth Kent 12 C3
Paddlesworth Kent 13 N8
Paddock Wood Kent 12 C7
Paddolgreen Shrops 45 M7
Padfield Derbys 56 F7
Padgate Warrtn 55 P9
Padhams Green Essex 22 F8
Padiham Lancs 62 F13
Padside N York 63 P8
Padstow Cnwll 3 N1
Padworth W Berk 19 T7
Page Bank Dur 69 R5
Pagham W Susx 10 D11
Paglesham Essex 23 M9
Paignton Torbay 6 A12
Pailton Warwks 37 N4
Paine's Cross E Susx 11 U6
Painleyhill Staffs 46 D7
Painscastle Powys 34 E11
Painshawfield Nthumb 77 M13
Painsthorpe E R Yk 64 J8
Painswick Gloucs 28 G6
Painter's Forstal Kent 12 J4
Paisley Rens 89 L13
Pakefield Suffk 41 T2
Pakenham Suffk 40 F7
Pale Gwynd 43 U6
Pale Green Essex 39 U12
Palestine Hants 19 L12
Paley Street W & M 20 E7
Palfrey Wsall 36 D1
Palgrave Suffk 40 K5
Pallington Dorset 7 U6
Palmarsh Kent 13 M9
Palmers Green Gt Lon 21 P4
Palmerston E Ayrs 81 Q9
Palmerstown V Glam 16 F3
Palnackie D & G 73 U8
Palnure D & G 73 M7
Palterton Derbys 57 Q13
Pamber End Hants 19 T9
Pamber Green Hants 19 T9
Pamber Heath Hants 19 T8
Pamington Gloucs 36 B14
Pamphill Dorset 8 D8
Pampisford Cambs 39 Q11
Panborough Somset 17 N7
Panbride Angus 91 S4
Pancrasweek Devon 14 G11
Pancross V Glam 16 D3
Pandy Gwynd 43 M13
Pandy Gwynd 43 S8
Pandy Mons 27 Q3
Pandy Powys 43 T13
Pandy Wrexhm 44 E6
Pandy Wrexhm 44 H3
Pandy'r Capel Denbgs 44 C3
Pandy Tudur Conwy 53 Q10
Panfield Essex 22 H2
Pangbourne W Berk 19 T5
Pangdean W Susx 11 M8
Panks Bridge Herefs 35 P11
Pannal N York 63 S9
Pannal Ash N York 63 R9
Pant Shrops 44 G9
Pantasaph Flints 54 E11
Panteg Pembks 24 F4
Pantersbridge Cnwll 4 F7
Pant-ffrwyth Brdgnd 26 G11
Pant Glas Gwynd 42 J4
Pantglas Powys 43 Q14
Pant-Gwyn Carmth 25 U5
Pant-lasau Swans 26 B7
Pant Mawr Powys 33 R4
Panton Lincs 59 L11
Pant-pastynog Denbgs 53 T10
Pantperthog Gwynd 43 P13
Pantside Caerph 27 N8
Pant-y-caws Carmth 24 K5
Pant-y-dwr Powys 33 U6
Pant-y-ffridd Powys 44 E13
Pantyffynnon Carmth 25 V8
Pantygaseg Torfn 27 P8
Pantygelli Mons 27 Q4
Pant-y-gog Brdgnd 26 G9
Pantymwyn Flints 54 E14
Panxworth Norfk 51 Q11
Papa Stour Shet 106 r7
Papa Stour Airport Shet 106 r8
Papa Westray Ork 106 t14
Papa Westray Airport Ork 106 t14
Papcastle Cumb 66 H6
Papigoe Highld 112 J6
Papple E Loth 84 F4
Papplewick Notts 47 P3
Papworth Everard Cambs 39 L8
Papworth St Agnes Cambs 39 L8
Par Cnwll 3 R6
Paramour Street Kent 13 Q3
Parbold Lancs 55 L4
Parbrook Somset 17 Q9
Parbrook W Susx 10 H5
Parc Gwynd 43 S7
Parcllyn Cerdgn 32 D10
Parc Seymour Newpt 27 S9
Pardown Hants 19 S11
Pardshaw Cumb 66 G8
Parham Suffk 41 P8
Park D & G 74 H7
Park Nthumb 76 D13
Park Bottom Cnwll 2 H8
Park Bridge Tamesd 56 D6
Park Corner E Susx 11 S3
Park Corner Oxon 19 U3
Park Corner W & M 20 E6
Park End Bed 38 E10
Parkend Gloucs 28 B6
Park End Nthumb 76 H10
Parker's Green Kent 12 B6
Parkeston Essex 23 T1
Parkeston Quay Essex 41 M14
Park Farm Kent 12 K8
Parkgate Ches W 54 G11
Parkgate Cumb 66 K3
Parkgate D & G 74 K8
Parkgate E Susx 12 D13
Parkgate Essex 22 G2
Park Gate Hants 9 Q7
Parkgate Kent 12 G9
Parkgate Kent 21 T10
Park Gate Leeds 63 P11
Parkgate Surrey 11 L2
Park Gate Worcs 36 B6
Park Green Essex 22 C2
Park Green Suffk 40 K8
Park Hall Shrops 44 H7
Parkhall W Duns 89 L11
Parkham Devon 14 J8
Parkham Ash Devon 14 J8
Park Head Derbys 47 L3
Parkhill Dur 70 D5
Park Hill Gloucs 27 V8
Parkhouse Mons 27 U7
Parkmill Swans 25 T13
Park Royal Gt Lon 21 L6
Parkside Dur 70 F3
Parkside N Lans 82 F7
Parkside Wrexhm 44 J2
Parkstone BCP 8 E10
Park Street Herts 31 P12
Park Street W Susx 10 J4
Parkway Herefs 35 R13
Parley Green BCP 8 G9
Parmoor Bucks 20 C5
Parracombe Devon 15 Q3
Parrog Pembks 24 J3
Parsonby Cumb 66 H5
Parson Cross Sheff 57 M8
Parson Drove Cambs 49 N12
Parson's Heath Essex 23 P2
Parson's Hill Derbys 46 J8
Partick C Glas 89 M12
Partington Traffd 55 R8
Partney Lincs 59 R13
Parton Cumb 66 E8
Partridge Green W Susx 10 K7
Partrishow Powys 27 P3
Parwich Derbys 46 G3
Paslow Wood Common Essex 22 E7
Passenham W Nthn 30 G5
Passfield Hants 10 C4
Passingford Bridge Essex 22 D8
Paston C Pete 48 J13
Paston Norfk 51 P7
Pasturefields Staffs 46 C9
Patchacott Devon 15 L13
Patcham Br & H 11 N9
Patchetts Green Herts 20 K3
Patching W Susx 10 H9
Patchole Devon 15 P4
Patchway S Glos 28 B11
Pateley Bridge N York 63 P6
Paternoster Heath Essex 23 M4
Pathe Somset 17 L10
Pathhead Fife 91 L13
Pathhead Mdloth 83 S6
Pathlow Warwks 36 G9
Path of Condie P & K 90 G9
Patmore Heath Herts 22 B2
Patna E Ayrs 81 N10
Patney Wilts 18 G9
Patrick IoM 60 c6
Patrick Brompton N York 63 Q1
Patricroft Salfd 55 S7
Patrington E R Yk 59 P2
Patrington Haven E R Yk 59 P2
Patrixbourne Kent 13 N4
Patterdale W & F 67 N9
Pattingham Staffs 45 T14
Pattishall W Nthn 37 S10
Pattiswick Green Essex 22 K3
Patton Shrops 35 N1
Patton Bridge W & F 67 S13
Paul Cnwll 2 D11
Paulerspury W Nthn 37 T11
Paull E R Yk 59 L1
Paulton BaNES 17 S5
Paultons Park Hants 9 L5
Paunton Herefs 35 Q10
Pauperhaugh Nthumb 77 N6
Pave Lane Wrekin 45 S10
Pavenham Bed 38 E9
Pawlett Somset 16 J8
Pawston Nthumb 85 M12
Paxford Gloucs 36 G13
Paxton Border 85 N8
Payden Street Kent 12 H5
Payhembury Devon 6 E4
Paynter's Lane End Cnwll 2 H8
Paythorne Lancs 62 G9
Paytoe Herefs 34 K6
Peacehaven E Susx 11 Q10
Peak Dale Derbys 56 G11
Peak District National Park 56 J8
Peak Forest Derbys 56 H11
Peak Hill Lincs 49 L10
Peakirk C Pete 48 J12
Pearson's Green Kent 12 C7
Peartree Green Herefs 35 N14
Peasedown St John BaNES 17 T5
Peasehill Derbys 47 M4
Peaseland Green Norfk 50 J10
Peasemore W Berk 19 Q5
Peasenhall Suffk 41 Q7
Pease Pottage W Susx 11 M4
Pease Pottage Services W Susx 11 M4
Peaslake Surrey 10 H2
Peasley Cross St Hel 55 M8
Peasmarsh E Susx 12 G11
Peasmarsh Somset 6 K2
Peasmarsh Surrey 20 G13
Peathill Abers 105 Q2
Peat Inn Fife 91 Q10
Peatling Magna Leics 37 Q2
Peatling Parva Leics 37 Q3
Peaton Shrops 35 M3
Pebmarsh Essex 40 E14
Pebsham E Susx 12 E14
Pebworth Worcs 36 F11
Pecket Well Calder 62 K14
Peckforton Ches E 45 M2
Peckham Gt Lon 21 P7
Peckleton Leics 47 N13
Pedairffordd Powys 44 D9
Pedlinge Kent 13 M8
Pedmore Dudley 36 B4
Pedwell Somset 17 M9
Peebles Border 83 Q10
Peel IoM 60 c6
Peel Lancs 61 R13
Peel Common Hants 9 R8
Peene Kent 13 N8
Peening Quarter Kent 12 G10
Peggs Green Leics 47 M10
Pegsdon C Beds 31 P6
Pegswood Nthumb 77 Q8
Pegwell Kent 13 S3
Peinchorran Highld 100 e6
Peinlich Highld 100 d4
Pelcomb Pembks 24 F7
Pelcomb Bridge Pembks 24 F7
Pelcomb Cross Pembks 24 F7
Peldon Essex 23 N4
Pell Green E Susx 12 B9
Pelsall Wsall 46 D13
Pelsall Wood Wsall 46 D13
Pelton Dur 69 S2
Pelton Fell Dur 69 S2
Pelutho Cumb 66 H3
Pelynt Cnwll 4 G9
Pemberton Carmth 25 T10
Pemberton Wigan 55 N6
Pembles Cross Kent 12 G6
Pembrey Carmth 25 R10
Pembridge Herefs 34 J9
Pembroke Pembks 24 G10
Pembroke Dock Pembks 24 G10
Pembrokeshire Coast National Park Pembks 24 D6
Pembury Kent 12 B7
Pen-allt Herefs 27 V2
Penallt Mons 27 U5
Penally Pembks 24 K11
Penare Cnwll 3 P8
Penarth V Glam 16 G2
Penblewin Pembks 24 K7
Pen-bont Rhydybeddau Cerdgn 33 N4
Penbryn Cerdgn 32 E10
Pencader Carmth 25 R3
Pencaenewydd Gwynd 42 H5
Pencaitland E Loth 84 C5
Pencarnisiog IoA 52 E8
Pencarreg Carmth 32 K11
Pencarrow Cnwll 4 E4
Pencelli Powys 26 K2
Penclawdd Swans 25 T11
Pencoed Brdgnd 26 H11
Pencombe Herefs 35 N10
Pencoyd Herefs 27 U2
Pencraig Herefs 27 V3
Pencraig Powys 44 B8
Pendeen Cnwll 2 B10
Penderyn Rhondd 26 G6
Pendine Carmth 25 M9
Pendlebury Salfd 55 S6
Pendleton Lancs 62 F12
Pendock Worcs 35 S14
Pendoggett Cnwll 4 C5
Pendomer Somset 7 P2
Pendoylan V Glam 26 K12
Penegoes Powys 43 Q13
Penelewey Cnwll 3 L8
Pen-ffordd Pembks 24 J6
Pengam Caerph 27 M8
Pengam Cardif 27 N12
Penge Gt Lon 21 Q8
Pengelly Cnwll 4 D4
Pengenffordd Powys 27 M2
Pengorffwysfa IoA 52 G4
Pengover Green Cnwll 4 H7
Pen-groes-oped Mons 27 Q6
Pengwern Denbgs 53 T7
Penhale Cnwll 2 H13
Penhale Cnwll 3 N5
Penhale Cnwll 3 R4
Penhale Cnwll 5 L10
Penhallow Cnwll 2 K6
Penhalurick Cnwll 2 J9
Penhalvean Cnwll 2 J9
Penhill Swindn 29 N10
Penhow Newpt 27 S9
Penhurst E Susx 12 C12
Peniarth Gwynd 43 M12
Penicuik Mdloth 83 P7
Peniel Carmth 25 R6
Peniel Denbgs 53 T10
Penifiler Highld 100 d5
Peninver Ag & B 79 P11
Penisarwaun Gwynd 52 J10
Penistone Barns 56 K6
Penjerrick Cnwll 2 K10
Penketh Warrtn 55 N9
Penkill S Ayrs 80 J13
Penkridge Staffs 46 B11
Penlean Cnwll 14 F13
Penleigh Wilts 18 C10
Penley Wrexhm 44 K5
Penllergaer Swans 25 V11
Pen-llyn IoA 52 E6
Penllyn V Glam 26 H12
Pen-lôn IoA 52 F9
Penmachno Conwy 43 Q3
Penmaen Caerph 27 M8
Penmaen Swans 25 T13
Penmaenan Conwy 53 M7
Penmaenmawr Conwy 53 M7
Penmaenpool Gwynd 43 N10
Penmark V Glam 16 E3
Penmon IoA 52 K6
Penmorfa Gwynd 42 K5
Penmynydd IoA 52 H8
Penn Bucks 20 F4
Penn Wolves 35 U1
Pennal Gwynd 43 N13
Pennan Abers 105 N2
Pennant Cerdgn 32 K8
Pennant Denbgs 44 B7
Pennant Powys 43 S14
Pennant-Melangell Powys 44 B8
Pennar Pembks 24 G10
Pennard Swans 25 U13
Pennerley Shrops 44 J14
Pennicott Devon 15 U12
Pennines 62 K12
Pennington Hants 9 L9
Pennington W & F 61 P4
Pennington Green Wigan 55 P5
Pennorth Powys 27 L2
Penn Street Bucks 20 F3
Pennsylvania S Glos 28 D13
Penny Bridge W & F 61 Q3
Pennycross Ag & B 93 N13
Pennygate Norfk 51 P9
Pennyghael Ag & B 93 N13
Pennyglen S Ayrs 80 K10
Penny Green Derbys 57 R11
Penny Hill Lincs 49 N8
Pennymoor Devon 15 U10
Pennywell Sundld 70 E1
Penparc Cerdgn 32 D11
Penparcau Cerdgn 33 L4
Penpedairheol Caerph 27 L8
Penpedairheol Mons 27 Q7
Penpergwm Mons 27 Q5
Penperlleni Mons 27 Q7
Penpethy Cnwll 4 D3
Penpillick Cnwll 3 R5
Penpol Cnwll 3 L9
Penpoll Cnwll 4 E10
Penponds Cnwll 2 G9
Penpont Cnwll 3 R2
Penpont D & G 74 F7
Penpont Powys 26 H2
Penquit Devon 5 Q10
Penrest Cnwll 4 J5
Penrherber Carmth 25 N3
Pen-rhiw Pembks 32 D12
Penrhiwceiber Rhondd 26 K8
Pen Rhiwfawr Neath 26 C5
Penrhiwgoch Carmth 25 U7
Penrhiwllan Cerdgn 32 G12
Penrhiwpal Cerdgn 32 F11
Penrhos Gwynd 42 F7
Penrhos IoA 52 C6
Penrhos Mons 27 S5
Penrhos Powys 26 E5
Penrhos garnedd Gwynd 52 J8
Penrhyn Bay Conwy 53 P6
Penrhyn-coch Cerdgn 33 M4
Penrhyndeudraeth Gwynd 43 M6
Penrhyn-side Conwy 53 P6
Penrhyn Slate Landscape Gwynd 52 K9
Penrhys Rhondd 26 J9
Penrice Swans 25 S13
Penrioch N Ayrs 79 R7
Penrith W & F 67 R6
Penrose Cnwll 3 M2
Penruddock W & F 67 P7
Penryn Cnwll 2 K10
Pensarn Conwy 53 S7
Pensax Worcs 35 R7
Pensby Wirral 54 G10
Penselwood Somset 17 U10
Pensford BaNES 17 R4
Pensham Worcs 36 B12
Penshaw Sundld 70 D2
Penshurst Kent 11 S2
Penshurst Station Kent 21 T13
Pensilva Cnwll 4 H6
Pensnett Dudley 36 B3
Penstone Devon 15 S12
Penstrowed Powys 34 C2
Pentewan Cnwll 3 Q7
Pentir Gwynd 52 J9
Pentire Cnwll 2 K4
Pentlepoir Pembks 24 K9
Pentlow Essex 40 D12
Pentlow Street Essex 40 D11
Pentney Norfk 50 B11
Pentonbridge Cumb 75 T10
Penton Grafton Hants 19 M11
Penton Mewsey Hants 19 M11
Pentraeth IoA 52 H7
Pentre Denbgs 54 C14
Pentre Flints 54 H13
Pentre Mons 27 Q6
Pentre Mons 27 S7
Pentre Powys 34 C3
Pentre Powys 34 E3
Pentre Powys 34 G2
Pentre Rhondd 26 H8
Pentre Shrops 44 J10
Pentre Wrexhm 44 G5
Pentre-bâch Cerdgn 33 L11
Pentre Bach Flints 54 F11
Pentrebach Myr Td 26 K7
Pentre-bach Powys 33 T14
Pentrebeirdd Powys 44 E11
Pentre Berw IoA 52 G8
Pentre-bont Conwy 43 P3
Pentre-cagel Carmth 32 F12
Pentrecelyn Denbgs 44 D3
Pentre-celyn Powys 43 S12
Pentre-chwyth Swans 26 B9
Pentre-clawdd Shrops 44 G7
Pentre-cwrt Carmth 25 Q3
Pentredwr Denbgs 44 E4
Pentrefelin Gwynd 42 K6
Pentrefelin IoA 52 F4
Pentre Ffwrndan Flints 54 G12
Pentrefoelas Conwy 43 S3
Pentregalar Pembks 25 L4
Pentregat Cerdgn 32 G10
Pentre-Gwenlais Carmth 25 V7
Pentre Gwynfryn Gwynd 43 L8
Pentre Halkyn Flints 54 F12
Pentre Hodrey Shrops 34 H5
Pentre Isaf Conwy 53 S8
Pentre Llanrhaeadr Denbgs 54 C14
Pentre Llifior Powys 44 E14
Pentrellwyn Cerdgn 32 H12
Pentre-llwyn-llwyd Powys 33 U10
Pentre-llyn Cerdgn 33 M5
Pentre-llyn-cymmer Conwy 43 U3
Pentre-Maw Powys 43 S13
Pentre Meyrick V Glam 26 H12
Pentre-piod Torfn 27 P7
Pentre-poeth Newpt 27 P10
Pentre'rbryn Cerdgn 32 G10
Pentre'r-felin Cerdgn 33 M11
Pentre'r Felin Conwy 53 P9
Pentre'r-felin Powys 26 G1
Pentre Saron Denbgs 53 T10
Pentre-tafarn-y-fedw Conwy 53 P10
Pentre ty gwyn Carmth 33 R13
Pentrich Derbys 47 L3
Pentridge Dorset 8 E5
Pen-twyn Caerph 27 N7
Pentwyn Cardif 27 N11
Pen-twyn Mons 27 U6
Pen-twyn Torfn 27 P7
Pentwynmaur Caerph 27 M8
Pentyrch Cardif 27 L11
Penwithick Cnwll 3 Q5
Penwood Hants 19 P8
Penwyllt Powys 26 F4
Penybanc Carmth 25 V6
Penybont Powys 34 D8
Pen-y-bont Powys 44 F9
Penybontfawr Powys 44 C9
Pen-y-bryn Pembks 32 C12
Pen-y-cae Powys 26 E5
Penycae Wrexhm 44 G4
Pen-y-cae-mawr Mons 27 S8
Penycaerau Gwynd 42 C8
Pen-y-cefn Flints 54 D11
Pen-y-clawdd Mons 27 T6
Pen-y-coedcae Rhondd 26 K10
Penycwn Pembks 24 E6
Pen-y-fai Brdgnd 26 F11
Pen-y-felin Flints 54 E13
Penyffordd Flints 44 H1
Pen-y-ffordd Flints 54 D10
Penyffridd Gwynd 52 H11
Pen-y-garn Cerdgn 33 M3
Pen-y-Garnedd Powys 44 D9
Pen-y-graig Gwynd 42 D7
Penygraig Rhondd 26 J9
Penygroes Carmth 25 U8
Penygroes Gwynd 52 G12
Penygroeslon Gwynd 42 D7
Pen-y-Gwryd Gwynd 53 L11
Pen-y-lan V Glam 26 H12
Pen-y-Mynydd Carmth 25 S10
Penymynydd Flints 44 H1
Pen-y-pass Gwynd 52 K11
Pen-yr-Heol Mons 27 S5
Penysarn IoA 52 G4
Pen-y-stryt Denbgs 44 F3
Penywaun Rhondd 26 H7
Penzance Cnwll 2 D10
Peopleton Worcs 36 B10
Peover Heath Ches E 55 S12
Peper Harow Surrey 10 E2
Peplow Shrops 45 P9
Pepper's Green Essex 22 F5
Pepperstock C Beds 31 N9
Perceton N Ayrs 81 M4
Percyhorner Abers 105 R2
Perelle Guern 6 c3
Perham Down Wilts 19 L11
Periton Somset 16 C7
Perivale Gt Lon 21 L6
Perkins Village Devon 6 D6
Perkinsville Dur 69 S2
Perlethorpe Notts 57 T12
Perranarworthal Cnwll 2 K9
Perranporth Cnwll 2 K6
Perranuthnoe Cnwll 2 E11
Perranwell Cnwll 2 K6
Perranwell Cnwll 2 K9
Perran Wharf Cnwll 2 K9
Perranzabuloe Cnwll 2 K6
Perrott's Brook Gloucs 28 K6
Perry Birm 36 E2
Perry Cambs 38 H7
Perry Barr Birm 36 E2
Perry Green Essex 22 K3
Perry Green Herts 22 B4
Perry Green Wilts 28 J10
Perrystone Hill Herefs 28 B2
Perry Street Somset 6 K3
Pershall Staffs 45 T8
Pershore Worcs 36 B11
Pertenhall Bed 38 G7
Perth P & K 90 H7
Perthy Shrops 44 J7
Perton Herefs 35 N12
Perton Staffs 45 U14
Pertwood Wilts 18 C13
Peterborough C Pete 48 J14
Peterborough Services Cambs 38 H2
Peterchurch Herefs 34 H13
Peterculter C Aber 99 Q3
Peterhead Abers 105 U6
Peterlee Dur 70 F4
Petersfield Hants 9 U4
Peter's Green Herts 31 P9
Petersham Gt Lon 21 L8
Peters Marland Devon 15 L10
Peterstone Wentlooge Newpt 27 P12
Peterston-super-Ely V Glam 26 K12
Peterstow Herefs 27 V3
Peters Village Kent 12 D3
Peter Tavy Devon 5 N5
Petham Kent 13 M5
Petherwin Gate Cnwll 4 H3
Petrockstow Devon 15 M11
Petsoe End M Keyn 38 C11
Pet Street Kent 13 L6
Pett E Susx 12 G13
Pettaugh Suffk 41 L9
Pett Bottom Kent 13 N5
Petterden Angus 91 P4
Pettinain S Lans 82 J10
Pettistree Suffk 41 P9
Petton Devon 16 D12
Petton Shrops 44 K8
Petts Wood Gt Lon 21 S9
Pettycur Fife 83 Q1
Petty France S Glos 28 E10
Pettymuk Abers 105 Q11
Petworth W Susx 10 F6
Pevensey E Susx 11 U9
Pevensey Bay E Susx 11 V10
Pewsey Wilts 18 J8
Pewsham Wilts 18 D6
Pheasant's Hill Bucks 20 C5
Phepson Worcs 36 B9
Philadelphia Sundld 70 D2
Philham Devon 14 G8
Philiphaugh Border 84 C13
Phillack Cnwll 2 F9
Philleigh Cnwll 3 M9
Philpot End Essex 22 F4
Philpstoun W Loth 82 K3
Phocle Green Herefs 28 B2
Phoenix Green Hants 20 C11
Pibsbury Somset 17 M11
Pica Cumb 66 F8
Piccadilly Warwks 46 H14
Piccotts End Herts 31 M11
Pickburn Donc 57 R5
Pickering N York 64 H3
Picket Piece Hants 19 N11
Picket Post Hants 8 H7
Picket Twenty Hants 19 N11
Pickford Covtry 36 J4
Pickford Green Covtry 36 J4
Pickhill N York 63 S3
Picklescott Shrops 44 K14
Pickmere Ches E 55 Q11
Pickney Somset 16 G11
Pickstock Wrekin 45 R9
Pickup Bank Bl w D 55 R2
Pickwell Devon 15 L4
Pickwell Leics 47 U11
Pickwick Wilts 18 C6
Pickworth Lincs 48 F7
Pickworth Rutlnd 48 E11
Picton Ches W 54 K12
Picton Flints 54 D10
Picton N York 70 F11
Piddinghoe E Susx 11 Q10
Piddington Bucks 20 D4
Piddington Oxon 30 D9
Piddington W Nthn 38 B10
Piddlehinton Dorset 7 T5
Piddletrenthide Dorset 7 T5
Pidley Cambs 39 M5
Piercebridge Darltn 69 R9
Pierowall Ork 106 t15
Piff's Elm Gloucs 28 H2
Pigdon Nthumb 77 P8
Pigeon Green Warwks 36 H8
Pig Oak Dorset 8 E8
Pig Street Herefs 34 J11
Pikehall Derbys 46 G2
Pilford Dorset 8 E8
Pilgrims Hatch Essex 22 E8
Pilham Lincs 58 E8
Pill N Som 27 U12
Pillaton Cnwll 4 K8
Pillatonmill Cnwll 4 K8
Pillerton Hersey Warwks 36 J11
Pillerton Priors Warwks 36 J11
Pilleth Powys 34 G7
Pilley Barns 57 M6
Pilley Hants 9 L9
Pilley Bailey Hants 9 L9
Pillgwenlly Newpt 27 Q10
Pillhead Devon 15 L7
Pilling Lancs 61 S10
Pilling Lane Lancs 61 R10
Pilning S Glos 27 V10
Pilot Inn Kent 13 L12
Pilsbury Derbys 56 H14
Pilsdon Dorset 7 M5
Pilsgate C Pete 48 G12
Pilsley Derbys 47 M1
Pilsley Derbys 56 K12
Pilson Green Norfk 51 Q11
Piltdown E Susx 11 Q6
Pilton Devon 15 N6
Pilton N Nthn 38 F4
Pilton Rutlnd 48 D13
Pilton Somset 17 Q8
Pilton Green Swans 25 R13
Pimbo Lancs 55 L6
Pimlico Herts 31 N11
Pimlico Lancs 62 E11
Pimlico W Nthn 30 D4
Pimperne Dorset 8 C7
Pinchbeck Lincs 48 K8
Pinchbeck Bars Lincs 48 J8
Pincheon Green Donc 57 U3
Pinchinthorpe R & Cl 70 J10
Pincock Lancs 55 M3
Pinfold Lancs 54 J4
Pinford End Suffk 40 D9
Pinged Carmth 25 R10
Pingewood W Berk 19 U7
Pin Green Herts 31 S7
Pinhoe Devon 6 C6
Pinkett's Booth Covtry 36 J4
Pinkney Wilts 28 G10
Pinkneys Green W & M 20 E6
Pinley Covtry 37 L5
Pinley Green Warwks 36 H7
Pin Mill Suffk 41 M13
Pinminnoch S Ayrs 80 H14
Pinmore S Ayrs 72 G1
Pinn Devon 6 F7
Pinner Gt Lon 20 K5
Pinner Green Gt Lon 20 K4
Pinsley Green Ches E 45 N4
Pinvin Worcs 36 C11
Pinwherry S Ayrs 72 G2
Pinxton Derbys 47 N3
Pipe and Lyde Herefs 35 M12
Pipe Aston Herefs 35 L6
Pipe Gate Shrops 45 R5
Pipehill Staffs 46 E12
Piperdam Angus 91 M5
Piperhill Highld 103 N5
Pipers Pool Cnwll 4 H4
Pipewell N Nthn 38 B3
Pippacott Devon 15 M5
Pippin Street Lancs 55 N2
Pipton Powys 34 E13
Pirbright Surrey 20 F11
Pirbright Camp Surrey 20 F11
Pirnie Border 84 H13
Pirnmill N Ayrs 79 R7
Pirton Herts 31 P6
Pirton Worcs 35 U11
Pisgah Cerdgn 33 N5
Pishill Oxon 20 B5
Pistyll Gwynd 42 F5
Pitblae Abers 105 R3
Pitcairngreen P & K 90 G6
Pitcalnie Highld 109 Q10
Pitcaple Abers 105 L10
Pitcarity Angus 98 E10
Pitchcombe Gloucs 28 G6
Pitchcott Bucks 30 G8
Pitcher Row Lincs 49 L7
Pitchford Shrops 45 M13
Pitch Green Bucks 30 G12
Pitch Place Surrey 10 D3
Pitch Place Surrey 20 G12
Pitchroy Moray 103 U8
Pitcombe Somset 17 S10
Pitcot V Glam 26 F13
Pitcox E Loth 84 G3
Pitfichie Abers 104 K12
Pitglassie Abers 104 K7
Pitgrudy Highld 109 P6
Pitlessie Fife 91 M10
Pitlochry P & K 97 Q12
Pitmachie Abers 104 K10
Pitmain Highld 97 L3
Pitmedden Abers 105 P10
Pitmedden Garden Abers 105 P10
Pitminster Somset 16 H13
Pitmuies Angus 91 S2
Pitmunie Abers 104 K13
Pitney Somset 17 N11
Pitroddie P & K 90 K6
Pitscottie Fife 91 P9
Pitsea Essex 22 H10
Pitses Oldham 56 D6
Pitsford W Nthn 37 U7
Pitstone Bucks 30 K9
Pitt Devon 16 D13
Pitt Hants 9 P3
Pittarrow Abers 99 N9
Pitt Court Gloucs 28 D8
Pittentrail Highld 109 N4
Pittenweem Fife 91 S11
Pitteuchar Fife 91 L12
Pittodrie House Hotel Abers 104 K11
Pitton Wilts 8 J2
Pitt's Wood Kent 12 B6
Pittulie Abers 105 R2
Pityme Cnwll 3 P1
Pity Me Dur 69 S3
Pivington Kent 12 H6
Pixey Green Suffk 41 M5
Pixham Surrey 21 L12
Plains N Lans 82 E5
Plain Street Cnwll 4 B5
Plaish Shrops 35 M1
Plaistow Gt Lon 21 R6
Plaistow W Susx 10 G4
Plaitford Hants 8 K5
Plank Lane Wigan 55 P7
Plas Cymyran IoA 52 C7
Plastow Green Hants 19 R8
Platt Bridge Wigan 55 P6
Platt Lane Shrops 45 M6
Platts Heath Kent 12 G5
Plawsworth Dur 69 S3
Plaxtol Kent 12 B5
Playden E Susx 12 H11
Playford Suffk 41 M11
Play Hatch Oxon 20 B7
Playing Place Cnwll 3 L8
Playley Green Gloucs 28 E1
Plealey Shrops 44 K12
Plean Stirlg 89 T8
Pleasance Fife 90 K9
Pleasington Bl w D 55 P1
Pleasley Derbys 57 R14
Pleasleyhill Notts 57 R14
Pleasurewood Hills Suffk 41 T1
Pleck Dorset 7 T2
Pledgdon Green Essex 22 E2
Pledwick Wakefd 57 M3
Pleinheaume Guern 6 d2
Plemont Jersey 7 a1
Plemstall Ches W 55 L12
Plenmeller Nthumb 76 E13
Pleshey Essex 22 G5
Plockton Highld 100 h6
Plowden Shrops 34 J3
Plox Green Shrops 44 J13
Pluckley Kent 12 H6
Pluckley Station Kent 12 H7
Pluckley Thorne Kent 12 H7
Plucks Gutter Kent 13 Q3
Plumbland Cumb 66 J5
Plumgarths W & F 67 Q14
Plumley Ches E 55 R12
Plump Hill Gloucs 28 C4
Plumpton E Susx 11 P8
Plumpton W & F 61 Q4
Plumpton W & F 67 Q5
Plumpton W Nthn 37 Q11
Plumpton End W Nthn 30 F4
Plumpton Green E Susx 11 P7
Plumpton Head W & F 67 R5
Plumstead Gt Lon 21 R7
Plumstead Norfk 50 K7
Plumstead Green Norfk 50 K6
Plumtree Notts 47 R7
Plumtree Green Kent 12 F6
Plungar Leics 47 U7
Plurenden Kent 12 H8
Plush Dorset 7 T4
Plusha Cnwll 4 H4
Plushabridge Cnwll 4 J6
Plwmp Cerdgn 32 G10
Plymouth C Plym 5 M10
Plympton C Plym 5 N9
Plymstock C Plym 5 N10
Plymtree Devon 6 E4
Pockley N York 64 E2
Pocklington E R Yk 64 J10
Pode Hole Lincs 48 K9
Podimore Somset 17 P12
Podington Bed 38 D8
Podmore Staffs 45 S6
Point Clear Essex 23 R5
Pointon Lincs 48 H7
Pokesdown BCP 8 G10
Polbain Highld 107 S2
Polbathic Cnwll 4 J9
Polbeth W Loth 82 K6
Polbrock Cnwll 3 Q3
Poldark Mine Cnwll 2 H10
Polebrook N Nthn 38 G3
Pole Elm Worcs 35 T10
Polegate E Susx 11 T10
Pole Moor Kirk 56 G3
Polesden Lacey Surrey 20 K12
Polesworth Warwks 46 J13
Polgigga Cnwll 2 B12
Polglass Highld 107 T3
Polgooth Cnwll 3 P6
Polgown D & G 74 D5
Poling W Susx 10 G10
Poling Corner W Susx 10 G9
Polkerris Cnwll 3 R6
Pollard Street Norfk 51 P7
Pollington E R Yk 57 T3
Polloch Highld 93 T5
Pollok C Glas 89 M13
Pollokshaws C Glas 89 N13
Pollokshields C Glas 89 N13
Polmassick Cnwll 3 P7
Polmear Cnwll 3 R6
Polmont Falk 82 H3
Polnish Highld 93 T2
Polperro Cnwll 4 G10
Polruan Cnwll 4 E10
Polsham Somset 17 P8
Polstead Suffk 40 G13
Polstead Heath Suffk 40 G12
Poltalloch Ag & B 87 Q6
Poltescoe Cnwll 2 J13
Poltimore Devon 6 C5
Polton Mdloth 83 Q6
Polwarth Border 84 J8
Polyphant Cnwll 4 H4
Polzeath Cnwll 4 A5
Pomathorn Mdloth 83 P7
Pomeroy Derbys 56 H13
Ponde Powys 34 D13
Pondersbridge Cambs 39 L2
Ponders End Gt Lon 21 Q3
Ponsanooth Cnwll 2 K9
Ponsonby Cumb 66 G11
Ponsongath Cnwll 2 K13
Ponsworthy Devon 5 S6
Pont Abraham Services Carmth 25 U9
Pontac Jersey 7 e4
Pontamman Carmth 26 A5
Pontantwn Carmth 25 R8
Pontardawe Neath 26 C7
Pontarddulais Swans 25 U10
Pont-ar-gothi Carmth 25 T6
Pont-ar-Hydfer Powys 26 F2
Pont-ar-llechau Carmth 26 C3
Pontarsais Carmth 25 R5
Pontblyddyn Flints 44 G1
Pont Cyfyng Conwy 53 M11
Pontcysyllte Aqueduct Wrexhm 44 G5
Pont Dolgarrog Conwy 53 N9
Pontdolgoch Powys 34 B2
Pont-Ebbw Newpt 27 P10
Pontefract Wakefd 57 Q2
Ponteland Nthumb 77 P11
Ponterwyd Cerdgn 33 P4
Pontesbury Shrops 44 J12
Pontesbury Hill Shrops 44 J12
Pontesford Shrops 44 K12
Pontfadog Wrexhm 44 F6
Pontfaen Pembks 24 H4
Pont-faen Powys 33 U14
Pontgarreg Cerdgn 32 F10
Pontgarreg Pembks 32 B12
Pont Henri Carmth 25 S9
Ponthir Torfn 27 Q9
Ponthirwaun Cerdgn 32 E11
Pontllanfraith Caerph 27 M8
Pontlliw Swans 25 V10
Pontllyfni Gwynd 42 H3
Pontlottyn Caerph 27 L6
Pont Morlais Carmth 25 T9
Pontnêddféchan Neath 26 G6
Pontnewydd Torfn 27 P8
Pontnewynydd Torfn 27 P7
Pont Pen-y-benglog Gwynd 53 L10
Pontrhydfendigaid Cerdgn 33 P7
Pont Rhyd-sarn Gwynd 43 S8
Pont Rhyd-y-cyff Brdgnd 26 F10
Pontrhydyfen Neath 26 D9
Pont-rhyd-y-groes Cerdgn 33 P6
Pontrhydyrun Torfn 27 P8
Pontrilas Herefs 27 R2
Pont Robert Powys 44 D11
Pont-rug Gwynd 52 H10
Ponts Green E Susx 12 C12
Pontshill Herefs 28 B3
Pontsian Cerdgn 32 H11
Pontsticill Myr Td 26 K5
Pont Walby Neath 26 F6
Pontwelly Carmth 32 H12
Pontyates Carmth 25 S9
Pontyberem Carmth 25 T8
Pont-y-blew Wrexhm 44 H6
Pontybodkin Flints 44 G2
Pontyclun Rhondd 26 J11
Pontycymer Brdgnd 26 G9
Pontyglasier Pembks 24 K3
Pontygwaith Rhondd 26 J9
Pontygynon Pembks 24 K3
Pontymister Caerph 27 N9
Pont-y-pant Conwy 53 N12
Pontypool Torfn 27 P7
Pontypridd Rhondd 26 K10
Pont-yr-hafod Pembks 24 F5
Pont-yr-Rhyl Brdgnd 26 G10
Pontywaun Caerph 27 N9
Pool Cnwll 2 H8
Poole BCP 8 E10
Poole Keynes Gloucs 28 J8
Poolewe Highld 107 Q8
Pooley Bridge W & F 67 Q8
Pooley Street Norfk 40 J4
Poolfold Staffs 45 U2
Pool Head Herefs 35 N10
Poolhill Gloucs 28 D2
Pool in Wharfedale Leeds 63 Q10
Pool of Muckhart Clacks 90 F11
Pool Quay Powys 44 G11
Pool Street Essex 40 C13
Pootings Kent 21 S13
Popes Hill Gloucs 28 C5
Popham Hants 19 S12
Poplar Gt Lon 21 Q6
Poplar Street Suffk 41 R7
Porchfield IoW 9 N10
Poringland Norfk 51 N13
Porkellis Cnwll 2 H10
Porlock Somset 15 U3
Porlock Weir Somset 15 U3
Portachoillan Ag & B 79 P4
Port-an-Eorna Highld 100 g6
Port Appin Ag & B 94 C9
Port Askaig Ag & B 86 G12
Portavadie Ag & B 87 S12
Port Bannatyne Ag & B 88 C12
Portbury N Som 27 U12
Port Carlisle Cumb 75 P13
Port Charlotte Ag & B 78 D4
Portchester Hants 9 S7
Port Clarence S on T 70 G8
Port Driseach Ag & B 87 T11
Port Ellen Ag & B 78 F6
Port Elphinstone Abers 105 M11
Portencalzie D & G 72 C5
Portencross N Ayrs 80 H3
Port Erin IoM 60 b9
Portesham Dorset 7 R7
Portessie Moray 104 E2
Port e Vullen IoM 60 h4
Port Eynon Swans 25 S13
Portfield Gate Pembks 24 F7
Portgate Devon 5 L3
Port Gaverne Cnwll 4 C4
Port Glasgow Inver 88 H11
Portgordon Moray 104 D3
Portgower Highld 109 U2
Porth Cnwll 3 L4
Porth Rhondd 26 J9
Porthallow Cnwll 2 K12
Porthallow Cnwll 4 G10
Porthcawl Brdgnd 26 E12
Porthcothan Cnwll 3 M2
Porthcurno Cnwll 2 B12
Porthdinllaen Gwynd 42 E5
Port Henderson Highld 107 N10
Porthgain Pembks 24 D4
Porthgwarra Cnwll 2 B12
Porthill Staffs 45 T4
Porthkea Cnwll 3 L8
Porthkerry V Glam 16 E3
Porthleven Cnwll 2 G11
Porthmadog Gwynd 43 L6
Porthmadog Gwynd 43 L6
Porthmeor Cnwll 2 C9
Porth Navas Cnwll 2 K11
Portholland Cnwll 3 P8
Porthoustock Cnwll 3 L12
Porthpean Cnwll 3 Q6
Porthtowan Cnwll 2 H7
Porthwgan Wrexhm 44 J4
Porthyrhyd Carmth 25 T7
Porth-y-Waen Shrops 44 G9
Portincaple Ag & B 88 F7
Portinfer Jersey 7 a1
Portington E R Yk 64 H13
Portinnisherrich Ag & B 87 T3
Portinscale Cumb 67 L8
Port Isaac Cnwll 4 B4
Portishead N Som 27 T12
Portknockie Moray 104 F2
Portland Dorset 7 S10
Portlethen Abers 99 S4
Portling D & G 66 C2
Portloe Cnwll 3 N9
Port Logan D & G 72 D11
Portlooe Cnwll 4 G10
Portmahomack Highld 109 S8
Port Mary D & G 73 S10
Portmeirion Gwynd 43 L6
Portmellon Cnwll 3 Q8
Port Mòr Highld 93 L3
Portmore Hants 9 L9
Port Mulgrave N York 71 N9
Portnacroish Ag & B 94 C9
Portnaguran W Isls 106 k5
Portnahaven Ag & B 78 B5
Portnalong Highld 100 c6
Portnancon Highld 110 J4
Port nan Giùran W Isls 106 k5
Port nan Long W Isls 106 d11
Port Nis W Isls 106 k2
Portobello C Edin 83 R4
Portobello Gatesd 69 S1
Portobello Wolves 46 C14
Port of Menteith Stirlg 89 N5
Port of Ness W Isls 106 k2
Porton Wilts 18 J13
Portontown Devon 5 L5
Portpatrick D & G 72 B9
Port Quin Cnwll 4 B4
Port Ramsay Ag & B 94 B9
Portreath Cnwll 2 H7
Portreath Harbour Cnwll 2 H7
Portree Highld 100 d5
Port Righ Ag & B 79 Q8
Port St Mary IoM 60 c9
Portscatho Cnwll 3 M9
Portsea C Port 9 S8
Portskerra Highld 111 T3
Portskewett Mons 27 T10
Portslade Br & H 11 M9
Portslade-by-Sea Br & H 11 M9
Portslogan D & G 72 B8
Portsmouth C Port 9 S9
Portsmouth Calder 56 D1
Portsmouth Arms Devon 15 P9
Portsmouth Historic Dockyard C Port 9 S8
Port Soderick IoM 60 e8
Port Solent C Port 9 S7
Portsonachan Hotel Ag & B 88 B1
Portsoy Abers 104 H2
Port Sunlight Wirral 54 H10
Portswood C Sotn 9 N6
Port Talbot Neath 26 D10
Port Tennant Swans 26 B9
Portuairk Highld 93 L5
Portway Herefs 35 L12
Portway Herefs 35 L13
Portway Sandw 36 C3
Portway Worcs 36 E6
Port Wemyss Ag & B 78 B5
Port William D & G 72 J11
Portwrinkle Cnwll 4 K10
Portyerrock D & G 73 M12
Posbury Devon 15 T13
Posenhall Shrops 45 Q13
Poslingford Suffk 40 C11
Posso Border 83 P12
Postbridge Devon 5 R5
Postcombe Oxon 30 F12
Post Green Dorset 8 D10
Postling Kent 13 M8
Postwick Norfk 51 N12
Potarch Abers 99 L4
Potsgrove C Beds 31 L6
Potten End Herts 31 M11
Potten Street Kent 13 Q2
Potter Brompton N York 65 M4
Pottergate Street Norfk 41 L2
Potterhanworth Lincs 58 J13
Potterhanworth Booths Lincs 58 J13
Potter Heigham Norfk 51 R10
Potterne Wilts 18 E9
Potterne Wick Wilts 18 E9
Potter Row Bucks 30 K12
Potters Bar Herts 31 R12
Potters Brook Lancs 61 T9
Potters Corner Kent 12 J7
Potter's Cross Staffs 35 T4
Potters Crouch Herts 31 P11
Potter's Forstal Kent 12 G6
Potters Green Covtry 37 L4
Potter's Green E Susx 11 S6
Potter's Green Herts 31 U8
Pottersheath Herts 31 R9
Potters Marston Leics 37 N1
Potter Somersal Derbys 46 F6
Potterspury W Nthn 30 G4
Potter Street Essex 22 C6
Potterton Abers 105 Q12
Potterton Leeds 63 U12
Potthorpe Norfk 50 F9
Pottle Street Wilts 18 B12
Potto N York 70 G12
Potton C Beds 38 K11
Pott Row Norfk 50 B9
Pott's Green Essex 23 M3
Pott Shrigley Ches E 56 D11
Poughill Cnwll 14 F11
Poughill Devon 15 U11
Poulner Hants 8 H7
Poulshot Wilts 18 E9
Poulton Gloucs 29 L7
Poulton Wirral 54 H8
Poulton-le-Fylde Lancs 61 Q12
Poulton Priory Gloucs 29 L8
Pound Bank Worcs 35 R6
Poundbury Dorset 7 S6
Poundffald Swans 25 U12
Poundgate E Susx 11 R5
Pound Green E Susx 11 S6
Pound Green Suffk 40 B10
Pound Green Worcs 35 S5
Pound Hill W Susx 11 M3
Poundon Bucks 30 D7
Poundsbridge Kent 11 S2
Poundsgate Devon 5 S6
Poundstock Cnwll 14 F13
Pound Street Hants 19 Q8
Pounsley E Susx 11 S6
Pouton D & G 73 M10
Pouy Street Suffk 41 Q6
Povey Cross Surrey 11 M2
Powburn Nthumb 77 M2
Powderham Devon 6 C8
Powerstock Dorset 7 P5
Powfoot D & G 75 M12
Pow Green Herefs 35 R12
Powhill Cumb 66 K1
Powick Worcs 35 T10
Powmill P & K 90 F12
Poxwell Dorset 7 T8
Poyle Slough 20 H7
Poynings W Susx 11 M8
Poyntington Dorset 17 S12
Poynton Ches E 56 D10
Poynton Wrekin 45 N10
Poynton Green Wrekin 45 N10
Poyston Cross Pembks 24 G7
Poystreet Green Suffk 40 G9
Praa Sands Cnwll 2 F11
Pratt's Bottom Gt Lon 21 S10
Praze-an-Beeble Cnwll 2 G9
Predannack Wollas Cnwll 2 H13
Prees Shrops 45 N7
Preesall Lancs 61 R10
Prees Green Shrops 45 N7
Preesgweene Shrops 44 G6
Prees Heath Shrops 45 N6
Prees Higher Heath Shrops 45 N6
Prees Lower Heath Shrops 45 N7
Prendwick Nthumb 77 L3
Pren-gwyn Cerdgn 32 H12
Prenteg Gwynd 43 L5
Prenton Wirral 54 H9
Prescot Knows 55 L8
Prescott Devon 6 E2
Prescott Shrops 35 Q4
Prescott Shrops 44 K9
Presnerb Angus 98 B10
Pressen Nthumb 85 L11
Prestatyn Denbgs 54 C10
Prestbury Ches E 56 C11
Prestbury Gloucs 28 J3
Presteigne Powys 34 H8

Prestleigh Somset 17 R8
Prestolee Bolton 55 S5
Preston Border 84 K7
Preston Br & H 11 N9
Preston Devon 5 V6
Preston Dorset 7 T8
Preston E R Yk 65 R13
Preston Gloucs 28 K7
Preston Herts 31 Q8
Preston Kent 12 K3
Preston Kent 13 P3
Preston Lancs 61 U14
Preston Nthumb 85 T13
Preston Rutlnd 48 C13
Preston Shrops 45 M11
Preston Somset 16 E9
Preston Torbay 6 A12
Preston Wilts 18 F5
Preston Wilts 19 L6
Preston Bagot Warwks 36 G7
Preston Bissett Bucks 30 E7
Preston Bowyer Somset 16 F11
Preston Brockhurst Shrops 45 M9
Preston Brook Halton 55 N10
Preston Candover Hants 19 T12
Preston Capes W Nthn 37 Q10
Preston Crowmarsh Oxon 19 T2
Preston Deanery W Nthn 37 U9
Preston Green Warwks 36 G7
Preston Gubbals Shrops 45 L10
Preston Montford Shrops 44 K11
Preston on Stour Warwks 36 H11
Preston on Tees S on T 70 F9
Preston on the Hill Halton 55 N10
Preston on Wye Herefs 34 J12
Prestonpans E Loth 83 S4
Preston Patrick W & F 61 U3
Preston Plucknett Somset 17 P13
Preston St Mary Suffk 40 F10
Preston Street Kent 13 Q3
Preston-under-Scar N York 63 M1
Preston upon the Weald Moors Wrekin 45 Q10
Preston Wynne Herefs 35 N11
Prestwich Bury 55 T6
Prestwick Nthumb 77 P11
Prestwick S Ayrs 81 M7
Prestwick Airport S Ayrs 81 M7
Prestwood Bucks 30 J12
Prestwood Staffs 35 U3
Price Town Brdgnd 26 G9
Prickwillow Cambs 39 S4
Priddy Somset 17 P6
Priestacott Devon 14 K11
Priestcliffe Derbys 56 H12
Priestcliffe Ditch Derbys 56 H12
Priest Hutton Lancs 61 U5
Priestland E Ayrs 81 R5
Priestley Green Calder 56 H1
Priest Weston Shrops 34 G1
Priestwood Green Kent 12 C3
Primethorpe Leics 37 P2
Primrose Green Norfk 50 J10
Primrosehill Border 84 K7
Primrose Hill Cambs 39 N3
Primrose Hill Derbys 47 M2
Primrose Hill Dudley 36 B3
Primrose Hill Lancs 54 J5
Primsidemill Border 85 L13
Prince of Wales Bridge Mons 27 U10
Princes Gate Pembks 24 K8
Princes Risborough Bucks 30 H12
Princethorpe Warwks 37 M6
Princetown Devon 5 P6
Prinsted W Susx 10 B9
Prion Denbgs 44 C1
Prior Rigg Cumb 75 U12
Priors Halton Shrops 35 L5
Priors Hardwick Warwks 37 N9
Priorslee Wrekin 45 R11
Priors Marston Warwks 37 N9
Priors Norton Gloucs 28 G3
Priors Park Gloucs 28 G1
Priory Wood Herefs 34 G11
Prisk V Glam 26 J12
Priston BaNES 17 S4
Pristow Green Norfk 40 K3
Prittlewell Sthend 23 L10
Privett Hants 9 T3
Prixford Devon 15 N5
Probus Cnwll 3 M7
Prora E Loth 84 E3
Prospect Cumb 66 H4
Prospidnick Cnwll 2 G10
Protstonhill Abers 105 N3
Prudhoe Nthumb 77 M13
Prussia Cove Cnwll 2 F11
Pubil P & K 95 P10
Publow BaNES 17 R4
Puckeridge Herts 31 U8
Puckington Somset 17 L13
Pucklechurch S Glos 28 C12
Puckrup Gloucs 35 U13
Puddinglake Ches W 55 R13
Puddington Ches W 54 H12
Puddington Devon 15 T10
Puddledock Norfk 40 J2
Puddletown Dorset 7 U6
Pudleston Herefs 35 N9
Pudsey Leeds 63 Q13
Pulborough W Susx 10 G7
Puleston Wrekin 45 R9
Pulford Ches W 44 J2
Pulham Dorset 7 T3
Pulham Market Norfk 41 L3
Pulham St Mary Norfk 41 M3
Pullens Green S Glos 28 B9
Pulloxhill C Beds 31 N6
Pulverbatch Shrops 44 K13
Pumpherston W Loth 83 L5
Pumsaint Carmth 33 N12
Puncheston Pembks 24 H5
Puncknowle Dorset 7 P7
Punnett's Town E Susx 11 U6
Purbrook Hants 9 T7
Purfleet-on-Thames Thurr 22 E12
Puriton Somset 16 K8
Purleigh Essex 22 K7
Purley Gt Lon 21 P10
Purley on Thames W Berk 19 U5
Purlogue Shrops 34 G5
Purlpit Wilts 18 C7
Purls Bridge Cambs 39 Q3
Purse Caundle Dorset 17 S13
Purshull Green Worcs 35 U6
Purslow Shrops 34 J4
Purston Jaglin Wakefd 57 P3
Purtington Somset 7 L3
Purton Gloucs 28 C6
Purton Gloucs 28 C7
Purton Wilts 29 L10
Purton Stoke Wilts 29 L9
Pury End W Nthn 37 T11
Pusey Oxon 29 S8
Putley Herefs 35 P13
Putley Green Herefs 35 P13
Putloe Gloucs 28 E6
Putney Gt Lon 21 M8
Putsborough Devon 14 K4
Puttenham Herts 30 J10
Puttenham Surrey 20 F13
Puttock End Essex 40 D12
Putton Dorset 7 R8
Putts Corner Devon 6 F5
Puxley W Nthn 30 G4
Puxton N Som 17 M4
Pwll Carmth 25 S10
Pwllcrochan Pembks 24 F10
Pwll-du Mons 27 N5
Pwll-glâs Denbgs 44 D3
Pwllgloyw Powys 34 B14
Pwllheli Gwynd 42 G6
Pwllmeyric Mons 27 U9
Pwll-trap Carmth 25 N7
Pwll-y-glaw Neath 26 D9
Pye Bridge Derbys 47 M3
Pyecombe W Susx 11 M8
Pye Corner Newpt 27 Q10
Pye Green Staffs 46 C11
Pyle Brdgnd 26 E11
Pyleigh Somset 16 F10
Pylle Somset 17 R9
Pymoor Cambs 39 Q3
Pymore Dorset 7 N6
Pyrford Surrey 20 H11
Pyrton Oxon 30 E13
Pytchley N Nthn 38 C6
Pyworthy Devon 14 H12

Q

Quabbs Shrops 34 F4
Quadring Lincs 48 K7
Quadring Eaudike Lincs 48 K7
Quainton Bucks 30 F8
Quaker's Yard Myr Td 26 K8
Quaking Houses Dur 69 Q2
Quantock Hills Somset 16 G9
Quarff Shet 106 u10
Quarley Hants 19 L12
Quarndon Derbys 46 K5
Quarr Hill IoW 9 R10
Quarrier's Village Inver 88 J12
Quarrington Lincs 48 G5
Quarrington Hill Dur 70 D5
Quarrybank Ches W 55 N13
Quarry Bank Dudley 36 B3
Quarrywood Moray 103 U3
Quarter N Ayrs 88 E13
Quarter S Lans 82 D8
Quatford Shrops 35 R2
Quatt Shrops 35 S3
Quebec Dur 69 Q4
Quedgeley Gloucs 28 F5
Queen Adelaide Cambs 39 S4
Queenborough Kent 23 M13
Queen Camel Somset 17 Q12
Queen Charlton BaNES 17 R3
Queen Dart Devon 15 T9
Queen Elizabeth Forest Park Stirlg 89 M5
Queen Elizabeth II Bridge Thurr 22 E12
Queenhill Worcs 35 U13
Queen Oak Dorset 17 U10
Queen's Bower IoW 9 R12
Queensbury C Brad 63 N13
Queensferry Flints 54 H13
Queensferry Crossing Fife 83 M2
Queen's Head Shrops 44 H8
Queen's Hills Norfk 51 L11
Queenslie C Glas 89 Q12
Queen's Park Bed 38 F11
Queen's Park Essex 22 G8
Queen's Park W Nthn 37 U8
Queen Street Kent 12 C6
Queen Street Wilts 28 K10
Queenzieburn N Lans 89 Q10
Quendon Essex 22 D1
Queniborough Leics 47 R11
Quenington Gloucs 29 M7
Quernmore Lancs 61 U8
Queslett Birm 36 E2
Quethiock Cnwll 4 J8
Quick's Green W Berk 19 S5
Quidenham Norfk 40 H3
Quidhampton Hants 19 R10
Quidhampton Wilts 8 G2
Quina Brook Shrops 45 M7
Quinbury End W Nthn 37 R10
Quinton Dudley 36 C4
Quinton W Nthn 37 U10
Quinton Green W Nthn 37 U10
Quintrell Downs Cnwll 3 L4
Quixhall Staffs 46 F5
Quixwood Border 84 K6
Quoditch Devon 14 K13
Quoig P & K 90 B7
Quorn Leics 47 Q10
Quothquan S Lans 82 J11
Quoyburray Ork 106 u19
Quoyloo Ork 106 r17

R

Raasay Highld 100 e5
Rabbit's Cross Kent 12 E6
Rableyheath Herts 31 R9
Raby Cumb 66 J2
Raby Wirral 54 H11
Rachan Mill Border 83 M12
Rachub Gwynd 52 K9
Rackenford Devon 15 U9
Rackham W Susx 10 G8
Rackheath Norfk 51 N11
Racks D & G 74 K11
Rackwick Ork 106 r20
Radbourne Derbys 46 J6
Radcliffe Bury 55 S5
Radcliffe Nthumb 77 R5
Radcliffe on Trent Notts 47 R6
Radclive Bucks 30 E6
Radcot Oxon 29 Q8
Raddery Highld 102 K4
Raddington Somset 16 D11
Radernie Fife 91 Q10
Radford Covtry 36 K4
Radford Semele Warwks 36 K8
Radlet Somset 16 H9
Radlett Herts 31 Q12
Radley Devon 15 R8
Radley Oxon 30 B13
Radley W Berk 19 N7
Radley Green Essex 22 F6
Radmore Green Ches E 45 N2
Radnage Bucks 20 C3
Radstock BaNES 17 S6
Radstone W Nthn 30 C4
Radway Warwks 37 L11
Radwell Bed 38 F9
Radwell Herts 31 R5
Radwinter Essex 39 T13
Radwinter End Essex 39 T13
Radyr Cardif 27 L11
RAF College (Cranwell) Lincs 48 F4
Rafford Moray 103 S4
RAF Museum Cosford Shrops 45 S12
RAF Museum London Gt Lon 21 M4
Ragdale Leics 47 S10
Ragdon Shrops 35 L2
Raginnis Cnwll 2 D11
Raglan Mons 27 S6
Ragnall Notts 58 D12
Raigbeg Highld 103 M10
Rainbow Hill Worcs 35 U9
Rainford St Hel 55 L6
Rainford Junction St Hel 55 L6
Rainham Gt Lon 22 D11
Rainham Medway 12 F2
Rainhill St Hel 55 L8
Rainhill Stoops St Hel 55 M8
Rainow Ches E 56 D11
Rainsough Bury 55 T6
Rainton N York 63 T4
Rainworth Notts 47 Q2
Raisbeck W & F 68 D11
Raise W & F 68 F3
Raisthorpe N York 64 K7
Rait P & K 90 K6
Raithby Lincs 59 P10
Raithby Lincs 59 Q13
Raithwaite N York 71 Q10
Rake Hants 10 C5
Rakewood Rochdl 56 D4
Ralia Highld 97 L4
Ram Carmth 33 L11
Ramasaig Highld 100 a5
Rame Cnwll 2 J10
Rame Cnwll 5 L11
Ram Hill S Glos 28 C12
Ram Lane Kent 12 J6
Rampisham Dorset 7 Q4
Rampside W & F 61 N6
Rampton Cambs 39 P7
Rampton Notts 58 D11
Ramsbottom Bury 55 S3
Ramsbury Wilts 19 L6
Ramscraigs Highld 112 D11
Ramsdean Hants 9 U4
Ramsdell Hants 19 S9
Ramsden Oxon 29 S4
Ramsden Worcs 36 B11
Ramsden Bellhouse Essex 22 H9
Ramsden Heath Essex 22 H8
Ramsey Cambs 39 L3
Ramsey Essex 23 T1
Ramsey IoM 60 h4
Ramsey Forty Foot Cambs 39 M3
Ramsey Heights Cambs 38 K4
Ramsey Island Pembks 24 B6
Ramsey Mereside Cambs 39 L3
Ramsey St Mary's Cambs 39 L3
Ramsgate Kent 13 S2
Ramsgill N York 63 N5
Ramshaw Dur 69 L3
Ramshaw Dur 69 P7
Ramsholt Suffk 41 P12
Ramshope Nthumb 76 E5
Ramshorn Staffs 46 E4
Ramsley Devon 5 R2
Ramsnest Common Surrey 10 E4
Ranby Lincs 59 M11
Ranby Notts 57 U10
Rand Lincs 58 K11
Randwick Gloucs 28 F6
Ranfurly Rens 88 J12
Rangemore Staffs 46 G9
Rangeworthy S Glos 28 C10
Rankinston E Ayrs 81 P10
Ranksborough Rutlnd 48 B11
Rank's Green Essex 22 H4
Rannoch Station P & K 95 N7
Ranscombe Somset 16 B8
Ranskill Notts 57 U9
Ranton Staffs 45 U9
Ranton Green Staffs 45 T9
Ranworth Norfk 51 Q11
Raploch Stirlg 89 S7
Rapness Ork 106 u15
Rapps Somset 16 K13
Rascarrel D & G 73 T10
Rashfield Ag & B 88 D9
Rashwood Worcs 36 B7
Raskelf N York 64 B5
Rassau Blae G 27 M5
Rastrick Calder 56 H2
Ratagan Highld 101 N8
Ratby Leics 47 P12
Ratcliffe Culey Leics 46 K14
Ratcliffe on Soar Notts 47 N8
Ratcliffe on the Wreake Leics 47 R11
Rathen Abers 105 R3
Rathillet Fife 91 N7
Rathmell N York 62 G8
Ratho C Edin 83 M4
Ratho Station C Edin 83 M4
Rathven Moray 104 E2
Ratlake Hants 9 N4
Ratley Warwks 37 L11
Ratling Kent 13 P5
Ratlinghope Shrops 34 K1
Rattar Highld 112 G2
Ratten Row Cumb 67 M4
Ratten Row Cumb 67 N3
Ratten Row Lancs 61 S11
Rattery Devon 5 S8
Rattlesden Suffk 40 G9
Ratton Village E Susx 11 T10
Rattray P & K 90 J2
Raughton Cumb 67 N3
Raughton Head Cumb 67 N3
Raunds N Nthn 38 E6
Ravenfield Rothm 57 Q7
Ravenglass Cumb 66 G13
Ravenhills Green Worcs 35 R10
Raveningham Norfk 41 Q1
Ravenscar N York 71 S12
Ravenscraig N Lans 82 E7
Ravensdale IoM 60 f4
Ravensden Bed 38 G10
Ravenseat N York 68 J12
Ravenshead Notts 47 Q3
Ravensmoor Ches E 45 P3
Ravensthorpe Kirk 56 K2
Ravensthorpe W Nthn 37 S6
Ravenstone Leics 47 M11
Ravenstone M Keyn 38 B10
Ravenstonedale W & F 68 F12
Ravenstruther S Lans 82 H9
Ravensworth N York 69 P11
Raw N York 71 R11
Rawcliffe C York 64 D9
Rawcliffe E R Yk 57 U2
Rawcliffe Bridge E R Yk 57 U2
Rawdon Leeds 63 Q12
Rawling Street Kent 12 H4
Rawmarsh Rothm 57 P7
Rawnsley Staffs 46 D11
Rawreth Essex 22 J9
Rawridge Devon 6 H3
Rawtenstall Lancs 55 T2
Raydon Suffk 40 H13
Raylees Nthumb 76 J7
Rayleigh Essex 22 K9
Raymond's Hill Devon 6 K5
Rayne Essex 22 H3
Raynes Park Gt Lon 21 M9
Reach Cambs 39 S7
Read Lancs 62 F13
Reading Readg 20 B8
Reading Services W Berk 19 U7
Reading Street Kent 12 H9
Reading Street Kent 13 S2
Reagill W & F 68 D9
Rearquhar Highld 109 N6
Rearsby Leics 47 S11
Rease Heath Ches E 45 P3
Reawla Cnwll 2 G9
Reay Highld 111 V4
Reculver Kent 13 P2
Red Ball Devon 16 E13
Redberth Pembks 24 J10
Redbourn Herts 31 P10
Redbourne N Linc 58 G7
Redbrook Gloucs 27 U6
Redbrook Wrexhm 45 M5
Redbrook Street Kent 12 H8
Redburn Highld 103 P6
Redburn Nthumb 76 F13
Redcar R & Cl 70 K8
Redcastle D & G 74 F12
Redcastle Highld 102 G6
Red Dial Cumb 67 L3
Redding Falk 82 H3
Reddingmuirhead Falk 82 H3
Reddish Stockp 56 C8
Redditch Worcs 36 D7
Rede Suffk 40 D9
Redenhall Norfk 41 N4
Redenham Hants 19 M11
Redesmouth Nthumb 76 H9
Redford Abers 99 P9
Redford Angus 91 S3
Redford W Susx 10 D5
Redfordgreen Border 75 S2
Redgate Rhondd 26 J10
Redgorton P & K 90 G6
Redgrave Suffk 40 H5
Redhill Abers 99 P3
Red Hill BCP 8 F9
Redhill Herts 31 T6
Redhill N Som 17 N4
Redhill Surrey 21 N12
Red Hill Warwks 36 F9
Redisham Suffk 41 R4
Redland Bristl 28 A12
Redland Ork 106 s17
Redlingfield Suffk 41 L6
Redlingfield Green Suffk 41 L6
Red Lodge Suffk 40 B6
Red Lumb Rochdl 55 T3
Redlynch Somset 17 T10
Redlynch Wilts 8 J4
Redmain Cumb 66 H6
Redmarley Worcs 35 S7
Redmarley D'Abitot Gloucs 28 E1
Redmarshall S on T 70 E8
Redmile Leics 47 U6
Redmire N York 63 L1
Redmyre Abers 99 P8
Rednal Birm 36 D5
Rednal Shrops 44 J8
Redpath Border 84 F11
Red Point Highld 107 M11
Red Post Cnwll 14 G11
Red Rice Hants 19 M12
Red Rock Wigan 55 N5
Red Roses Carmth 25 M8
Red Row Nthumb 77 R6
Redruth Cnwll 2 H8
Redstocks Wilts 18 D8
Redstone P & K 90 J5
Redstone Cross Pembks 24 K7
Red Street Staffs 45 T3
Redvales Bury 55 T5
Red Wharf Bay IoA 52 H6
Redwick Newpt 27 S11
Redwick S Glos 27 V10
Redworth Darltn 69 R8
Reed Herts 31 U5
Reedham Norfk 51 R13
Reedness E R Yk 58 C2
Reeds Beck Lincs 59 M13
Reeds Holme Lancs 55 T2
Reepham Lincs 58 H12
Reepham Norfk 50 K9
Reeth N York 69 M13
Reeves Green Solhll 36 J5
Regaby IoM 60 g3
Regil N Som 17 P4
Reiff Highld 107 S2
Reigate Surrey 21 N12
Reighton N York 65 Q4
Reinigeadal W Isls 106 h8
Reisque Abers 105 P12
Reiss Highld 112 H6
Rejerrah Cnwll 2 K5
Releath Cnwll 2 H10
Relubbus Cnwll 2 F10
Relugas Moray 103 Q6
Remenham Wokham 20 C6
Remenham Hill Wokham 20 C6
Rempstone Notts 47 Q9
Rendcomb Gloucs 28 K6
Rendham Suffk 41 P8
Rendlesham Suffk 41 P10
Renfrew Rens 89 M12
Renhold Bed 38 G10
Renishaw Derbys 57 Q11
Rennington Nthumb 77 Q2
Renton W Duns 88 J10
Renwick W & F 67 S4
Repps Norfk 51 R10
Repton Derbys 46 K8
Reraig Highld 100 h7
Resaurie Highld 102 K6
Rescassa Cnwll 3 P8
Rescorla Cnwll 3 P7
Resipole Burn Highld 93 S6
Reskadinnick Cnwll 2 G8
Resolis Highld 102 J2
Resolven Neath 26 E7
Rest and be thankful Ag & B 88 F4
Reston Border 85 M6
Restronguet Cnwll 3 L9
Reswallie Angus 98 J13
Reterth Cnwll 3 N4
Retford Notts 58 B10
Retire Cnwll 3 Q4
Rettendon Common Essex 22 J8
Rettendon Village Essex 22 J8
Retyn Cnwll 3 M5
Revesby Lincs 49 L1
Rew Devon 5 S13
Rew Devon 5 T6
Rewe Devon 6 B5
Rew Street IoW 9 P10
Rexon Devon 5 L3
Reydon Suffk 41 S5
Reymerston Norfk 50 H12
Reynalton Pembks 24 J9
Reynoldston Swans 25 S13
Rezare Cnwll 4 K5
Rhadyr Mons 27 R7
Rhandirmwyn Carmth 33 Q12
Rhayader Powys 33 U7
Rheindown Highld 102 F6
Rhenigidale W Isls 106 h8
Rhes-y-cae Flints 54 E12
Rhewl Denbgs 44 D1
Rhewl Denbgs 44 E5
Rhewl Mostyn Flints 54 E10
Rhicarn Highld 110 B11
Rhiconich Highld 110 F6
Rhicullen Highld 109 M10
Rhigos Rhondd 26 G6
Rhives Highld 109 Q4
Rhiwbina Cardif 27 M11
Rhiwbryfdir Gwynd 43 N4
Rhiwderyn Newpt 27 P10
Rhiwen Gwynd 52 J10
Rhiwinder Rhondd 26 J10
Rhiwlas Gwynd 43 T6
Rhiwlas Gwynd 52 J9
Rhiwlas Powys 44 E7
Rhiwsaeson Rhondd 26 K11
Rhode Somset 16 J10
Rhoden Green Kent 12 C6
Rhodesia Notts 57 S11
Rhodes Minnis Kent 13 N7
Rhodiad-y-brenin Pembks 24 C5
Rhonehouse D & G 74 D14
Rhoose V Glam 16 E3
Rhos Carmth 25 Q3
Rhos Denbgs 44 D1
Rhos Neath 26 C7
Rhosaman Carmth 26 C5
Rhosbeirio IoA 52 E4
Rhoscefnhir IoA 52 H7
Rhoscolyn IoA 52 C7
Rhoscrowther Pembks 24 F10
Rhosesmor Flints 54 F13
Rhos-fawr Gwynd 42 G6
Rhosgadfan Gwynd 52 H11
Rhosgoch IoA 52 F5
Rhosgoch Powys 34 E11
Rhos Haminiog Cerdgn 32 K8
Rhoshill Pembks 32 C12
Rhoshirwaun Gwynd 42 D8
Rhoslan Gwynd 42 J5
Rhoslefain Gwynd 43 L12
Rhosllanerchrugog Wrexhm 44 G4
Rhôs Lligwy IoA 52 G5
Rhosmaen Carmth 26 A3
Rhosmeirch IoA 52 G7
Rhosneigr IoA 52 D8
Rhosnesni Wrexhm 44 J3
Rhôs-on-Sea Conwy 53 P6
Rhosrobin Wrexhm 44 H3
Rhossili Swans 25 R13
Rhostrehwfa IoA 52 F8
Rhostryfan Gwynd 52 G11
Rhostyllen Wrexhm 44 H4
Rhosybol IoA 52 F5
Rhos-y-brithdir Powys 44 D9
Rhosygadfa Shrops 44 H7
Rhos-y-garth Cerdgn 33 M6
Rhos-y-gwaliau Gwynd 43 T7
Rhos-y-llan Gwynd 42 D6
Rhosymedre Wrexhm 44 G5
Rhos-y-meirch Powys 34 G7
RHS Garden Harlow Carr N York 63 R9
RHS Garden Wisley Surrey 20 J11
Rhu Ag & B 88 G9
Rhuallt Denbgs 54 C11
Rhubodach Ag & B 88 B11
Rhuddall Heath Ches W 45 N1
Rhuddlan Cerdgn 32 J12
Rhuddlan Denbgs 53 T7
Rhue Highld 107 V5
Rhulen Powys 34 D11
Rhunahaorine Ag & B 79 N6
Rhyd Gwynd 43 M5
Rhydargaeau Carmth 25 R5
Rhydcymerau Carmth 25 U3
Rhydd Worcs 35 T11
Rhyd-Ddu Gwynd 52 J12
Rhydding Neath 26 C8
Rhydgaled Conwy 53 S10
Rhydlanfair Conwy 53 P12
Rhydlewis Cerdgn 32 F11
Rhydlios Gwynd 42 C8
Rhydlydan Conwy 43 S3
Rhydowen Cerdgn 32 H11
Rhydroser Cerdgn 33 L7
Rhydspence Herefs 34 F11
Rhydtalog Flints 44 F3
Rhyd-uchaf Gwynd 43 T6
Rhyd-y-clafdy Gwynd 42 F7
Rhydycroesau Shrops 44 F7
Rhydyfelin Cerdgn 33 L5
Rhydyfelin Rhondd 26 K10
Rhyd-y-foel Conwy 53 R7
Rhydyfro Neath 26 C6
Rhyd-y-groes Gwynd 52 J9
Rhydymain Gwynd 43 R9
Rhyd-y-meirch Mons 27 Q6
Rhydymwyn Flints 54 F13
Rhyd-y-pennau Cerdgn 33 M3
Rhyd-yr-onnen Gwynd 43 M13
Rhyd-y-sarn Gwynd 43 N5
Rhyl Denbgs 53 T6
Rhymney Caerph 27 L6
Rhynd P & K 90 J7
Rhynie Abers 104 F10
Rhynie Highld 109 Q9
Ribbesford Worcs 35 S6
Ribbleton Lancs 62 B13
Ribby Lancs 61 S13
Ribchester Lancs 62 D12
Riber Derbys 46 K2
Riby Lincs 59 L5
Riccall N York 64 E12
Riccarton Border 76 A7
Riccarton E Ayrs 81 N5
Richards Castle Herefs 35 L7
Richings Park Bucks 20 H7
Richmond Gt Lon 21 L8
Richmond N York 69 Q12
Richmond Sheff 57 P9
Richmond Park Kent 13 R6
Rich's Holford Somset 16 F10
Rickerscote Staffs 46 B9
Rickford N Som 17 N5
Rickham Devon 5 T13
Rickinghall Suffk 40 H5
Rickling Essex 22 C1
Rickling Green Essex 22 D2
Rickmansworth Herts 20 J4
Riddell Border 84 E14
Riddings Derbys 47 M3
Riddlecombe Devon 15 P10
Riddlesden C Brad 63 M11
Ridge BaNES 17 Q5
Ridge Dorset 8 C11
Ridge Herts 31 R12
Ridge Wilts 8 D2
Ridgebourne Powys 34 C8
Ridge Green Surrey 21 P13
Ridge Lane Warwks 36 J2
Ridge Row Kent 13 P7
Ridgeway Derbys 57 P10
Ridgeway Worcs 36 D8
Ridgeway Cross Herefs 35 R11
Ridgewell Essex 40 B12
Ridgewood E Susx 11 R7
Ridgmont C Beds 31 L5
Riding Mill Nthumb 77 L13
Ridley Kent 12 B3
Ridley Nthumb 76 F13
Ridley Green Ches E 45 N3
Ridlington Norfk 51 P7
Ridlington Rutlnd 48 B13
Ridlington Street Norfk 51 P7
Ridsdale Nthumb 76 J9
Rievaulx N York 64 D2
Rigg D & G 75 Q12
Riggend N Lans 82 E4
Righoul Highld 103 N5
Rigmadon Park W & F 62 C3
Rigsby Lincs 59 R11
Rigside S Lans 82 G11
Riley Green Lancs 55 P1
Rileyhill Staffs 46 F11
Rilla Mill Cnwll 4 H6
Rillaton Cnwll 4 H6
Rillington N York 64 K5
Rimington Lancs 62 G10
Rimpton Somset 17 R12
Rimswell E R Yk 65 U14
Rinaston Pembks 24 G5
Rindleford Shrops 35 R1
Ringford D & G 73 R8
Ringinglow Sheff 57 L10
Ringland Norfk 50 K11
Ringles Cross E Susx 11 R6
Ringlestone Kent 12 G4
Ringley Bolton 55 S5
Ringmer E Susx 11 Q8
Ringmore Devon 5 R11
Ringmore Devon 6 B10
Ringorm Moray 104 B7
Ring's End Cambs 49 N13
Ringsfield Suffk 41 R3
Ringsfield Corner Suffk 41 R3
Ringshall Herts 31 L10
Ringshall Suffk 40 H10
Ringshall Stocks Suffk 40 J10
Ringstead N Nthn 38 E5
Ringstead Norfk 50 B5
Ringwood Hants 8 H7
Ringwould Kent 13 S6
Rinmore Abers 104 E12
Rinsey Cnwll 2 F11
Rinsey Croft Cnwll 2 G11
Ripe E Susx 11 S8
Ripley Derbys 47 L3
Ripley Hants 8 H9
Ripley N York 63 R7
Ripley Surrey 20 J11
Riplingham E R Yk 65 M13
Riplington Hants 9 T4
Ripon N York 63 S5
Rippingale Lincs 48 G8
Ripple Kent 13 S5
Ripple Worcs 35 U13
Ripponden Calder 56 F3
Risabus Ag & B 78 E7
Risbury Herefs 35 M10
Risby N Linc 58 F4
Risby Suffk 40 D7
Risca Caerph 27 N9
Rise E R Yk 65 R11
Riseden E Susx 11 U4
Riseden Kent 12 D8
Risegate Lincs 48 K8
Riseholme Lincs 58 G11
Risehow Cumb 66 F6
Riseley Bed 38 F8
Riseley Wokham 20 B10
Rishangles Suffk 41 L7
Rishton Lancs 62 E13
Rishworth Calder 56 F3
Rising Bridge Lancs 55 S1
Risley Derbys 47 N6
Risley Warrtn 55 Q8
Risplith N York 63 Q6
Rivar Wilts 19 M8
Rivenhall End Essex 22 K4
River Kent 13 Q7
River W Susx 10 E6
River Bank Cambs 39 R7
Riverford Highld 102 F5
Riverhead Kent 21 T11
Rivers Corner Dorset 7 U2
Rivington Lancs 55 P4
Rivington Services Lancs 55 P4
Roachill Devon 15 U8
Roade W Nthn 37 U10
Road Green Norfk 41 N2
Roadhead Cumb 75 V11
Roadmeetings S Lans 82 G9
Roadside E Ayrs 81 R9
Roadside Highld 112 E4
Roadwater Somset 16 D9
Roag Highld 100 b5
Roa Island W & F 61 N6
Roan of Craigoch S Ayrs 80 K12
Roast Green Essex 39 Q14
Roath Cardif 27 M12
Roberton Border 75 T3
Roberton S Lans 82 H13
Robertsbridge E Susx 12 D11
Roberttown Kirk 56 J2
Robeston Wathen Pembks 24 J7
Robgill Tower D & G 75 P11
Robin Hill Staffs 46 B2
Robin Hood Lancs 55 M4
Robin Hood Leeds 57 M1
Robinhood End Essex 40 B13
Robin Hood's Bay N York 71 S11
Roborough Devon 5 N8
Roborough Devon 15 N9
Robroyston C Glas 89 P12
Roby Knows 54 K8
Roby Mill Lancs 55 M5
Rocester Staffs 46 F6
Roch Pembks 24 E6
Rochdale Rochdl 56 C4
Roche Cnwll 3 P4
Rochester Medway 12 D2
Rochester Nthumb 76 G6
Rochford Essex 23 L9
Rochford Worcs 35 P7
Roch Gate Pembks 24 E6
Rock Cnwll 3 N1
Rock Neath 26 D9
Rock Nthumb 77 Q1
Rock W Susx 10 J8
Rock Worcs 35 R6
Rockbeare Devon 6 D6
Rockbourne Hants 8 G5
Rockcliffe Cumb 75 S13
Rockcliffe D & G 66 B2
Rockcliffe Cross Cumb 75 R13
Rock End Staffs 45 U2
Rockend Torbay 6 B12
Rock Ferry Wirral 54 H9
Rockfield Highld 109 S8
Rockfield Mons 27 T5
Rockford Devon 15 S3
Rockford Hants 8 H7
Rockgreen Shrops 35 M5
Rockhampton S Glos 28 C9
Rockhead Cnwll 4 D4
Rockhill Shrops 34 G5
Rock Hill Worcs 36 C7
Rockingham N Nthn 38 C2
Rockland All Saints Norfk 40 G1
Rockland St Mary Norfk 51 P13
Rockland St Peter Norfk 40 G1
Rockley Notts 58 B12
Rockley Wilts 18 J6
Rockliffe Lancs 56 C2
Rockville Ag & B 88 F7
Rockwell End Bucks 20 C5
Rockwell Green Somset 16 F12
Rodborough Gloucs 28 F7
Rodbourne Swindn 29 M10
Rodbourne Wilts 28 H11
Rodd Herefs 34 H8
Roddam Nthumb 77 L1
Rodden Dorset 7 R8
Roddymoor Dur 69 Q5
Rode Somset 18 B10
Rode Heath Ches E 45 T2
Rode Heath Ches E 56 C13
Rodel W Isls 106 f10
Roden Wrekin 45 N10
Rodhuish Somset 16 D9
Rodington Wrekin 45 N11
Rodington Heath Wrekin 45 N11
Rodley Gloucs 28 D5
Rodley Leeds 63 Q12
Rodmarton Gloucs 28 H8
Rodmell E Susx 11 Q9
Rodmersham Kent 12 H3
Rodmersham Green Kent 12 H3
Rodney Stoke Somset 17 N7
Rodsley Derbys 46 H5
Rodway Somset 16 J8
Rodway Wrekin 45 Q10
Roecliffe N York 63 T6
Roe Cross Tamesd 56 E7
Roe Green Herts 31 R11
Roe Green Herts 31 T6
Roe Green Salfd 55 R6
Roehampton Gt Lon 21 M8
Roffey W Susx 10 K4
Rogart Highld 109 N4
Rogate W Susx 10 C6
Roger Ground W & F 67 N13
Rogerstone Newpt 27 P10
Roghadal W Isls 106 f10
Rogiet Mons 27 T10
Roke Oxon 19 T2
Roker Sundld 77 U14
Rollesby Norfk 51 R10
Rolleston Leics 47 T13
Rolleston Notts 47 T3
Rollestone Wilts 18 G11
Rolleston on Dove Staffs 46 H8
Rolston E R Yk 65 S11
Rolstone N Som 17 L4
Rolvenden Kent 12 F9
Rolvenden Layne Kent 12 G9
Romaldkirk Dur 69 L8
Romanby N York 70 E14
Romanno Bridge Border 83 N9
Romansleigh Devon 15 R8
Romden Castle Kent 12 G7
Romesdal Highld 100 d4
Romford Dorset 8 F7
Romford Gt Lon 22 D10
Romiley Stockp 56 D8
Romney Street Kent 21 U10
Romsey Cambs 39 Q9
Romsey Hants 9 M4
Romsley Shrops 35 S4
Romsley Worcs 36 C4
Rona Highld 100 f4
Ronachan Ag & B 79 N5
Rood Ashton Wilts 18 C9
Rookhope Dur 68 K4
Rookley IoW 9 Q12
Rookley Green IoW 9 Q12
Rooks Bridge Somset 17 L6
Rooks Nest Somset 16 E10
Rookwith N York 63 Q2
Roos E R Yk 65 T13
Roose W & F 61 N6
Roosebeck W & F 61 P6
Roothams Green Bed 38 G9
Ropley Hants 9 S2
Ropley Dean Hants 9 S2
Ropley Soke Hants 9 T2
Ropsley Lincs 48 E7
Rora Abers 105 T5
Rorrington Shrops 44 H13
Rosarie Moray 104 D5
Rose Cnwll 2 K6
Roseacre Lancs 61 S12
Rose Ash Devon 15 S8
Rosebank S Lans 82 F9
Rosebush Pembks 24 J5
Rosecare Cnwll 14 E13
Rosecliston Cnwll 3 L5
Rosedale Abbey N York 71 M13
Rose Green Essex 23 M2
Rose Green Suffk 40 F13
Rose Green Suffk 40 G12
Rose Green W Susx 10 E11
Rosehall Highld 108 H4
Rosehearty Abers 105 Q2
Rose Hill E Susx 11 R7
Rose Hill Lancs 62 G13
Rosehill Shrops 45 L10
Roseisle Moray 103 T2
Roselands E Susx 11 U10
Rosemarket Pembks 24 G9
Rosemarkie Highld 102 K4
Rosemary Lane Devon 6 G2
Rosemount P & K 90 J3
Rosenannon Cnwll 3 P3
Rosenithon Cnwll 3 L12
Roser's Cross E Susx 11 S6
Rosevean Cnwll 3 Q5
Rosevine Cnwll 3 M9
Rosewarne Cnwll 2 G9
Rosewell Mdloth 83 Q6
Roseworth S on T 70 F8
Roseworthy Cnwll 2 G9
Rosgill W & F 67 R9
Roskestal Cnwll 2 B12
Roskhill Highld 100 b5
Roskorwell Cnwll 2 K12
Rosley Cumb 67 M3
Roslin Mdloth 83 Q6
Rosliston Derbys 46 H10
Rosneath Ag & B 88 G9
Ross D & G 73 Q11
Ross Nthumb 85 S11
Rossett Wrexhm 44 J2
Rossett Green N York 63 R9
Rossington Donc 57 T7
Ross-on-Wye Herefs 28 A3
Roster Highld 112 G9
Rostherne Ches E 55 R10
Rosthwaite Cumb 67 L10
Roston Derbys 46 F5
Rosudgeon Cnwll 2 F11
Rosyth Fife 83 M2
Rothbury Nthumb 77 M5
Rotherby Leics 47 S10
Rotherfield E Susx 11 T5
Rotherfield Greys Oxon 20 B6
Rotherfield Peppard Oxon 20 B6
Rotherham Rothm 57 P8
Rothersthorpe W Nthn 37 T9
Rotherwick Hants 20 B11
Rothes Moray 104 B6
Rothesay Ag & B 88 C13
Rothiebrisbane Abers 105 L8
Rothiemurchus Lodge Highld 97 R2
Rothienorman Abers 105 L8
Rothley Leics 47 Q11
Rothley Nthumb 77 L8
Rothmaise Abers 104 K9
Rothwell Leeds 63 S14
Rothwell Lincs 58 K7
Rothwell N Nthn 38 B4
Rotsea E R Yk 65 P9
Rottal Lodge Angus 98 F10
Rottingdean Br & H 11 P10
Rottington Cumb 66 E10
Roucan D & G 74 K10
Roud IoW 9 Q12
Rougham Norfk 50 D9
Rougham Suffk 40 F8
Rough Close Staffs 46 B6
Rough Common Kent 13 M4
Roughlee Lancs 62 G11
Roughpark Abers 104 C13
Roughton Lincs 59 M14
Roughton Norfk 51 M6
Roughton Shrops 35 S2
Roughway Kent 12 B5
Roundbush Essex 23 L7
Round Bush Herts 20 K3
Roundbush Green Essex 22 E5
Round Green Luton 31 P8
Roundham Somset 7 M3
Roundhay Leeds 63 S12
Rounds Green Sandw 36 C3
Round Street Kent 12 C2
Roundstreet Common W Susx 10 H5
Roundswell Devon 15 M6
Roundway Wilts 18 F8
Roundyhill Angus 98 F13
Rousay Ork 106 s16
Rousdon Devon 6 J6
Rousham Oxon 29 U3
Rous Lench Worcs 36 D10
Routenburn N Ayrs 88 E13
Routh E R Yk 65 P11
Rout's Green Bucks 20 C3
Row Cnwll 3 R1
Row W & F 61 T2
Row W & F 68 D6
Rowanburn D & G 75 T10
Rowardennan Stirlg 88 J6
Rowarth Derbys 56 F9
Row Ash Hants 9 Q6
Rowberrow Somset 17 N5
Rowborough IoW 9 P12
Rowde Wilts 18 E8
Rowden Devon 15 P13
Rowen Conwy 53 N8
Rowfield Derbys 46 G4
Rowfoot Nthumb 76 D13
Rowford Somset 16 H11
Row Green Essex 22 H3
Rowhedge Essex 23 P3
Rowhook W Susx 10 J4
Rowington Warwks 36 H7
Rowland Derbys 56 K12
Rowland's Castle Hants 9 U6
Rowlands Gill Gatesd 77 P14
Rowledge Surrey 10 C2
Rowley Dur 69 N3
Rowley E R Yk 65 M13
Rowley Shrops 44 H12
Rowley Hill Kirk 56 J4
Rowley Regis Sandw 36 C3
Rowlstone Herefs 27 R2
Rowly Surrey 10 G2
Rowner Hants 9 R8
Rowney Green Worcs 36 D6
Rownhams Hants 9 M5
Rownhams Services Hants 9 M5
Rowrah Cumb 66 G9
Rowsham Bucks 30 H9
Rowsley Derbys 57 L13
Rowstock Oxon 29 U10
Rowston Lincs 48 G2
Rowthorne Derbys 57 Q14
Rowton Ches W 54 K14
Rowton Shrops 34 K4
Rowton Shrops 44 J11
Rowton Wrekin 45 P10
Row Town Surrey 20 H10
Roxburgh Border 84 H12
Roxby N Linc 58 F3
Roxby N York 71 N9
Roxton Bed 38 J10
Roxwell Essex 22 F6
Royal Botanic Garden Edinburgh C Edin 83 P3
Royal Leamington Spa Warwks 36 K7
Royal Oak Darltn 69 R8
Royal Oak Lancs 54 K6
Royal's Green Ches E 45 P5
Royal Sutton Coldfield Birm 36 F1
Royal Tunbridge Wells Kent 11 T3
Royal Wootton Bassett Wilts 29 L11
Royal Yacht Britannia C Edin 83 Q3
Roy Bridge Highld 96 B7
Roydhouse Kirk 56 K4
Roydon Essex 22 B5
Roydon Norfk 40 K4
Roydon Norfk 50 B9
Roydon Hamlet Essex 22 B6
Royston Barns 57 N4
Royston Herts 31 U4
Royton Oldham 56 D5
Rozel Jersey 7 e2
Ruabon Wrexhm 44 H5
Ruaig Ag & B 92 D9
Ruan High Lanes Cnwll 3 N9
Ruan Lanihorne Cnwll 3 M8
Ruan Major Cnwll 2 J13
Ruan Minor Cnwll 2 J13
Ruardean Gloucs 28 B4
Ruardean Hill Gloucs 28 B4
Ruardean Woodside Gloucs 28 B4
Rubery Birm 36 C5
Rubha Ban W Isls 106 c17
Ruckcroft W & F 67 R4
Ruckhall Herefs 35 L13
Ruckinge Kent 12 K9
Ruckland Lincs 59 P11
Ruckley Shrops 45 M13
Rudbaxton Pembks 24 G6
Rudby N York 70 G11
Rudchester Nthumb 77 N12
Ruddington Notts 47 Q7
Ruddle Gloucs 28 C5
Ruddlemoor Cnwll 3 Q6
Rudford Gloucs 28 E3
Rudge Somset 18 B10
Rudgeway S Glos 28 B10
Rudgwick W Susx 10 H4
Rudhall Herefs 28 B2
Rudheath Ches W 55 Q12
Rudheath Woods Ches E 55 R12
Rudley Green Essex 22 K7
Rudloe Wilts 18 B6
Rudry Caerph 27 N10
Rudston E R Yk 65 P6
Rudyard Staffs 46 C2
Ruecastle Border 76 C1
Rufford Lancs 55 L3
Rufford Abbey Notts 57 T14
Rufforth C York 64 C9
Rug Denbgs 44 C5
Rugby Warwks 37 P5
Rugby Services Warwks 37 P5
Rugeley Staffs 46 D10
Ruigh'riabhach Highld 107 T5
Ruisgarry W Isls 106 e10
Ruishton Somset 16 J11
Ruisigearraidh W Isls 106 e10
Ruislip Gt Lon 20 J5
Rùm Highld 100 c10
Rumbach Moray 104 D5
Rumbling Bridge P & K 90 F12
Rumburgh Suffk 41 P4
Rumby Hill Dur 69 Q6
Rumford Cnwll 3 M2
Rumford Falk 82 H3
Rumney Cardif 27 N12
Rumwell Somset 16 G12
Runcorn Halton 55 M10
Runcton W Susx 10 D10
Runcton Holme Norfk 49 T12
Runfold Surrey 20 E13
Runhall Norfk 50 J12
Runham Norfk 51 S11
Runham Norfk 51 T12
Runnington Somset 16 F12
Runsell Green Essex 22 J6
Runshaw Moor Lancs 55 M3
Runswick N York 71 P9
Runtaleave Angus 98 D10
Runwell Essex 22 J9
Ruscombe Wokham 20 C7
Rushall Herefs 35 P13
Rushall Norfk 41 L4
Rushall Wilts 18 H9
Rushall Wsall 46 D13
Rushbrooke Suffk 40 E8
Rushbury Shrops 35 M2
Rushden Herts 31 T6
Rushden N Nthn 38 E7
Rushenden Kent 23 M13
Rusher's Cross E Susx 11 U5
Rushford Devon 5 M5
Rushford Norfk 40 F4
Rush Green Essex 23 S4
Rush Green Gt Lon 22 D10
Rush Green Herts 31 R8
Rush Green Warrtn 55 Q9
Rushlake Green E Susx 11 U7
Rushmere Suffk 41 S3
Rushmere St Andrew Suffk 41 L11
Rushmoor Surrey 10 D2
Rushock Herefs 34 H9
Rushock Worcs 35 U6
Rusholme Manch 56 C8
Rushton Ches W 55 N14
Rushton N Nthn 38 B4
Rushton Shrops 45 P12
Rushton Spencer Staffs 46 B1
Rushwick Worcs 35 T10
Rushyford Dur 69 S7
Ruskie Stirlg 89 P5
Ruskington Lincs 48 G3
Rusland Cross W & F 61 Q2
Rusper W Susx 11 L3
Ruspidge Gloucs 28 C5
Russell Green Essex 22 H5
Russell's Water Oxon 20 B5
Russel's Green Suffk 41 N6
Russ Hill Surrey 11 L2
Rusthall Kent 11 T3
Rustington W Susx 10 G10
Ruston N York 65 M3
Ruston Parva E R Yk 65 P7
Ruswarp N York 71 Q11
Ruthall Shrops 35 N2
Rutherford Border 84 G12
Rutherglen S Lans 89 P13
Ruthernbridge Cnwll 3 Q3
Ruthin Denbgs 44 D2
Ruthrieston C Aber 99 S3
Ruthven Abers 104 G6
Ruthven Angus 91 L2
Ruthven Highld 97 M4
Ruthven Highld 103 M9
Ruthvoes Cnwll 3 N4
Ruthwaite Cumb 66 K5
Ruthwell D & G 75 L12
Ruxley Gt Lon 21 S8
Ruxton Green Herefs 27 U4
Ruyton-XI-Towns Shrops 44 J9
Ryal Nthumb 77 L11
Ryall Dorset 7 M5
Ryall Worcs 35 U12
Ryarsh Kent 12 C3
Rycote Oxon 30 E11
Rydal W & F 67 N11
Ryde IoW 9 R10
Rye E Susx 12 H11
Ryebank Shrops 45 M7
Ryeford Herefs 28 B3
Rye Foreign E Susx 12 G11
Rye Harbour E Susx 12 H12
Ryehill E R Yk 59 M1
Ryeish Green Wokham 20 B9
Rye Street Worcs 35 S13
Ryhall Rutlnd 48 F11
Ryhill Wakefd 57 N4
Ryhope Sundld 70 F2
Rylah Derbys 57 Q13
Ryland Lincs 58 H11
Rylands Notts 47 P6
Rylstone N York 62 K8
Ryme Intrinseca Dorset 7 Q2
Ryther N York 64 D12
Ryton Gatesd 77 P13
Ryton N York 64 H4
Ryton Shrops 45 S13
Ryton Warwks 37 M3
Ryton-on-Dunsmore Warwks 37 L6
Ryton Woodside Gatesd 77 N13
RZSS Edinburgh Zoo C Edin 83 P4

S

Sabden Lancs 62 F12
Sabine's Green Essex 22 D8
Sacombe Herts 31 T9
Sacombe Green Herts 31 T9
Sacriston Dur 69 R3
Sadberge Darltn 70 D9
Saddell Ag & B 79 P9
Saddington Leics 37 S2
Saddlebow Norfk 49 T10
Saddlescombe W Susx 11 M8
Sadgill W & F 67 Q11
Saffron Walden Essex 39 R13
Sageston Pembks 24 J10
Saham Hills Norfk 50 F13
Saham Toney Norfk 50 E13
Saighton Ches W 44 K1
St Abbs Border 85 N5
St Agnes Border 84 H6
St Agnes Cnwll 2 J6
St Agnes IoS 2 b3
St Agnes Mining District Cnwll 2 J7
St Albans Herts 31 P11
St Allen Cnwll 3 L6
St Andrew Guern 6 d3
St Andrews Fife 91 R8
St Andrews Botanic Garden Fife 91 R8
St Andrews Major V Glam 16 F2
St Andrews Well Dorset 7 N6
St Anne's Lancs 61 Q14
St Ann's D & G 75 L7
St Ann's Chapel Cnwll 5 L6
St Ann's Chapel Devon 5 R11
St Anthony-in-Meneage Cnwll 2 K11
St Anthony's Hill E Susx 11 U10
St Arvans Mons 27 U8
St Asaph Denbgs 53 T8
St Athan V Glam 16 D3
St Aubin Jersey 7 c3
St Austell Cnwll 3 Q6
St Bees Cumb 66 E10
St Blazey Cnwll 3 R6
St Blazey Gate Cnwll 3 R6
St Boswells Border 84 F12
St Brelade Jersey 7 b3
St Brelade's Bay Jersey 7 b3
St Breock Cnwll 3 P2
St Breward Cnwll 3 R1
St Briavels Gloucs 27 V7
St Brides Pembks 24 D8
St Brides Major V Glam 26 F13
St Brides Netherwent Mons 27 S10
St Brides-super-Ely V Glam 26 K12
St Brides Wentlooge Newpt 27 P11
St Budeaux C Plym 5 M9
Saintbury Gloucs 36 F13
St Buryan Cnwll 2 C11
St Catherine BaNES 17 U3
St Catherines Ag & B 88 D4
St Chloe Gloucs 28 F7
St Clears Carmth 25 N7
St Cleer Cnwll 4 G7
St Clement Cnwll 3 M8
St Clement Jersey 7 e4
St Clether Cnwll 4 G4
St Colmac Ag & B 88 B12
St Columb Major Cnwll 3 N4
St Columb Minor Cnwll 3 L4
St Columb Road Cnwll 3 N5
St Combs Abers 105 T3
St Cross South Elmham Suffk 41 N4
St Cyrus Abers 99 N11
St David's P & K 90 D7
St Davids Pembks 24 C5
St Davids Cathedral Pembks 24 C5
St Day Cnwll 2 J8
St Decumans Somset 16 E8
St Dennis Cnwll 3 P5
St Devereux Herefs 27 S1
St Dogmaels Pembks 32 C11
St Dogwells Pembks 24 G5
St Dominick Cnwll 5 L7
St Donats V Glam 16 B3
St Edith's Marsh Wilts 18 E8
St Endellion Cnwll 4 B5
St Enoder Cnwll 3 M5
St Erme Cnwll 3 L7
St Erney Cnwll 4 K9
St Erth Cnwll 2 F9
St Erth Praze Cnwll 2 F9
St Ervan Cnwll 3 M2
St Eval Cnwll 3 M3
St Ewe Cnwll 3 P7
St Fagans Cardif 27 L12
St Fagans National Museum of History Cardif 27 L12
St Fergus Abers 105 T5
St Fillans P & K 95 T14
St Florence Pembks 24 J10
St Gennys Cnwll 14 D13
St George Conwy 53 S7
St Georges N Som 17 L4
St George's V Glam 27 L12
St George's Hill Surrey 20 J10
St Germans Cnwll 4 K9
St Giles in the Wood Devon 15 M9
St Giles-on-the-Heath Devon 4 K2
St Gluvia's Cnwll 2 K10
St Harmon Powys 33 U6
St Helen Auckland Dur 69 Q7
St Helens Cumb 66 F6
St Helen's E Susx 12 F13
St Helens IoW 9 S11
St Helens St Hel 55 M7
St Helier Gt Lon 21 N9
St Helier Jersey 7 d3
St Hilary Cnwll 2 E10
St Hilary V Glam 26 J13
Saint Hill Devon 6 E3
Saint Hill W Susx 11 P3
St Illtyd Blae G 27 N7
St Ippolyts Herts 31 Q7
St Ishmael's Pembks 24 D9
St Issey Cnwll 3 N2
St Ive Cnwll 4 J7
St Ive Cross Cnwll 4 J7
St Ives Cambs 39 M6
St Ives Cnwll 2 E8
St Ives Dorset 8 G8
St James Norfk 51 N9
St James's End W Nthn 37 T8
St James South Elmham Suffk 41 P4
St Jidgey Cnwll 3 N3
St John Cnwll 5 L10
St John Jersey 7 c1
St Johns Dur 69 N6
St John's E Susx 11 S4
St John's IoM 60 d6
St John's Kent 21 T11
St Johns Surrey 20 G11
St Johns Worcs 35 T10
St John's Chapel Devon 15 M7
St John's Chapel Dur 68 J5
St John's Fen End Norfk 49 R11
St John's Highway Norfk 49 R11
St John's Kirk S Lans 82 J11
St John's Town of Dalry D & G 73 Q3
St John's Wood Gt Lon 21 N6
St Judes IoM 60 f3
St Just Cnwll 2 B10
St Just-in-Roseland Cnwll 3 L9
St Just Mining District Cnwll 2 B10
St Katherines Abers 105 M9
St Keverne Cnwll 2 K12
St Kew Cnwll 3 Q1
St Kew Highway Cnwll 3 Q1
St Keyne Cnwll 4 G8
St Lawrence Cnwll 3 Q3
St Lawrence Essex 23 N7
St Lawrence IoW 9 Q13
St Lawrence Jersey 7 c2
St Lawrence Kent 13 S2
St Lawrence Bay Essex 23 N6
St Leonards Bucks 30 K11
St Leonards Dorset 8 G8
St Leonards E Susx 12 F14
St Leonard's Street Kent 12 C4
St Levan Cnwll 2 B12
St Luke's Park Essex 22 J8
St Lythans V Glam 27 L13
St Mabyn Cnwll 3 Q2
St Madoes P & K 90 J7
St Margarets Herefs 34 J14
St Margarets Herts 31 U10
St Margaret's at Cliffe Kent 13 S7
St Margaret's Hope Ork 106 t20
St Margaret South Elmham Suffk 41 P4
St Marks IoM 60 d8
St Martin Cnwll 2 J12
St Martin Cnwll 4 H9
St Martin Guern 6 d3
St Martin Jersey 7 e2
St Martin's IoS 2 c1
St Martin's P & K 90 J5
St Martin's Shrops 44 H6
St Martin's Moor Shrops 44 H6
St Mary Jersey 7 c2
St Mary Bourne Hants 19 P10
St Marychurch Torbay 6 B11
St Mary Church V Glam 16 D2
St Mary Cray Gt Lon 21 S9
St Mary Hill V Glam 26 H12
St Mary in the Marsh Kent 13 L10
St Mary's IoS 2 c2
St Mary's Ork 106 t19

St Mary's Bay Kent 13 L10
St Mary's Hoo Medway 22 K12
St Mary's Platt Kent 12 B4
St Maughans Mons 27 T4
St Maughans Green Mons 27 T4
St Mawes Cnwll 3 L10
St Mawgan Cnwll 3 M3
St Mellion Cnwll 4 K7
St Mellons Cardif 27 N11
St Merryn Cnwll 3 M2
St Mewan Cnwll 3 P6
St Michael Caerhays Cnwll 3 P8
St Michael Church Somset 16 K10
St Michael Penkevil Cnwll 3 M8
St Michaels Kent 12 G8
St Michaels Worcs 35 N7
St Michael's Mount Cnwll 2 E11
St Michael's on Wyre Lancs 61 T11
St Michael South Elmham Suffk 41 P4
St Minver Cnwll 4 B5
St Monans Fife 91 R11
St Neot Cnwll 4 F7
St Neots Cambs 38 J8
St Newlyn East Cnwll 3 L5
St Nicholas Pembks 24 F3
St Nicholas V Glam 26 K13
St Nicholas-at-Wade Kent 13 Q2
St Ninians Stirlg 89 S7
St Olaves Norfk 51 S14
St Osyth Essex 23 R4
St Ouen Jersey 7 b2
St Owen's Cross Herefs 27 U3
St Paul's Cray Gt Lon 21 S9
St Paul's Walden Herts 31 Q8
St Peter Jersey 7 b2
St Peter Port Guern 6 e3
St Peter's Guern 6 c3
St Peter's Kent 13 S2
St Peter's Hill Cambs 38 K6
St Petrox Pembks 24 G11
St Pinnock Cnwll 4 G8
St Quivox S Ayrs 81 M8
St Ruan Cnwll 2 J13
St Sampson Guern 6 e2
St Saviour Guern 6 c3
St Saviour Jersey 7 d3
St Stephen Cnwll 3 N6
St Stephens Cnwll 4 J3
St Stephens Cnwll 5 L9
St Teath Cnwll 4 D4
St Thomas Devon 6 B6
St Margaret's Bay Kent 13 S7
St Tudy Cnwll 3 R1
St Twynnells Pembks 24 G11
St Veep Cnwll 4 E9
St Vigeans Angus 91 T3
St Wenn Cnwll 3 P4
St Weonards Herefs 27 T3
St Winnow Cnwll 4 E9
St y-Nyll V Glam 26 K12
Salcombe Devon 5 S13
Salcombe Regis Devon 6 G7
Salcott-cum-Virley Essex 23 M5
Sale Traffd 55 S8
Saleby Lincs 59 S11
Sale Green Worcs 36 B9
Salehurst E Susx 12 E11
Salem Carmth 25 V5
Salem Cerdgn 33 N4
Salen Ag & B 93 P10
Salen Highld 93 R6
Salesbury Lancs 62 D13
Salford C Beds 30 K5
Salford Oxon 29 Q2
Salford Salfd 55 T7
Salford Priors Warwks 36 E10
Salfords Surrey 21 N13
Salhouse Norfk 51 P11
Saline Fife 90 F13
Salisbury Wilts 8 G2
Salisbury Plain Wilts 18 G12
Salkeld Dykes W & F 67 R5
Sallachy Highld 108 J3
Salle Norfk 50 K9
Salmonby Lincs 59 P12
Salperton Gloucs 29 L3
Salph End Bed 38 G10
Salsburgh N Lans 82 F6
Salt Staffs 46 C8
Salta Cumb 66 G3
Saltaire C Brad 63 N12
Saltaire C Brad 63 N12
Saltash Cnwll 5 L9
Saltburn Highld 109 N10
Saltburn-by-the-Sea R & Cl 71 L8
Saltby Leics 48 C8
Salt Coates Cumb 66 J2
Saltcoats Cumb 66 G13
Saltcoats N Ayrs 80 J4
Saltcotes Lancs 61 R14
Saltdean Br & H 11 P10
Salterbeck Cumb 66 E7
Salterforth Lancs 62 H10
Salterswall Ches W 55 P13
Salterton Wilts 18 H13
Saltfleet Lincs 59 S8
Saltfleetby All Saints Lincs 59 S8
Saltfleetby St Clement Lincs 59 S8
Saltfleetby St Peter Lincs 59 R9
Saltford BaNES 17 S3
Salthouse Norfk 50 J5
Saltley Birm 36 F3
Saltmarsh Newpt 27 Q11
Saltmarshe E R Yk 58 C2
Saltney Flints 54 J14
Salton N York 64 G4
Saltrens Devon 15 L8
Saltwick Nthumb 77 P9
Saltwood Kent 13 N8
Salvington W Susx 10 J9
Salwarpe Worcs 35 U8
Salway Ash Dorset 7 N5
Sambourne Warwks 36 E8
Sambrook Wrekin 45 R9
Samlesbury Lancs 62 B13
Samlesbury Bottoms Lancs 62 C14
Sampford Arundel Somset 16 F13
Sampford Brett Somset 16 E8
Sampford Courtenay Devon 15 P12
Sampford Moor Somset 16 F13
Sampford Peverell Devon 6 D2
Sampford Spiney Devon 5 N6
Samsonlane Ork 106 v17
Samson's Corner Essex 23 Q4
Samuelston E Loth 84 D4
Sanaigmore Ag & B 86 C11
Sancreed Cnwll 2 C11
Sancton E R Yk 64 K12
Sand Somset 17 M7
Sandaig Highld 100 g9
Sandale Cumb 66 K4
Sandal Magna Wakefd 57 M3
Sanday Ork 106 v15
Sanday Airport Ork 106 v15
Sandbach Ches E 45 S1
Sandbach Services Ches E 45 S1
Sandbank Ag & B 88 E9
Sandbanks BCP 8 E11
Sandend Abers 104 H2
Sanderstead Gt Lon 21 P10
Sandford Devon 15 T12
Sandford Dorset 8 C11
Sandford Hants 8 H8
Sandford IoW 9 Q12
Sandford N Som 17 M5
Sandford S Lans 82 D10
Sandford Shrops 44 H9
Sandford Shrops 45 N7
Sandford W & F 68 F9
Sandford-on-Thames Oxon 30 B12
Sandford Orcas Dorset 17 R12
Sandford St Martin Oxon 29 T2
Sandgate Kent 13 P8
Sandhaven Abers 105 R2
Sandhead D & G 72 D10
Sandhill Rothm 57 P7
Sandhills Dorset 7 Q4
Sandhills Dorset 7 S2
Sand Hills Leeds 63 T12
Sandhills Oxon 30 C11
Sandhills Surrey 10 E3
Sandhoe Nthumb 76 K12
Sandhole Ag & B 87 U6
Sand Hole E R Yk 64 J12
Sandholme E R Yk 64 J13
Sandholme Lincs 49 M6
Sandhurst Br For 20 D10
Sandhurst Gloucs 28 F3
Sandhurst Kent 12 F10
Sandhurst Cross Kent 12 E10
Sandhutton N York 63 T3
Sand Hutton N York 64 F8
Sandiacre Derbys 47 N6
Sandilands Lincs 59 T10
Sandiway Ches W 55 P12
Sandleheath Hants 8 G5
Sandleigh Oxon 29 U7
Sandley Dorset 17 U12
Sandling Kent 12 E4
Sandlow Green Ches E 55 S13
Sandness Shet 106 r8
Sandon Essex 22 H7
Sandon Herts 31 T6
Sandon Staffs 46 B8
Sandon Bank Staffs 46 B8
Sandown IoW 9 R12
Sandplace Cnwll 4 H9
Sandridge Herts 31 Q10
Sandridge Wilts 18 D7
Sandringham Norfk 49 U8
Sands Bucks 20 D4
Sandsend N York 71 Q10
Sand Side W & F 61 N3
Sandside W & F 61 T3
Sandtoft N Linc 58 B5
Sandway Kent 12 G5
Sandwich Kent 13 R4
Sandwich Bay Kent 13 S4
Sandwick Shet 106 u11
Sandwick W & F 67 P9
Sandwick W Isls 106 j5
Sandwith Cumb 66 E10
Sandwith Newtown Cumb 66 E10
Sandy C Beds 38 J11
Sandy Bank Lincs 49 L2
Sandycroft Flints 54 H13
Sandy Cross E Susx 11 T6
Sandy Cross Herefs 35 Q9
Sandyford D & G 75 P7
Sandygate Devon 5 V6
Sandygate IoM 60 f3
Sandy Haven Pembks 24 E9
Sandyhills D & G 66 C1
Sandylands Lancs 61 S7
Sandy Lane C Brad 63 N12
Sandylane Staffs 45 R6
Sandylane Swans 25 U13
Sandy Lane Wilts 18 E7
Sandy Lane Wrexhm 44 K5
Sandy Park Devon 5 S3
Sandysike Cumb 75 S12
Sandyway Herefs 27 T2
Sangobeg Highld 110 J3
Sangomore Highld 110 J3
Sankey Bridges Warrtn 55 N9
Sankyn's Green Worcs 35 S7
Sanna Highld 93 L5
Sanndabhaig W Isls 106 j5
Sannox N Ayrs 80 E3
Sanquhar D & G 74 E4
Santon Cumb 66 H12
Santon IoM 60 e8
Santon Bridge Cumb 66 H12
Santon Downham Suffk 40 D3
Sapcote Leics 37 N2
Sapey Common Herefs 35 R8
Sapiston Suffk 40 F5
Sapley Cambs 38 K6
Sapperton Derbys 46 G7
Sapperton Gloucs 28 H7
Sapperton Lincs 48 F7
Saracen's Head Lincs 49 M8
Sarclet Highld 112 H8
Sarisbury Hants 9 Q7
Sarn Brdgnd 26 G11
Sarn Powys 34 F2
Sarnau Carmth 25 P7
Sarnau Cerdgn 32 F10
Sarnau Gwynd 43 U6
Sarnau Powys 34 B14
Sarnau Powys 44 F10
Sarn Bach Gwynd 42 F8
Sarnesfield Herefs 34 J10
Sarn Mellteyrn Gwynd 42 D7
Sarn Park Services Brdgnd 26 G11
Sarn-wen Powys 44 G10
Saron Carmth 25 Q3
Saron Carmth 25 V8
Saron Gwynd 52 G11
Saron Gwynd 52 H9
Sarratt Herts 20 H3
Sarre Kent 13 Q2
Sarsden Oxon 29 Q3
Sarson Hants 19 M12
Satley Dur 69 P4
Satmar Kent 13 Q8
Satron N York 68 K13
Satterleigh Devon 15 Q8
Satterthwaite W & F 61 Q1
Satwell Oxon 20 B6
Sauchen Abers 105 L13
Saucher P & K 90 J5
Sauchieburn Abers 99 M10
Saughall Ches W 54 J13
Saul Gloucs 28 D6
Saundby Notts 58 C9
Saundersfoot Pembks 24 K10
Saunderton Bucks 30 G12
Saunderton Station Bucks 20 D3
Saunton Devon 15 L5
Sausthorpe Lincs 59 Q13
Saverley Green Staffs 46 C6
Savile Town Kirk 56 K2
Sawbridge Warwks 37 P7
Sawbridgeworth Herts 22 C5
Sawdon N York 65 L3
Sawley Derbys 47 N7
Sawley Lancs 62 F10
Sawley N York 63 Q6
Sawston Cambs 39 Q11
Sawtry Cambs 38 J4
Saxby Leics 48 B10
Saxby Lincs 58 H9
Saxby All Saints N Linc 58 G3
Saxelbye Leics 47 S9
Saxham Street Suffk 40 J8
Saxilby Lincs 58 E11
Saxlingham Norfk 50 H6
Saxlingham Green Norfk 41 M1
Saxlingham Nethergate Norfk 41 M1
Saxlingham Thorpe Norfk 41 M1
Saxmundham Suffk 41 Q8
Saxondale Notts 47 S6
Saxon Street Cambs 39 U9
Saxtead Suffk 41 N7
Saxtead Green Suffk 41 N8
Saxtead Little Green Suffk 41 M7
Saxthorpe Norfk 50 K7
Saxton N York 64 B12
Sayers Common W Susx 11 M7
Scackleton N York 64 E5
Scadabay W Isls 106 g9
Scadabhagh W Isls 106 g9
Scafell Pike Cumb 66 K11
Scaftworth Notts 57 U8
Scagglethorpe N York 64 J5
Scalasaig Ag & B 86 F7
Scalby E R Yk 64 J14
Scalby N York 65 N1
Scald End Bed 38 F9
Scaldwell W Nthn 37 U6
Scaleby Cumb 75 T13
Scalebyhill Cumb 75 T13
Scale Houses W & F 67 S3
Scales W & F 61 P5
Scales W & F 67 M7
Scalesceugh Cumb 67 P3
Scalford Leics 47 U9
Scaling N York 71 M10
Scaling Dam R & Cl 71 M10
Scalloway Shet 106 u10
Scalpay Highld 100 f6
Scalpay W Isls 106 h9
Scamblesby Lincs 59 N11
Scammonden Kirk 56 G3
Scamodale Highld 93 U4
Scampston N York 64 K4
Scampton Lincs 58 G11
Scaniport Highld 102 H8
Scapegoat Hill Kirk 56 G3
Scarba Ag & B 87 M5
Scarborough N York 65 N2
Scarcewater Cnwll 3 N6
Scarcliffe Derbys 57 Q13
Scarcroft Leeds 63 T11
Scarfskerry Highld 112 G2
Scargill Dur 69 N10
Scarinish Ag & B 92 C10
Scarisbrick Lancs 54 J4
Scarness Cumb 66 K6
Scarning Norfk 50 G11
Scarrington Notts 47 T5
Scarth Hill Lancs 54 K5
Scarthingwell N York 64 B12
Scartho NE Lin 59 N5
Scatsta Airport Shet 106 t6
Scaur D & G 66 B2
Scawby N Linc 58 G5
Scawsby Donc 57 R6
Scawthorpe Donc 57 S5
Scawton N York 64 C3
Scayne's Hill W Susx 11 P6
Scethrog Powys 27 L2
Scholar Green Ches E 45 T2
Scholes Kirk 56 J1
Scholes Kirk 56 J5
Scholes Leeds 63 T12
Scholes Rothm 57 N7
Scholes Wigan 55 N5
School Aycliffe Dur 69 S8
School Green C Brad 63 N13
School Green Ches W 55 P14
Schoolgreen Wokham 20 B9
School House Dorset 7 L4
Scissett Kirk 56 K4
Scleddau Pembks 24 F4
Scofton Notts 57 T10
Scole Norfk 41 L5
Scone P & K 90 H6
Sconser Highld 100 e6
Scoonie Fife 91 N11
Scopwick Lincs 48 G2
Scoraig Highld 107 T5
Scorborough E R Yk 65 N10
Scorrier Cnwll 2 J8
Scorriton Devon 5 S7
Scorton Lancs 61 U10
Scorton N York 69 S12
Sco Ruston Norfk 51 N9
Scotby Cumb 67 P1
Scotch Corner N York 69 R11
Scotch Corner Rest Area N York 69 R11
Scotforth Lancs 61 T8
Scot Hay Staffs 45 S4
Scothern Lincs 58 H11
Scotland Lincs 48 F7
Scotland Gate Nthumb 77 R9
Scotlandwell P & K 90 J11
Scot Lane End Bolton 55 P5
Scotscalder Station Highld 112 C5
Scotsdike Cumb 75 S11
Scot's Gap Nthumb 77 L8
Scotsmill Abers 104 H12
Scotstoun C Glas 89 M12
Scotswood N u Ty 77 Q13
Scotter Lincs 58 E6
Scotterthorpe Lincs 58 E6
Scottish Seabird Centre E Loth 84 F1
Scottlethorpe Lincs 48 G9
Scotton Lincs 58 E7
Scotton N York 63 S8
Scotton N York 69 Q13
Scottow Norfk 51 N9
Scott Willoughby Lincs 48 G6
Scoulton Norfk 50 G13
Scounslow Green Staffs 46 E8
Scourie Highld 110 D8
Scourie More Highld 110 C8
Scousburgh Shet 106 t12
Scouthead Oldham 56 E5
Scrabster Highld 112 D2
Scraesburgh Border 76 D2
Scrafield Lincs 59 P13
Scrainwood Nthumb 76 K4
Scrane End Lincs 49 N5
Scraptoft Leics 47 R12
Scratby Norfk 51 T10
Scrayingham N York 64 G8
Scrays E Susx 12 E12
Scredington Lincs 48 G5
Scremby Lincs 59 R13
Scremerston Nthumb 85 Q9
Screveton Notts 47 T5
Scrivelsby Lincs 59 N13
Scriven N York 63 S8
Scrooby Notts 57 U8
Scropton Derbys 46 G7
Scrub Hill Lincs 48 K2
Scruton N York 63 R1
Scuggate Cumb 75 T11
Scullomie Highld 111 N4
Sculthorpe Norfk 50 E7
Scunthorpe N Linc 58 E4
Scurlage Swans 25 S13
Sea Somset 6 K2
Seaborough Dorset 7 M3
Seabridge Staffs 45 T5
Seabrook Kent 13 N8
Seaburn Sundld 77 U14
Seacombe Wirral 54 H8
Seacroft Leeds 63 T12
Seacroft Lincs 49 S1
Seadyke Lincs 49 M6
Seafield W Loth 82 K5
Seaford E Susx 11 R11
Seaforth Sefton 54 H7
Seagrave Leics 47 R10
Seagry Heath Wilts 18 E4
Seaham Dur 70 F3
Seahouses Nthumb 85 U12
Seal Kent 21 U11
Sealand Flints 54 J13
Seale Surrey 20 E13
Seamer N York 65 N3
Seamer N York 70 G10
Seamill N Ayrs 80 J3
Sea Palling Norfk 51 R8
Searby Lincs 58 J5
Seasalter Kent 13 L3
Seascale Cumb 66 F12
Seathwaite Cumb 66 K10
Seathwaite W & F 66 K13
Seatle W & F 61 R3
Seatoller Cumb 66 K10
Seaton Cnwll 4 J10
Seaton Cumb 66 F6
Seaton Devon 6 H6
Seaton Dur 70 E3
Seaton E R Yk 65 R10
Seaton Kent 13 P4
Seaton Nthumb 77 S10
Seaton Rutlnd 48 D14
Seaton Burn N Tyne 77 Q11
Seaton Carew Hartpl 70 H7
Seaton Delaval Nthumb 77 S10
Seaton Ross E R Yk 64 H11
Seaton Sluice Nthumb 77 S10
Seatown Dorset 7 M6
Seatown Moray 104 A1
Seave Green N York 70 J12
Seaview IoW 9 S10
Seaville Cumb 66 J2
Seavington St Mary Somset 7 M2
Seavington St Michael Somset 17 M13
Sebastopol Torfn 27 P8
Sebergham Cumb 67 N4
Seckington Warwks 46 J12
Second Severn Crossing Mons 27 U10
Sedbergh W & F 62 D1
Sedbury Gloucs 27 U9
Sedbusk N York 62 H1
Sedgeberrow Worcs 36 D13
Sedgebrook Lincs 48 C6
Sedge Fen Suffk 39 U4
Sedgefield Dur 70 E7
Sedgeford Norfk 50 B6
Sedgehill Wilts 8 B3
Sedgemoor Services Somset 17 L6
Sedgley Dudley 36 B2
Sedgley Park Bury 55 T6
Sedgwick W & F 61 U2
Sedlescombe E Susx 12 E12
Sedrup Bucks 30 H10
Seed Kent 12 H4
Seend Wilts 18 D8
Seend Cleeve Wilts 18 D8
Seer Green Bucks 20 G4
Seething Norfk 41 P1
Sefton Sefton 54 J6
Seghill Nthumb 77 R11
Seighford Staffs 45 U8
Seion Gwynd 52 H9
Seisdon Staffs 35 T1
Selattyn Shrops 44 G7
Selborne Hants 9 U2
Selby N York 64 E13
Selham W Susx 10 E6
Selhurst Gt Lon 21 P9
Selkirk Border 84 D13
Sellack Herefs 27 V2
Sellafield Station Cumb 66 F12
Sellafirth Shet 106 v4
Sellan Cnwll 2 C10
Sellick's Green Somset 16 H13
Sellindge Kent 13 L8
Selling Kent 12 K4
Sells Green Wilts 18 D8
Selly Oak Birm 36 D4
Selmeston E Susx 11 S9
Selsdon Gt Lon 21 Q10
Selsey W Susx 10 D12
Selsfield Common W Susx 11 N4
Selside N York 62 F4
Selside W & F 67 R13
Selsley Gloucs 28 F7
Selsted Kent 13 P7
Selston Notts 47 N3
Selworthy Somset 16 B7
Semer Suffk 40 G11
Semington Wilts 18 C8
Semley Wilts 8 B3
Sempringham Lincs 48 H7
Send Surrey 20 H11
Send Marsh Surrey 20 H11
Senghenydd Caerph 27 L9
Sennen Cnwll 2 B11
Sennen Cove Cnwll 2 B11
Sennybridge Powys 26 G2
Serlby Notts 57 T9
Sessay N York 64 B4
Setchey Norfk 49 T11
Setley Hants 9 L8
Seton Mains E Loth 84 C3
Settle N York 62 G7
Settrington N York 64 J5
Seven Ash Somset 16 G10
Sevenhampton Gloucs 28 K3
Sevenhampton Swindn 29 P9
Seven Kings Gt Lon 21 S5
Sevenoaks Kent 21 T11
Sevenoaks Weald Kent 21 T12
Seven Sisters Neath 26 E6
Seven Springs Gloucs 28 J4
Seven Star Green Essex 23 M2
Severn Beach S Glos 27 U11
Severn Bridge S Glos 27 V9
Severn Stoke Worcs 35 U12
Severn View Services S Glos 27 V10
Sevick End Bed 38 G10
Sevington Kent 12 K7
Sewards End Essex 39 S13
Sewardstonebury Essex 21 Q3
Sewell C Beds 31 L8
Sewerby E R Yk 65 R6
Seworgan Cnwll 2 J10
Sewstern Leics 48 C9
Sexhow N York 70 G11
Sgalpaigh W Isls 106 h9
Sgiogarstaigh W Isls 106 k2
Shabbington Bucks 30 E11
Shackerley Shrops 45 T12
Shackerstone Leics 47 L12
Shacklecross Derbys 47 M7
Shackleford Surrey 20 F13
Shade Calder 56 D2
Shader W Isls 106 i3
Shadforth Dur 70 D4
Shadingfield Suffk 41 R4
Shadoxhurst Kent 12 J8
Shadwell Leeds 63 S12
Shadwell Norfk 40 F4
Shaftenhoe End Herts 39 P13
Shaftesbury Dorset 8 B4
Shaftholme Donc 57 S5
Shafton Barns 57 N4
Shafton Two Gates Barns 57 N4
Shakerley Wigan 55 Q6
Shalbourne Wilts 19 M8
Shalcombe IoW 9 M11
Shalden Hants 19 U12
Shalden Green Hants 19 V12
Shaldon Devon 6 B10
Shalfleet IoW 9 N11
Shalford Essex 22 H2
Shalford Surrey 20 H13
Shalford Green Essex 22 H2
Shallowford Staffs 45 U8
Shalmsford Street Kent 13 L5
Shalstone Bucks 30 D5
Shamley Green Surrey 10 G2
Shandford Angus 98 H11
Shandon Ag & B 88 G8
Shandwick Highld 109 R9
Shangton Leics 37 T1
Shankhouse Nthumb 77 R10
Shanklin IoW 9 R12
Shantron Ag & B 88 H8
Shap W & F 67 S9
Shapinsay Ork 106 u18
Shapwick Dorset 8 C8
Shapwick Somset 17 M9
Shard End Birm 36 G3
Shardlow Derbys 47 M7
Shareshill Staffs 46 B12
Sharlston Wakefd 57 N3
Sharlston Common Wakefd 57 N3
Sharmans Cross Solhll 36 F5
Sharnal Street Medway 22 J13
Sharnbrook Bed 38 E9
Sharneyford Lancs 56 C2
Sharnford Leics 37 N2
Sharnhill Green Dorset 7 T3
Sharoe Green Lancs 61 U13
Sharow N York 63 S5
Sharpenhoe C Beds 31 N6
Sharperton Nthumb 76 K5
Sharp Green Norfk 51 Q9
Sharpness Gloucs 28 C7
Sharpthorne W Susx 11 P4
Sharptor Cnwll 4 H6
Sharpway Gate Worcs 36 C7
Sharrington Norfk 50 H6
Shatterford Worcs 35 S4
Shatterling Kent 13 Q4
Shatton Derbys 56 K10
Shaugh Prior Devon 5 N8
Shave Cross Dorset 7 M5
Shavington Ches E 45 Q3
Shaw C Brad 63 L12
Shaw Oldham 56 D5
Shaw Swindn 29 M10
Shaw W Berk 19 Q7
Shaw Wilts 18 C7
Shawbirch Wrekin 45 P11
Shawbost W Isls 106 h4
Shawbury Shrops 45 N9
Shawclough Rochdl 56 C4
Shaw Common Gloucs 28 C2
Shawdon Hill Nthumb 77 M3
Shawell Leics 37 P4
Shawford Hants 9 P3
Shawforth Lancs 56 C2
Shaw Green Herts 31 T6
Shaw Green Lancs 55 M3
Shaw Green N York 63 R9
Shawhead D & G 74 G10
Shaw Mills N York 63 R7
Shawsburn S Lans 82 E8
Shear Cross Wilts 18 C12
Shearington D & G 74 K12
Shearsby Leics 37 R2
Shearston Somset 16 J10
Shebbear Devon 14 K11
Shebdon Staffs 45 S8
Shebster Highld 112 B4
Shedfield Hants 9 R6
Sheen Staffs 46 F1
Sheepbridge Derbys 57 N12
Sheep Hill Dur 69 Q1
Sheepridge Kirk 56 J3
Sheepscar Leeds 63 S13
Sheepscombe Gloucs 28 G5
Sheepstor Devon 5 P7
Sheepwash Devon 15 L11
Sheepwash Nthumb 77 R8
Sheepway N Som 27 T12
Sheepy Magna Leics 46 K13
Sheepy Parva Leics 46 K13
Sheering Essex 22 D5
Sheerness Kent 23 M13
Sheerwater Surrey 20 H10
Sheet Hants 10 B6
Sheffield Cnwll 2 D11
Sheffield Sheff 57 N9
Sheffield Bottom W Berk 19 T7
Sheffield Green E Susx 11 Q5
Sheffield Park & Garden E Susx 11 Q6
Shefford C Beds 31 P5
Shefford Woodlands W Berk 19 N6
Sheigra Highld 110 D4
Sheinton Shrops 45 P13
Shelderton Shrops 34 K5
Sheldon Birm 36 G4
Sheldon Derbys 56 J13
Sheldon Devon 6 F3
Sheldwich Kent 12 K4
Sheldwich Lees Kent 12 K4
Shelf Calder 63 N14
Shelfanger Norfk 40 K4
Shelfield Warwks 36 F8
Shelfield Wsall 46 D13
Shelfield Green Warwks 36 F8
Shelford Notts 47 S5
Shelford Warwks 37 M3
Shellacres Nthumb 85 M10
Shelley Essex 22 E6
Shelley Kirk 56 K4
Shelley Suffk 40 H13
Shelley Far Bank Kirk 56 K4
Shellingford Oxon 29 R9
Shellow Bowells Essex 22 F6
Shelsley Beauchamp Worcs 35 R8
Shelsley Walsh Worcs 35 R8
Shelton Bed 38 F7
Shelton Norfk 41 M2
Shelton Notts 47 U5
Shelton Shrops 45 L11
Shelton Green Norfk 41 M2
Shelton Lock C Derb 47 L7
Shelton Under Harley Staffs 45 T6
Shelve Shrops 44 H14
Shelwick Herefs 35 M12
Shenfield Essex 22 F8
Shenington Oxon 37 L12
Shenley Herts 31 Q12
Shenley Brook End M Keyn 30 H5
Shenleybury Herts 31 Q12
Shenley Church End M Keyn 30 H5
Shenmore Herefs 34 J13
Shennanton D & G 72 J7
Shenstone Staffs 46 F13
Shenstone Worcs 35 U6
Shenstone Woodend Staffs 46 F13
Shenton Leics 47 L14
Shenval Moray 103 V10
Shepeau Stow Lincs 49 M11
Shephall Herts 31 S8
Shepherd's Bush Gt Lon 21 M6
Shepherd's Green Oxon 20 B6
Shepherds Patch Gloucs 28 D7
Shepherdswell Kent 13 Q6
Shepley Kirk 56 J5
Shepperdine S Glos 28 B8
Shepperton Surrey 20 J9
Shepperton Green Surrey 20 J9
Shepreth Cambs 39 N11
Shepshed Leics 47 N10
Shepton Beauchamp Somset 17 M13
Shepton Mallet Somset 17 R8
Shepton Montague Somset 17 S10
Shepway Kent 12 E5
Sheraton Dur 70 F5
Sherborne Dorset 17 R13
Sherborne Gloucs 29 N5
Sherborne Somset 17 Q5
Sherborne St John Hants 19 T9
Sherbourne Warwks 36 J8
Sherburn Dur 70 D4
Sherburn N York 65 M4
Sherburn Hill Dur 70 D4
Sherburn in Elmet N York 64 B13
Shere Surrey 20 J13
Shereford Norfk 50 E8
Sherfield English Hants 8 K4
Sherfield on Loddon Hants 19 U9
Sherfin Lancs 55 S1
Sherford Devon 5 N10
Sherford Devon 5 T12
Sherford Dorset 8 C10
Sheriffhales Shrops 45 S11
Sheriff Hutton N York 64 F6
Sheringham Norfk 51 L5
Sherington M Keyn 38 C11
Shermanbury W Susx 11 L7
Shernborne Norfk 50 B7
Sherrington Wilts 18 E13
Sherston Wilts 28 G10
Sherwood C Nott 47 Q5
Sherwood Forest Notts 47 R1
Shetland Islands Shet 106 u8
Shettleston C Glas 89 P13
Shevington Wigan 55 M5
Shevington Moor Wigan 55 M4
Shevington Vale Wigan 55 M5
Sheviock Cnwll 4 K9
Shibden Head C Brad 63 M14
Shide IoW 9 Q11
Shidlaw Nthumb 85 L11
Shiel Bridge Highld 101 N8
Shieldaig Highld 107 P14
Shieldhill D & G 74 K8
Shieldhill Falk 82 G3
Shieldhill House Hotel S Lans 82 K10
Shields N Lans 82 E7
Shielfoot Highld 93 R4
Shielhill Angus 98 G12
Shielhill Inver 88 F11
Shifford Oxon 29 S7
Shifnal Shrops 45 R12
Shilbottle Nthumb 77 P4
Shildon Dur 69 R7
Shillford E Rens 81 P1
Shillingford Devon 16 C12
Shillingford Oxon 19 S2
Shillingford Abbot Devon 6 B7
Shillingford St George Devon 6 B7
Shillingstone Dorset 8 A6
Shillington C Beds 31 P6
Shillmoor Nthumb 76 H4
Shilton Oxon 29 Q6
Shilton Warwks 37 M4
Shimpling Norfk 41 L4
Shimpling Suffk 40 E10
Shimpling Street Suffk 40 E10
Shincliffe Dur 69 S4
Shiney Row Sundld 70 D2
Shinfield Wokham 20 B9
Shingay Cambs 39 M11
Shingle Street Suffk 41 Q12
Shinnersbridge Devon 5 T8
Shinness Highld 108 J2
Shipbourne Kent 21 U12
Shipdham Norfk 50 G12
Shipham Somset 17 M5
Shiphay Torbay 6 A11
Shiplake Oxon 20 C7
Shiplake Row Oxon 20 B7
Shiplate N Som 17 L5
Shipley C Brad 63 P12
Shipley Derbys 47 M5
Shipley Shrops 35 T1
Shipley W Susx 10 J6
Shipley Bridge Surrey 11 N2
Shipley Hatch Kent 12 K8
Shipmeadow Suffk 41 Q2
Shippea Hill Station Cambs 39 T4
Shippon Oxon 29 U8
Shipston-on-Stour Warwks 36 J12
Shipton Bucks 30 G7
Shipton Gloucs 28 K4
Shipton N York 64 D8
Shipton Shrops 35 N2
Shipton Bellinger Hants 18 K11
Shipton Gorge Dorset 7 N6
Shipton Green W Susx 10 C11
Shipton Moyne Gloucs 28 G10
Shipton-on-Cherwell Oxon 29 U4
Shiptonthorpe E R Yk 64 K11
Shipton-under-Wychwood Oxon 29 Q4
Shirburn Oxon 30 E13
Shirdley Hill Lancs 54 J4
Shire W & F 68 D5
Shirebrook Derbys 57 R13
Shiregreen Sheff 57 N8
Shirehampton Bristl 27 U12
Shiremoor N Tyne 77 S11
Shirenewton Mons 27 T9
Shire Oak Wsall 46 E13
Shireoaks Notts 57 S10
Shirkoak Kent 12 H8
Shirland Derbys 47 M2
Shirlett Shrops 45 P14
Shirley C Sotn 9 N6
Shirley Derbys 46 H5
Shirley Gt Lon 21 Q9
Shirley Solhll 36 F5
Shirl Heath Herefs 34 K9
Shirrell Heath Hants 9 R6
Shirwell Devon 15 P5
Shiskine N Ayrs 79 S10
Shittlehope Dur 69 M5
Shobdon Herefs 34 K8
Shobley Hants 8 H7
Shobrooke Devon 15 U12
Shoby Leics 47 S9
Shocklach Ches W 44 K4
Shocklach Green Ches W 44 K4
Shoeburyness Sthend 23 M10
Sholden Kent 13 S5
Sholing C Sotn 9 P6
Shoot Hill Shrops 44 K11
Shop Cnwll 3 M2
Shop Cnwll 14 F10
Shopwyke W Susx 10 D9
Shore Rochdl 56 D3
Shoreditch Gt Lon 21 P6
Shoreditch Somset 16 H12
Shoreham Kent 21 T10
Shoreham-by-Sea W Susx 11 L9
Shoreswood Nthumb 85 N9
Shorley Hants 9 R3
Shorncote Gloucs 28 K8
Shorne Kent 22 G13
Shortacross Cnwll 4 H9
Shortbridge E Susx 11 R6
Shortfield Common Surrey 10 C2
Shortgate E Susx 11 R7
Short Heath Birm 36 E2
Shortheath Hants 10 B3
Short Heath Wsall 46 C13
Shortlanesend Cnwll 3 L7
Shortlees E Ayrs 81 N5
Shortstown Bed 38 G11
Shorwell IoW 9 P12
Shoscombe BaNES 17 T5
Shotesham Norfk 51 M14
Shotgate Essex 22 J9
Shotley Suffk 41 M13
Shotley Bridge Dur 69 N2
Shotleyfield Nthumb 69 N2
Shotley Gate Suffk 41 M14
Shottenden Kent 12 K5
Shottermill Surrey 10 D4
Shottery Warwks 36 G10
Shotteswell Warwks 37 M11
Shottisham Suffk 41 P12
Shottle Derbys 46 K4
Shottlegate Derbys 46 K4
Shotton Dur 70 E7
Shotton Dur 70 F5
Shotton Flints 54 H13
Shotton Nthumb 77 Q10
Shotton Nthumb 85 L12
Shotton Colliery Dur 70 E4
Shotts N Lans 82 G7
Shotwick Ches W 54 H12
Shougle Moray 103 V4
Shouldham Norfk 49 U12
Shouldham Thorpe Norfk 49 U12
Shoulton Worcs 35 T9
Shover's Green E Susx 12 C9
Shraleybrook Staffs 45 S4
Shrawardine Shrops 44 J10
Shrawley Worcs 35 T7
Shreding Green Bucks 20 H6
Shrewley Warwks 36 H7
Shrewsbury Shrops 45 L11
Shrewton Wilts 18 G12
Shripney W Susx 10 E10
Shrivenham Oxon 29 P10
Shropham Norfk 40 G2
Shroton Dorset 8 B6
Shrub End Essex 23 N3
Shucknall Herefs 35 N12
Shudy Camps Cambs 39 T12
Shuna Ag & B 87 P4
Shurdington Gloucs 28 H4
Shurlock Row W & M 20 D8
Shurnock Worcs 36 D8
Shurrery Highld 112 B5
Shurrery Lodge Highld 112 B5
Shurton Somset 16 H8
Shustoke Warwks 36 H2
Shute Devon 6 J5
Shute Devon 15 U12
Shutford Oxon 37 L12
Shut Heath Staffs 45 U9
Shuthonger Gloucs 35 U13
Shutlanger W Nthn 37 T11
Shutterton Devon 6 C9
Shutt Green Staffs 45 U12
Shuttington Warwks 46 J12
Shuttlewood Derbys 57 Q12
Shuttleworth Bury 55 T3
Siabost W Isls 106 h4
Siadar W Isls 106 i3
Sibbertoft W Nthn 37 S4
Sibdon Carwood Shrops 34 K4
Sibford Ferris Oxon 37 L13
Sibford Gower Oxon 37 L13
Sible Hedingham Essex 40 C14
Sibley's Green Essex 22 F2
Siblyback Cnwll 4 G6
Sibsey Lincs 49 N3
Sibsey Fenside Lincs 49 M3
Sibson Cambs 38 G1
Sibson Leics 47 L13
Sibster Highld 112 H6
Sibthorpe Notts 47 U4
Sibthorpe Notts 58 B12
Sibton Suffk 41 Q7
Sicklesmere Suffk 40 E8
Sicklinghall N York 63 T10
Sidbrook Somset 16 J11
Sidbury Devon 6 F6
Sidbury Shrops 35 Q3
Sid Cop Barns 57 N5
Sidcot N Som 17 M5
Sidcup Gt Lon 21 S8
Siddick Cumb 66 F6
Siddington Ches E 55 T12
Siddington Gloucs 28 K8
Sidemoor Worcs 36 C6
Sidestrand Norfk 51 N6
Sidford Devon 6 F6
Sidlesham W Susx 10 D11
Sidlesham Common W Susx 10 D11
Sidley E Susx 12 D14
Sidmouth Devon 6 F7
Siefton Shrops 35 L4
Sigford Devon 5 T6
Sigglesthorne E R Yk 65 R10
Sigingstone V Glam 16 C2
Signet Oxon 29 P5
Silchester Hants 19 T8
Sileby Leics 47 R10
Silecroft Cumb 61 L3
Silfield Norfk 50 K14
Silian Cerdgn 33 L10
Silkstead Hants 9 N4
Silkstone Barns 57 L5
Silkstone Common Barns 57 L6
Silk Willoughby Lincs 48 G5
Silloth Cumb 66 H2
Silpho N York 65 M1
Silsden C Brad 63 L10
Silsoe C Beds 31 N5
Silton Dorset 17 U11
Silverburn Mdloth 83 P6
Silverdale Lancs 61 T5
Silverdale Staffs 45 T4
Silver End Essex 22 K4
Silverford Abers 105 M3
Silvergate Norfk 51 L8
Silver Jubilee Bridge Halton 55 M10
Silverlace Green Suffk 41 P8
Silverley's Green Suffk 41 N5
Silverstone W Nthn 30 E4
Silver Street Kent 12 G3
Silver Street Somset 17 P10
Silverton Devon 6 C4
Silverwell Cnwll 2 J7
Silvington Shrops 35 P5
Simister Bury 55 T5
Simmondley Derbys 56 F8
Simonburn Nthumb 76 H11
Simonsbath Somset 15 S5
Simonsburrow Devon 16 F13
Simonstone Lancs 62 F13
Simonstone N York 62 H1
Simprim Border 85 L9
Simpson M Keyn 30 J5
Simpson Cross Pembks 24 E7
Sinclair's Hill Border 85 L8
Sinclairston E Ayrs 81 P9
Sinderby N York 63 S3
Sinderhope Nthumb 68 H2
Sinderland Green Traffd 55 R9
Sindlesham Wokham 20 C9
Sinfin C Derb 46 K7
Singleborough Bucks 30 G6
Single Street Gt Lon 21 R11
Singleton Kent 12 K7
Singleton Lancs 61 R12
Singleton W Susx 10 D8
Singlewell Kent 22 G13
Sinkhurst Green Kent 12 F7
Sinnahard Abers 104 F13
Sinnington N York 64 G2
Sinope Leics 47 M10
Sinton Worcs 35 T8
Sinton Worcs 35 T8
Sinton Green Worcs 35 T8
Sipson Gt Lon 20 J7
Sirhowy Blae G 27 L5
Sissinghurst Kent 12 E8
Siston S Glos 28 C12
Sitcott Devon 4 K2
Sithney Cnwll 2 G11
Sithney Common Cnwll 2 G11
Sithney Green Cnwll 2 G11
Sittingbourne Kent 12 H3
Six Ashes Shrops 35 S3
Six Bells Blae G 27 N7
Six Hills Leics 47 R9
Sixhills Lincs 59 L9
Six Mile Bottom Cambs 39 S9
Sixmile Cottages Kent 13 M7
Sixpenny Handley Dorset 8 D5
Six Rues Jersey 7 c2
Sizewell Suffk 41 S8
Skaill Ork 106 u19
Skara Brae Ork 106 r18
Skares E Ayrs 81 Q9
Skateraw Abers 99 S5
Skateraw E Loth 84 J3
Skeabost Highld 100 d5
Skeeby N York 69 Q12
Skeffington Leics 47 T13
Skeffling E R Yk 59 Q3
Skegby Notts 47 N1
Skegby Notts 58 C13
Skegness Lincs 59 U14
Skelbo Highld 109 P5
Skelbo Street Highld 109 P6
Skelbrooke Donc 57 R4
Skeldyke Lincs 49 M6
Skellingthorpe Lincs 58 F12
Skellorn Green Ches E 56 D10
Skellow Donc 57 R4
Skelmanthorpe Kirk 56 K4
Skelmersdale Lancs 55 L5
Skelmorlie N Ayrs 88 E12
Skelpick Highld 111 Q5
Skelston D & G 74 F8
Skelton C York 64 D8
Skelton E R Yk 58 C1
Skelton N York 69 N12
Skelton R & Cl 71 L9
Skelton W & F 67 P5
Skelton on Ure N York 63 T6
Skelwith Bridge W & F 67 M12
Skendleby Lincs 59 R13
Skene House Abers 105 M13
Skenfrith Mons 27 T3
Skerne E R Yk 65 N8
Skerray Highld 111 P4
Skerricha Highld 110 E6
Skerton Lancs 61 T7
Sketchley Leics 37 M2
Sketty Swans 25 V12
Skewen Neath 26 C8
Skewsby N York 64 E5
Skeyton Norfk 51 M8
Skeyton Corner Norfk 51 N8
Skiall Highld 112 B3
Skidbrooke Lincs 59 R8
Skidbrooke North End Lincs 59 R7
Skidby E R Yk 65 N13
Skigersta W Isls 106 k2
Skilgate Somset 16 C11
Skillington Lincs 48 C8
Skinburness Cumb 66 H1
Skinflats Falk 82 H2
Skinidin Highld 100 b5
Skinners Green W Berk 19 P7
Skinningrove R & Cl 71 M9
Skipness Ag & B 79 S4
Skipper's Bridge D & G 75 S9
Skiprigg Cumb 67 N3
Skipsea E R Yk 65 R9
Skipsea Brough E R Yk 65 R9
Skipton N York 62 K9
Skipton-on-Swale N York 63 T4
Skipwith N York 64 F12
Skirbeck Lincs 49 M5
Skirlaugh E R Yk 65 Q12
Skirling Border 83 L11
Skirmett Bucks 20 C4
Skirpenbeck E R Yk 64 G8
Skirwith N York 62 E5
Skirwith W & F 68 D6
Skirza Highld 112 J3
Skitby Cumb 75 T12
Skittle Green Bucks 30 G12
Skokholm Island Pembks 24 B10
Skomer Island Pembks 24 B9
Skulamus Highld 100 f7
Skyborry Green Shrops 34 G6
Skye Green Essex 23 L3
Skye of Curr Highld 103 Q11
Skyreholme N York 63 M7
Slack Calder 62 K14
Slackbuie Highld 102 J7
Slackcote Oldham 56 E5
Slack Head W & F 61 T4
Slackholme End Lincs 59 T12
Slacks of Cairnbanno Abers 105 N6
Slad Gloucs 28 G6
Slade Devon 6 F3
Slade Devon 15 M3
Slade Devon 15 T7
Slade End Oxon 19 S2
Slade Green Gt Lon 22 D12
Slade Heath Staffs 46 B12
Slade Hooton Rothm 57 R9
Sladesbridge Cnwll 3 Q2
Slades Green Worcs 35 T14
Slaggyford Nthumb 68 E2
Slaidburn Lancs 62 E9
Slaithwaite Kirk 56 G4
Slaley Derbys 46 J2
Slaley Nthumb 76 K14
Slamannan Falk 82 G4
Slapton Bucks 30 K8
Slapton Devon 5 U11
Slapton W Nthn 37 R11
Slattocks Rochdl 56 C5
Slaugham W Susx 11 M5
Slaughterford Wilts 18 B6
Slawston Leics 37 U2
Sleaford Hants 10 C3
Sleaford Lincs 48 G4
Sleagill W & F 67 S9
Sleap Shrops 45 L8
Sleapford Wrekin 45 P10
Sleapshyde Herts 31 Q11
Sleasdairidh Highld 109 L5
Slebech Pembks 24 H7
Sledge Green Worcs 35 T14
Sledmere E R Yk 65 L7
Sleetbeck Cumb 75 V10
Sleight Dorset 8 D9
Sleightholme Dur 69 L10
Sleights N York 71 Q11
Slepe Dorset 8 C10
Slickly Highld 112 G3
Sliddery N Ayrs 79 S11
Sligachan Highld 100 d7
Sligrachan Ag & B 88 E7
Slimbridge Gloucs 28 D7
Slindon Staffs 45 T7
Slindon W Susx 10 F9
Slinfold W Susx 10 J4
Sling Gloucs 28 A6
Sling Gwynd 52 K9
Slingsby N York 64 F5
Slip End C Beds 31 N9
Slip End Herts 31 S5
Slipton N Nthn 38 E5
Slitting Mill Staffs 46 D10
Slochd Highld 103 M11
Slockavullin Ag & B 87 Q6
Sloley Norfk 51 N9
Sloncombe Devon 5 S3
Sloothby Lincs 59 S12
Slough Slough 20 G7
Slough Green Somset 16 J13
Slough Green W Susx 11 M5
Slumbay Highld 101 M4
Slyfield Surrey 20 G12
Slyne Lancs 61 T6
Smailholm Border 84 G11
Smallbridge Rochdl 56 D3
Smallbrook Devon 15 U13
Smallbrook Gloucs 28 A7
Smallburgh Norfk 51 P9
Smallburn E Ayrs 82 C13
Smalldale Derbys 56 G11
Smalldale Derbys 56 J10
Small Dole W Susx 11 L8
Smalley Derbys 47 M5
Smalley Common Derbys 47 M5
Smalley Green Derbys 47 M5
Smallfield Surrey 11 N2
Smallford Herts 31 Q11
Small Heath Birm 36 F3
Small Hythe Kent 12 G9
Smallridge Devon 6 K4
Smallthorne C Stke 45 U3
Smallways N York 69 P10
Smallwood Ches E 45 T1
Small Wood Hey Lancs 61 R10
Smallworth Norfk 40 H4
Smannell Hants 19 N11
Smardale W & F 68 F11
Smarden Kent 12 G7
Smarden Bell Kent 12 G7
Smart's Hill Kent 11 S2
Smeafield Nthumb 85 R11
Smeatharpe Devon 6 G2
Smeeth Kent 13 L8
Smeeton Westerby Leics 37 S2
Smelthouses N York 63 P7
Smerral Highld 112 E10
Smestow Staffs 35 U2
Smethwick Sandw 36 D3
Smethwick Green Ches E 55 T14
Smirisary Highld 93 Q3
Smisby Derbys 46 K10
Smith End Green Worcs 35 S10
Smithfield Cumb 75 T12
Smith Green Lancs 61 T8
Smithies Barns 57 M5
Smithincott Devon 6 E2
Smith's End Herts 39 P13
Smith's Green Essex 22 E3
Smith's Green Essex 39 U12
Smithstown Highld 107 N9
Smithton Highld 102 K6
Smithy Bridge Rochdl 56 D3
Smithy Green Ches E 55 R12
Smithy Green Stockp 56 C9
Smithy Houses Derbys 47 L4
Smockington Leics 37 N3
Smoo Highld 110 J3
Smythe's Green Essex 23 M4
Snade D & G 74 F8
Snailbeach Shrops 44 J13
Snailwell Cambs 39 T7
Snainton N York 65 L3
Snaith E R Yk 57 T2
Snake Pass Inn Derbys 56 H8
Snape N York 63 R3
Snape Suffk 41 Q9
Snape Green Lancs 54 J4
Snape Street Suffk 41 Q9
Snaresbrook Gt Lon 21 R5
Snarestone Leics 46 K12
Snarford Lincs 58 H10
Snargate Kent 12 J10
Snave Kent 12 K10
Sneachill Worcs 36 B10
Snead Powys 34 H2
Sneath Common Norfk 41 L3
Sneaton N York 71 Q11
Sneatonthorpe N York 71 R11
Snelland Lincs 58 J10
Snelson Ches E 55 T12
Snelston Derbys 46 G5
Snetterton Norfk 40 G2
Snettisham Norfk 49 U7
Snibston Leics 47 M11
Snig's End Gloucs 28 E2
Snitter Nthumb 77 L5
Snitterby Lincs 58 G8
Snitterfield Warwks 36 H9
Snitterton Derbys 46 J1
Snitton Shrops 35 N5
Snoadhill Kent 12 H7
Snodhill Herefs 34 H12
Snodland Kent 12 D3
Snoll Hatch Kent 12 C6
Snowden Hill Barns 57 L6
Snowdon Gwynd 52 K12
Snowdon Kent 13 P5
Snowdonia National Park 43 R8
Snow End Herts 22 B1
Snowshill Gloucs 36 E14
Snow Street Norfk 40 J4
Soake Hants 9 T6
Soar Cardif 26 K11
Soar Devon 5 S13
Soar Powys 26 H1
Soay Highld 100 d8
Soberton Hants 9 S5
Soberton Heath Hants 9 S6
Sockbridge W & F 67 Q7
Sockburn Darltn 70 D11
Sodom Denbgs 54 C12
Sodylt Bank Shrops 44 H6
Soham Cambs 39 S6
Soham Cotes Cambs 39 S5
Solas W Isls 106 d11
Solbury Pembks 24 E8
Soldon Devon 14 H10
Soldon Cross Devon 14 H10
Soldridge Hants 19 U13
Sole Street Kent 12 C2
Sole Street Kent 13 L6
Solihull Solhll 36 G5
Sollas W Isls 106 d11
Sollers Dilwyn Herefs 34 K9
Sollers Hope Herefs 35 P14
Sollom Lancs 55 L3
Solva Pembks 24 D6
Solwaybank D & G 75 R10
Somerby Leics 47 U11
Somerby Lincs 58 J5
Somercotes Derbys 47 M3
Somerford BCP 8 H10
Somerford Keynes Gloucs 28 K8
Somerley W Susx 10 C11
Somerleyton Suffk 41 S1
Somersal Herbert Derbys 46 F6
Somersby Lincs 59 P12
Somersham Cambs 39 N5
Somersham Suffk 40 J11
Somerton Oxon 29 U2
Somerton Somset 17 N11
Somerton Suffk 40 D10
Somerwood Shrops 45 N11
Sompting W Susx 10 K9
Sompting Abbotts W Susx 10 K9
Sonning Wokham 20 C7
Sonning Common Oxon 20 B6
Sonning Eye Oxon 20 B7
Sontley Wrexhm 44 H4
Sopley Hants 8 H9
Sopwell Herts 31 Q11
Sopworth Wilts 28 F10
Sorbie D & G 73 L10
Sordale Highld 112 D4
Sorisdale Ag & B 92 H6
Sorn E Ayrs 81 R7
Sornhill E Ayrs 81 Q6
Sortat Highld 112 G4
Sotby Lincs 59 M11
Sots Hole Lincs 58 K14
Sotterley Suffk 41 R4
Soughton Flints 54 F13
Soulbury Bucks 30 J7
Soulby W & F 67 Q7
Soulby W & F 68 F10
Souldern Oxon 30 B6
Souldrop Bed 38 E8
Sound Ches E 45 P4
Sound Muir Moray 104 D5
Soundwell S Glos 28 C12
Sourton Devon 5 N2
Soutergate W & F 61 N3
South Acre Norfk 50 D11
South Alkham Kent 13 P7
Southall Gt Lon 20 K7
South Allington Devon 5 T13
South Alloa Falk 90 C13
Southam Gloucs 28 J2
Southam Warwks 37 M8
South Ambersham W Susx 10 E6
Southampton C Sotn 9 N6
Southampton Airport Hants 9 P5
South Anston Rothm 57 R10
South Ascot W & M 20 F9
South Ashford Kent 12 K7
South Baddesley Hants 9 M9
South Bank C York 64 D9
South Bank R & Cl 70 H8
South Barrow Somset 17 R11
South Beddington Gt Lon 21 N10
South Beer Cnwll 4 J2
South Benfleet Essex 22 J10
South Bockhampton BCP 8 H9
Southborough Gt Lon 21 R9
Southborough Kent 11 T2
Southbourne BCP 8 G10
Southbourne W Susx 10 B9
South Bowood Dorset 7 M5
South Bramwith Donc 57 T4
South Brent Devon 5 R8
South Brewham Somset 17 T9
South Broomhill Nthumb 77 Q6
Southburgh Norfk 50 H12
South Burlingham Norfk 51 Q12
Southburn E R Yk 65 M9
South Cadbury Somset 17 R11
South Carlton Lincs 58 F11
South Carlton Notts 57 S10
South Cave E R Yk 65 L13
South Cerney Gloucs 28 K8
South Chailey E Susx 11 P7
South Chard Somset 6 K3
South Charlton Nthumb 77 P1
South Cheriton Somset 17 S12
South Church Dur 69 R7
Southchurch Sthend 23 M10
South Cleatlam Dur 69 P9
South Cliffe E R Yk 64 K12
South Clifton Notts 58 D12
South Cockerington Lincs 59 Q9
South Cornelly Brdgnd 26 E11
Southcott Cnwll 14 E13
Southcott Devon 5 T4
Southcott Devon 14 K9
Southcott Devon 15 M13
Southcott Wilts 18 J9
Southcourt Bucks 30 H10
South Cove Suffk 41 S4
South Creake Norfk 50 E6
South Crosland Kirk 56 H4
South Croxton Leics 47 S11
South Dalton E R Yk 65 M10
South Darenth Kent 21 U9
South Dell W Isls 106 j2
South Downs National Park 11 P9
South Duffield N York 64 F13
South Earlswood Surrey 21 N13
Southease E Susx 11 Q9
South Elkington Lincs 59 N9
South Elmsall Wakefd 57 Q4
Southend Ag & B 79 M14
South End E R Yk 59 Q3
South End Hants 8 G5
South End Herefs 35 R12
South End N Linc 58 K2
South End Norfk 40 G2
Southend Wilts 18 J6
Southend Airport Essex 23 L10
Southend-on-Sea Sthend 23 L10
Southernby W & F 67 N5
Southernden Kent 12 G6
Southerndown V Glam 26 F13
Southerness D & G 66 E2
South Erradale Highld 107 M10
Southerton Devon 6 E6
Southery Norfk 39 T2
South Fambridge Essex 23 L9
South Fawley W Berk 19 N4
South Ferriby N Linc 58 G2
South Field E R Yk 58 H1
Southfield Falk 82 F4
Southfleet Kent 22 F13
Southford IoW 9 Q13
Southgate Gt Lon 21 N4
Southgate Norfk 49 U7
Southgate Norfk 50 E6
Southgate Norfk 50 K9
Southgate Swans 25 U13
South Godstone Surrey 21 Q13
South Gorley Hants 8 H6
South Gosforth N u Ty 77 Q12

Tannington Suffk 41 M7
Tannochside N Lans 82 D6
Tansley Derbys 46 K2
Tansor N Nthn 38 G2
Tantobie Dur 69 Q2
Tanton N York 70 H10
Tanwood Worcs 36 B6
Tanworth in Arden Warwks 36 F6
Tan-y-Bwlch Gwynd 43 N5
Tan-y-fron Conwy 53 S10
Tan-y-fron Wrexhm 44 G3
Tan-y-grisiau Gwynd 43 N4
Tan-y-groes Cerdgn 32 E11
Taobh Tuath W Isls 106 e10
Taplow Bucks 20 F6
Tarbert Ag & B 79 M5
Tarbert Ag & B 87 R12
Tarbert W Isls 106 g8
Tarbet Ag & B 88 H5
Tarbet Highld 100 g10
Tarbet Highld 110 D7
Tarbock Green Knows 55 L9
Tarbolton S Ayrs 81 N7
Tarbrax S Lans 82 K7
Tardebigge Worcs 36 C7
Tarfside Angus 98 H8
Tarland Abers 98 H3
Tarleton Lancs 55 L2
Tarlscough Lancs 54 K4
Tarlton Gloucs 28 J8
Tarnock Somset 17 L6
Tarns Cumb 66 H3
Tarnside W & F 61 S1
Tarporley Ches W 55 N14
Tarr Somset 15 U6
Tarrant Crawford Dorset 8 C8
Tarrant Gunville Dorset 8 C6
Tarrant Hinton Dorset 8 C6
Tarrant Keyneston Dorset 8 C8
Tarrant Launceston Dorset 8 C7
Tarrant Monkton Dorset 8 C7
Tarrant Rawston Dorset 8 C7
Tarrant Rushton Dorset 8 C7
Tarring Neville E Susx 11 Q10
Tarrington Herefs 35 P12
Tarskavaig Highld 100 e8
Tarves Abers 105 P9
Tarvin Ches W 55 L13
Tarvin Sands Ches W 55 L13
Tasburgh Norfk 41 M1
Tasley Shrops 35 Q2
Taston Oxon 29 S3
Tatenhill Staffs 46 H9
Tathall End M Keyn 38 B11
Tatham Lancs 62 C6
Tathwell Lincs 59 P10
Tatsfield Surrey 21 R11
Tattenhall Ches W 45 L2
Tatterford Norfk 50 E8
Tattersett Norfk 50 D8
Tattershall Lincs 48 K2
Tattershall Bridge Lincs 48 J2
Tattershall Thorpe Lincs 48 K2
Tattingstone Suffk 40 K13
Tattingstone White Horse Suffk 40 K13
Tatton Park Ches E 55 R10
Tatworth Somset 6 K3
Tauchers Moray 104 D6
Taunton Somset 16 H12
Taunton Deane Services Somset 16 G12
Taverham Norfk 51 L11
Taverners Green Essex 22 E4
Tavernspite Pembks 25 L8
Tavistock Devon 5 M6
Tavistock Devon 5 M6
Taw Green Devon 15 Q13
Tawstock Devon 15 N7
Taxal Derbys 56 F11
Tay Bridge C Dund 91 P6
Taychreggan Hotel Ag & B 88 B1
Tay Forest Park P & K 97 M11
Tayinloan Ag & B 79 M6
Taynton Gloucs 28 D3
Taynton Oxon 29 P5
Taynuilt Ag & B 94 E12
Tayport Fife 91 Q6
Tayvallich Ag & B 87 N8
Tealby Lincs 59 L8
Tealing Angus 91 P4
Team Valley Gatesd 77 Q14
Teangue Highld 100 f9
Teanord Highld 102 G3
Tebay W & F 68 D12
Tebay Services W & F 68 D11
Tebworth C Beds 31 L7
Tedburn St Mary Devon 5 U2
Teddington Gloucs 36 C14
Teddington Gt Lon 21 L8
Tedstone Delamere Herefs 35 Q9
Tedstone Wafer Herefs 35 Q9
Teesport R & Cl 70 H8
Teesside International Airport S on T 70 E10
Teesside Park S on T 70 G9
Teeton W Nthn 37 S6
Teffont Evias Wilts 8 D2
Teffont Magna Wilts 8 D2
Tegryn Pembks 25 M4
Teigh Rutlnd 48 C10
Teigncombe Devon 5 R3
Teigngrace Devon 5 V6
Teignmouth Devon 6 B10
Teindside Border 75 T4
Telford Wrekin 45 Q12
Telford Services Shrops 45 R12
Telham E Susx 12 E13
Tellisford Somset 18 B9
Telscombe E Susx 11 Q10
Telscombe Cliffs E Susx 11 Q10
Tempar P & K 95 T7
Templand D & G 75 L8
Temple Cnwll 4 E6
Temple Mdloth 83 R7
Temple Balsall Solhll 36 H5
Temple Bar Cerdgn 32 K10
Temple Cloud BaNES 17 R5
Templecombe Somset 17 T12
Temple End Suffk 39 U10
Temple Ewell Kent 13 Q7
Temple Grafton Warwks 36 F9
Temple Guiting Gloucs 29 L2
Temple Herdewyke Warwks 37 L10
Temple Hirst N York 57 T2
Temple Normanton Derbys 57 P13
Temple of Fiddes Abers 99 Q7
Temple Sowerby W & F 68 D7
Templeton Devon 15 U10
Templeton Pembks 24 K8
Templetown Dur 69 P2
Tempsford C Beds 38 J10
Tenbury Wells Worcs 35 N7
Tenby Pembks 24 K10
Tendring Essex 23 R3
Tendring Green Essex 23 R2
Tendring Heath Essex 23 R2
Ten Mile Bank Norfk 39 S1
Tenpenny Heath Essex 23 Q3
Tenterden Kent 12 G9
Terling Essex 22 J4
Tern Wrekin 45 P10
Ternhill Shrops 45 P7
Terregles D & G 74 H10
Terrington N York 64 F5
Terrington St Clement Norfk 49 S9
Terrington St John Norfk 49 R11
Terry's Green Warwks 36 F6
Teston Kent 12 D5
Testwood Hants 9 M6
Tetbury Gloucs 28 G9
Tetbury Upton Gloucs 28 G8
Tetchill Shrops 44 J7
Tetcott Devon 14 H13
Tetford Lincs 59 P12
Tetney Lincs 59 P6
Tetney Lock Lincs 59 P6
Tetsworth Oxon 30 E12
Tettenhall Wolves 45 U13
Tettenhall Wood Wolves 45 U14
Teversal Notts 47 N1
Teversham Cambs 39 Q9
Teviothead Border 75 T4
Tewin Herts 31 S10
Tewin Wood Herts 31 S9
Tewkesbury Gloucs 35 U14
Teynham Kent 12 J3
Thackley C Brad 63 P12
Thackthwaite Cumb 66 H8
Thackthwaite W & F 67 P7
Thainstone Abers 105 M12
Thakeham W Susx 10 J7
Thame Oxon 30 F11
Thames Ditton Surrey 21 L9
Thamesmead Gt Lon 21 S6
Thamesport Medway 23 L13
Thanington Kent 13 M4
Thankerton S Lans 82 J11
Tharston Norfk 41 L2
Thatcham W Berk 19 R7
Thatto Heath St Hel 55 M8
Thaxted Essex 22 F1
Theakston N York 63 S2
Thealby N Linc 58 E3
Theale Somset 17 N7
Theale W Berk 19 T6
Thearne E R Yk 65 P12
The Bank Ches E 45 T2
The Beeches Gloucs 28 K7
Theberton Suffk 41 R7
The Blythe Staffs 46 D8
The Bog Shrops 44 J14
The Bourne Worcs 36 C9
The Braes Highld 100 e6
The Bratch Staffs 35 U2
The Bridge Kent 22 D12
The Broad Herefs 35 L8
The Broads 51 S12
The Brunt E Loth 84 H4
The Bryn Mons 27 Q6
The Bungalow IoM 60 f5
The Burf Worcs 35 T7
The Camp Gloucs 28 H6
The Chequer Wrexhm 45 L5
The City Bed 38 H9
The City Bucks 20 C3
The Common Oxon 29 Q2
The Common Wilts 8 J2
The Common Wilts 28 K10
The Corner Kent 12 D7
The Cronk IoM 60 e3
Theddingworth Leics 37 S3
Theddlethorpe All Saints Lincs 59 S9
Theddlethorpe St Helen Lincs 59 S9
The Deep C KuH 65 P14
The Den N Ayrs 81 L2
The Forge Herefs 34 H9
The Forstal Kent 12 K8
The Fouralls Shrops 45 Q7
The Green Cumb 61 M3
The Green Essex 22 J4
The Green N York 71 N11
The Green Wilts 8 B2
The Grove Dur 69 N2
The Grove Worcs 35 U12
The Haven W Susx 10 H4
The Haw Gloucs 28 F2
The Hendre Mons 27 T5
The Hill Cumb 61 M3
The Holt Wokham 20 D7
The Hundred Herefs 35 M8
Thelbridge Cross Devon 15 S10
The Leacon Kent 12 J9
The Lee Bucks 30 K12
The Lhen IoM 60 f2
Thelnetham Suffk 40 H5
The Lochs Moray 104 C3
Thelveton Norfk 41 L4
Thelwall Warrtn 55 Q9
The Marsh Powys 44 H14
Themelthorpe Norfk 50 J9
The Middles Dur 69 R2
The Moor Kent 12 E10
The Mumbles Swans 25 V13
The Murray S Lans 81 S2
The Mythe Gloucs 35 U14
The Narth Mons 27 U6
The Neuk Abers 99 N4
Thenford W Nthn 30 B4
Theobald's Green Wilts 18 F7
The Quarry Gloucs 28 D8
The Quarter Kent 12 G7
The Reddings Gloucs 28 H3
Therfield Herts 31 T5
The Rhôs Powys 27 M1
The Ross P & K 89 S1
The Sands Surrey 20 E13
The Shoe Wilts 18 B6
The Smithies Shrops 45 Q14
The Spring Warwks 36 J6
The Square Torfn 27 P8
The Stair Kent 12 B6
The Stocks Kent 12 H10
The Straits Hants 10 B3
The Strand Wilts 18 D9
Thetford Norfk 40 E4
Thetford Forest Park 40 D3
Thethwaite Cumb 67 N4
The Towans Cnwll 2 F9
The Town IoS 2 b1
The Vauld Herefs 35 M11
The Wyke Shrops 45 R12
Theydon Bois Essex 21 R3
Theydon Mount Essex 21 S3
Thicket Priory N York 64 F11
Thickwood Wilts 18 B6
Thimbleby Lincs 59 M12
Thimbleby N York 70 F13
Thingwall Wirral 54 G10
Thirkleby N York 64 B4
Thirlby N York 64 B3
Thirlestane Border 84 F9
Thirn N York 63 Q2
Thirsk N York 63 U3
Thirtleby E R Yk 65 R13
Thistleton Lancs 61 S12
Thistleton Rutlnd 48 D10
Thistley Green Suffk 39 U5
Thixendale N York 64 J7
Thockrington Nthumb 76 K10
Tholomas Drove Cambs 49 P12
Tholthorpe N York 64 B6
Thomas Chapel Pembks 24 K9
Thomas Close W & F 67 P4
Thomastown Abers 104 H8
Thompson Norfk 40 F1
Thomshill Moray 103 V4
Thong Kent 22 G13
Thongsbridge Kirk 56 J5
Thoralby N York 63 L2
Thoresby Notts 57 T12
Thoresthorpe Lincs 59 S11
Thoresway Lincs 59 L7
Thorganby Lincs 59 M7
Thorganby N York 64 F11
Thorgill N York 71 M13
Thorington Suffk 41 R6
Thorington Street Suffk 40 H13
Thorlby N York 62 K9
Thorley Herts 22 C4
Thorley IoW 9 M11
Thorley Houses Herts 22 C3
Thorley Street IoW 9 M11
Thormanby N York 64 B5
Thornaby-on-Tees S on T 70 G9
Thornage Norfk 50 J6
Thornborough Bucks 30 F6
Thornborough N York 63 R4
Thornbury C Brad 63 P13
Thornbury Devon 14 K11
Thornbury Herefs 35 P9
Thornbury S Glos 28 B9
Thornby Cumb 67 L2
Thornby W Nthn 37 S5
Thorncliff Staffs 46 D2
Thorncombe Dorset 7 L4
Thorncombe Street Surrey 10 F2
Thorncott Green C Beds 38 J11
Thorncross IoW 9 N12
Thorndon Suffk 40 K7
Thorndon Cross Devon 5 N2
Thorne Donc 57 U4
Thorne Coffin Somset 17 P13
Thornecroft Devon 5 T7
Thornehillhead Devon 14 K9
Thorner Leeds 63 T11
Thornes Staffs 46 E13
Thornes Wakefd 57 M3
Thorne St Margaret Somset 16 F12
Thorney Bucks 20 H7
Thorney C Pete 49 L13
Thorney Notts 58 E12
Thorney Somset 17 M12
Thorney Hill Hants 8 J9
Thorney Island W Susx 10 B10
Thorney Toll Cambs 49 M13
Thornfalcon Somset 16 J12
Thornford Dorset 7 R2
Thorngrafton Nthumb 76 F12
Thorngrove Somset 17 L10
Thorngumbald E R Yk 59 M1
Thornham Norfk 50 B5
Thornham Magna Suffk 40 K6
Thornham Parva Suffk 40 K6
Thornhaugh C Pete 48 G13
Thornhill C Sotn 9 P6
Thornhill Caerph 27 M11
Thornhill Cumb 66 F11
Thornhill D & G 74 G6
Thornhill Derbys 56 J10
Thornhill Kirk 57 L3
Thornhill Stirlg 89 Q5
Thornhill Lees Kirk 56 K3
Thornhills Calder 56 J2
Thornholme E R Yk 65 Q7
Thornicombe Dorset 8 B8
Thornington Nthumb 85 M12
Thornley Dur 69 P5
Thornley Dur 70 E5
Thornley Gate Nthumb 68 H1
Thornliebank E Rens 89 N14
Thorns Suffk 40 B9
Thornsett Derbys 56 F9
Thorns Green Ches E 55 S10
Thornthwaite Cumb 66 K7
Thornthwaite N York 63 P8
Thornton Angus 91 N2
Thornton Bucks 30 F5
Thornton C Brad 63 M13
Thornton E R Yk 64 H10
Thornton Fife 91 L12
Thornton Lancs 61 Q11
Thornton Leics 47 N12
Thornton Lincs 59 M13
Thornton Middsb 70 G10
Thornton Nthumb 85 P9
Thornton Pembks 24 F9
Thornton Sefton 54 H6
Thornton Curtis N Linc 58 J3
Thorntonhall S Lans 81 R1
Thornton Heath Gt Lon 21 P9
Thornton Hough Wirral 54 H10
Thornton-in-Craven N York 62 J10
Thornton in Lonsdale N York 62 D5
Thornton-le-Beans N York 63 T1
Thornton-le-Clay N York 64 F6
Thornton-le-Dale N York 64 J3
Thornton le Moor Lincs 58 H7
Thornton-le-Moor N York 63 T2
Thornton-le-Moors Ches W 54 K12
Thornton-le-Street N York 63 U2
Thorntonloch E Loth 84 K4
Thornton Rust N York 62 K2
Thornton Steward N York 63 P2
Thornton Watlass N York 63 Q2
Thornwood Common Essex 22 C7
Thornydykes Border 84 G9
Thornythwaite W & F 67 N8
Thoroton Notts 47 U5
Thorp Arch Leeds 63 U10
Thorpe Derbys 46 G3
Thorpe E R Yk 65 M10
Thorpe Lincs 59 S10
Thorpe N York 63 L7
Thorpe Norfk 51 R14
Thorpe Notts 47 U4
Thorpe Surrey 20 H9
Thorpe Abbotts Norfk 41 L5
Thorpe Acre Leics 47 P10
Thorpe Arnold Leics 47 U9
Thorpe Audlin Wakefd 57 Q3
Thorpe Bassett N York 64 K5
Thorpe Bay Sthend 23 M10
Thorpe by Water Rutlnd 38 C1
Thorpe Common Rothm 57 N7
Thorpe Constantine Staffs 46 J12
Thorpe End Norfk 51 N11
Thorpe Green Essex 23 S3
Thorpe Green Lancs 55 N2
Thorpe Green Suffk 40 F10
Thorpe Hesley Rothm 57 N7
Thorpe in Balne Donc 57 S4
Thorpe Langton Leics 37 T2
Thorpe Larches Dur 70 E7
Thorpe Lea Surrey 20 H8
Thorpe le Fallows Lincs 58 F10
Thorpe-le-Soken Essex 23 S3
Thorpe le Street E R Yk 64 J11
Thorpe Malsor N Nthn 38 B5
Thorpe Mandeville W Nthn 30 B4
Thorpe Market Norfk 51 M6
Thorpe Marriot Norfk 51 L10
Thorpe Morieux Suffk 40 F10
Thorpeness Suffk 41 S9
Thorpe on the Hill Leeds 57 M1
Thorpe on the Hill Lincs 58 F13
Thorpe Park Resort Surrey 20 H9
Thorpe St Andrew Norfk 51 N12
Thorpe St Peter Lincs 49 Q1
Thorpe Salvin Rothm 57 R10
Thorpe Satchville Leics 47 T11
Thorpe Thewles S on T 70 E8
Thorpe Tilney Lincs 48 H2
Thorpe Underwood N Nthn 37 U4
Thorpe Underwood N York 64 B8
Thorpe Waterville N Nthn 38 F4
Thorpe Willoughby N York 64 D13
Thorpland Norfk 49 T12
Thorrington Essex 23 Q4
Thorverton Devon 6 B4
Thrales End C Beds 31 P9
Thrandeston Suffk 40 K5
Thrapston N Nthn 38 E5
Threapland Cumb 66 J5
Threapland N York 62 K7
Threapwood Ches W 44 K4
Threapwood Staffs 46 D5
Threapwood Head Staffs 46 D5
Threave S Ayrs 81 L11
Three Ashes Herefs 27 U3
Three Bridges W Susx 11 M3
Three Burrows Cnwll 2 K7
Three Chimneys Kent 12 F8
Three Cocks Powys 34 E13
Three Crosses Swans 25 U12
Three Cups Corner E Susx 11 U6
Three Gates Worcs 35 Q8
Threehammer Common Norfk 51 P10
Three Hammers Cnwll 4 G3
Three Holes Norfk 49 R13
Threekingham Lincs 48 G6
Three Leg Cross E Susx 12 C9
Three Legged Cross Dorset 8 F7
Three Mile Cross Wokham 20 B9
Threemilestone Cnwll 2 K7
Threemiletown W Loth 83 L3
Three Oaks E Susx 12 F13
Threlkeld W & F 67 M7
Threshers Bush Essex 22 C6
Threshfield N York 62 K7
Thrigby Norfk 51 S11
Thringarth Dur 68 K8
Thringstone Leics 47 M10
Thrintoft N York 70 D14
Thriplow Cambs 39 P11
Throapham Rothm 57 R9
Throckenhalt Lincs 49 N12
Throcking Herts 31 T6
Throckley N u Ty 77 P12
Throckmorton Worcs 36 C10
Throop BCP 8 G9
Throop Dorset 8 A10
Throphill Nthumb 77 N8
Thropton Nthumb 77 L5
Throsk Stirlg 90 C13
Througham Gloucs 28 H6
Throughgate D & G 74 G9
Throwleigh Devon 5 R2
Throwley Kent 12 J4
Throwley Forstal Kent 12 J5
Thrumpton Notts 47 P7
Thrumpton Notts 58 B10
Thrumster Highld 112 H7
Thrunscoe NE Lin 59 P5
Thrunton Nthumb 77 M3
Thrup Oxon 29 Q8
Thrupp Gloucs 28 G7
Thrupp Oxon 29 U4
Thrushelton Devon 5 L3
Thrussington Leics 47 S10
Thruxton Hants 19 L11
Thruxton Herefs 34 K14
Thrybergh Rothm 57 Q7
Thulston Derbys 47 M7
Thundersley Essex 22 J10
Thurcaston Leics 47 Q11
Thurcroft Rothm 57 Q9
Thurdon Cnwll 14 G10
Thurgarton Norfk 51 L7
Thurgarton Notts 47 S4
Thurgoland Barns 57 L6
Thurlaston Leics 47 P14
Thurlaston Warwks 37 N6
Thurlbear Somset 16 J12
Thurlby Lincs 48 D1
Thurlby Lincs 48 G10
Thurlby Lincs 59 S11
Thurleigh Bed 38 G9
Thurlestone Devon 5 R12
Thurloxton Somset 16 J10
Thurlstone Barns 56 K6
Thurlton Norfk 51 R14
Thurlwood Ches E 45 T2
Thurmaston Leics 47 R12
Thurnby Leics 47 R13
Thurne Norfk 51 R10
Thurnham Kent 12 F4
Thurning N Nthn 38 G4
Thurning Norfk 50 J8
Thurnscoe Barns 57 Q5
Thurrock Services Thurr 22 E12
Thursby Cumb 67 M2
Thursden Lancs 62 J13
Thursford Norfk 50 G7
Thursley Surrey 10 E3
Thurso Highld 112 D3
Thurstaston Wirral 54 F10
Thurston Suffk 40 F7
Thurston Clough Oldham 56 E5
Thurstonfield Cumb 67 M1
Thurstonland Kirk 56 J4
Thurston Planche Suffk 40 F8
Thurton Norfk 51 P13
Thurvaston Derbys 46 H6
Thuxton Norfk 50 H12
Thwaite N York 68 J13
Thwaite Suffk 40 K7
Thwaite Head W & F 61 Q1
Thwaites C Brad 63 M11
Thwaite St Mary Norfk 41 P1
Thwaites Brow C Brad 63 M11
Thwing E R Yk 65 N5
Tibbermore P & K 90 F7
Tibbers D & G 74 G6
Tibberton Gloucs 28 E3
Tibberton Worcs 36 B9
Tibberton Wrekin 45 Q9
Tibenham Norfk 40 K3
Tibshelf Derbys 47 M1
Tibshelf Services Derbys 47 M1
Tibthorpe E R Yk 65 M8
Ticehurst E Susx 12 C9
Tichborne Hants 9 R2
Tickencote Rutlnd 48 E12
Tickenham N Som 17 N2
Tickford End M Keyn 30 J4
Tickhill Donc 57 S8
Ticklerton Shrops 35 L2
Ticknall Derbys 47 L9
Tickton E R Yk 65 P11
Tidbury Green Solhll 36 F5
Tidcombe Wilts 19 L9
Tiddington Oxon 30 D12
Tiddington Warwks 36 H9
Tiddleywink Wilts 18 C5
Tidebrook E Susx 11 U4
Tideford Cnwll 4 K9
Tideford Cross Cnwll 4 J8
Tidenham Gloucs 27 V8
Tideswell Derbys 56 J11
Tidmarsh W Berk 19 T6
Tidmington Warwks 36 J13
Tidpit Hants 8 F5
Tidworth Wilts 18 K11
Tiers Cross Pembks 24 F8
Tiffield W Nthn 37 T10
Tigerton Angus 98 J11
Tigh a' Ghearraidh W Isls 106 c11
Tigharry W Isls 106 c11
Tighnabruaich Ag & B 87 T11
Tigley Devon 5 T8
Tilbrook Cambs 38 G7
Tilbury Thurr 22 F12
Tibury Dock Thurr 22 F12
Tilbury Green Essex 40 B12
Tilbury Juxta Clare Essex 40 C12
Tile Cross Birm 36 G3
Tile Hill Covtry 36 J5
Tilehouse Green Solhll 36 G5
Tilehurst Readg 19 U6
Tilford Surrey 10 D2
Tilgate W Susx 11 M4
Tilgate Forest Row W Susx 11 M4
Tilham Street Somset 17 Q9
Tillers Green Gloucs 35 Q14
Tilley Shrops 45 M8
Tillicoultry Clacks 90 D12
Tillietudlem S Lans 82 F9
Tillingham Essex 23 N7
Tillington Herefs 35 L12
Tillington W Susx 10 F6
Tillington Common Herefs 35 L11
Tillybirloch Abers 99 M2
Tillyfourie Abers 104 J13
Tillygreig Abers 105 P11
Tillyrie P & K 90 H10
Tilmanstone Kent 13 R5
Tilney All Saints Norfk 49 S10
Tilney High End Norfk 49 S10
Tilney St Lawrence Norfk 49 R11
Tilshead Wilts 18 F11
Tilstock Shrops 45 M6
Tilston Ches W 45 L3
Tilstone Bank Ches W 45 N2
Tilstone Fearnall Ches W 45 N1
Tilsworth C Beds 31 L8
Tilton on the Hill Leics 47 T12
Tiltups End Gloucs 28 F8
Tilty Essex 22 E2
Timberland Lincs 48 H2
Timbersbrook Ches E 56 C14
Timberscombe Somset 16 C8
Timble N York 63 P9
Timewell Devon 16 C11
Timpanheck D & G 75 R11
Timperley Traffd 55 S9
Timsbury BaNES 17 S5
Timsbury Hants 9 L4
Timsgarry W Isls 106 f5
Timsgearraidh W Isls 106 f5
Timworth Suffk 40 E7
Timworth Green Suffk 40 E7
Tincleton Dorset 7 U6
Tindale Cumb 76 C14
Tingewick Bucks 30 E6
Tingley Leeds 57 L1
Tingrith C Beds 31 M6
Tingwall Airport Shet 106 u9
Tingwell Ork 106 t17
Tinhay Devon 4 K3
Tinker's Hill Hants 19 P11
Tinkersley Derbys 57 L14
Tinsley Sheff 57 P8
Tinsley Green W Susx 11 M3
Tintagel Cnwll 4 D3
Tintern Mons 27 U7
Tintinhull Somset 17 N13
Tintwistle Derbys 56 F7
Tinwald D & G 74 K9
Tinwell Rutlnd 48 F12
Tippacott Devon 15 S3
Tipp's End Norfk 39 R1
Tiptoe Hants 8 K9
Tipton Sandw 36 C2
Tipton Green Sandw 36 C2
Tipton St John Devon 6 E6
Tiptree Essex 23 L4
Tiptree Heath Essex 23 L4
Tirabad Powys 33 S12
Tircoed Swans 25 V10
Tiree Ag & B 92 C10
Tiree Airport Ag & B 92 C10
Tiretigan Ag & B 79 N3
Tirley Gloucs 28 F2
Tiroran Ag & B 93 M13
Tirphil Caerph 27 L7
Tirril W & F 67 R7
Tir-y-fron Flints 44 G2
Tisbury Wilts 8 C3
Tisman's Common W Susx 10 H4
Tissington Derbys 46 G3
Titchberry Devon 14 F7
Titchfield Hants 9 Q7
Titchfield Common Hants 9 Q7
Titchmarsh N Nthn 38 F5
Titchwell Norfk 50 C5
Tithby Notts 47 S6
Tithebarn Devon 6 C6
Titley Herefs 34 H8
Titmore Green Herts 31 R7
Titsey Surrey 21 R12
Titson Cnwll 14 F12
Tittensor Staffs 45 U6
Tittleshall Norfk 50 E9
Titton Worcs 35 T7
Tiverton Ches W 45 N1
Tiverton Devon 6 C2
Tivetshall St Margaret Norfk 41 L3
Tivetshall St Mary Norfk 41 L3
Tivington Somset 16 B7
Tivy Dale Barns 57 L5
Tixall Staffs 46 C9
Tixover Rutlnd 48 E13
Toab Shet 106 t12
Toadhole Derbys 47 L2
Toadmoor Derbys 46 K3
Tobermory Ag & B 93 N7
Toberonochy Ag & B 87 N4
Tobha Mòr W Isls 106 c15
Tocher Abers 104 K9
Tochieneal Moray 104 G2
Tockenham Wilts 18 F5
Tockenham Wick Wilts 18 F4
Tocketts R & Cl 70 K9
Tockholes Bl w D 55 Q2
Tockington S Glos 28 B10
Tockwith N York 64 B9
Todber Dorset 17 U13
Todburn Nthumb 77 N6
Toddington C Beds 31 M7
Toddington Gloucs 28 K1
Toddington Services C Beds 31 M7
Todds Green Herts 31 R7
Todenham Gloucs 36 H13
Todhills Angus 91 P4
Todhills Cumb 75 S13
Todhills Dur 69 R6
Todhills Rest Area Cumb 75 S13
Todmorden Calder 56 D2
Todwick Rothm 57 Q10
Toft Cambs 39 N9
Toft Ches E 55 S11
Toft Lincs 48 G10
Toft Shet 106 u6
Toft Warwks 37 N6
Toft Hill Dur 69 Q7
Toft Hill Lincs 48 K1
Toft Monks Norfk 41 R2
Toft next Newton Lincs 58 H9
Toftrees Norfk 50 E8
Toftwood Norfk 50 G11
Togston Nthumb 77 Q5
Tokavaig Highld 100 f8
Tokers Green Oxon 20 B7
Tolastadh bho Thuath W Isls 106 k4
Toldish Cnwll 3 N5
Tolland Somset 16 F10
Tollard Farnham Dorset 8 D5
Tollard Royal Wilts 8 C5
Toll Bar Donc 57 S5
Tollbar End Covtry 37 L5
Toller Fratrum Dorset 7 Q5
Toller Porcorum Dorset 7 Q5
Tollerton N York 64 C7
Tollerton Notts 47 R7
Toller Whelme Dorset 7 P4
Tollesbury Essex 23 N5
Tolleshunt D'Arcy Essex 23 M5
Tolleshunt Knights Essex 23 M5
Tolleshunt Major Essex 23 M5
Tollingham E R Yk 64 J12
Toll of Birness Abers 105 S9
Tolpuddle Dorset 7 U6
Tolworth Gt Lon 21 L9
Tomatin Highld 103 M10
Tomchrasky Highld 101 V9
Tomdoun Highld 101 T11
Tomich Highld 102 B10
Tomich Highld 102 F6
Tomich Highld 109 L3
Tomich Highld 109 M10
Tomintoul Moray 103 U12
Tomlow Warwks 37 N8
Tomnacross Highld 102 F7
Tomnavoulin Moray 103 V10
Tompkin Staffs 46 B3
Ton Mons 27 Q7
Ton Mons 27 R8
Tonbridge Kent 21 U13
Tondu Brdgnd 26 F11
Tonedale Somset 16 F12
Tonfanau Gwynd 43 L13
Tong C Brad 63 Q13
Tong Kent 12 J4
Tong Shrops 45 S12
Tong W Isls 106 j5
Tonge Leics 47 M9
Tong Green Kent 12 J5
Tongham Surrey 20 E13
Tongland D & G 73 R9
Tong Norton Shrops 45 S12
Tongue Highld 111 M5
Tongue End Lincs 48 J10
Tongwynlais Cardif 27 L11
Tonmawr Neath 26 E8
Tonna Neath 26 D8
Ton-teg Rhondd 26 K10
Tonwell Herts 31 T9
Tonypandy Rhondd 26 H9
Tonyrefail Rhondd 26 J10
Toot Baldon Oxon 30 C12
Toot Hill Essex 22 D7
Toothill Hants 9 M5
Toothill Swindn 29 M11
Tooting Gt Lon 21 N8
Tooting Bec Gt Lon 21 N8
Topcliffe N York 63 T4
Topcroft Norfk 41 N2
Topcroft Street Norfk 41 N2
Top End Bed 38 F8
Topham Donc 57 T3
Top of Hebers Rochdl 56 C5
Toppesfield Essex 40 B13
Toprow Norfk 51 L14
Topsham Devon 6 C7
Top-y-rhos Flints 44 G2
Torbeg N Ayrs 79 R10
Torboll Highld 109 P5
Torbreck Highld 102 H7
Torbryan Devon 5 U7
Torcastle Highld 94 G3
Torcross Devon 5 U12
Tore Highld 102 H5
Torfrey Cnwll 4 E10
Torinturk Ag & B 79 Q3
Torksey Lincs 58 D11
Torlundy Highld 94 G3
Tormarton S Glos 28 E12
Tormore N Ayrs 79 R9
Tornagrain Highld 103 L5
Tornaveen Abers 99 L2
Torness Highld 102 G10
Toronto Dur 69 Q6
Torpenhow Cumb 66 K5
Torphichen W Loth 82 J4
Torphins Abers 99 L3
Torpoint Cnwll 5 L9
Torquay Torbay 6 B12
Torquhan Border 84 C9
Torr Devon 5 P10
Torran Highld 100 e5
Torrance E Duns 89 P11
Torranyard N Ayrs 81 M4
Torre Somset 16 D9
Torridon Highld 107 R13
Torridon House Highld 107 Q13
Torrin Highld 100 e7
Torrisdale Ag & B 79 P8
Torrisdale Highld 111 P4
Torrish Highld 111 V13
Torrisholme Lancs 61 T7
Torrobull Highld 108 K4
Torry C Aber 99 S2
Torryburn Fife 82 K1
Torteval Guern 6 b4
Torthorwald D & G 74 K10
Tortington W Susx 10 G9
Torton Worcs 35 T6
Tortworth S Glos 28 D9
Torvaig Highld 100 d5
Torver W & F 67 L14
Torwood Falk 89 T9
Torwoodlee Border 84 D11
Torworth Notts 57 U9
Tosberry Devon 14 G8
Toscaig Highld 100 g6
Toseland Cambs 38 K8
Tosside Lancs 62 F8
Tostock Suffk 40 G8
Totaig Highld 100 b4
Tote Highld 100 d5
Tote Highld 100 e3
Tote Hill W Susx 10 D6
Totford Hants 19 S13
Tothill Lincs 59 R10
Totland IoW 9 L11
Totley Sheff 57 M11
Totley Brook Sheff 57 M10
Totnes Devon 5 U8
Toton Notts 47 P7
Totronald Ag & B 92 F7
Totscore Highld 100 c3
Tottenham Gt Lon 21 P4
Tottenhill Norfk 49 T11
Totteridge Gt Lon 21 M4
Totternhoe C Beds 31 L8
Tottington Bury 55 S4
Tottleworth Lancs 62 E13
Totton Hants 9 M6
Touchen End W & M 20 E7
Toulston N York 64 B11
Toulton Somset 16 G10
Toulvaddie Highld 109 R8
Tovil Kent 12 E5
Towan Cnwll 3 M2
Towan Cnwll 3 Q7
Toward Ag & B 88 D12
Toward Quay Ag & B 88 D12
Towcester W Nthn 37 S11
Towednack Cnwll 2 D9
Tower of London Gt Lon 21 P6
Towersey Oxon 30 F11
Towie Abers 104 E13
Tow Law Dur 69 P5
Town End Cambs 39 P1
Town End W & F 61 S3
Town End W & F 67 M11
Town End W & F 68 D7
Townend W Duns 88 J10
Towngate Lincs 48 H11
Towngate W & F 67 R3
Town Green Lancs 54 K5
Town Green Norfk 51 Q11
Townhead Barns 56 J6
Townhead Cumb 66 G5
Townhead D & G 74 K8
Town Head N York 62 G8
Town Head W & F 67 P12
Townhead W & F 68 D6
Townhead of Greenlaw D & G 74 D13
Townhill Fife 90 H14
Town Kelloe Dur 70 E5
Townlake Devon 5 L6
Town Lane Wigan 55 Q7
Town Littleworth E Susx 11 Q7
Town of Lowton Wigan 55 P7
Town Row E Susx 11 T4
Towns End Hants 19 S9
Townsend Somset 7 L2
Townshend Cnwll 2 F10
Town Street Suffk 40 C3
Townwell S Glos 28 D9
Town Yetholm Border 85 L13
Towthorpe C York 64 E8
Towthorpe E R Yk 64 K7
Towton N York 64 B12
Towyn Conwy 53 S7
Toxteth Lpool 54 J9
Toynton All Saints Lincs 59 Q14
Toynton Fen Side Lincs 49 N1
Toynton St Peter Lincs 59 R14
Toy's Hill Kent 21 S12
Trabboch E Ayrs 81 N8
Trabbochburn E Ayrs 81 P8
Traboe Cnwll 2 J12
Tracebridge Somset 16 E12
Tradespark Highld 103 N4
Trafford Park Traffd 55 S7
Trallong Powys 26 H2
Tranent E Loth 83 T4
Tranmere Wirral 54 H9
Trantelbeg Highld 111 T6
Trantlemore Highld 111 T6
Tranwell Nthumb 77 P9
Trap Carmth 26 B4
Traprain E Loth 84 F3
Trap's Green Warwks 36 F7
Trapshill W Berk 19 N8
Traquair Border 83 R12
Trash Green W Berk 19 U7
Trawden Lancs 62 J12
Trawscoed Cerdgn 33 N6
Trawsfynydd Gwynd 43 P6
Trealaw Rhondd 26 J9
Treales Lancs 61 S13
Trearddur Bay IoA 52 C7
Treator Cnwll 3 N1
Tre Aubrey V Glam 16 D2
Trebanog Rhondd 26 J9
Trebanos Neath 26 C7
Trebartha Cnwll 4 H5
Trebarwith Cnwll 4 D3
Trebeath Cnwll 4 H3
Trebetherick Cnwll 4 A5
Treborough Somset 16 D9
Trebudannon Cnwll 3 M4
Trebullett Cnwll 4 J5
Treburgett Cnwll 4 D5
Treburley Cnwll 4 J5
Treburrick Cnwll 3 M2
Trebyan Cnwll 3 R4
Trecastle Powys 26 F2
Trecogo Cnwll 4 J4
Trecott Devon 15 P12
Trecwn Pembks 24 G4
Trecynon Rhondd 26 H7
Tredaule Cnwll 4 G4
Tredavoe Cnwll 2 D11
Tredegar Blae G 27 L6
Tredethy Cnwll 3 R2
Tredington Gloucs 28 H2
Tredington Warwks 36 J12
Tredinnick Cnwll 3 N2
Tredinnick Cnwll 3 Q5
Tredinnick Cnwll 4 F7
Tredinnick Cnwll 4 G9
Tredinnick Cnwll 4 H9
Tredomen Powys 27 L1
Tredrizzick Cnwll 4 B5
Tredunnock Mons 27 R9
Tredustan Powys 27 L1
Treen Cnwll 2 B12
Treen Cnwll 2 C9
Treesmill Cnwll 3 R5
Treeton Rothm 57 P9
Trefasser Pembks 24 E3
Trefdraeth IoA 52 F8
Trefecca Powys 27 L1
Trefechan Myr Td 26 J6
Trefeglwys Powys 33 U2
Trefenter Cerdgn 33 M7
Treffgarne Pembks 24 G6
Treffgarne Owen Pembks 24 E5
Treffynnon Pembks 24 E5
Trefil Blae G 27 L5
Trefilan Cerdgn 32 K9
Trefin Pembks 24 D4
Treflach Shrops 44 G8
Trefnannau Powys 44 F10
Trefnant Denbgs 54 C12
Trefonen Shrops 44 G8
Trefor Gwynd 42 G4
Trefor IoA 52 E6
Treforest Rhondd 26 K10
Trefrew Cnwll 4 E4
Trefriw Conwy 53 N10
Tregadillett Cnwll 4 H4
Tre-gagle Mons 27 U6
Tregaian IoA 52 G6
Tregare Mons 27 S5
Tregarne Cnwll 2 K12
Tregaron Cerdgn 33 N9
Tregarth Gwynd 52 K9
Tregaswith Cnwll 3 M4
Tregatta Cnwll 4 D3
Tregawne Cnwll 3 Q3
Tregeare Cnwll 4 G3
Tregeiriog Wrexhm 44 E7
Tregele IoA 52 E4
Tregellist Cnwll 4 C5
Tregenna Cnwll 3 M8
Tregeseal Cnwll 2 B10
Tregew Cnwll 3 L10
Tre-Gibbon Rhondd 26 H6
Tregidden Cnwll 2 K12
Tregiskey Cnwll 3 Q7
Treglemais Pembks 24 D5
Tregole Cnwll 14 E13
Tregolls Cnwll 2 J9
Tregonce Cnwll 3 N2
Tregonetha Cnwll 3 P4
Tregonning & Gwinear Mining District Cnwll 2 F10
Tregony Cnwll 3 N8
Tregoodwell Cnwll 4 E4
Tregorrick Cnwll 3 Q6
Tregoss Cnwll 3 P4
Tregoyd Powys 34 E13
Tregrehan Mills Cnwll 3 Q6
Tre-groes Cerdgn 32 H12
Tregullon Cnwll 3 R4
Tregunna Cnwll 3 P2
Tregunnon Cnwll 4 G4
Tregurrian Cnwll 3 M3
Tregynon Powys 44 C14
Tre-gynwr Carmth 25 R7
Trehafod Rhondd 26 J9
Trehan Cnwll 5 L9
Treharris Myr Td 26 K8
Treharrock Cnwll 4 C5
Trehemborne Cnwll 3 M2
Treherbert Carmth 33 L11
Treherbert Rhondd 26 G8
Trehunist Cnwll 4 J8
Trekenner Cnwll 4 J5
Treknow Cnwll 4 D3
Trelan Cnwll 2 J13
Trelash Cnwll 4 F2
Trelassick Cnwll 3 M6
Trelawne Cnwll 4 G10
Trelawnyd Flints 54 C11
Treleague Cnwll 2 K12
Treleaver Cnwll 2 K13
Trelech Carmth 25 N4
Trelech a'r Betws Carmth 25 P5
Treleddyd-fawr Pembks 24 C5
Trelew Cnwll 3 L9
Trelewis Myr Td 27 L8
Treligga Cnwll 4 C4
Trelights Cnwll 4 B5
Trelill Cnwll 4 C5
Trelinnoe Cnwll 4 J4
Trelion Cnwll 3 N6
Trelissick Cnwll 3 L9
Trellech Mons 27 U6
Trelleck Grange Mons 27 T7
Trelogan Flints 54 D10
Trelow Cnwll 3 N3
Trelowarren Cnwll 2 J12
Trelowia Cnwll 4 H9
Treluggan Cnwll 3 M9
Trelystan Powys 44 G13
Tremadog Gwynd 43 L6
Tremail Cnwll 4 F3
Tremain Cerdgn 32 D11
Tremaine Cnwll 4 G3
Tremar Cnwll 4 H7
Trematon Cnwll 4 K9
Trembraze Cnwll 4 H7
Tremeirchion Denbgs 54 C12
Tremethick Cross Cnwll 2 C10
Tremore Cnwll 3 Q4
Tre-Mostyn Flints 54 D11
Trenance Cnwll 3 L12
Trenance Cnwll 3 M3
Trenance Cnwll 3 N2
Trenarren Cnwll 3 Q7
Trench Wrekin 45 Q11
Trench Green Oxon 19 U5
Trendeal Cnwll 3 M6
Trendrine Cnwll 2 D9
Treneague Cnwll 3 P2
Trenear Cnwll 2 H10
Treneglos Cnwll 4 G3
Trenerth Cnwll 2 G9
Trenewan Cnwll 4 F10
Trenewth Cnwll 4 D5
Trengune Cnwll 4 F2
Treninnick Cnwll 3 L4
Trenowah Cnwll 2 K5
Trenoweth Cnwll 2 K10
Trent Dorset 17 Q13
Trentham C Stke 45 U5
Trentishoe Devon 15 P3
Trentlock Derbys 47 N7
Trent Port Lincs 58 D10
Trent Vale C Stke 45 U5
Trenwheal Cnwll 2 G10
Treoes V Glam 26 G12
Treorchy Rhondd 26 H8
Trequite Cnwll 4 C5
Tre'r-ddol Cerdgn 33 N2
Trerhyngyll V Glam 26 J12
Trerulefoot Cnwll 4 J9
Tresaith Cerdgn 32 E10
Tresawle Cnwll 3 M7
Tresco IoS 2 b2
Trescott Staffs 35 U1
Trescowe Cnwll 2 F10
Tresean Cnwll 2 K5
Tresham Gloucs 28 E9
Treshnish Isles Ag & B 92 G10
Tresillian Cnwll 3 M7
Tresinney Cnwll 4 E4
Treskinnick Cross Cnwll 14 F13
Tresmeer Cnwll 4 G3
Tresparrett Cnwll 4 E2
Tressait P & K 97 N11
Tresta Shet 106 t8
Tresta Shet 106 w4
Treswell Notts 58 C11
Treswithian Cnwll 2 G8
Tre Taliesin Cerdgn 33 N2
Trethevey Cnwll 4 D3
Trethewey Cnwll 2 B12
Trethomas Caerph 27 M10
Trethosa Cnwll 3 N6
Trethurgy Cnwll 3 Q5
Tretio Pembks 24 C5
Tretire Herefs 27 U3
Tretower Powys 27 M3
Treuddyn Flints 44 G2
Trevadlock Cnwll 4 H5
Trevalga Cnwll 4 D2
Trevalyn Wrexhm 44 J2
Trevanger Cnwll 4 B5
Trevanson Cnwll 3 P2
Trevarrack Cnwll 2 D10
Trevarren Cnwll 3 N4
Trevarrian Cnwll 3 M3
Trevarrick Cnwll 3 P8
Trevarth Cnwll 2 J8
Trevaughan Carmth 25 M7
Tre-vaughan Carmth 25 Q6
Treveal Cnwll 2 D8
Treveal Cnwll 2 K5
Treveighan Cnwll 4 D5
Trevellas Downs Cnwll 2 J6
Trevelmond Cnwll 4 G8
Trevemper Cnwll 3 L5
Treveor Cnwll 3 P8
Treverbyn Cnwll 3 M7
Treverbyn Cnwll 3 Q5
Treverva Cnwll 2 K10
Trevescan Cnwll 2 B12
Trevethin Torfn 27 P7
Trevia Cnwll 4 D4
Trevigro Cnwll 4 J7
Trevilla Cnwll 3 L9
Trevilson Cnwll 3 L5
Treviscoe Cnwll 3 N5
Treviskey Cnwll 3 N8
Trevithick Cnwll 3 M4
Trevithick Cnwll 3 P7
Trevoll Cnwll 3 L5
Trevone Cnwll 3 M1
Trevor Wrexhm 44 G5
Trevorgans Cnwll 2 C11
Trevorrick Cnwll 3 N2
Trevose Cnwll 3 M1
Trew Cnwll 2 G11
Trewalder Cnwll 4 D4
Trewalkin Powys 27 M1
Trewarmett Cnwll 4 D3
Trewassa Cnwll 4 E3
Trewavas Cnwll 2 F11
Trewavas Mining District Cnwll 2 F11
Treween Cnwll 4 G4
Trewellard Cnwll 2 B10
Trewen Cnwll 4 H4
Trewennack Cnwll 2 H11
Trewent Pembks 24 H11
Trewern Powys 44 G11
Trewetha Cnwll 4 C4
Trewethern Cnwll 3 Q1
Trewidland Cnwll 4 H9
Trewillis Cnwll 2 K13
Trewint Cnwll 4 G4
Trewint Cnwll 4 H8
Trewithian Cnwll 3 M9
Trewoodloe Cnwll 4 J6
Trewoon Cnwll 2 H13
Trewoon Cnwll 3 P6
Treworga Cnwll 3 M8
Treworgan Cnwll 3 L7
Treworlas Cnwll 3 M9
Treworld Cnwll 4 E2
Treworthal Cnwll 3 M9
Tre-wyn Mons 27 Q3
Treyarnon Cnwll 3 M2
Treyford W Susx 10 C7
Trickett's Cross Dorset 8 F8
Triermain Cumb 76 B12
Triffleton Pembks 24 G6
Trillacott Cnwll 4 H3
Trimdon Dur 70 E6
Trimdon Colliery Dur 70 E5
Trimdon Grange Dur 70 E5
Trimdon Station Dur 70 E5
Trimingham Norfk 51 N6
Trimley Lower Street Suffk 41 N13
Trimley St Martin Suffk 41 N13
Trimley St Mary Suffk 41 N13
Trimpley Worcs 35 S5
Trimsaran Carmth 25 S10
Trims Green Herts 22 C4
Trimstone Devon 15 M4
Trinafour P & K 95 U6
Trinant Caerph 27 N8
Tring Herts 30 K10
Tringford Herts 30 K10
Tring Wharf Herts 30 K10
Trinity Angus 99 L11
Trinity Jersey 7 d2
Trinity Gask P & K 90 E8
Triscombe Somset 16 G9
Trislaig Highld 94 F4
Trispen Cnwll 3 L6
Tritlington Nthumb 77 Q7
Troan Cnwll 3 M5
Trochry P & K 90 E3
Troedrhiwfuwch Caerph 27 L7
Troedyraur Cerdgn 32 F11
Troedyrhiw Myr Td 26 K7
Trofarth Conwy 53 Q8
Trois Bois Jersey 7 c2
Troon Cnwll 2 H9
Troon S Ayrs 81 L6
Tropical World Leeds Leeds 63 S12
Trossachs Stirlg 89 M4
Trossachs Pier Stirlg 89 L4
Troston Suffk 40 E6
Troswell Cnwll 4 H2
Trotshill Worcs 35 U9
Trottiscliffe Kent 12 B3
Trotton W Susx 10 C6
Troughend Nthumb 76 H7
Trough Gate Lancs 56 C2
Troutbeck W & F 67 N7
Troutbeck W & F 67 P12
Troutbeck Bridge W & F 67 P12
Troway Derbys 57 N11
Trowbridge Wilts 18 C9
Trowell Notts 47 N6
Trowell Services Notts 47 N5
Trowle Common Wilts 18 B9
Trowley Bottom Herts 31 N10
Trowse Newton Norfk 51 M12
Troy Leeds 63 Q12
Trudoxhill Somset 17 T8
Trull Somset 16 H12
Trumfleet Donc 57 T4
Trumpan Highld 100 b3
Trumpet Herefs 35 Q13
Trumpington Cambs 39 P10
Trumpsgreen Surrey 20 G9
Trunch Norfk 51 N7
Trunnah Lancs 61 Q11
Truro Cnwll 3 L8
Truscott Cnwll 4 H3
Trusham Devon 5 V4
Trusley Derbys 46 J6
Trusthorpe Lincs 59 T10
Trysull Staffs 35 U2
Tubney Oxon 29 T8
Tuckenhay Devon 5 U9
Tuckhill Shrops 35 S3
Tuckingmill Cnwll 2 H8
Tuckingmill Wilts 8 C3
Tuckton BCP 8 G10
Tucoyse Cnwll 3 P7
Tuddenham Suffk 40 B6
Tuddenham St Martin Suffk 41 L11
Tudeley Kent 12 B6
Tudhoe Dur 69 S5
Tudorville Herefs 28 A3
Tudweiliog Gwynd 42 D6
Tuesley Surrey 10 F2
Tuffley Gloucs 28 F5
Tufton Hants 19 Q11
Tufton Pembks 24 H5
Tugby Leics 47 U13
Tugford Shrops 35 N3
Tughall Nthumb 85 U13
Tullibody Clacks 90 C12
Tullich Abers 98 F4
Tullich Highld 102 H10
Tullich Highld 109 R9
Tulliemet P & K 97 S13
Tulloch Abers 105 N9
Tullochgorm Ag & B 87 T6
Tulloch Station Highld 96 D7
Tullymurdoch P & K 98 B13
Tullynessle Abers 104 H12
Tulse Hill Gt Lon 21 P8
Tumble Carmth 25 T8
Tumbler's Green Essex 22 K2
Tumby Lincs 48 K2
Tumby Woodside Lincs 49 L2
Tummel Bridge P & K 95 V7
Tunbridge Wells Kent 11 T3
Tundergarth D & G 75 N9
Tunga W Isls 106 j5
Tungate Norfk 51 N8
Tunley BaNES 17 S5
Tunstall C Stke 45 U3
Tunstall E R Yk 65 U13
Tunstall Kent 12 G3
Tunstall Lancs 62 C5
Tunstall N York 69 R13
Tunstall Norfk 51 R12
Tunstall Staffs 45 S8
Tunstall Suffk 41 Q9
Tunstall Sundld 70 E2
Tunstead Derbys 56 H12
Tunstead Norfk 51 N9
Tunstead Milton Derbys 56 F10
Tunworth Hants 19 U11
Tupsley Herefs 35 M12
Turgis Green Hants 19 U9
Turkdean Gloucs 29 M4
Tur Langton Leics 37 T2
Turleigh Wilts 18 B8
Turleygreen Shrops 35 S3
Turn Lancs 55 T3
Turnastone Herefs 34 J13
Turnberry S Ayrs 80 J11
Turnchapel C Plym 5 M10
Turnditch Derbys 46 J4
Turner Green Lancs 62 C13
Turner's Green E Susx 11 U7
Turner's Green Warwks 36 G7
Turners Hill W Susx 11 N3
Turners Puddle Dorset 8 A10
Turnford Herts 31 U12
Turnhouse C Edin 83 N4
Turnworth Dorset 7 V3
Turriff Abers 105 L5
Turton Bottoms Bl w D 55 R3
Turves Cambs 39 M1
Turvey Bed 38 D10
Turville Bucks 20 C4
Turville Heath Bucks 20 B4
Turweston Bucks 30 D5
Tushielaw Inn Border 75 R2
Tutbury Staffs 46 H8
Tutnall Worcs 36 C6
Tutshill Gloucs 27 U9
Tuttington Norfk 51 M8
Tutts Clump W Berk 19 S6
Tutwell Cnwll 4 K5
Tuxford Notts 58 B12
Twatt Ork 106 r17
Twatt Shet 106 t8
Twechar E Duns 89 Q10
Tweedbank Border 84 E12
Tweedmouth Nthumb 85 P8
Tweedsmuir Border 83 M14
Twelveheads Cnwll 2 K8
Twelve Oaks E Susx 12 C11
Twemlow Green Ches E 55 S13
Twenty Lincs 48 J9
Twerton BaNES 17 T4
Twickenham Gt Lon 21 L8
Twigworth Gloucs 28 F3
Twineham W Susx 11 M7
Twineham Green W Susx 11 M6
Twinhoe BaNES 17 U5
Twinstead Essex 40 E13
Twitchen Devon 15 S6
Twitchen Shrops 34 J5
Twitham Kent 13 Q4
Two Bridges Devon 5 Q6
Two Dales Derbys 57 L14
Two Gates Staffs 46 H13
Two Mile Ash W Susx 10 J5
Two Mile Oak Cross Devon 5 U7
Two Pots Devon 15 M4
Two Waters Herts 31 N11
Twycross Leics 46 K13
Twycross Zoo Leics 46 K12
Twyford Bucks 30 E7
Twyford Hants 9 P4
Twyford Leics 47 T11
Twyford Lincs 48 D9
Twyford Norfk 50 H9
Twyford Wokham 20 C7
Twyford Common Herefs 35 M13
Twyn-carno Caerph 27 L6
Twynholm D & G 73 R9
Twyning Gloucs 35 U13
Twynllanan Carmth 26 D3
Twyn-yr-Odyn V Glam 27 L13
Twyn-y-Sheriff Mons 27 S6
Twywell N Nthn 38 E5
Tyberton Herefs 34 J13
Tyburn Birm 36 F2
Tycroes Carmth 25 V8
Ty Croes IoA 52 D8
Tycrwyn Powys 44 D10
Tydd Gote Lincs 49 Q10
Tydd St Giles Cambs 49 P10
Tydd St Mary Lincs 49 P10
Tye Hants 9 U8
Tye Green Essex 22 D3
Tye Green Essex 22 J3
Tye Green Essex 39 S13
Tyersal C Brad 63 P13
Tyldesley Wigan 55 Q6
Tyler Hill Kent 13 M3
Tylers Green Bucks 20 F4
Tyler's Green Essex 22 D6
Tylers Green Surrey 21 Q12
Tylorstown Rhondd 26 J8
Tylwch Powys 33 U4
Ty-nant Conwy 43 U5
Ty-nant Gwynd 43 T8
Tyncelyn Cerdgn 33 M8
Tyndrum Stirlg 95 L12
Ty'n-dwr Denbgs 44 F5
Tyneham Dorset 8 B12
Tynemouth N Tyne 77 T12
Tyne Tunnel S Tyne 77 S12
Tynewydd Rhondd 26 G8
Tyninghame E Loth 84 G3
Tynron D & G 74 F7
Ty'n-y-bryn Rhondd 26 J10
Ty'n-y-coedcae Caerph 27 M10
Tynygongl IoA 52 H6
Tynygraig Cerdgn 33 N7
Ty'n-y-Groes Conwy 53 N8
Tyn-y-nant Rhondd 26 K10
Tyrie Abers 105 Q3
Tyringham M Keyn 38 C11
Tyseley Birm 36 F4
Tythegston Brdgnd 26 F12
Tytherington Ches E 56 D11
Tytherington S Glos 28 C10
Tytherington Somset 17 U8
Tytherington Wilts 18 D12
Tytherleigh Devon 6 K4
Tytherton Lucas Wilts 18 D6
Tyttenhanger Herts 31 Q11
Tywardreath Cnwll 3 R6
Tywardreath Highway Cnwll 3 R5
Tywyn Conwy 53 N7
Tywyn Gwynd 43 L13

U

Ubbeston Green Suffk 41 P6
Ubley BaNES 17 P5
Uckerby N York 69 R12
Uckfield E Susx 11 R6
Uckinghall Worcs 35 U13
Uckington Gloucs 28 H3
Uckington Shrops 45 N11
Uddingston S Lans 82 C6
Uddington S Lans 82 G12
Udimore E Susx 12 G12
Udny Green Abers 105 P10
Udny Station Abers 105 Q11
Uffcott Wilts 18 H5
Uffculme Devon 6 E2
Uffington Lincs 48 G12
Uffington Oxon 29 R10

Uffington Shrops 45 M11
Ufford C Pete 48 G13
Ufford Suffk 41 N10
Ufton Warwks 37 L8
Ufton Nervet W Berk 19 T7
Ugadale Ag & B 79 P10
Ugborough Devon 5 R9
Uggeshall Suffk 41 R4
Ugglebarnby N York 71 Q11
Ughill Sheff 57 L8
Ugley Essex 22 D2
Ugley Green Essex 22 D2
Ugthorpe N York 71 N10
Uibhist A Deas W Isls 106 d15
Uibhist A Tuath W Isls 106 c11
Uig Ag & B 92 F8
Uig Highld 100 a1
Uig Highld 100 c3
Uig Highld 100 d5
Uigshader Highld 100 d5
Uisken Ag & B 86 P2
Ulbster Highld 112 H8
Ulcat Row W & F 67 P8
Ulceby Lincs 59 Q11
Ulceby N Linc 58 K4
Ulceby Skitter N Linc 58 K3
Ulcombe Kent 12 F6
Uldale Cumb 66 J6
Uley Gloucs 28 E8
Ulgham Nthumb 77 Q7
Ullapool Highld 108 A6
Ullenhall Warwks 36 G7
Ullenwood Gloucs 28 H4
Ulleskelf N York 64 C12
Ullesthorpe Leics 37 P3
Ulley Rothm 57 Q9
Ullingswick Herefs 35 N11
Ullock Cumb 66 G8
Ullswater W & F 67 N7
Ullswater 'Steamers' W & F 67 N7
Ulpha Cumb 66 J14
Ulpha W & F 61 T3
Ulrome E R Yk 65 R8
Ulsta Shet 106 u5
Ulting Wick Essex 22 K6
Ulva Ag & B 86 K6
Ulverley Green Solhll 36 F4
Ulverston W & F 61 P4
Ulwell Dorset 8 E12
Ulzieside D & G 74 E4
Umberleigh Devon 15 P8
Unapool Highld 110 E10
Underbarrow W & F 61 T1
Under Burnmouth Border 75 U9
Undercliffe C Brad 63 P13
Underdale Shrops 45 M11
Underling Green Kent 12 E6
Underriver Kent 21 U12
Underwood Newpt 27 R10
Underwood Notts 47 N3
Undley Suffk 39 S4
Undy Mons 27 S10
Union Mills IoM 60 f7
Union Street E Susx 12 D9
Unst Shet 106 v3
Unstone Derbys 57 N11
Unstone Green Derbys 57 N11
Unthank Cumb 67 N3
Unthank Cumb 67 M11
Unthank Nthumb 85 P9
Unthank W & F 67 Q5
Unthank W & F 68 D4
Upavon Wilts 18 H10
Up Cerne Dorset 7 S4
Upchurch Kent 12 F2
Upcott Devon 15 S7
Upcott Herefs 34 H10
Upend Cambs 40 B9
Up Exe Devon 6 B4
Upgate Norfk 50 K10
Upgate Street Norfk 40 J2
Upgate Street Norfk 41 N2
Uphall Dorset 7 P3
Uphall W Loth 83 L4
Upham Devon 15 U11
Upham Hants 9 Q4
Uphampton Herefs 34 J8
Uphampton Worcs 35 T7
Uphill N Som 16 K5
Up Holland Lancs 55 M5
Uplawmoor E Rens 81 N2
Upleadon Gloucs 28 E2
Upleatham R & Cl 70 K9
Uplees Kent 12 K3
Uploders Dorset 7 P6
Uplowman Devon 16 D13
Uplyme Devon 6 K6
Up Marden W Susx 10 B8
Upminster Gt Lon 22 E10
Up Mudford Somset 17 Q13
Up Nately Hants 19 U10
Upottery Devon 6 H3
Upper Affcot Shrops 34 K3
Upper Arley Worcs 35 S4
Upper Arncott Oxon 30 D9
Upper Astrop W Nthn 30 B5
Upper Badcall Highld 110 D8
Upper Basildon W Berk 19 S5
Upper Batley Leeds 56 K1
Upper Beeding W Susx 10 K8
Upper Benefield N Nthn 38 F2
Upper Bentley Worcs 36 C7
Upper Bighouse Highld 111 T5
Upper Birchwood Derbys 47 M2
Upper Boat Rhondd 27 L10
Upper Boddington W Nthn 37 N10
Upper Borth Cerdgn 33 M3
Upper Brailes Warwks 36 K13
Upper Breinton Herefs 35 L12
Upper Broadheath Worcs 35 T9
Upper Broughton Notts 47 S8
Upper Bucklebury W Berk 19 R7
Upper Burgate Hants 8 H5
Upper Bush Medway 12 C2
Upperby Cumb 67 P2
Upper Caldecote C Beds 38 J11
Upper Canada N Som 17 L5
Upper Canterton Hants 8 K6
Upper Catesby W Nthn 37 P9
Upper Catshill Worcs 36 C6
Upper Chapel Powys 34 B12
Upper Cheddon Somset 16 H11
Upper Chicksgrove Wilts 8 D3
Upper Chute Wilts 19 L9
Upper Clapton Gt Lon 21 P5
Upper Clatford Hants 19 N12
Upper Coberley Gloucs 28 J4
Upper Cotton Staffs 46 E4
Upper Cound Shrops 45 N12
Upper Cudworth Barns 57 N5
Upper Cumberworth Kirk 56 K5
Upper Dallachy Moray 104 D3
Upper Deal Kent 13 S5
Upper Dean Bed 38 G7
Upper Denby Kirk 56 K5
Upper Denton Cumb 76 C12
Upper Dicker E Susx 11 S8
Upper Dinchope Shrops 35 L4
Upper Dounreay Highld 112 B3
Upper Dovercourt Essex 23 T1
Upper Drumbane Stirlg 89 Q4
Upper Dunsforth N York 63 U7
Upper Eashing Surrey 10 F2
Upper Eathie Highld 103 L3
Upper Egleton Herefs 35 P12
Upper Elkstone Staffs 46 E2
Upper Ellastone Staffs 46 F5
Upper End Derbys 56 G11
Upper Enham Hants 19 N10
Upper Farmcote Shrops 35 S2
Upper Farringdon Hants 19 V13
Upper Framilode Gloucs 28 E5
Upper Froyle Hants 10 B2
Upper Godney Somset 17 N8
Upper Gravenhurst C Beds 31 P5
Upper Green Mons 27 R4
Upper Green Suffk 40 B8
Upper Green W Berk 19 N8
Upper Grove Common Herefs 27 V2
Upper Hackney Derbys 46 J1
Upper Hale Surrey 20 D13
Upper Halliford Surrey 20 J9
Upper Halling Medway 12 C3
Upper Hambleton Rutlnd 48 D12
Upper Hardres Court Kent 13 M4
Upper Hardwick Herefs 34 K9
Upper Hartfield E Susx 11 S3
Upper Hartshay Derbys 47 L3
Upper Hatherley Gloucs 28 H3
Upper Hatton Staffs 45 T6
Upper Haugh Rothm 57 N7
Upper Hayton Shrops 35 M4
Upper Heaton Kirk 56 H3
Upper Helmsley N York 64 F8
Upper Hergest Herefs 34 G10
Upper Heyford Oxon 29 U3
Upper Heyford W Nthn 37 S9
Upper Hill Herefs 35 L10
Upper Hockenden Kent 21 S9
Upper Hopton Kirk 56 J3
Upper Howsell Worcs 35 S11

Upper Hulme Staffs 46 D1
Upper Ifold Surrey 10 G4
Upper Inglesham Swindn 29 P8
Upper Kilcott Gloucs 28 E10
Upper Killay Swans 25 U12
Upper Kinchrackine Ag & B 94 H13
Upper Knockando Moray 103 U7
Upper Lambourn W Berk 19 M4
Upper Landywood Staffs 46 C12
Upper Langford N Som 17 N5
Upper Langwith Derbys 57 R13
Upper Largo Fife 91 P11
Upper Layham Suffk 40 H12
Upper Leigh Staffs 46 D6
Upper Littleton N Som 17 P4
Upper Lochton Abers 99 M4
Upper Longdon Staffs 46 D11
Upper Ludstone Shrops 35 T1
Upper Lybster Highld 112 G9
Upper Lydbrook Gloucs 28 B4
Upper Lyde Herefs 35 L12
Upper Lye Herefs 34 J7
Upper Maes-coed Herefs 34 H14
Upper Marham Norfk 50 B12
Upper Midhope Sheff 56 K6
Upper Milton Worcs 35 T5
Upper Minety Wilts 28 K9
Upper Moor Worcs 36 C11
Upper Moor Side Leeds 63 Q13
Upper Mulben Moray 104 B6
Upper Netchwood Shrops 35 P2
Upper Nobut Staffs 46 D6
Upper Norwood W Susx 10 E7
Upper Oddington Gloucs 29 P2
Upper Padley Derbys 56 K11
Upper Pennington Hants 9 L9
Upper Pollicott Bucks 30 F10
Upper Poppleton C York 64 D9
Upper Quinton Warwks 36 G11
Upper Ratley Hants 9 L4
Upper Rissington Gloucs 29 P4
Upper Rochford Worcs 35 Q8
Upper Ruscoe D & G 73 P7
Upper Sapey Herefs 35 Q8
Upper Saxondale Notts 47 S5
Upper Seagry Wilts 18 D4
Upper Shelton C Beds 38 D4
Upper Sheringham Norfk 50 K5
Upper Skelmorlie N Ayrs 88 F12
Upper Slaughter Gloucs 28 C5
Upper Soudley Gloucs 28 C5
Upper Spond Herefs 34 H10
Upper Standen Kent 13 P7
Upper Staploe Bed 38 H9
Upper Stoke Norfk 51 N13
Upper Stondon C Beds 31 P5
Upper Stowe W Nthn 37 R9
Upper Street Hants 8 H5
Upper Street Norfk 41 L5
Upper Street Norfk 51 P10
Upper Street Suffk 40 G10
Upper Street Suffk 40 C10
Upper Street Suffk 41 K10
Upper Strensham Worcs 35 U13
Upper Sundon C Beds 31 N7
Upper Swell Gloucs 29 N2
Upper Tankersley Barns 57 M7
Upper Tasburgh Norfk 41 M2
Upper Tean Staffs 46 D6
Upperthong Kirk 56 H5
Upperthorpe Derbys 57 Q10
Upperthorpe N Linc 58 C6
Upper Threapwood Ches W 44 J4
Upperton W Susx 10 F6
Upper Town Dur 69 N4
Upper Town Derbys 46 H3
Upper Town Herefs 35 N11
Upper Town N Som 17 P3
Upper Town Suffk 40 E8
Uppertown Highld 112 J1
Upper Tumble Carmth 25 T8
Upper Tysoe Warwks 36 K12
Upper Ufford Suffk 41 N11
Upperup Gloucs 28 K8
Upper Upham Wilts 18 K5
Upper Upnor Medway 22 J13
Upper Victoria Angus 91 R4
Upper Vobster Somset 17 T7
Upper Weald M Keyn 30 H5
Upper Weedon W Nthn 37 R9
Upper Wellingham E Susx 11 Q8
Upper Welland Worcs 35 S12
Upper Weston BaNES 17 U3
Upper Weybread Suffk 41 M5
Upper Wick Worcs 35 T10
Upper Wield Hants 19 T13
Upper Winchendon Bucks 30 F10
Upperwood Derbys 46 J2
Upper Woodford Wilts 18 H13
Upper Woolhampton W Berk 19 S7
Upper Wraxall Wilts 18 B6
Upper Wyche Worcs 35 S12
Uppincott Devon 6 B3
Uppingham Rutlnd 48 C14
Uppington Dorset 8 D7
Uppington Shrops 45 N12
Upsall N York 64 B2
Upsettlington Border 85 M9
Upshire Essex 22 B7
Upstreet Kent 13 P3
Up Sydling Dorset 7 R4
Upthorpe Suffk 40 G6
Upton Bucks 30 H11
Upton C Pete 48 H13
Upton Ches W 54 K13
Upton Cnwll 14 H6
Upton Cnwll 14 F12
Upton Cumb 67 M5
Upton Devon 5 S12
Upton Devon 6 E7
Upton Dorset 8 B10
Upton Dorset 8 D10
Upton E R Yk 65 Q9
Upton Halton 55 L9
Upton Hants 9 L5
Upton Hants 19 N9
Upton Leics 37 L2
Upton Lincs 58 E9
Upton Norfk 51 Q11
Upton Notts 47 U2
Upton Notts 58 B11
Upton Oxon 19 R3
Upton Oxon 29 U5
Upton Pembks 24 H10
Upton R & Cl 71 L9
Upton Slough 20 G7
Upton Somset 16 C11
Upton Somset 17 N11
Upton Wakefd 57 P4
Upton Warwks 36 F9
Upton Wilts 18 C13
Upton Wirral 54 F10
Upton Bishop Herefs 28 C2
Upton Cheyney S Glos 17 S3
Upton Cressett Shrops 35 Q2
Upton Crews Herefs 28 C2
Upton Cross Cnwll 4 H6
Upton End C Beds 31 P6
Upton Grey Hants 19 U11
Upton Heath Ches W 54 K13
Upton Hellions Devon 15 T12
Upton Lovell Wilts 18 D12
Upton Magna Shrops 45 N11
Upton Noble Somset 17 T9
Upton Pyne Devon 6 B5
Upton St Leonards Gloucs 28 G4
Upton Scudamore Wilts 18 C11
Upton Snodsbury Worcs 36 B10
Upton-upon-Severn Worcs 35 T12
Upton Warren Worcs 36 B7
Upwaltham W Susx 10 E7
Upware Cambs 39 R6
Upwell Norfk 49 Q13
Upwey Dorset 7 S7
Upwick Green Herts 22 C3
Upwood Cambs 39 L4
Urchfont Wilts 18 F9
Urdimarsh Herefs 35 M11
Ure Bank N York 63 S5
Urlay Nook S on T 70 F10
Urmston Traffd 55 S8
Urquhart Moray 104 B3
Urquhart Castle Highld 102 F10
Urra N York 70 J12
Urray Highld 102 F5
Usan Angus 99 N13
Ushaw Moor Dur 69 R4
Usk Mons 27 R6
Usselby Lincs 58 J7
Usworth Sundld 77 S14

Utkinton Ches W 55 M13
Utley C Brad 63 M11
Uton Devon 15 T13
Utterby Lincs 59 P8
Uttoxeter Staffs 46 E7
Uwchmynydd Gwynd 42 C8
Uxbridge Gt Lon 20 J6
Uyeasound Shet 106 v3
Uzmaston Pembks 24 G8

V

Vale Guern 6 e2
Valley IoA 52 C7
Valley End Surrey 20 G10
Valley Truckle Cnwll 4 D4
Valtos Highld 100 e3
Valtos W Isls 106 h5
Vange Essex 22 H10
Varteg Torfn 27 P6
Vatsetter Shet 106 v5
Vatten Highld 100 b5
Vaynor Myr Td 26 J6
Vazon Bay Guern 6 c2
Veensgarth Shet 106 u9
Velindre Powys 34 E13
Vellow Somset 16 E9
Velly Devon 14 G8
Venngreen Devon 14 J11
Vennington Shrops 44 H12
Venn Ottery Devon 6 E6
Venny Tedburn Devon 15 T13
Venterdon Cnwll 4 J6
Ventnor IoW 9 R13
Venton Devon 5 P9
Vernham Dean Hants 19 M9
Vernham Street Hants 19 M9
Vernolds Common Shrops 35 L4
Verwood Dorset 8 F8
Veryan Cnwll 3 N9
Veryan Green Cnwll 3 N8
Vicarage Devon 6 G7
Vickerstown W & F 61 M6
Victoria Barns 56 J5
Victoria Blae G 27 M6
Victoria Cnwll 3 N4
Vidlin Shet 106 u7
Viewfield Moray 104 B3
Viewpark N Lans 82 C6
Vigo Kent 12 B3
Village de Putron Guern 6 e3
Ville la Bas Jersey 7 a1
Villiaze Guern 6 c3
Vinehall Street E Susx 12 E11
Vines Cross E Susx 11 T7
Virginia Water Surrey 20 H9
Virginstow Devon 4 J2
Vobster Somset 17 T7
Voe Shet 106 u7
Vowchurch Herefs 34 J13
Vulcan Village St Hel 55 N8

W

Waberthwaite Cumb 66 H14
Wackerfield Dur 69 Q8
Wacton Norfk 41 L2
Wadborough Worcs 36 B11
Waddesdon Bucks 30 F9
Waddeton Devon 6 A13
Waddicar Sefton 54 J7
Waddingham Lincs 58 G7
Waddington Lancs 62 F11
Waddington Lincs 58 G14
Waddon Devon 6 A9
Waddon Dorset 7 S7
Waddon Gt Lon 21 N10
Wadebridge Cnwll 3 P2
Wadeford Somset 6 K2
Wadenhoe N Nthn 38 F4
Wadesmill Herts 31 U9
Wadhurst E Susx 12 B9
Wadshelf Derbys 57 M12
Wadswick Wilts 18 B7
Wadworth Donc 57 S7
Waen Denbgs 53 S10
Waen Denbgs 54 D13
Waen Powys 44 F10
Waen Fach Powys 44 F10
Waen-pentir Gwynd 52 J9
Waen-wen Gwynd 52 J9
Wagbeach Shrops 44 J13
Wainfelin Torfn 27 P7
Wainfleet All Saints Lincs 49 Q2
Wainfleet Bank Lincs 49 Q2
Wainfleet St Mary Lincs 49 Q2
Wainhouse Corner Cnwll 14 E13
Wainscott Medway 22 H13
Wain's Hill N Som 17 L2
Wainstalls Calder 63 L14
Waitby W & F 68 G11
Waithe Lincs 59 N6
Wakefield Wakefd 57 M2
Wake Green Birm 36 E4
Wakerley N Nthn 48 E14
Wakes Colne Essex 23 L2
Walberswick Suffk 41 S6
Walberton W Susx 10 F9
Walbottle N u Ty 77 P12
Walbutt D & G 74 D12
Walby Cumb 75 T13
Walcombe Somset 17 P7
Walcot Lincs 48 G6
Walcot N Linc 58 E2
Walcot Shrops 34 J4
Walcot Shrops 45 N3
Walcot Swindn 29 N11
Walcot Warwks 36 G10
Walcot Green Norfk 40 K4
Walcote Leics 37 Q3
Walcote Warwks 36 F10
Walcott Lincs 48 H2
Walcott Norfk 51 Q7
Walden N York 63 L3
Walden Head N York 62 K3
Walden Stubbs N York 57 S3
Walderslade Medway 12 E3
Walderton W Susx 10 B8
Walditch Dorset 7 N6
Waldley Derbys 46 F6
Waldridge Dur 69 S2
Waldringfield Suffk 41 N11
Waldron E Susx 11 S7
Wales Rothm 57 Q10
Wales Somset 17 Q12
Walesby Lincs 58 K8
Walesby Notts 57 U12
Walford Herefs 27 V3
Walford Herefs 34 J7
Walford Shrops 44 K9
Walford Staffs 45 T7
Walford Heath Shrops 44 K10
Walgherton Ches E 45 Q4
Walgrave W Nthn 38 B6
Walhampton Hants 9 L8
Walkden Salfd 55 R6
Walker N u Ty 77 R12
Walkerburn Border 83 R11
Walker Fold Lancs 62 D11
Walkeringham Notts 58 C8
Walkerith Lincs 58 C8
Walkern Herts 31 S8
Walker's Green Herefs 35 M11
Walker's Heath Birm 36 E5
Walkerton Fife 90 K11
Walkford Dorset 8 J10
Walkhampton Devon 5 N7
Walkington E R Yk 65 M12
Walkley Sheff 57 M9
Walk Mill Lancs 62 H13
Walkwood Worcs 36 D8
Wall Nthumb 76 J12
Wall Staffs 46 E12
Wallacetown S Ayrs 80 K9
Wallacetown S Ayrs 81 L7
Wallands Park E Susx 11 Q8
Wallasey Wirral 54 G8
Wallasey (Kingsway) Tunnel Wirral 54 H8
Wall End Herefs 34 K10
Wall End W & F 61 N3
Wallend Medway 23 L12
Waller's Green Herefs 35 P13
Wallhead Cumb 75 U13
Wall Heath Dudley 35 U3
Wall Houses Nthumb 77 L12
Wallingford Oxon 19 R3
Wallington Gt Lon 21 N10
Wallington Hants 9 R7
Wallington Herts 31 S6
Wallington Heath Wsall 46 C13
Wallis Pembks 24 H6
Wallisdown BCP 8 F10
Walliswood Surrey 10 H4
Wall Mead BaNES 17 S5
Walls Shet 106 s9
Wallsend N Tyne 77 R12
Wall under Haywood Shrops 35 M2
Wallyford E Loth 83 S4
Walmer Kent 13 S5
Walmer Bridge Lancs 55 L2
Walmersley Bury 55 S4
Walmestone Kent 13 Q4
Walmley Birm 36 F2
Walmley Ash Birm 36 F2
Walmsgate Lincs 59 Q11
Walpole Somset 16 K8
Walpole Suffk 41 Q6
Walpole Cross Keys Norfk 49 R10
Walpole Highway Norfk 49 R11
Walpole St Andrew Norfk 49 R10
Walpole St Peter Norfk 49 R10
Walrow Somset 16 K7
Walsall Wsall 46 D14
Walsall Wood Wsall 46 D13
Walsden Calder 56 D2
Walsgrave on Sowe Covtry 37 L4
Walsham le Willows Suffk 40 H6
Walshford N York 63 U9
Walsoken Norfk 49 Q11
Walston S Lans 83 L9
Walsworth Herts 31 Q6
Walter's Ash Bucks 20 D3
Walters Green Kent 11 S2
Walterston V Glam 16 E2
Walterstone Herefs 27 Q2
Waltham Kent 13 L6
Waltham NE Lin 59 N6
Waltham Abbey Essex 31 U12
Waltham Chase Hants 9 Q5
Waltham Cross Herts 31 U12
Waltham on the Wolds Leics 48 B9
Waltham St Lawrence W & M 20 D7
Waltham's Cross Essex 22 G1
Walthamstow Gt Lon 21 Q5
Walton C Pete 48 J13
Walton Cumb 75 T13
Walton Derbys 57 N13
Walton Leeds 63 U10
Walton Leics 37 Q3
Walton M Keyn 30 J5
Walton Powys 34 G9
Walton Shrops 34 K3
Walton Somset 17 N9
Walton Staffs 45 U7
Walton Suffk 41 N13
Walton W Susx 10 C10
Walton Wakefd 57 N3
Walton Warwks 36 H10
Walton Wrekin 45 M11
Walton Cardiff Gloucs 28 H1
Walton East Pembks 24 H6
Walton Elm Dorset 17 U13
Walton Grounds W Nthn 30 B6
Walton Highway Norfk 49 Q11
Walton-in-Gordano N Som 17 M2
Walton-le-Dale Lancs 62 B14
Walton-on-Thames Surrey 20 K9
Walton-on-the-Hill Staffs 46 C9
Walton-on-the-Hill Surrey 21 M11
Walton on the Wolds Leics 47 Q10
Walton-on-Trent Derbys 46 H10
Walton Park N Som 17 M2
Walton West Pembks 24 E8
Walwen Flints 54 E11
Walwen Flints 54 E12
Walwick Nthumb 76 J11
Walworth Darltn 69 R9
Walworth Gt Lon 21 P7
Walworth Gate Darltn 69 R8
Walwyn's Castle Pembks 24 E8
Wambrook Somset 6 K3
Wampool Cumb 66 K2
Wanborough Surrey 20 F12
Wanborough Swindn 29 P11
Wandon End Herts 31 P8
Wandsworth Gt Lon 21 N8
Wangford Suffk 41 S5
Wangford Suffk 40 B4
Wanlockhead D & G 74 G3
Wannock E Susx 11 T10
Wansford C Pete 48 G14
Wansford E R Yk 65 N8
Wanshurst Green Kent 12 E6
Wanstead Gt Lon 21 R5
Wanstrow Somset 17 T8
Wanswell Gloucs 28 D7
Wantage Oxon 29 S10
Wants Green Worcs 35 S9
Wapley S Glos 28 D12
Wappenbury Warwks 37 L7
Wappenham W Nthn 37 R11
Warbleton E Susx 11 U6
Warblington Hants 10 B10
Warborough Oxon 19 S2
Warboys Cambs 39 M4
Warbreck Bpool 61 Q12
Warbstow Cnwll 14 G2
Warburton Traffd 55 R9
Warcop W & F 68 F9
Warden Kent 23 P13
Warden Nthumb 76 J12
Ward End Birm 36 F3
Warden Street C Beds 31 P4
Ward Green Suffk 40 J8
Wardhedges C Beds 31 N5
Wardington Oxon 37 N11
Wardle Ches E 45 P2
Wardle Rochdl 56 D4
Wardley Gatesd 77 S13
Wardley Rutlnd 48 B13
Wardlow Derbys 56 J12
Wardsend Ches E 56 D10
Wardy Hill Cambs 39 Q4
Ware Herts 31 U10
Ware Kent 13 P3
Wareham Dorset 8 C11
Warehorne Kent 12 J9
Warenford Nthumb 85 T13
Waren Mill Nthumb 85 S12
Wareside Herts 31 U10
Waresley Cambs 39 L10
Waresley Worcs 35 T7
Ware Street Kent 12 E4
Warfield Br For 20 E8
Warfleet Devon 5 V11
Wargate Lincs 48 K6
Wargrave Wokham 20 C7
Warham Herefs 35 L13
Warham Norfk 50 F5
Wark Nthumb 76 H11
Wark Nthumb 85 L11
Warkleigh Devon 15 P8
Warkton N Nthn 38 C5
Warkworth N Nthn 37 N11
Warkworth Nthumb 77 Q4
Warlaby N York 63 S1
Warland Calder 56 D2
Warleggan Cnwll 4 F7
Warleigh BaNES 17 U3
Warley Town Calder 63 L14
Warlingham Surrey 21 Q11
Warmbrook Derbys 46 H3
Warmfield Wakefd 57 N2
Warmingham Ches E 45 R1
Warmington N Nthn 38 G2
Warmington Warwks 37 M11
Warminster Wilts 18 C12
Warmley S Glos 28 C13
Warmsworth Donc 57 R6
Warmwell Dorset 7 U7
Warndon Worcs 35 U9
Warner Bros. Studio Tour London Herts 31 N12
Warnford Hants 9 S3
Warnham W Susx 10 J4
Warningcamp W Susx 10 G9
Warninglid W Susx 11 L5
Warren Ches E 56 C12
Warren Pembks 24 F11
Warrenby R & Cl 70 K7
Warren Row W & M 20 C6
Warren Street Kent 12 J5
Warrington M Keyn 38 C9
Warrington Warrtn 55 P9
Warriston C Edin 83 Q4
Warsash Hants 9 P7
Warslow Staffs 46 E2
Warsop Vale Notts 57 R13
Warter E R Yk 64 K9
Warthermarske N York 63 Q4
Warthill N York 64 F8
Wartling E Susx 11 U9
Wartnaby Leics 47 U9
Warton Lancs 61 S13
Warton Lancs 61 T5
Warton Nthumb 77 M4
Warton Warwks 46 J13
Warwick Warwks 36 J8
Warwick Bridge Cumb 67 Q1
Warwick Castle Warwks 36 J8

Warwick-on-Eden Cumb 67 Q1
Warwick Services Warwks 36 K9
Warwickland Cumb 75 U10
Wasbister Ork 106 s16
Wasdale Head Cumb 66 J11
Wash Derbys 56 G10
Washall Green Herts 22 B1
Washaway Cnwll 3 Q2
Washbourne Devon 5 T10
Washbrook Somset 17 M6
Washbrook Suffk 40 K12
Washfield Devon 16 B13
Washfold N York 69 N11
Washford Somset 16 E8
Washford Pyne Devon 15 T10
Washingborough Lincs 58 H12
Washington Sundld 70 D1
Washington W Susx 10 J8
Washington Services 69 S1
Washwood Heath Birm 36 F3
Wasing W Berk 19 S8
Waskerley Dur 69 M3
Wasperton Warwks 36 J9
Wasps Nest Lincs 58 J14
Wass N York 64 D4
Wast Water Cumb 66 J11
Watchet Somset 16 E8
Watchfield Oxon 29 P9
Watchfield Somset 16 K7
Watchgate W & F 67 R13
Watcombe Torbay 6 B11
Watendlath Cumb 67 L9
Water Devon 5 T4
Water Lancs 62 H2
Waterbeach Cambs 39 Q7
Waterbeach W Susx 10 D9
Waterden Norfk 50 E6
Water Eaton Oxon 30 B10
Water Eaton Staffs 46 B11
Water End Bed 38 H11
Water End C Beds 31 N6
Water End E R Yk 64 H12
Water End Essex 39 S12
Water End Herts 31 M11
Water End Herts 31 Q11
Waterfall Staffs 46 E3
Waterfoot Ag & B 79 Q8
Waterfoot E Rens 81 R2
Waterfoot Lancs 55 T2
Water Fryston Wakefd 57 Q1
Watergate Cnwll 4 F5
Waterhead W & F 67 P12
Waterheads Border 83 P8
Waterhouses Dur 69 Q4
Waterhouses Staffs 46 E3
Wateringbury Kent 12 C5
Waterlane Gloucs 28 H7
Waterloo Cnwll 4 E6
Waterloo Derbys 47 M1
Waterloo Highld 100 g6
Waterloo N Lans 82 F8
Waterloo Pembks 24 G9
Waterloo Sefton 54 H7
Waterloo Cross Devon 6 E2
Waterloo Port Gwynd 52 G10
Waterlooville Hants 9 T7
Watermead Bucks 30 H9
Watermillock W & F 67 P8
Water Newton Cambs 38 H1
Water Orton Warwks 36 G2
Waterperry Oxon 30 D11
Waterrow Somset 16 E11
Watersfield W Susx 10 G7
Waterside Bl w D 55 R3
Waterside Bucks 31 L12
Waterside Cumb 66 K3
Waterside Donc 57 U4
Waterside E Ayrs 81 N4
Waterside E Ayrs 81 N11
Waterside E Duns 89 Q10
Water's Nook Bolton 55 Q5
Waterstock Oxon 30 D11
Waterston Pembks 24 F9
Water Stratford Bucks 30 E6
Water Street Neath 26 E11
Waters Upton Wrekin 45 P10
Watford Herts 20 K3
Watford W Nthn 37 R7
Watford Gap Services W Nthn 37 R7
Wath N York 63 R5
Wath N York 63 U3
Wath upon Dearne Rothm 57 P6
Watlington Norfk 49 R11
Watlington Oxon 19 U2
Watnall Notts 47 P4
Watten Highld 112 F6
Wattisfield Suffk 40 H6
Wattisham Suffk 40 H10
Wattlesborough Heath Shrops 44 H11
Watton Dorset 7 N6
Watton E R Yk 65 N9
Watton Norfk 50 F13
Watton-at-Stone Herts 31 T9
Watton Green Norfk 50 F13
Wattons Green Essex 22 D8
Wattston N Lans 82 E5
Wattstown Rhondd 26 J9
Wattsville Caerph 27 N8
Wauldby E R Yk 65 M14
Waulkmill Abers 99 L5
Waunarlwydd Swans 26 A9
Waun Fach Powys 27 M2
Waunfawr Cerdgn 33 M4
Waunfawr Gwynd 52 H11
Waungron Swans 25 U10
Waunlwyd Blae G 27 M6
Wavendon M Keyn 30 K5
Waverbridge Cumb 66 K3
Waverton Ches W 54 K13
Waverton Cumb 66 K3
Wavertree Lpool 54 J9
Wawne E R Yk 65 P12
Waxham Norfk 51 S8
Waxholme E R Yk 65 U14
Way Kent 13 R2
Wayford Somset 7 M3
Waytown Dorset 7 N5
Way Village Devon 15 U10
Way Wick N Som 17 L4
Weacombe Somset 16 F8
Weald Oxon 29 R7
Wealdstone Gt Lon 21 L5
Weardley Leeds 63 R11
Weare Somset 17 M6
Weare Giffard Devon 15 L8
Wearhead Dur 68 J5
Wearne Somset 17 M11
Weasdale W & F 68 D12
Weasenham All Saints Norfk 50 E9
Weasenham St Peter Norfk 50 E9
Weaste Salfd 55 S7
Weatheroak Hill Worcs 36 D6
Weaverham Ches W 55 P12
Weaverslake Staffs 46 F10
Weaverthorpe N York 65 L5
Webbington Somset 17 L5
Webb's Heath S Glos 28 C13
Webheath Worcs 36 D7
Webton Herefs 34 K13
Wedderlairs Abers 105 P9
Weddington Warwks 37 L2
Wedhampton Wilts 18 F9
Wedmore Somset 17 M7
Wednesbury Sandw 36 C1
Wednesfield Wolves 46 B13
Weecar Notts 58 C13
Weedon Bucks 30 H9
Weedon Lois W Nthn 37 R11
Weeford Staffs 46 F13
Week Devon 5 S8
Week Devon 15 T7
Week Devon 15 U9
Week Somset 16 B9
Weeke Hants 9 P2
Weekley N Nthn 38 C4
Week St Mary Cnwll 14 G13
Weel E R Yk 65 P12
Weeley Essex 23 R2
Weeley Heath Essex 23 R2
Weem P & K 90 B2
Weeping Cross Staffs 46 B9
Weethley Warwks 36 E9
Weeting Norfk 40 B3
Weeton E R Yk 59 R1
Weeton Lancs 61 R13
Weeton N York 63 R10
Weetwood Leeds 63 R12
Weir Lancs 56 C2
Weirbrook Shrops 44 H9

Weir Quay Devon 5 L7
Weisdale Shet 106 t8
Welborne Norfk 50 J11
Welbourn Lincs 48 E3
Welburn N York 64 G6
Welburn N York 64 F12
Welbury N York 70 E12
Welby Lincs 48 D6
Welches Dam Cambs 39 Q3
Welcombe Devon 14 F9
Weldon N Nthn 38 D3
Welford W Berk 19 P6
Welford W Nthn 37 R4
Welford-on-Avon Warwks 36 F10
Welham Leics 37 U2
Welham Notts 58 B11
Welham Green Herts 31 R11
Well Hants 20 B12
Well Lincs 59 R12
Well N York 63 R2
Welland Worcs 35 S12
Wellbank Angus 91 N4
Well End Bucks 20 E5
Well End Herts 21 M3
Wellesbourne Warwks 36 J9
Wellesbourne Mountford Warwks 36 J9
Well Head Herts 31 Q7
Well Hill Kent 21 S10
Wellhouse W Berk 19 R6
Welling Gt Lon 21 S8
Wellingborough N Nthn 38 C7
Wellingham Norfk 50 E9
Wellingore Lincs 48 E2
Wellington Cumb 66 G12
Wellington Herefs 35 L11
Wellington Somset 16 F12
Wellington Wrekin 45 P11
Wellington Heath Herefs 35 R12
Wellington Marsh Herefs 35 L11
Wellow BaNES 17 T5
Wellow IoW 9 M11
Wellow Notts 57 U13
Wellpond Green Herts 22 B3
Wells Somset 17 P7
Wellsborough Leics 47 L13
Wells Green Ches E 45 Q3
Wells Head C Brad 63 L13
Wells-next-the-Sea Norfk 50 F5
Wellstye Green Essex 22 F4
Welltown Cnwll 4 E6
Wellwood Fife 90 F14
Welney Norfk 39 R2
Welshampton Shrops 44 K6
Welsh Bicknor Herefs 28 A4
Welsh End Shrops 45 M6
Welsh Frankton Shrops 44 J6
Welsh Hook Pembks 24 F5
Welsh Newton Herefs 27 T3
Welshpool Powys 44 F12
Welsh St Donats V Glam 16 D2
Welton Cumb 67 M3
Welton E R Yk 65 M14
Welton Lincs 58 H10
Welton W Nthn 37 Q8
Welton le Marsh Lincs 59 S13
Welton le Wold Lincs 59 N9
Welwick E R Yk 59 P1
Welwyn Herts 31 R9
Welwyn Garden City Herts 31 R10
Wem Shrops 45 M8
Wembdon Somset 16 J9
Wembley Gt Lon 21 L5
Wembury Devon 5 N11
Wembworthy Devon 15 Q10
Wemyss Bay Invclyd 88 E11
Wenallt Cerdgn 33 N6
Wendens Ambo Essex 39 R13
Wendlebury Oxon 30 C9
Wendling Norfk 50 F11
Wendover Bucks 30 K11
Wendron Cnwll 2 H10
Wendron Mining District Cnwll 2 H10
Wendy Cambs 39 M11
Wenfordbridge Cnwll 4 D5
Wenhaston Suffk 41 R5
Wennington Cambs 38 K5
Wennington Gt Lon 22 E10
Wennington Lancs 62 C6
Wensley Derbys 46 J1
Wensley N York 63 L1
Wentbridge Wakefd 57 P4
Wentnor Shrops 34 J2
Wentworth Cambs 39 Q5
Wentworth Rothm 57 N7
Wenvoe V Glam 16 F2
Weobley Herefs 34 K10
Weobley Marsh Herefs 35 L10
Wepham W Susx 10 G9
Wereham Norfk 49 S13
Wergs Wolves 45 U13
Wern Gwynd 42 K4
Wern Powys 27 N3
Wern Powys 44 F11
Wern Powys 44 G9
Wernffrwd Swans 25 T12
Wern-Gifford Mons 27 Q4
Wernington Staffs 46 D3
Wern-y-gaer Flints 54 F13
Werrington C Pete 48 J12
Werrington Cnwll 4 J3
Werrington Staffs 46 B4
Wervin Ches W 54 K12
Wesham Lancs 61 S13
Wessington Derbys 47 L1
West Aberthaw V Glam 16 D3
West Acre Norfk 50 B10
West Allerdean Nthumb 85 P9
West Alvington Devon 5 S12
West Amesbury Wilts 18 H12
West Anstey Devon 15 U7
West Appleton N York 69 R14
West Ashby Lincs 59 M12
West Ashling W Susx 10 C9
West Ashton Wilts 18 C9
West Auckland Dur 69 Q7
West Ayton N York 65 L2
West Bagborough Somset 16 G10
West Bank Blae G 27 N6
West Bank Halton 55 M10
West Barkwith Lincs 58 K9
West Barnby N York 71 P10
West Barns E Loth 84 H3
West Barsham Norfk 50 F7
West Bay Dorset 7 N6
West Beckham Norfk 50 K6
West Bedfont Surrey 20 J8
Westbere Kent 13 N3
West Bergholt Essex 23 N2
West Bilney Norfk 50 B11
West Blatchington Br & H 11 N9
Westborough Lincs 48 C4
Westbourne BCP 8 F10
Westbourne W Susx 10 B9
West Bourton Dorset 17 U11
West Bowling C Brad 63 P13
West Bradenham Norfk 50 F12
West Bradford Lancs 62 F11
West Bradley Somset 17 Q9
West Bretton Wakefd 57 L4
West Bridgford Notts 47 Q6
West Briscoe Dur 68 K8
West Bromwich Sandw 36 D2
West Buckland Devon 15 Q6
West Buckland Somset 16 F12
West Burrafirth Shet 106 s8
West Burton N York 63 L2
West Burton W Susx 10 G8
Westbury Bucks 30 E6
Westbury Shrops 44 J12
Westbury Wilts 18 C10
Westbury Leigh Wilts 18 C10
Westbury-on-Severn Gloucs 28 D4
Westbury on Trym Bristl 27 V12
Westbury-sub-Mendip Somset 17 P7
West Butsfield Dur 69 P3
West Butterwick N Linc 58 D5
Westby Lancs 61 R13
West Byfleet Surrey 20 J10
West Cairngaan D & G 72 E12
West Caister Norfk 51 T11
West Calder W Loth 82 K6
West Camel Somset 17 Q11
West Chaldon Dorset 7 U8
West Challow Oxon 29 S10
West Charleton Devon 5 S12
West Chelborough Dorset 7 P3
West Chevington Nthumb 77 Q6
West Chiltington W Susx 10 H7
West Chinnock Somset 7 N2
West Chisenbury Wilts 18 H10
West Clandon Surrey 20 H12
West Cliffe Kent 13 R7
Westcliff-on-Sea Sthend 23 L10
West Clyst Devon 6 C5

West Coker Somset 7 P2
Westcombe Somset 17 S8
West Compton Somset 17 P8
West Compton Dorset 7 Q6
Westcote Gloucs 29 P3
Westcote Barton Oxon 29 T2
Westcott Bucks 30 F9
Westcott Devon 6 D4
Westcott Surrey 20 K13
West Cottingwith N York 64 F11
Westcourt Wilts 18 K8
West Cowick E R Yk 57 T2
West Cranmore Somset 17 S8
West Cross Swans 25 V13
West Curry Cnwll 14 H2
West Curthwaite Cumb 67 M3
West Dean Wilts 8 K3
West Dean W Susx 10 D8
West Deeping Lincs 48 H12
West Derby Lpool 54 J8
West Dereham Norfk 49 S13
West Ditchburn Nthumb 77 N1
West Down Devon 15 M4
Westdown Camp Wilts 18 F11
Westdowns Cnwll 4 D4
West Drayton Gt Lon 20 J7
West Drayton Notts 57 U12
West Dunnet Highld 112 F2
Wested Kent 21 S10
West Ella E R Yk 65 N14
West End Bed 38 E10
West End Caerph 27 N8
West End E R Yk 65 L13
West End E R Yk 65 N13
West End E R Yk 65 R11
West End Essex 23 L9
West End Gloucs 28 D9
West End Hants 9 P6
West End Hants 19 T4
West End Herts 31 S11
West End Lancs 62 C9
West End Leeds 63 R12
West End Lincs 59 N6
West End N Som 17 N3
West End N York 63 N9
West End Norfk 50 H12
West End Norfk 51 T11
West End Oxon 19 S4
West End S Glos 28 E10
West End Somset 17 R8
West End Surrey 20 G11
West End Surrey 20 K10
West End W & F 61 T3
West End Wilts 8 C3
West End Wilts 8 D4
West End Wilts 18 E5
West End W Susx 11 L7
West End Green Hants 19 U8
Westenhanger Kent 13 M8
Wester Aberchalder Highld 102 G11
Wester Balblair Highld 102 G6
Westerdale Highld 112 D6
Westerdale N York 71 L11
Westerfield Suffk 41 L11
Westergate W Susx 10 F9
Westerham Kent 21 R12
Westerhope N u Ty 77 P12
Westerland Devon 5 V8
Wester Ochiltree W Loth 82 K4
Wester Pitkierie Fife 91 R10
Wester Ross Highld 107 S9
Westerton W Susx 10 D9
Westerton of Rossie Angus 99 M13
Westerwick Shet 106 s9
West Farleigh Kent 12 D5
West Farndon W Nthn 37 P10
West Felton Shrops 44 H9
Westfield BaNES 17 S6
Westfield Cumb 66 F7
Westfield E Susx 12 F12
Westfield Highld 112 C4
Westfield N Lans 82 E4
Westfield Norfk 50 G12
Westfield Surrey 20 H11
Westfield W Loth 82 H4
Westfields Dorset 7 S3
Westfields of Rattray P & K 90 H3
Westgate Dur 68 K4
Westgate N Linc 58 C5
Westgate Norfk 50 G5
Westgate Hill C Brad 63 Q14
Westgate-on-Sea Kent 13 R1
Westgate Street Norfk 51 L9
West Ginge Oxon 19 Q3
West Grafton Wilts 18 K8
West Green Hants 20 B11
West Grimstead Wilts 8 J3
West Grinstead W Susx 10 K6
West Haddlesey N York 57 S1
West Haddon W Nthn 37 R6
West Hagbourne Oxon 19 R3
West Hagley Worcs 35 U4
West Hallam Derbys 47 M4
West Hallam Common Derbys 47 M5
West Halton N Linc 58 F2
Westham Dorset 7 S9
West Ham Gt Lon 21 Q6
Westham E Susx 11 U9
Westham Somset 17 L7
Westhampnett W Susx 10 D9
West Handley Derbys 57 N11
West Hanney Oxon 19 Q2
West Hanningfield Essex 22 H8
West Hardwick Wakefd 57 P3
West Harnham Wilts 8 G3
West Harptree BaNES 17 Q5
West Harting W Susx 10 B7
West Hatch Somset 16 J12
West Hatch Wilts 8 C3
West Haven Angus 91 R4
Westhay Somset 17 M8
Westhead Lancs 54 K5
West Head Norfk 49 R12
West Heath Birm 36 D5
West Heath Hants 19 S9
West Helmsdale Highld 109 U2
West Hendred Oxon 19 Q3
West Heslerton N York 65 L4
West Hewish N Som 17 L4
Westhide Herefs 35 N12
Westhill Abers 99 Q2
West Hill Devon 6 E6
Westhill Highld 102 K6
West Hoathly W Susx 11 P3
West Holme Dorset 8 B11
Westhope Herefs 35 L10
Westhope Shrops 35 L3
West Horndon Essex 22 F10
Westhorp W Nthn 37 P11
Westhorpe Lincs 48 K7
Westhorpe Suffk 40 J8
West Horrington Somset 17 Q7
West Horsley Surrey 20 J12
West Horton Nthumb 85 R12
West Hougham Kent 13 Q7
Westhoughton Bolton 55 Q5
West Houlland Shet 106 s8
Westhouse N York 62 C5
Westhouses Derbys 47 M2
West Howe BCP 8 F9
West Howetown Somset 16 B9
Westhumble Surrey 20 K12
West Huntspill Somset 16 K8
West Hyde C Beds 31 N8
West Hyde Herts 20 H4
West Hythe Kent 13 M8
West Ilkerton Devon 15 R3
West Ilsley W Berk 19 Q4
West Itchenor W Susx 10 B10
West Keal Lincs 59 P14
West Kennett Wilts 18 H7
West Kilbride N Ayrs 80 J3
West Kingsdown Kent 21 U10
West Kington Wilts 18 B5
West Kirby Wirral 54 F9
West Knapton N York 64 K5
West Knighton Dorset 7 T7
West Knoyle Wilts 8 B2
West Kyloe Nthumb 85 R10
West Lambrook Somset 17 M13
West Langdon Kent 13 R6
West Lavington W Susx 10 D7
West Lavington Wilts 18 F10
West Layton N York 69 P10
West Leake Notts 47 P8
West Learmouth Nthumb 85 L11
West Lees N York 70 H11

West Leigh Devon 15 Q11
Westleigh Devon 15 L8
West Leigh Devon 5 S10
Westleigh Somset 16 E12
Westleigh Wigan 55 Q6
West Lexham Norfk 50 D10
Westley Shrops 44 J12
Westley Suffk 40 D8
Westley Waterless Cambs 39 T9
West Lilling N York 64 E7
Westlington Bucks 30 G10
West Linton Border 83 N8
West Littleton S Glos 28 E12
West Lockinge Oxon 29 T10
West Lulworth Dorset 8 A11
West Lutton N York 65 L6
West Lydford Somset 17 Q10
West Lyng Somset 16 K11
West Lynn Norfk 49 T10
West Malling Kent 12 C4
West Malvern Worcs 35 S11
West Marden W Susx 10 B8
West Markham Notts 58 B12
Westmarsh Kent 13 Q3
West Marsh NE Lin 59 N5
West Marton N York 62 H9
West Meon Hants 9 S4
West Meon Hut Hants 9 T3
West Meon Woodlands Hants 9 S3
West Mersea Essex 23 P5
Westmeston E Susx 11 N8
West Midland Safari Park Worcs 35 T5
Westmill Herts 31 T7
Westmill Herts 31 R6
West Milton Dorset 7 P5
West Minster Kent 23 L13
Westminster Gt Lon 21 N7
Westminster Abbey & Palace Gt Lon 21 N7
West Molesey Surrey 20 K9
West Monkton Somset 16 J11
West Moors Dorset 8 F8
West Morden Dorset 8 C9
West Morriston Border 84 F10
West Morton C Brad 63 M11
West Mudford Somset 17 Q12
Westmuir Angus 98 F13
Westness Ork 106 s17
West Newbiggin Darltn 70 D10
Westnewton Cumb 66 H4
West Newton E R Yk 65 S12
West Newton Norfk 49 U8
West Newton Somset 16 J11
Westnewton Nthumb 85 M12
West Norwood Gt Lon 21 P8
Westoe S Tyne 77 T12
West Ogwell Devon 5 U7
Weston BaNES 17 T3
Weston Ches E 45 R2
Weston Ches E 45 S4
Weston Devon 6 E4
Weston Devon 6 F7
Weston Dorset 7 S10
Weston Halton 55 M10
Weston Hants 9 U3
Weston Herefs 34 J9
Weston Herts 31 S6
Weston Lincs 49 L8
Weston N York 63 P10
Weston Notts 58 B13
Weston Shrops 34 K3
Weston Shrops 45 N8
Weston Staffs 46 B8
Weston W Berk 19 P6
Weston Beggard Herefs 35 N12
Westonbirt Gloucs 28 F10
Weston by Welland N Nthn 37 U2
Weston Colley Hants 19 R13
Weston Colville Cambs 39 T10
Weston Corbett Hants 19 U11
Weston Coyney C Stke 46 B5
Weston Favell W Nthn 37 U8
Weston Green Cambs 39 T10
Weston Heath Shrops 45 S11
Weston Hills Lincs 49 L9
Westoning C Beds 31 M5
Weston-in-Gordano N Som 27 S13
Westoning Woodend C Beds 31 M6
Weston Jones Staffs 45 S9
Weston Longville Norfk 50 K10
Weston Lullingfields Shrops 44 K9
Weston-on-Avon Warwks 36 G10
Weston-on-the-Green Oxon 30 B9
Weston Patrick Hants 19 U11
Weston Rhyn Shrops 44 G6
Weston-sub-Edge Gloucs 36 F12
Weston-super-Mare N Som 16 K4
Weston Turville Bucks 30 J10
Weston-under-Lizard Staffs 45 T11
Weston under Penyard Herefs 28 B3
Weston-under-Redcastle Shrops 45 N8
Weston under Wetherley Warwks 37 L7
Weston Underwood Derbys 46 J5
Weston Underwood M Keyn 38 C10
Westonzoyland Somset 16 K10
West Orchard Dorset 17 V13
West Overton Wilts 18 H7
West Panson Devon 14 J2
West Park Abers 99 P4
West Parley Dorset 8 F9
West Peckham Kent 12 B5
West Peeke Devon 14 J2
West Pelton Dur 69 R2
West Pennard Somset 17 P9
West Pentire Cnwll 3 L4
West Perry Cambs 38 H7
West Pinchbeck Lincs 48 K8
West Porlock Somset 15 U3
Westport Somset 17 L12
West Pulham Dorset 7 T3
West Putford Devon 14 J9
West Quantoxhead Somset 16 F8
Westquarter Falk 82 H3
West Raddon Devon 15 T12
West Rainton Dur 70 D3
West Rasen Lincs 58 J9
West Ravendale NE Lin 59 L7
Westray Ork 106 t15
Westray Airport Ork 106 t14
West Raynham Norfk 50 F8
West Retford Notts 57 U11
Westridge Green W Berk 19 R5
Westrigg W Loth 82 H5
West Rounton N York 70 G12
West Row Suffk 39 T5
West Rudham Norfk 50 D8
West Runton Norfk 51 L5
Westruther Border 84 F9
Westry Cambs 49 N14
West Saltoun E Loth 84 D5
West Sandford Devon 15 T12
West Sandwick Shet 106 u5
West Scrafton N York 63 L3
West Sleekburn Nthumb 77 R9
West Somerton Norfk 51 S10
West Stafford Dorset 7 T7
West Stockwith Notts 58 C7
West Stoke W Susx 10 C9
West Stonesdale N York 68 K12
West Stoughton Somset 17 M7
West Stour Dorset 17 U12
West Stourmouth Kent 13 P3
West Stow Suffk 40 D6
West Stowell Wilts 18 H8
West Stratton Hants 19 R12
West Street Kent 12 K5
West Street Medway 22 J13
West Street Suffk 40 G6
West Tanfield N York 63 R4
West Taphouse Cnwll 4 F8
West Tarbert Ag & B 79 Q5
West Tarring W Susx 10 J10
West Thirston Nthumb 77 P5
West Thorney W Susx 10 B10
West Thorpe Notts 47 R8
West Thurrock Thurr 22 E12
West Tilbury Thurr 22 G13
West Tisted Hants 9 T3
West Torrington Lincs 58 K10
West Town BaNES 17 P4
West Town Hants 9 U9

Place	County	Page	Grid
West Town	Herefs	34	K8
West Town	N Som	17	N3
West Town	Somset	17	P9
West Tytherley	Hants	8	K3
West Walton	Norfk	49	Q11
Westward	Cumb	67	L4
Westward Ho!	Devon	14	K7
Westwell	Kent	12	J6
Westwell	Oxon	29	P6
Westwell Leacon	Kent	12	J6
West Wellow	Hants	9	N11
West Wembury	Devon	5	L11
West Wemyss	Fife	91	M13
Westwick	Cambs	39	N8
Westwick	Dur	69	M4
West Wick	N Som	17	L4
Westwick	Norfk	51	N8
West Wickham	Cambs	39	T11
West Wickham	Gt Lon	21	P9
Westwood	Devon	6	D5
Westwood	Kent	13	S2
Westwood	Notts	47	N3
West Woodburn	Nthumb	76	H8
West Woodhay	W Berk	19	N8
Westwood Heath	Covtry	36	J5
West Woodlands	Somset	17	U8
Westwoodside	N Linc	58	B6
West Worldham	Hants	10	A3
West Worlington	Devon	15	R9
West Worthing	W Susx	10	J10
West Wratting	Cambs	39	T10
West Wycombe	Bucks	20	D4
West Wylam	Nthumb	77	N14
West Yatton	Wilts	18	B5
West Yoke	Kent	12	B2
West Youlstone	Cnwll	14	G9
Wetham Green	Kent	12	F2
Wetheral	Cumb	67	Q2
Wetherby	Leeds	63	U10
Wetherby Services	N York	63	U9
Wetherden	Suffk	40	H8
Wetheringsett	Suffk	40	K7
Wethersfield	Essex	22	H1
Wetherup Street	Suffk	40	K8
Wetley Rocks	Staffs	46	C4
Wettenhall	Ches E	45	P1
Wetton	Staffs	46	F2
Wetwang	E R Yk	65	L9
Wetwood	Staffs	45	S7
Wexcombe	Wilts	19	L9
Wexham	Slough	20	G6
Wexham Street	Bucks	20	G6
Weybourne	Norfk	50	K5
Weybourne	Surrey	20	F13
Weybread	Suffk	41	M4
Weybread Street	Suffk	41	M5
Weybridge	Surrey	20	J9
Weycroft	Devon	6	K5
Weydale	Highld	112	E4
Weyhill	Hants	19	M11
Weymouth	Dorset	7	S9
Whaddon	Bucks	30	H6
Whaddon	Cambs	39	N11
Whaddon	Gloucs	28	F5
Whaddon	Wilts	8	H3
Whaddon	Wilts	18	C8
Whaley	Derbys	57	R12
Whaley Bridge	Derbys	56	F10
Whaley Thorns	Derbys	57	R12
Whaligoe	Highld	112	H8
Whalley	Lancs	62	E12
Whalley Banks	Lancs	62	E12
Whalsay	Shet	106	v7
Whalton	Nthumb	77	N9
Whaplode	Lincs	49	M9
Whaplode Drove	Lincs	49	M11
Wharf	Warwks	37	L10
Wharles	Lancs	61	S12
Wharley End	C Beds	30	K4
Wharncliffe Side	Sheff	57	L8
Wharram-le-Street	N York	64	K6
Wharton	Ches W	45	Q13
Wharton	Herefs	35	M9
Whashton	N York	69	Q11
Whasset	W & F	61	U3
Whatcote	Warwks	36	K12
Whatfield	Suffk	40	H11
Whatley	Somset	7	L3
Whatley	Somset	17	T7
Whatley's End	S Glos	28	C11
Whatlington	E Susx	12	E12
Whatsole Street	Kent	13	M7
Whatstandwell	Derbys	46	K3
Whatton-in-the-Vale	Notts	47	T6
Whauphill	D & G	73	L10
Whaw	N York	69	L12
Wheal Peevor	Cnwll	2	J8
Wheal Rose	Cnwll	2	J8
Wheatacre	Norfk	41	S2
Wheatfield	Oxon	30	E13
Wheathampstead	Herts	31	Q10
Wheathill	Shrops	35	P4
Wheathill	Somset	17	Q10
Wheatley	Hants	10	B2
Wheatley	Oxon	30	C12
Wheatley Hill	Dur	70	E5
Wheatley Hills	Donc	57	S6
Wheatley Lane	Lancs	62	G12
Wheaton Aston	Staffs	45	U11
Wheddon Cross	Somset	16	B9
Wheelbarrow Town	Kent	13	M6
Wheeler End	Bucks	20	D4
Wheeler's Green	Wokham	20	C8
Wheelerstreet	Surrey	10	F2
Wheelock	Ches E	45	S2
Wheelock Heath	Ches E	45	S2
Wheeldale	Wakefd	57	P4
Wheldrake	C York	64	F11
Whelford	Gloucs	29	N8
Whelpley Hill	Bucks	31	L12
Whelpo	Cumb	67	M5
Whelston	Flints	54	F11
Whempstead	Herts	31	T8
Whenby	N York	64	E6
Whepstead	Suffk	40	D9
Wherstead	Suffk	41	L12
Wherwell	Hants	19	N12
Wheston	Derbys	56	H12
Whetsted	Kent	12	C6
Whetstone	Gt Lon	21	N4
Whetstone	Leics	37	Q1
Wheyrigg	Cumb	66	J3
Whicham	Cumb	61	L3
Whichford	Warwks	36	K14
Whickham	Gatesd	77	Q13
Whiddon	Devon	5	R3
Whiddon Down	Devon	5	R2
Whigstreet	Angus	91	Q3
Whilton	Nhants	37	R8
Whimble	Devon	14	J12
Whimple	Devon	6	D5
Whimpwell Green	Norfk	51	Q8
Whinburgh	Norfk	50	H12
Whin Lane End	Lancs	61	R11
Whinnyfold	Abers	105	T9
Whinny Hill	S on T	70	E9
Whippingham	IoW	9	Q10
Whipsnade	C Beds	31	M9
Whipsnade Zoo ZSL	C Beds	31	M9
Whipton	Devon	6	B6
Whirlow	Sheff	57	M9
Whisby	Lincs	58	F13
Whissendine	Rutlnd	48	B11
Whissonsett	Norfk	50	F9
Whistlefield	Ag & B	88	F6
Whistlefield Inn	Ag & B	88	D7
Whistley Green	Wokham	20	C8
Whiston	Knows	55	L8
Whiston	Nhants	38	C8
Whiston	Rothm	57	P9
Whiston	Staffs	45	U8
Whiston	Staffs	46	D4
Whiston Cross	Shrops	35	S13
Whiston Eaves	Staffs	46	D4
Whitacre Fields	Warwks	36	J2
Whitbeck	Cumb	61	L3
Whitbourne	Herefs	35	R9
Whitburn	S Tyne	77	U13
Whitburn	W Loth	82	H6
Whitby	Ches W	54	J11
Whitby	N York	71	Q10
Whitbyheath	Ches W	54	J11
Whitchester	Border	84	J8
Whitchurch	BaNES	17	R3
Whitchurch	Bucks	30	G8
Whitchurch	Cardif	27	L11
Whitchurch	Devon	5	N6
Whitchurch	Hants	19	Q11
Whitchurch	Herefs	27	V4
Whitchurch	Oxon	19	T5
Whitchurch	Pembks	24	D5
Whitchurch	Shrops	45	M5
Whitchurch Canonicorum	Dorset	7	L5
Whitchurch Hill	Oxon	19	T5
Whitcombe	Somset	7	T7
Whitcot	Shrops	34	J3
Whitcott Keysett	Shrops	34	G4
Whiteacre	Kent	13	M6
Whiteash Green	Essex	22	J1
White Ball	Somset	16	F13
Whitebridge	Highld	102	E12
Whitebrook	Mons	27	U6
Whitebushes	Surrey	11	M2
Whitecairns	Abers	105	Q12
Whitechapel	Gt Lon	21	P6
White Chapel	Lancs	62	B11
Whitecliff	Gloucs	27	V6
White Colne	Essex	23	L2
White Coppice	Lancs	55	P3
Whitecraig	E Loth	83	R4
Whitecroft	Gloucs	28	B6
Whitecross	Cnwll	2	E10
White Cross	Cnwll	2	H12
Whitecross	Falk	82	H3
White End	Worcs	35	S14
Whiteface	Highld	109	N7
Whitefarland	N Ayrs	79	R7
Whitefaulds	S Ayrs	80	K11
Whitefield	Bury	55	T5
Whitefield	Devon	15	R5
Whitefield	Somset	16	E11
Whitefield Lane End	Knows	55	L9
Whiteford	Abers	105	L10
Whitegate	Ches W	55	P13
Whitehall	Hants	20	B12
Whitehall	Ork	106	u17
Whitehall	W Susx	10	J6
Whitehaven	Cumb	66	E9
Whitehill	Kent	12	K4
Whitehill	Leics	47	M11
Whitehills	Abers	104	K2
Whitehills	Angus	98	J13
Whitehouse	Abers	104	J13
Whitehouse	Ag & B	79	Q3
Whitehouse Common	Birm	36	F1
Whitekirk	E Loth	84	F2
White Ladies Aston	Worcs	36	B10
Whiteleaf	Bucks	30	H12
White-le-Head	Dur	69	Q2
Whiteley	Hants	9	Q7
Whiteley Bank	IoW	9	R12
Whiteley Green	Ches E	56	D11
Whiteley Village	Surrey	20	J10
Whitemans Green	W Susx	11	N5
White Mill	Carmth	25	S6
Whitemire	Moray	103	Q5
Whitemoor	C Nott	47	Q5
Whitemoor	Cnwll	3	N5
Whitemoor	Derbys	47	L4
Whitemoor	Staffs	45	U2
Whiteness	Shet	106	u9
White Notley	Essex	22	J4
Whiteoak Green	Oxon	29	R5
White Ox Mead	BaNES	17	T5
Whiteparish	Wilts	8	J3
Whiterashes	Abers	105	P11
White Roding	Essex	22	E5
Whiterow	Highld	112	J7
Whiterow	Moray	103	R4
Whiteshill	Gloucs	28	F6
Whiteside	E Susx	11	S8
Whitesmith	E Susx	11	S8
Whitestaunton	Somset	6	J2
Whitestone	Cnwll	4	F6
Whitestone	Devon	5	V2
Whitestone	Warwks	36	K3
Whitestone Cross	Devon	5	V3
Whitestreet Green	Suffk	40	G13
White Waltham	W & M	20	D7
Whiteway	BaNES	17	T4
Whiteway	Gloucs	28	H5
Whitewell	Lancs	62	C10
Whiteworks	Devon	5	Q8
Whitfield	C Dund	91	P5
Whitfield	Kent	13	R6
Whitfield	Nhants	30	E5
Whitfield	Nthumb	76	F14
Whitfield	S Glos	28	C9
Whitfield Hall	Nthumb	76	F14
Whitford	Devon	6	J5
Whitford	Flints	54	D11
Whitgift	E R Yk	58	D2
Whitgreave	Staffs	46	B8
Whithorn	D & G	73	L11
Whiting Bay	N Ayrs	79	S9
Whitkirk	Leeds	63	T13
Whitland	Carmth	25	L7
Whitleigh	C Plym	5	M9
Whitletts	S Ayrs	81	M8
Whitley	N York	57	T1
Whitley	Readg	20	B8
Whitley	Sheff	57	M8
Whitley	Wilts	18	C7
Whitley Bay	N Tyne	77	T11
Whitley Chapel	Nthumb	76	K14
Whitley Heath	Staffs	45	T9
Whitley Lower	Kirk	56	K3
Whitley Row	Kent	21	S12
Whitlock's End	Solhll	36	F5
Whitminster	Gloucs	28	E6
Whitmore	Dorset	8	F7
Whitmore	Staffs	45	T5
Whitnage	Devon	16	D13
Whitnash	Warwks	36	K8
Whitney-on-Wye	Herefs	34	G11
Whitrigg	Cumb	66	K1
Whitrigg	Cumb	67	M3
Whitrigglees	Cumb	66	K1
Whitsbury	Hants	8	G5
Whitsome	Border	85	M8
Whitson	Newpt	27	R11
Whitstable	Kent	13	M2
Whitstone	Cnwll	14	G13
Whittingham	Nthumb	77	M2
Whittingslow	Shrops	34	K3
Whittington	Derbys	57	N12
Whittington	Gloucs	28	K3
Whittington	Lancs	62	C4
Whittington	Norfk	50	B14
Whittington	Shrops	44	H7
Whittington	Staffs	35	U3
Whittington	Staffs	46	G12
Whittington	Warwks	36	G14
Whittington	Worcs	35	U9
Whittington Moor	Derbys	57	N12
Whittlebury	Nhants	30	E4
Whittle-le-Woods	Lancs	55	N2
Whittlesey	Cambs	39	L1
Whittlesford	Cambs	39	Q11
Whittlestone Head	Bl w D	55	R3
Whitton	N Linc	58	F2
Whitton	Nthumb	77	M4
Whitton	Powys	34	G7
Whitton	S on T	70	E8
Whitton	Shrops	35	N6
Whitton	Suffk	40	K11
Whittonditch	Wilts	19	L6
Whittonstall	Nthumb	69	N1
Whitway	Hants	19	Q9
Whitwell	Derbys	57	R11
Whitwell	Herts	31	Q8
Whitwell	IoW	9	Q13
Whitwell	N York	69	S13
Whitwell	Rutlnd	48	D12
Whitwell-on-the-Hill	N York	64	G6
Whitwell Street	Norfk	50	K9
Whitwick	Leics	47	M10
Whitwood	Wakefd	57	P2
Whitworth	Lancs	56	C4
Whixall	Shrops	45	M7
Whixley	N York	63	U8
Whorlton	Dur	69	P9
Whorlton	N York	70	G12
Whyle	Herefs	35	N8
Whyteleafe	Surrey	21	P11
Wibdon	Gloucs	27	V8
Wibsey	C Brad	63	N13
Wibtoft	Warwks	37	N4
Wichelstowe	Swindn	29	M11
Wichenford	Worcs	35	S8
Wichling	Kent	12	J4
Wick	Bmouth	8	H10
Wick	Devon	6	G4
Wick	Highld	112	H6
Wick	S Glos	28	C13
Wick	Somset	16	K8
Wick	Somset	17	M11
Wick	V Glam	16	B2
Wick	W Susx	10	G10
Wick	Worcs	36	C11
Wick Airport	Highld	112	H6
Wicken	Cambs	39	S6
Wicken	Nhants	30	F5
Wicken Bonhunt	Essex	39	Q14
Wickenby	Lincs	58	J10
Wick End	Bed	38	E10
Wicken Green Village	Norfk	50	D7
Wickersley	Rothm	57	Q8
Wicker Street Green	Suffk	40	G12
Wickford	Essex	22	H9
Wickham	Hants	9	R6
Wickham	W Berk	19	N6
Wickham Bishops	Essex	23	L5
Wickhambreaux	Kent	13	P4
Wickhambrook	Suffk	40	B10
Wickhamford	Worcs	36	E12
Wickham Green	Suffk	40	J7
Wickham Green	W Berk	19	N6
Wickham Heath	W Berk	19	P7
Wickham Market	Suffk	41	P9
Wickhampton	Norfk	51	R12
Wickham St Paul	Essex	40	D13
Wickham Skeith	Suffk	40	J7
Wickham Street	Suffk	40	C10
Wickham Street	Suffk	40	J7
Wickhurst Green	W Susx	10	J4
Wicklewood	Norfk	50	J13
Wickmere	Norfk	51	L7
Wick St Lawrence	N Som	17	L3
Wicksteed Park	N Nthn	38	C5
Wickstreet	E Susx	11	S8
Wickwar	S Glos	28	D10
Widcombe	BaNES	17	T4
Widdington	Essex	22	D1
Widdop	Calder	62	J13
Widdrington	Nthumb	77	R7
Widdrington Station	Nthumb	77	Q7
Widecombe in the Moor	Devon	5	S6
Widegates	Cnwll	4	H9
Widemouth Bay	Cnwll	14	F12
Wideopen	N Tyne	77	Q11
Widford	Essex	22	G7
Widford	Herts	22	B5
Widford	Oxon	29	P5
Widley	Hants	9	T7
Widmer End	Bucks	20	E3
Widmerpool	Notts	47	R8
Widmore	Gt Lon	21	Q9
Widnes	Halton	55	M9
Widworthy	Devon	6	H5
Wigan	Wigan	55	N6
Wigborough	Somset	17	M13
Wiggaton	Devon	6	F6
Wiggenhall St Germans	Norfk	49	S11
Wiggenhall St Mary Magdalen	Norfk	49	S11
Wiggenhall St Mary the Virgin	Norfk	49	S11
Wiggenhall St Peter	Norfk	49	T11
Wiggens Green	Essex	39	U12
Wiggenstall	Staffs	46	E2
Wigginton	Herts	30	K10
Wigginton	Oxon	37	L14
Wigginton	Shrops	44	H6
Wigginton	Staffs	46	H11
Wigginton	C York	64	E8
Wigginton Bottom	Herts	30	K11
Wigglesworth	N York	62	G8
Wiggonby	Cumb	67	L2
Wiggonholt	W Susx	10	H7
Wighill	N York	64	B10
Wighton	Norfk	50	F6
Wigley	Hants	9	L5
Wigmore	Herefs	34	K7
Wigmore	Medway	12	E3
Wigsley	Notts	58	D12
Wigsthorpe	N Nhants	38	F4
Wigston	Leics	47	R14
Wigston Fields	Leics	47	R13
Wigston Parva	Leics	37	N3
Wigthorpe	Notts	57	S10
Wigtoft	Lincs	49	L6
Wigton	Cumb	67	L3
Wigtown	D & G	73	L8
Wike	Leeds	63	S11
Wilbarston	Nhants	38	B3
Wilberfoss	E R Yk	64	G9
Wilburton	Cambs	39	Q5
Wilby	Nhants	38	C8
Wilby	Norfk	40	H3
Wilby	Suffk	41	M6
Wilcot	Wilts	18	H8
Wilcott	Shrops	44	J10
Wilcove	Cnwll	5	L9
Wilcrick	Newpt	27	S10
Wilday Green	Derbys	57	M12
Wildboarclough	Ches E	56	E13
Wilden	Bed	38	G9
Wilden	Worcs	35	T6
Wildhern	Hants	19	N10
Wildhill	Herts	31	S11
Wildmanbridge	S Lans	82	F8
Wildmill	Brdgnd	26	G11
Wildmoor	Hants	20	B10
Wildmoor	Worcs	36	C5
Wildsworth	Lincs	58	C7
Wilford	C Nott	47	Q6
Wilkesley	Ches E	45	P5
Wilkhaven	Highld	109	S7
Wilkieston	W Loth	83	M5
Wilkin's Green	Herts	31	R11
Wilksby	Lincs	59	N14
Willand	Devon	6	D2
Willards Hill	E Susx	12	D11
Willaston	Ches E	45	R3
Willaston	Ches W	54	H11
Willen	M Keyn	30	J5
Willenhall	Covtry	37	L5
Willenhall	Wsall	46	C14
Willerby	E R Yk	65	N13
Willerby	N York	65	N4
Willersey	Gloucs	36	F13
Willersley	Herefs	34	H11
Willesborough	Kent	12	K7
Willesborough Lees	Kent	13	L7
Willesden	Gt Lon	21	M6
Willesleigh	Devon	15	N6
Willesley	Wilts	18	B10
Willett	Somset	16	F10
Willey	Shrops	45	Q14
Willey	Warwks	37	N4
Willey Green	Surrey	20	G12
Williamscote	Oxon	37	M11
Williamstown	Rhondd	26	J9
Willian	Herts	31	S6
Willicote	Warwks	36	G11
Willingale	Essex	22	E6
Willingdon	E Susx	11	U10
Willingham	Cambs	39	P6
Willingham by Stow	Lincs	58	E10
Willingham Green	Cambs	39	T10
Willingham St Mary	Suffk	41	R4
Willington	Bed	38	H10
Willington	Derbys	46	J8
Willington	Dur	69	Q5
Willington	Kent	12	E5
Willington	Warwks	36	J13
Willington Corner	Ches W	55	M13
Willitoft	E R Yk	64	G13
Williton	Somset	16	E8
Willoughby	Lincs	59	S12
Willoughby	Warwks	37	P7
Willoughby Hills	Lincs	49	N3
Willoughby-on-the-Wolds	Notts	47	R8
Willoughby Waterleys	Leics	37	Q2
Wilton	N York	64	K3
Wilton	R & Cl	70	J9
Wilton	Wilts	19	L8
Wilton	Wilts	8	F2
Wilton Dean	Border	75	U3
Wimbish	Essex	39	S13
Wimbish Green	Essex	39	T13
Wimbledon	Gt Lon	21	M8
Wimblington	Cambs	39	P2
Wimboldsley	Ches W	55	Q13
Wimborne Minster	Dorset	8	E9
Wimborne St Giles	Dorset	8	E6
Wimbotsham	Norfk	49	T12
Wimpole	Cambs	39	N11
Wimpstone	Warwks	36	H11
Wincanton	Somset	17	T11
Winceby	Lincs	59	P13
Wincham	Ches W	55	Q11
Winchburgh	W Loth	83	L3
Winchcombe	Gloucs	28	K2
Winchelsea	E Susx	12	H12
Winchelsea Beach	E Susx	12	H12
Winchester	Hants	9	P2
Winchester Services	Hants	9	P3
Winchet Hill	Kent	12	D7
Winchfield	Hants	20	C12
Winchmore Hill	Bucks	20	F4
Winchmore Hill	Gt Lon	21	P4
Wincle	Ches E	56	E13
Wincobank	Sheff	57	N8
Winder	Cumb	66	G11
Windermere	Cumb	67	P13
Windermere Jetty Museum	W & F	67	P13
Winderton	Warwks	36	K12
Windhill	Highld	102	G6
Windlehurst	Stockp	56	E9
Windlesham	Surrey	20	F10
Windmill	Cnwll	3	M2
Windmill	Derbys	56	J11
Windmill Hill	E Susx	11	U8
Windmill Hill	Somset	16	K13
Windrush	Gloucs	29	N5
Windsole	Abers	104	F3
Windsor	W & M	20	G7
Windsor Castle	W & M	20	G7
Windsoredge	Gloucs	28	F7
Windsor Green	Suffk	40	E10
Windy Arbour	Warwks	36	J6
Windygates	Fife	91	M11
Windyharbour	Ches E	56	C12
Windy Hill	Wrexhm	44	H3
Wineham	W Susx	11	L6
Winestead	E R Yk	59	L1
Winewall	Lancs	62	J11
Winfarthing	Norfk	40	K3
Winford	IoW	9	R12
Winford	N Som	17	P4
Winforton	Herefs	34	G11
Winfrith Newburgh	Dorset	7	V8
Wing	Bucks	30	J8
Wing	Rutlnd	48	C13
Wingate	Dur	70	F5
Wingates	Bolton	55	P5
Wingates	Nthumb	77	M6
Wingerworth	Derbys	57	M13
Wingfield	C Beds	31	M7
Wingfield	Suffk	41	M5
Wingfield	Wilts	18	B9
Wingfield Green	Suffk	41	M5
Wingham	Kent	13	P4
Wingland	Lincs	49	R9
Wingmore	Kent	13	N6
Wingrave	Bucks	30	J9
Winkburn	Notts	47	T2
Winkfield	Br For	20	F8
Winkfield Row	Br For	20	E8
Winkhill	Staffs	46	E3
Winkhurst Green	Kent	21	S13
Winkleigh	Devon	15	P10
Winksley	N York	63	R5
Winkton	BCP	8	H9
Winlaton	Gatesd	77	P13
Winlaton Mill	Gatesd	77	P13
Winless	Highld	112	H6
Winllan	Powys	44	F9
Winmarleigh	Lancs	61	T10
Winnall	Hants	9	P2
Winnersh	Wokham	20	C8
Winnington	Ches W	55	Q12
Winscales	Cumb	66	F7
Winsford	Ches W	55	Q13
Winsford	Somset	16	B10
Winsham	Devon	15	L5
Winsham	Somset	7	L3
Winshill	Staffs	46	J9
Winshwen	Swans	26	B8
Winskill	W & F	67	S6
Winslade	Hants	19	U11
Winsley	Wilts	18	B8
Winslow	Bucks	30	G7
Winsor	Hants	9	L5
Winstanley	Wigan	55	N6
Winster	Derbys	46	J1
Winster	W & F	67	P13
Winston	Dur	69	P9
Winston	Suffk	41	L8
Winstone	Gloucs	28	H6
Winswell	Devon	15	L9
Winterborne Came	Dorset	7	T7
Winterborne Clenston	Dorset	8	A8
Winterborne Herringston	Dorset	7	S7
Winterborne Houghton	Dorset	8	A7
Winterborne Kingston	Dorset	8	B8
Winterborne Monkton	Dorset	7	S7
Winterborne Stickland	Dorset	8	A8
Winterborne Tomson	Dorset	8	B8
Winterborne Whitechurch	Dorset	8	A8
Winterborne Zelston	Dorset	8	B9
Winterbourne	S Glos	28	B11
Winterbourne	W Berk	19	Q6
Winterbourne Abbas	Dorset	7	R6
Winterbourne Bassett	Wilts	18	H5
Winterbourne Dauntsey	Wilts	8	H2
Winterbourne Earls	Wilts	8	H2
Winterbourne Gunner	Wilts	8	H2
Winterbourne Monkton	Wilts	18	H5
Winterbourne Steepleton	Dorset	7	R7
Winterbourne Stoke	Wilts	18	G12
Winterbrook	Oxon	19	T3
Winterburn	N York	62	J8
Winteringham	N Linc	58	F2
Wintersett	Wakefd	57	N3
Winterslow	Wilts	8	J2
Winterton	N Linc	58	F3
Winterton-on-Sea	Norfk	51	S10
Winthorpe	Lincs	59	T13
Winthorpe	Notts	48	B2
Winton	BCP	8	F9
Winton	Cumb	68	H10
Winton	E Susx	11	S10
Winton	N York	70	G13
Wintringham	N York	64	K5
Winwick	Cambs	38	H4
Winwick	Nhants	37	R6
Winwick	Warrtn	55	P7
Wirksworth	Derbys	46	J3
Wirral		54	F9
Wirswall	Ches E	45	M4
Wisbech	Cambs	49	Q12
Wisbech St Mary	Cambs	49	P12
Wisborough Green	W Susx	10	H5
Wiseman's Bridge	Pembks	25	L10
Wiseton	Notts	58	B9
Wishanger	Gloucs	28	H6
Wishaw	N Lans	82	E7
Wishaw	Warwks	36	G2
Wisley	Surrey	20	J11
Wispington	Lincs	59	L12
Wissenden	Kent	12	J7
Wissett	Suffk	41	Q5
Wissington	Suffk	40	G13
Wistanstow	Shrops	34	K4
Wistanswick	Shrops	45	Q8
Wistaston	Ches E	45	Q3
Wistaston Green	Ches E	45	Q3
Wisterfield	Ches E	56	C12
Wiston	Pembks	24	H7
Wiston	S Lans	82	J12
Wiston	W Susx	10	J8
Wistow	Cambs	39	L4
Wistow	Leics	37	S1
Wistow	N York	64	D13
Wiswell	Lancs	62	E12
Witcham	Cambs	39	Q3
Witchampton	Dorset	8	D7
Witchford	Cambs	39	R4
Witcombe	Somset	17	N12
Witham	Essex	22	K5
Witham Friary	Somset	17	T8
Witham on the Hill	Lincs	48	G10
Witham St Hughs	Lincs	48	C1
Withcall	Lincs	59	N10
Withdean	Br & H	11	N9
Witherenden Hill	E Susx	12	B10
Witheridge	Devon	15	T9
Witherley	Leics	36	K1
Withern	Lincs	59	R10
Withernsea	E R Yk	65	U14
Withernwick	E R Yk	65	R10
Withersdale Street	Suffk	41	N4
Withersfield	Suffk	39	U11
Witherslack	W & F	61	S3
Withiel	Cnwll	3	N3
Withiel Florey	Somset	16	C10
Withielgoose	Cnwll	3	Q3
Withington	Gloucs	28	K5
Withington	Herefs	35	N12
Withington	Manch	55	T8
Withington	Shrops	45	N11
Withington	Staffs	46	D6
Withington Green	Ches E	56	C12
Withington Marsh	Herefs	35	N12
Withleigh	Devon	16	B12
Withnell	Lancs	55	P2
Withnell Fold	Lancs	55	P2
Withybed Green	Worcs	36	D6
Withybrook	Warwks	37	M4
Withycombe	Somset	16	D8
Withyham	E Susx	11	S3
Withy Mills	BaNES	17	S5
Withypool	Somset	15	U7
Withywood	Brist	17	Q3
Witley	Surrey	10	E3
Witnesham	Suffk	41	L10
Witney	Oxon	29	S5
Wittering	C Pete	48	G13
Wittersham	Kent	12	H10
Witton	Birm	36	E2
Witton	Norfk	51	N11
Witton	Norfk	51	P12
Witton Gilbert	Dur	69	R3
Witton Green	Norfk	51	R13
Witton le Wear	Dur	69	Q5
Witton Park	Dur	69	Q6
Wiveliscombe	Somset	16	E11
Wivelrod	Hants	19	U13
Wivelsfield	E Susx	11	N6
Wivelsfield Green	E Susx	11	N7
Wivelsfield Station	W Susx	11	N7
Wivenhoe	Essex	23	P3
Wivenhoe Cross	Essex	23	P3
Wiveton	Norfk	50	H5
Wix	Essex	23	R2
Wixams	Bed	38	F11
Wixford	Warwks	36	E10
Wixhill	Shrops	45	N8
Wixoe	Suffk	40	B12
Woburn	C Beds	31	L6
Woburn Safari Park	C Beds	31	L6
Woburn Sands	M Keyn	30	K5
Wokefield Park	W Berk	19	U8
Woking	Surrey	20	H11
Wokingham	Wokham	20	D9
Wolborough	Devon	5	V6
Woldingham	Surrey	21	P11
Wold Newton	E R Yk	65	N5
Wold Newton	NE Lin	59	M7
Wolfclyde	S Lans	82	K12
Wolferlow	Herefs	35	Q8
Wolferton	Norfk	49	T8
Wolfhampcote	Warwks	37	P7
Wolfhill	P & K	90	J4
Wolf Hills	Nthumb	76	E14
Wolf's Castle	Pembks	24	G5
Wolfsdale	Pembks	24	F6
Wollaston	Dudley	35	U4
Wollaston	Nhants	38	D8
Wollaston	Shrops	44	J11
Wollaton	C Nott	47	P6
Wollaton Hall	C Nott	47	P6
Wollerton	Shrops	45	P8
Wollescote	Dudley	35	U4
Wolseley Bridge	Staffs	46	D9
Wolsingham	Dur	69	N5
Wolstanton	Staffs	45	T4
Wolston	Warwks	37	M5
Wolsty	Cumb	66	H2
Wolvercote	Oxon	29	U6
Wolverhampton	Wolves	46	B14
Wolverhampton Halfpenny Green Airport	Staffs	35	U3
Wolverley	Shrops	45	L7
Wolverley	Worcs	35	T6
Wolverton	Hants	19	R9
Wolverton	Kent	13	N7
Wolverton	M Keyn	30	H4
Wolverton	Warwks	36	J8
Wolverton	Wilts	17	U10
Wolverton Common	Hants	19	R9
Wolvesnewton	Mons	27	T8
Wolvey	Warwks	37	M4
Wolvey Heath	Warwks	37	M4
Wolviston	S on T	70	G7
Wombleton	N York	64	F3
Wombourne	Staffs	35	U2
Wombwell	Barns	57	N5
Womenswold	Kent	13	P5
Womersley	N York	57	R3
Wonastow	Mons	27	S5
Wonersh	Surrey	20	H13
Wonford	Devon	6	B6
Wonson	Devon	5	R3
Wonston	Dorset	7	U3
Wonston	Hants	19	Q13
Wooburn	Bucks	20	F5
Wooburn Green	Bucks	20	F5
Wooburn Moor	Bucks	20	F5
Woodacott	Devon	14	J11
Woodale	N York	69	L14
Woodall	Rothm	57	Q9
Woodall Services	Rothm	57	Q10
Woodbank	Ches W	54	H12
Woodbastwick	Norfk	51	P11
Woodbeck	Notts	58	C11
Wood Bevington	Warwks	36	E10
Woodborough	Notts	47	R4
Woodborough	Wilts	18	H9
Woodbridge	Devon	6	G5
Woodbridge	Dorset	8	B5
Woodbridge	Suffk	41	N11
Wood Burcote	Nhants	30	E4
Woodbury	Devon	6	D7
Woodbury Salterton	Devon	6	D7
Woodchester	Gloucs	28	F7
Woodchurch	Kent	12	J8
Woodchurch	Wirral	54	G10
Woodcombe	Somset	16	C7
Woodcote	Gt Lon	21	N10
Woodcote	Oxon	19	T4
Woodcote	Wrekin	45	S10
Woodcote Green	Worcs	36	C6
Woodcott	Hants	19	Q10
Woodcroft	Gloucs	27	V9
Wood Dalling	Norfk	50	J8
Woodditton	Cambs	39	U9
Woodeaton	Oxon	30	B10
Wood Eaton	Staffs	45	T10
Wood End	Bed	38	F8
Wood End	Bed	38	F9
Woodend	Cumb	66	K13
Wood End	Gt Lon	20	K6
Wood End	Herts	31	T7
Woodend	Nhants	30	D4
Woodend	Highld	93	S6
Woodend	Staffs	46	G9
Woodend	W Loth	82	H4
Woodend	W Susx	10	C9
Wood End	Warwks	36	G5
Wood End	Warwks	36	H4
Wood End	Warwks	36	J2
Wood End	Wolves	46	C14
Wood Enderby	Lincs	59	M14
Woodend Green	Essex	22	D2
Woodfalls	Wilts	8	H4
Woodfield	Oxon	29	U3
Woodfield	S Ayrs	81	L7
Woodford	Cnwll	14	F9
Woodford	Devon	5	T9
Woodford	Gloucs	28	C8
Woodford	Gt Lon	21	R4
Woodford	Nhants	38	E5
Woodford	Stockp	56	D10
Woodford Bridge	Gt Lon	21	R4
Woodford Green	Gt Lon	21	R4
Woodford Halse	Nhants	37	P10
Woodford Wells	Gt Lon	21	R4
Woodgate	Birm	36	C4
Woodgate	Devon	16	F13
Woodgate	Norfk	50	H10
Woodgate	Norfk	50	J9
Woodgate	W Susx	10	F10
Woodgate	Worcs	36	C7
Wood Green	Gt Lon	21	P4
Woodgreen	Hants	8	H5
Woodgreen	Oxon	29	S5
Woodhall	Herts	31	S9
Woodhall Hill	Leeds	63	Q12
Woodhall Spa	Lincs	59	L14
Woodham	Dur	69	S7
Woodham	Surrey	20	J10
Woodham Ferrers	Essex	22	J8
Woodham Mortimer	Essex	22	K7
Woodham Walter	Essex	22	K6
Woodhaven	Fife	91	P6
Wood Hayes	Wolves	46	B13
Woodhead	Abers	105	M8
Woodhill	Shrops	35	S3
Woodhill	Somset	17	L11
Woodhorn	Nthumb	77	R8
Woodhouse	Leeds	63	R13
Woodhouse	Leics	47	P11
Woodhouse	Sheff	57	P9
Woodhouse	Wakefd	57	N2
Woodhouse Eaves	Leics	47	P10
Woodhouse Green	Staffs	56	D14
Woodhouselee	Mdloth	83	P6
Woodhouselees	D & G	75	R10
Woodhouse Mill	Sheff	57	P9
Woodhouses	Cumb	67	L2
Woodhouses	Oldham	56	D6
Woodhouses	Staffs	46	G11
Woodhouses	Staffs	46	F10
Woodhuish	Devon	6	B14
Woodhurst	Cambs	39	M5
Woodingdean	Br & H	11	P9
Woodkirk	Leeds	57	L1
Woodland	Devon	5	T7
Woodland	Devon	5	U9
Woodland	Dur	69	N7
Woodland	Kent	13	M7
Woodland	S Ayrs	80	K10
Woodland Head	Devon	5	S13
Woodlands	Donc	57	Q5
Woodlands	Dorset	8	F7
Woodlands	Hants	9	L6
Woodlands	Kent	21	U10
Woodlands	N York	63	S8
Woodlands	Somset	16	G8
Woodlands Park	W & M	20	E7
Woodlands St Mary	W Berk	19	M5
Woodland Street	Somset	17	Q9
Woodland View	Sheff	57	M9
Woodlane	Staffs	46	F9
Woodleigh	Devon	5	S11
Woodlesford	Leeds	57	M1
Woodley	Stockp	56	E8
Woodley	Wokham	20	C8
Woodmancote	Gloucs	28	J2
Woodmancote	Gloucs	28	E7
Woodmancote	Gloucs	28	J6
Woodmancote	W Susx	9	U8
Woodmancote	W Susx	11	L8
Woodmancott	Hants	19	S12
Woodmansey	E R Yk	65	N12
Woodmansgreen	W Susx	10	D5
Woodmansterne	Surrey	21	N11
Woodmanton	Devon	6	D7
Woodmarsh	Wilts	18	B9
Woodmill	Staffs	46	F9
Woodminton	Wilts	8	E3
Woodnesborough	Kent	13	R4
Woodnewton	N Nhants	38	G2
Wood Norton	Norfk	50	H8
Woodplumpton	Lancs	61	T13
Woodrising	Norfk	50	G12
Wood Row	Leeds	57	M1
Wood's Corner	E Susx	11	V7
Woods Eaves	Herefs	34	G11
Woodseaves	Shrops	45	Q8
Woodseaves	Staffs	45	S8
Woodsend	Wilts	18	K5
Woodsetts	Rothm	57	R10
Woodsford	Dorset	7	U6
Wood's Green	E Susx	12	B8
Woodside	Br For	20	F8
Woodside	Cumb	66	F6
Woodside	Fife	91	Q10
Woodside	Gt Lon	21	Q9
Woodside	Hants	9	L10
Woodside	Herts	31	R11
Woodside	P & K	90	J4
Woodside Green	Kent	12	J5
Woodstock	Oxon	29	U4
Woodstock	Pembks	24	H6
Woodston	C Pete	38	J1
Wood Street	Norfk	51	Q9
Wood Street Village	Surrey	20	G12
Woodthorpe	Derbys	57	Q12
Woodthorpe	Leics	47	P10
Woodthorpe	Lincs	59	R10
Woodthorpe	Notts	47	Q5
Woodton	Norfk	41	N2
Woodtown	Devon	14	K8
Woodtown	Devon	14	K8
Woodvale	Sefton	54	H4
Woodville	Derbys	46	K10
Woodwall Green	Staffs	45	S7
Wood Walton	Cambs	39	L4
Woodyates	Dorset	8	E5
Woofferton	Shrops	35	M7
Wookey	Somset	17	P7
Wookey Hole	Somset	17	P7
Wool	Dorset	8	A10
Woolacombe	Devon	15	L3
Woolage Green	Kent	13	P6
Woolage Village	Kent	13	P5
Woolaston	Gloucs	27	V7
Woolaston Common	Gloucs	28	A7
Woolavington	Somset	16	K8
Woolbeding	W Susx	10	D5
Woolbrook	Devon	6	F7
Wooldale	Kirk	56	J5
Wooler	Nthumb	85	N12
Woolfardisworthy	Devon	14	H8
Woolfardisworthy	Devon	15	T10
Woolfold	Bury	55	S5
Woolfords	S Lans	82	K7
Woolhampton	W Berk	19	S7
Woolhope	Herefs	35	P13
Woolland	Dorset	7	U3
Woollard	BaNES	17	R4
Woollaton	Devon	14	K10
Woolley	BaNES	17	T4
Woolley	Cambs	38	J6
Woolley	Cnwll	14	F9
Woolley	Derbys	57	M14
Woolley	Wakefd	57	M4
Woolley Bridge	Derbys	56	F8
Woolley Edge Services	Wakefd	57	M4
Woolmere Green	Worcs	36	C8
Woolmer Green	Herts	31	S9
Woolminstone	Somset	7	M3
Woolpack	Kent	12	H8
Woolpit	Suffk	40	G8
Woolscott	Warwks	37	N7
Woolsgrove	Devon	15	T11
Woolsington	N u Ty	77	P12
Woolstaston	Shrops	35	L2
Woolsthorpe	Lincs	48	C7
Woolsthorpe by Colsterworth	Lincs	48	D9
Woolston	C Sotn	9	P6
Woolston	Devon	5	S11
Woolston	Shrops	34	J6
Woolston	Shrops	44	J9
Woolston	Somset	16	E10
Woolston	Somset	17	R10
Woolston	Warrtn	55	P8
Woolstone	Gloucs	28	J1
Woolstone	M Keyn	30	J5
Woolstone	Oxon	29	Q10
Woolston Green	Devon	5	T7
Woolton	Lpool	54	K9
Woolton Hill	Hants	19	P8
Woolverstone	Suffk	41	L13
Woolverton	Somset	17	U5
Woolwich	Gt Lon	21	R7
Woonton	Herefs	34	J10
Woonton	Herefs	35	N8
Wooperton	Nthumb	85	P13
Woore	Shrops	45	R5
Wootten Green	Suffk	41	M6
Wootton	Bed	38	F11
Wootton	Hants	8	K9
Wootton	Kent	13	P6
Wootton	N Linc	58	H3
Wootton	N Nhants	37	U9
Wootton	Oxon	29	T5
Wootton	Oxon	29	U7
Wootton	Shrops	44	H8
Wootton	Staffs	45	T8
Wootton	Staffs	46	F5
Wootton Bassett	Wilts	18	G4
Wootton Bridge	IoW	9	R10
Wootton Broadmead	Bed	31	M4
Wootton Common	IoW	9	R10
Wootton Courtenay	Somset	16	B8
Wootton Fitzpaine	Dorset	7	L5
Wootton Rivers	Wilts	18	J8
Wootton St Lawrence	Hants	19	S10
Wootton Wawen	Warwks	36	G8
Worcester	Worcs	35	U10
Worcester Park	Gt Lon	21	M9
Wordsley	Dudley	35	U3
Worfield	Shrops	35	S2
Worgret	Dorset	8	C11
Workhouse End	Bed	38	G10
Workhouse Green	Suffk	40	G13
Workington	Cumb	66	E8
Worksop	Notts	57	S11
Worlaby	Lincs	59	L11
Worlaby	N Linc	58	H4
Worlds End	Bucks	30	J11
World's End	Hants	9	T6
World's End	W Berk	19	Q5
Worlds End	W Susx	11	M6
Worleston	Ches E	45	Q3
Worlingham	Suffk	41	R3
Worlington	Devon	15	T10
Worlington	Suffk	39	U6
Worlingworth	Suffk	41	M7
Wormald Green	N York	63	S6
Wormbridge	Herefs	27	R1
Wormegay	Norfk	49	T11
Wormelow Tump	Herefs	27	T1
Wormhill	Derbys	56	H12
Wormhill	Herefs	34	K12
Wormingford	Essex	23	N2
Worminghall	Bucks	30	D11
Wormington	Gloucs	36	D13
Worminster	Somset	17	Q8
Wormit	Fife	91	P6
Wormleighton	Warwks	37	N10
Wormley	Herts	31	U11
Wormley	Surrey	10	E3
Wormleybury	Herts	31	U11
Wormley Hill	Donc	57	T3
Wormshill	Kent	12	G4
Wormsley	Herefs	34	K11
Worplesdon	Surrey	20	G12
Worrall	Sheff	57	M8
Worsbrough	Barns	57	N5
Worsbrough Bridge	Barns	57	N5
Worsbrough Dale	Barns	57	N5
Worsley	Salfd	55	S6
Worstead	Norfk	51	P8
Worsthorne	Lancs	62	H13
Worston	Devon	5	N10
Worston	Lancs	62	F11
Worth	Kent	13	R4
Worth	Somset	17	N7
Worth	W Susx	11	M3
Wortham	Suffk	40	J5
Worthen	Shrops	44	J12
Worthenbury	Wrexhm	44	K4
Worthing	Norfk	50	G10
Worthing	W Susx	10	J10
Worthington	Leics	47	M9
Worth Matravers	Dorset	8	D13
Worthybrook	Mons	27	T5
Worting	Hants	19	T9
Wortley	Barns	57	M7
Wortley	Leeds	63	R13
Worton	N York	63	L1
Worton	Wilts	18	E9
Wortwell	Norfk	41	N3
Wotherton	Shrops	44	G13
Wothorpe	C Pete	48	F13
Wotter	Devon	5	P8
Wotton	Surrey	20	K13
Wotton Underwood	Bucks	30	D10
Wotton-under-Edge	Gloucs	28	D9
Woughton on the Green	M Keyn	30	J5
Wouldham	Kent	12	D3
Woundale	Shrops	35	S2
Wrabness	Essex	23	R1
Wrafton	Devon	15	L5
Wragby	Lincs	58	K11
Wragby	Wakefd	57	N3
Wramplingham	Norfk	50	K12
Wrangaton	Devon	5	R9
Wrangbrook	Wakefd	57	Q4
Wrangle	Lincs	49	P2
Wrangle Common	Lincs	49	P2
Wrangle Lowgate	Lincs	49	P2
Wrangway	Somset	16	F13
Wrantage	Somset	16	K12
Wrawby	N Linc	58	H5
Wraxall	N Som	17	N2
Wraxall	Somset	17	R9
Wray	Lancs	62	C6
Wraysbury	W & M	20	H7
Wrayton	Lancs	62	C5
Wrea Green	Lancs	61	R13
Wreaks End	Cumb	61	N2
Wreay	Cumb	67	P3
Wreay	Cumb	67	N4
Wrecclesham	Surrey	10	D2
Wrekenton	Gatesd	77	R14
Wrelton	N York	64	G2
Wrenbury	Ches E	45	N4
Wrench Green	N York	65	L2
Wreningham	Norfk	41	L1
Wrentham	Suffk	41	S4
Wrenthorpe	Wakefd	57	M2
Wrentnall	Shrops	44	K12
Wressle	E R Yk	64	G13
Wressle	N Linc	58	F5
Wrestlingworth	C Beds	39	L11
Wretham	Norfk	40	F3
Wretton	Norfk	49	U13
Wrexham	Wrexhm	44	H3
Wrexham Industrial Estate	Wrexhm	44	K3
Wribbenhall	Worcs	35	S6
Wrickton	Shrops	35	P3
Wrightington Bar	Lancs	55	M4
Wright's Green	Essex	22	D4
Wrinehill	Staffs	45	S4
Wrington	N Som	17	N4
Writhlington	BaNES	17	T5
Writtle	Essex	22	G6
Wrockwardine	Wrekin	45	P11
Wroot	N Linc	58	B5
Wrose	C Brad	63	P12
Wrotham	Kent	12	B3
Wrotham Heath	Kent	12	B4
Wrottesley	Staffs	45	T13
Wroughton	Swindn	18	H4
Wroxall	IoW	9	R13
Wroxall	Warwks	36	H6
Wroxeter	Shrops	45	N12
Wroxham	Norfk	51	P11
Wroxton	Oxon	37	M12
Wyaston	Derbys	46	G5
Wyatt's Green	Essex	22	F8
Wyberton	Lincs	49	M5
Wyboston	Bed	38	J9
Wybunbury	Ches E	45	R4
Wychbold	Worcs	36	B8
Wych Cross	E Susx	11	Q3
Wychnor	Staffs	46	G10
Wychnor Bridges	Staffs	46	G10
Wyck	Hants	10	B3
Wyck Rissington	Gloucs	29	N4
Wycliffe	Dur	69	P10
Wycoller	Lancs	62	J12
Wycomb	Leics	47	U9
Wycombe Marsh	Bucks	20	E4
Wyddial	Herts	31	U5
Wye	Kent	13	L6
Wyesham	Mons	27	U5
Wyfordby	Leics	47	U10
Wyke	C Brad	63	P14
Wyke	Devon	5	V2
Wyke	Devon	6	J4
Wyke	Shrops	45	P12
Wyke	Surrey	20	F12
Wyke Champflower	Somset	17	S10
Wykeham	N York	64	H3
Wykeham	N York	65	L3
Wyken	Covtry	37	L4
Wyken	Shrops	35	S2
Wyke Regis	Dorset	7	S9
Wykey	Shrops	44	J9
Wykin	Leics	47	M14
Wylam	Nthumb	77	N13
Wylde Green	Birm	36	F2
Wyllie	Caerph	27	M8
Wylye	Wilts	18	F13
Wymering	C Port	9	S7
Wymeswold	Leics	47	R9
Wymington	Bed	38	E8
Wymondham	Leics	48	B11
Wymondham	Norfk	50	K13
Wyndham	Brdgnd	26	H9
Wynford Eagle	Dorset	7	P5
Wynyard Park	S on T	70	F7
Wynyard Village	S on T	70	F7
Wyre Piddle	Worcs	36	C11
Wysall	Notts	47	R8
Wyson	Herefs	35	M7
Wythall	Worcs	36	E5
Wytham	Oxon	29	U6
Wythburn	Cumb	67	M10
Wythenshawe	Manch	55	T9
Wythop Mill	Cumb	66	J7
Wyton	Cambs	39	L7
Wyton	E R Yk	65	R13
Wyverstone	Suffk	40	H7
Wyverstone Street	Suffk	40	H7
Wyville	Lincs	48	C8

Y

Place	County	Page	Grid
Yaddlethorpe	N Linc	58	E5
Yafford	IoW	9	N12
Yafforth	N York	70	D14
Yalberton	Torbay	6	A13
Yalding	Kent	12	C5
Yanwath	W & F	67	Q7
Yanworth	Gloucs	29	L5
Yapham	E R Yk	64	H9
Yapton	W Susx	10	F10
Yarburgh	Lincs	59	Q8
Yarcombe	Devon	6	H3
Yard	Devon	15	S8
Yardley	Birm	36	F3
Yardley Gobion	Nhants	30	G4
Yardley Hastings	N Nhants	38	C9
Yardley Wood	Birm	36	F4
Yardro	Powys	34	F9
Yarford	Somset	16	H10
Yarkhill	Herefs	35	P12
Yarley	Somset	17	P8
Yarlet	Staffs	45	U8
Yarlington	Somset	17	R11
Yarm	S on T	70	F10
Yarmouth	IoW	9	M11
Yarnacott	Devon	15	N6
Yarnbrook	Wilts	18	C9
Yarnfield	Staffs	45	U7
Yarnscombe	Devon	15	N8
Yarnton	Oxon	29	U5
Yarpole	Herefs	35	L8
Yarrow	Border	83	R13
Yarrow	Somset	17	L8
Yarrow Feus	Border	83	Q13
Yarrowford	Border	83	S13
Yarsop	Herefs	34	K11
Yarwell	N Nhants	38	G1
Yate	S Glos	28	D11
Yateley	Hants	20	D10
Yatesbury	Wilts	18	G6
Yattendon	W Berk	19	S6
Yatton	Herefs	34	K7
Yatton	N Som	17	M4
Yatton Keynell	Wilts	18	C5
Yaverland	IoW	9	S12
Yawl	Devon	6	K6
Yaxham	Norfk	50	H11
Yaxley	Cambs	38	J2
Yaxley	Suffk	40	K6
Yazor	Herefs	34	K11
Yeading	Gt Lon	20	K6
Yeadon	Leeds	63	Q11
Yealand Conyers	Lancs	61	U4
Yealand Redmayne	Lancs	61	U4
Yealand Storrs	Lancs	61	T4
Yealmbridge	Devon	5	P10
Yealmpton	Devon	5	P10
Yearby	R & Cl	70	J8
Yearngill	Cumb	66	J4
Yearsley	N York	64	E5
Yeaton	Shrops	44	K10
Yeaveley	Derbys	46	G5
Yeavering	Nthumb	85	M12
Yedingham	N York	64	K4
Yelford	Oxon	29	S7
Yell	Shet	106	u5
Yelland	Devon	15	L5
Yelling	Cambs	39	L8
Yelvertoft	Nhants	37	Q6
Yelverton	Devon	5	N7
Yelverton	Norfk	51	N13
Yenston	Somset	17	T12
Yeoford	Devon	5	S13
Yeolmbridge	Cnwll	4	J3
Yeo Mill	Devon	15	U8
Yeo Vale	Devon	14	K8
Yeovil	Somset	17	P13
Yeovil Marsh	Somset	17	P13
Yeovilton	Somset	17	Q12
Yerbeston	Pembks	24	J9
Yesnaby	Ork	106	r18
Yetlington	Nthumb	77	L4
Yetminster	Dorset	7	Q2
Yetts o'Muckhart	Clacks	90	F12
Yews Green	C Brad	63	M13
Yew Tree	Sandw	36	D2
Yielden	Bed	38	F7
Yieldshields	S Lans	82	G8
Yiewsley	Gt Lon	20	J6
Y Nant	Wrexhm	44	G3
Ynysboeth	Rhondd	26	K8
Ynysddu	Caerph	27	M8
Ynysforgan	Swans	26	B8
Ynyshir	Rhondd	26	J8
Ynyslas	Cerdgn	33	M2
Ynysmaerdy	Rhondd	26	J10
Ynysmeudwy	Neath	26	C7
Ynystawe	Swans	26	B7
Ynyswen	Powys	26	E6
Ynyswen	Rhondd	26	G8
Ynysybwl	Rhondd	26	K8
Yockenthwaite	N York	62	H4
Yockleton	Shrops	44	J11
Yokefleet	E R Yk	58	D1
Yoker	C Glas	89	M12
Yonder Bognie	Abers	104	H6
York	C York	64	E9
York	Lancs	62	E13
Yorkletts	Kent	13	L3
Yorkley	Gloucs	28	B6
Yorkshire Dales National Park		62	H4
York Town	Surrey	20	E10
Yorton Heath	Shrops	45	M9
Youlgreave	Derbys	56	J14
Youlthorpe	E R Yk	64	H8
Youlton	N York	64	C7
Youngsbury	Herts	31	U9
Young's End	Essex	22	H4
Yoxall	Staffs	46	F10
Yoxford	Suffk	41	R7
Y Rhiw	Gwynd	42	D8
Yr Wyddfa	Gwynd	52	K11
Ysbyty Cynfyn	Cerdgn	33	P6
Ysbyty Ifan	Conwy	43	Q4
Ysbyty Ystwyth	Cerdgn	33	P6
Ysceifiog	Flints	54	E12
Ysgubor-y-Coed	Cerdgn	33	N2
Ystalyfera	Neath	26	D6
Ystrad	Rhondd	26	H8
Ystrad Aeron	Cerdgn	33	L9
Ystradfellte	Powys	26	F5
Ystradffin	Carmth	33	P11
Ystradgynlais	Powys	26	E5
Ystradmeurig	Cerdgn	33	P7
Ystradowen	V Glam	26	J12
Ystradowen	Carmth	26	D5
Ystumtuen	Cerdgn	33	N5
Ythanbank	Abers	105	Q8
Ythanwells	Abers	104	J8
Ythsie	Abers	105	P9

Z

Place	County	Page	Grid
Zeal Monachorum	Devon	15	R12
Zeals	Wilts	17	U10
Zelah	Cnwll	2	J5
Zennor	Cnwll	2	C9
Zoar	Cnwll	2	J14
Zouch	Notts	47	P9
ZSL London Zoo	Gt Lon	21	N6
ZSL Whipsnade Zoo	C Beds	31	M9